P9-CFD-843

A Simplified Approach to S/370 Assembly Language Programming

barbara j. burian

A Simplified Approach to S/370 Assembly Language Programming

Prentice-Hall, Inc. Englewood Cliffs, New Jersey 07632

Library of Congress Cataloging in Publication Data

BURIAN, BARBARA J
A simplified approach to S/370 assembly language programming.

Includes index.
1. IBM 370 (Computer)—Programming. 2. Assembler language (Computer program language) I. Title.
QA76.8.I123B87 001.6′424 76-41894
ISBN 0-13-810119-1

Englewood Cliffs, New Jersey 07632

10 9 8 7 6

Printed in the United States of America

PRENTICE-HALL INTERNATIONAL, INC., London
PRENTICE-HALL OF AUSTRALIA PTY. LIMITED, Sydney
PRENTICE-HALL OF CANADA, LTD., Toronto
PRENTICE-HALL OF INDIA PRIVATE LIMITED, New Delhi
PRENTICE-HALL OF JAPAN, INC., Tokyo
PRENTICE-HALL OF SOUTHEAST ASIA PTE. LTD., Singapore
WHITEHALL BOOKS LIMITED, Wellington, New Zealand

To my Uncle, George D. Woods
and his wife, Louise

Contents

SECTION IV—OPERATING SYSTEM CONCEPTS

The topics grouped here are related to the operating system used, but may be introduced at any point within Section III

Preface

NEED

Why another assembly language text? Because this is a difficult subject and as such has been presented in books directed to the reader with some programming experience, rather than to the student who may only have encountered an elementary programming course.

The usual approach to the assembly languages treats such hardware related concepts as the interrupt system, the program status word, and establishing addressability in introductory chapters. The student is often confused because these topics involve a 'theory of' rather than a 'hands on' approach to learning. The 'hands on' approach gives the student programming exercises from the first, making the computer alive, and completely involving the reader in the fun and challenge of programming.

Can the assembly language be presented on a level that an inexperienced programmer can grasp, and still involve hands on computer experience? Yes, if the more difficult concepts are not examined until the student has acquired some programming background. We use business and binary subsets of the assembly language, and then expand these subsets into a full understanding of the language.

OBJECTIVE The objective of this text is to introduce the assembly language to the reader in the *simplest manner possible*, to build his or her confidence in his own ability to program, and *then* to educate him toward a complete understanding of assembly language programming.

METHOD Most inexperienced readers can grasp the COBOL statement

```
SUBTRACT DEPOSIT FROM BAL
IF BAL IS NEGATIVE GO TO
OVERDRAFT-ROUTINE
```

They might also accept the symbolic statements

```
SP   BAL,DEPOSIT
BM   OVRDRAFT
```

but probably could not understand the explicit instructions

```
SP   0(4,3),4(4,3)
BC   4,0(6)
```

The assembly language is introduced at the symbolic level. A business subset is presented first to enable the reader to grasp basic concepts using familiar decimal numbers. The student is given sufficient knowledge to code simple computer exercises—the hands on approach—before being introduced to the binary instructions using a subset involving fullword add, subtract, move, and compare instructions. The text emphasizes basic programming techniques, including loop control and total breaks. The book is not only an assembly language text, but a basic programming text as well.

I have found that students spend a great deal of time grasping the *purpose* of problems illustrating new instructions. Often they never really understand the problem statement, and as a result never understand the coded solution. I have tried to eliminate this confusion by using the same examples throughout the text. Once a student understands the problem statement, he or she can turn full attention to the code as new instructions and concepts are presented using the same familiar problem statement. The student feels secure as new instructions solve the already familiar problem.

ORGANIZATION Section I serves as a review of the computer and programming environment, and introduces background topics including storage concepts, S/370 instruction formats, and computer arithmetic. The first two chapters in this section should be presented before introducing the business subset. Chapters 3 and 4 should be discussed before presenting the binary subset in Chapter 8.

Section II presents both a business and a binary subset of the assembly language, introducing arithmetic, move, compare, and branching instructions.

Implied addressing is used in all programs, using symbols to reference storage locations. The extended mnemonics are used rather than introducing the BC instruction and the condition code in the PSW. The GET and PUT macros, which are identical in OS and DOS, are presented to show the flow of data from input through process to output. The concept of the BALR/USING pair is not presented until Chapter 9. A macro is used to establish addressability as the subsets are developed. The emphasis—until Chapter 9—is on programming rather than on architecture and addressing.

The programs used in Section II are expanded in Section III to illustrate masking and testing the condition code in the PSW, loop control, and address modification. New concepts are introduced including table handling, logical arithmetic, and character and bit manipulation. The business subset introduced in Section II is expanded to include the TRT, EX, TR, and EDMK instructions, as well as the new S/370 instructions MVCL, CLCL, and SRP.

Section IV relates to the operating system environment. Both OS and DOS are referenced. This section includes chapters on sequential I/O coding, linkage conventions, job control relating to the testing environment, and debugging techniques. These chapters may be introduced at any point after the reader understands addressing.

FLEXIBILITY

Both OS and DOS are treated equally. The programs presented in Sections II and III are operating system independent. By contrast, the reader is given examples of both OS and DOS macro coding, job control statements, and debugging techniques in Section IV. No one operating system is emphasized.

Two options are available to the instructor. The material in Sections III and IV is completely modular and may be presented in one of two ways. The more standard (computer science) approach would include a full discussion of the binary instructions (Chapter 10), sequence control (Chapter 11), address modification and table handling (Chapter 12), followed by logical arithmetic and bit and byte handling (Chapter 13). The material on subroutines (Chapter 16), job control statements (Chapter 17), and testing and debugging (Chapter 18) could be placed anywhere within these topics.

A business approach might include sequence control (Chapter 11), possibly address modification and table handling (Chapter 12), and the extended business subset (Chapter 14). The I/O macros, material on job control, linkages, testing and debugging could be presented as desired.

ACKNOWLEDGEMENTS

I am grateful to my students at New York University for their cooperation and enthusiasm in evaluating this book, for reading and reviewing the chapters, and for their criticisms and suggestions, and to my colleagues on the staff and faculty of the Data Processing Institute of the Division of Business and Management for their help and encouragement.

I especially want to thank Bob Strauss for his criticisms and editorial comments, Dr. Richard L. Wexelblat of Bell Labs, Professor Henry Austin of Oakland Community College, Karl Karlstrom and Phyllis Springmeyer of Prentice-Hall, whose comments and criticisms were invaluable, and my friends and colleagues at IBM who patiently taught me assembly language programming.

Finally, I wish to thank my husband, Bob, and my children Pamela and Susie, for their patience, encouragement, and help.

BARBARA J. BURIAN

section one

Background Topics

1

Introductory Concepts

This text serves as an introduction to the IBM Assembly Language. We assume that the reader has some knowledge of basic data processing concepts, including numbering systems and computer architecture. This chapter serves to review these concepts, and to discuss these ideas in the context in which they are referenced in the text.

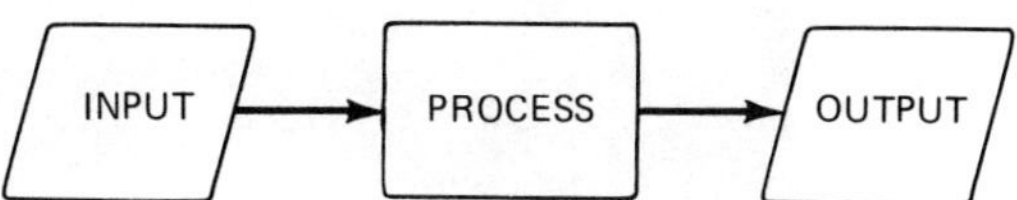

Figure 1-1 The basic data processing pattern.

COMPUTING SYSTEMS FUNDAMENTALS

We use the basic data processing pattern (Figure 1-1) to illustrate many of our programming problems. The basic data processing pattern simply states that most data processing problems can be represented in terms of information called *input* which enters the computer to be *processed.* The results are then *output*, often in the form of a printed report.

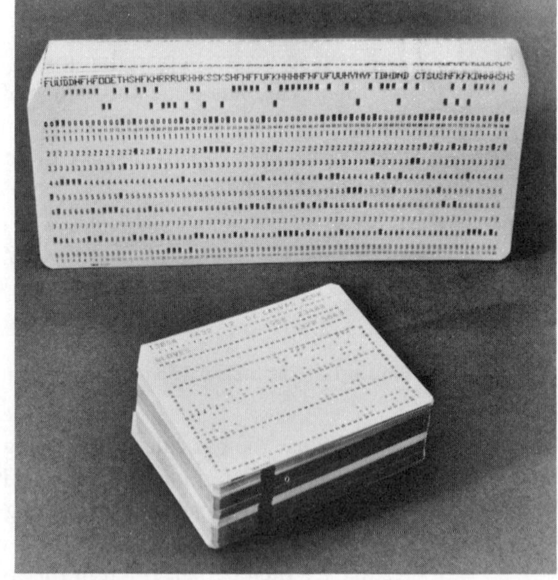

Figure 1-2 Data recording media (*Courtesy* of International Business Machines Corporation.)

Data

We use the term data to describe the input and output in the computer system. The word data is plural. Thus we say data *are* rather than data *is*. Data are facts. Data are not always associated with the computer. You use data in your day-to-day activities. The radio provides you with data concerning the day's weather. Your mail provides you with data concerning bills, checking accounts, and so forth. The input and output of the computer environment are just another form of data.

Data Recording Media. In our every day activities we usually record data on paper. We refer to this paper as a data recording medium. Paper may be used as a data recording medium in the computer environment, but other methods are more common, as illustrated in Figure 1-2. The card is the data recording medium most often associated with computers. The familiar "do not fold, spindle or mutilate" refers to the punched card. Information is recorded on the punched card in 80 vertical columns. One or more punches are required to represent a single letter (A–Z), digit (0–9), or a special character (%$&¢*, etc.). (See Figure 1-3.)

Data may be recorded on magnetic tape or on magnetic disk. We refer to data recorded on magnetic tape as *sequential* data. We read the records on magnetic tape one at a time. In order to process the last record, we must first process the preceding records.

Data also may be recorded on magnetic disk. We often use the analogy of a phonograph record. The data are recorded as magnetic spots arranged in concentric circles (Figure 1-4). Just as we can go directly to a section of music on a phonograph record, we can go directly to a piece of data on the magnetic disk. We do not have to process all the preceding records. We call this concept *random* or *direct access*. But, just as we can listen to the music on a phonograph record from the beginning to the end, or from the first note to the last note, we also can process the data recorded on a magnetic disk from beginning to end, one piece of data at a time. Thus, data on the disk may be processed sequentially or by using the technique called random access.

The Hierarchy of Data. The data used in the computer environment may be broken down into three levels. We refer to this division of data as the hierarchy of data (Figure 1-5). Let's consider a collection of punched cards. Each card contains payroll information about an individual within a company. We call this card the payroll *record*. Each piece of information within the record is called a *field*. The collection of all the payroll record cards is called a *file*.

The file is the highest or most inclusive level in the hierarchy of data. The file is comprised of individual records which, in turn, may be divided into fields. Let's consider a single payroll record (Figure 1-5). The first six positions of this record contain the employee number field. The next twenty positions contain the employee name. This becomes the employee name field, and so on.

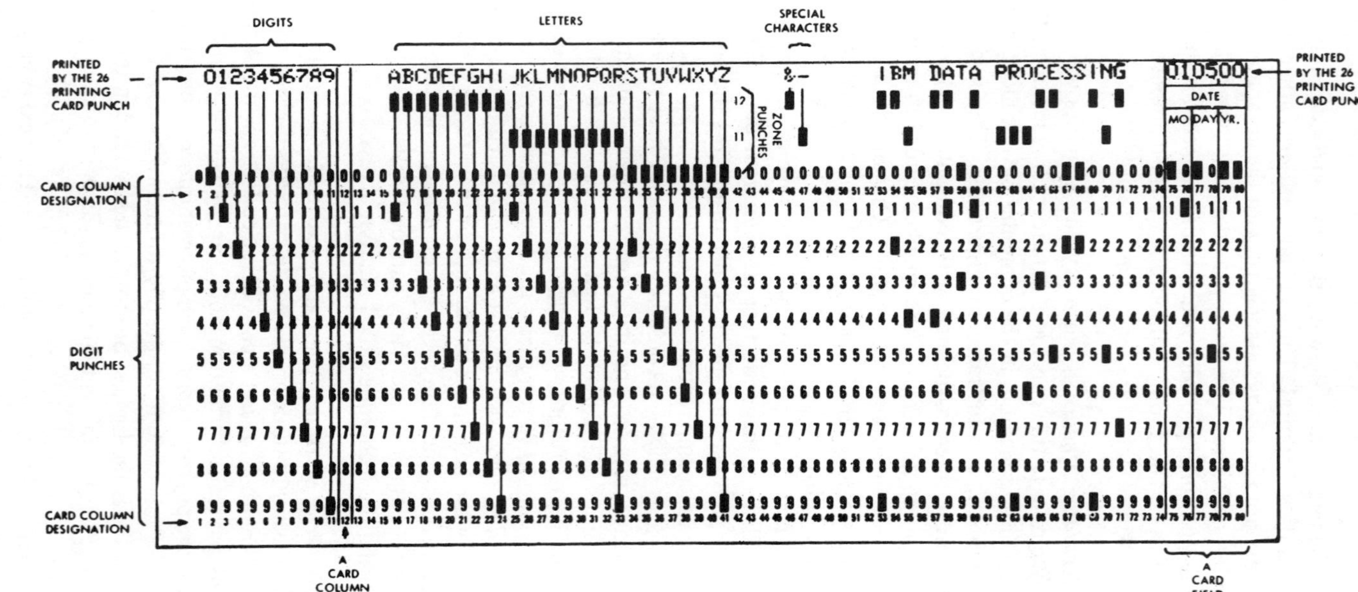

Figure 1-3 Data recorded on a punched card. (*Courtesy* of International Business Machines Corporation.)

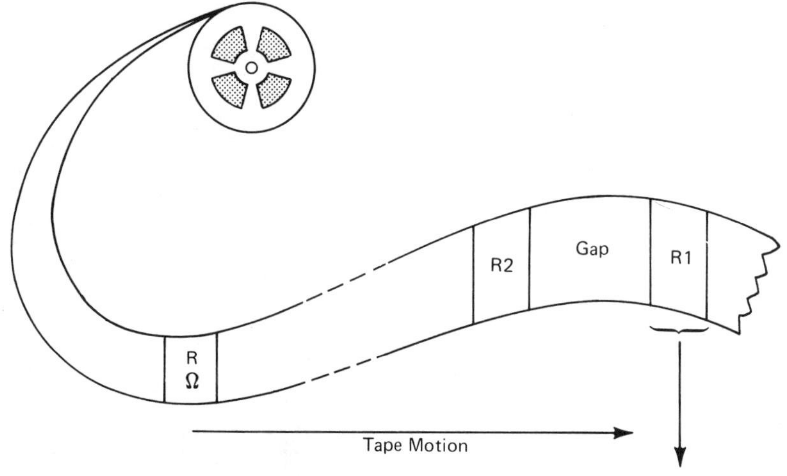

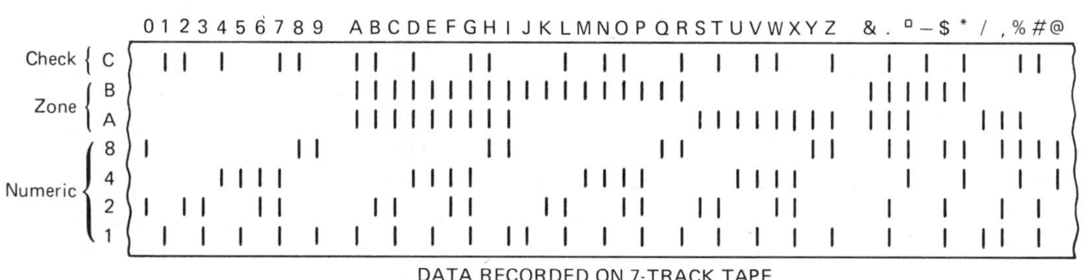

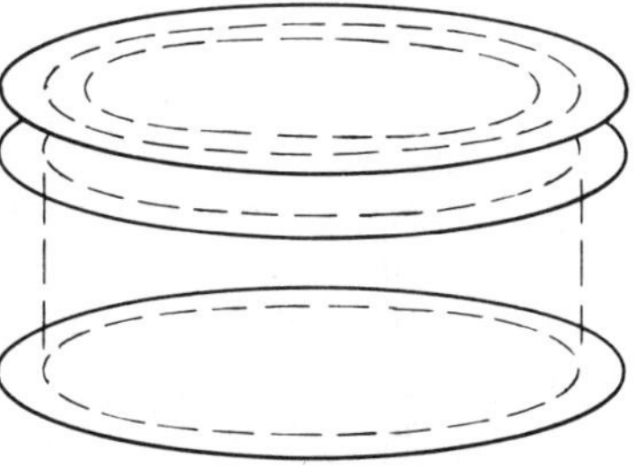

Figure 1-4 Recording data on magnetic tape and disk. (Photo *courtesy* of International Business Machines Corporation.)

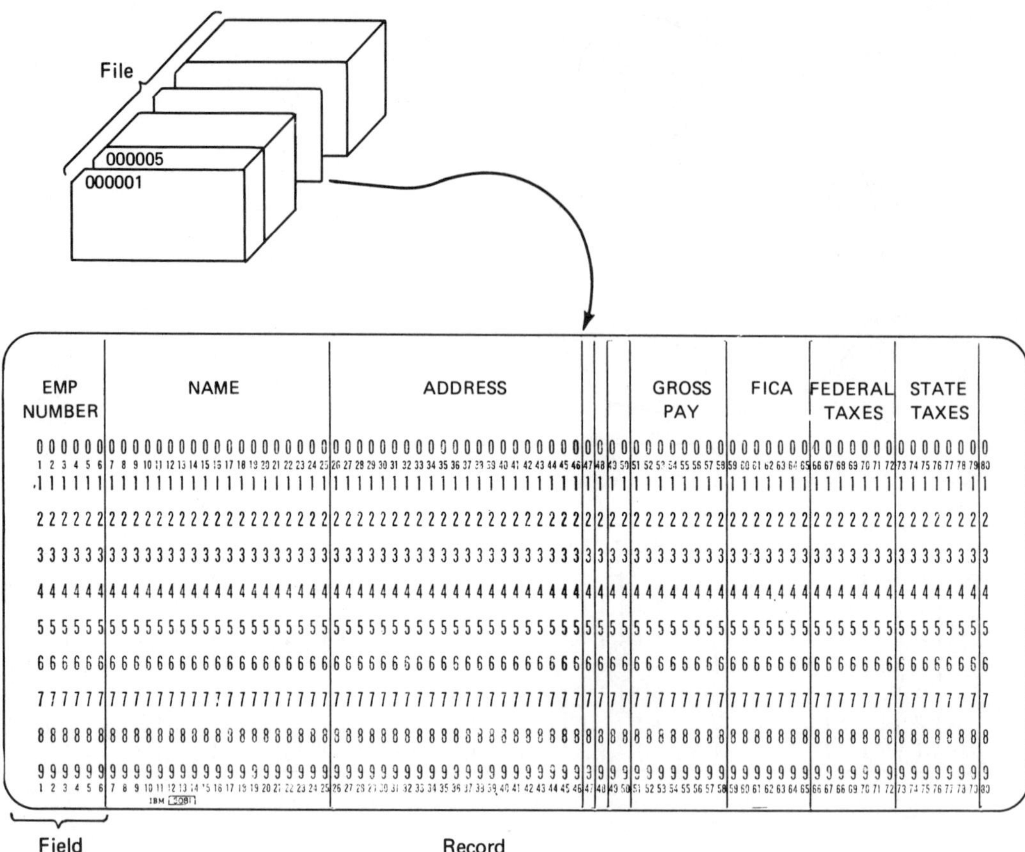

Figure 1-5 The hierarchy of data.

Some fields within a record have special significance. The employee number field identifies the employee. Most of us would rather be identified by our name, but the simple fact of modern business is that we are identified by numbers—employee numbers, account numbers, social security numbers, and so on. We call these identifying fields *key* fields or *sequence* fields. Files are usually arranged in sequence based not on the name field, but on the number or key field. Notice the payroll file in Figure 1-5. The first record is employee 000001. The next record is employee 000005. We say that the file is arranged in ascending sequence by employee number. Although the employee numbers are increasing, they are not necessarily consecutive.

Another special type of field is the code field. The payroll record must indicate the marital status of the employee for tax purposes. If we were to use the words *single*, *married*, *divorced*, or *other* on our record, we would use too much space. Eight columns would be needed to represent the word *divorced*. Instead, we use a numeric code requiring only one column to represent the marital status. For example, a code of 1 indicates that the employee is single, a code of 2 that the employee is married, and so on. The use of a code saves space on the employee record card.

We have seen that data may be recorded on different media such as card, disk, and tape. Before the data are processed, they first must be input. Notice that we use the word *input* as a verb. We also use the word *output* as a verb. We call the machines which input data input devices.

Input

Two of the most frequently used input devices are the card reader and the magnetic tape reader. These devices are sequential devices. The magnetic disk is a random access device with the capability to read data sequentially or at random.

Other input devices read data recorded on punched paper tape, printed documents, or documents marked with a special magnetic ink. Special input devices called teleprocessing terminals input data over telephone lines.

Processing

Regardless of the input device used, the data arrive at the computer. We are now involved with the processing function. This is the operation involving the computer itself. The processing box in our basic data processing pattern may be expanded to include storage and the Central Processing Unit (CPU). When data are input, they reside in storage, but the actual computing (or processing) occurs in the CPU (Figure 1-6). The CPU itself is divided into two sections—the Control Section and the Arithmetic and Logic Unit (ALU). The Control Section oversees the operation of the entire computer. The ALU is responsible for arithmetic calculations and logical operations.

Let's explore these important concepts in more detail. Data are read by an input device and are transmitted to storage. No matter what the input medium, the data appear in storage in the same form. In order to understand how the data are stored, we must examine the storage medium itself.

Storage. One type of storage consists of rings which may be magnetized in either a clockwise or counter-clockwise direction. We refer to these rings as bits. A bit may be either *on* or *off*, depending upon the direction in which it is magnetized. Different computers employ different storage techniques. Our discussion is related to the IBM S/360 and S/370 computers. These computers use eight bits to represent a single letter, digit, or special character. We call this group of eight bits a *byte*. One byte of storage is required to represent a character.

The Control Section. The Control Section is responsible for executing the instructions which comprise the computer program. In order to understand how

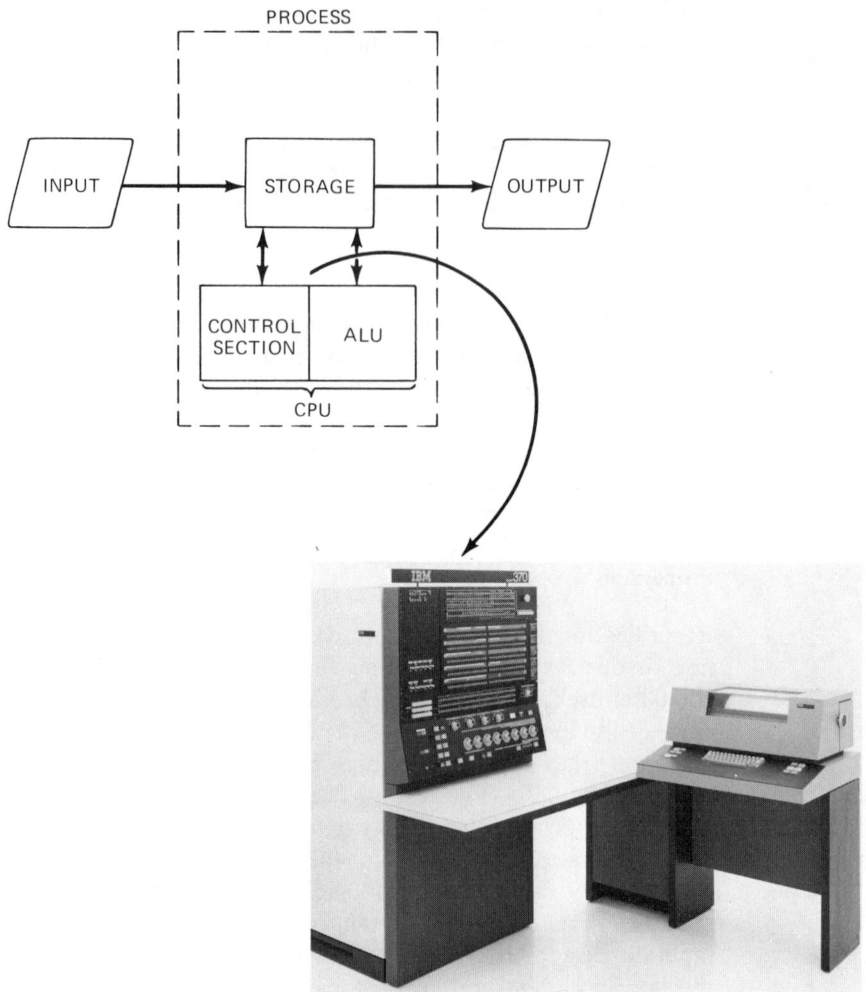

Figure 1-6 The CPU. (Photo *courtesy* of International Business Machines Corporation.)

the Control Section operates, let's examine a hypothetical instruction (Figure 1-7). Let's assume the instruction FA 4000 5000 tells us to add two numbers. The instruction must specify the operation to be performed (add, subtract, compare) and must refer to the data. Most computer instructions do not contain the data itself, but contain the address of the data. The instruction shown in Figure 1-7 consists of two parts—the operation code, or *op-code* (FA), and the *address* of the data involved. By address we mean the location of the data in storage. The op-code FA specifies an add operation, an operation requiring two operands. The number 4000 specifies the address of one operand. The number 5000 specifies the address of the second operand. In order to find the value of the data, we

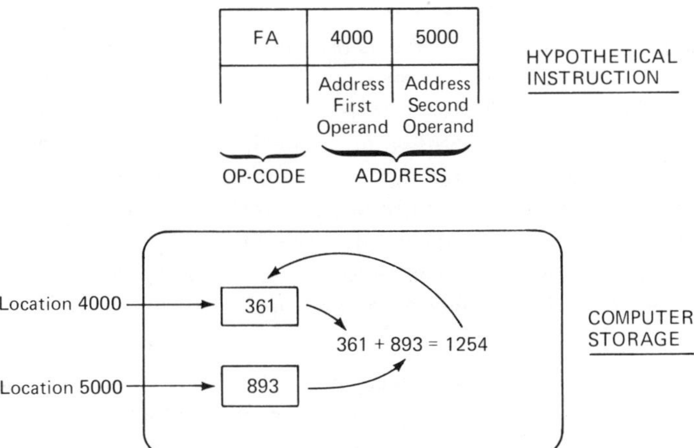

Figure 1-7 Execution of an ADD instruction.

must examine the data at storage location 4000 and storage location 5000. We find that the data at location 4000 contains the number 361 and the data at location 5000 contains the number 893. The result of the add operation is 1254. The computer places this result in the first operand location—location 4000. The contents of the second operand location in location 5000 are unchanged. It is important to remember that the instruction does not contain the data itself, only the *address* of the data. The result of the add operation shown in Figure 1-7 is *not* 9000. We must examine the data at location 4000 and location 5000 to determine the result of the add operation.

The Control Section is responsible for executing the instructions which comprise the computer program. It is important to remember that the instructions executed by the Control Section contain the addresses of data, not the actual data. The instructions reference storage locations which contain the data to be processed. The instructions comprising the program also reside in computer storage

The ALU. The ALU performs the arithmetic and logical operations requested by the program. We might refer to the ALU as the "think box." When we see the complex circuitry of the modern computer adapted to fictional television or movie stories, it is the ALU that is most often represented.

Output

Once an operation or series of operations is complete, the result usually is returned to a main storage location. The next step is to output the result. The output devices accept data from computer storage and record them on the correct media. The card punch records the data on punched cards. The printer records the data on a continuous roll of paper. The card punch and the printer are output devices only. Other devices, however, such as the magnetic disk drive and magnetic tape drive serve as both input and output devices.

The computer environment consists of input devices, the computer itself consisting of the CPU and storage units, and the output devices. We have seen how data are read by the appropriate input device into main storage. The storage unit also contains the instructions comprising the computer program. These instructions are executed one at a time by the Control Section of the CPU. Instruction execution often involves the ALU. Once the data are processed, the results are output from main storage. The output devices accept data from main storage and write the data to the appropriate medium.

DATA PROCESSING ENVIRONMENT

The computer environment is only one part of the entire data processing environment. Let's examine some of its other aspects.

Hardware and Software

We use the term *hardware* to refer to the input devices, the computer itself, and the output devices. The term hardware is synonymous with machine. But the machine must be told what to do. The instructions comprising the computer program tell the machine what to do. We use the term *software* to describe the computer programs.

The programs written in a customer or user installation are considered to be software. We often use the term application programs when referring to all programs comprising a particular user function. The term software, however, more accurately describes a special type of program—the *control programs* or *operating systems.*

Operating Systems. An operating system is a collection of programs, usually written by the computer manufacturer. The operating system performs many functions. Let's consider one—an area called I/O operations or input/output operations.

When the programmer wishes to read a record into the computer—remember, we must input data before we can process it—he (or she) issues a read statement in the program. A single command. But many hundreds of computer instructions are required to read a single record from an input device. The operating system—once it knows the programmer needs a record—performs the necessary instructions to transfer the record from the input device to the computer. Without the operating system, the programmer would have to code hundreds of instructions to read data.

NUMBERING SYSTEMS

Our daily activities involve the decimal numbering system. However, there are many other numbering systems available. Two of these systems, the binary and the hexadecimal numbering systems, are essential to our understanding of assembly language. Let's first review our understanding of the decimal numbering system, and then go on to develop the binary and hexadecimal numbering systems.

The Decimal System

The decimal system has ten distinct symbols—the digits 0–9. All decimal numbers are expressed using these ten digits. For example, the number 1976, familiar to all of us, uses four of the ten possible digits. Let's look at the number 1976 in a different way.

$$1 \times 10^3 + 9 \times 10^2 + 7 \times 10^1 + 6 \times 10^0$$

We call this means of expressing a number *expanded notation*. Let's calculate the value of the expanded notation.

$$1 \times 10^3 + 9 \times 10^2 + 7 \times 10^1 + 6 \times 10^0$$

$$\begin{aligned} 6 \times 1 &= 6 \\ 7 \times 10 &= 70 \\ 9 \times 100 &= 900 \\ 1 \times 1000 &= \underline{1000} \\ & 1976 \end{aligned}$$

Notice that when we expand the value 6×10^0 we assume that the expression 10^0 is equivalent to 1. Any number, raised to the zero power, is equal to 1.

When we express a number in expanded notation, we are expressing the number in terms of a coefficient times the base (ten in this case) raised to a power. The rightmost digit is the units digit (ten raised to the zero power is one), the next rightmost digit is the tens digit (ten raised to the first power is ten), and so on. Notice that the exponents increase by one each time we move to the left.

The value of the base is determined by the number of distinct symbols. We call decimal numbers base ten numbers, and decimal arithmetic base ten arithmetic.

As we discuss the different numbering systems, we use the subscript notation to indicate the base. Thus the number 11100_2 is represented in the binary system, and the number 28_{10} is represented in the decimal system. In subsequent chapters we omit the decimal subscript and subscript only nondecimal numbers.

The Binary Numbering System

The binary numbering system has only two symbols—zero and one (0 and 1). Thus binary numbers are base two numbers. Let's develop the binary numbers. The first two numbers are easy.

zero—0_2

one —1_2

Now the number two—but we are out of symbols. We now must go to the next column, setting the first column back to zero (this is exactly what we do in decimal numbers when we go from nine to ten). Thus

two —10_2

three—11_2

and into another column for the number four. The binary numbers from one to sixteen now appear as

decimal	binary
0	0
1	1
2	10
3	11
4	100
5	101
6	110
7	111
8	1000
9	1001
10	1010
11	1011
12	1100
13	1101
14	1110
15	1111
16	10000

Expanded Notation. Binary numbers also may be expressed in expanded notation—remember the base is different. The number 101010_2 may be written as:

$$1 \times 2^5 + 0 \times 2^4 + 1 \times 2^3 + 0 \times 2^2 + 1 \times 2^1 + 0 \times 2^0$$

$$\begin{aligned} 0 \times 1 &= 0 \\ 1 \times 2 &= 2 \\ 0 \times 4 &= 0 \\ 1 \times 8 &= 8 \\ 0 \times 16 &= 0 \\ 1 \times 32 &= 32 \\ \hline & \quad 42 \end{aligned}$$

The use of expanded notation provides a means of converting binary numbers to their decimal equivalent. Use expanded notation to verify that the binary number 11100_2 is equivalent to the decimal number 28.

Binary Arithmetic. In decimal arithmetic we add the numbers 1_{10} and 1_{10} to obtain the result 2_{10}. In binary arithmetic we add the numbers 1_2 and 0_2 to obtain the result 1_2. Both of these examples are simple additions which do not involve a carry.

Now consider the decimal addition

$$\begin{array}{r} 18_{10} \\ +18_{10} \\ \hline 36_{10} \end{array}$$

The addition of the first two numbers in the units position results in a number greater than nine. We must carry into the tens position.

We must also consider the carry in binary arithmetic. For example

$$\begin{array}{r} 1001_2 \\ +1001_2 \\ \hline 10010_2 \end{array}$$

The addition of the two right-hand digits results in a number equal to the base of two. Our result is zero and a carry into the next column. It is also possible to have a result of one, and a carry into the next column.

$$\begin{array}{r} 1011_2 \\ +1011_2 \\ \hline 10110_2 \end{array}$$

The addition of the two rightmost digits results in a zero with a carry of one into the next column. The addition of the two digits—1_2 and 1_2—plus the carry of one results in a one in the second position and a carry into the next position.

We always can verify that the result of binary addition is correct by converting the binary operands to their familiar decimal equivalents. Thus

$$\begin{array}{r} 1101_2 \\ +1101_2 \\ \hline 11010_2 \end{array} \qquad \begin{array}{r} 13_{10} \\ +13_{10} \\ \hline 26_{10} \end{array}$$

The reader should verify that the number 11010_2 is equivalent to the number 26_{10}.

Now let's consider subtraction. The decimal subtraction

$$\begin{array}{r} 987_{10} \\ -362_{10} \\ \hline 625_{10} \end{array}$$

should cause no problem. Now consider this subtraction as a special type of addition. The subtrahend 362_{10} is converted to its complement and is added to the minuend (987_{10}). The complement of a number is the number which must be added to the number to equal the next power of the base. Or—the result obtained when the number is subtracted from the next power of the base. For example, the complement of the number 362_{10} is 638_{10}. We can either add 362_{10} and 638_{10} to obtain 1000_{10}, or we can subtract 362_{10} from 1000_{10} to obtain the complement 638_{10}.*

Now let's use the complement to perform subtraction. We can either *subtract* the subtrahend 362_{10} from the minuend 987_{10}, or we can convert the subtrahend to its complement and *add*. The results are identical!

subtract subtrahend	*add complement of subtrahend*
987_{10}	987_{10}
-362_{10}	$+638_{10}$
625_{10}	625_{10} a carry of 1

The carry out of the leftmost position indicates that the result is positive and is carried in uncomplemented or true form.

Let's consider an example which yields a negative result.

$$\begin{array}{r} 362_{10} \\ -987_{10} \\ \hline -625_{10} \end{array}$$

If we approach the same example by taking the complement of 987_{10} and adding we obtain the following result.

$$\begin{array}{r} 362_{10} \\ +013_{10} \\ \hline 375_{10} \end{array}$$

It appears that the results are not the same. But wait a minute! What about the carry out of the leftmost position, indicating that the number is positive and in true form? There is no carry in this example! This means that the result is *negative* and is carried in complement form. The answer must be recomplemented to verify the result. The complement of 375_{10} is 625_{10}. Expressed as a negative number the answer becomes -625_{10}.

*A quick approach to complementing a decimal number; subtract each digit from nine and the last or rightmost non-zero digit from ten. Thus the complement of 345 becomes 655.

We approach binary subtraction using the complement approach. In decimal arithmetic we take the ten's complement of the subtrahend and add. In binary arithmetic we take the two's complement of the subtrahend and add.

The two's complement of a number is the number which, when added to the original number, results in the next higher power of the base. For example, the two's complement of the number 1010_2 is 0110_2. We add these two numbers to verify that the complement is correct.

$$\begin{array}{r} 1010_2 \\ +0110_2 \\ \hline 10000_2 \end{array}$$

We obtain the two's complement of a number by reversing the digits and adding one. For example, the number 1010_2 reverses to 0101_2. We now add one

$$\begin{array}{r} 0101_2 \\ +0001_2 \\ \hline 0110_2 \end{array}$$

to obtain the correct complement of 1010_2.

Now let's use the complement approach in binary arithmetic and verify our results using decimal arithmetic. To perform the subtraction

$$\begin{array}{r} 1010_2 \\ -0110_2 \\ \hline \end{array}$$

we must first complement the subtrahend. We reverse the digits, and add one.

$$\begin{array}{rr} 0110_2 \text{ reverses to} & 1001_2 \\ \text{and add 1} & 0001_2 \\ \hline & 1010_2 \end{array}$$

We *add* the complement of the subtrahend to the minuend.

$$\begin{array}{rl} 1010_2 & \\ +1010_2 & \\ \hline 0100_2 & \text{and a carry of 1} \end{array}$$

The carry out of the leftmost position tells us the result is positive and is carried in true form. We can verify the result using decimal equivalents of the binary operands.

$$\begin{array}{rr} 1010_2 & 10_{10} \\ -0110_2 & -\ 6_{10} \\ \hline 0100_2 & 4_{10} \end{array}$$

The binary number 0100_2 is indeed equivalent to the decimal number 4_{10}.

Binary subtraction also may result in negative results. Consider the example

$$\begin{array}{r} 0101_2 \\ -1100_2 \\ \hline \end{array}$$

Again, we complement the subtrahend and add

$$\begin{array}{r} 0101_2 \\ +0100_2 \\ \hline 1001_2 \end{array}$$

There is no carry. This means that the result is negative and is carried in complement form. We must recomplement. We find the answer is -0111_2. We can use decimal arithmetic to verify the result.

$$\begin{array}{rr} 0101_2 & 5_{10} \\ -1100_2 & -12_{10} \\ \hline -0111_2 & -\ 7_{10} \end{array}$$

The Hexadecimal Numbering System

The use of binary numbers becomes awkward when large numbers are involved. Yet the binary numbering system is tied to the computer environment. Remember how data are stored in the computer. Each storage unit, or bit, may be on or off. One of two possible states—0 or 1. We use the binary notation to represent data in computer storage. For example, the bit pattern

$$10100000_2$$

represents the number 160_{10}.

The use of binary numbers to represent data stored in computer storage is confusing. Therefore, we use a notation to condense these binary digits into a more usable form. This notation is called the *hexadecimal numbering system.*

The hexadecimal, or base sixteen, numbering system has sixteen distinct symbols—including digits and letters. A letter can have a numeric equivalent! This is a difficult concept for the beginning programmer. The symbols used in the hexadecimal numbering system, together with their decimal and binary equivalents, are shown in Table 1-1.

Table 1-1 Three Numbering Systems

decimal	hexadecimal	binary
0	0	0
1	1	1
2	2	10
3	3	11
4	4	100
5	5	101
6	6	110
7	7	111
8	8	1000
9	9	1001
10	A	1010
11	B	1011
12	C	1100
13	D	1101
14	E	1110
15	F	1111
16	10	10000

To express the number sixteen in the hexadecimal numbering system, we must set the symbol in the units position back to zero and carry one into the next position, the *sixteens* position. Why sixteens position? Let's look at a hexadecimal number in expanded notation to see why.

The hexadecimal number $13C_{16}$ (again we use a subscript to denote the base) may be expressed as

$$1_{10} \times 16^2_{10} + 3_{10} \times 16^1_{10} + 12_{10} \times 16^0_{10}$$

The place value of the digit in the rightmost column is one*—we call this column the units position. The place value of the next column is equivalent to 16^1_{10} or a place value of sixteen. We call this column the sixteens position.

We may use the expanded notation to convert a hexadecimal number to its decimal equivalent. For example, the decimal equivalent of the number $13C_{16}$ is 316_{10}. Let's see why.

$$1_{10} \times 16^2_{10} + 3_{10} \times 16^1_{10} + 12_{10} \times 16^0_{10}$$

$$\begin{aligned} 12_{10} \times 1_{10} &= 12_{10} \\ 3_{10} \times 16_{10} &= 48_{10} \\ 1_{10} \times 256_{10} &= \underline{256_{10}} \\ & \quad\; 316_{10} \end{aligned}$$

*Again, the number 16^0 is equal to one.

Use expanded notation to verify that the decimal equivalent of the number $203D_{16}$ is 8253_{10}.

A simpler approach to converting hexadecimal numbers to their decimal equivalents involves the use of a conversion table (Figure 1-8). Let's use this table to convert the number $203D_{16}$ to its decimal equivalent.

HEX	DEC	HEX	DEC	HEX		HEX	DEC	HEX	DEC	HEX	DEC	HEX	DEC	HEX	DEC
0	0	0	0	0	0	0	0	0	0	0	0	0	0	0	0
1	268,435,456	1	16,777,216	1	1,048,576	1	65,536	1	4,096	1	256	1	16	1	1
2	536,870,912	2	33,554,432	2	2,097,152	2	131,072	2	8,192	2	512	2	32	2	2
3	805,306,368	3	50,331,648	3	3,145,728	3	196,608	3	12,288	3	768	3	48	3	3
4	1,073,741,824	4	67,108,864	4	4,194,304	4	262,144	4	16,384	4	1,024	4	64	4	4
5	1,342,177,280	5	83,886,080	5	5,242,880	5	327,680	5	20,480	5	1,280	5	80	5	5
6	1,610,612,736	6	100,663,296	6	6,291,456	6	393,216	6	24,576	6	1,536	6	96	6	6
7	1,879,048,192	7	117,440,512	7	7,340,032	7	458,752	7	28,672	7	1,792	7	112	7	7
8	2,147,483,648	8	134,217,728	8	8,388,608	8	524,288	8	32,768	8	2,048	8	128	8	8
9	2,415,919,104	9	150,994,944	9	9,437,184	9	589,824	9	36,864	9	2,304	9	144	9	9
A	2,684,354,560	A	167,772,160	A	10,485,760	A	655,360	A	40,960	A	2,560	A	160	A	10
B	2,952,790,016	B	184,549,376	B	11,534,336	B	720,896	B	45,056	B	2,816	B	176	B	11
C	3,221,225,472	C	201,326,592	C	12,582,912	C	786,432	C	49,152	C	3,072	C	192	C	12
D	3,489,660,928	D	218,103,808	D	13,631,488	D	851,968	D	53,248	D	3,328	D	208	D	13
E	3,758,096,384	E	234,881,024	E	14,680,064	E	917,504	E	57,344	E	3,584	E	224	E	14
F	4,026,531,840	F	251,658,240	F	15,728,640	F	983,040	F	61,440	F	3,840	F	240	F	15
Hexadecimal Positions	8		7		6		5		4		3		2		1

Figure 1-8 Hexadecimal conversion table.

The values in each column in this table are equivalent to the values used in the expanded notation in the previous example. For example, the digit 2 in the fourth column is equivalent to the number 2×16^3 or 8192_{10}. If we search the fourth column we find that the hexadecimal number associated with the digit 2 is 8192_{10}. Now let's use this conversion table to develop the decimal equivalent of $203D_{16}$ (Figure 1-9). We obtain a result of 8253_{10}—the same result we found using expanded notation.

This same table may be used to convert decimal numbers to their hexadecimal equivalents. To find the hexadecimal equivalent of the decimal number 1976_{10}, we search the table for the number closest to *but less than* the decimal number. We find the number 1792_{10} in the third column. We now know that the hexadecimal equivalent has three digits, and a 7_{16} in the leftmost digit. We *subtract* the number 1792_{10} from the number 1976_{10}. The result is 184_{10}. Now we search for the number closest to, but less than, the number 184_{10}. We find the number 176_{10} in the second column. The second digit in our answer is B_{16}. We subtract the number 176_{10} from 184_{10} to obtain the result 8_{10}, the last digit in our answer. Thus the hexadecimal equivalent of the number 1976_{10} is $7B8_{16}$. Figure 1-10 shows just how this conversion is accomplished. Can you use this

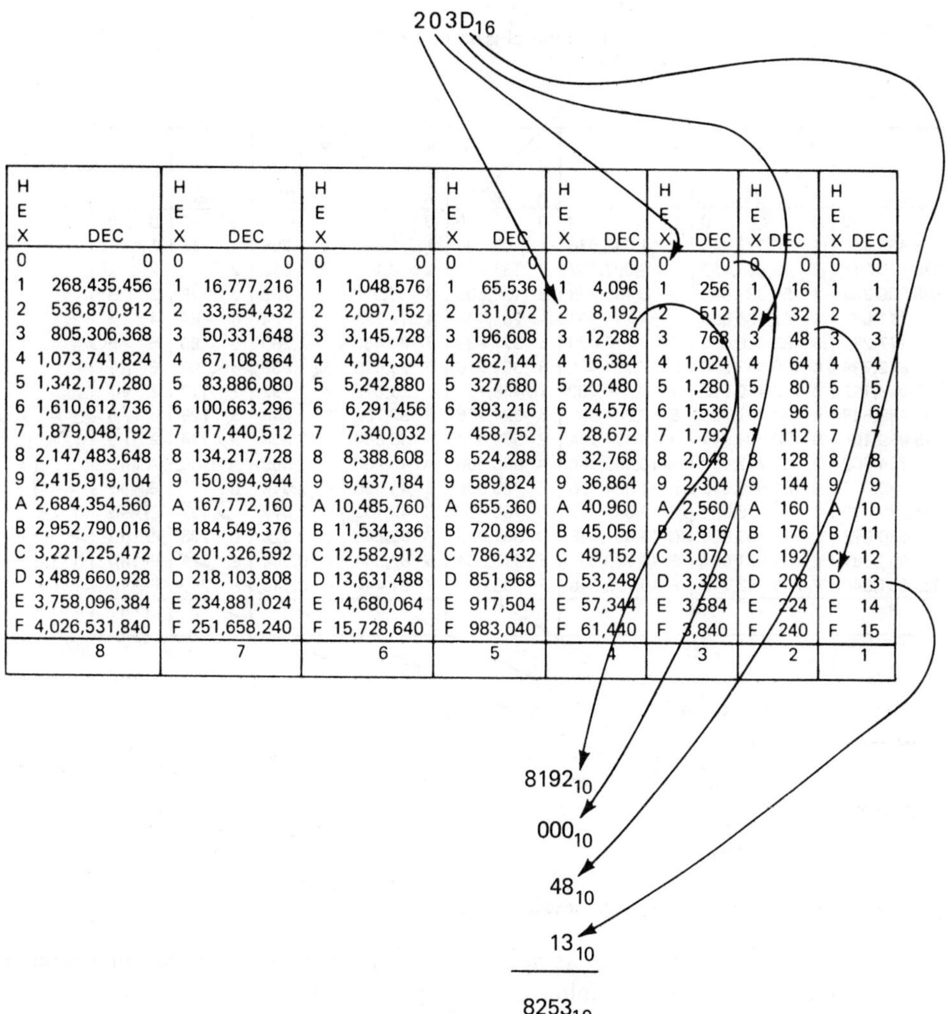

HEX	DEC	HEX	DEC	HEX	DEC	HEX	DEC	HEX	DEC	HEX	DEC	HEX	DEC	HEX	DEC
0	0	0	0	0	0	0	0	0	0	0	0	0	0	0	0
1	268,435,456	1	16,777,216	1	1,048,576	1	65,536	1	4,096	1	256	1	16	1	1
2	536,870,912	2	33,554,432	2	2,097,152	2	131,072	2	8,192	2	512	2	32	2	2
3	805,306,368	3	50,331,648	3	3,145,728	3	196,608	3	12,288	3	768	3	48	3	3
4	1,073,741,824	4	67,108,864	4	4,194,304	4	262,144	4	16,384	4	1,024	4	64	4	4
5	1,342,177,280	5	83,886,080	5	5,242,880	5	327,680	5	20,480	5	1,280	5	80	5	5
6	1,610,612,736	6	100,663,296	6	6,291,456	6	393,216	6	24,576	6	1,536	6	96	6	6
7	1,879,048,192	7	117,440,512	7	7,340,032	7	458,752	7	28,672	7	1,792	7	112	7	7
8	2,147,483,648	8	134,217,728	8	8,388,608	8	524,288	8	32,768	8	2,048	8	128	8	8
9	2,415,919,104	9	150,994,944	9	9,437,184	9	589,824	9	36,864	9	2,304	9	144	9	9
A	2,684,354,560	A	167,772,160	A	10,485,760	A	655,360	A	40,960	A	2,560	A	160	A	10
B	2,952,790,016	B	184,549,376	B	11,534,336	B	720,896	B	45,056	B	2,816	B	176	B	11
C	3,221,225,472	C	201,326,592	C	12,582,912	C	786,432	C	49,152	C	3,072	C	192	C	12
D	3,489,660,928	D	218,103,808	D	13,631,488	D	851,968	D	53,248	D	3,328	D	208	D	13
E	3,758,096,384	E	234,881,024	E	14,680,064	E	917,504	E	57,344	E	3,584	E	224	E	14
F	4,026,531,840	F	251,658,240	F	15,728,640	F	983,040	F	61,440	F	3,840	F	240	F	15
8		7		6		5		4		3		2		1	

Figure 1-9 Using the conversion table.

same approach to verify that the hexadecimal equivalent of the decimal number 3768_{10} is $EB8_{16}$?

Why hexadecimal? We use hexadecimal symbols to represent binary numbers, or we convert binary numbers to their hexadecimal equivalents for ease of handling.

Consider the binary number 1010101111001101_2. Surely a large number. We could determine its decimal equivalent using expanded notation but this method is time consuming and quite prone to error. If, however, we could

1976_{10}

Number closest to 1976_{10}

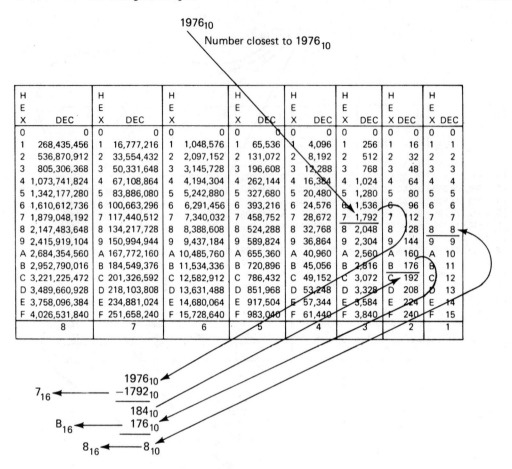

HEX	DEC	HEX	DEC	HEX	DEC	HEX	DEC	HEX	DEC	HEX	DEC	HEX	DEC	HEX	DEC
0	0	0	0	0	0	0	0	0	0	0	0	0	0	0	0
1	268,435,456	1	16,777,216	1	1,048,576	1	65,536	1	4,096	1	256	1	16	1	1
2	536,870,912	2	33,554,432	2	2,097,152	2	131,072	2	8,192	2	512	2	32	2	2
3	805,306,368	3	50,331,648	3	3,145,728	3	196,608	3	12,288	3	768	3	48	3	3
4	1,073,741,824	4	67,108,864	4	4,194,304	4	262,144	4	16,384	4	1,024	4	64	4	4
5	1,342,177,280	5	83,886,080	5	5,242,880	5	327,680	5	20,480	5	1,280	5	80	5	5
6	1,610,612,736	6	100,663,296	6	6,291,456	6	393,216	6	24,576	6	1,536	6	96	6	6
7	1,879,048,192	7	117,440,512	7	7,340,032	7	458,752	7	28,672	7	1,792	7	112	7	7
8	2,147,483,648	8	134,217,728	8	8,388,608	8	524,288	8	32,768	8	2,048	8	128	8	8
9	2,415,919,104	9	150,994,944	9	9,437,184	9	589,824	9	36,864	9	2,304	9	144	9	9
A	2,684,354,560	A	167,772,160	A	10,485,760	A	655,360	A	40,960	A	2,560	A	160	A	10
B	2,952,790,016	B	184,549,376	B	11,534,336	B	720,896	B	45,056	B	2,816	B	176	B	11
C	3,221,225,472	C	201,326,592	C	12,582,912	C	786,432	C	49,152	C	3,072	C	192	C	12
D	3,489,660,928	D	218,103,808	D	13,631,488	D	851,968	D	53,248	D	3,328	D	208	D	13
E	3,758,096,384	E	234,881,024	E	14,680,064	E	917,504	E	57,344	E	3,584	E	224	E	14
F	4,026,531,840	F	251,658,240	F	15,728,640	F	983,040	F	61,440	F	3,840	F	240	F	15
8		7		6		5		4		3		2		1	

1976_{10}

$7_{16} \leftarrow -1792_{10}$

184_{10}

$B_{16} \leftarrow 176_{10}$

$8_{16} \leftarrow 8_{10}$

Figure 1-10 Converting decimal numbers to hexadecimal.

convert this number to its hexadecimal equivalent and use the conversion table our task would be simplified. (See Figure 1-11.)

We use one hexadecimal symbol to represent four bits. Thus the hexadecimal equivalent of the binary number 1010101111001101_2 is $ABCD_{16}$. We

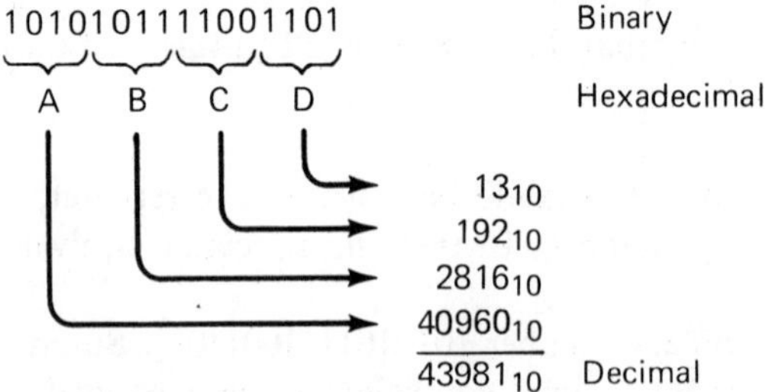

Figure 1-11 Converting binary numbers to hexadecimal.

use the conversion table to find that the decimal equivalent of the number $ABCD_{16}$ is $43{,}981_{10}$.

We can reverse this process to find the binary equivalent of a decimal number. First we take the hexadecimal equivalent of the decimal number and convert the result to binary. For example, the binary equivalent of the number 1976_{10} is 011110111000_2. To obtain this result, we use the hexadecimal equivalent of 1976_{10}. Our previous example showed this number to be $7B8_{16}$. Now we convert each single hexadecimal digit to four bits. The result is 011110111000_2. It is not necessary to represent the leftmost zero—we do it by convention.

The hexadecimal numbering system provides a convenient means of representing cumbersome binary numbers. If this numbering system is to aid us in understanding how the computer operates, we must develop the concept of hexadecimal arithmetic.

Hexadecimal Arithmetic. Hexadecimal addition is straightforward as long as we do not have to consider a carry. For example, the operation

$$\begin{array}{r} 32D_{16} \\ +191_{16} \\ \hline 4BE_{16} \end{array}$$

is not difficult, providing you remember that a decimal eleven is equivalent to the hexadecimal digit B.

A carry is involved when the result of an addition is equal to or greater than the base of sixteen. For example

$$\begin{array}{r} 32D_{16} \\ +804_{16} \\ \hline B31_{16} \end{array}$$

The addition of the first two digits results in the number seventeen (thirteen plus four). We represent a one in the rightmost position and a carry into the sixteens position. We can state this another way. The result is seventeen, we subtract the base to obtain one, and add sixteen to the operand.

$$\begin{array}{r} 32D_{16} \\ +804_{16} \\ \hline \end{array}$$

seventeen or sixteen plus 1, thus

$$\begin{array}{r} 3\phantom{D_{16}} \\ 3\not{2}D_{16} \\ +804_{16} \\ \hline B31_{16} \end{array}$$

The confusing aspect of hexadecimal arithmetic is the use of letters as symbols. For example

$$\begin{array}{r} 813D_{16} \\ +79AE_{16} \\ \hline FAEB_{16} \end{array}$$

Not only does this example involve a carry

$$\begin{array}{r} 813D_{16} \\ +79AE_{16} \\ \hline 27\ (16 + 11)\ \text{thus} \end{array}$$

$$\begin{array}{r} 4\ \ \ \\ 81\not{3}D_{16} \\ +79AE_{16} \\ \hline FAEB_{16} \end{array}$$

but each digit in the answer is represented by a letter. This new concept becomes very comfortable with practice.

Hexadecimal subtraction, like addition, is not difficult until we must borrow. Consider the example

$$\begin{array}{r} A9C3_{16} \\ -1022_{16} \\ \hline 99A1_{16} \end{array}$$

We find we can subtract a letter from a letter; remembering, of course, that the letters represent digits in the hexadecimal numbering system.

$$\begin{array}{r} AF8B_{16} \\ -0C2A_{16} \\ \hline A361_{16} \end{array}$$

Now let's examine a situation where we must borrow.

$$\begin{array}{r} 9815_{16} \\ -7391_{16} \\ \hline \end{array}$$

We proceed from right to left. We subtract one from five—the result is four.

$$\begin{array}{r} 9815_{16} \\ -7391_{16} \\ \hline 4_{16} \end{array}$$

Proceeding to the next digit, we find that we cannot subtract nine from one. We must borrow from the next position, thus

$$
\begin{array}{rrrr}
 & 7 & 11 & \\
9 & \not{8} & \not{1} & 5_{16} \\
-7 & 3 & 9 & 1_{16} \\
\hline
 & & & 4_{16}
\end{array}
$$

In this example we are not borrowing ten, but *sixteen*. As we approach the second column, we are not subtracting nine from eleven but nine from *seventeen*! A hexadecimal 11_{16} is equivalent to a decimal seventeen! Thus

$$
\begin{array}{rrrr}
 & 7 & 11 & \\
9 & \not{8} & \not{1} & 5_{16} \\
-7 & 3 & 9 & 1_{16} \\
\hline
2 & 4 & 8 & 4_{16}
\end{array}
$$

See if you can use the same approach to verify the following example.

$$
\begin{array}{r}
903C_{16} \\
-0CDE_{16} \\
\hline
835E_{16}
\end{array}
$$

We also can use the complement approach to hexadecimal subtraction. Let's consider our first subtraction example.

$$
\begin{array}{r}
A9C3_{16} \\
-1022_{16} \\
\hline
99A1_{16}
\end{array}
$$

Using the complement approach, we take the sixteen's complement of the subtrahend and add. The sixteen's complement of 1022_{16} is $EFDE_{16}$. We obtain the complement by subtracting the left digits from fifteen, and the rightmost non-zero digit from sixteen, and use the complement in hexadecimal addition.

$$
\begin{array}{rl}
A9C3_{16} & \\
+EFDE_{16} & \\
\hline
99A1_{16} & \text{and a carry}
\end{array}
$$

The carry tells us the answer is positive and is carried in true form.

As a last example, let's consider a subtraction which gives a negative result.

$$
\begin{array}{r}
907B_{16} \\
-ABCO_{16} \\
\hline
\end{array}
$$

We take the complement of the subtrahend and add.

$$\begin{array}{r} 907B_{16} \\ +5440_{16} \\ \hline E4BB_{16} \end{array}$$

There is no carry. The result is negative and is carried in complement form. We must recomplement to find that our answer is $-1B45_{16}$.

PROBLEMS

1.1 Use the basic data processing pattern to discuss the components of the computer environment. Distinguish between input and output devices, CPU and Storage, Control Section and ALU.

1.2 Discuss the concept of data as it applies to the computer environment. Include the hierarchy of data, data recording media, and the data recording methods in your discussion.

1.3 Express the following numbers in expanded notation.

- a. 1984_{10}
- b. 1984_{16}
- c. 10111_2
- d. $A345B_{16}$
- e. 127_8

1.4 Give the binary and hexadecimal equivalents of following decimal numbers.

decimal	binary	hexadecimal
10		
15		
16		
27		
89		
189		

1.5 Convert the following decimal numbers to their hexadecimal equivalents.

- a. 163
- b. 1984
- c. 13,908
- d. 15,889
- e. 123,997

1.6 Convert the following hexadecimal numbers to their decimal equivalents.

a. 10_{16}
b. 16_{16}
c. $12C5_{16}$
d. $A3C7_{16}$
e. $12AB0_{16}$

1.7 Convert the following numbers to complement form.

a. 123_{10}
b. 10111_2
c. 1010111_2
d. $108A_{16}$
e. $90CDE_{16}$

1.8 Perform the following arithmetic operations.

a. $\begin{array}{r} 10111_2 \\ +11011_2 \\ \hline \end{array}$ **b.** $\begin{array}{r} 10111_2 \\ -01111_2 \\ \hline \end{array}$ **c.** $\begin{array}{r} 11000_2 \\ -11110_2 \\ \hline \end{array}$

d. $\begin{array}{r} 129A_{16} \\ +2271_{16} \\ \hline \end{array}$ **e.** $\begin{array}{r} 603D_{16} \\ +ABCD_{16} \\ \hline \end{array}$ **f.** $\begin{array}{r} 90A6_{16} \\ -347C_{16} \\ \hline \end{array}$

g. $\begin{array}{r} 790C_{16} \\ -8330_{16} \\ \hline \end{array}$

2

S/370 Programming Concepts

A program is a series of instructions telling the computer how to input, process, and output data. These instructions are executed, one at a time, by the Control Section of the CPU.

The instructions the computer executes consist of an operation or op-code, and usually the addresses of one or more operands. A typical instruction might appear as

0001101001000001

This is a machine-language instruction. The computer interprets the bits comprising the op-code and the operand addresses, and knows what it is to do. We find machine language cumbersome, and often use hexadecimal notation for clarity. The instruction shown above is represented in hexadecimal as

1A41

But even this notation is awkward for the programmer to use. He must remember which op-code is associated with which operation. He must remember how to address each operand. For these reasons, we do not use machine language, but code our programs at another language level.

LANGUAGE LEVELS

The machine language is the lowest level of programming language—the language closest to the computer itself. It also is the most difficult level for the programmer to use. But consider the instruction

```
AR 4,1
```

This is a symbolic instruction (using symbols to replace bits) which tells the computer to add the contents of register 1—a register is a storage unit within the CPU—to the contents of register 4 and to place the result in register 4. Rather than use the hexadecimal or binary op-code, the programmer uses the notation AR (Add Register). We call this notation a *mnemonic*.

The symbolic instructions constitute the second level of computer languages. The S/370 Assembly Language is a symbolic language. Each type of computer has its own symbolic language. The rules of the symbolic language are closely tied to the design of the computer itself. For this reason, a program written in S/370 Assembly Language usually cannot be executed on another manufacturer's computer, or even on another IBM computer.*

The third level of languages is often called high-level or problem-oriented languages. The instructions comprising these languages are more closely related to the problem than to the computer involved. COBOL (Common Business Oriented Language) is designed to solve business data processing problems. FORTRAN (FORmula TRANslator) is related to scientific problems.

Although the rules for coding high-level languages may vary among manufacturers, the languages are very similar. A program written in Honeywell COBOL will run on an IBM S/370 with only minor changes.

There are, then, three levels of computer languages—machine language, symbolic language, and high-level language. The computer only understands the bits comprising the machine language instruction. As programmers, we find the machine language awkward. We write our instructions to the computer in either symbolic or high-level languages.

The instructions comprising the symbolic or high-level language (*the source module*) must be translated to machine language, before the computer can execute these instructions (*the object module*). We call this process of translation *assembling* or *compiling* the program (Figure 2-1). We usually associate the term *assembly* with the translation of a symbolic language to machine language, and the term *compiling* or *compilation* with the translation of high-level languages to machine languages.

*The S/360 and S/370 Assembler Languages are upward compatible.

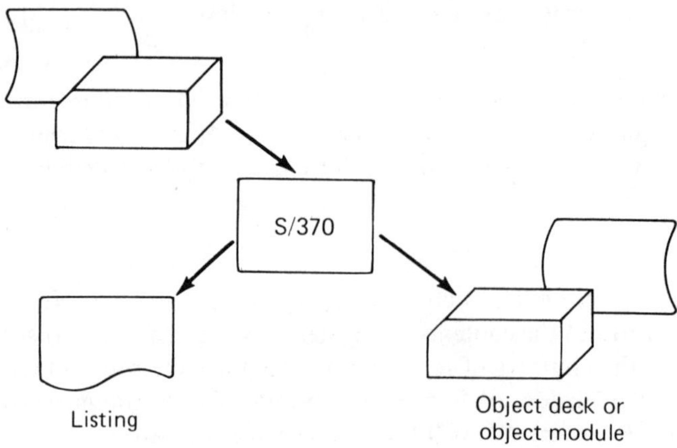

Figure 2-1 Translating source programs to object programs.

An operating system program, supplied by the vendor, performs this translation. This text is concerned with the symbolic language for the IBM S/360 and S/370 computers. We use the term *assembler* to refer to the translation program supplied by IBM. The assembler is the operating system program which translates symbolic source statements into machine-language object statements.

THE FLOWCHART

The programmer must know what his (or her) program is to accomplish before he codes the instructions comprising the program. He usually receives a description of the purpose of the program, the *program specifications*, from the systems designer. He must carefully examine the program specifications, determining how he will approach the solution to the problem. Often the programmer documents the program logic using a flowchart.

A flowchart is a graphic representation of a process. We can flowchart almost any operation. Let's consider the processes and decisions involved in getting up in the morning. The symbol at the top of Figure 2-2 tells us where the flowchart begins. We use the oval to mark the beginning (and end) of the flowchart.

The alarm rings. The rectangle is used to show a process—something is happening. We then make a decision. The diamond is the symbol for a decision. Is it 7:00? There are two exits from the decision. If it is not seven o'clock we reset the alarm and go back to sleep. If it is seven o'clock, we get up and listen to the news.

Now another decision. Is it cold? If it is cold we dress warmly; otherwise wear light clothes. And the final process, leave for school.

The steps employed in solving a programming problem involve processes and decisions. In addition, we must show how data are input and how data are output. We use different symbols to represent these operations.

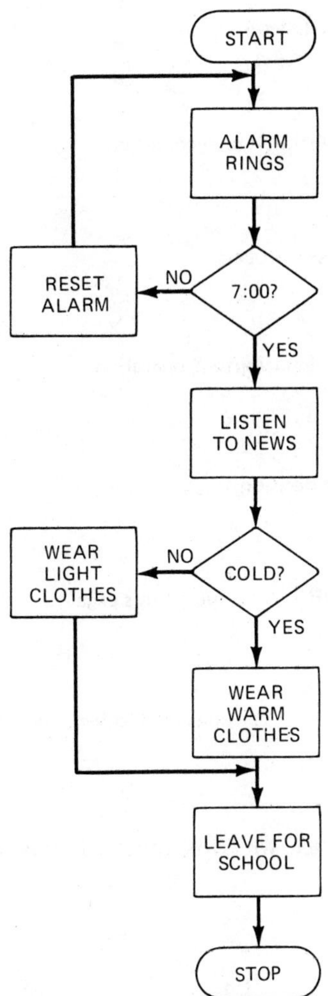

Figure 2-2 The flowchart.

Flowcharting Symbols

There are about two dozen symbols used in program and system flowcharts. The most frequently used are shown in Figure 2-3 on page 32.

The Arrow. The arrow is used to show the order or sequence in which the instructions are executed. The solid arrow shows a sequence which must be followed.

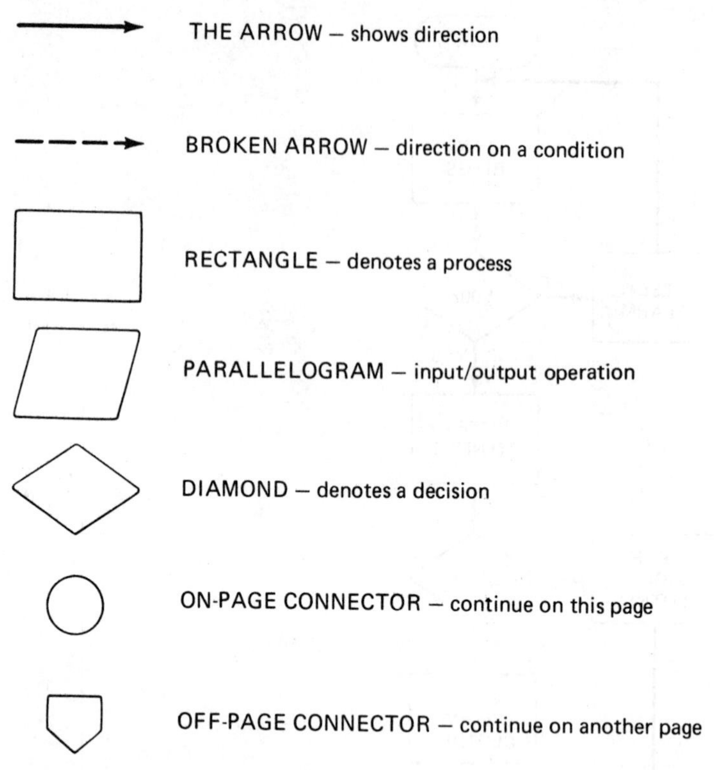

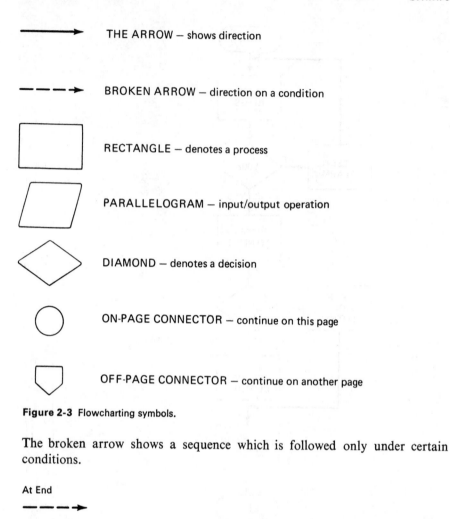

Figure 2-3 Flowcharting symbols.

The broken arrow shows a sequence which is followed only under certain conditions.

At End

─ ─ ─ ➤

The Rectangle. The rectangle is the most frequently used symbol. The rectangle is used for any operation other than a decision. All arithmetic operations and move operations are shown in a rectangle.

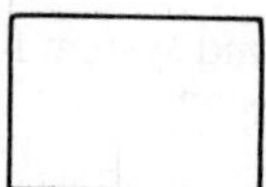

The Parallelogram. The parallelogram is used to show the movement of data from an input device to the computer, and from main storage to the output device. We often call the parallelogram an I/O (input/output) symbol.

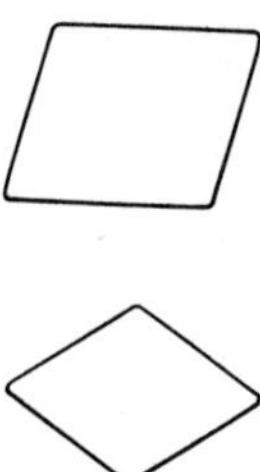

The Diamond. The diamond is used to show that a decision must be made. One of two (or three) paths may be taken depending upon a condition. For example, if the quantity A is greater than the quantity B, we go to ROUTINE 1; otherwise we go to ROUTINE 2.

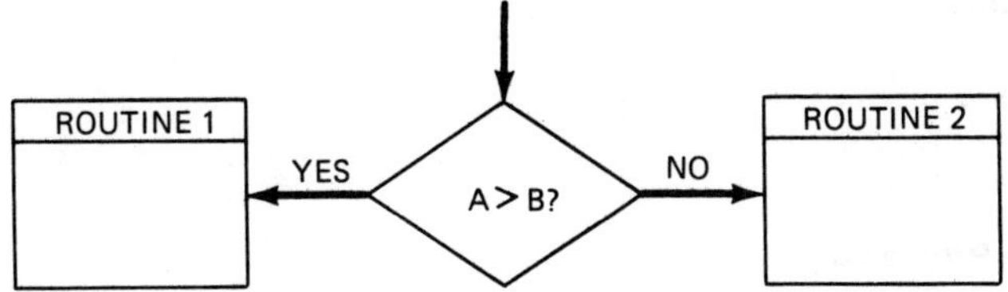

Can you think of a situation where three alternatives are possible? To a programmer this would be a decision which requires three exits. Suppose we are examining a number. The quantity *X* might be positive, negative, or zero. This condition requires three possible directions. Notice that the arrow shows where we enter the decision, and the direction of flow when we leave the decision box.

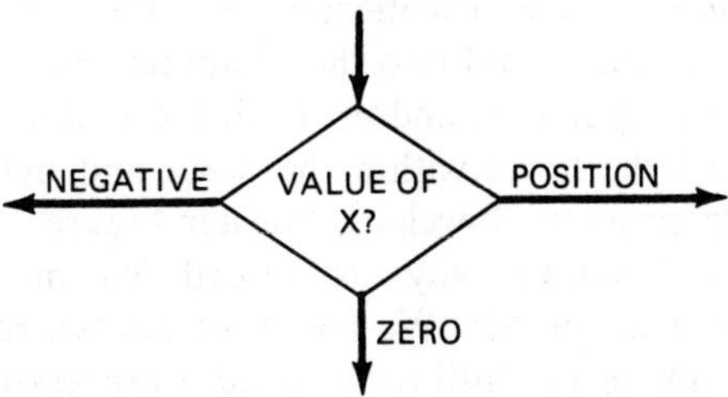

The Connector. The small circle, the on-page connector, shows that the sequence of symbols is interrupted and is continued on another section of the page.

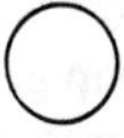

Usually we label the connectors to show were the flowchart continues.

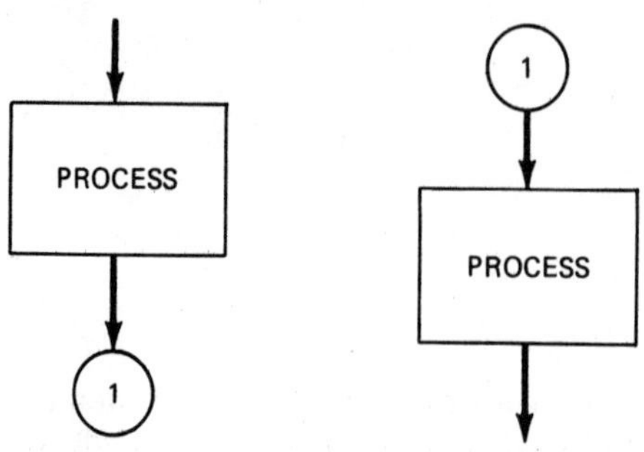

If we must continue the flowchart on another page, we use the off-page connector.

Sample Problems

Let's see how these flowcharting symbols may be used in a simple problem. The examples we will discuss are programs which are solved using the Assembly Language later in the text. A complete description of each problem is found in Appendix C.

Program 1 Program 1 asks us to print certain fields from the employee master file. One line is to be printed for each record. Figure 2-4 illustrates this problem. We call the graphic in Figure 2-4 a *memory map*. The memory map shows the movement of data through storage. A record is read into the computer, the fields are moved from the input area to the output area, and the record is written.

Notice that we label the fields within the input and output areas. We reference these fields in the program flowchart shown in Figure 2-5. At this point we have read, moved, and written only one record. We must repeat these operations for each record in the file. We could, of course, repeat the three symbols again and again and again until each record is processed. If there were 100 records within the file, we would have to repeat the symbols 100 times. We would, of course, always need to know how many records comprised the file.

A more satisfactory approach is to show graphically that we repeat these *same* three operations. We do this by bringing the directional arrow back to the READ operation (Figure 2-6). We say we *loop* back to the READ statement.

Now we have another problem. How many times do we repeat these operations? We cannot continue indefinitely. We want to stop processing when a certain condition occurs—when all the cards have been processed. We call this condition end-of-file time and use the broken arrow to show the direction we

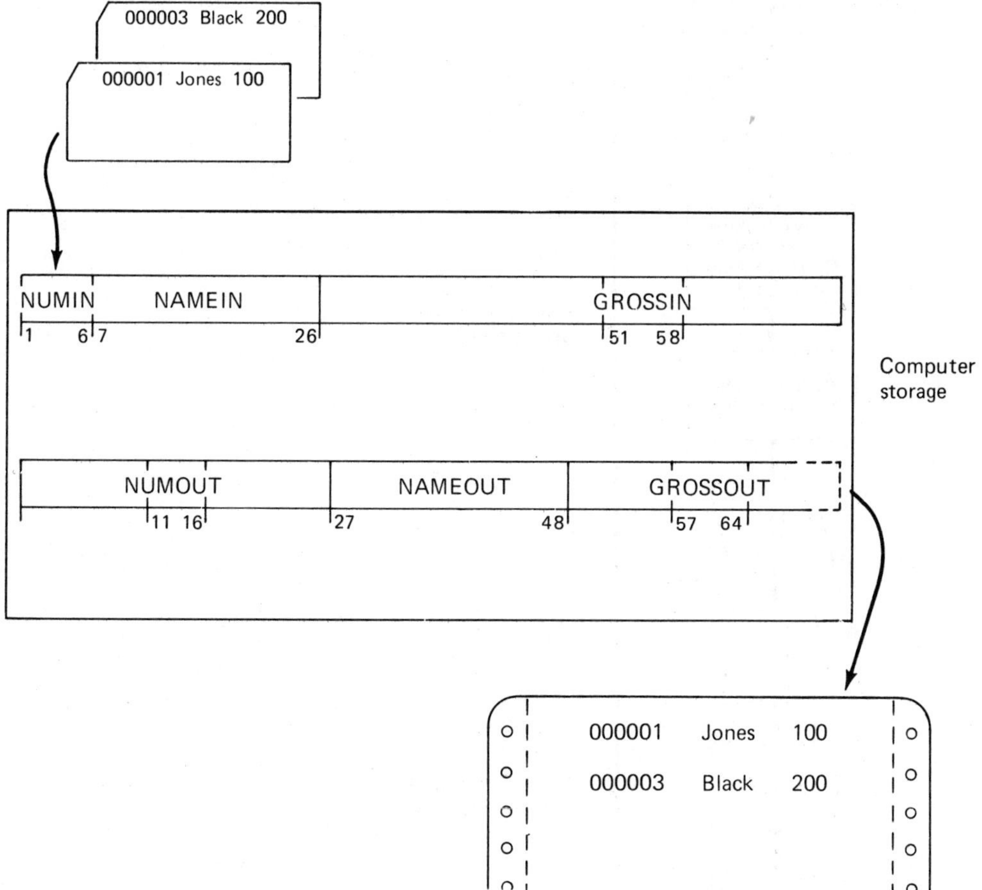

Figure 2-4 Program 1—memory map.

are to follow when the *end-of-file* condition occurs (Figure 2-7). At this point the program is complete and we stop processing. The oval marks the end of the program.

A Decision. Now let's assume that we are to print only certain records—perhaps only the records of those employees earning more than $10,000 a year. This flowchart involves a decision. Let's follow the logic shown in Figure 2-8.

The oval marks the beginning of the program. First, we read a card. Remember, before we process or make a decision, the data must be in storage. We then examine the earnings field. If the earnings are more than $10,000, we move the record to the output area and write the record. We then return to read the next card.

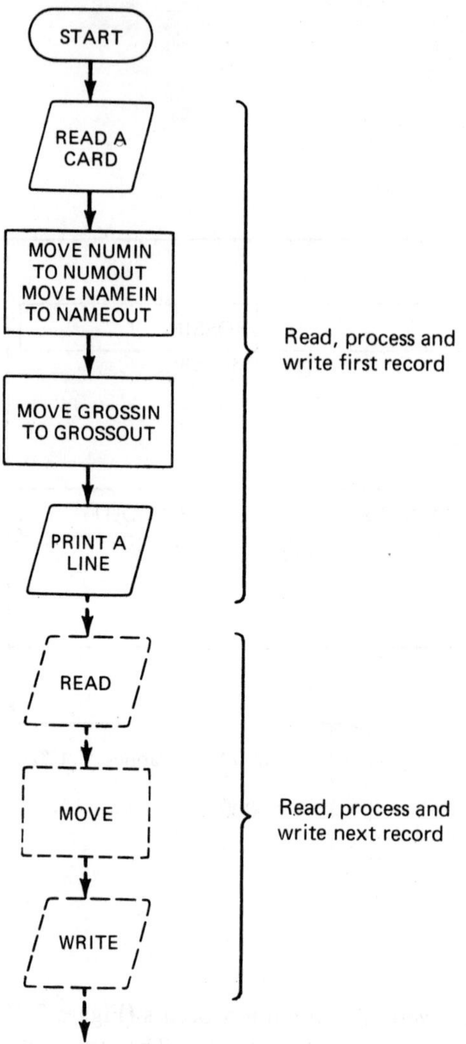

Figure 2-5 Program 1—flowchart.

If, however, the earnings are not greater than $10,000, we do not process the record, but loop back to read another card. In this example we use the on-page connectors, rather than extend the arrow back to the READ box.

When all the records have been processed, the program is complete. The oval marks the end of the program.

The flowchart is a tool which allows the programmer to represent the logical operations involved in solving a given problem. Now let's examine some programming techniques and see how the flowchart helps us understand the operations involved.

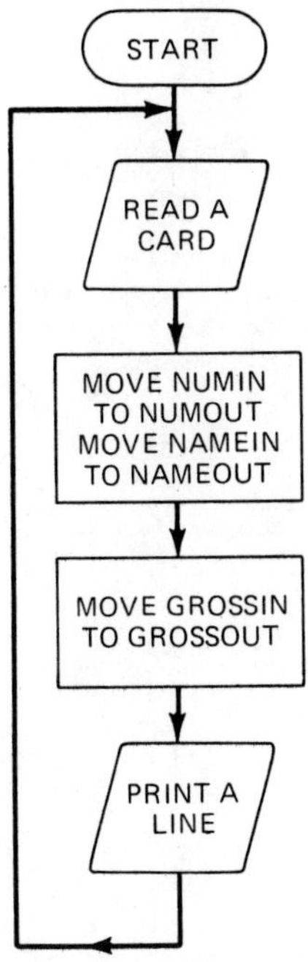

Figure 2-6 Program 1—flowchart showing the use of a loop.

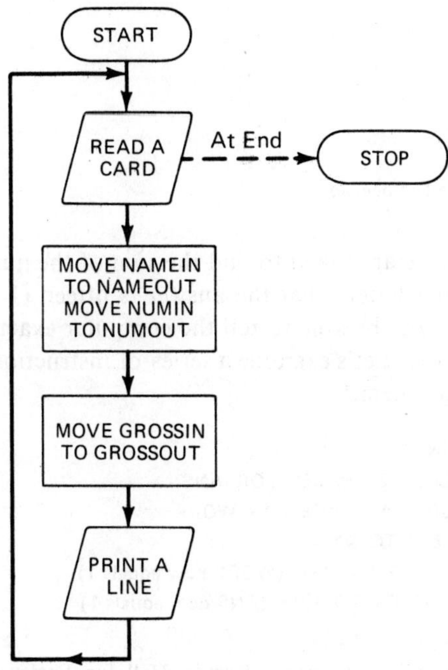

Figure 2-7 Program 1—flowchart with end-of-file condition.

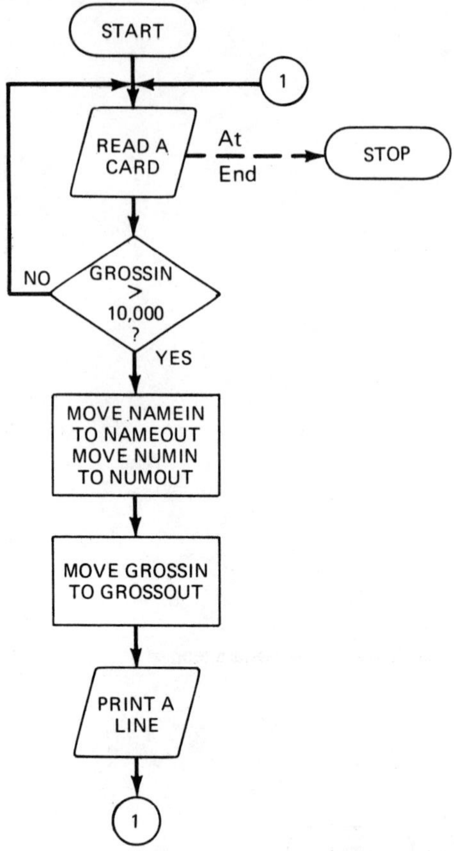

Figure 2-8 Program 1—flowchart; a decision.

PROGRAMMING CONCEPTS

In our next problem, we are asked to find the sum of the numbers from 1 to 5. We can see immediately that the answer is fifteen (1 + 2 + 3 + 4 + 5). We must, however, be able to tell the computer exactly what steps to take to arrive at this answer. Let's examine a series of instructions which represents a solution to this problem.*

```
BEGIN
RESERVE 2 SPACES FOR ANS
RESERVE 1 SPACE FOR WORK
MOVE 0 TO ANS
MOVE 1 TO WORK (WORK now equals 1)
ADD WORK TO ANS (ANS now equals 1)
```

*Fink and Burian, *Business Data Processing*, Prentice-Hall, Inc. Englewood Cliffs, N.J., 1974.

```
7  ADD 1 TO WORK (WORK now equals 2)
8  ADD WORK TO ANS (ANS now equals 3)
9  ADD 1 TO WORK (WORK now equals 3)
10 ADD WORK TO ANS (ANS now equals 6)
11 ADD 1 TO WORK (WORK now equals 4)
12 ADD WORK TO ANS (ANS now equals 10)
13 ADD 1 TO WORK (WORK now equals 5)
14 ADD WORK TO ANS (ANS now equals 15)
15 PRINT ANS
16 STOP
```

This program (Figure 2-9) is correct in that it does produce the right answer. However, we find we are repeating the same instructions again and again. We must try to make the program more efficient.

We can code a programming loop, instructing the computer to go back to a certain instruction.*

```
   BEGIN
   RESERVE 2 SPACES FOR ANS
   RESERVE 1 SPACE FOR WORK
   MOVE 0 TO ANS
   MOVE 1 TO WORK
6  ADD WORK TO ANS
   ADD 1 TO WORK
   GO TO 6
   PRINT ANS
   STOP
```

It is not necessary to number each statement. Usually, we label only those statements we wish to reference in the program.

When we flowchart this solution, we find we are caught in a never-ending loop (see Figure 2-10). We need a decision to tell us when to stop executing these instructions. Our program becomes

```
   BEGIN
   RESERVE 2 SPACES FOR ANS
   RESERVE 1 SPACE FOR WORK
   MOVE 0 TO ANS
   MOVE 1 TO WORK
6  ADD WORK TO ANS
   IF WORK EQUALS 5 GO TO 10 ELSE
   ADD 1 TO WORK
   GO TO 6
10 PRINT ANS
   STOP
```

*Fink and Burian, *Business Data Processing*, Prentice-Hall, Inc., Englewood Cliffs, N.J., 1974.

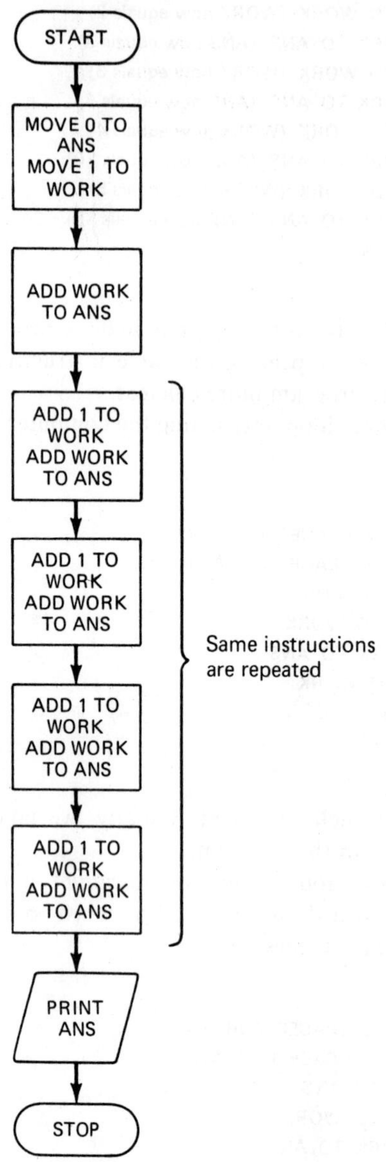

Figure 2-9 Sum of the numbers from 1–4.

We have added a very special instruction. The statement

```
IF WORK EQUALS 5 GO TO 10 ELSE
ADD 1 TO WORK
GO TO 6
```

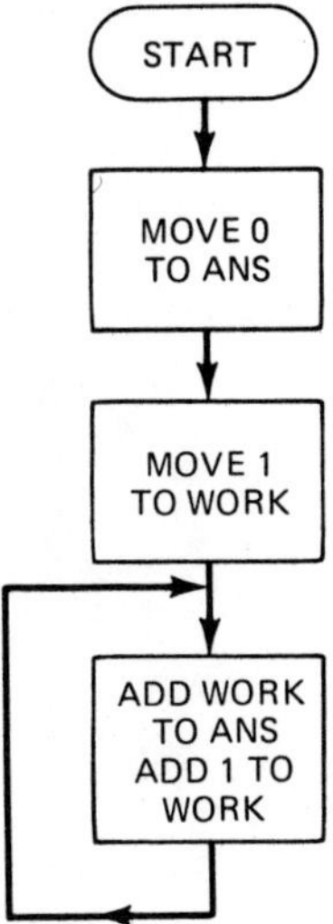

Figure 2-10 Sum problem—flowcharting a loop.

is a *branching* instruction. A branching instruction changes the order in which the instructions are executed. In this instance, the next instruction executed depends upon the value of WORK. We say that we branch *conditionally*, thus this is a conditional branch instruction.

Some branching instructions are unconditional. For example

```
GO TO PRINT
```

In this example, we go to PRINT under any circumstances. We branch *unconditionally* to PRINT. A conditional branch would appear as

```
IF ANS IS NEGATIVE GO TO PRINT
```

When we use a conditional branch instruction, we must use a decision diamond when we flowchart the solution (Figure 2-11).

This solution works because we have a means of controlling the number of times we increment WORK and ANS. We *count* the number of times we execute these instructions. We are using the storage area WORK as a *counter*. Each time we execute the instructions, we add 1 to WORK. When WORK equals 5, we exit from the loop and the program is complete.

Our program consists of four phases—the initialization phase, the body, the test, and the exit. We set initial values to ANS and WORK during the initialization phase:

```
MOVE 0 TO ANS
MOVE 1 TO WORK
```

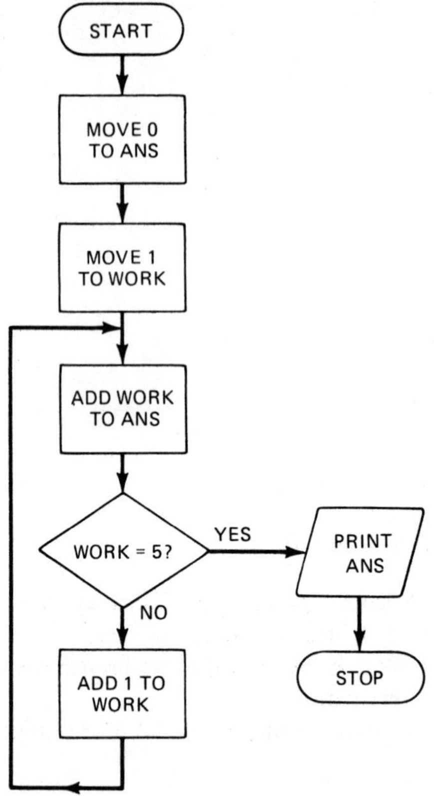

Figure 2-11 Sum problem—flowcharting a conditional branch.

The body of the loop consists of the instruction

```
ADD WORK TO ANS
```

The test phase consists of the instruction

```
IF WORK EQUALS 5 GO TO 10
ELSE ADD 1 TO WORK
GO TO 6
```

We do not enter the exit phase

```
PRINT ANS
STOP
```

until WORK is equal to 5.

All programming loops follow this same general pattern and are controlled in the same way. We need a counter to keep track of the number of times we execute the instructions comprising the body of the loop. We must initialize this counter at the beginning of the loop, increment the value in the counter each time we execute the loop and, finally, test the value of the counter against a constant. We call this constant the *limit*.

In our program we initialize the counter WORK to a value of 1. We increment the counter by 1 each time we execute the loop, and test the counter against the limit of 5. When the value in the counter equals the limit of 5, we exit from the loop, print the answer, and stop.

Suppose we now are asked to find the sum of the numbers from 1 to 10. We must modify our program. We must change the limit from 5 to 10. The solution to our program is not flexible—each time the limit changes, we must make a change to the program.

We can improve our program if we accept the limit from a punched card. Up until now we have been testing the counter WORK against a *constant* such as 5 or 10. If we accept the limit from a card, the limit becomes *variable*.

Let's assume that the first two columns of a card specify the limit of the series. If we punch the number 5 in the card, we are to find the sum of the numbers from 1 to 5. If we punch the number 99 in the card, we are to find the sum of the numbers from 1 to 99. We must, of course, allow for a larger answer. The sum of the numbers from 1 to 99 is quite large.

We now must include the instructions to read a card into computer storage. We will use the instruction

```
READ CARD,LIMIT
```

to read a card into memory and to place the data from the first two columns of that card in an area of storage called LIMIT. Our program now becomes

```
   BEGIN
   RESERVE 4 SPACES FOR ANS
   RESERVE 2 SPACES FOR WORK
   RESERVE 2 SPACES FOR LIMIT
   MOVE 0 TO ANS
   MOVE 1 TO WORK
   READ CARD, LIMIT
 6 ADD WORK TO ANS
   IF WORK EQUALS LIMIT GO TO 10 ELSE
   ADD 1 TO WORK
   GO TO 6
10 PRINT ANS
   STOP
```

The value developed in ANS depends upon the number of times we execute the instructions comprising the loop, and consequently on the value in LIMIT. If we punch a 05 in the card, the value in LIMIT becomes 5 and we find the sum of the numbers from 1 to 5. If however, we punch a 27 in the card, we find the sum of the numbers from 1 to 27. Notice that we do not change the program each time we change the limit—we merely change the data card.

The instructions we have used in our programs are not assembly language instructions. They are hypothetical instructions used to illustrate certain programming techniques. In later chapters, we will develop the assembly language solutions to these same problems.

We have developed the flowchart as a tool the programmer uses to plan the steps that must be taken in coding a program. We have examined some basic programming techniques, developing the concept of a loop, and the need for loop conrol.

PROBLEMS

2.1 Indicate the purpose of the following flowcharting symbols

a. ⟶

b.  - - - ⟶

c. 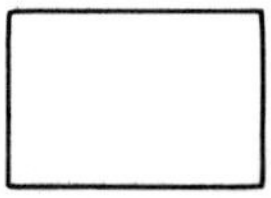 (rectangle)

d. 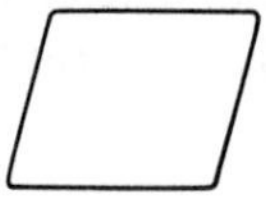 (parallelogram)

e. 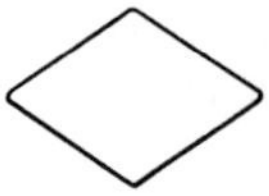 (diamond)

f. 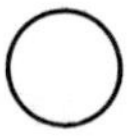 (circle)

g.  (pentagon)

2.2 Develop a flowchart to find the sum of a series. The limit of the series is entered on a punched card. The first four columns of the card contain the limit. Write the result to the printer.

2.3 Assume a computer has as its output device a printer capable of printing 120 characters per line. Our input is a deck of 80-column cards, some of which have a 1-punch (a punch in row 1) in column 80. List those cards with a 1-punch in column 80. Bypass all other cards. Remember, we are to use only 80 out of the 120 spaces on each line of the printed sheet. The rest are to remain blank. Develop a flowchart to solve the problem.

2.4 Develop flowcharts to solve the following variations of Program 6 in Appendix C.

a. Program 6a
b. Program 6b
c. Program 6c
d. Program 6d
e. Program 6e
f. Program 6f
g. Program 6g

2.5 Answer the following questions with respect to the program shown below. Notice that we use names called symbolic labels rather than numbers to label the instructions.

```
         BEGIN
         RESERVE 2 SPACES FOR ANS
         RESERVE 1 SPACE FOR WORK
         MOVE 0 TO ANS
         MOVE 1 TO WORK
LOOP     ADD WORK TO ANS
         IF WORK EQUALS 4 GO TO EXIT ELSE
         ADD 1 TO WORK
         GO TO LOOP
EXIT     PRINT ANS
         STOP
```

a. Which of the following are examples of branching instructions?

```
1. STOP
2. GO TO LOOP
3. IF WORK EQUALS 4 GO TO EXIT
4. ADD WORK TO ANS
```

b. What would happen if we changed the statement IF WORK EQUALS 4 GO TO EXIT to the statement IF WORK EQUALS 10 GO TO EXIT.

c. The statement, IF WORK EQUALS 4 GO TO EXIT is an example of

1. an exit statement
2. an unconditional branching instruction
3. a conditional branching instruction
4. none of these

d. Which of the following statements are true and which are false?

1. All instructions in a program must be labeled.

2. The number 4 in the statement, IF WORK EQUALS 4, is used as a limit.

3. The language used in this program somewhat resembles high-level languages such as COBOL.

4. Before we could test this program, it would have to be translated into machine language.

5. If we change the value of the number 4 in the statement IF WORK EQUALS 4, our answer remains the same.

6. The instruction PRINT ANS is part of the processing loop.

7. The instruction MOVE 0 TO ANS is considered to be an output instruction.

3

S/370 Hardware Concepts

We have used the basic data processing pattern to introduce the terms input, processing, and output. This chapter examines the processing function, discussing how we represent data in storage, and how the CPU functions.

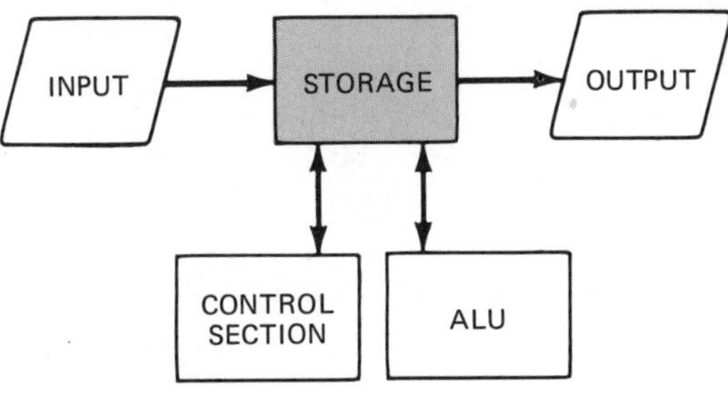

Figure 3-1 The basic data processing pattern.

MAIN STORAGE The computer consists of two parts—the storage unit and the CPU. (See Figure 3-1.) We use the terms *main* or *primary* storage to reference the storage unit. Main storage is used to store information. This information includes both the data to be processed and the instructions telling the computer how to process the data.

Divisions of Storage

We have seen that the smallest unit in storage is the bit. The bit is useful for representing binary numbers. Each bit corresponds to a single binary digit. But we also must represent letters and special characters. To do this we use a special code* which requires a group of eight bits to represent a single character. We call this group of eight bits a *byte*.

Bytes are often grouped together. We use the term *fullword* to reference a group of four bytes, the term *halfword* to reference a group of two bytes, and the term *double word* to reference a group of eight bytes. Remember, we are now talking about bytes *not* bits.

Addressing Main Storage

The computer instruction references data. Remember, the instruction does not contain the data itself, but the *address* of each operand.

Data residing in computer storage is addressed using a 24-bit (six hexadecimal digit) address. We address bytes, not bits. You might think of storage as a series of houses on a street. Each house (byte) contains eight rooms (bits). The address of each house contains six digits. The address of the first house is 000001_{16}, the second 000002_{16}, and so on, until the tenth house. We include leading zeros to bring the address to six digits. The address of the tenth house is $00000A_{16}$—a hexadecimal ten. We continue in this manner until each house on the street has an address. The highest possible address is $FFFFFF_{16}$—the largest number we can express in six hexadecimal digits.

We usually do not address data in storage using the absolute address. We use three numbers to determine the absolute, or effective address, of data in storage. For example

$$\begin{array}{r} 004000_{16} \\ +005000_{16} \\ +\quad 200_{16} \\ \hline 009200_{16} \end{array}$$

We add three numbers to find the absolute address of the operand in storage. In this instance, the effective address of the operand is 009200_{16}. Remember, this is a hexadecimal number.

Where do these numbers come from? Two of these numbers are held in storage areas within the CPU called *registers*. There are sixteen registers available. A register contains 32 bits or a fullword of data. For example, register 3

*We use the EBCDIC code to represent decimal numbers, letters, and special characters.

might contain the number $00000000000000000100000000000000_2$. This notation is cumbersome. We use hexadecimal shorthand to express the same number as 00004000_{16}. One hexadecimal digit for each group of four binary bits.

Registers can hold numbers which may be used to determine storage addresses. If register 3 contains the number 00004000_{16} and register 4 contains the number 00005000_{16}, then we could use these two numbers to locate data in storage.

But what about the third number in our example, the number 200_{16}? This is also a hexadecimal number, but it is not contained in a register. It is part of the computer instruction itself.

Let's return for a moment to the instruction. We said that the instruction contains the *address* of the data to be processed. In a previous example, we considered the hypothetical instruction FA40005000. We said the operation code FA specified an add operation. The instruction tells the computer to add the contents of location 5000 to the contents of location 4000 and to place the result at location 4000.

We now know that the computer instruction does not carry the absolute (effective) address of the data. We know, also, that the effective address is determined by three numbers—two of which are contained in registers. Let's assume that register 2 contains the number 00001500_{16}, register 3 contains the number 00002000_{16}, and register 4 contains the number 00002500_{16}. Now let's examine the instruction FA2350034500 (Figure 3-2). The op-code FA specifies an add operation. The address of the first operand is determined by the contents of registers 2 and 3 plus the number 500_{16} contained within the instruction itself. We know that register 2 contains the number 00001500_{16}, and that the number 00002000_{16} is in register 3. The effective address of the first operand becomes $00003A00_{16}$. When we follow the same approach, we find that the effective address of the second operand becomes $00004A00_{16}$.

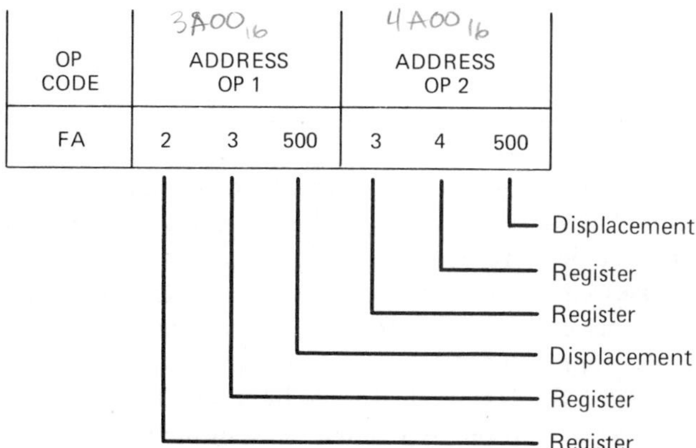

Figure 3-2 An S/370 instruction.

In determining storage addresses, we do not use the entire 32-bit number in the register. We use only the low-order or rightmost 24 bits. Thus, in the example shown in Figure 3-2, if register 2 contains 99001500_{16}, the effective address is unchanged. We are only interested in the number 001500_{16}. We ignore the first two hexadecimal digits.

We call the 3-digit number contained in the instruction the *displacement*. We now can say that the effective address of data in main storage is determined by the contents of two registers (the *index register* and the *base register*) and a displacement.

Storage Boundaries

Some addresses within main storage are special. We call these special addresses storage boundaries. Any storage boundary that is divisible by two is called a halfword boundary. To determine if an address lies on a halfword boundary, we need only examine the last digit. If the last digit of the *hexadecimal* address is divisible by two, the address lies on a halfword boundary. For example, the address 009876_{16} lies on a halfword boundary. The address $00987E_{16}$ is also on a halfword boundary—the digit E_{16} is a decimal 14, divisible by two. The address 009879_{16} is not on a halfword boundary. Can you see why?

Fullword boundaries are storage addresses which are divisible by four. Double word boundaries are addresses which are divisible by eight. Let's look at some examples.

	boundary		
address	**halfword**	**fullword**	**double word**
$00987C_{16}$	x	x	
009080_{16}	x	x	x
$00ABCD_{16}$			
009088_{16}	x	x	x
909084_{16}	x	x	

Notice that addresses which are on doubleword boundaries also are on halfword and fullword boundaries. If the last digit of an address is zero, the address resides on a double word boundary.

Addresses which are on fullword boundaries also are on halfword boundaries. Any number divisible by four also is divisible by two! (See Figure 3-3.)

Another approach to boundaries involves looking at the bit configuration (binary digits) of the last digit. The address 008032_{16} resides on a halfword boundary. If we look at the bit configuration of the last digit—that is, 0010_2—we see one low-order or rightmost zero. Halfword boundaries must have a low-order zero in the *binary* representation of the address. Remember, the computer

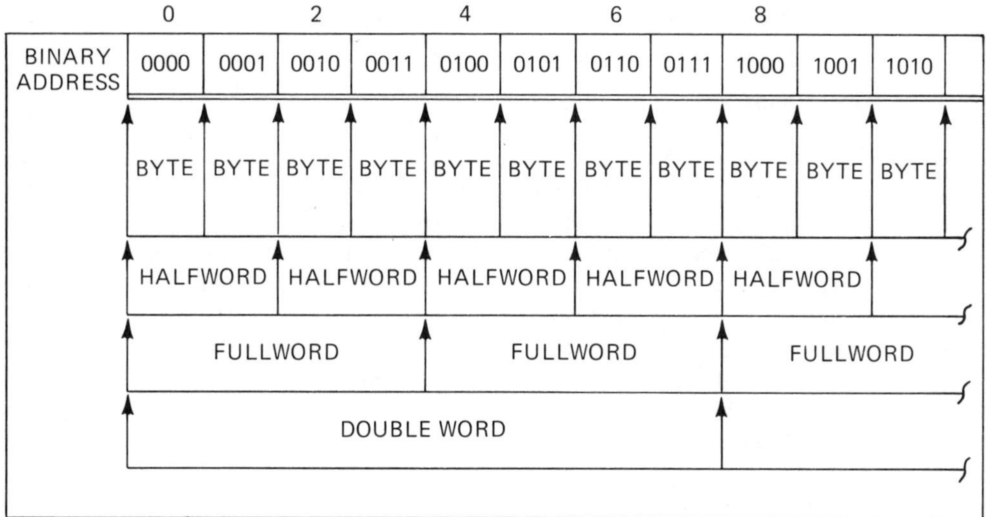

Figure 3-3 Integral storage boundaries.

address may be expressed either as a 6-digit hexadecimal address, or as a 24-bit binary address. Now we are looking at the low-order zeros in the binary address.

Halfword boundaries require one low-order zero in the binary representation of the address. Fullword boundaries require two low-order zeros. The address $90987C_{16}$ is a fullword boundary. Let's look at the low-order digit C_{16}. The bit configuration is 1100_2. Two low-order zeros! Of course, this is also a halfword boundary.

As you might imagine, double word boundaries require three low-order zeros. The address $00A098_{16}$ resides on a double word boundary. The bit configuration of the last digit is 1000_2—three low-order zeros! Can you see why any hexadecimal address ending in zero must reside on a double word boundary? The bit configuration for a hexadecimal zero is 0000_2—four low-order zeros!

A Review

We have introduced some important concepts. Let's pause to review them. We have learned that the smallest unit in storage is a bit. A bit may be used to represent one binary digit. The term byte refers to a group of eight bits. Other common groupings include the halfword (two bytes), the fullword (four bytes), and the double word (eight bytes).

Each byte is addressed by a 24-bit binary (6-hexadecimal digit) address. The instruction, however, does not contain the actual or effective address. The effective address is determined by the contents of two registers and a displacement value specified in the instruction.

Some addresses within computer storage are special. We say these addresses reside on main storage boundaries. Addresses divisible by two reside on halfword boundaries, addresses divisible by four reside on fullword boundaries, and addresses divisible by eight reside on double word boundaries.

Representing Data in Storage

Data residing in main storage may be either numeric (consisting only of numbers) or alphanumeric (consisting of numbers, letters, and special characters). Numeric data may be represented in various ways.

Let's consider the number fifteen. We may express this number as the decimal number 15_{10} or as the binary number 1111_2. Or, we could use another notation known as scientific or exponential notation. In this notation, the number fifteen appears as $.15 \times 10^2$.

These different means of expressing the same number are like codes or languages. The S/370 has the ability to handle numbers expressed in any of these codes. Let's see how each of these numbers appears in computer storage.

Decimal Numbers. When we express the decimal number 15_{10} in computer storage we are expressing a 2-digit number. We require two bytes of main storage—one byte for each digit.

The number fifteen appears in storage as 1111000111110101_2. We are using the symbols 0 and 1 to represent bits which are either on or off. We use a total of sixteen bits or to bytes. But how does this string of sixteen bits possibly represent the simple number fifteen? Let's examine this string of bits.

BYTE		BYTE	
ZONE	DIGIT	ZONE	DIGIT
1111	0001	1111	0101

Each byte consists of four zone bits and four digit bits. The zone bits distinguish between numeric or alphabetic data. The zone configuration for numeric data is 1111_2. Notice that the first four bits of each byte contain 1111_2—we are representing numeric data.

The second four bits in each byte are called the digit bits. These bits tell us which digit we are representing. The configuration 0001_2 represents the digit one. The configuration 0101_2—a binary five—represents the digit five.

We use hexadecimal notation to represent decimal numbers. Remember, this notation is used to represent the contents of storage. The number fifteen is represented as $F1F5_{16}$.

When we represent decimal numbers in storage, we require one byte for each digit. We need four bytes to represent the number 1984. The number appears as $F1F9F8F4_{16}$. Notice that the zone bits are repeated in each byte.

Decimal numbers may be positive or negative. Again, the zone bits help us here. The low-order (rightmost) zone bits determine the sign of the number.

Positive numbers have a zone configuration of 1100_2 (C_{16}). Negative numbers have a zone configuration of 1101_2 (D_{16}). Numbers with a zone configuration of 1111_2 (F_{16}) are considered to be unsigned and are treated as positive. The computer also accepts zone configurations of 1010_2 and 1110_2 as positive, and 1011_2 as negative.

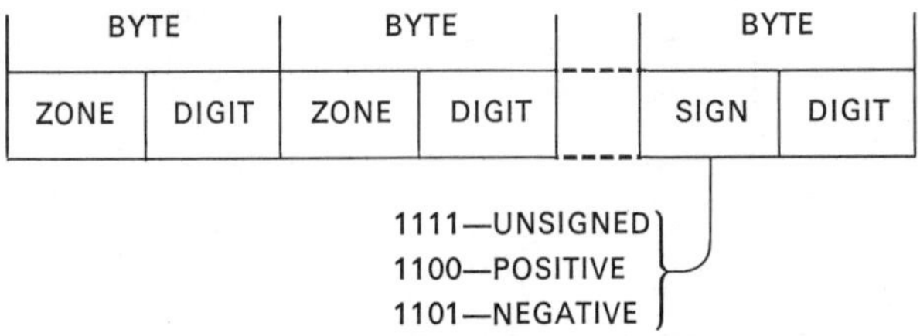

The larger the number, the more storage is required. The number 1984 requires four bytes of storage. The number 6,000,000,000,000, representing the approximate number of miles light travels in a year, requires thirteen bytes (104 bits). We can reduce the amount of storage required to express decimal numbers by eliminating the redundant zone bits. For example, the number 1984 could be represented in only two bytes if we eliminated the zone bits. But, as shown in Figure 3-4, we would have no means of determining the sign of the number. We must leave the low-order zone bits which determine the sign.

BYTE		BYTE		BYTE		BYTE	
ZONE	DIGIT	ZONE	DIGIT	ZONE	DIGIT	SIGN	DIGIT
1111	0001	1111	1001	1111	1000	1100	0100

BYTE		BYTE	
DIGIT	DIGIT	DIGIT	DIGIT
0001	1001	1000	0100

No sign bits

Figure 3-4 Stripping zone bits.

We call the process of stripping the zone bits and squeezing the remaining digit bits *packing*. Notice that when we pack a number, we retain the sign bits (Figure 3-5). The sign bits now occupy the rightmost four bits of the rightmost byte. We use the term low-order bits to refer to the rightmost bits, and the term nibble to refer to a group of four bits. Thus, the sign bits occupy the low-order *nibble*. The remaining digits are squeezed together. Sometimes it is necessary to supply leftmost or high-order zeros. We call this zero fill. We fill the high-order

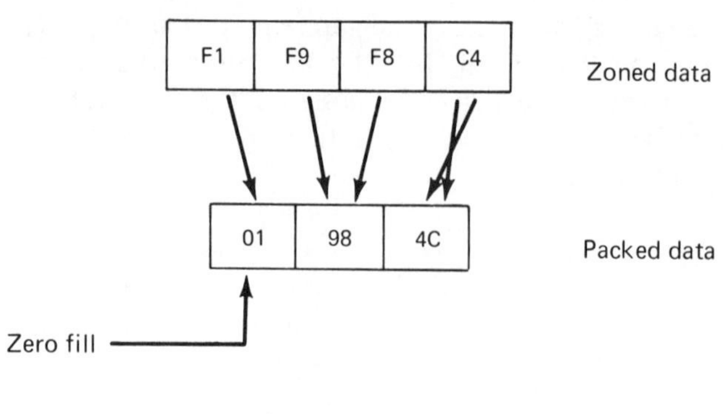

BYTE		BYTE		BYTE	
DIGIT	DIGIT	DIGIT	DIGIT	DIGIT	SIGN
0000	0001	1001	1000	0100	1100

Figure 3-5 Packing decimal data.

nibble with zeros. Zero fill is always required when we pack numbers with an even number of digits. Can you see why?

Decimal numbers, then, may be represented in either of two ways. We can use one byte for each decimal digit. We say this number appears in *zoned format*. Or, a decimal number may be squeezed into fewer bytes, stripping the zone bits, and saving only the four sign bits. We say this number appears in *packed format*. The size of the decimal number is variable. We may use from 1 to 16 bytes to represent decimal data, thus, we refer to decimal data as variable-length data.

Binary Numbers. Numbers also may be represented in storage using the binary code. In this case, each binary digit requires one bit. The number fifteen—expressed in binary as 1111_2—requires four bits. In this example, the notation 1 corresponds to the on condition. The number fifteen may be represented in storage by four on bits.

The design of the computer requires that numbers represented in the binary code contain a fixed number of bits. Binary numbers may be represented as either a halfword of data, or as a fullword of data. Thus the number fifteen may appear as 0000000000001111_2 or as the 32-bit fullword 0000000000000000-0000000000001111_2. We refer to binary data as fixed-length data.

We also must consider the sign of binary data. The first bit—the high-order bit—determines the sign of the number. If the first bit is off, the number is positive and is carried in true form. The halfword 0000000000001111_2 represents a positive fifteen. If the first bit is on, the number is negative and is carried in *complement* form.* The number 1111111111110001_2 represents a negative fifteen.

*Please reference Chapter 1 for a review of true and complement form.

As always, the binary notation is awkward. We find the hexadecimal notation less cumbersome. The number fifteen appears in storage as 0000000000001111_2 but may be written as $000F_{16}$. Similarly, the binary code for a negative fifteen may be written as $FFF1_{16}$. These same numbers could be expressed as fullword operands appearing as $0000000F_{16}$ and $FFFFFFF1_{16}$. Notice that when we expand from a halfword to a fullword we extend the sign bit to the left. We say we propogate the sign bit sixteen bit positions to the left.

Let's look at some additional examples.

number (in decimal)	bit configuration (halfword operand)	hexadecimal shorthand
5	0000000000000101	0005
10	0000000000001010	000A
20	0000000000010100	0014
35	0000000000100011	0023
255	0000000011111111	00FF
32,767	0111111111111111	7FFF
−5	1111111111111011	FFFB
−10	1111111111110110	FFF6
−20	1111111111101100	FFEC
−35	1111111111011101	FFDD
−255	1111111100000001	FF01
−32,767	1000000000000001	8001

The small positive numbers have many high-order zeros. The small negative numbers have many high-order ones. Notice that the negative number is the complement of the positive number. We do not merely change the sign bit to change the sign. We must complement the entire number. The sign bit is also changed as we complement.

The hexadecimal notation provides a convenient means for handling these awkward numbers. Notice that the hexadecimal representation of the negative numbers is the *sixteens* complement of the positive number. When you look at the hexadecimal notation, remember that it is not the first hexadecimal digit, but the first binary bit which determines the sign. Look at the following examples.

halfword operand (in hexadecimal)	sign
007C	positive
100C	positive
800B	negative
FF67	negative
7FFF	positive

In summary, numbers may be represented in the binary code as halfword or fullword operands. We refer to binary data as fixed-length data. We will see that the S/360 (but not the S/370) computer requires binary data to reside on either a halfword (for halfword operands) or a fullword (for fullword operands) boundary.

The sign of the number represented in the binary code is determined by the high-order bit. If this bit is off, the number is positive and is carried in true form. If this bit is on, the number is negative and is carried in complement form.

Floating-Point Numbers. We use the exponential notation to express very large or very small numbers. For example, the large number 6,000,000,000,000 can also be written as $.6 \times 10^{13}$. The number is expressed as a fraction times the base raised to a power. The power, or exponent, is used to move the decimal point. In this example, the exponent moves the decimal point thirteen positions to the right (Figure 3-6).

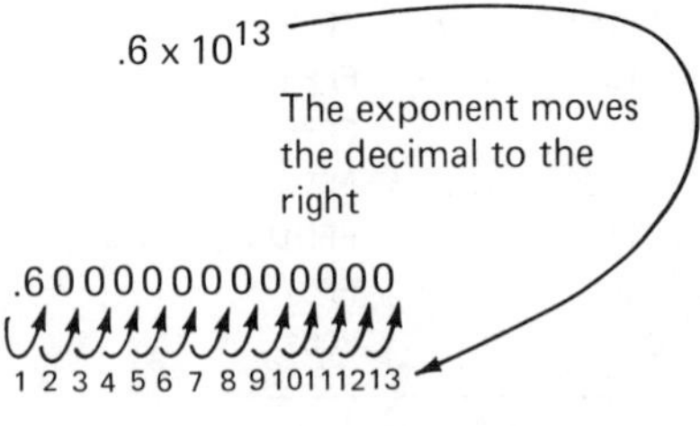

6,000,000,000,000

Figure 3-6 Exponential notation.

We can also use the exponent to move the decimal point to the left. The number .00976 may be written as $.976 \times 10^{-2}$. The negative exponent moves the decimal point to the left.

Let's see how the exponential notation is used to represent large or very small numbers in storage. The number 6,000,000,000,000 requires thirteen bytes if represented in zoned decimal format. Suppose however, we represent only the fraction and the exponent. We can then represent this number in only one byte. The first four bits represent the exponent and the last four bits represent the fraction.

6,000,000,000,000

expressed in exponential notation as

$.6 \times 10^{13}$

can be represented as

BYTE	
EXPONENT	FRACTION
1101	0110

We call this concept *floating-point* notation. It is used mainly in scientific programming.

The EBCDIC Code. We have seen that numeric data may be placed in storage as zoned or packed decimal numbers, as fixed-length binary numbers, or by using floating-point notation. We now will examine the code used to represent alphabetic data, including the special characters.

The EBCDIC (Extended Binary Coded Decimal Interchange Code) uses eight bits or one byte to represent a character. The EBCDIC code is similar to the Hollerith code. The Hollerith (punched card) code requires a combination of zone and digit punches for each letter as shown below.

letters	zone punch	digit punches
A to I	12-punch	1 to 9
J to R	11-punch	1 to 9
S to Z	0-punch	2 to 9

The EBCDIC code divides the alphabet in the same manner, assigning four zone bits and four digit bits to each letter.

letters	zone bits	digit bits
A to I	1100	0001 to 1001
J to R	1101	0001 to 1001
S to Z	1110	0010 to 1001

The letter A, for example, is represented in storage as 11000001_2. We also may use the notation $C1_{16}$ to represent these same eight bits.

BYTE	
ZONE	DIGIT
1100	0001

11000001	in binary
C 1	in hexadecimal

Note: 11000001_2 also represents the number 193_{10} in binary! The interpretation of the bits—an alphabetic A or the number 193_{10} expressed in binary—is a function of the program.

The bit configuration and hexadecimal representation of some letters are given below. You should also examine your IBM System/370 Reference Data Card to find the bit configuration of all the letters.*

letter	bit configuration	hexadecimal representation
B	11000010	C2
I	11001001	C9
K	11010010	D2
R	11011001	D9
S	11100010	E2

The EBCDIC code also is used to represent numbers. The code requires one byte for each digit. Again, four zone bits and four digit bits are required for each digit. The zone bits used to represent the digits are 1111_2. The number five appears in storage as 11110101_2 or $F5_{16}$. Yes, unsigned *zoned* decimal numbers are really represented in the EBCDIC code. The EBCDIC code may be used to represent both alpha and unsigned numeric data.

digit	bit configuration	hexadecimal representation
0	11110000	F0
1	11110001	F1
2	11110010	F2
.	.	.
.	.	.
.	.	.
8	11111000	F8
9	11111001	F9

The EBCDIC code also is used to represent special characters. The special characters do not follow the zone—digit format. Refer to Appendix A for the bit configuration of the special characters.

Summary

Numeric data may be represented as variable-length zoned (EBCDIC) or packed decimal numbers, fixed-length binary numbers, or floating-point numbers.

*Refer to Appendix A for a reproduction of the IBM System/370 Reference Card, from X20–1703.

Alphabetic data is represented using the EBCDIC code. One byte—four zone bits and four digit bits—is required to represent a single character. The EBCDIC code also is used to represent the special characters.

THE ALU (ARITHMETIC-LOGIC UNIT)

We continue our discussion of S/370 hardware concepts with the CPU—examining first the ALU. The ALU is responsible for executing the arithmetic and logical functions requested by the computer program.

Let's see just what we mean by the terms arithmetic and logical. Any instructions involving the four basic arithmetic operations—addition, subtraction, multiplication, division—are called arithmetic operations. A logical operation, on the other hand, usually involves a decision. We might ask the computer to determine which of two numbers is larger, or if a number is positive or negative.

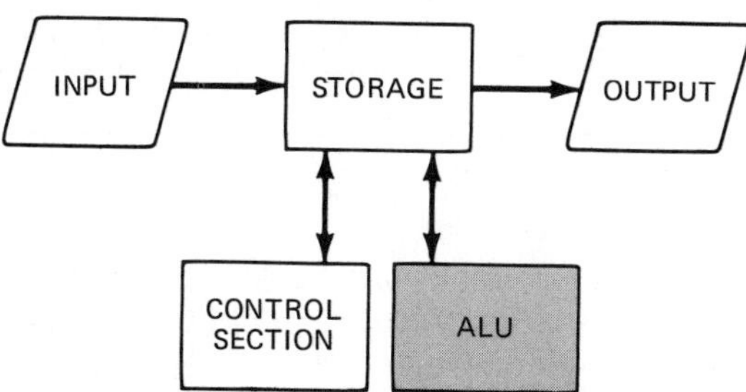

Figure 3-7 The basic data processing pattern.

Both arithmetic and logical operations involve numeric data. Numeric data may be stored as variable-length decimal data, fixed-length binary data, or floating-point numbers. The ALU must have the ability to perform arithmetic and logical operations on *each* of the three types of numeric data.

For this reason the ALU (Figure 3-8) has three sections. Each section is designed to perform arithmetic and logical operations on a specific kind of data—decimal, binary, or floating-point.

Let's pause for a moment. The computer processes data. Data are recorded on external media. These data are read by the input device into main storage. Numeric data may be stored as decimal, binary, or floating-point operands. When the computer program requires an arithmetic or logical operation, the circuitry of the ALU is required. Each type—decimal, binary, or floating-point—of operation is handled differently.

Decimal Operations

Decimal operations—both arithmetic and logical—are performed on operands residing in main storage. Notice that the section of the ALU which performs decimal operations does not have any registers associated with it.

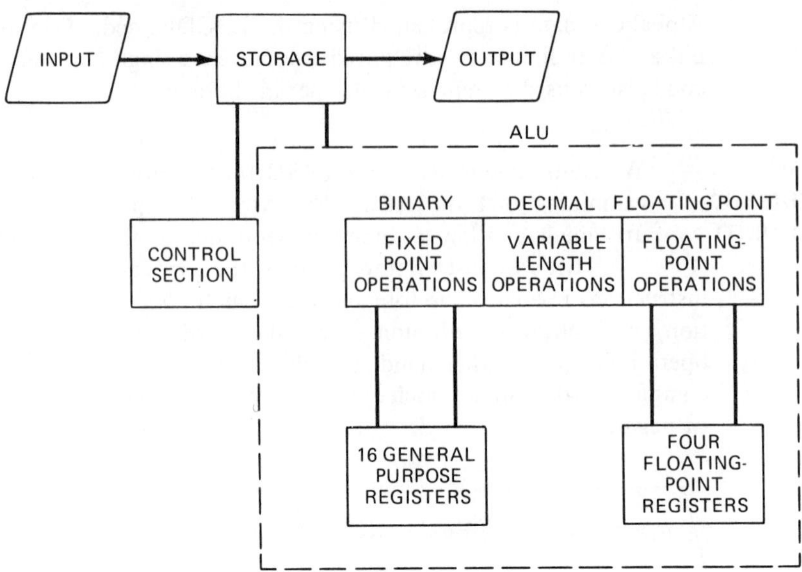

Figure 3-8 The ALU.

We refer to decimal operations as variable-length operations. The operands do not have a required length—they may vary from 1 to 16 bytes. In many cases, however, the decimal operands must be in packed format. All arithmetic operations and some logical operations require that the decimal operands be packed.

Binary Operations

At least one binary operand must be in a register before any arithmetic or logical operations may be perfomed on binary data. There are sixteen general-purpose registers available. Each of these registers may contain a fullword, or 32 bits, of data. The programmer must code the instructions to move the data from storage to a register *before* the arithmetic or logical instruction is issued.

The registers associated with the section of the ALU performing binary operations may also be used in addressing. Thus the registers serve two purposes. They may hold numbers used in developing the effective address of data in main storage, or they may hold fixed-length binary operands.

Floating-Point Operations

Floating-point operations are similar to binary operations in that at least one operand must be placed in a register. There are four floating-point registers available. These registers hold floating-point data. Floating-point data may be fullword, double word or extended (double-double word) operands. The floating-point registers must be large enough to hold a double word operand—that is, 64 bits. Extended operands are held in adjacent registers.

Summary

The ALU is divided into three sections—each section has the circuitry to perform arithmetic and logical operations on a different type of data. Decimal or variable-length operations are performed on variable-length operands residing in main storage. Many operations require that the data be packed.

Binary or fixed-length operations are performed on halfword or fullword binary operands. At least one operand must be moved to one of sixteen fullword general-purpose registers.

Floating-point operations are performed on fullword, double word, or extended floating-point operands. At least one operand must be moved to one of four floating-point registers.

THE CONTROL SECTION

The Control Section (Figure 3-9) of the CPU is responsible for controlling the execution of the instructions comprising the computer program.

The program resides in main storage. The instructions are fetched, one at a time, and executed by the Control Section. The Control Section must first locate the instruction, then decode the instruction to determine what operation is to be performed. The Control Section then must locate the data. Are the operands both in main storage (decimal operations) or are one or both operands in a register (binary operations)? Once the Control Section locates the data, the instruction is executed.

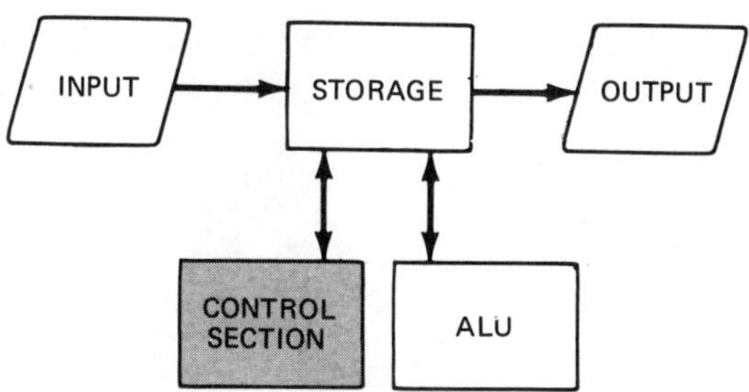

Figure 3-9 The basic data processing pattern.

The time cycle required to fetch, decode, and execute a single instruction is broken into two distinct times—*I-time* and *E-time*. During I-time, the Control Section fetches and decodes the instruction. During E-time the instruction is executed.

PROBLEMS

3.1 Effective addresses of data are determined by adding the contents of two registers (using only the low-order 24 bits) and a displacement contained within the instruction. Given the following instruction format

op-code	R1	R1	D1	R2	R2	D2
	first operand			second operand		

where the notation R1 refers to the registers used to address the first operand, the notation D1 references the 12-bit displacement (coded in hexadecimal notation), the notation R2 references the registers used to address the second operand, and the notation D2 references the 12-bit displacement, develop the effective addresses for each operand in each of the following instructions. The contents of the registers involved are:

registers	**instruction**
R3: 00009000	FA 3 4 000 4 5 000
R4: 00003000	FA 3 3 003 4 4 004
R5: 80004000	FA 5 6 100 3 3 FFF
R6: FF00000A	FA 3 4 000 6 5 FF0

For example, in the first instruction, the effective address of the first operand is $0000C000_{16}$ and of the second operand is 00007000_{16}.

3.2 Indicate which of the following hexadecimal addresses are halfword boundaries (H), fullword boundaries (F), or double word boundaries (D). Some addresses do not reside on any boundaries.

a. 009900
b. 007002
c. FFFFFF
d. 00900C
e. 00789D
f. 00BBBB
g. 00900C
h. 907894

3.3 The characteristics of an address may be determined by examining the bit configuration of the last hexadecimal digit in the address. Given the following bit configurations, indicate which represent halfword, fullword, double word, or no valid boundary.

a. 0000
b. 1000
c. 1100
d. 1010
e. 0001
f. 0010
g. 0100
h. 0110

3.4 Represent the following decimal numbers in both zoned and packed format. Remember, two hexadecimal digits are equivalent to one byte of storage. You may use either binary or hexadecimal notation in your answer.

	zoned		packed	
number	**binary**	**hexadecimal**	**binary**	**hexadecimal**
+9	11001001	C9	10011100	9C
+10				
-27				
-99				
+12				
100(unsigned)				
328(unsigned)				

3.5 Represent the following decimal numbers as halfword binary numbers. Remember, negative numbers are carried in complement form.

+9
+10
−27
−99
+12
+100
−328

3.6 Code your name using the EBCDIC code. How many bytes of storage will you use? What about the space between your first and last name? Use the table in Appendix A.

3.7 Discuss the differences between decimal, binary, and floating-point operations.

4

An Introduction to the Assembly Language

There are three levels of programming languages —machine language, symbolic language, and high-level languages. The computer only understands machine language.

MACHINE LANGUAGE

A single high-level language instruction may be translated into many machine instructions. A single symbolic instruction however, is translated into only one machine-language instruction. The symbolic instruction is quite similar to the machine instruction. Both instructions contain an operation code and the address of each operand. The machine instruction contains this information in a binary code the computer understands. For example

$$0001101000110010_2$$

The symbolic instruction contains this same information expressed in symbols the programmer can understand,

```
AR    3,2
```

The Instruction

The instruction specifies the operation to be performed. By operation we mean a process such as addition, subtraction, multiplication, division, comparing, and so forth. The instruction also specifies the type of data—remember, the S/370 is capable of performing operations on decimal, binary, or floating-point numbers. The computer must know if it is adding two binary numbers or two decimal numbers. Note that the data types must be the same. The program cannot tell the computer to add a decimal number to a binary number.

Not only must the instruction specify the type of data, but it must specify the size or length of each operand. Binary bumbers may be halfword (2 bytes) or fullword (4 bytes) operands. Decimal numbers may be from one to sixteen bytes. The computer must know the length of each operand field.

The computer also must know the address of each operand. Is the operand in a register or in main storage? Most instructions involve two operands. Both operands might be in registers, one operand might be in a register and one operand might be in main storage, or both operands might be in main storage.

The instruction must provide all this information. Let's begin to develop or *format* the instruction.

Operation Code. All instructions must contain an operation code telling the computer what process is to be performed. Let's assume the operation code is the first piece of information in the instruction.

We must reserve a certain number of bits for the operation code. If we reserve four bits for the op-code, we have a possibility of only sixteen instructions. That is, we can have sixteen combinations of one and zero in four bits. Certainly we need an op-code which gives us more flexibility.

All S/370 instructions contain an 8-bit op-code, giving us the possibility of 256 different instructions. We now can indicate the number of bits reserved for the op-code in the instruction format.

Notice that we start numbering with bit zero, not with bit one. An 8-bit op-code occupies bits 0–7 of the instruction.

Type Data. The instruction also must specify the type of data to be processed. The op-code itself specifies the type of data referenced. There is a different op-code for each type of data. Let's consider the add operation. The op-code 5A (we are using hexadecimal notation to represent an 8-bit op-code) tells the computer to add two binary numbers while the op-code FA tells the computer to add two decimal operands.

Length Data. The computer also must know the length of each operand. Binary operands may contain either two (halfword operands) or four (fullword operands) bytes. Decimal operands may contain from 1 to 16 bytes.
The length of binary operands is specified in the op-code itself.

operation	operand	binary op-code	hexadecimal op-code
Add	halfword binary	01001010	4A
	fullword binary	01011010	5A

The op-code does not specify the length of the data when decimal operands are involved. The instruction itself must specify the length of each operand. Our instruction format must allow for the length of the first operand, and for the length of the second operand. Thus

op-code	length OP1	length OP2	
0 7			

We know that the op-code requires 8 bits. How many bits are required to specify the length of each operand?

The largest decimal operand used in an arithmetic operation is 16 bytes in length. To represent the number 16 in binary we require five bits. The number appears as 10000_2. It appears that we need five bits for each length field.

But wait a moment! We never can have a length field of zero. An operand must be at least one byte long to exist. Let's assume that the length code in the instruction is *one less* than the length of the operand. Then, for an operand of sixteen bytes, we specify a length code of fifteen. The computer knows the operand is sixteen bytes long. And we can fit the number fifteen into *four* binary bits! Our instruction format becomes

op-code	length OP1	length OP2	
0 7	8 11	12 15	

The instruction does not contain the actual length of the decimal operand. The length in the instruction is *one less* than the length of the operand. In this way we use four bits for each operand length, still allowing a maximum operand length of sixteen.

At this point, we begin to see the need for two different types of instructions. Instructions involving binary operands do not require fields specifying the length of each operand. The op-code itself specifies the length of the operands involved. Instructions involving decimal operands do require fields specifying the length of each operand. Thus we have two different instruction formats.

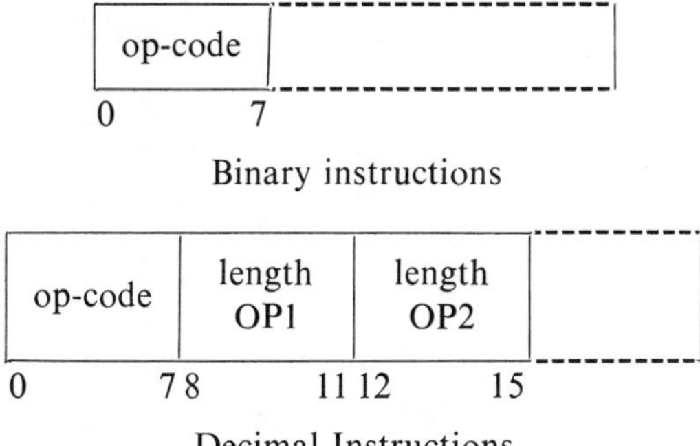

Binary instructions

Decimal Instructions

Operand Addresses. All instructions must specify the address of each operand. The way we specify the operand address depends upon where the operand resides. Both operands may reside in main storage, both operands may reside in registers, or one operand may reside in a register and the other in storage.

Let's first consider an add operation where both operands reside in registers. Remember, there are sixteen general-purpose registers. A binary operand may reside in any of these sixteen registers. We address registers by number. Register 3 is addressed as 0011_2 (a three in binary). Register 12 is addressed as register 1100_2 (a twelve in binary). The sixteen registers are numbered 0 to 15, thus the highest address is 1111_2, addressing register 15. We need four bits to address any of the sixteen general-purpose registers.

If both operands reside in registers, we need four bits to address the first operand register, and four bits to address the second operand register. The instruction format for binary operations where both operands reside in a register becomes

op-code	first operand address	second operand address
0 7	8 11	12 15

It is possible, however, that one binary operand resides in main storage. Let's review the means for addressing main storage. Each byte in main storage may be addressed with a 24-bit or six hexadecimal digit address.

It appears that if one operand resides in a register, and one operand resides in storage, we must reserve 24 bits for the storage operand address *in addition to* the four bits specifying the register operand address. But wait a moment! We do not address storage using the actual address, but by specifying two registers and a displacement. The sum of the contents of each register, together with the value of the displacement, determines the effective address of the storage operand.

When we address storage, we must provide four bits for each register address in addition to the bits required for the displacement. The displacement is a 12-bit number. Thus, to address storage

register number	register number	displacement
4 bits	4 bits	12 bits

we need only four bits to address an operand in a register, but we need a total of twenty bits to address an operand residing in main storage.

Let's pause for a moment and review the instruction formats we are building. All instructions require an op-code. The S/370 instruction has an 8-bit op-code. All instructions contain the address of each operand. But here we have an additional consideration. If the operand resides in a register, we need only four bits to address any of the sixteen general-purpose registers. If the operand resides in main storage, we need a total of twenty bits to specify two registers and a 12-bit displacement used to address data in storage. We also must remember that we are dealing with two operands. Both operands may reside in registers, one operand may reside in a register and one operand may reside in storage, or both operands may reside in storage. Let's see if we can summarize.

condition	bits required for OP1	bits required for OP2	total bits for operand addresses
both operands in registers	4	4	8
one operand in a register; one operand in storage	4	20	24
both operands in storage	20	20	40

It becomes apparent that a single instruction format is not practical. We need at least three different instruction formats to account for the number of bits required to address the operands. And one more consideration must enter this discussion. When we talk about variable-length decimal data residing in storage, we again encounter the length attribute of each operand. The S/370 provides five different instruction formats to handle these situations.

S/370 Instruction Formats

The five instruction formats available to the S/370 programmer are given in Figure 4-1.

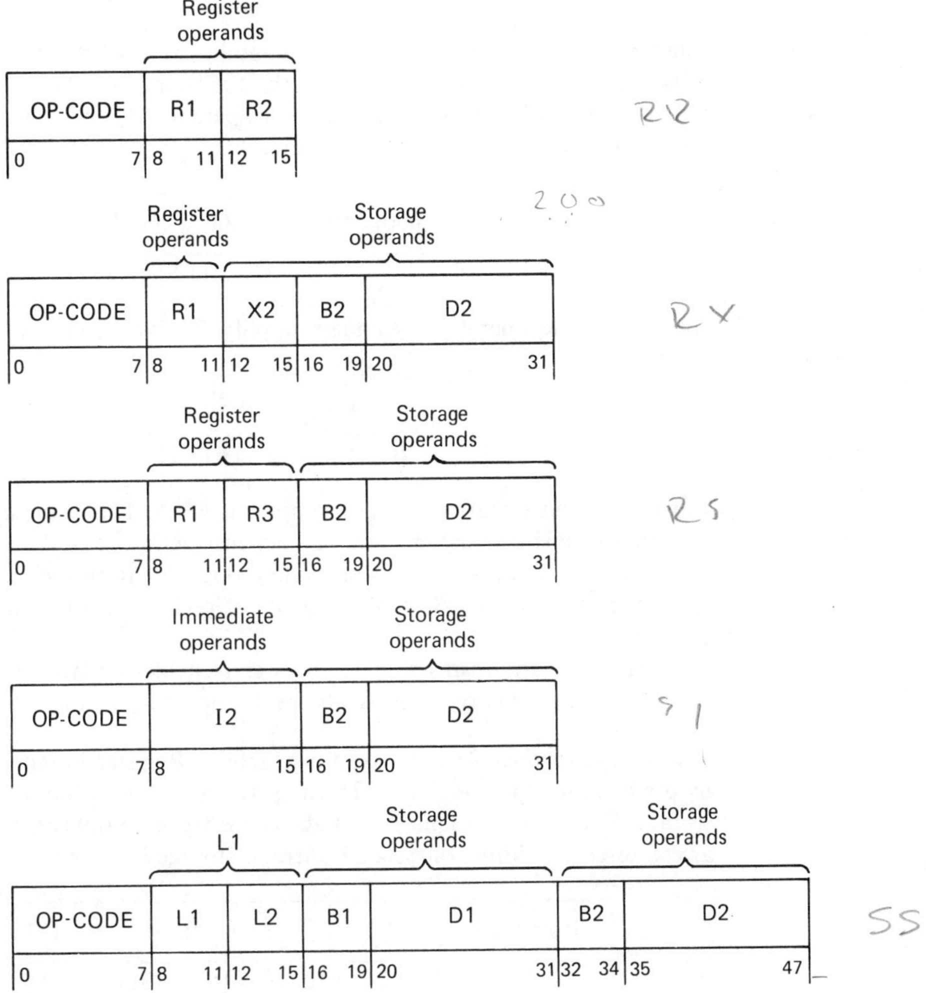

Figure 4-1 Instruction formats.

Two factors affect these formats. First, operand addresses require varying numbers of bits, depending on their location (register or main storage). Second, instructions concerned with decimal operands must provide for a length attribute for each operand.

The RR Instruction. Most RR-type instructions (Register-to-Register) are concerned with fullword binary operands residing in registers. There is no need to worry about length attributes—operands in registers contain 32 bits. Let's look at the format of the RR-type instruction.

op-code	R1	R2
0 7	8 11	12 15

The first eight bits of the instruction contain the op-code. The next four bits (bits 8–11) of the instruction specify the first operand (R1) register. The last four bits (bits 12–15) specify the second operand (R2) register. Let's examine an RR-type instruction. The instruction

00011010	0100	0011
0 7	8 11	12 15

specifies an add operation. We may simplify the instruction as

1A	4	3
0 7	8 11	12 15

using the hexadecimal notation. The op-code is 1A. This is the op-code for the add register instruction. The add register instruction adds the contents of the second operand to the contents of the first operand. In this instruction, we add the contents of register 3 to the contents of register 4. The result is placed in register 4.

The RR-type instruction requires sixteen bits or two bytes of storage. Don't forget, the instructions as well as the operands reside in storage.

The RX Instruction. The RX-type instruction (Register-to-indeXed storage) is used when one operand resides in a register, and one operand resides in main storage. Four bits are required to address the first operand register. Twenty bits are required to address the second operand storage location.

op-code	R1	X2	B2	D2
0 7	8 11	12 15	16 19	20 31
	4 bits	20 bits		

Bits 0–7 represent the op-code.

Bits 8–11 specify the first operand (R1) register. Bits 12–31 specify the two registers and displacement required to address the second operand storage location. The two registers required to address storage are called the *index register* and the *base register*. Bits 12–15 specify the index register (X2), bits 16–19 specify the base register (B2), and bits 20–31 contain the 12-bit displacement.

Consider, for example, the instruction

01011010	0100	1100	0010	000000000100
0 7	8 11	12 15	16 19	20 31

This 32-bit instruction may be expressed in hexadecimal as

5A	4	C	2	004
0 7	8 11	12 15	16 19	20 31

The op-code 5A specifies an add operation. This instruction adds the contents of a fullword operand in storage to the contents of register 4. Register 4 is the first operand. The result of the operation is placed in register 4.

Bits 12–15 specify the index register. The index register is register 12 (a C_{16} is equivalent to a decimal 12). Bits 16–19 specify the base register. The base register is register 2. Bits 20–31 specify the displacement. The displacement is 004_{16}. We cannot, however, determine the effective address of the second operand until we know the contents of registers 12 and 2. Let's assume register 12 contains 00009000_{16}, and register 2 contains 00001000_{16}. The effective address of the storage operand now becomes 00A004.

Contents index register (12)	009000_{16}
+Contents base register (2)	001000_{16}
+displacement	004_{16}
effective address	$00A004_{16}$

The instruction 5A4C2004 adds the fullword contents of location $00A004_{16}$ to the contents of register 4. The result is placed in register 4.

How do we know that we are working with fullword operands and not with halfword operands? There is a different op-code when we are involved with halfword operands. The op-code 01001010_2 ($4A_{16}$) specifies the addition of a halfword of data residing in storage to the operand residing in the register.

The RX-type instruction requires four bytes or a fullword of storage. The instruction must contain the information required to address the second operand in main storage. That is, the RX-type instruction must specify the index register, the base register, and the 12-bit displacement used to locate the second operand in storage.

The SS Instruction. The SS-type instruction (Storage-to-Storage) instruction involves two operands residing in storage. The SS-type instructions are concerned with variable-length decimal operands and must also provide the length attribute of each operand.

The format of the SS-type instruction is

op-code	L1	L2	B1	D1	B2	D2
0 7	8 11	12 15	16 19	20 31	32 35	36 47

The instruction provides for the length attribute of each operand, and for a base register and displacement for each storage operand. The instruction does not provide for index registers. Decimal operands are addressed only by a base register and displacement. The index register is not used.

There are two means of addressing main storage. We may take the sum of the contents of two registers, the base register and the index register, plus the 12-bit displacement. Or, we may take the sum of the base register alone, using no index register, plus the 12-bit displacement. RX-type instructions use an index register. SS-type instructions do not.

Let's examine an SS-type instruction. The instruction

11111010	0001	0010	1100	000000000000	1100	000000001000
0 7	8 11	12 15	16 19	20 31	32 35	36 47

may be expressed in hexadecimal as

FA	1	2	C	000	C	008
0 7	8 11	12 15	16 19	20 31	32 35	36 47

The op-code FA specifies a decimal add operation. We are adding two decimal operands residing in main storage. We now must determine the length and address of each operand.

The first operand contains two bytes. The length attribute of the first operand is contained in bits 8–11 of the instruction. Bits 8–11 contain 0001_2. But this number is *one less* than the actual number of bytes in the operand.

The second operand in our SS-type instruction contains three bytes. Again, the length attribute in bits 12–15 is *one less* than the length of the operand.

Bits 16–31 address the first operand in storage. Bits 16–19 specify the base register. Bit 20–31 specify the 12-bit displacement. In the example, the first operand is addressed by register 12 and a displacement of 000_{16}.

Bits 32–47 address the second operand. Bits 32–35 specify the base register. Bits 36–47 specify the 12-bit displacement. Notice that we may use the same base register to address different operands. The value of the displacements are different. If register 12 contains 007000_{16}. then the address of the first operand becomes 007000_{16}, and the address of the second operand becomes 007008_{16}.

The SS-type instruction is the longest S/370 instruction, requiring 48 bits of storage. This is because the SS-type instruction must address two storage operands and specify the length of each operand.

RS and SI Instructions. The RS (Register-to-Storage) and SI (Storage Immediate) instructions both contain 32 bits. The formats of these instructions are given in Figure 4-1. The RS-type instruction is used when more than one register operand is required.

The SI instruction, like the RR-type, RS-type, and SS-type instructions involves two operands. One operand resides in storage and is addressed by a base register and 12-bit displacement. The second operand is contained within the instruction itself.

The instruction formats we have introduced are machine language formats. We are looking at the instructions exactly as they appear in storage. As programmers, however, we do not want to be bothered by the combersome binary notation. We do not want to be concerned with assigning base registers, index registers, and displacements; if, indeed, we could understand just what determines the choice of base, index, and displacement. As programmers, we do not code at the machine level, but at the symbolic level. We use symbols for the binary op-codes and addresses.

SYMBOLIC LANGUAGE

The computer understands the instruction

```
0001101000110001
```

and knows that it is to add the contents of register 1 to the contents of register 3. We code this instruction using symbolic notation as

```
AR   3,1
```

The assembler translates this symbolic instruction into a single machine instruction.

A program written in assembly language consists of symbolic instructions. The program is assembled into machine language and executed by the computer. Each symbolic instruction generates a single machine instruction. The machine instruction, however, may be two, four, or six bytes in length, depending upon the type of machine instruction generated.

Symbolic Code—Examples

Let's examine some symbolic instructions, working from the machine instruction to the symbolic level, and then examine the format for the symbolic instructions.

The machine instruction

1A	31

is generated from the symbolic instruction

```
AR   3,1
```

The format for this symbolic instruction is

AR	R1,R2
mnemonic	operands

The mnemonic is the symbol we use to specify the operation. The mnemonic AR (Add Register) tells the computer to add the contents of the second operand register to the contents of the first operand register, and to place the result in the first operand register. Since both operands reside in registers, we need only name the registers involved to address each operand.

The machine code

5A	4C	20	04

is generated from the symbolic instruction

```
A   4,4(12,2)
```

This is an example of the RX-type instruction. The format for this instruction is

A	R1,D2(X2,B2)
mnemonic	operands

The meaning of each operand symbol or number is determined by its *position* in the instruction. We call these operands *positional operands*. In the example we use the mnemonic A (Add fullword) to specify that we are adding the contents of a fullword residing in storage to the contents of the R1 register. When we work with a halfword operand, we use the mnemonic AH (Add Halfword).

The operands must specify the first operand register, and the base register, index register, and displacement required to address the second operand in storage. The format of the instruction tells us where to place the numbers specifying the first operand (R1) register, and the base register (B2), index register (X2), and displacement (D2) used in addressing the second operand.

We call this symbolic notation the *explicit notation*. We explicitly state the base register, index register, and displacement used to address the storage operand. In the example, the second operand storage location is addressed using register 12 as the index register, register 2 as the base register, and a displacement of 004_{16}. The effective address of the storage operand depends on the contents of registers 12 and 2.

We can use another notation called *implicit* addressing. For example

```
A  4,FLDA
```

Here we use the mnemonic A to specify the fullword add operation. The number 4 tells the computer the first operand register. We use the *label* FLDA to specify the second operand storage location. FLDA is the name of a fullword storage location.

FLDA is a label—a label which refers to data in storage. Labels are easy for the programmer to work with. But the computer can locate data in storage only in terms of a base register, an index register, and a displacement. How does the computer locate the data stored at FLDA?

It is important to remember that the implicit code is *source* code. This code must be assembled to machine code. The assembler must translate the symbolic instruction

```
A  4,FLDA
```

to the corresponding machine instruction. This means that the programmer is *implying*—thus the term implicit addressing—that the assembler knows which base register, index register, and displacement to use in the RX-type machine format. More on this later.

Let's examine one final instruction, an SS-type instruction. The machine instruction

FA	12	C0	00	C0	08

is generated from the symbolic instruction

```
AP  0(2,12),8(3,12)
```

The format for the SS-type symbolic instruction is

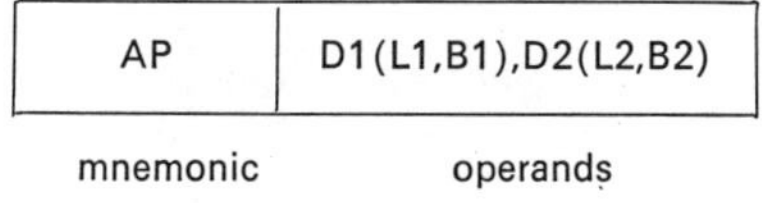

The mnemonic AP (Add Packed) tells the computer we are adding two variable-length decimal operands residing in storage. The instruction specifies the length

(L1), the base (B1), the displacement (D1) of the first operand, and the length (L2), the base (B2), and the displacement (D2) of the second operand. Remember the assembled value for each length attribute is one less than the actual length of the operand.

We also can use the implicit notation. For example

```
AP    FLDA,FLDB
```

This instruction tells us to add the contents of FLDB to the contents of FLDA. The result is placed in FLDA.

Symbolic Code—A Review

The computer understands machine code. We code at the source level using symbolic instructions. We code assembly instructions using either implicit or explicit notation. In either case, the assembler translates the single source statement into a machine language instruction.

We always use decimal numbers in the source statements. If hexadecimal or binary numbers are used we must use a special notation. For example, the instruction

```
AR    14,15
```

tells the computer to add the contents of register 15 to the contents of register 14.

The machine instruction generated from this symbolic statement appears as

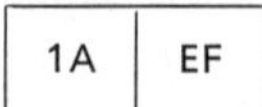

The decimal numbers used to specify the first operand register and the second operand register are translated into binary. These register addresses are represented in binary in the machine instruction. We use the hexadecimal notation for simplicity.

```
AR    14,15
```

symbolic instruction

00011010	1110	1111	machine instruction—binary
OPCODE	OP1	OP2	

1A	E	F	machine instruction—hexadecimal
OPCODE	OP1	OP2	

THE ASSEMBLY PROCESS

The statements comprising the source program are coded by the programmer. The programmer follows the format given for each symbolic instruction and writes the instructions on an assembly language coding sheet. These instructions are punched into cards. These cards are input, the statements

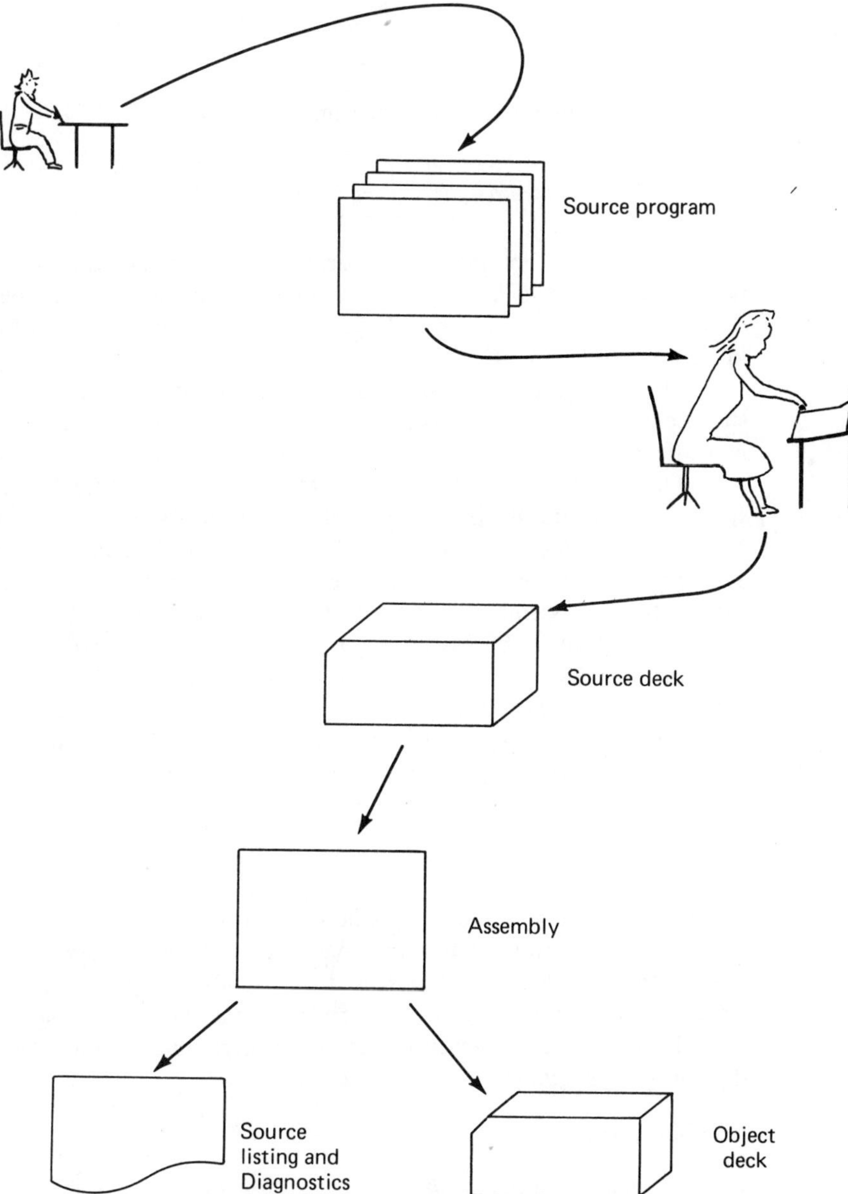

Figure 4-2 The assembly process.

translated into machine instructions, and the object program produced. (See Figure 4-2.)

Format

All assembly statements follow the same general format:

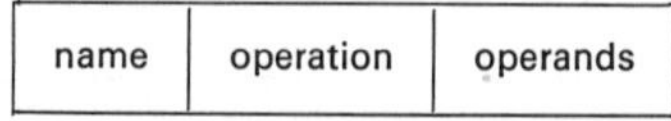

The name field is optional. The operation field specifies the operation to be performed (AR, A AP, etc.). The programmer supplies information about the operands in the operand field. A typical programmer's coding form is shown in Figure 4-3.

The name field, if used, must begin in the first position of the source statement. The operation field must be separated by at least one space from the name field. Most programmers start the operation field in position ten.

The operand fields are separated from the operation field by at least one space. The operand fields usually start in position sixteen and may not exceed position 71 on the card. Occasionally the operand field requires more space. The operand must be continued on the next card. A punch in column 72 is often used to tell the assembler that the statement is continued.

The operand subfields are separated by commas. *There are no spaces in the operand fields*. Any statement following a space after the operand field is regarded as a *comment* and ignored by the computer.

The assembly program may not contain blank cards. A special card, consisting of an asterisk (*) in position 1 may be used for spacing or for additional comments.

Labels

The programmer may label fields he (or she) references in the program, and also may label certain statements. We label statements we wish to reference later in the program. The labels used in assembly programs are from 1 to 8 alpha or numeric characters. The special characters $, # or @ also may be used. These characters however, often have special meaning and we do not use them in our programs.

A Sample Listing

The assembler gives the programmer a *listing*. This listing (Figure 4-4) contains the statements comprising the symbolic program as well as the generated object instructions. If the programmer makes any coding errors, a diagnostic listing also is included. The diagnostic listing documents coding or language errors, but not logic errors. We will discuss both types of errors in a later chapter.

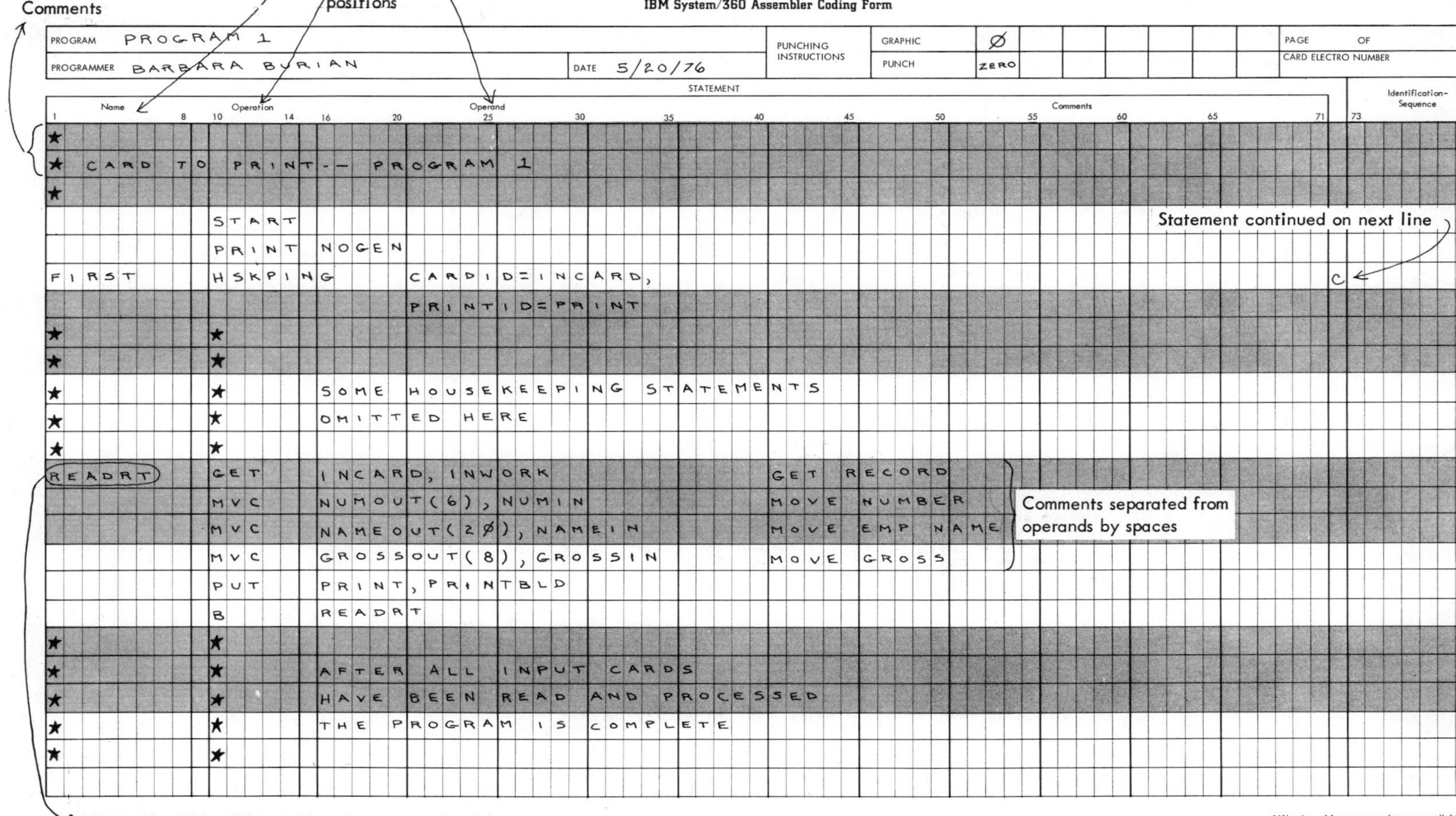

IBM

GX28-6509-4 U/M 050**
Printed in U.S.A.

IBM System/360 Assembler Coding Form

PROGRAM	PROGRAM 1		PUNCHING INSTRUCTIONS	GRAPHIC	Ø	PAGE OF
PROGRAMMER	BARBARA BURIAN	DATE 5/20/76		PUNCH	ZERO	CARD ELECTRO NUMBER *

```
STATEMENT
Name     Operation  Operand                              Comments          Identification-Sequence
1      8 10     14 16                                                   71 73                  80
*
* CARD TO PRINT-- PROGRAM 1
*
         START
         PRINT  NOGEN
FIRST    HSKPING      CARDID=INCARD,                                      C
                      PRINTID=PRINT
*        *
*        *
*        *      SOME HOUSEKEEPING STATEMENTS
*        *      OMITTED HERE
*        *
READRT   GET    INCARD,INWORK                        GET RECORD
         MVC    NUMOUT(6),NUMIN                      MOVE NUMBER
         MVC    NAMEOUT(20),NAMEIN                   MOVE EMP NAME
         MVC    GROSSOUT(8),GROSSIN                  MOVE GROSS
         PUT    PRINT,PRINTBLD
         B      READRT
*        *
*        *      AFTER ALL INPUT CARDS
*        *      HAVE BEEN READ AND PROCESSED
*        *      THE PROGRAM IS COMPLETE
*        *
```


* A standard card form, IBM electro 6509, is available for punching source statements from this form. Instructions for using this form are in any IBM System/360 assembler language reference manual. Address comments concerning this form to IBM Nordic Laboratory, Publications Development, Box 962, S-181 09 Lidingö 9, Sweden.

**Number of forms per pad may vary slightly

Figure 4-3 Assembly Language source program.

```
                                                                                     PAGE    1
  (4)    (3)                         (2)          (1)
  LOC  OBJECT CODE    ADDR1 ADDR2   STMT    SOURCE STATEMENT                                F04MAR74    6/17/76

                                       1 *
                                       2 * PROGRAM 1
                                       3 * CARD TO PRINT
                                       4 *
CCC000                                 5           START
                                       6           PRINT NOGEN
                                       7 FIRST     HSKPING CARDID=INCARD,PRINTID=PRINT         NAME FILES
                                     151 *         *
                                     152 *         *     SOME
                                     153 *         *     HOUSEKEEPING
                                     154 *         *     STATEMENTS
                                     155 *         *     ARE
                                     156 *         *     OMITTED
                                     157 *         *     HERE
                                     158 *         *
                                     159 READRT    GET   INCARD,INWORK                        GET RECORD INTO INWORK
00016A D205 C1E2 C188 001E8 0018E    164           MVC   NUMOUT(6),NUMIN                      MOVE EMP NUMBER
0CC170 D213 C1F2 C18E 001F8 00194    165           MVC   NAMEOUT(20),NAMEIN                   EMP NAME
000176 D207 C210 C1BA 00216 001C0    166           MVC   GROSSOUT(8),GROSSIN                  AND GROSS
                                     167           PUT   PRINT,PRINTBLD                       THEN WRITE RECORD
00018A 47F0 C156             0015C   172           B     READRT                               AND LOOP BACK
                                     173 *         *
                                     174 *         *     AFTER ALL INPUT CARDS
                                     175 *         *     HAVE BEEN READ AND PROCESSED
                                     176 *         *     THE PROGRAM IS COMPLETE
                                     177 *         *
                                     178 *
                                     179 * DATA AREAS
                                     180 *
00C18E                               181 INWORK    DS    0CL80                                INPUT AREA
0CC18E                               182 NUMIN     DS    CL6                                  *
00C194                               183 NAMEIN    DS    CL20                                 *
00C1A8                               184           DS    CL24                                 *
00C1C0                               185 GROSSIN   DS    CL8                                  *
00C1C8                               186           DS    CL22                                 *
00C1DE                               187 PRINTBLD  DS    0CL120                               OUTPUT AREA
0001DE 4040404040404040              188           DC    10CL1' '                             *
0001E8                               189 NUMOUT    DS    CL6                                  *
00C1EE 4040404040404040              190           DC    10CL1' '                             *
00C1F8                               191 NAMEOUT   DS    CL20                                 *
00020C 4040404040404040              192           DC    10CL1' '                             *
000216                               193 GROSSOUT  DS    CL8                                  *
00021E 4040404040404040              194           DC    56CL1' '                             *
0CC000                               195           END   FIRST
```

(1) Source statements as coded

(2) The assembler numbers each statement

(3) Generated object code

(4) Relative location of each statement is given in hexadecimal

Figure 4-4 A sample program.

PROBLEMS

4.1 Discuss the considerations involved in designing an instruction format. What are the advantages of the variable-length instruction formats used on the S/370? What would be the advantages of a 6-bit op-code. The disadvantages?

4.2 Give the machine language instructions for each of the following operations. The hexadecimal op-code is supplied. Indicate the format (RR, RX, SS) of the instruction (Reference the information in Appendix A.)

a. Add ($1A_{16}$) the contents of register 2 to the contents of register 3. The result is in register 3.
b. Subtract ($1B_{16}$) the contents of register 12 from the contents of register 14. The result is in register 14.
c. Add ($4A_{16}$) the contents of a halfword operand in storage to register 10. The storage operand is addressed by register 2 as the base, register 8 as the index, and a *decimal* displacement of 22.
d. Subtract (FB_{16}) the contents of a two byte decimal operand from the contents of a twelve byte decimal operand. Use register 12 as the base register. The first and second operands have *decimal* displacements of 8 and 12 respectively.

Give your answers in hexadecimal notation.

4.3 Give the symbolic language instruction for each of the operations in Problem 4.2. Which notation should you use—implicit or explicit? Why?

4.4 Examine the mnemonics and generated operation code in Appendix A.

a. The first two bits of each instruction identify the instruction type. What are the first two bits of the following instruction types?
   1. RR
   2. RX
   3. SS
   4. RS
   5. SI
b. Bits 2 and 3 of the op-code usually indicate the length of the operand. What do bits 2–3 contain for
   1. halfword operands
   2. fullword operands
   3. double word (long form floating-point) operands
   4. variable-length operands (decimal)
c. Bits 4–7 of the op-code often specify the operation itself. What do bits 4–7 contain for each of the following operations?
   1. addition
   2. subtraction
   3. multiplication
   4. division

4.5 The contents of five registers are:

register	contents (hexadecimal)
1	0000987C
4	FF00000A
8	0000ABC0
12	80009000
14	00005000

Give the effective address of each of the following.

base	index	displacement (hexadecimal)
1	4	008
1	1	FF0
4	—	000
12	12	004
14	12	900
1	—	000
8	12	100

4.6 Which of the following are valid assembly language labels?

a. FIRST
b. 1
c. LABEL#1
d. &&FIRST
e. # 4
f. MYFIELD
g. STOCK-NUM
h. STOCKNUMBER

section two

A Subset Approach to the Assembly Language

5

Decimal Instructions

Computer programs process data. Remember the basic data processing pattern (Figure 5-1). Data are input. Data are processed. Data are output.

We must define the data to be processed in the computer program. We must describe the input and the output files. We must tell the computer the characteristics of the records within each file.

But not all data are contained on files. For example, an employee is entitled to overtime pay if he works more than forty hours in a week. We calculate overtime by multiplying base pay by 1.5. This is the familiar time and a half for overtime. The number 1.5 is a *constant*. A constant is another type of data.

Let's pause for a moment. The computer processes data. Data may be contained as fields and records within a file. Data also may be constants. Data

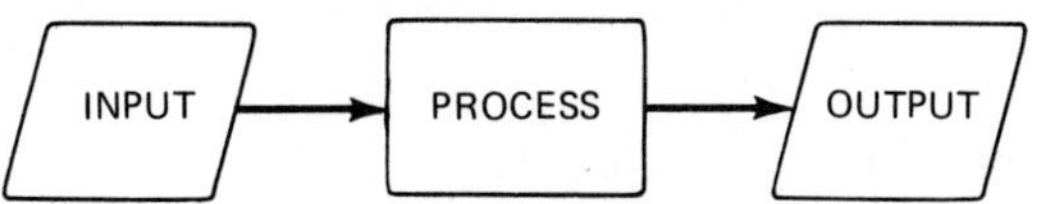

Figure 5-1 The basic data processing pattern.

files are recorded on external media such as punched cards and magnetic tapes. Constants are different. Constants are defined as part of the computer program.

The computer program consists of two elements—data descriptions and instructions (Figure 5-2). The instructions manipulate the data, following the basic data processing pattern. Input instructions *read* data recorded on external media. (Constants are part of the program and are already in computer storage.) Processing instructions *process* the data, and output instructions *write* the processed data.

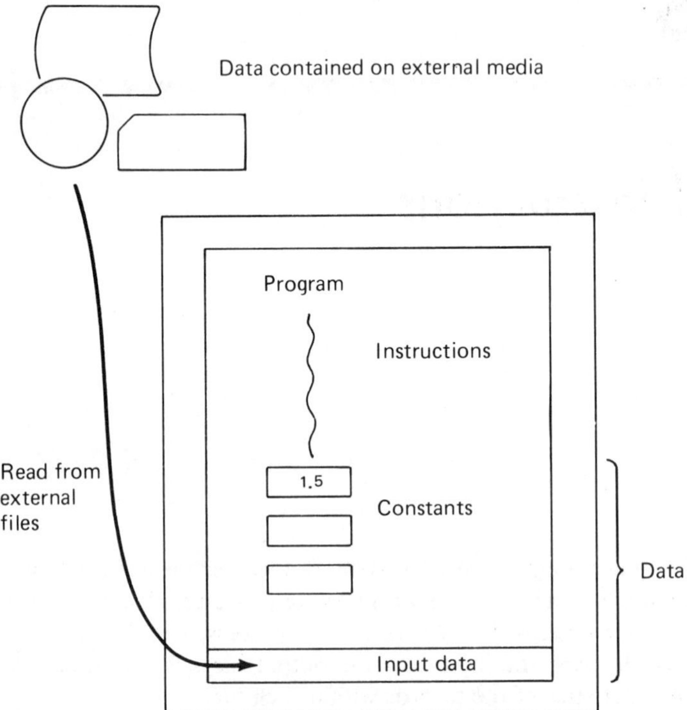

Figure 5-2 Instructions and data in the computer program.

Before we can process *any* data, we must define the data. We must describe all files and all the constants the computer program will use. We will reserve the file descriptions for a later chapter and begin our study of assembly language with a discussion of constants, examining decimal data first.

DEFINING DATA

These are two types of decimal data—zoned and packed. Let's review these concepts now.

Representing Decimal Data

The number 12345 may be represented in two ways. We may represent 12345 as the zoned decimal number

F1	F2	F3	F4	C5

When we represent a number in zoned format, each digit requires one byte of storage.

The zone bits are repetitive. The number 12345 is a 5-digit number. We require five bytes of storage to represent the number. Packing allows us to strip the extra zone bits and to squeeze the number into fewer bytes. We must, however, save the low-order zone bits. These are the bits that tell us the sign of the number (Figure 5-3).

We save two bytes when we pack the number 12345. We need only three bytes to represent the number in packed decimal format. We need five bytes to represent the number in zoned format. We pack decimal data to save storage. We also must pack decimal data before performing decimal arithmetic.

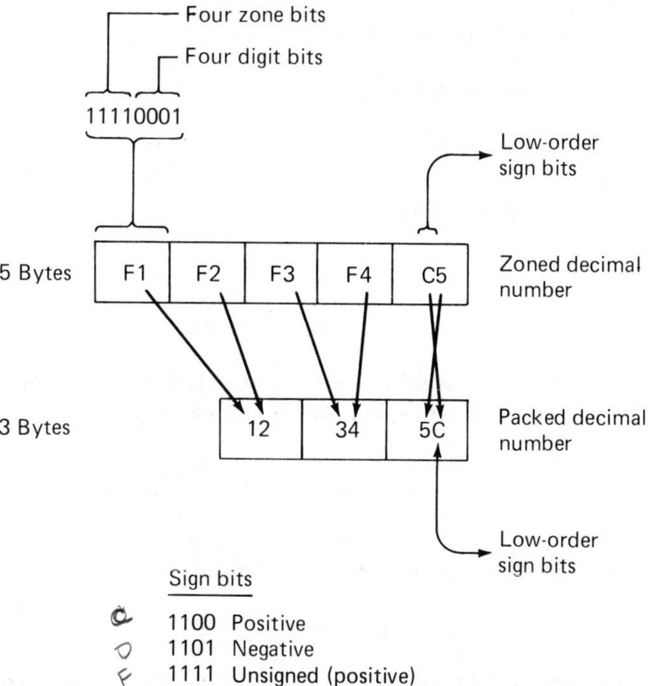

Figure 5-3 Representing decimal numbers.

The DC Instruction

Assembly language instructions tell the computer what operations to perform. Assembly instructions are also used to describe data. The DC (Define Constant) instruction is used to define the constants in a program.*

*A summary of the constants and their characteristics is found in Table B-2, Appendix B.

We must tell the computer everything about the constant; its length, its type, and, most important, its *value*. Is it 1 or 256 bytes long? Is it a numeric or a non-numeric constant? Is it a binary or a decimal constant? What is the value of the constant?

Figure 5-4 illustrates the DC instruction. The name of the constant is CON1. The term DC states that we are defining a constant. The letter Z tells the computer we are defining a zoned decimal constant. The entry L5 specifies a length of 5. The number in quotes—12345—is the value of the constant.

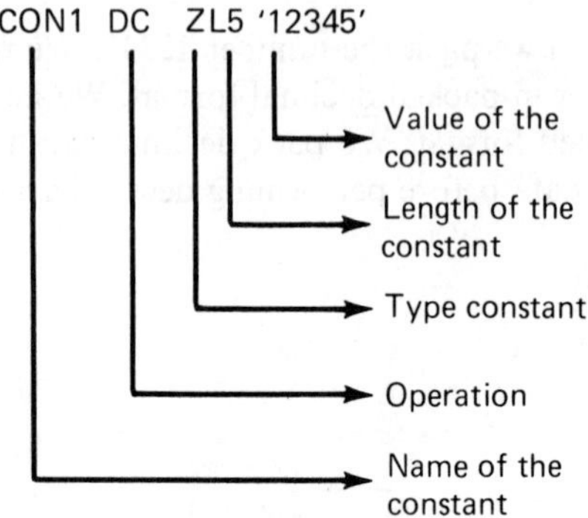

Figure 5-4 Use of the DC statement.

The statement

```
CON1    DC    ZL5'12345'
```

defines a 5-byte zoned constant whose value is 12345. We use the labed CON1 to represent this constant which appears in main storage as

F1	F2	F3	F4	C5

We also can define a packed constant. The statement

```
CON2    DC    PL3'12345'
```

defines a 3-byte packed constant whose value is 12345. The constant appears in main storage as

12	34	5C

We can repeat the constant any number of times. The statement

```
CON3    DC    2PL3'12345'
```

repeats the packed constant 12345 once. We are, in total, defining a 6-byte area of storage. The constant appears in storage as

12	34	5C	12	34	5C

All DC statements follow the same format (Figure 5-5). The name field is optional. The operation DC is required. The operand field consists of four subfields.

name	operation	operands
Optional name	DC	One or more operand fields

```
D T M 'constant'
| | |   └──►Value of constant, required
| | └──────►Modifiers, optional
| └────────►Type of data, required
└──────────►Duplication factor, optional
```

Figure 5-5 Format of the DC statement.

DC Operand Subfields. The duplication factor causes the constant to be generated a specified number of times. The type subfield tells the type of constant—zoned or packed, for example. The modifier subfield supplies the length of the constant. (There are additional modifiers which are not discussed in this chapter.) The constant subfield supplies the value of the constant. The constant subfield is required and must be enclosed in quotes.

Use of the DC Instruction. We define decimal constants as signed or unsigned decimal numbers. The maximum length of the constant is 16 bytes. If the length modifier is omitted, the length of zoned (Z) constants is determined by the number of digits in the constant. The statement

```
ZONED1   DC   Z'123'
```

generates a 3-byte constant.

The length of packed (P) constants is determined by the number of *pairs* of digits. Padding occurs in the leftmost digit. For example, the statement

```
PACK1   DC   P'123'
```

generates a 2-byte constant appearing as

12	3C

The statement

```
PACK2  DC  P'1234'
```

generates a 3-byte constant appearing as

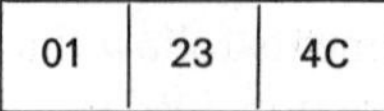

01	23	4C

Table 5-1 shows the use of the DC instruction to define zoned and packed data. Sometimes the specified length is more than required to represent the constant. The assembler fills the additional bytes with leading zeros.

Table 5-1 Examples of the DC Statement

generated code	constant			
F1F2F3F4C5	ZONED1	DC	ZL5'12345'	5-BYTE ZONED CONSTANT—POSITIVE
F1F2F3F4D5	ZONED2	DC	ZL5'-12345'	5-BYTE ZONED CONSTANT—NEGATIVE
12345C	PACKED1	DC	PL3'12345'	3-BYTE PACKED CONSTANT—POSITIVE
12345D	PACKED2	DC	PL3'-12345'	3-BYTE PACKED CONSTANT—NEGATIVE
F0F1F2F3F4C5	ZONED3	DC	ZL6'12345'	LEFTMOST BYTE PADDED
0012345C	PACKED3	DC	PL4'12345'	LEFTMOST BYTE PADDED
F2F3F4C5	ZONED4	DC	ZL4'12345'	LEFTMOST BYTE TRUNCATED
345D	PACKED4	DC	PL2'-12345'	LEFTMOST BYTE TRUNCATED
F1F2C3F1F2C3	DUP1	DC	2ZL3'123'	USE OF DUPLICATION FACTOR
123C123C123C	DUP2	DC	3PL2'123'	USE OF DUPLICATION FACTOR
123C	PACKED5	DC	P'123'	ASSEMBLER ASSUMES 2 BYTES

When the specified length is too small, the constant is *truncated.* Significant digits are eliminated from the high-order position of the constant, *the generated constant is incorrect.*

If the length attribute is omitted, the length is determined by the value of the constant itself.

Representing Alphanumeric Data

We also can use the DC statement to describe alphanumeric data

```
DATA1  DC CL3'CAT'
```

In this example the type submodifier is C. We are defining a new type of constant, the character constant. The character constant may contain numeric or alphabetic data. Special characters are also allowed.

The character constant may contain any of the 256 bit combinations available in an 8-bit byte. *An exception*—if we wish to represent an ampersand (&) or a single quote (') we must represent the character by a *pair* of ampersands or quotes. For example

```
CHAR1   DC   CL12'VALUE IS &&27'
```

The length attribute is 12, although 13 characters (each space requires one position) are contained between quotes. The double ampersand appears only once in the generated constant.

The maximum length of the character constant is 256 bytes. Each character, with the exception of the double ampersand or quote, is assembled into a single byte. No boundary alignment is performed.

Table 5-2 Generating Character Constants

generated code	constant			
C140C3C8C1D9C1C3	CHAR1	DC	C'A CHARACTER CONSTANT'	ASSEMBLER ASSUMES A
E3C5D940C3D6D5E2				
E3C1D5E3				
	*			LENGTH OF 20 BYTES
C140D7C1C4C4C5C4	CHAR2	DC	CL20'A PADDED CONSTANT'	ASSEMBLER PADS THREE
40C3D6D5E2E3C1D5				
F3404040				
	*			RIGHTMOST BYTES
C140E3D9E4D5C3C1	CHAR3	DC	CL10'A TRUNCATED CONSTANT'	ASSEMBLER TRUNCATES TEN
F3C5				
	*			RIGHTMOST BYTES
E4E2C540D6C64050	CHAR4	DC	CL14'USE OF && AND '''	ASSEMBLER GENERATES
40C1D5C4407D				SINGLE & AND '
	*			
C3C1E3C3C1E3	CHAR5	DC	2CL3'CAT'	USE OF DUPLICATION FACTOR
C3C1C3C1	CHAR6	DC	2CL2'CAT'	RIGHTMOST BYTE LOST
C3C1E340C3C1E340	CHAR7	DC	2CL4'CAT'	RIGHTMOST BYTE PADDED
F1F2F3	CHAR8	DC	CL3'123'	NUMERIC CONSTANT

Notice that one of two situations may occur if the length modifier provided is not equal to the character constant. The rightmost digits are dropped if the number of characters specified is greater than the length modifier. On the other hand, if the number of characters specified is less than the length modifier, blanks are added. We say the rightmost bytes are *padded* with blanks. Each symbol in the character constant requires one byte of storage. The data are represented using the EBCDIC code*. Note that the EBCDIC code for a blank

*Refer to Appendix A for the Extended Binary Coded Decimal Interchange Code representation of the digits, letters, and special characters.

is 40_{16}. Digits coded as character constants are represented in the EBCDIC code, not as zoned or packed constants. Thus the constant

```
CHAR1   DC   CL3'123'
```

appears in storage as

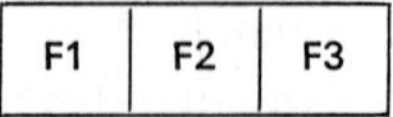

The zoned decimal constant

```
ZONED1   DC   ZL3'123'
```

appears in storage as

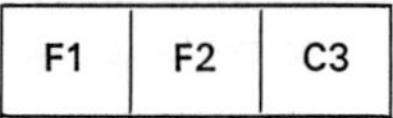

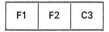

while the packed constant

```
PACKED1   DC   PL2'123'
```

appears in storage as

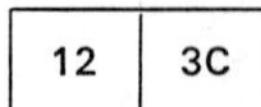

Different type modifiers generate different data in storage. We use the DC statement to define and initialize constants defined in the program. But we also need a means of reserving space for data read into storage.

The DS Statement

The DS (Define Storage) statement provides a means of reserving storage without defining a value for that storage area. For example

```
CARDIN   DS   CL80
```

This statement reserves 80 bytes of storage for CARDIN. The area is not set to an initial value. After the card is read, CARDIN contains the data represented in the punched card.

The format of the DS statement, illustrated in Figure 5-6, is similar to the format of the DC statement.

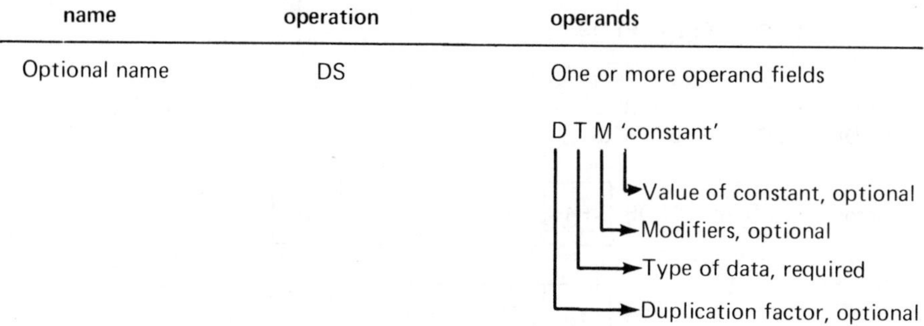

Figure 5-6 Format of the DS statement.

DECIMAL CONVERSION INSTRUCTIONS

We have seen how the DC statement may be used to define a constant. We will now examine the assembly language instructions used to process data. First we will see how data may be converted from zoned to packed format, then examine the instructions which perform arithmetic operations on decimal data. First, the decimal conversion instructions. The PACK instruction converts from 1 to 16 bytes of zoned decimal data to packed format. The UNPK (UNPacK) instruction converts packed decimal data to zoned decimal format.

The PACK Instruction

The instruction

```
PACK   FLDA,FLDB
```

takes the data at the second operand location, FLDB, and packs it into the first operand location (Figure 5-7). The assembler must know the length of the each operand field. The maximum length of either operand is sixteen bytes. The instruction shown in Figure 5-7 does not specify a length. In this case the assembler assumes the length attribute to be the length of the field itself. FLDB is defined as a 5-byte constant. The assembler assumes a length of five for the second operand field.

FLDA is defined as a 3-byte field in Figure 5-7. The assembler assumes a length of three for the first operand. We can, however, change the length attributes of the data by coding a length operand in the symbolic instruction. For example,

```
        PACK   FLDA(5),FLDB(3)
          .
          .
          .
FLDA    DS     CL5
FLDB    DC     ZL5'12345'
```

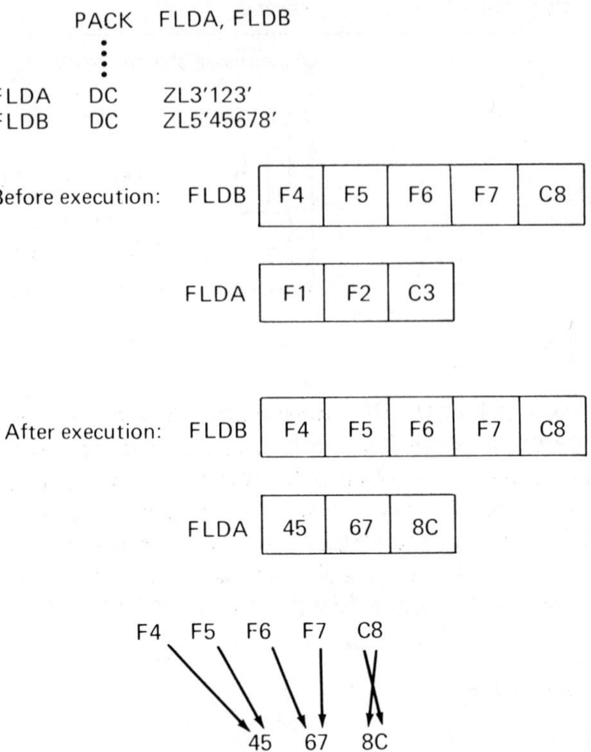

Figure 5-7 Execution of the PACK instruction.

In this instance we pack only the *first* three bytes of FLDB into the five byte field FLDA. We need only two bytes to represent the number 123 in packed format. The additional bytes are padded with zeros (Figure 5-8).

The PACK instruction proceeds from right to left. If the length of the first operand (receiving) field is too small, the leftmost positions of the second operand (sending) field are truncated. If the length of the first operand field is too large, the field is padded with zeros. Table 5-3 illustrates this principle.

Table 5-3 Execution of the PACK Instruction

location	instruction	first operand after execution
FLDA: C1	PACK FLDE(4),FLDA(1)	FLDE: 0000001C
FLDB: F1D2	PACK FLDC(3),FLDB(2)	FLDC: 00012D
FLDC: F1F2C3	PACK FLDD(4),FLDC(3)	FLDC: 0000123C
FLDD: F1F2F3C4	PACK FLDC(3),FLDC(2)	FLDD: 00012F
FLDE: F0F0F0D1	PACK FLDB(2),FLDD(4)	FLDB: 234C

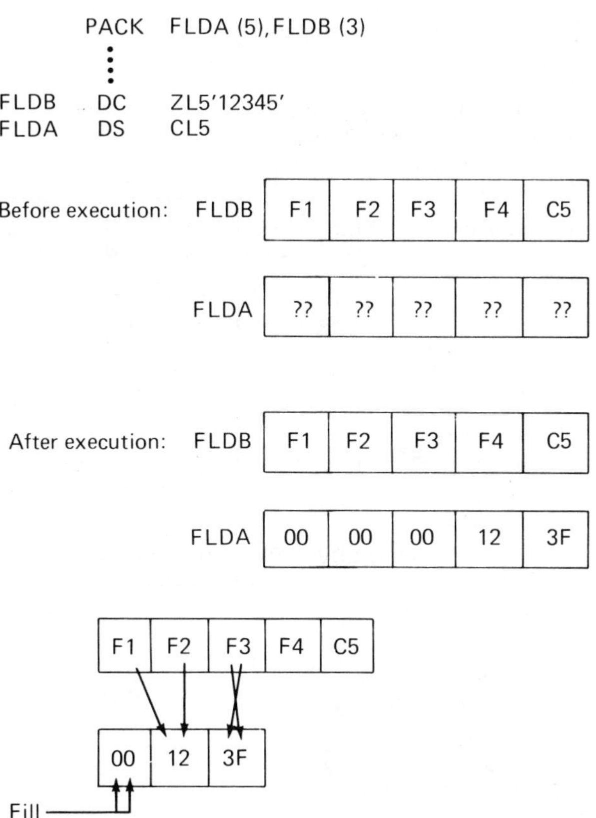

Figure 5-8 Execution of the PACK instruction.

The UNPK Instruction

The UNPK instruction converts packed decimal data to zoned form. The instruction

```
UNPK   FLDA(5),FLDB(3)
```

converts the packed data in FLDB to zoned form in FLDA (Figure 5-9). The assembler must know the length of each operand. Execution proceeds from right to left. If the first operand (receiving) field is too small, the high-order positions of the second operand (sending) field are truncated. If the receiving field is too large, decimal zeros are added. We see examples of the UNPK instruction in Table 5-4.

Packing a decimal number saves storage. The redundant zone positions are eliminated. There is another reason for packing data. The S/370 *requires* data to be packed before decimal arithmetic is performed.

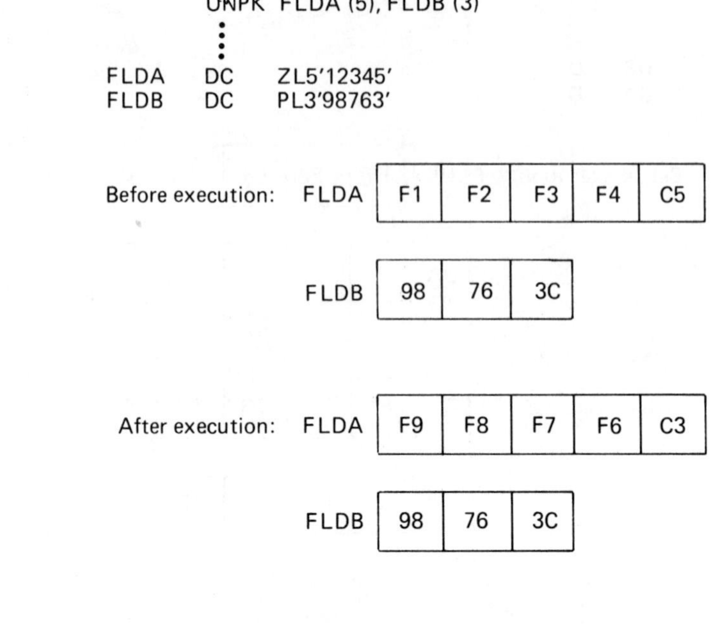

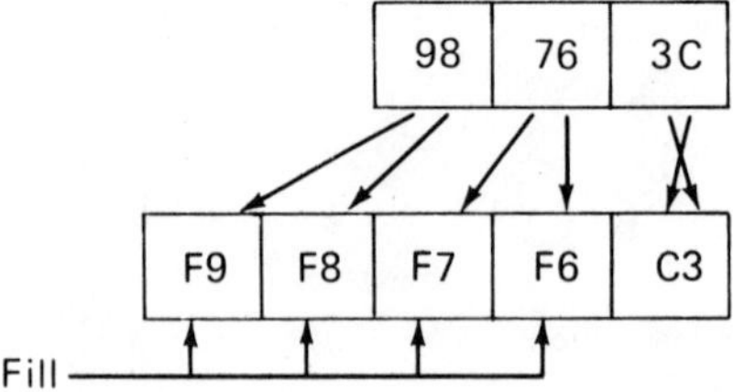

Figure 5-9 Execution of the UNPK instruction.

Table 5-4 Execution of the UNPK Instruction

location	instruction	first operand after execution
FLDA: 1C	UNPK FLDB(1),FLDA(1)	FLDB: C1
FLDB: 2D	UNPK FLDD(2),FLDC(2)	FLDD: F1D2
FLDC: 012D	UNPK FLDE(3),FLDB(1)	FLDE: F0F0D2
FLDD: 345C	UNPK FLDD(2),FLDE(3)	FLDD: F9C6
FLDE: 12896C	UNPK FLDD(2),FLDE(2)	FLDD: F298

DECIMAL ARITHMETIC

The decimal arithmetic instructions perform arithmetic operations—addition, subtraction, multiplication, and division—on *packed* decimal operands. Both operands reside in main storage.

Decimal Add and Subtract Instructions

The decimal add instruction, the AP (Add Packed) instruction, adds two packed decimal numbers. The maximum operand length is sixteen bytes. The result of the addition is placed in the first operand location.

In the example shown below

```
        AP    FLDA(3),FLDB(3)
        .
        .
        .
FLDA    DC    PL3'123'
FLDB    DC    PL3'345'
```

FLDA will contain the result, the sum of the contents of FLDA and FLDB. After the instruction is executed, FLDA contains

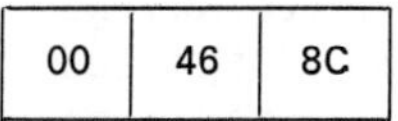

The contents of FLDB are unchanged.

The first operand field must be large enough to hold the *result* of the addition. For example, the code

```
        AP    FLDA(3),FLDB(3)
        .
        .
        .
FLDA    DC    PL3'99999'
FLDB    DC    PL3'99999'
```

generates a packed result of

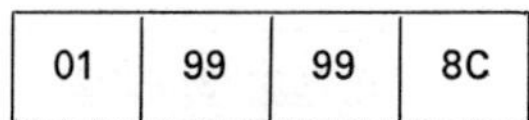

The result requires *four* bytes of storage. The instruction specifies a length of three bytes for the first operand. The computer realizes that an error has occurred. We refer to this type of error—the answer is too big for the first operand location—as an *overflow condition.* In some cases the computer stops when an overflow condition occurs. In other cases, the programmer must include instructions to test for the overflow error. We will examine this type of error in Chapter 18.

An overflow is one type of error which may occur during execution of the AP instruction. Another error, called a *data exception,* occurs if one of the fields in an AP operation does not contain packed data. For example,

```
        AP ONE, TWO
        .
        .
        .
ONE DC ZL3'001'
TWO DC ZL3'002'
```

We are attempting to add two *zoned* constants. A data exception occurs. The computer stops processing the program when a data exception occurs.

Table 5-5 shows the use of the AP instruction. Some of the examples given result in errors. It is the programmer's responsibility to allow sufficient storage for the answer, and to make certain that all data fields contain packed data.

Table 5-5 Execution of the AP Instruction

location	instruction	first operand after execution
FLD1: 01238C	AP FLD1(3),FLD2(2)	FLD1: 02135C
FLD2: 897C	AP FLD1(3),FLD3(2)	FLD1: 02237C
FLD3: 999C	AP FLD3(2),FLD4(2)	FLD3: 962C
FLD4: 037D	AP FLD2(2),FLD4(2)	FLD2: 860C
	AP FLD2(2),FLD3(2)	OVERFLOW
	AP FLD1(2),FLD2(2)	DATA EXCEPTION

The SP (Subtract Packed) instruction subtracts the contents of the second operand location from the contents of the first operand location. The result is placed in the first operand location. Both operands must contain packed data. The maximum length of each operand is sixteen bytes.

Table 5-6 Execution of the SP Instruction

location	instruction	first operand after execution
FLD1: 01238C	SP FLD1(3),FLD2(2)	FLD1: 00341C
FLD2: 897C	SP FLD1(3),FLD3(2)	FLD1: 00239C
FLD3: 999C	SP FLD1(3),FLD4(2)	FLD1: 01275C
FLD4: 037D	SP FLD3(2),FLD2(2)	FLD3: 102C
	SP FLD2(2),FLD3(2)	FLD2: 102D
	SP FLD2(2),FLD4(2)	FLD2: 934C
	SP FLD4(2),FLD2(2)	FLD4: 934D
	SP FLD3(2),FLD4(2)	OVERFLOW

A Sample Program

We have seen examples of the decimal add and subtract instructions. We now will examine the use of one of these instructions, the AP instruction, in a sample program.

Program 2 ***Problem Statement.**** Find the sum of four 4-byte packed decimal constants in main storage. Store the sum in zoned format in an area of storage called RESULT.

Solution. We begin our solution by defining the data:

0000010C	4 PACKED CONSTANTS
0000020C	
0000030C	
0000040C	

four packed constants in storage. The values assigned these constants are arbitrary. Any valid decimal number would serve our purpose. We must define these constants, and then develop the instructions to find their sum.

We use the DC instruction to define the constants.

```
CON1  DC  PL4'10'
CON2  DC  PL4'20'
CON3  DC  PL4'30'
CON4  DC  PL4'40'
```

We also must set aside storage for the answer. We name this storage space RESULT.

```
RESULT DS CL4
```

Our program must add the contents of CON1, CON2, CON3, and CON4. We need an area of storage in which to build the answer. This additional area of storage is called a work area. We use work areas for *temporary* storage of data. Our program requires one work area

```
ANS DC PL4'0'
```

We must initialize ANS since we will be *adding* packed data to this field. Remember, both operands in a decimal add instruction must contain packed data. If we did not initialize ANS, the computer would add the contents of CON1 to whatever data is still in the storage area provided for ANS. Our result would obviously be wrong. Also the data already in ANS would probably not be packed, which would cause the computer to stop after the first add.

We now are ready to develop the processing instructions. We will build the answer in ANS. We add the first constant to ANS

```
AP      ANS,CON1
```

It is not necessary to code a length attribute for either field. We specified the length of each operand in the DC instruction.

*A description of all the programs used in the text is found in Appendix C.

We repeat the AP instruction for each of the three remaining constants. We must then UNPK the sum contained in ANS into RESULT. The complete solution to Program 2 is given in Figure 5-10.

```
*
* PROGRAM 2
* SUM OF FOUR DECIMAL CONSTANTS
*
         PRINT NOGEN
FIRST    HSKPING
*        *
*        *      SOME
*        *      HOUSEKEEPING
*        *      STATEMENTS
*        *      ARE
*        *      OMITTED
*        *      HERE
*        *
         AP     ANS,CON1                 ADD FIRST CONSTANT
         AP     ANS,CON2                 ADD SECOND CONSTANT
         AP     ANS,CON3                 ADD THIRD CONSTANT
         AP     ANS,CON4                 ADD FOURTH CONSTANT
         UNPK   RESULT,ANS               UNPACK ANSWER INTO RESULT
*        *
*        *      THE PROGRAM IS COMPLETE
*        *      THE RETURN STATEMENT
*        *      SIGNIFIES END-OF-JOB
*        *
         RETURN (14,12)                  RETURN
*
* DATA AREAS
*
CON1     DC     PL4'10'
CON2     DC     PL4'20'                  * FOUR
CON3     DC     PL4'30'                  * PACKED
CON4     DC     PL4'40'                  * DECIMAL
ANS      DC     PL4'0'                   * CONSTANTS
RESULT   DS     CL4
         END    FIRST
```

Figure 5-10 Program 2—solution.

In this, and in subsequent programs, we must use certain statements to simplify the solution. Our programs all follow the general pattern

```
      PRINT   NOGEN
FIRST HSKPING
      .                 processing
      .                 instructions
      .
      RETURN  (14,12)
      .                 data areas
      .
      .
      END     FIRST
```

The PRINT statement eliminates printing the instructions associated with the HSKPING and RETURN statements.

The HSKPING statement performs certain initializing functions. Operands following the HSKPING statement may be used to name files. For example,

```
HSKPING  CARDID=INCARD,PRINTID=PRINT
```

This statement names an input card file INCARD and a print file PRINT.

The HSKPING statement also may be used to name a section of code to be entered when all the records in an input file have been read.

```
HSKPING  CARDID=INCARD,EOFID=EOJRT
```

The RETURN statement is the last instruction in the program. This statement tells the operating system that the program is complete.

The data areas usually follow the RETURN statement. And finally, the END statement marks the end of the program. The label in the END statement is the name associated with the first instruction in the program.

We begin the program (see Figure 5-10) with the PRINT and HSKPING statements. We do not use files in this program so there are no operands in the HSKPING statement. We then add the first constant to ANS. We repeat this instruction for the remaining constants. The sum is now in ANS in packed format. The problem statement asks us to store the sum in zoned format. The UNPK instruction takes the packed sum in ANS and unpacks it into RESULT. The program is now complete. The RETURN statement tells the operating system that this program is finished.

We have seen the use of the decimal add instruction in a sample program. We now will introduce the decimal multiply and divide instructions, and examine the use of the divide instruction in a sample program.

Decimal Multiply and Divide Instructions

The decimal multiply and divide instructions operate on packed operands in storage. The instructions are storage-to-storage instructions. In both the multiply and divide instructions, the result is placed in the first operand location.

The MP (Multiply Decimal) Instruction. The statement

```
MP  FLDA(6),FLDB(3)
```

multiplies the contents of FLDA by the contents of FLDB. Both operands must be in packed format. An error called a data exception occurs if one or both operands do not contain valid packed data. The result of the operation is placed in FLDA (Figure 5-11).

We refer to FLDB, the second operand field, as the *multiplier*. FLDA, the first operand field, is the *multiplicand.* The multiplier may contain only fifteen digits. We need eight bytes of storage to represent a packed number containing fifteen digits and a sign. If the length of the multiplier exceeds eight bytes, an

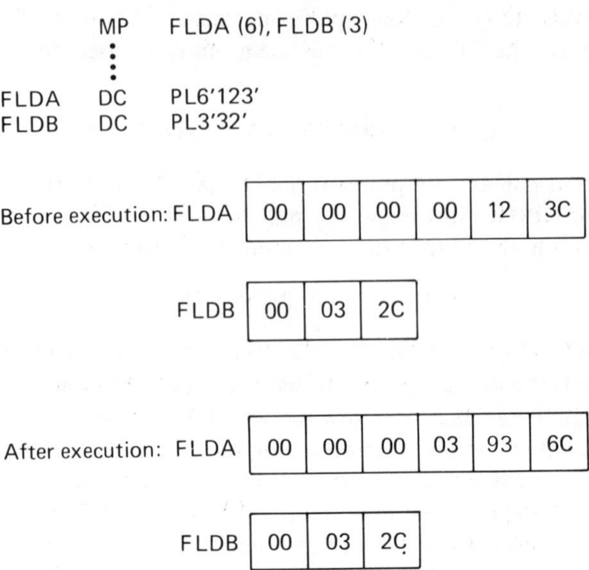

Figure 5-11 Execution of the MP instruction.

error called a specification exception occurs. The computer stops processing the program.

In a multiplication operation, the sum of the number of digits in the product (the answer) is equal to the sum of the digits in *both* operands. The product must fit into the first operand location. The multiplicand must have high-order zeros equal to the number of digits plus sign in the multiplier, otherwise the computer stops processing. An error called a data exception is recognized. This rule ensures that the product always fits into the first operand location. (See Figure 5-12).

Both operands in the multiplication operation are signed or treated as positive. The sign of the product follows the rules of algebra. The reader should examine the examples in Table 5-7, and verify that the sign of each product is correct.

Table 5-7 Execution of the MP Instruction

location	instruction	first operand after execution
FLDA: 2C	MP FLDC(3),FLDA(1)	FLDC: 00246C
FLDB: 2D	MP FLDC(3),FLDB(1)	FLDC: 00246D
FLDC: 00123C	MP FLDD(3),FLDA(1)	FLDD: 00246D
FLDD: 00123D	MP FLDD(3),FLDB(1)	FLDD: 00246C
	MP FLDD(3),FLDC(2)	DATA EXCEPTION
	MP FLDD(3),FLDC(3)	DATA EXCEPTION

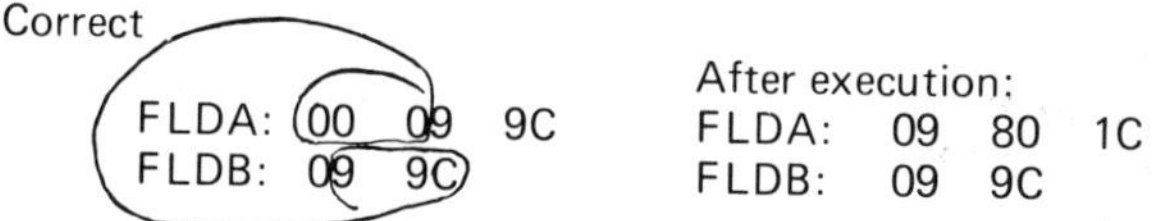

MP FLDA (3), FLDB (2)

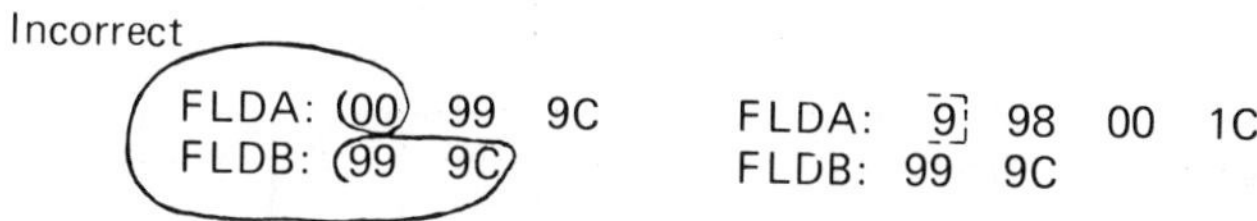

Answer does not fit!

Figure 5-12 Field size considerations.

The DP (Divide Packed) Instruction. The DP instruction divides the contents of the first operand (the dividend) by the contents of the second operand (the divisor). The result is placed in the first operand location. Both operands must be in packed format. An error called a data exception occurs if one or both operands does not contain packed data.

The result obtained in division is unique. We must consider both the quotient and the remainder. In the program segment shown below, we are

```
         DP  TOP(6),BOTTOM(2)
          .
          .
          .
BOTTOM   DC  PL2'3'
TOP      DC  PL6'127'
```

dividing the number 127 by the number 3. The quotient is 42. The remainder is 1.

We must represent both the quotient of 42 and the remainder of 1 in the area of storage called TOP. The quotient is placed in the high-order bytes of TOP. The remainder is placed in the low-order bytes. The length of the remainder is equal to the length of the divisor (the second operand). The remaining bytes contain the quotient (Figure 5-13). If the quotient and remainder do not fit into the first operand location, an error called a decimal divide exception occurs. An attempt to divide by zero also causes a decimal divide exception.

We also must consider the *signs* of the quotient and remainder. The sign of the quotient is determined by the rules of algebra. The remainder takes the sign of the dividend.

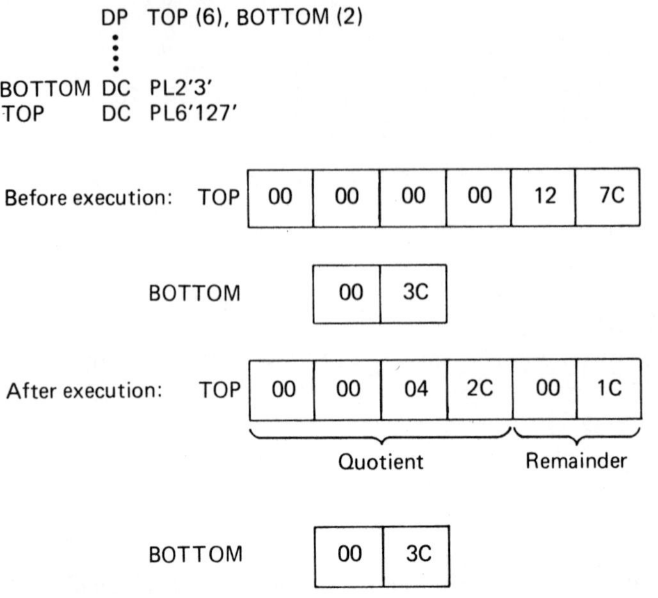

Figure 5-13 The DP instruction.

Table 5-8 Execution of the DP Instruction

location	instruction	first operand after execution
FLDA: 2C	DP FLDC(3),FLDA(1)	FLDC: 061C1C
FLDB: 2D	DP FLDC(3),FLDB(1)	FLDC: 061D1C
FLDC: 00123C	DP FLDD(3),FLDA(1)	FLDD: 061D1D
FLDD: 00123D	DP FLDD(3),FLDB(1)	FLDD: 061C1D
	DP FLDC(3),FLDD(2)	DATA EXCEPTION
	DP FLDA(1),FLDC(3)	DECIMAL DIVIDE EXCEPTION

Two Sample Programs

We have seen examples of the decimal multiply and divide instructions. We will now develop sample programs using some of these instructions.

Program 3 ***Problem Statement.*** Find the average of four 4-byte constants. You must define a value for each constant. Store the quotient in an area of storage called RESULT. You may ignore the remainder.

Solution. The reader should begin to anticipate the steps involved in solving a programming problem. We first define our data. We must define the four constants and the work areas we will need.

```
CON1    DC  PL4'10'
CON2    DC  PL4'20'
CON3    DC  PL4'30'
CON4    DC  PL4'40'
ANS     DC  PL4'0'
RESULT  DS  CL4
```

We need one additional constant for Program 3. We are to find the average of four numbers. To find the average, we first find the sum and then divide by 4. We must define a constant whose value is 4.

```
FOUR  DC  PL1'4'
```

Can you explain why the constant was defined as a packed constant rather than a zoned constant? Since the constant is used in an arithmetic operation, it must appear in packed format. If we define a zoned constant, we must code an extra pack instruction. It is more efficient to define the data as packed from the start.

The processing instructions are similar to the instructions in Program 2. We develop the sum of the constants in ANS. We divide the number in ANS by the constant FOUR. The quotient is now in the first three bytes of ANS. The last byte of ANS contains the remainder. (See Figure 5-14.)

Let's pause for a moment to make certain we understand the concept of quotient and remainder. We are dividing a 4-byte number (ANS) by a 1-byte number (FOUR). The result is in the first operand field, ANS. The high-order bytes of ANS contain the quotient; the low-order bytes contain the remainder. The size of the remainder is governed by the size of the second operand, the constant FOUR. The remainder is one byte in length. The remaining three bytes constitute the quotient.

We must unpack the first three bytes of ANS into RESULT. We must specify the length attribute in the UNPK instruction. The instruction

```
UNPK  RESULT,ANS(3)
```

takes the first three bytes of ANS, ignoring the remainder, and unpacks the data into RESULT.

We have examined the use of the decimal add and divide instructions in a simple program. We will now develop the solution to a slightly more complex problem.

Program 4 ***Problem Statement.*** The formula for the volume of a sphere is $(4/3)\pi R^3$. Write a program to find the volume of a sphere with a radius of 10. Use the integer 3 as the value of π. Store the answer in RESULT.

Solution. We begin the solution of Program 4 by defining data. We must define a constant for π, a constant for the radius, a constant for the integer 4, and a

```
*
* PROGRAM 3
* AVERAGE FOUR DECIMAL CONSTANTS
*
          PRINT NOGEN
FIRST     HSKPING
*         *
*         *       SOME
*         *       HOUSEKEEPING
*         *       STATEMENTS
*         *       ARE
*         *       OMITTED
*         *       HERE
*         *
          AP      ANS,CON1                   ADD FIRST CONSTANT
          AP      ANS,CON2                   ADD SECOND CONSTANT
          AP      ANS,CON3                   ADD THIRD CONSTANT
          AP      ANS,CON4                   ADD FOURTH CONSTANT
          DP      ANS,FOUR                   AND FIND AVERAGE
          UNPK    RESULT,ANS(3)              UNPACK QUOTIENT - IGNORE REMAINDER
*         *
*         *       THE PROGRAM IS COMPLETE
*         *       THE RETURN STATEMENT
*         *       SIGNIFIES END-OF-JOB
*         *
          RETURN (14,12)                     RETURN
*
* DATA AREAS
*
FOUR      DC      PL1'4'
CON1      DC      PL4'10'
CON2      DC      PL4'20'                    * FOUR
CON3      DC      PL4'30'                    * PACKED
CON4      DC      PL4'40'                    * DECIMAL
ANS       DC      PL4'0'                     * CONSTANTS
RESULT    DS      CL4
          END     FIRST
```

Figure 5-14 Program 3—solution.

constant for the integer 3. We must also define a work area where we will build the answer (RCUBE).

```
FOUR     DC   PL1'4'
THREE    DC   PL1'3'
RADIUS   DC   PL2'10'
RCUBE    DC   PL6'10'
PI       DC   PL1'3'
RESULT   DS   PL5
```

The solution to Program 4 is given in Figure 5-15. The program first finds the cube of the radius. The initial value of RCUBE is ten. We multiply RCUBE by RADIUS. The result in RCUBE is the square of the radius. We now multiply RCUBE by RADIUS to obtain the cube of the radius.

The next statement multiplies the value in RCUBE by the value in π. The result in RCUBE is then multiplied by 4. The last arithmetic statement, the DP instruction, divides the number in RCUBE by 3.

```
*
* PROGRAM 4
* VOLUME OF A SPHERE
* VOLUME=(4/3)PI(R**3)
* DECIMAL INTEGER ARITHMETIC
* SOLUTION BY JUDY ADCOCK
*
         PRINT NOGEN
BEGIN    HSKPING
*        *
*        *      SOME
*        *      HOUSEKEEPING
*        *      STATEMENTS
*        *      ARE
*        *      OMITTED
*        *      HERE
*        *
         MP     RCUBE,RADIUS              SQUARE RADIUS
         MP     RCUBE,RADIUS              CUBE RADIUS
         MP     RCUBE,PI                  MULTIPLY BY PI
         MP     RCUBE,FOUR                MULTIPLY BY 4
         DP     RCUBE,THREE               DIVIDE BY 3
         UNPK   RESULT(5),RCUBE(3)        STORE RESULT IGNORING REMAINDER
*        *
*        *      THE PROGRAM IS COMPLETE
*        *      THE RETURN STATEMENT
*        *      SIGNIFIES END-OF-JOB
*        *
         RETURN (14,12)                   RETURN
*
* DATA AREAS
*
FOUR     DC     PL1'4'
THREE    DC     PL1'3'
RADIUS   DC     PL2'10'
RCUBE    DC     PL6'10'
PI       DC     PL1'3'
RESULT   DS     PL5
         END    BEGIN
```

Figure 5-15 Program 4—solution.

We are asked to store the quotient—the remainder is zero—in RESULT. We must unpack the first three bytes of RCUBE into RESULT. The instruction

```
UNPK   RESULT(5),RCUBE(3)
```

unpacks the first three bytes of RCUBE into result. The answer, the volume of a sphere with a radius of ten, is stored in zoned format in RESULT. The program is not yet complete. The RETURN statement tells the operating system that this program is finished.

PROBLEMS **5.1** Write the assembly language instructions (DC) to define the following constants.

1. A 4-byte zoned decimal constant (CON1) with a value of 6789.
2. A 4-byte zoned decimal constant (CON2) with a value of 4.
3. A 10-byte packed decimal constant (CON3) with a value of zero.

4. An 80-byte character constant (CON4) with a value of spaces.
5. A 4-byte zoned decimal constant (CON5) with a value of 1212. Use a duplication factor.

5.2 How many bytes of computer storage are reserved by each of the following statements?

```
a. FLDA   DC   CL1'1'          f. FLDF   DC   ZL1'1'
b. FLDB   DS   CL1'1'          g. FLDG   DC   PL1'1'
c. FLDC   DS   2CL3'123'       h. FLDH   DC   CL4'CAT'
d. FLDD   DC   3PL3'123'       i. FLDI   DC   CL2'CAT'
e. FLDE   DC   80CL1'1'        j. FLDJ   DC   PL4'12'
```

5.3 Give the contents of each of the storage areas defined in Problem 5.2. Please indicate if you do not know the contents of a field.

5.4 The contents of six computer storage locations are given below. Give the contents of the first operand location after each of the following instructions is executed.

storage location	contents	instruction	
FLDA	00123C	PACK	FLDA(3),FLDF(3)
FLDB	000000127C	AP	FLDB(5),FLDA(3)
FLDC	2C	AP	FLDA(3),FLDD(1)
FLDD	2D	SP	FLDA(3),FLDD(1)
FLDE	3C	MP	FLDB(5),FLDE(1)
FLDF	F1F2F3	MP	FLDA(3),FLDD(1)
		SP	FLDC(1),FLDD(1)
		DP	FLDA(3),FLDE(1)
		DP	FLDA(3),FLDD(1)
		DP	FLDA(3),FLDC(1)
		UNPK	FLDB(5),FLDA(3)

5.5 The following instructions reference the data described in Problem 5.4. The execution of some of these instructions causes an error. Indicate the type of error (data exception, divide exception, overflow, or specification exception). Please indicate if no error occurs.

```
a. INST1   AP   FLDF(3),FLDA(3)
b. INST2   AP   FLDC(1),FLDD(1)
c. INST3   AP   FLDC(1),FLDB(5)
d. INST4   MP   FLDF(3),FLDE(1)
e. INST5   MP   FLDD(1),FLDE(1)
f. INST6   MP   FLDA(3),FLDB(3)
g. INST7   AP   FLDA(3),FLDB(3)
h. INST8   DP   FLDA(3),FLDB(5)
```

5.6 Write a program to find the sum of four 4-byte *zoned* constants in storage.

5.7 Write a program to find the sum of the numbers from 1 to 5. Do not attempt any loop control.

5.8 Write an assembly language program to calculate the value of the following expression:

$$X = \frac{(A + B) - C}{(D + E)}$$

Use the following constants in your program.

```
A   DC   PL3'123'
B   DC   PL3'001'
C   DC   PL3'3'
D   DC   PL2'2'
E   DC   PL3'3'
```

Store the quotient (you may ignore the remainder) in zoned format in an area of storage called RESULT.

5.9 Decimal arithmetic performs operations on integers. Placing decimal points and rounding becomes the programmer's responsibility. When we round a number, we add 5 to the last digit we wish to drop and divide by the appropriate power of ten. Develop the instructions to round the following numbers as shown.

```
a. DEC1   DC   P'123.456'   round to one decimal place
b. DEC2   DC   Z'123.456'   round to two decimal places
c. BIN3   DC   P'1.23456'   round to three decimal places
```

Note: Although the decimal point is shown in the constant, the constants are assembled as integers.

5.10 How would you go about determining if the data in an area of storage called RESULT is an even or odd number? Develop as much of the code to test your answer as you can. What instructions must you know before your can complete the code?

6

Data Transfer and Sequence Control

We have learned to define decimal data and to perform arithmetic operations on decimal data. We now will examine the instructions which transfer data, and then develop the basic concepts of sequence control.

DATA TRANSFER

There are two types of data transfer as illustrated in Figure 6-1. We may transfer data between two storage locations using the MVC (MoVe Characters) instruction. We may also transfer data between the I/O devices and computer storage. We use the GET and PUT statements to transfer data in and out of storage. The GET and PUT instructions are special instructions called *macros*. These instructions are abbreviations for large groups of instructions.

The MVC Instruction

The MVC instruction is used to move variable-length decimal data from one main storage location to another. The instruction may be used to move from 1 to 256 bytes of data. The MVCL (MoVe Characters Long) instruction can be used to move more than 256 bytes of data. This instruction, discussed in Chapter 14, is available only on the S/370.

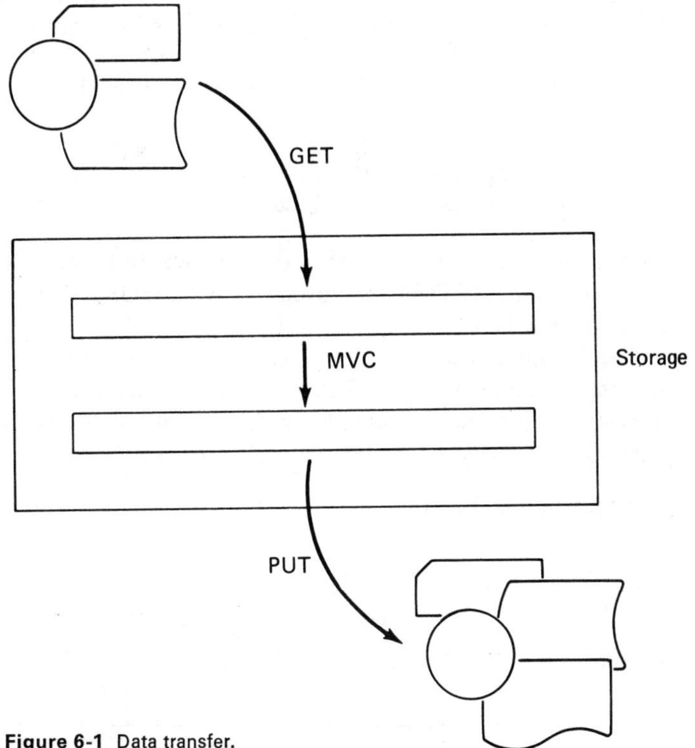

Figure 6-1 Data transfer.

Let's consider an example of the MVC instruction. The statement

```
MVC   CARDWORK,CARDIN
```

moves data from an area of storage called CARDIN to an area of storage called CARDWORK. The MVC instruction moves data from the second operand location to the first operand location.

The instruction does not specify how many bytes of data we are moving. Let's see how we tell the computer the length of the data. The statement

```
MVC   CARDWORK(80),CARDIN
```

tells the computer we are moving 80 bytes of data from an area of storage called CARDIN to an area of storage called CARDWORK. The number specifying the length of the field we are moving follows the first operand. The length field is enclosed in parenthesis. If we wished to move 100 bytes of data, we would code the statement

```
MVC   CARDWORK(100),CARDIN
```

But remember, before we can process data, we must define the data. Both CARDIN and CARDWORK must be defined. For example

```
          MVC  CARDWORK(80),CARDIN
          .
          .
          .
CARDWORK  DS   CL80
CARDIN    DS   CL80
```

We do not know the value of CARDIN. We do know, however, that the 80 bytes of data at CARDIN are moved to CARDWORK. The data previously in CARDWORK is destroyed.

What about the contents of CARDIN? After execution of the MVC instruction, the contents of CARDIN remains unchanged. Only the contents of the first operand location are changed. We can use the DC statement in a program segment to clarify this concept (Figure 6-2).

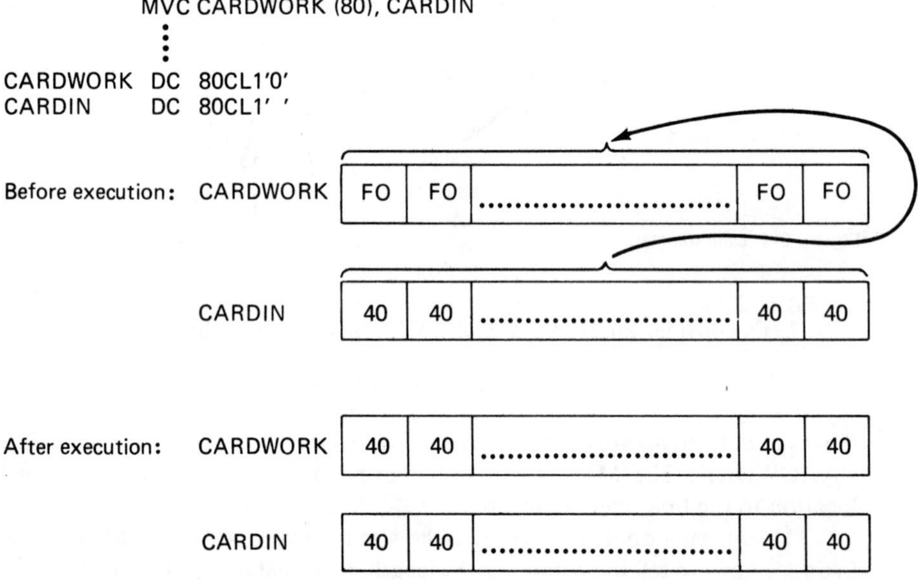

Figure 6-2 Execution of the MVC instruction.

CARDIN is set to blanks (a hexadecimal 40 (40_{16}) is the EBCDIC code for a blank). CARDWORK is set to decimal zeros. The MVC statement moves 80 blanks from CARDIN to CARDWORK. The zeros in CARDWORK are destroyed. CARDIN still contains 80 blanks.

The MVC statement moves data, a character at a time, from the second operand location to the first operand location. Data movement proceeds from left to right. If the specified length is less than the length of the second operand, the low-order bytes of data are lost. We see an example of this in Figure 6-3.

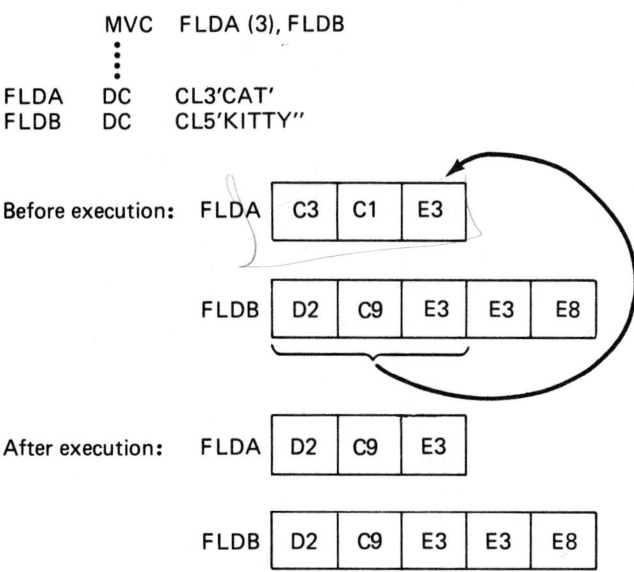

Figure 6-3 Low-order bytes can be lost in the MVC instruction.

FLDB is a 5-byte field containing the character constant KITTY. FLDA is a 3-byte field containing the chatacter constant CAT. The last two bytes of FLDB are not moved when the MVC instruction is executed.

A Sample Program

We know the use of the DC and DS instructions to define data and to reserve storage. We have learned that the MVC instruction is used to move data from one area of storage to another. We now will see how this instruction may be used in a computer program. Let's examine the problem statement for program 1, and then develop the assembly language program.

Program 1 ***Problem Statement.*** A payroll file resides on punched cards. Each card contains the payroll record of an employee. The format of the record is given in Figure 6-4. Write a program to print the employee number, employee name, and gross pay. All other fields are ignored. The format of the printed report is also in Figure 6-4.

The solution to Program 1 follows the basic data processing pattern. Data are input. Data are processed. Data are output. A general flowchart for Program 1 is shown in Figure 6-5.

Solution. The solution to Program 1 consists to data descriptions and instructions. We must describe the format of the input record and the output record. We also must describe the input card file and the output print file. At this point, however, we will present the solution without the file descriptions.

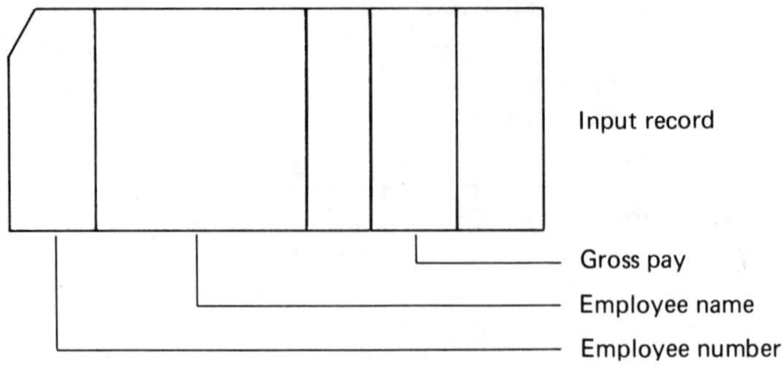

Input positions	Field	Output positions
1-6	Employee number	11-16
7-26	Employee name	27-46
51-58	Gross pay	57-64

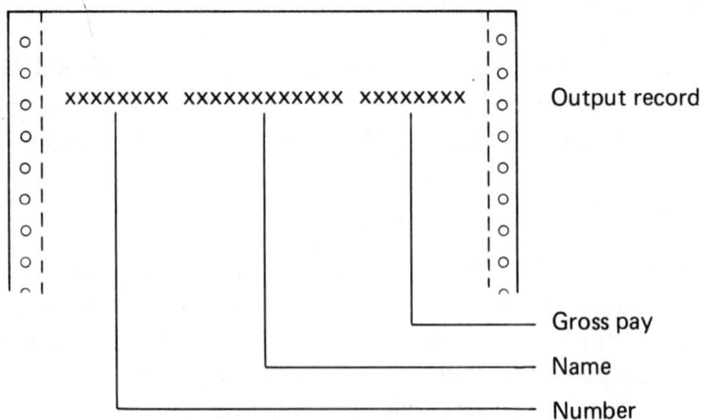

Figure 6-4 Program 1—problem statement.

Let's examine the description of the input record. We must tell the computer the name of each field. We also must specify the length of the field, and the type of data the field contains. We do not assign a value to the field. The values—the data we are processing—are contained on the punched card. We use the DS statement to set aside storage for each field within a single punched card record. The storage is not initialized until the data record is read into the computer.

We must reserve 80 bytes of storage for the input record.

```
INWORK  DS  CL80
```

We now must format or describe the fields comprising INWORK.

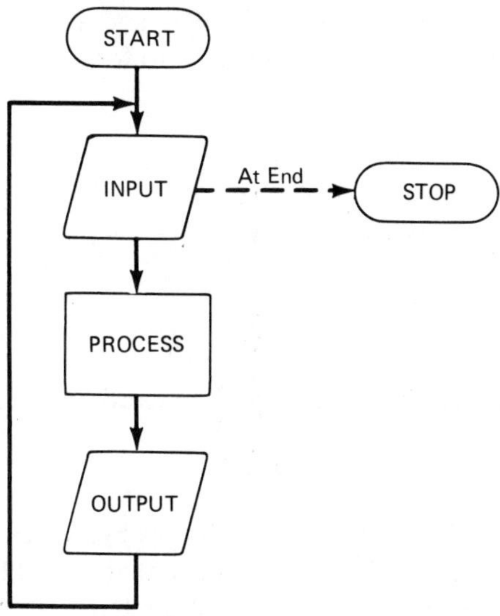

Figure 6-5 Program 1—flowchart.

The first field is the employee number field. We chose the symbolic name NUMIN for the employee number. NUMIN is a 6-position field. We reserve storage for NUMIN using the statement

```
NUMIN  DS  CL6
```

Notice that we do not assign a value for NUMIN. NUMIN is not a constant. It is a variable. The value of NUMIN changes each time a new data card is read.

The next field is the 20-position employee name field. We reserve storage for the name field as follows

```
NAMEIN  DS  CL20
```

Let's examine the input record description at this point.

```
INWORK  DS  CL80
NUMIN   DS  CL6
NAMEIN  DS  CL20
```

Our description is not correct. We have reserved a total of 106 positions of storage. We are not giving the assembler the correct information. We want to tell the assembler that we are reserving 80 bytes for INWORK, and that we are formating these 80 bytes into the fields comprising the payroll record.

We can use the duplication factor in the DC statement to solve our problem. Remember, the duplication factor tells the assembler the number of times the data description is to be duplicated. A duplication factor of zero reserves no storage. For example

```
INWORK  DS  0CL80
```

But this statement does define the label INWORK and associates a length of 80 with the label INWORK. We can now proceed to format the 80 bytes comprising INWORK.

```
INWORK   DS  0CL80
NUMIN    DS  CL6
NAMEIN   DS  CL20
         DS  CL24
GROSSIN  DS  CL8
         DS  CL22
```

We select the label INWORK for the input record.

```
INWORK  DS  0CL80
```

The next five DS statements total 80 bytes. The first six bytes are called NUMIN. The next twenty bytes are called NAMEIN. Notice that not all the fields in the input record are labeled. We label only those fields referenced in our program.

We also must describe the output record. The conventional size of the printed line is 120 characters. We use the DS and DC statements to format the 120 characters of the output record PRINTBLD.

```
PRINTBLD   DS  0CL120
           DC  10CL1' '
NUMOUT     DS  CL6
           DC  10CL1' '
NAMEOUT    DS  CL20
           DC  10CL1' '
GROSSOUT   DS  CL8
           DC  56CL1' '
```

We use the DC statement in PRINTBLD to initialize certain areas of storage to spaces. The program moves data into the remaining areas—NAMEOUT, NUMOUT, and GROSSOUT. The programmer must ensure that the areas between these output fields contain blanks. If he does not, the printed report may contain meaningless information appropriately called garbage.

We have just described the input record INWORK and the output record PRINTBLD (Figure 6-6). We now are ready to develop the instructions themselves.

Let's see what the instructions must do. First we must read a record into INWORK. We must move the number field from INWORK to the correct position in PRINTBLD. We must move the name field and the gross salary field, and we must write the data from PRINTBLD to the printer.

We will use the statement

```
GET   INCARD,INWORK
```

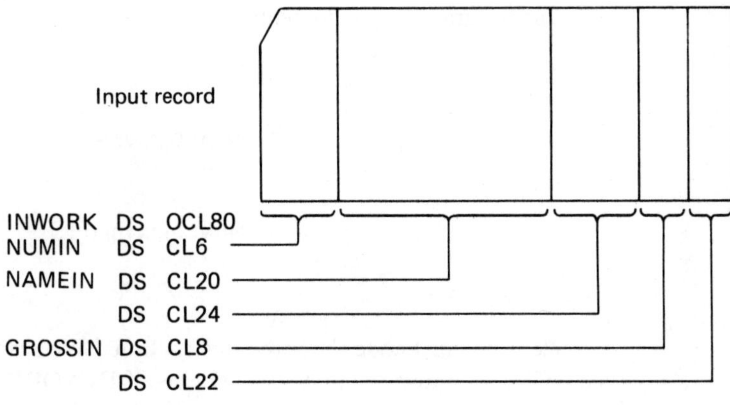
Input record
INWORK DS OCL80
NUMIN DS CL6
NAMEIN DS CL20
DS CL24
GROSSIN DS CL8
DS CL22

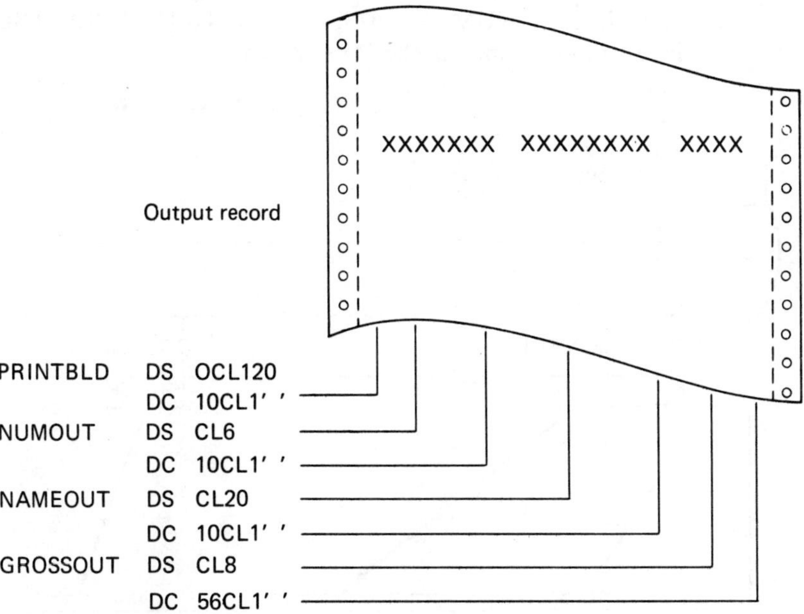
XXXXXXX XXXXXXXX XXXX
Output record
PRINTBLD DS OCL120
DC 10CL1' '
NUMOUT DS CL6
DC 10CL1' '
NAMEOUT DS CL20
DC 10CL1' '
GROSSOUT DS CL8
DC 56CL1' '

Figure 6-6 Program 1—data formats.

to read a single data card. This statement takes a record from the file called INCARD and places it in an area of storage called INWORK. We will use the statement

```
PUT   PRINT,PRINTBLD
```

to write the data from an area of storage called PRINTBLD to the file called PRINT.

Our program begins to evolve.

```
        .
        .
        .
        GET   INCARD,INWORK
        .
        .
        .
        PUT   PRINT,PRINTBLD
        .
        .
        .
```

We now must code the move instructions. We read a single record into INWORK. We move the first six positions of INWORK to positions 11–16 of PRINTBLD (the output description in Figure 6-7 specifies that the employee number field occupies positions 11–16 on the report). We have associated the symbolic name NUMIN with the first six positions of INWORK, and the symbolic name NUMOUT with positions 11–16 of PRINTBLD. We can use these symbolic names in the MVC statement

```
        MVC   NUMOUT(6),NUMIN
```

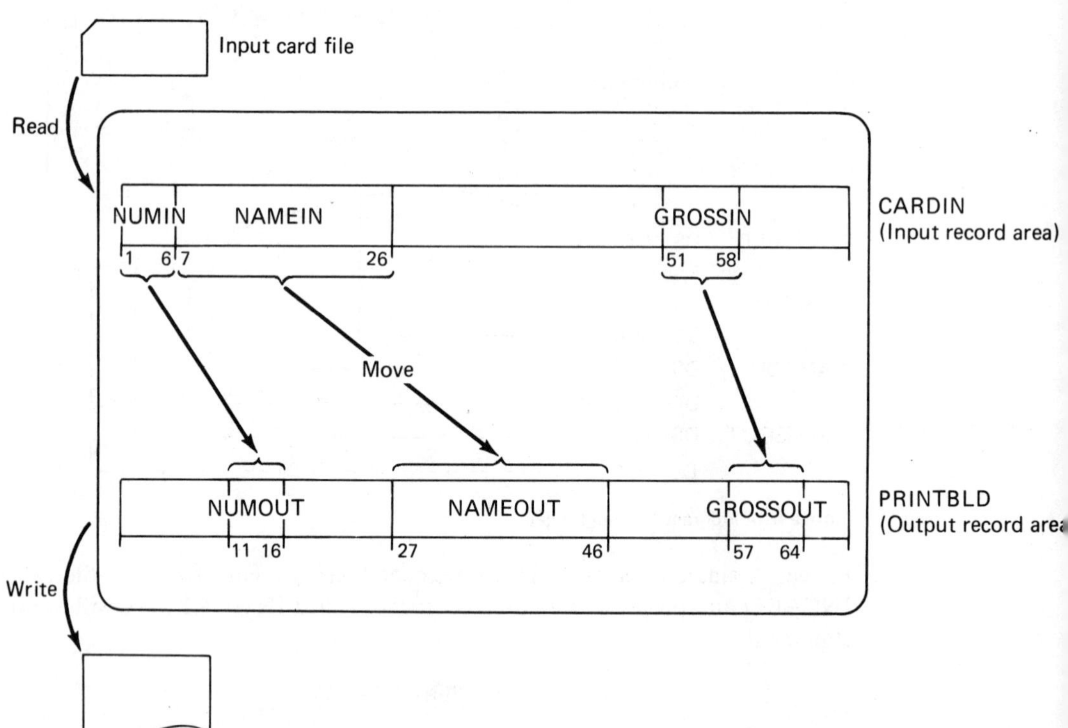

Figure 6-7 Program 1—schematic.

The length attribute associated with the first operand tells the assembler that six bytes of data are being moved.

The other move statements are coded in the same way. Our program now appears as

```
        .
        .
        .
        GET   INCARD,INWORK
        MVC   NUMOUT(6),NUMIN
        MVC   NAMEOUT(20),NAMEIN
        MVC   GROSSOUT(8),GROSSIN
        PUT   PRINT,PRINTBLD
        .
        .
        .
```

The program is not complete. We have read only one card. There may be other cards remaining in the card reader. We could code successive GET, MVC, and PUT instructions to process each remaining data card. We know, however, that this type of programming is unwieldy. We would have to know the exact number of cards in the file, and we would have to change the program every time the number of cards in the file were changed.

We execute the GET, MVC, and PUT statements over and over. These statements comprise a loop. After we process the first card, we loop back to the GET statement. We must code an unconditional branch statement. The code becomes

```
READRT  GET   INCARD INWORK
        .
        .
        .
        PUT   PRINT,PRINTBLD
        B     READRT
```

The statement

```
        B     READRT
```

returns us to the GET statement labeled READRT. At what point do we exit from the loop? There is no counter to be incremented and tested as a means of controlling the number of times we execute the instructions within the loop. We want to exit from this loop when all the cards in the reader have been processed. We say we exit from the loop at end-of-file .The operating system knows when all the cards have been processed and terminates the program. The complete solution for Program 1 is given in Figure 6-8.

We have used the PRINT and HSKPING statements before. They perform certain required functions and are used to simplify the solution. In this

```
*
* PROGRAM 1
* CARD TO PRINT
*
         START
         PRINT NOGEN
FIRST    HSKPING CARDID=INCARD,PRINTID=PRINT       NAME FILES
*        *
*        *        SOME
*        *        HOUSEKEEPING
*        *        STATEMENTS
*        *        ARE
*        *        OMITTED
*        *        HERE
*        *
READRT   GET      INCARD,INWORK                    GET RECORD INTO INWORK
         MVC      NUMOUT(6),NUMIN                  MOVE EMP NUMBER
         MVC      NAMEOUT(20),NAMEIN               EMP NAME
         MVC      GROSSOUT(8),GROSSIN              AND GROSS
         PUT      PRINT,PRINTBLD                   THEN WRITE RECORD
         B        READRT                           AND LOOP BACK
*        *
*        *        AFTER ALL INPUT CARDS
*        *        HAVE BEEN READ AND PROCESSED
*        *        THE PROGRAM IS COMPLETE
*        *
*
* DATA AREAS
*
INWORK   DS       0CL80                            INPUT AREA
NUMIN    DS       CL6                              *
NAMEIN   DS       CL20                             *
         DS       CL24                             *
GROSSIN  DS       CL3                              *
         DS       CL22                             *
PRINTBLD DS       0CL120                           OUTPUT AREA
         DC       10CL1' '                         *
NUMOUT   DS       CL6                              *
         DC       10CL1' '                         *
NAMEOUT  DS       CL20                             *
         DC       10CL1' '                         *
GROSSOUT DS       CL8                              *
         DC       56CL1' '                         *
         END      FIRST
```

Figure 6-8 Program 1—solution.

example, we name the files in the HSKPING statement. The input card file is called INCARD. The output print file is called PRINT.

The main program loop starts with the label READRT. We read a record into INWORK. We move three fields from INWORK to PRINTBLD. And we print the record. We then loop back to the GET statement. When all the cards have been processed the program is complete.

We have seen the use of the MVC instruction in a program. Now let's examine another move instruction; one which moves only a single byte of data.

The MVI Instruction

The MVC instruction may be used to move from 1 to 256 bytes of data from one storage location to another. The MVI (Move Immediate) instruction is used to move a single byte of data to a storage location. The data to be moved is contained within the instruction itself. We call this byte of data the *immediate operand.*

The instruction

```
MVI   LOCA,C' A'
```

moves the character A to the first byte of LOCA. LOCA is the first operand. The second operand is the immediate data to be moved.

We may specify the immediate data as a character (EBCDIC code) operand, a hexadecimal operand, or as a binary operand. For example, the following three instructions provide identical results.

```
MVI   LOCA,C' A'
MVI   LOCA,X' C1'
MVI   LOCA,B' 11000001'
```

Let's pause for a moment. We can describe a byte of data as a single character (C′ A′), as two hexadecimal digits (X′ C1′), or as eight binary bits (B′11000001′). We must tell the assembler which notation we are using. The letter C specifies character notation, the letter X specifies hexadecimal notation, and the letter B specifies binary notation.

Table 6-1 gives some examples of the MVI instruction.

Table 6-1 The MVI Instruction

location	instruction	first operand after execution
LOCA: 00F1F2	MVI LOCA,C' 1'	LOCA: F1F1F2
LOCB: C3C1E2	MVI LOCB,C' A'	LOCB: C1C1E2
LOCC: C4D6C7	MVI LOCC,X' 40'	LOCC: 40D6C7
	MVI LOCA,C' '	LOCA: 40F1F2
	MVI LOCB,B' 00000000'	LOCB: 00C1E2
	MVI LOCC,X' C4'	LOCC: C4D6C7

The MVI and MVC instructions are often used together to propagate a single character throughout a storage area. Assume we want to clear the five bytes of storage labeled AREA to blanks. A single EBCDIC character—a blank—is moved into the first byte of AREA

```
MVI    AREA,X' 40'
```

and is then propagated through the remaining four bytes of AREA

```
         MVC   AREA+1(4),AREA
```

The notation

```
         AREA+1
```

is called *relative* addressing—we are addressing bytes *relative* to the first byte in AREA. In this instance, AREA+1 references the second byte in AREA. This technique works because the MVC instruction moves data a byte at a time from left to right (Figure 6-9), from the sending field to the receiving field. In this example AREA is both the sending and receiving field.

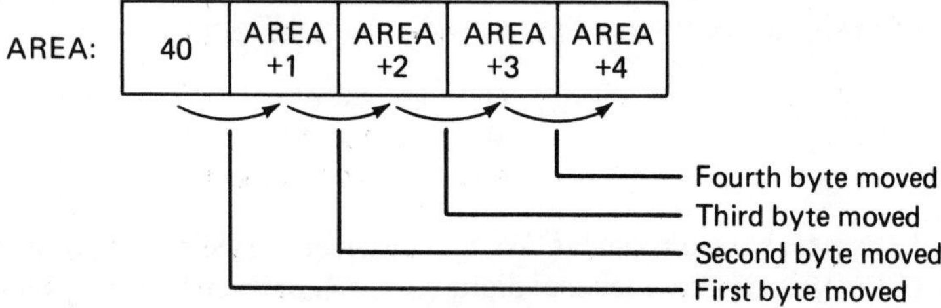

Figure 6-9 Propagating a single byte using the MVC instruction.

We can eliminate the MVI instruction by setting the storage byte preceding AREA to the desired fill character.

```
         MVC   AREA(5),AREA-1
          .
          .
          .
         DC    C' '
AREA     DS    CL5
```

We use relative addressing to reference the fill character, and propagate this byte through the five bytes of AREA.

We used the character constant to initialize the byte preceding AREA to a blank. Some programmers prefer to use hexadecimal or binary notation to specify storage data. For example

```
HEX1     DC    X'40'
```

We are describing a 1-position area of storage called HEX1 and initializing it to a blank. We use hexadecimal notation to describe the value of the constant. We could also use binary notation.

```
BIN1   DC   B'01000000'
```

We use X(hexadecimal) or B(binary) as the type attribute to tell the assembler which notation we are using. Let's look at hexadecimal and binary constants in more detail.

Hexadecimal and Binary Constants

The hexadecimal constant (X) may contain up to 256 hexadecimal digits. The constant is assembled as one byte for each pair of digits. When no length attribute is specified, the assembler calculates the length from the value of the constant. If the length of the constant exceeds the specified length, the leftmost bits or bytes are truncated. If, however, the length of the constant is less than the specified length, the leftmost positions are filled with hexadecimal zeros.

Table 6-2 Generating Hexadecimal Constants

generated code	constant			
C3C1E3	HEX1	DC	X'C3C1E3'	ASSEMBLER ASSUMES LENGTH OF THREE
00C3C1E3	HEX2	DC	XL4'C3C1E3'	ASSEMBLER PADS LEFTMOST BYTE
C1E3	HEX3	DC	XL2'C3C1E3'	ASSEMBLER TRUNCATES LEFTMOST BYTE
C3C1E3C3C1E3	HEX4	DC	2XL3'C3C1E3'	USE OF DUPLICATION FACTOR
00C3C1E300C3C1E3	HEX5	DC	2XL4'C3C1E3'	ASSEMBLER PADS LEFTMOST BYTE
C1E3C1E3	HEX6	DC	2XL2'C3C1E3'	LEFTMOST BYTE TRUNCATED

A binary constant is defined using only 1's and 0's. The maximum length is 256 bytes. The implied length is the number of bytes occupied by the constant, plus any necessary bits required to generate byte alignment. Padding occurs on the left, using binary zeros.

Table 6-3 Generating Binary Constants

generated code	constant			
C1	BIN1	DC	B'11000001'	ASSEMBLER ASSUMES ONE BYTE
1F	BIN2	DC	BL1'110000011111'	FOUR LEFTMOST BITS TRUNCATED
0C	BIN3	DC	BL1'1100'	LEFT FOUR BITS PADDED

Before we leave our discussion of data transfer, let's examine a move instruction used only on packed decimal data.

The ZAP Instruction

The MVC and MVI instructions move data without considering the format of the data. We have used these instructions to move zoned, packed, or character data. The ZAP (Zero and Add Packed) instruction moves only packed decimal data.

The ZAP instruction places the second operand in the first operand location. For example

```
         ZAP   FIRST(5),SECOND
         .
         .
         .
FIRST    DC    CL5'12345'
SECOND   DC    PL3'1'
```

The instruction proceeds as if FIRST contained packed zeros. We are adding SECOND to a field containing zeros. The contents of the second operand field remains unchanged. The result is placed in the first operand location. After execution of this instruction, the field FIRST contains $000000001C_{16}$. (See Figure 6-10.)

The ZAP instruction is useful in initializing fields used in decimal arithmetic instructions. Assume we are asked to multiply two 4-byte fields. The first

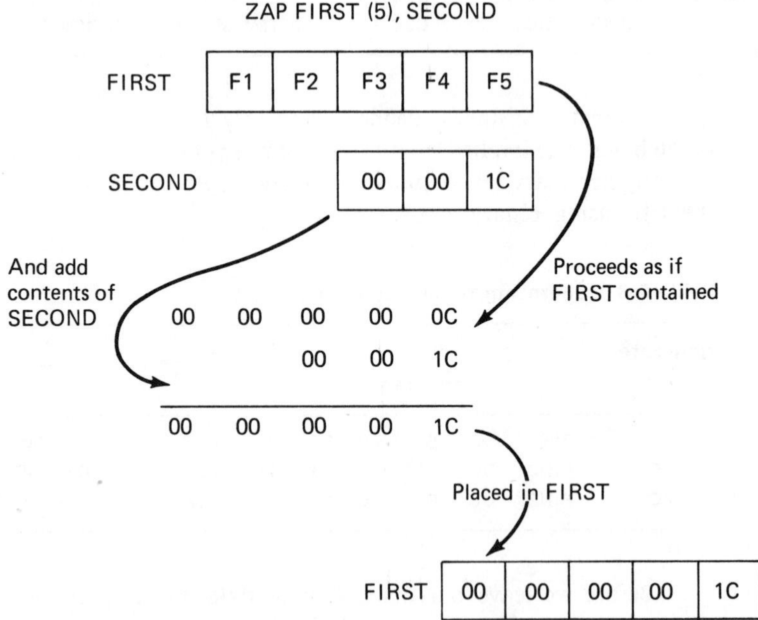

Figure 6-10 The ZAP instruction.

operand must contain high-order zeros equal to the number of packed digits plus sign. The code

```
         MP  FIRST(4),SECOND(4)
         .
         .
         .
FIRST    DC  PL4'1234567'
SECOND   DC  PL4'0098765'
```

is incorrect. FIRST must have 6 high-order zeros. We use the ZAP instruction to move FIRST to a work area and clear the high-order positions to zeros.

```
         ZAP  WORK(7),FIRST(4)
         MP   WORK(7),SECOND(4)
         .
         .
         .
FIRST    DC   PL4'1234567'
SECOND   DC   PL4'0098765'
WORK     DS   PL7
```

The examples presented in this section involved sequential instruction execution. Now let's examine the concept of nonsequential programs—programs involving branching instructions.

SEQUENCE CONTROL

In our earlier discussion of programming concepts, we touched upon sequential and nonsequential program execution. We learned that there are two types of branching instructions—conditional and unconditional. We learned that programming a loop helps us execute certain instructions over and over again. We learned that we need a counter to control the number of times we execute the instructions within a loop. And finally, we learned that we must initialize the loop control counter before we enter the loop, increment the counter within the loop, and test the counter to determine when to exit from the loop.

We developed the solution to a program to find the sum of the numbers from 1–5 to illustrate these looping concepts. We saw how we could find the sum of any series of numbers when the limit of the series is contained as data on a punched card.

We did not, however, use assembly language instructions in our discussion. We developed our own instructions to illustrate these new concepts. Now that we have begun to understand the assembly language, we will see how the compare and branching operations are handled in assembly language.

We will consider first the sum of the numbers from 1 to 5. Figure 6-11 is a flowchart for this program, which shows the need for two types of instructions. We must code a *compare instruction* to test the value of the counter, and we must code a *branch instruction* to direct the flow of instruction execution.

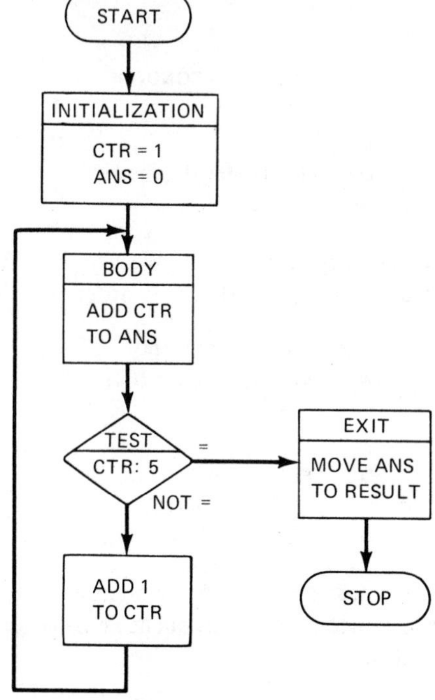

Figure 6-11 Program 5—flowchart.

We also must code an arithmetic instruction to increment the counter. This is no problem. We know the arithmetic instructions for decimal operands.

The Compare Instruction

The CP (Compare Packed) instruction tests the relation of two numbers. They may be equal to one another, the first operand may be greater than the second operand, or the first operand may be less than the second operand. There are three possible conditions.

The CP instruction compares two decimal operands. The operands must both be in packed format. The maximum size of each operand is sixteen bytes. Both operands reside in main storage.

Let's consider an example of the CP instruction. Assume OP1 contains 00010C (+10) and OP2 contains 020C(+20). The instruction

```
CP   OP1(3),OP2(2)
```

asks us to compare the number ten to the number twenty. OP1 is a 3-byte field containing the number ten in packed decimal format. OP2 is a 2-byte field containing the number twenty in packed decimal format. The first operand is less than the second operand. When the compare instruction is executed an indicator within the CPU is set recording the result of the compare. At some later point we may want to test this indicator. In this example, the indicator is set to show that the first operand is less than the second operand.

The CP instruction is an arithmetic compare instruction. The sign of each operand is considered in determining the result of the compare. Remember, the sign of the decimal number is determined by the low-order sign position. Let's assume that OP1 contains 00010C (+10) and OP2 contains 020D (−20). When the instruction

```
CP   OP1(3),OP2(2)
```

is executed, the indicator is set to show that the first operand is greater than the second operand (+10 > −20). But when the instruction

```
CP   OP2(2),OP1(3)
```

is executed, the indicator is set to show that the first operand is *less* than the second operand (−20 < +10). The sign of the numbers involved must be considered in determining the result of the compare operation.

The rules of algebra determine the setting of the indicator after the compare operation. Table 6-4 shows the results when two positive number, two negative numbers and two numbers having different signs are compared. Notice that the larger the *magnitude* (actual value) of the negative number, the smaller the number is.

Table 6-4 The Arithmetic Compare

first operand	second operand	result
+10	+20	OP1 < OP2
+15	+ 7	OP1 > OP2
+10	−10	OP1 > OP2
−11	+ 3	OP1 < OP2
−11	− 3	OP1 < OP2
−24	−37	OP1 > OP2

Table 6-5 gives examples of the CP instruction involving both positive and negative numbers. The result of each compare is given at the right.

In summary, the CP instruction is used to compare two packed decimal numbers in main storage. The length of each operand may vary from one to sixteen bytes. The compare is algebraic—the signs of the numbers affects the result of the compare. If one of the operands does not contain packed data, a data exception occurs.

Table 6-5 The CP Instruction

location	instruction	result
POS1 : 00138C	CP POS1(3),POS2(2)	$Op_1 > Op_2$
POS2 : 006C	CP POS2(2),POS1(3)	$Op_1 < Op_2$
NEG1 : 099D	CP POS1(3),NEG1(2)	$Op_1 > Op_2$
NEG2 : 001D	CP NEG1(2),NEG1(2)	$Op_1 = Op_2$
	CP NEG1(2),NEG2(2)	$Op_1 < Op_2$
	CP NEG2(2),NEG1(2)	$Op_1 > Op_2$
	CP POS1(2),NEG1(2)	Error

The Branching Instructions

We have just introduced the CP instruction. We have seen that the CP instruction examines the relation between two numbers. The result of the compare usually affects the subsequent logic of instructions. Let's consider the solution to Program 5 as an example. Program 5 finds the sum of the numbers from 1 to 5. The flowchart in Figure 6-11 shows that we must compare the value in a counter to the constant 5. If the counter is equal to 5, the program exits from the loop. If, however, the counter is less than five, the counter is updated and the loop continues. In programming, we first must test the counter and then code a branch instruction.

The branch instruction is *the most important part of programming*. What type of branch instruction will we code? The logic of our program requires that we determine the relation between two numbers—a counter and the constant 5—and then branch depending upon the result of the compare. We must code a *conditional* branch instruction. The branch is conditional upon the result of the compare!

The conditional branch instruction must consider the three possible results of the compare. Remember, the compare instruction sets an indicator in the CPU according to the result of the compare. The conditional branch instruction tests this indicator. For example, the instructions

```
CP    CTR,LIM
BE    EXIT
```

compare the contents of an area of storage called CTR with the contents of an area of storage called LIM. If CTR *equals* LIM a branch to EXIT is taken.

The BE (Branch Equal) instruction is only one example of a conditional branch instruction. The BH (Branch High) instruction causes a branch if the first operand is greater than the second operand. The BL (Branch Low) instruction causes a branch if the first operand is less than the second operand.

Another type of branch instruction—the *unconditional* branch instruction

```
B    RTA
```

causes a branch to RTA *regardless* of the result of the preceding compare instruction.

A Sample Program

Let's return to Program 5. We know that we must compare the contents of a counter with the limit. In this case, the number five. When the contents of the counter are equal to the limit, we exit from the loop. If, however, the contents of the counter are less than the limit, we increment the counter and return to the loop. We code these instructions as follows

```
BODY   .
       .
       .
TEST   CP   CTR,LIMIT
       BE   EXIT
       AP   CTR,ONE
       B    BODY
EXIT   .
       .
       .
LIMIT  DC   PL1'5'
ONE    DC   PL1'1'
CTR    DS   CL1
```

Notice that we defined ONE and LIMIT as packed constants. It is not necessary to issue a PACK instruction before the CP instruction. The data being compared is already in packed format.

Our discussion of loop control in Chapter 2 introduced the four components of a loop. The initialization, the body, the test, and the exit. Let's develop Program 5 according to these specifications.

We already have coded the test instructions. We compare LIMIT to CTR and branch to the instruction labeled EXIT when they are equal. Let's go back to the initialization instructions.

We are going to find the sum of the numbers from 1 to 5. We will build the result in an area of storage called ANS. We also must define and initialize an area of storage called CTR. We will increment CTR each time we execute the instructions within the loop.

```
INIT  MVC  CTR,ONE
      MVC  ANS,ZERO
      .
      .
      .
CTR   DS   CL1
ANS   DS   CL2
```

The body of the loop consists of adding the contents of CTR to ANS,

```
BODY  AP  ANS,CTR
```

```
*
* PROGRAM 5
* SUM OF THE NUMBERS FROM 1 - 5
* DECIMAL ARITHMETIC
*
         PRINT NOGEN
SUM      HSKPING
*        *
*        *     SOME
*        *     HOUSEKEEPING
*        *     STATEMENTS
*        *     ARE
*        *     OMITTED
*        *     HERE
*        *
INIT     MVC   CTR,ONE                INITIALIZE CTR
         MVC   ANS,ZERO               AND ANS
BODY     AP    ANS,CTR                ADD TO ANS
TEST     CP    CTR,LIMIT              TEST FOR EXIT
         BE    EXIT                   EXIT IF EQUAL
         AP    CTR,ONE                ELSE INCREMENT CTR
         B     BODY                   AND GO TO BODY
EXIT     UNPK  RESULT,ANS             WHEN FINISHED UNPACK ANS
*                                     INTO RESULT
*        *
*        *     THE PROGRAM IS COMPLETE
*        *     THE RETURN STATEMENT
*        *     SIGNIFIES END-OF-JOB
*        *
EOJ      RETURN (14,12)               END OF JOB
*
* DATA AREAS
*
LIMIT    DC    PL1'5'                 DEFINE LIMIT
ONE      DC    PL1'1'                 DEFINE CONSTANTS USED TO
ZERO     DC    PL2'0'                 INITIALIZE CTR AND ANS
ANS      DS    CL2                    PACKED SUM BUILT IN ANS
CTR      DS    CL1                    CTR IS INCREMENTED BY 1
RESULT   DS    CL2                    RESULT CONTAINS ZONED ANSWER
         END   SUM
```

Values of ANS and CTR as program executes

CTR = 1

ANS = 0

ANS = 1	ANS = 3	ANS = 6	ANS = 10	ANS = 15
1:5	2:5	3:5	4:5	5:5
NO	NO	NO	NO	YES-EXIT
CTR=2	CTR=3	CTR=4	CTR=5	

Figure 6-12 Program 5—solution using decimal arithmetic.

and, finally, the instruction labeled EXIT unpacks the sum accumulated in ANS into an area of storage called RESULT. The complete solution to Program 5 using decimal arithmetic is given in Figure 6-12.

The figures to the right of the code show the values of CTR and ANS as the program is executed. We can see that when CTR equals LIMIT, the correct value is developed in ANS. In this way, we check the logic of the program. We now can use this code to find the sum of the numbers to any limit—provided we change the value of LIMIT. For example, if we define LIMIT as

```
LIMIT  DC  PL3'100'
```

we find the sum of the numbers from 1–100. We must, of course, change the sizes of ANS and RESULT. The sum of the numbers from 1 to 100 will obviously require more than two bytes of storage.

LOGICAL COMPARE

The compare instructions used in the solution to Program 5 are arithmetic or algebraic compares. The *sign* of each operand affects the result of the compare.

The *logical compare* instructions are not concerned with the sign of each operand. Let's consider an example. The arithmetic compare

```
         CP  FIRST,SECOND
         .
         .
         .
FIRST    DC  PL2'123'      APPEARS AS 123C
SECOND   DC  PL2'-456'     APPEARS AS 456D
```

results in the indicator being set to show that the first operand is greater than the second operand ($+123 > -456$). The corresponding logical compare instruction gives a different result.

```
         CLC FIRST,SECOND
```

In this example, the first operand is *less than* the second operand. The number $123C_{16}$ is less than the number $456D_{16}$. The sign of each operand is unimportant. We are not comparing a positive number with a negative number. We are comparing the value of the number—regardless of sign.

The CLC Instruction

The CLC (Compare Logical Characters) instruction compares two operands in main storage. The length of the operands is determined by the length of the first operand. From 1 to 256 bytes may be compared. Table 6-6 gives examples of the CLC instruction. Remember, the result of the compare is not affected by the sign of the numbers involved.

Table 6-6 The CLC Instruction

location	instruction	result
FIRST: 003C	CLC FIRST(2),SECOND	$Op_1 < Op_2$
SECOND: 019D	CLC FIRST(2),FOURTH	$Op_1 < Op_2$
THIRD: ABC080	CLC THIRD(3),FIFTH	$Op_1 > Op_2$
FOURTH: FFC3	CLC FOURTH(2),SECOND	$Op_1 > Op_2$
FIFTH: 009D3C	CLC FIFTH(3),THIRD	$Op_1 < Op_2$
	CLC FIRST(1),FIFTH(1)	$Op_1 = Op_2$

The CLI Instruction

The CLI (Compare Logical Immediate) instruction compares one byte of immediate data (an operand coded within the instruction itself) with one byte of data residing in main storage. For example, the instruction

```
         CLI   FIRST,C'A'
          .
          .
          .
FIRST    DC    XL1'C1'
```

compares the data at FIRST with the immediate operand, a character A. The operands are equal. A character A is equivalent to a hexadecimal C1.

Table 6-7 The CLI Instruction

location	instruction	result
FLDA: C3	CLI FLDA,C'C'	$Op_1 = I_2$
FLDB: F8	CLI FLDB,X'F8'	$Op_1 = I_2$
FLDC: 0000D9	CLI FLDB,C'8'	$Op_1 = I_2$
	CLI FLDA,C'A'	$Op_1 > I_2$
	CLI FLDA,C'8'	$Op_1 < I_2$
	CLI FLDC,X'D9'	$Op_1 < I_2$
	CLI FLDC,B'00000000'	$Op_1 = I_2$

A Sample Program

The logical compare instructions most often are used in problems involving non-numeric data. For example, the employee number in the sample payroll record in Figure 6-13 reflects both department number and employee within department. This field is not necessarily numeric, although we refer to it as the employee *number* field. The following are valid employee numbers.

001000
03A003
D1C009

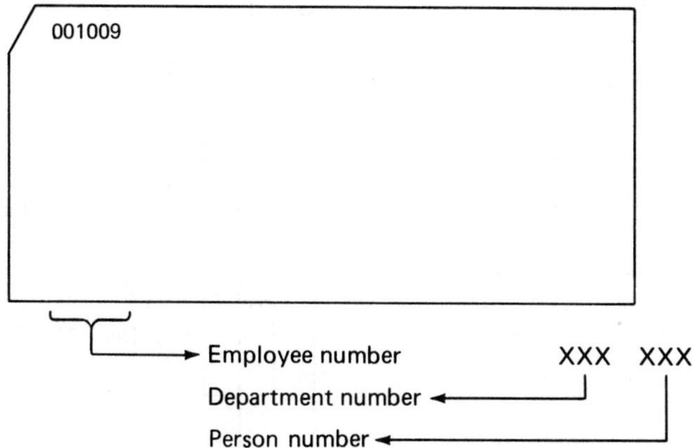

Figure 6-13 A non-numeric department number.

Now let's see how the logical compare instructions are used in a program involving these non-numeric fields.

Program 6 ***Program Statement.*** An employee file is recorded on punched cards. Find the total gross earnings for all the employees in Department A30. Store the total earnings in an area of storage called TOTGROSS.

Table 6-8 Program 6—I/O Specifications

input positions	field
1–6	Employee Number
1–3	Department Number
4–6	Person Number
51–58	Gross Pay

Let's use a sample data deck in an effort to understand the problem statement.

The data shown in Figure 6-14 are arranged in sequence. Each employee number is *higher* than the preceding employee number. Most files used in business data processing are arranged by key—the sequence key in this example is the employee number field.

We are interested only in the earnings figures of the employees in Department A30. Inspection tells us that the total amount earned by employees in

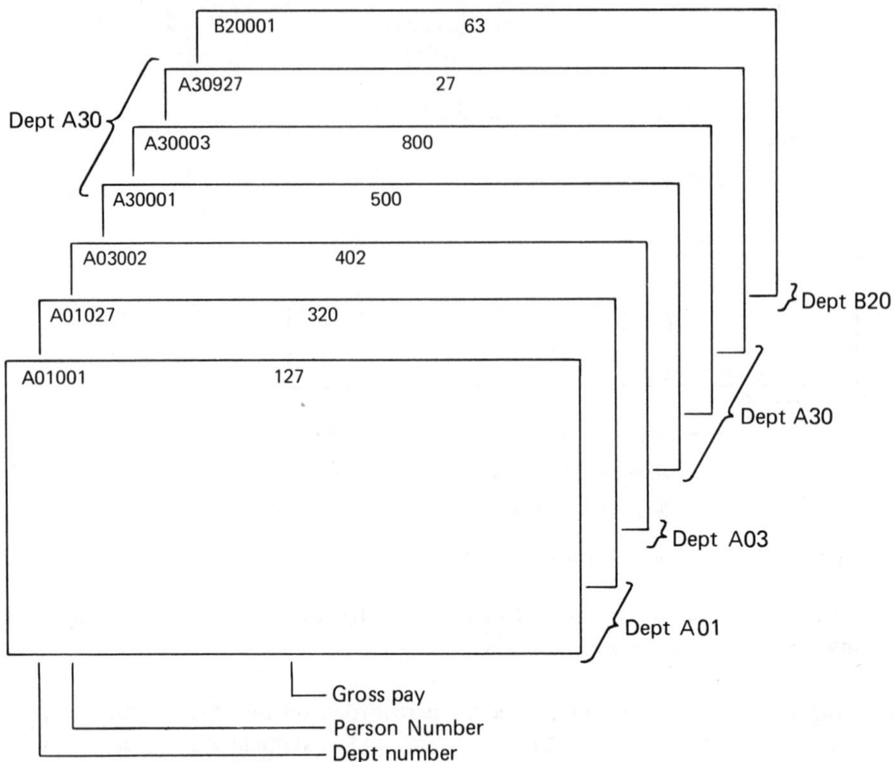

Figure 6-14 Program 6—sample data.

this department was $1,327.00. How do we arrive at this figure? We look at each card in order. When we arrive at a card containing A30 in positions 1–3, we record the gross pay. We examine the next card. It is still within Department A30. We add the gross pay of employee 003 to the previous earnings figure for this department. In this way we maintain a total. We continue examining the cards, adding each earnings figure until we find a card which is not within Department A30. We know we have accumulated the total earnings for Department A30. The cards are in sequence. There should be no more cards for Department A30.

We can represent this decision process graphically in a flowchart (Figure 6-15). The housekeeping (HSKP) box represents required statements which must always be coded. The read operation follows.

We read a card. We examine the department number. If the department number is not equal to A30, we loop back to read another card. If, however, the department number is equal to A30, we add the gross pay to an accumulator. When all the cards are read, the program is complete.

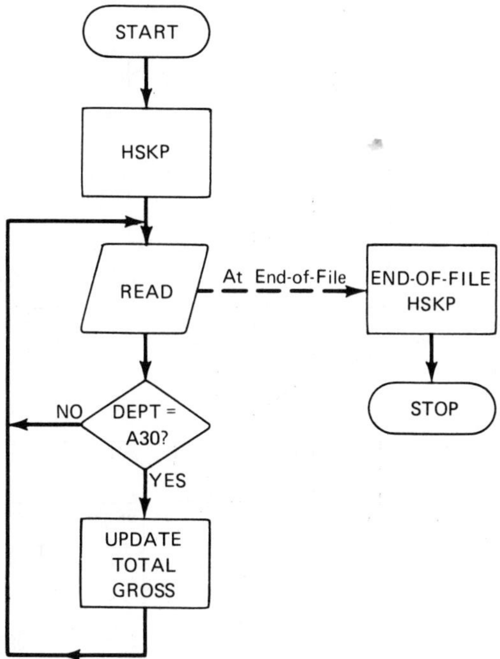

Figure 6-15 Program 6—flowchart.

We are actually finished with the program when we have processed all the cards within Department A30, but the computer does not let us stop at this point. There are still cards remaining in the input device, the card reader. We must continue reading these cards even though we do not process them. When all the cards have been read, we are finished with our program.

Solution. We will use the logical compare instruction to examine the department number in each card. We will compare the department number to the constant A30.

But before we can process any data, we must read that data into storage The statement,

```
GET  INCARD,CARDWK
```

reads a single card from the input card reader and places the data in an area of storage called CARDWK. We must define CARDWK, and describe the fields within CARDWK. We say that we are *formatting* the area of storage called CARDWK. We reference the department number field using the label DEPTIN. We can reference the gross pay field using the label GROSSIN. (See Figure 6-16.)

We now can use the logical compare instruction,

```
CLC  DEPTIN,DEPT
```

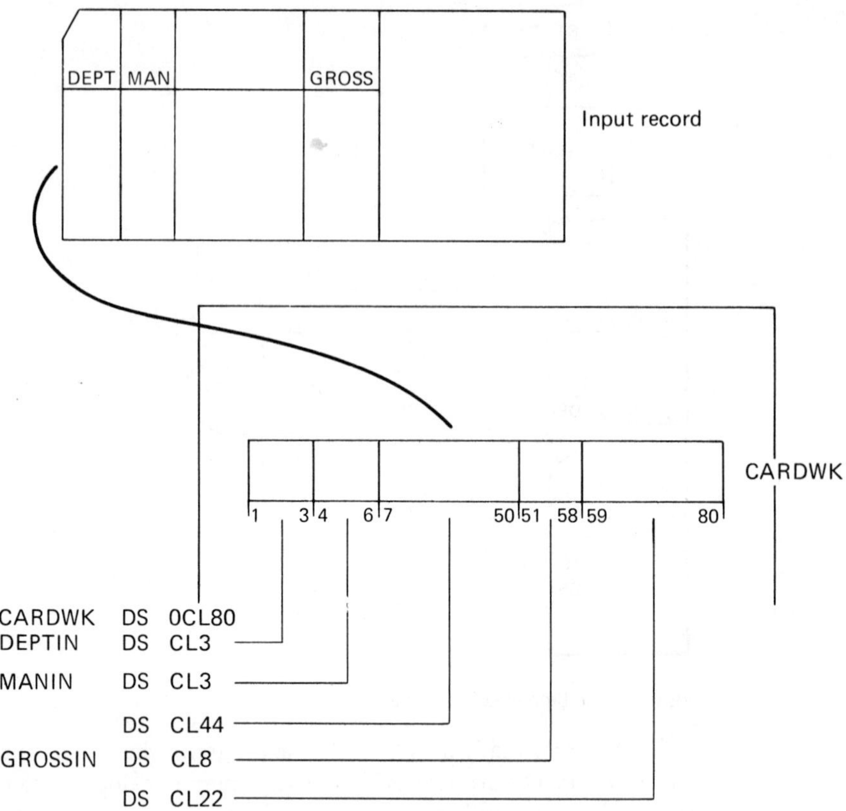

Figure 6-16 Program 6—format of the input area.

to examine DEPTIN. We must, of course, define the symbol DEPT. DEPT is a constant containing the value A30.

```
DEPT   DC   CL3'A30'
```

If the value of DEPTIN is equal to A30, we branch to the code to update or change the value of the accumulator

```
BE   UPDATE
```

otherwise we return to the read statement

```
B    READRT
```

Figure 6-17 gives the complete solution to Program 6. The PRINT and HSKPING statements perform certain required functions. We name the input file INCARD,

```
*
* PROGRAM 6
* SUMMARIZE EARNINGS IN DEPT A30
*
         START
         PRINT NOGEN
PROG6    HSKPING CARDID=INCARD          NAME INPUT FILE
*        *
*        *      SOME
*        *      HOUSEKEEPING
*        *      STATEMENTS
*        *      ARE
*        *      OMITTED
*        *      HERE
*        *
RDLOOP   GET    INCARD,CARDWK           READ A CARD INTO CARDWK
         CLC    DEPTIN,DEPT             COMPARE DEPARTMENT TO A30
         BE     UPDATE                  BRANCH IF EQUAL
         B      RDLOOP                  ELSE LOOP TO NEXT CARD
UPDATE   PACK   GROSSPK(5),GROSSIN      PACK GROSS FIELD
         AP     TOTGROSS(7),GROSSPK     ADD GROSS FIELD
         B      RDLOOP                  RETURN TO READ STATEMENT
*        *
*        *      AFTER ALL INPUT CARDS
*        *      HAVE BEEN READ AND PROCESSED
*        *      THE PROGRAM IS COMPLETE
*
*
* DATA AREAS
*
CARDWK   DS     0CL80                   INPUT AREA
DEPTIN   DS     CL3                     *
MANIN    DS     CL3                     *
         DS     CL44                    *
GROSSIN  DS     CL8                     *
         DS     CL22                    *
DEPT     DC     CL3'A30'                DEFINE CONSTANT 'A30'
GROSSPK  DS     CL5
TOTGROSS DC     PL7'0'                  TOTGROSS CONTAINS PACKED SUM
         END    PROG6
```

Figure 6-17 Program 6—solution.

The GET statement reads the first card into CARDWK. We reference the first 3 bytes of CARDWK (containing the department number) using the label DEPTIN. The instruction

```
CLC   DEPTIN,DEPT
```

compares the department number of the first record against a constant of A30. Using the data shown in Figure 6-14, we see that these fields are not equal. We do not branch to UPDATE,

```
BE UPDATE
B  READRT
```

but branch unconditionally to READRT. We continue in this manner until we read the first card in Department A30. After we execute the compare instruction, we branch to UPDATE. The instructions

```
UPDATE  PACK  GROSSPK(5),GROSSIN
        AP    TOTGROSS(7),GROSSPK
```

accumulate the earnings in the field TOTGROSS. We continue processing the cards within Department A30. Finally, we read the first card within department B0. We do not go to the update code, but branch back to the read statement. The program requires that we read all the cards in the file. When the last card, is read, the program is complete.

Program 6 shows how the CLC instruction may be used in a simple business application. Much of business data processing involves processing data files arranged in sequence. At this point, our knowledge of the assembly language is sufficient for us to explore these concepts in more depth—to develop, in fact, a business subset to the assembly language. The next chapter is devoted to just such a subset.

PROBLEMS

6.1 The record description developed in Program 1 defined only three fields, NUMIN, NAMEIN, and GROSSIN. Write the record description for the entire record given below. You must define a symbolic name and reserve storage for each field within the record. Why would you use the DS statement rather than the DC statement?

card columns	field	size
1–6	Employee Number	6
7–26	Employee Name	20
27–46	Employee Address	20
47	Income Blacket	1
48	Marital Status	1
49–50	Dependents	2
51–58	YTD Gross Pay	8
59–65	YTD FICA Deductions	7
66–72	YTD Federal Taxes	7
73–79	YTD State Taxes	7
80	Profile Code	1

6.2 The MVC instruction moves data from one storage area to another. The contents of five computer storage locations are given below. Give the contents of the first operand location after each of the following instructions is executed.

location	contents	instruction
FLDA	F1F2F3F4F5	MVC FLDA(5),FLDB
FLDB	F0F0F0F0F0	MVC FLDA(3),FLDB
FLDC	C1C2C3	MVC FLDC(3),FLDA
FLDD	C3C1E2	MVC FLDC,FLDA
FLDE	404040	MVC FLDD(2),FLDE
		MVC FLDD(1),FLDA
		MVC FLDA(3),FLDE

6.3 Give the assembled (generated value) for each of the following constants. You may use either binary or hexadecimal notation.

```
a. CHAR1   DC   CL4' DATA'
b. CHAR2   DC   CL6' DATA'
c. CHAR3   DC   CL2' DATA'
d. CHAR4   DC   C' DATA  AREA'
e. CHAR5   DC   C' 0078'
f. CHAR6   DC   CL2' 0078'
g. CHAR7   DC   CL4' 0078'
h. HEX1    DC   X' 404040'
i. HEX2    DC   XL4' 40'
j. HEX3    DC   XL2' C1C2C3C4'
k. BIN1    DC   B' 10101010'
l. BIN2    DC   BL2' 10101010'
m. BIN3    DC   B' 1010'
n. ZONE1   DC   Z' 123'
o. ZONE2   DC   ZL4' 789'
p. ZONE3   DC   ZL2' -12345'
q. PACK1   DC   PL3' 580'
r. PACK2   DC   P' -120'
s. PACK    DC   PL1' 123'
```

6.4 The contents of three storage locations are given below. After a compare operation, an indicator is set to show the result of the compare. The operands may be equal, the first operand may be less than the second operand, or the first operand may be greater than the second operand. Give the result of the compare for each of the following instructions.

location	contents	instruction
DATA1	001C	CP DATA1,DATA2
DATA2	009D	CP DATA2,DATA1
DATA3	F1C3	CP DATA1,DATA3
		CP DATA1(1),DATA2
		CP DATA1(1),DATA3

6.5 Examine the following code.

```
INIT     PACK  CTR,ONE
BODY     AP    ANS,CTR
         CP    CTR,LIMIT
         BE    EXIT
         AP    CTR,TWO
         B     BODY
EXIT     UNPK  RESULT,ANS
               .
               .
               .
CTR      DS    CL2
LIMIT    DC    PL2'10'
TWO      DC    PL1'2'
ONE      DC    ZL1'1'
ANS      DS    PL3'0'
RESULT   DS    CL6
```

How many times will the **AP** instruction be executed? Give a reason for your answer.

6.6 A branch instruction often follows a compare instruction. Indicate if a branch occurs after each of the following instruction pairs is executed.

location	contents	instruction	
DATA1	003C	CLI	DATA1,B'00000000'
DATA2	009D	BL	NEXT
DATA3	F1C3	CLI	DATA3,Z'-3'
		BE	NEXT
		CP	DATA1,DATA2
		BL	NEXT
		CP	DATA2,DATA1
		BH	NEXT

6.7 Program 5 asks us to find the sum of the numbers from 1 to 5. The solution given in Figure 6-12 uses the **BE** instruction. Develop another solution using the **BL** instruction in place of the **BE** instruction. This involves a change in logic.

6.8 Develop a solution to Program 5 placing the **TEST** routine *before* the **BODY** (reference Figure 6-12, p. 130). This involves a change in logic and may affect the initial setting of the counter.

6.9 The logical compare instructions are not concerned with the sign of the operands. Give the result of the compare for each of the following instructions.

location	contents	instruction
FULL1	00000020	CLC DATA1,DATA2
FULL2	FFFFFFEC	CLC DATA2,DATA1
DATA1	010C	CLC DATA3,DATA2
DATA2	009D	CLC DATA2(1),DATA3
DATA3	F1C3	CLC DATA3(1),DATA2
register 3	0000006A	CLI FULL1,X'00'
register 4	FFFFFF9C	CLI FULL2,X'00'
		CLI DATA3,C'1'
		CLI DATA3,X'D1'
		CLI DATA3,B'11110001'

6.10 Write a program to verify that the cards used in Program 6 are in sequence. List those cards which are not in sequence.

6.11 Write a program to flag the employees with an income of over $10,000. Use the I/O specifications provided in Figure 6-4 (p. 114). Use an asterisk (*) in position 66 of the print record to indicate those employees earning over $10,000.

6.12 Write a program to find the value of any constant NUM raised to a power EXP. The values of NUM and EXP are input on a card. Develop your own input format. What considerations are critical as you design your input format and set up work areas?

6.13 Write a program to find the average number of dependents of the employees in Department A30. Use the input specifications given in Table 6-8 (p. 133). The number of dependents is specified in columns 49–50 of each record.

6.14 Write a program to determine if the 4-byte zoned decimal constant DATA is odd or even. If the constant is odd, move it to an area of storage labeled ODD. If the constant is even, move it to an area of strage labeled EVEN.

7

A Business Subset

At this point the reader has a basic knowledge of how assembly language works. This chapter introduces a new instruction—the ED (EDit) instruction—and then summarizes the instructions introduced to this point into a business subset of the S/370 Assembly Language.

We have seen how the MVC instruction may be used to move data from one area of storage to another. We have not, however, been concerned with the appearance of the data in the printed report.

Figure 7-1 gives an example of the output obtained when Program 1 is executed. The gross pay field is unedited. The output does not contain decimal points, commas, or dollar signs. We will now introduce the assembly instruction used to edit numeric data.

THE ED(EDit) INSTRUCTION

We edit numeric data using a pattern that tells where dollar signs, decimal points, and commas belong. The pattern is called a *mask*, and we say that we "edit the data against the mask."

Consider the raw or unedited data

91	23	45	6F

```
001   MARY POLITE        12345678
003   POLLY GOERGEN      00000895
007   ARTHUR EHINGER     00670987
123   EDGAR JAMES        00000678
203   GRETCHEN ARTHUR    00980078
204   VERNIE MOUNT       00780090
310   N. P. BIGMAN       00089700
427   HANNAH PEAR        00987789
512   LOUISE HERNANDO    00980098
698   LOU ORGAN          89066788
789   BECKY SQUARE       00099874
882   SHARON RAHAM       90777884
990   JACK RUDE          00980056
998   KING WRONG         00890005
```

Figure 7-1 Program 7—sample output.

We want the edited result to appear as $91,234.56. We must code a mask which places the commas, decimal point, and dollar sign in the correct positions. For example, the mask

d d , d d d . d d

shows the relative position of the decimal point and comma within the seven digits comprising the data (Figure 7-2). The position of the dollar sign is not shown. We will discuss placement of the dollar sign later in this section.

Notice that the raw data field contains packed data. The ED instruction requires numeric data to be in packed format. The edited result appears in zoned format.

Zero Suppression

We refer to the zeros appearing to the left of the first significant (non-zero) digit as leading zeros. We will begin our discussion of the ED instruction by examining the mask used to suppress leading zeros. The number 00987 contains two

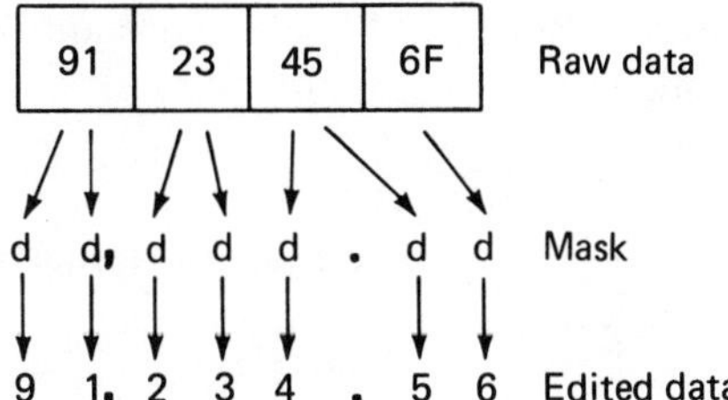

Figure 7-2 The edit mask.

leading zeros. The first significant digit is 9—the third digit in the number. If we suppress the leading zeros, the number 00987 would appear as   987.

The data we wish to edit must first be packed. The packed data is then edited against a hexadecimal mask containing a hexadecimal character for each digit within the packed field. This character is called a *digit selector*. The digit selector is represented by a hexadecimal 20 (20_{16}). The mask must also contain an additional character called the *fill character*. The fill character is always the first character of the edit mask (Figure 7-3). If we wish to suppress leading zeros—that is, replace leading zeros with a blank—the fill character is a hexadecimal 40 (40_{16}), the EBCDIC code for a blank. We use a single b to represent a blank.

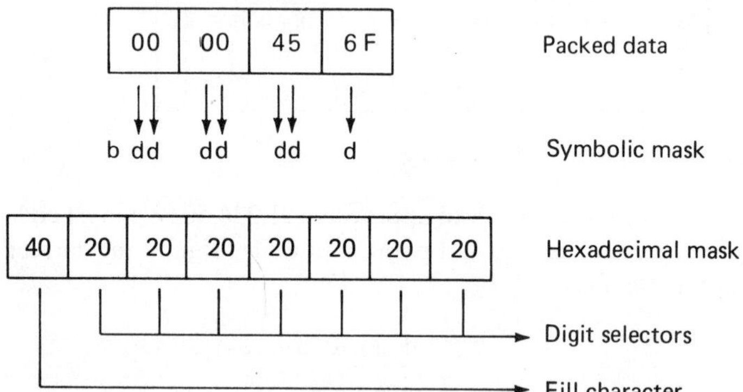

Figure 7-3 Hexadecimal edit mask.

The following code shows how the edit mask is used in the ED instruction.

```
         MVC   FLDOUT(6),MASK
         PACK  DATAPK(3),RAWDATA
         ED    FLDOUT(6),DATAPK
          .
          .
          .
MASK     DC    X'402020202020'
RAWDATA  DC    ZL5'00987'
DATAPK   DS    CL3
```

We cannot define the mask as a decimal or character constant. We define the mask as a hexadecimal constant. The description of the mask

```
MASK     DC    X'402020202020'
```

contains twelve hexadecimal digits. The mask appears in storage as

40	20	20	20	20	20

We are defining a 6-byte hexadecimal constant.

The mask is destroyed each time we edit data. We must move the mask to the edit field before each edit operation. We then pack the field RAWDATA. The result of the PACK instruction is $00987C_{16}$. There are five digits in the packed field. We need five digits in the edit mask, and we need a fill character. The format of the 6-position mask is *bddddd.* The b represents the fill character—a blank. The d represents a digit selector. The mask is coded as 402020202020_{16}. A 20_{16} represents the digit selector.

The ED instruction proceeds from left to right. The digit selectors in the mask are replaced by the digits in the packed data field. The fill character replaces leading zeros. (See Figure 7-4.)

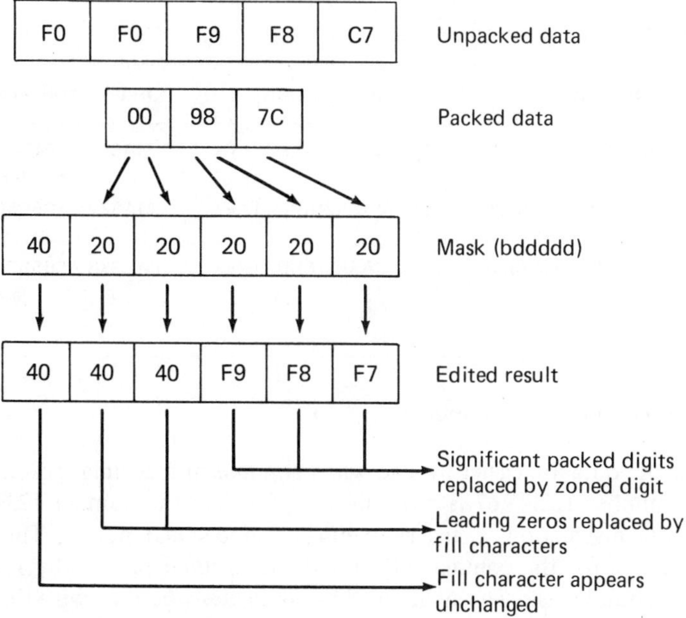

Figure 7-4 Suppressing leading zeros.

The first character of the mask is the fill character. It is not replaced. The first digit in the packed field is a leading zero. The first digit selector is replaced by the fill character. The second packed digit is also non-significant. The second digit selector is replaced by the fill character. The next digit is significant. The digit 9 replaces the third digit selector. Notice that the edited data appears in *zoned* format.

Replacement continues from left to right until all digit selectors in the mask have been replaced with *zoned* data.

The fill character replaces any zeros to the left of the first significant digit. Zeros to the right of the first significant digit appear unchanged—they are not replaced by the fill character.

We may choose any character as the fill character. Often the choice of a blank is not wise. Consider a check where leading zeros are replaced by a blank. The dollar amount might appear as $ 1.27. Surely an invitation for check alteration.

We often use an asterisk as a fill character, especially in accounting applications. The data shown above would appear as $***1.27. We need only change the first character of the edit mask from a 40_{16} to a $5C_{16}$.

```
MASK   DC   XL6'5C2020202020'
```

Table 7-1 shows the use of the blank, the asterisk, and the dollar sign as a fill character.

Table 7-1 Use of Fill Characters

location	instruction	mask after execution
DATAPK: 00987C	ED MASK1(6),DATAPK	MASK1: 404040F9F8F7 (bbb987)
MASK1: 402020202020	ED MASK2(6),DATAPK	MASK2: 5C5C5CF9F8F7 (***987)
MASK2: 5C2020202020	ED MASK3(6),DATAPK	MASK3: 5B5B5BF9F8F7 ($$$987)
MASK3: 5B2020202020		

Inserting Special Characters

Numeric data are easier to read when commas and decimal points are inserted. The number 12,345.67 is more meaningful than the number 1234567. We use the ED instruction to insert commas and decimal points. The hexadecimal characters for the comma ($6B_{16}$) and the decimal point ($4B_{16}$) appear in the hexadecimal mask. The symbolic mask indicates where we wish the commas and decimal point to appear in the edited result (Figure 7-5).

Commas and decimal points are represented in hexadecimal in the edit mask. These characters are called *message characters*. Message characters are not replaced by numeric data. They may, however, be replaced by the fill character. Any message character appearing to the left of the first significant digit is replaced by the fill character (Figure 7-6).

Significance Starter

Sometimes we want the message character to appear regardless of whether a significant digit has been encountered. We must insert a decimal point to indicate that the number 01 is a decimal .01. We can use a special edit control character called a *significance starter* to force the message character to appear. The code for the significance starter is 21_{16}. Except for this special use, 21_{16} behaves the same as 20_{16}. All digits and message characters to the right of the

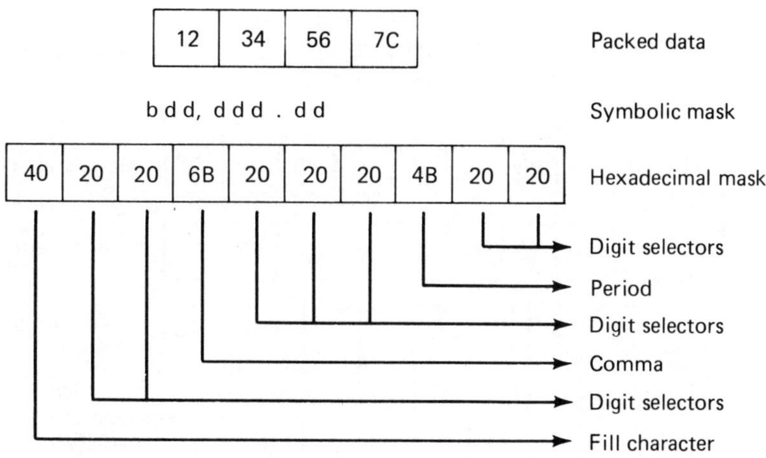

Figure 7-5 Inserting special characters.

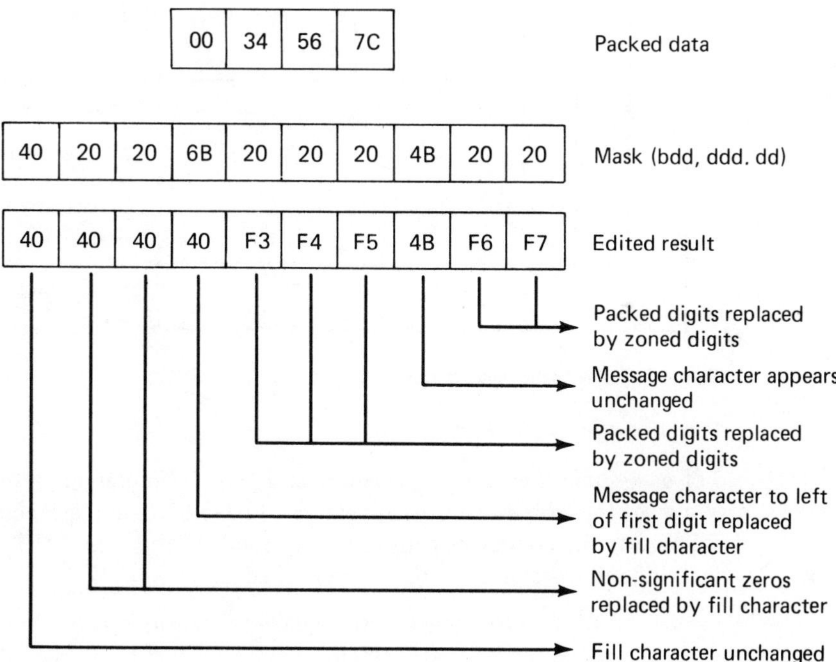

Figure 7-6 Inserting special characters.

significance starter appear in the edited result regardless of whether a significant digit has been encountered (Figure 7-7). We use an *s* in the symbolic mask to represent the significance starter. Notice that nonsignificant zeros to the right of the significance starter appear in the edited result. Editing proceeds as if a significant digit was found in the location of the significance starter.

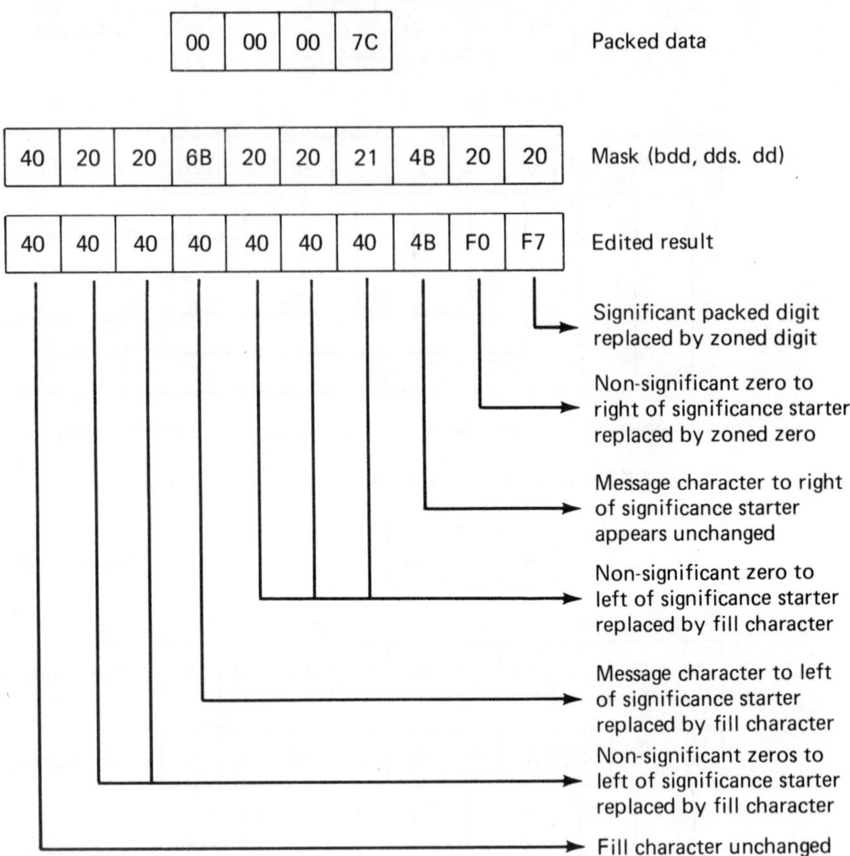

Figure 7-7 The significance starter.

Inserting the Dollar Sign

Let us assume that the packed number 1234567C represents a dollar amount. We want the edited result to appear as $12,345.67. The mask shown in Figure 7-7 inserts the comma and the decimal point. We use the MVI instruction to insert the dollar sign after the data is edited.

```
         MVC   EDITFLD(10),MASK          MOVE MASK
         PACK  DATAPK(4),DATA            PACK
         ED    EDITFLD(10),DATAPK        AND EDIT DATA THEN
         MVI   EDITFLD,C'$'              INSERT $
         .
         .
         .
MASK     DC    X'4020206B2020214B2020'   DEFINE MASK BDD,DDS.DD
EDITFLD  DS    CL10
DATAPK   DS    CL4
DATA     DC    ZL7'1234567
```

The MVI instruction inserts the dollar sign in the first position of the edited result. We do not have to be concerned about overlaying data with the dollar sign. The first position of the edited result is always occupied by the fill character, never by significant data.

Some applications require the use of the *floating dollar sign*; the dollar sign is to appear to the left of the first significant digit. The EDMK (EDit and MarK) instruction may be used to position the dollar sign. We will discuss this instruction in a later chapter.

Sign Control

The ED instruction examines the sign of the packed data. If the sign of the data is negative, any mask characters remaining after the sign position of the data is examined remain unchanged in the edited result (Figure 7-8).

If the sign of the second operand is positive, characters remaining in the edit mask are replaced by the fill character. Table 7-2 shows how the edit instruction is used to insert a minus sign or the accounting symbols DB and CR in

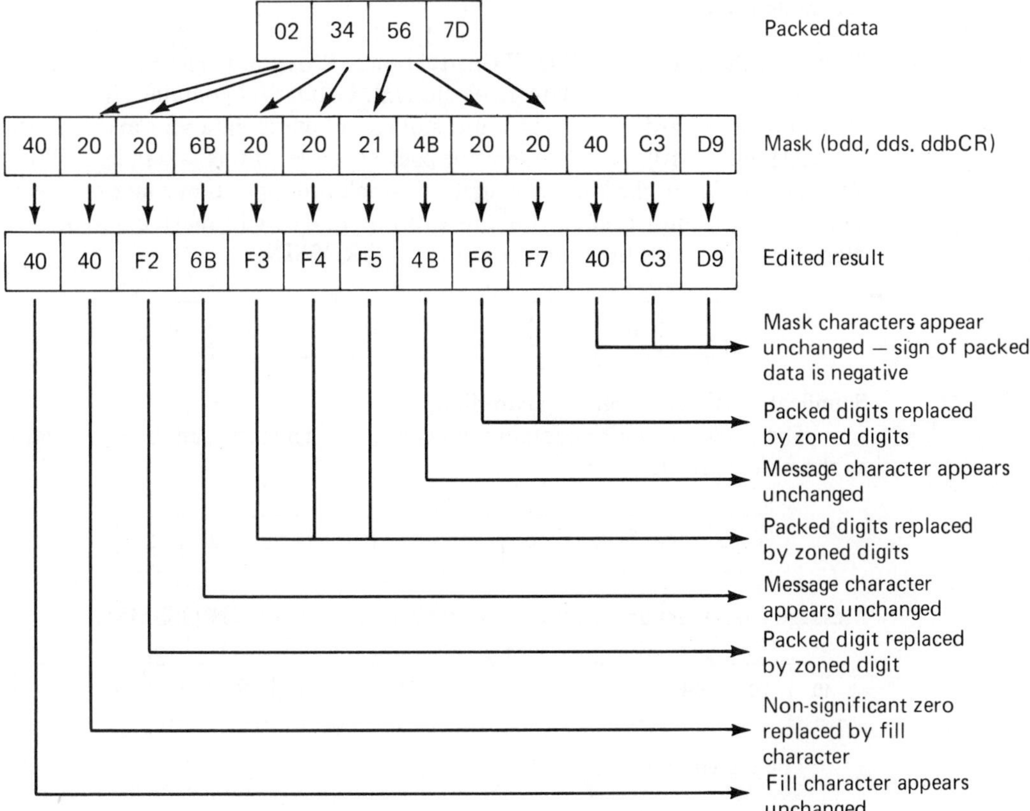

Figure 7-8 Editing negative numbers.

Table 7-2 Editing Negative Data

location		instruction	mask after editing
DATAPOS:	34567C	ED MASK1(10),DATAPOS	40F3F4F54BF6F7404040 (b345.67bbb)
DATANEG:	34567D	ED MASK1(10),DATANEG	40F3F4F54BF6F740C3D1 (b345.67bCR)
MASK1:	402020214B202040C3D1 (bdds.ddbCR)	ED MASK2(10),DATANEG	40F3F4F54BF6F740C4C2 (b345.67bDB)
MASK2:	402020214B202040C4C2 (bdds.ddbDB)	ED MASK3(8),DATANEG	40F3F4F54BF6F760 (b345.67–)
MASK3:	402020214B202060 (bdds.dd–)		

negative data. The symbols are all represented in hexadecimal. When the second operand is positive, the mask characters remaining after the sign position is examined are replaced by the fill character.

A Sample Program

Figure 7-9 shows the use of the ED instruction in Program 1. The ED instruction is used to edit the year-to-date gross amount. GROSSIN contains eight digits. When punched card data is read into storage, numeric data appears in zoned format (Figure 7-10). This data must be packed before editing takes place. When an 8-digit field is packed into five digits, the high-order position contains a zero. The edit mask must account for this extra digit. The edit mask contains *nine* digit selectors to edit the *eight*-position field GROSSIN.

20	20	20	20	20	21	20	20	20

Significance is started on the sixth digit.

The mask must also contain a fill character. This program uses the blank as the fill character.

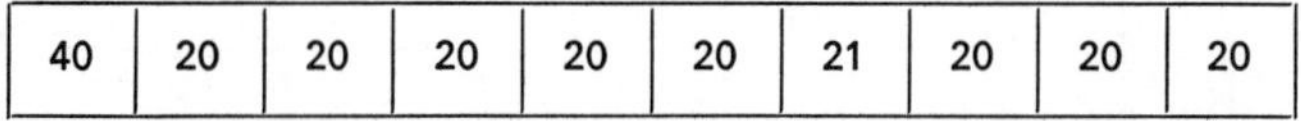

40	20	20	20	20	20	21	20	20	20

Message characters are inserted to complete the code for GROSSMSK.

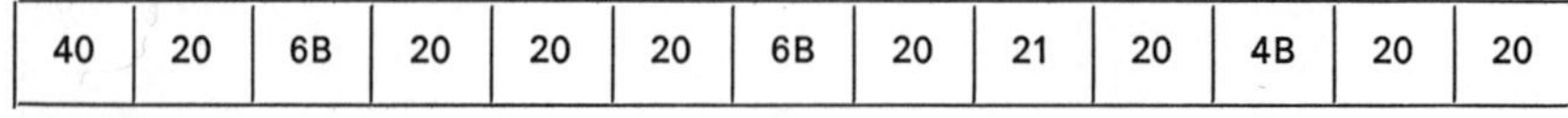

40	20	6B	20	20	20	6B	20	21	20	4B	20	20

The instruction

```
ED    GROSSOUT(13),GROSSPK
```

```
*
* PROGRAM 1
* CARD TO PRINT
* USE OF THE ED INSTRUCTION
*
         PRINT NOGEN
         START
FIRST    HSKPING CARDID=INCARD,PRINTID=PRINT      NAME FILES
*        *
*        *      SOME
*        *      HOUSEKEEPING
*        *      STATEMENTS
*        *      ARE
*        *      OMITTED
*        *      HERE
*        *
READRT   GET    INCARD,INWORK                     GET RECORD INTO INWORK
         MVC    NUMOUT(6),NUMIN                   MOVE EMP NUMBER
         MVC    NAMEOUT(20),NAMEIN                EMP NAME
         PACK   GROSSPK(5),GROSSIN                PACK GROSS
         MVC    GROSSOUT(13),GROSSMSK             MOVE MASK
         ED     GROSSOUT(13),GROSSPK              AND EDIT PACKED DATA
         MVI    GROSSOUT,C'$'                     MOVING $ TO FIRST POS
         PUT    PRINT,PRINTBLD                    THEN WRITE RECORD
         B      READRT                            AND LOOP BACK
*        *
*        *      AFTER ALL INPUT CARDS
*        *      HAVE BEEN READ AND PROCESSED
*        *      THE PROGRAM IS COMPLETE
*        *
*
* DATA AREAS
*
INWORK   DS     0CL80
NUMIN    DS     CL6                               INPUT AREA
NAMEIN   DS     CL20                              *
         DS     CL24                              *
GROSSIN  DS     CL8                               *
         DS     CL22                              *
PRINTBLD DS     0CL120                            OUTPUT AREA
         DC     10CL1' '                          *
NUMOUT   DS     CL6                               *
         DC     10CL1' '                          *
NAMEOUT  DS     CL20                              *
         DC     10CL1' '                          *
GROSSOUT DS     CL13                              *
         DS     CL51                              *
GROSSPK  DS     CL5                               PACK DATA BEFORE EDIT
GROSSMSK DC     XL13'40206B2020206B2021204B2020'  EDIT MASK
         END    FIRST
```

Figure 7-9 Program 1—solution with editing.

edits the data. The MVI instruction is then used to insert the dollar sign.

```
MVI   GROSSOUT,C'$'
```

Sample output data for Program 1 with editing is given in Figure 7-11.

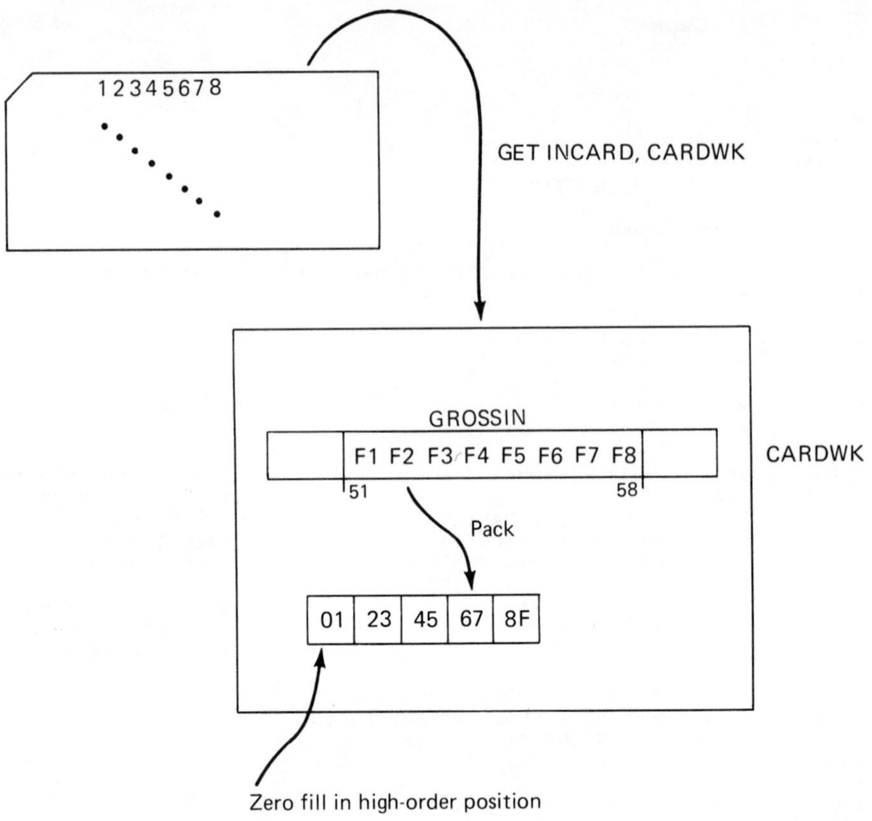

Figure 7-10 Numeric data representation.

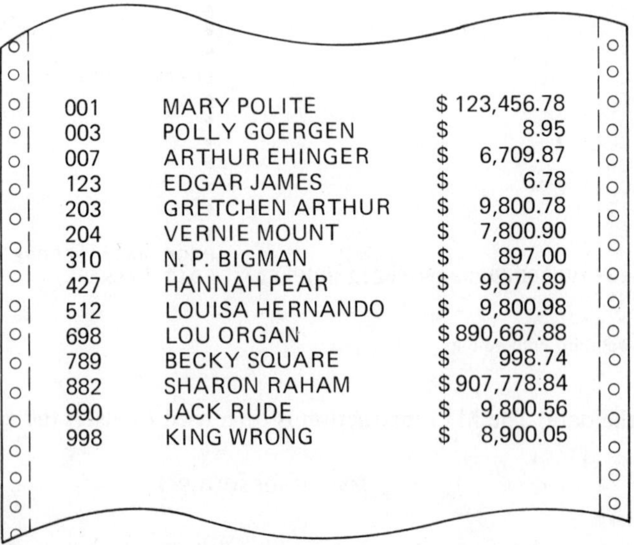

001 MARY POLITE $ 123,456.78
003 POLLY GOERGEN $ 8.95
007 ARTHUR EHINGER $ 6,709.87
123 EDGAR JAMES $ 6.78
203 GRETCHEN ARTHUR $ 9,800.78
204 VERNIE MOUNT $ 7,800.90
310 N. P. BIGMAN $ 897.00
427 HANNAH PEAR $ 9,877.89
512 LOUISA HERNANDO $ 9,800.98
698 LOU ORGAN $ 890,667.88
789 BECKY SQUARE $ 998.74
882 SHARON RAHAM $ 907,778.84
990 JACK RUDE $ 9,800.56
998 KING WRONG $ 8,900.05

Figure 7-11 Program 1—edited output.

A Review

The ED instruction is used to suppress leading zeros and to insert punctuation characters in numeric data. The data to be edited, the second operand, must be in packed format. The second operand is tested, a byte at a time, proceeding from left to right, against the first operand. The first operand—called the *pattern* or *edit* mask—contains edit-control characters (20_{16} and 21_{16}) and message characters. The first character of the mask is the fill character. The fill character replaces nonsignificant digits in the second operand. Significance may be forced by the presence of a significance starter (21_{16}). There is only one length attribute in the instruction, referring to the first operand, the pattern.

A BUSINESS SUBSET

Table 7-3 summarizes the decimal, logical, and I/O instructions we have used to this point. These instructions fit into the basic data processing pattern. The GET instruction is an input instruction. The arithmetic, compare, branching, and data manipulation instructions are processing instructions. The PUT instruction is an output instruction. Remember, the GET and PUT instructions are *macros*—abbreviations for large groups of instructions.

A Sample Program

Let's see how we solve a typical business problem using this subset.

Table 7-3 Instructions Comprising a Business Subset

function	instruction	operation
INPUT	GET	READ A RECORD
PROCESSING		
ARITHMETIC	AP	ADD PACKED
	SP	SUBTRACT PACKED
	MP	MULTIPLY PACKED
	DP	DIVIDE PACKED
COMPARE	CP	COMPARE PACKED
	CLC	COMPARE LOGICAL
	CLI	COMPARE LOGICAL IMMEDIATE
BRANCH	BE	BRANCH EQUAL
	BH	BRANCH HIGH
	BL	BRANCH LOW
	B	BRANCH
DATA MANIPULATION	MVC	MOVE CHARACTERS
	PACK	PACK
	UNPK	UNPACK
	ED	EDIT
	MVI	MOVE IMMEDIATE
	ZAP	ZERO AND ADD PACKED
OUTPUT	PUT	WRITE A RECORD

Program 6 ***Problem-Statement.*** An employee file is sorted by employee number. The employee number reflects the department and the employee within department. Summarize the gross employee earnings within each department. The input/output specifications are as follows:

input positions	field	output positions
1–6	Employee Number	
1–3	Department Number	1–3
4–6	Person Number	
51–58	Gross Pay	4–16

We are asked to summarize the file by department. Let's see if we understand the problem statement. Figure 7-12 shows a small sample data deck. Three departments are represented—Departments B01, B09, and B27. Each department contains a number of detail cards. There are three detail cards within Department B01. These cards represent the detail employee records for employees 001, 029 and 055. There is only one detail record within Department B09 and two detail records in Department B27.

Our problem is to find the cumulative or total gross earnings of all the employees within each department. The sum of employee earnings within Department B01 is $877. Let's see how we arrive at this figure. We look at the first detail record in Department B01. Employee 001 earned $300. The next card is also within Department B01. Employee 029 earned $500. The next card is still within Department B01. Employee 027 earned $77. Look at the next card. This card is the detail record from another department. At this point we want to record the total of the three preceding figures—giving us the total earnings for Department B01.

This point is critical! We do not work with the total earnings of a department until we reach a new department. We refer to this situation—finding a new department number—as a *department break*. Of course, the new department number must be higher than the preceding department number. Otherwise, the cards are not in sequence.

Let's see how we flowchart this process. We read a card and *compare* the department number of the card being read to the department number of the previous card. If the numbers are equal, we do not have a department break. We process the detail record. Detail processing involves adding the gross earnings amount to an accumulator. If, however, the new department number is greater than the preceding department number, we have a department break. We want to punch a summary card for the old department group and go on to process the detail card from the new department.

If the new department is less than the preceding department number, an error has occurred. The employee cards are out of sequence. We stop our program.

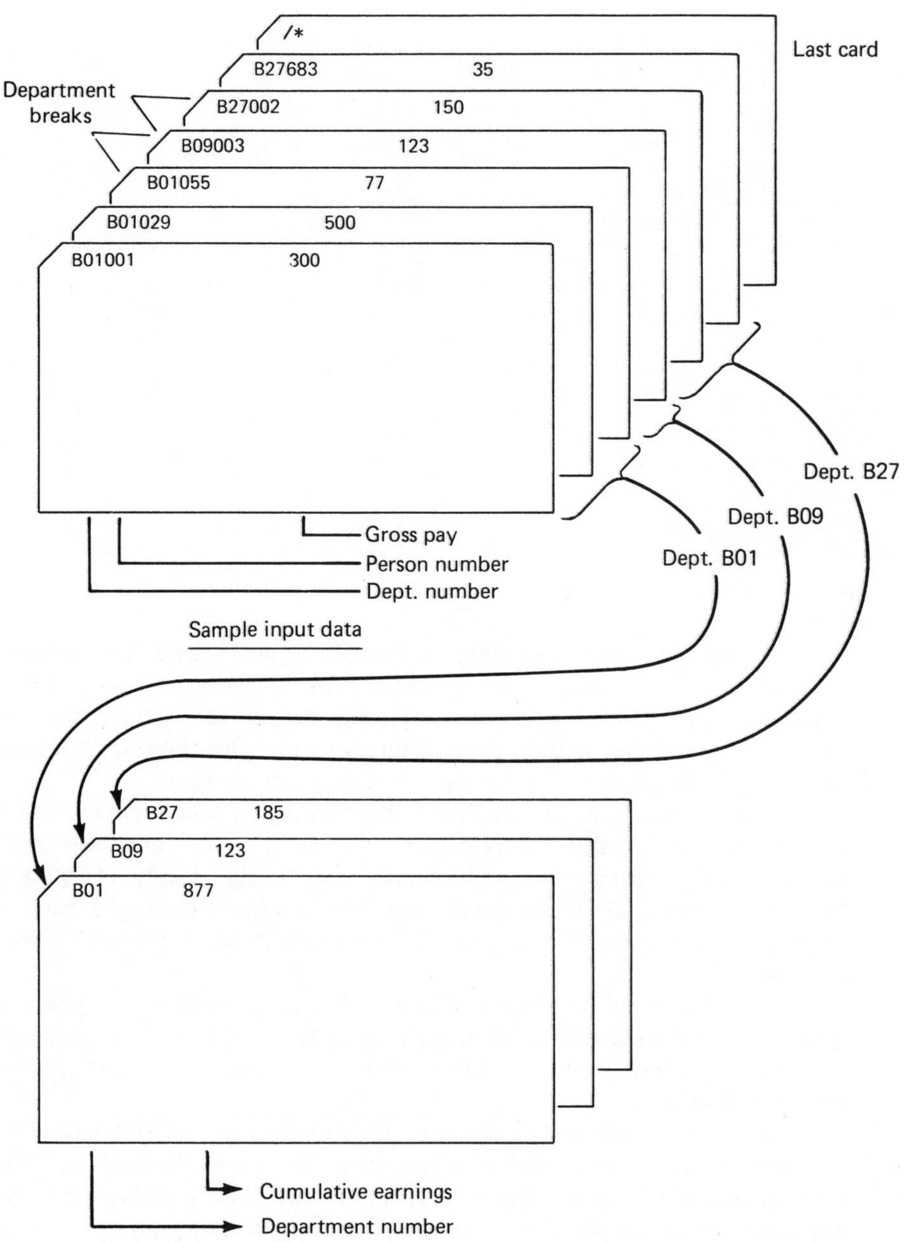

/*
Last card
B27683 35
Department breaks
B27002 150
B09003 123
B01055 77
B01029 500
B01001 300
Dept. B27
Dept. B09
Dept. B01
Gross pay
Person number
Dept. number
Sample input data
B27 185
B09 123
B01 877
Cumulative earnings
Department number

Figure 7-12 Sample data.

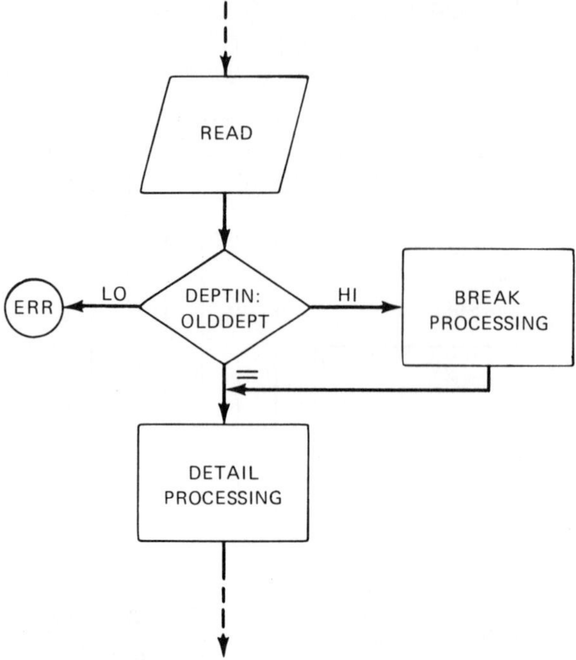

Figure 7-13 The sequence check.

We refer to the flowchart in Figure 7-13 as a sequence check. This concept is one of the most fundamental aspects of business data processing. Most business data is arranged in sequence by some key. In this example, the key is the employee number reflecting person number within department. Each time we read a detail card, we must examine the department number.

There are three possible conditions. The new department number is equal to the previous or old department number. We call this condition a *new-equal.* The new department number may be greater than the old department number. This is a *new-high* condition. Or the new department numer may be less than the old department number. This is a *new-low* condition. A new-low usually represents an error.

Let's check the data given in Figure 7-12 against the flowchart given in Figure 7-13. This process is called *desk checking.* We check sample data against our logic. Any errors we locate at this point are corrected before we write the symbolic program.

The flowchart tells us to read a card. We read the first detail card (Department B01—employee 001). The flowchart then tells us to compare the department number of this card to the department number of the previous card. But this is the first card read! There is no previous department number.

We refer to this circumstance as a *first-time* situation. Often we must treat the first card (and some-times the last card) in a special way. We do not want to enter the compare routine when we read the first card. We want to go directly to the detail processing. We will enter the compare routine on the next read.

We must add an additional read box to our flowchart (Figure 7-14). We refer to this special read statement as a first-time read. The first time we read a card we go to detail processing. All other cards are handled by the second read statement which is followed by the compare box.

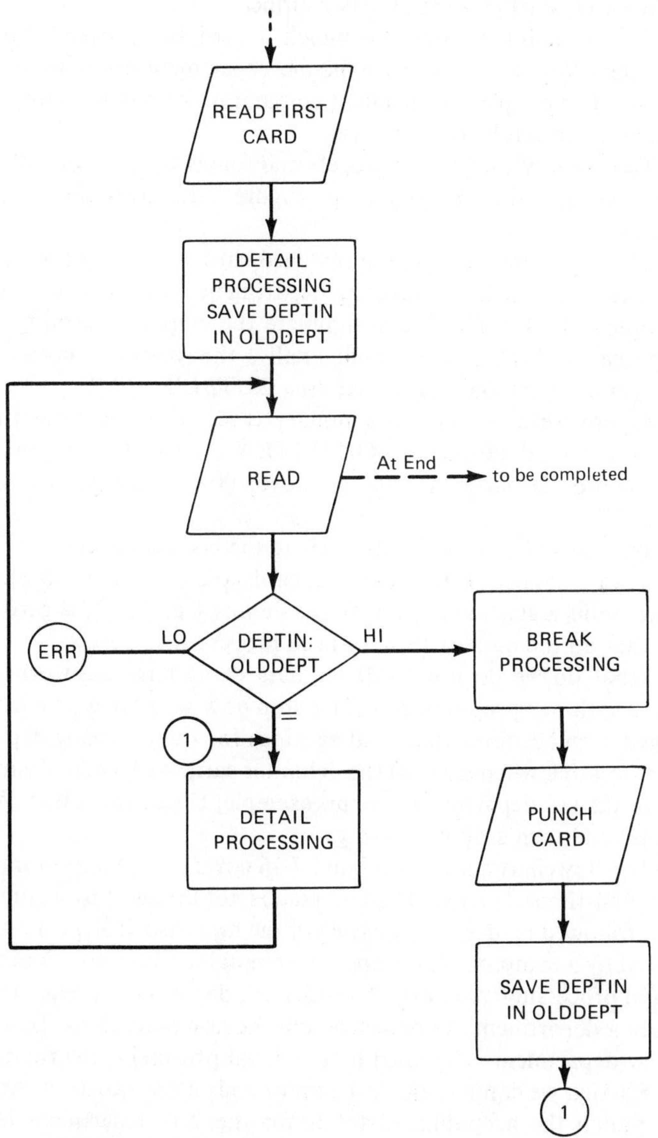

Figure 7-14 Program 6—flowchart.

Let's see how the new flowchart handles the data. We read the first card, save the department number, and add the employee earning amount to an accumulator. We read the second card and enter the compare routine. The department number is equal to the old department number. We add the second employee's earnings to the accumulator. We read the third card; still the same department. We add employee 055's earnings to the accumulator. The next card we read causes a department break. Department B09 is greater than Department B01. We now must go to the break routine.

At this point we want to punch a card summarizing the earnings for Department B01. We summarize the old department *before* we process the new department. We must punch a card containing the old department number and the cumulative employee earnings.

To help us visualize this process and follow the path of data through main storage, we use the memory map. Figure 7-15 gives the memory map for Problem 6.

The data contained on the punched card is read into an area of storage called the input area. We save the department number in another area of storage called OLDDEPT. We accumulate the employee earnings in an area of storage called TOTGROSS, and, finally, the output record—the summary card—is punched from the output area OUTBLD.

Before we can punch a summary card, we must move the department number and total earnings to OUTBLD. We must then return to process the detail record (Department B09, employee 003) which caused the department break.

We continue this way until we read the last card in the data deck. The last card is not a data card. It is a special card called a *delimiter* card. The delimiter card contains a slash-asterick (/*) in columns 1 and 2. This card tells the computer that all the data cards have been processed.

What do we do now? All the data cards have been processed. We are finished with our program. But if we stop now we have a problem. Remember, we have been accumulating total earnings for the *preceding* department. If we stop processing when we read the delimiter card, we have not punched the total card for the last department—in this example, Department B27. We must punch the total and then stop processing.

The flowchart shown in Figure 7-16 covers some important concepts. We have a first-time situation. The first read is not followed by a compare. The first read is followed by detail processing of the first card. The next read statement is followed by a compare. There are two acceptable situations. A new-equal results in detail processing. A new-high results in a department break. The totals of the preceding department are punched, and the flowchart shows that first record of the new department is handled by the detail processing instructions.

Finally, we come to the last card or end-of-file situation. At this point, we must punch the accumulated totals for the last department before we stop

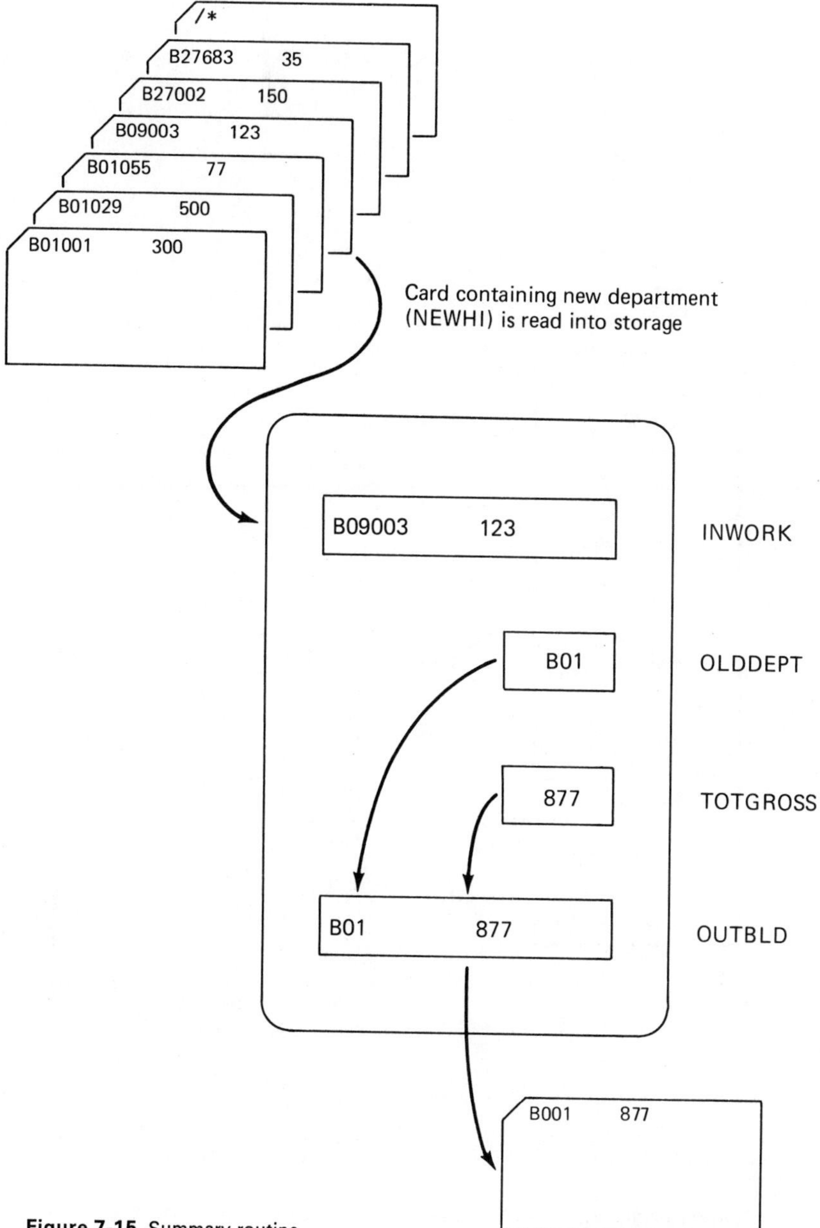

Figure 7-15 Summary routine.

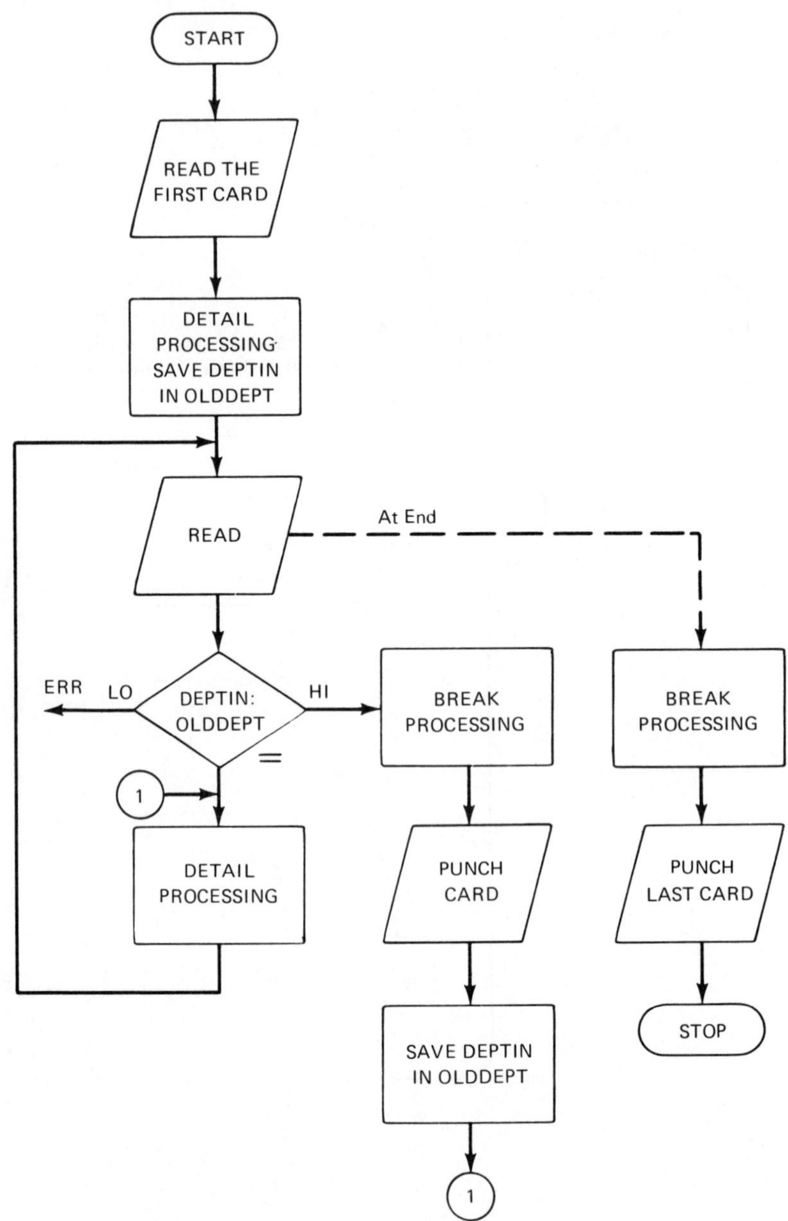

Figure 7-16 Program 6—flowchart.

processing. We must consider the end-of-file condition as a special department break.

We have one last consideration before we start coding Program 6. Each time the totals for a department are punched, we must clear the accumulator. If we do not do this, only the first department summarized is accurate. The second summary card would reflect the total earnings of Departments B01 and B09, and the third summary card would reflect the total earnings of all three departments. We will clear the accumulator after the totals for a department are moved to the output area.

Solution. Our first step is to define the areas of storage our program requires. We must define an input area and an output area (Figure 7-17).

```
INWORK    DS  0CL80
NUMIN     DS  0CL6
DEPTIN    DS  CL3
MANIN     DS  CL3
          DS  CL44
GROSSIN   DS  CL8
          DS  CL22
OUTBLD    DS  0CL80
DEPTOUT   DS  CL3
GROSSOUT  DS  CL13
          DC  64CL1' '
```

We call the input area INWORK, and give it a length attribute of 80

```
INWORK  DS  0CL80
```

but do not reserve any storage. The subsequent DS statements format and reserve storage. NUMIN consists of two fields, DEPTIN and MANIN, totalling 6 bytes. (We do not format the following 44 bytes as they are not referenced in this program.) GROSSIN contains 8 bytes. The remaining 22 bytes complete INWORK.

The first 3 bytes of OUTBLD are labeled DEPTOUT. The following 13 bytes contain GROSSOUT, the earnings total for a given department. Notice that the following 64 bytes have been initialized to blanks with a DC statement. If we do not initialize DEPTOUT, the contents of these 64 storage positions are punched into the output card. But we want the output card to contain only the department number and the earnings total. We must set the remaining positions to spaces.

We define two work areas

```
OLDDEPT   DS  CL3
TOTGROSS  DC  PL7'0'
```

TOTGROSS is initialized to packed zeros. Can you explain why?

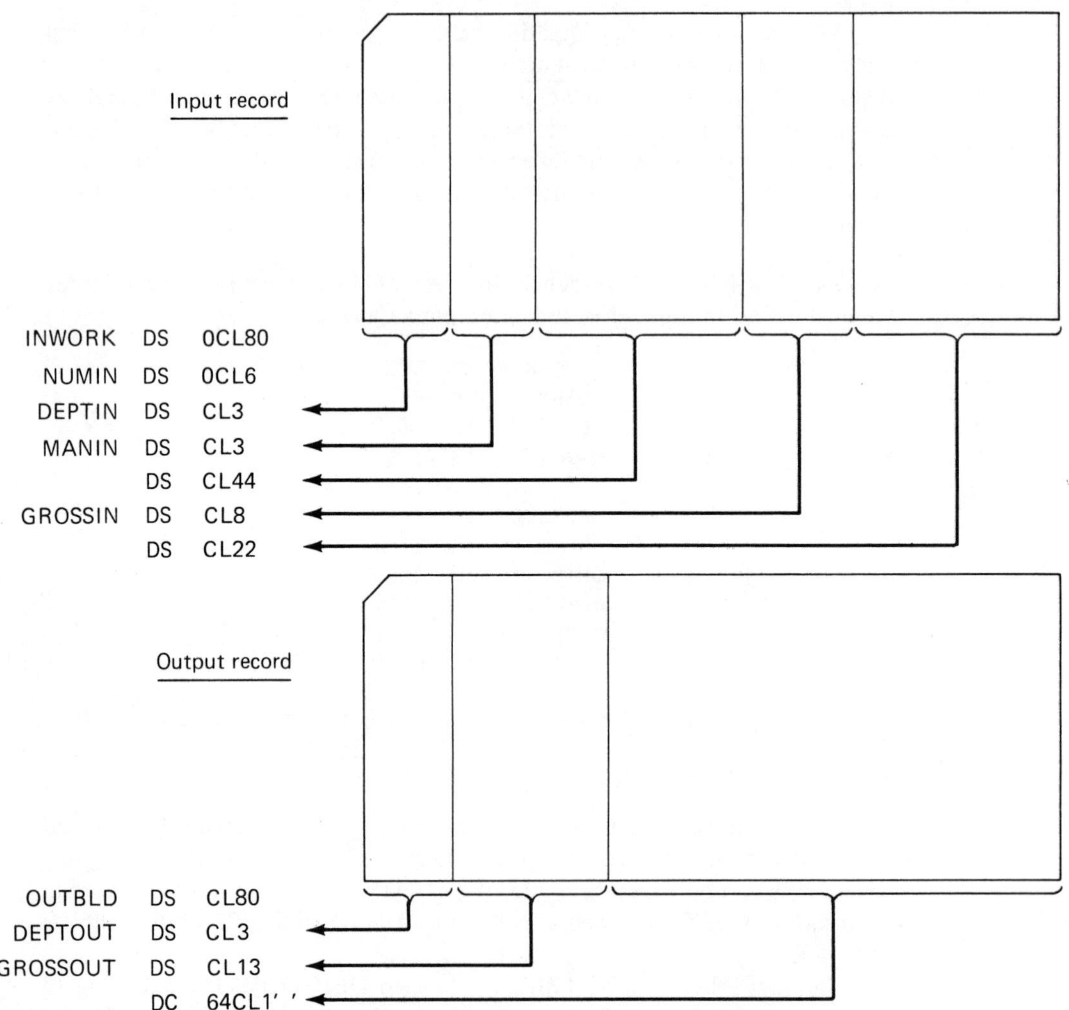

Figure 7-17 Program 6—data formats.

The program logic requires us to accumulate the input earnings field GROSSIN. Data referenced in a decimal add instruction must contain packed data. When numeric data recorded on a punched card is read into storage, it appears in zoned format (Figure 7-18). We must pack GROSSIN before we can add the data to the total field. We must define a work area into which we can pack the gross earnings figure.

```
GROSSPK  DS  CL5
```

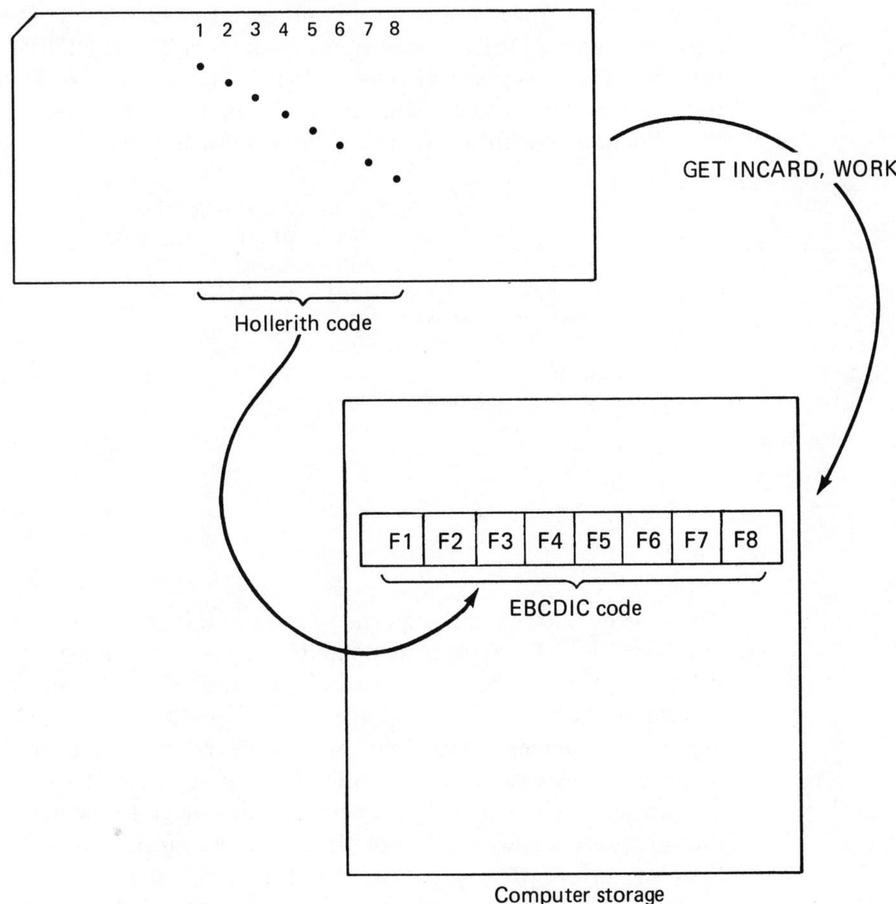

Figure 7-18 Data codes.

Now let's develop the symbolic instructions, referencing the flowchart given in Figure 7-16. We code the instructions to read the first card.

```
FIRSTRD  GET   INCARD,INWORK
         MVC   OLDDEPT(3),DEPTIN
         PACK  GROSSPK(5),GROSSIN
         AP    TOTGROSS(7),GROSSPK
```

The statement

```
GET   INCARD,INWORK
```

reads the first card into an area of storage called INWORK. We save the department number DEPTIN in an area of storage called OLDDEPT. We then add the employee gross salary GROSSIN to the total salary TOTGROSS. Remember, we must always pack data before we can add using decimal arithmetic.

We now code the compare and branch instructions.

```
READLOOP GET   INCARD,INWORK
         CLC   DEPTIN(3),OLDDEPT
         BH    BREAK
         BL    ERROR
DETAIL   .
         .
         .
         .
BREAK    .
         .
         .
         .
ERROR    .
         .
         .
         .
```

The sequence check is the important aspect of this code. We read the next card into INWORK. We want to compare the department number of this card with the department number of the card we just finished processing. We cannot ask the computer to look back at the previous card. But we can compare the department number of the input card (DEPTIN) with the department number of the previous card saved in OLDDEPT. If the new department number is greater than the previous department number, we go to the break routine, and then process the new detail card. Notice that we must process the card causing the break before we loop back to the read statement.

If the department number is less than the old department number, we recognize an error. A card is out of sequence. Otherwise, the new department number must be equal to the old department number. We continue with the detail processing of this card, and then loop to READLOOP.

Let's develop the code for the detail and break processing.

```
DETAIL PACK  GROSSPK(5),GROSSIN
       AP    TOTGROSS(7),GROSSPK
       B     READLOOP
```

We must pack the detail gross amount into a work area, and then add the packed figure to the cumulative total TOTGROSS. We then return to read the next card.

In the break processing we punch the cumulative total, clear the accumulator, and continue to process the new detail card.

```
BREAK  UNPK  GROSSOUT(13),TOTGROSS
       MVC   DEPTOUT(3),OLDDEPT
       PUT   PUNCH,OUTBLD
       MVC   OLDDEPT(3),DEPTIN
       SP    TOTGROSS(7),TOTGROSS
       B     DETAIL
```

Notice that we use the same instruction, PUT, to write a line or to punch a card. The output device is determined by the filename PUNCH as it appears in the HSKPING statement. (See Figure 7-19.)

Before we punch the summary card we must move the cumulative total to the output area. The UNPK statement accomplishes this. We then move the previous department number OLDDEPT to the output area. We now can punch the summary card. Before we return to process the first detail card of the new department grouping, we move the new department number to OLDDEPT and clear the accumulator by subtracting TOTGROSS from itself.

The only remaining consideration is the end-of-file code. When the delimiter card is read, we want to punch the summary card for the last department group. It is not necessary for the programmer to check for the delimiter card; the computer does this. The programmer need only name the code to be entered when the delimiter card is read. We call our end-of-file code ENDRT.

```
ENDRT  MVC   DEPTOUT(3),OLDDEPT
       UNPK  GROSSOUT(13),TOTGROSS
       PUT   PUNCH,OUTBLD
*      *
*      *     PROGRAM COMPLETE
*      *     FILES ARE NOW CLOSED
*      *     END OF JOB
*      *
```

The complete solution to Program 6 is given in Figure 7-19. Some of the necessary housekeeping statements are omitted to simplify the solution. The HSKPING statement names the input file, the output file, and in this example, specifies the name of the end-of-file code, ENDRT.

TESTING AND DEBUGGING

As the programmer writes, punches, and tests his (or her) program, he often encounters errors. We call these errors *bugs*. He may encounter errors when he assembles his program. Assembly time errors are usually careless mistakes. Consider the code

```
        MVC   FLDA(3),FLDB(3)
        .
        .
        .
FLDA    DC    CL3'-123'
FIELDB  DC    PL3'+789'
```

```
*
* PROGRAM 6
* SUMMARIZE EMPLOYEE EARNINGS BY DEPARTMENT
*
         START
         PRINT NOGEN
PROG7    HSKPING CARDID=INCARD,PUNCHID=OUTCARD,EOFID=ENDRT
*        *      SOME
*        *      HOUSEKEEPING
*        *      STATEMENTS
*        *      ARE
*        *      OMITTED
*        *      HERE
*        *
FIRSTRD  GET    INCARD,INWORK               READ FIRST RECORD
         MVC    OLDDEPT(3),DEPTIN           SAVE DEPT
         PACK   GROSSPK(5),GROSSIN          PACK INPUT EARNINGS
         AP     TOTGROSS(7),GROSSPK         ADD TO TOTAL
READLOOP GET    INCARD,INWORK               GET NEXT RECORD
         CLC    DEPTIN(3),OLDDEPT           TEST FOR BREAK
         BH     BREAK                       BRANCH IF BREAK
         BL     ERROR                       OR ERROR
DETAIL   PACK   GROSSPK(5),GROSSIN          ELSE PROCESS DETAIL
*                                           PACK GROSS AMOUNT
         AP     TOTGROSS(7),GROSSPK         AND ADD TO TOTAL
         B      READLOOP                    RETURN TO READ
BREAK    UNPK   GROSSOUT(13),TOTGROSS       UNPACK TOTAL
         MVC    DEPTOUT(3),OLDDEPT          MOVE DEPT TO OUTPUT
         PUT    OUTCARD,OUTBLD              PUNCH SUMMARY CARD
         MVC    OLDDEPT(3),DEPTIN           SAVE DEPARTMENT
         SP     TOTGROSS(7),TOTGROSS        CLEAR COUNTER
         B      DETAIL                      GO TO PROCESS DETAIL
ERROR    B      READLOOP                    ERROR - READ NEXT REC
*        *
*        *      WHEN ALL THE CARDS ARE PROCESSED
*        *      THE CODE AT EOJRT IS ENTERED
*        *
ENDRT    MVC    DEPTOUT(3),OLDDEPT          MOVE LAST DEPT
         UNPK   GROSSOUT(13),TOTGROSS       UNPACK LAST TOTAL
         PUT    OUTCARD,OUTBLD              PUNCH LAST SUMMARY
*        *      THE PROGRAM IS COMPLETE
*        *      THE RETURN STATEMENT
*        *      SIGNIFIES END-OF-JOB
*        *
         L      13,4(13)                    REQUIRED BY OPSYS
         RETURN (14,12)                     END-OF-JOB
*
* DATA AREAS
*
INWORK   DS     0CL80                       INPUT AREA
NUMIN    DS     0CL6                        *
DEPTIN   DS     CL3                         *
MANIN    DS     CL3                         *
         DS     CL44                        *
GROSSIN  DS     CL8                         *
         DS     CL22                        *
OUTBLD   DS     0CL80                       OUTPUT AREA
DEPTOUT  DS     CL3                         *
GROSSOUT DS     CL13                        *
         DC      64CL1' '                   *
OLDDEPT  DS     CL3
TOTGROSS DC     PL7'0'
GROSSPK  DS     CL5
         END
```

Figure 7-19 Program 6—solution.

There are three mistakes in this section of code. Notice the move statement. The programmer has coded two length attributes. But the format of the move statement requires one length attribute. The length attribute is associated with the first operand. The statement should appear as

```
MVC   FLDA(3),FLDB
```

The description of FLDA is in error. The programmer uses the type sub-modifier C to define signed numeric data. The constant should appear as

```
FLDA   DC   ZL3'-123'
```

And, finally, the programmer has misspelled the second operand label, FLDB. The MVC statement references FLDB. The constant describes FIELDB. The labels must be identical.

These errors are detected when the program is assembled. The programmer must correct these errors in the source program, and resubmit the program. The assembler provides a diagnostic listing specifying the statements which are in error.

Execution-Time Errors

When the programmer has eliminated the errors in his source program, he or she is ready to test the program. He must make certain the program produces the correct results. We encounter two types of errors during testing—*logic* errors and *language* errors.

Logic Errors. Logic errors occur when the programmer has not carefully planned the program. Consider the code

```
INIT     PACK   CTR,ONE
BODY     AP     ANS,CTR
         CP     CTR,LIMIT
         BE     EXIT
         AP     CTR,TWO
         B      BODY
EXIT     UNPK   ANS,RESULT
         .
         .
         .
CTR      DS     CL2
LIMIT    DC     PL2'10'
TWO      DC     PL1'2'
ONE      DC     ZL1'1'
ANS      DC     PL3'0'
RESULT   DS     CL6
```

We are caught in a never-ending loop. The program initializes CTR to 1, and increments CTR by 2 each time the body of the loop is executed. The test instruction compares CTR against a limit of 10. CTR never equals 10. We never exit from the loop.

Logic errors are hard to detect. Sometimes we execute the entire program without realizing a logic error has occurred. But when we examine the results of the program, we find that they are incorrect. We must then determine what went wrong. We say that we are *debugging* the program.

Language Errors. Language errors are caused when the programmer does not follow the rules of assembly language. The code

```
         AP    FLDA(3),FLDB(3)
         .
         .
         .
FLDA     DC    ZL3'123'
FLDB     DC    ZL3'456'
```

does not result in an assembly-time error. But when the computer executes the AP instruction, a data exception occurs. FLDA and FLDB do not contain packed data. This error is so severe that the computer cannot continue with this program. The program is cancelled. The programmer receives a printout of computer storage, and other information to aid him in locating the error. We call this listing a storage *dump*.

Analyzing a Storage Dump

The format of the storage dump returned to the programmer depends upon the operating system in use. We will discuss dumps from both OS/370 and DOS/370 systems.

OS/370 Storage Dump. Figure 7-20 gives a sample OS/370 storage dump. The operating system lists information (1) regarding execution of the job. Much of this information is not used in debugging. The *completion code* (2) is important. The completion code tells the reason for the error. A completion code of 0C7 indicates a data exception. Each operating system has a book of codes. The programmer references this manual to find the meaning of the completion code.

The dump tells us the cause of the error and the address of the instruction following the instruction in error (3). Remember, the program itself resides in storage and is addressable. Data and instructions are addressed using a six hexadecimal digit address. We see that a data exception occurred at location $1F97C4_{16}$.

The listing also contains the contents of the general purpose registers (4). The registers are part of the CPU and are used for storing addresses and binary numbers.

We must know where our program resides in storage. The listing gives us the entry point (5) in our program. The entry point is the address of the first instruction within the program. We use the entry address to locate the relative address of the instruction causing the error (6).

We subtract the entry address from the address of the instruction in error to determine the relative address of the instruction causing the problem. We find that the instruction following the error has a relative location of $00000C_{16}$. We now locate this instruction in the source listing (7). The first column on the source listing gives the relative location of all the instructions in the program. We are interested in the instruction preceding the instruction at location $00000C_{16}$. We find an AP instruction. We must now determine the cause of the error.

A program check occurs when an operand in a decimal arithmetic operation does not contain packed data. The instruction

```
AP   ANS,PKFLD
```

references two fields. PKFLD is initialized when the contents of CON1 are packed into PKFLD. The data in error resides at ANS. We did not initialize ANS when we defined it. ANS does not contain packed data. A data exception occured when the AP instruction was executed. We must either define ANS as a packed constant

```
ANS   DC   PL4'0'
```

or use the ZAP instruction

```
ZAP   ANS,CON1
```

We also are given a printout of computer storage. The printout contains the address of each section of storage (8), a hexadecimal representation of the data in storage (9), and an interpretation of storage (10).

The storage addresses are given in hexadecimal. The address given is the first byte of each line. There are 32 bytes of data in each line. Each byte of data is represented by two hexadecimal digits. The operating system represents each byte of storage in the rightmost section of the dump. Often a byte of storage does not contain a valid EBCDIC character. A period is printed. Any valid EBCDIC configuration is printed.

We can use the storage dump to examine the field named ANS and see why the error occurred. We locate ANS by adding the relative location value of ANS (000041_{16}) to the entry address ($1F97B8_{16}$). We determine that ANS resides at storage location $1F97F9_{16}$ (11). We locate ANS and see that it contains four bytes. It appears as

00	00	00	00

The low-order sign bits do not contain a valid sign. The field does not contain packed data. This is the reason the data exception occurred.

```
//ERRORS    JOB (GG38,4637,,,,3),'BB',CLASS=F                                  JOB 139
//DECDUMP EXEC ASMFCLG
XXASM       EXEC  PGM=IFUASM,PARM='LOAD,NODECK',REGION=50K,ROLL=(NO,YES)
XXSYSLIB DD     DSNAME=SYS1.MACLIB,DISP=SHR                             IEUD 00040016
XXSYSUT1    DD  DSNAME=&SYSUT1,UNIT=SYSSQ,SPACE=(1700,(400,50))
XXSYSUT2    DD  DSNAME=&SYSUT2,UNIT=SYSSQ,SPACE=(1700,(400,50))
XXSYSUT3    DD  DSNAME=&SYSUT3,SPACE=(1700,(400,50)),UNIT=SYSSQ
XXSYSPRINT DD   SYSOUT=A
XXSYSGO     DD  DSNAME=&LOADSET,UNIT=SYSSQ,SPACE=(80,(200,50)),         +
XX              DISP=(MOD,PASS)
//ASM.SYSIN DD *
IEF236I ALLOC. FOR ERRORS   ASM      DECDUMP
IEF237I 154   ALLOCATED TO SYSLIB
IEF237I 151   ALLOCATED TO SYSUT1
IEF237I 150   ALLOCATED TO SYSUT2
IEF237I 151   ALLOCATED TO SYSUT3
IEF237I 433   ALLOCATED TO SYSPRINT
IEF237I 150   ALLOCATED TO SYSGO
IEF237I 504   ALLOCATED TO SYSIN
IEF142I - STEP WAS EXECUTED - COND CODE 0000
IEF285I   SYS1.MACLIB                                     KEPT
IEF285I   VOL SER NOS= SYSRES.
IEF285I   SYS76169.T081651.RV000.ERRORS.SYSUT1            DELETED
IEF285I   VOL SER NOS= ACC004.
IEF285I   SYS76169.T081651.RV000.ERRORS.SYSUT2            DELETED
IEF285I   VOL SER NOS= MISC01.
IEF285I   SYS76169.T081651.RV000.ERRORS.SYSUT3            DELETED
IEF285I   VOL SER NOS= ACC004.
IEF285I   SYS76169.T081651.RV000.ERRORS.LOADSET           PASSED
IEF285I   VOL SER NOS= MISC01.
IEF373I STEP /ASM     / START 76169.1211
IEF374I STEP /ASM     / STOP  76169.1220 CPU   0MIN 17.99SEC MAIN 150K LCS   OK
IEFACTAI -                                     8.70 RESIDENT MIN       RC =     0 <-----<<
IEFACTBI - I/O UTILIZATION FOR STEP ASM       WAS -
IEFACTCI -        -DEVICE TYPE-    -EXCP COUNT-
IEFACTDI -         DASD                     462
IEFACTDI -         TAPE                       0
IEFACTDI -         UNIT RECORD               80
IEFACTDI -         OTHER                      0
IEFACTDI -         -----------     -----------
IEFACTDI -         TOTAL                    542
XXLKED      EXEC  PGM=IEWL,PARM='LIST,LET',COND=(9,LT,ASM),REGION=150K,
XX          ROLL=(NO,YES)
XXSYSLIN    DD  DSNAME=&LOADSET,DISP=(OLD,DELETE)
XX          DD  DDNAME=SYSIN
//LKED.SYSLMOD DD DSNAME=&GOSET(P6),UNIT=SYSDA,
//             SPACE=(1024,(50,20,1)),DISP=(MOD,PASS)
X/SYSLMOD  DD   DSNAME=&GOSET(GO),UNIT=SYSDA,                           +
XX              SPACE=(1024,(50,20,1)),DISP=(MOD,PASS)
XXSYSUT1    DD  DSNAME=&SYSUT1,UNIT=SYSDA,SPACE=(1024,(50,20))
XXSYSPRINT DD   SYSOUT=A
IEF236I ALLOC. FOR ERRORS   LKED     DECDUMP
IEF237I 150   ALLOCATED TO SYSLIN
IEF237I 150   ALLOCATED TO SYSLMOD
IEF237I 150   ALLOCATED TO SYSUT1
IEF237I 433   ALLOCATED TO SYSPRINT
IEF142I - STEP WAS EXECUTED - COND CODE 0000
IEF285I   SYS76169.T081651.RV000.ERRORS.LOADSET           DELETED
IEF285I   VOL SER NOS= MISC01.
IEF285I   SYS76169.T081651.RV000.ERRORS.GOSET             PASSED
IEF285I   VOL SER NOS= MISC01.
```

(1) OS/370 Job control messages

Figure 7-20 An OS/370 storage dump.

```
IEF285I    SYS76169.T081651.RV000.ERRORS.SYSUT1           DELETED
IEF285I    VOL SER NOS= MISC01.
IEF373I STEP /LKED    / START 76169.1220
IEF374I STEP /LKED    / STOP  76169.1221 CPU    0MIN 00.79SEC MAIN 136K LCS    OK
IEFACTAI -                                          0.77 RESIDENT MIN         RC =      0  <-----<<
IEFACTBI - I/O UTILIZATION FOR STEP LKED       WAS -
IEFACTCI -        -DEVICE TYPE-    -EXCP COUNT-
IEFACTCI -         DASD                      11
IEFACTDI -         TAPE                       0
IEFACTDI -         UNIT RECORD                5
IEFACTDI -         OTHER                      0
IEFACTDI -         -----------     ----------
IEFACTDI -         TOTAL                     16
XXGO        EXEC  PGM=*.LKED.SYSLMOD,COND=((8,LT,ASM),(4,LT,LKED)),
XX          ROLL=(NO,YES)
//GO.SYSUDUMP DD SYSOUT=A
//
IEF236I ALLOC. FOR ERRORS   GO        DECDUMP
IEF237I 150    ALLOCATED TO PGM=*.DD
IEF237I 430    ALLOCATED TO SYSUDUMP
COMPLETION CODE - SYSTEM=0C7  USER=0000                   (2) OS|370 Code - indicates data exception
IEF285I    SYS76169.T081651.RV000.ERRORS.GOSET           PASSED
IEF285I    VOL SER NOS= MISC01.
IEF373I STEP /GO      / START 76169.1221
IEF374I STEP /GO      / STOP  76169.1222 CPU    0MIN 01.84SEC MAIN   8K LCS    OK
IEFACTAI -                                          0.69 RESIDENT MIN         RC = ABEND  <-----<<
IEFACTBI - I/O UTILIZATION FOR STEP GO         WAS -
IEFACTCI -        -DEVICE TYPE-    -EXCP COUNT-
IEFACTDI -         DASD                       0
IEFACTDI -         TAPE                       0
IEFACTDI -         UNIT RECORD              232
IEFACTDI -         OTHER                      0
IEFACTDI -         -----------     -----------
IEFACTDI -         TOTAL                    232
IEF285I    SYS76169.T081651.RV000.ERRORS.GOSET           DELETED
IEF285I    VOL SER NOS= MISC01.
IEF375I    JOB /ERRORS  / START 76169.1211
IEF376I    JOB /ERRORS  / STOP  76169.1222 CPU    0MIN 20.62SEC
IEFACTBI - I/O UTILIZATION FOR THE JOB ERRORS    WAS -
IEFACTCI -        -DEVICE TYPE-    -EXCP COUNT-
IEFACTDI -         DASD                     473
IEFACTDI -         TAPE                       0
IEFACTDI -         UNIT RECORD              317
IEFACTDI -         OTHER                      0
IEFACTDI -         -----------     -----------
IEFACTDI -         TOTAL                    790

IEFACTFI - ACCOUNT GG384637 HAS USED     $4.25 TO DATE, AND HAS    $20.75 REMAINING  $ $ $ $
```

Figure 7-20 (Continued)

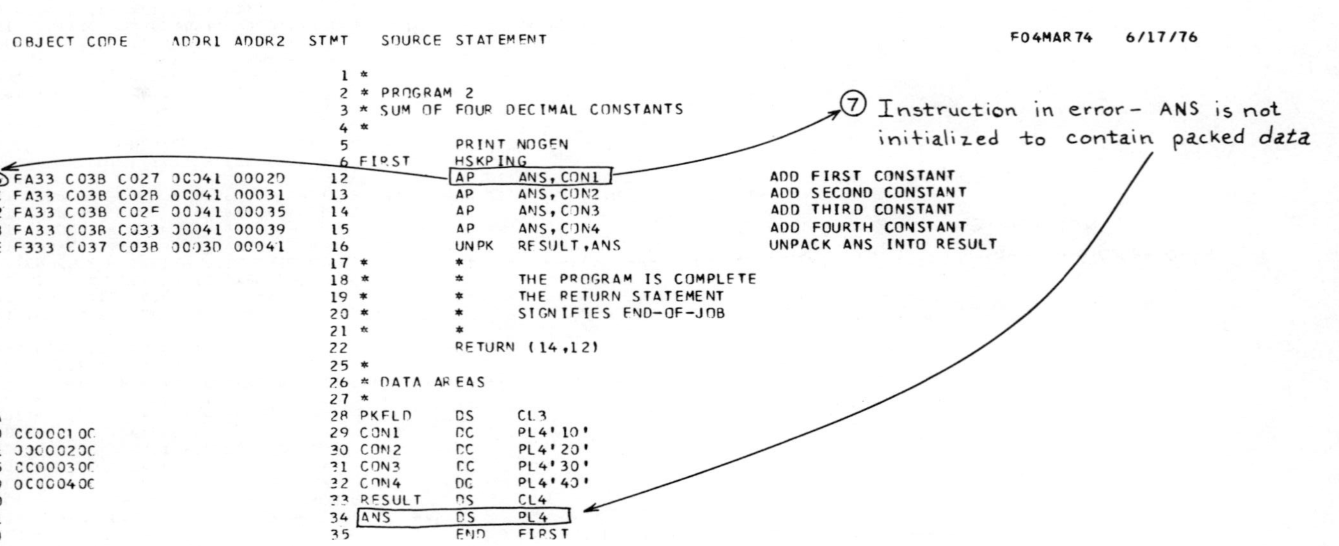

```
                                                                                  PAGE    1
  LOC  OBJECT CODE     ADDR1 ADDR2  STMT   SOURCE STATEMENT                        F04MAR74  6/17/76

                                       1 *
                                       2 * PROGRAM 2
                                       3 * SUM OF FOUR DECIMAL CONSTANTS
                                       4 *
                                       5          PRINT NOGEN
                                       6 FIRST    HSKPING
000006 FA33 C03B C027 00041 0002D     12          AP    ANS,CON1           ADD FIRST CONSTANT
00000C FA33 C03B C02B 00041 00031     13          AP    ANS,CON2           ADD SECOND CONSTANT
000012 FA33 C03B C02F 00041 00035     14          AP    ANS,CON3           ADD THIRD CONSTANT
000018 FA33 C03B C033 00041 00039     15          AP    ANS,CON4           ADD FOURTH CONSTANT
00001E F333 C037 C03B 0003D 00041     16          UNPK  RESULT,ANS         UNPACK ANS INTO RESULT
                                      17 *        *
                                      18 *        *     THE PROGRAM IS COMPLETE
                                      19 *        *     THE RETURN STATEMENT
                                      20 *        *     SIGNIFIES END-OF-JOB
                                      21 *        *
                                      22          RETURN (14,12)
                                      25 *
                                      26 * DATA AREAS
                                      27 *
00002A                                28 PKFLD    DS    CL3
00002D 0000010C                       29 CON1     DC    PL4'10'
000031 0000020C                       30 CON2     DC    PL4'20'
000035 0000030C                       31 CON3     DC    PL4'30'
000039 0000040C                       32 CON4     DC    PL4'40'
00003D                                33 RESULT   DS    CL4
000041                                34 ANS      DS    PL4
000000                                35          END   FIRST
```

(7) Instruction in error - ANS is not initialized to contain packed data

Figure 7-20 (Continued)

```
JOB ERRORS            STEP GO              TIME 122140   DATE 76169                                              PAGE 0001

COMPLETION CODE       SYSTEM = 0C7         OS|370 Error code (2)

PSW AT ENTRY TO ABEND   FF85000D C01F97C4   Location of instruction following error - (3)

TCB  028E70   RBP    000146C0   PIE      C0000000   DEB  0002BBA4   TIO 0002BFC0   CMP    800C7000   TRN   00000000
              MSS    02031D28   PK-FLG   00852400   FLG  00007F78   LLS 00018B28   JLB    00000000   JPQ   00017060
              FSA    0121DF68   TCB      C0000000   TMF  00000000   JST 0002BE70   NTC    00000000   OTC   0002CAE8
              LTC    C0000000   IQE      00000000   ECB  0002C994   TSF 20000000   D-PQE  00031A88   SQS   0002B360
              NSTAE  C0000000   TCT      80028988   USER 00000000   DAR 00000000   RESV   00000000   JSCB  8702C5D8
              RESV   C0000000   IOB      C0000000


ACTIVE RBS

PRB  0159F0   RESV   00000000   APSW     C01F97C4   WC-SZ-STAB 00040082   FL-CDE  00016FD0   PSW FF85000D C01F97C4
              Q/TTR  00000000   WT-LNK   C002BE70

SVRB 014630   TAB-LN 00080220   APSW     F9F0F1C3   WC-SZ-STAB 0012D002   TQN     00000000   PSW 00040033 50007CE2
              Q/TTR  00005212   WT-LNK   C00159F0
              RG 0-7   FD000008   0021DFF8   0002C728   5C02C998   0002CF30   0002CAE8   0002C004   0002E3E8
              RG 8-15  0C02C970   0002B988   0002C998   00000000   401F97BE   0021DF68   00010BDA   011F97B8
              EXTSA    000021BE   8F21DF10   C0000000   00000000   FF030000   000146AC   000146B4   E2E8E2C9
                       C5C1F0F1   C9C5C170   C1C2C5D5   C4F90C70

SVRB 0146C0   TAB-LN C04803D8   APSW     F1F0F5C1   WC-SZ-STAB 0012D002   TQN     00000000   PSW FF04000C 4021D7A6
              Q/TTR  00005321   WT-LNK   C0014630
              RG 0-7   0C1058B0   00014690   80007BFA   0000AA50   0002BE70   00014630   0402BE70   00014630
              RG 8-15  0002BE70   40007842   0002BE70   8F21DF10   0002BFF0   000146B4   4000A3D4   00000000
              EXTSA    E2E8F2C9   C5C1F0F1   C9C7C3F5   F4FCF3C4   00014630   00000000   E2E3C1C5   00000000
                       80014720   0CCC0000   00000000   0026AF52


LOAD LIST

          NE C0018D98   RSP-CDE 02017060        NE 00018C30   RSP-CDE 01015E00        NE 00018C98   RSP-CDE 01015E18
          NE C0C18C60   RSP-CDE 01015D88        NE 00000000   RSP-CDE 01015DA0

                                                                                  Entry point - load address (5)
CDE

     016FD0       ATR1 0B   NCDE 000000   ROC-RB 000159F0   NM P6         USE 01   EPA 1F97B8   ATR2 20   XL/MJ 017EF0
     017060       ATR1 30   NCDE 016FD0   ROC-RB 00000000   NM IGC0A05A   USE 02   EPA 21D058   ATR2 28   XL/MJ 017EB0
     C15E00       ATR1 B0   NCDE 015DE8   ROC-RB 00000000   NM IGG019CF   USE 02   EPA 27C3F0   ATR2 20   XL/MJ 017470
     015F18       ATR1 B0   NCDE 015FC0   ROC-RB 00000000   NM IGG019CL   USE 02   EPA 27E818   ATR2 20   XL/MJ 017480
     015D88       ATR1 B1   NCDE 015D70   ROC-RB 0C000000   NM IGG019BA   USE 02   EPA 27D018   ATR2 28   XL/MJ 017420
     015DA0       ATR1 B0   NCDE 015D88   ROC-RB 00000000   NM IGG019BB   USE 02   EPA 27C988   ATR2 20   XL/MJ 017430

XL                                              LN         ADR          LN         ADR          LN         ADR

     017EF0    SZ C0000010   NO 00000001     80000048   001F97B8                             (6) Address of error    1F97C4
     017EB0    SZ C0000010   NO 0C000001     800007A8   0021D058                                 Load address        1F97B8
                                                                                                 Relative address    00000C
                                                                                                 or location counter
                                                                                                 value of instruction
                                                                                                 following error
```

Figure 7-20 (Continued)

```
                                                                                                        PAGE 0003
          R1  0021DFF8   R2  0002C728   R3  5C02C998   R4  0002CF30   R5  0002CAE8   R6  0002C004
          R7  C002F3E8   R8  0002C970   R9  0002B9B8   R10 0002C998   R11 00000000   R12 4027DBD2

INTERRUPT AT 1F97C4

PROCEEDING BACK VIA REG 13

P6        WAS ENTERED VIA LINK

SA    21DF68   WD1 00000000   HSA 00000000   LSA 00000000   RET 00010BDA   EPA 011F97B8   R0  FD000008
               R1  0021DFF8   R2  0002C728   R3  5C02C998   R4  0002CF30   R5  0002CAE8   R6  0002C004
               R7  0002E3E8   R8  0002C970   R9  0002B9B8   R10 0002C998   R11 00000000   R12 4027DBD2

REGS AT ENTRY TO ABEND

    FLTR 0-6       4040404040400026      2469F000001770 43            DF414300F476169F      0000000000000000

    REGS 0-7       FD000008   0021DFF8   0002C728   5C02C998          0002CF30   0002CAE8   0002C004   0002E3E8
    REGS 8-15      C002C970   0002B9B8   C002C998   00000000          401F97BE   0021DF68   00010BDA   011F97B8

LOAD MODULE     P6

1F97A0                                                                          90ECD00C 05C0FA33   *..........D.....................*
1F97C0    C03BC027 FA33C03B C02BFA33 C03BC02F    FA33C03B C033F333 C037C03B 98ECD00C   *..........................3.........*
1F97EC    C7FFCC00 CC000001 0C000002 0C000003    0C000004 0C000000 00000000 00000000   *................................*

LOAD MODULE     IGC0A05A

21D040                                                                          4180D099 1B114313   *................................*
21D060    00001A81 41330001 95FF3000 47806068    1BEE1BFF 1B001B11 43E30000 43030001   *.......................T......*
21D080    8CE0C004 88F0001C 8C000004 8810001C    1A2C44E0 6070 1A1E 41818001 44F06076   *.....0.......................0..*
21D0A0    F384D069 D069DC07 D06962C6 41FFF001    44F0607C 47F066F8 413E3003 47F06010   *3..........F..0..0...0.8.....0..*
21D0C0    41330001 47F060E2 D2008000 3C02D200    D0692000 D2C08000 D0695050 D08C5000   *.....0.SK.....K.....K...........*
21D0E0    D12094FC D1235800 D1201A10 5800D120    41110003 5010D064 94FCD067 D703D06C   *J...J...J.....J...............P...*
21D100    D06C1810 54006290 19014780 60BC1B10    401CD06C 5810D064 4A10D06C 1B005D00   *...............  ...............*
21D120    668040C0 D06A1211 4770611C 4810D06A    12114770 60E85850 D08C5860 D12407F5   *.. ..................Y......J..5*
21D140    4120D121 45B06236 5820D120 413062C4    48A0D06A 48A0D06C 88A00002 45B0623E   *..J........J....D...............*
21D160    46A06104 9640D112 455062DA 94BFD112    47F060DE 18A15810 D1204B10 D06C5010   *..... J........J..0.......J.......*
21D180    D0704120 DC7145B0 62364810 D06C8810    10011A31 5820C120 45B0623E 5020D120   *.........................J........J.*
21D1A0    9640D112 455062DA 94BFD112 4810D06C    12114770 61984700 615E4110 0001191A   *. J........J....................*
21D1C0    47B061A6 18125B10 6680D51F 1C002000    477061A6 4810D06E 41110001 4010D06E   *...........N...................  ...*
21D1E0    41220020 5020D120 46A0615E 47F061B0    1B114010 D06C46A0 611E47F0 60D44810   *......J.......0.....  .........0.M..*
21D200    D06E1211 4780619E 5810D120 4800D06E    89C00005 1B105010 D0704120 D0714810   *...........J....................*
21D220    D06EC610 12114770 6202D203 D09F629D    41306294 45B0623E D20DD0AA 62A29640   *...........K...............K...... *
21D240    D1124550 62DA948F D112D701 D06ED06E    12AA4780 60D447F0 619ED204 D09F629D   *J........J.P............M.0..K.....*
21D260    413062 97 45B0623E 9260D0AB 5810D120    5B106680 5010D070 4120D071 4130629A   *.................J...............*
21D280    45B0623E D200D0B2 62A247F0 61F64130    62B047F0 65744180 D09995FF 30004780   *....K.......0.W.....0...............*
21D2A0    627C1B00 43030000 1B114313 0C011480    44106284 F384D070 D070DC07 D07062C6   *.......................3..........F*
21D2C0    41111001 4410628A 41330002 41220004    47F0623E 41330001 07FBD078 D200D070   *...................0...........K...*
21D2E0    20C0D20C 8000D070 FFFFFFE0 0B02FF0C    02FF1302 FFC3C9D5 C5E240E2 C1D4C540   *..K....................LINES SAME *
21D300    C1E240C1 C2D6F5C5 0002FF09 0312031B    03240330 03290342 034B03FF 0903FF12   *AS ABOVE........................*
21D32C    03FF1B03 FF2403FF 3003FF39 03FF4203    FF0098E0 D08012EE 47806310 D27CF000   *............................K.0.*
```

③ Address instruction following error

Entry address 1F97B8
Location ANS 000041
Address ANS 1F97F9 ⑪

General purpose requests ④

ANS in storage - does not contain packed data

Storage addresses ⑧

Data in storage using one less digit for four bits ⑨

OS/370 Attempts to print contents of storage ⑩

Figure 7-20 *(Concluded)*

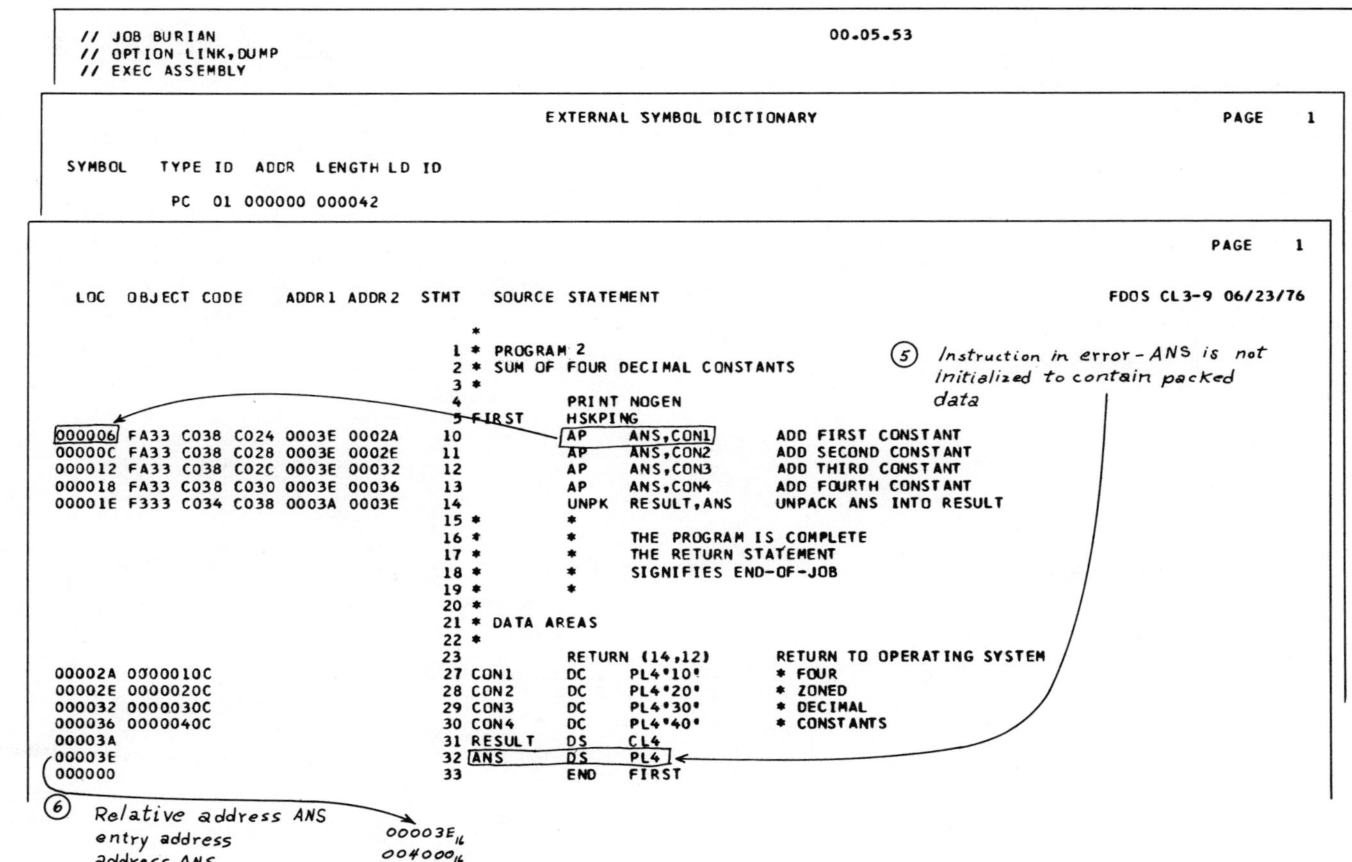

```
// JOB BURIAN                                                        00.05.53
// OPTION LINK,DUMP
// EXEC ASSEMBLY

                              EXTERNAL SYMBOL DICTIONARY                         PAGE    1

SYMBOL   TYPE ID  ADDR  LENGTH LD ID

          PC  01 000000 000042

                                                                                 PAGE    1

  LOC  OBJECT CODE    ADDR1 ADDR2  STMT   SOURCE STATEMENT                FDOS CL3-9 06/23/76

                                          *
                                        1 * PROGRAM 2
                                        2 * SUM OF FOUR DECIMAL CONSTANTS
                                        3 *
                                        4            PRINT NOGEN
                                        5 FIRST      HSKPING
000006 FA33 C038 C024 0003E 0002A      10            AP    ANS,CON1        ADD FIRST CONSTANT
00000C FA33 C038 C028 0003E 0002E      11            AP    ANS,CON2        ADD SECOND CONSTANT
000012 FA33 C038 C02C 0003E 00032      12            AP    ANS,CON3        ADD THIRD CONSTANT
000018 FA33 C038 C030 0003E 00036      13            AP    ANS,CON4        ADD FOURTH CONSTANT
00001E F333 C034 C038 0003A 0003E      14            UNPK  RESULT,ANS      UNPACK ANS INTO RESULT
                                       15 *          *
                                       16 *          *     THE PROGRAM IS COMPLETE
                                       17 *          *     THE RETURN STATEMENT
                                       18 *          *     SIGNIFIES END-OF-JOB
                                       19 *          *
                                       20 *
                                       21 * DATA AREAS
                                       22 *
                                       23            RETURN (14,12)        RETURN TO OPERATING SYSTEM
00002A 0000010C                        27 CON1       DC    PL4'10'         * FOUR
00002E 0000020C                        28 CON2       DC    PL4'20'         * ZONED
000032 0000030C                        29 CON3       DC    PL4'30'         * DECIMAL
000036 0000040C                        30 CON4       DC    PL4'40'         * CONSTANTS
00003A                                 31 RESULT     DS    CL4
00003E                                 32 ANS        DS    PL4
000000                                 33            END   FIRST
```


Figure 7-21 A DOS/370 storage dump.

```
                                        CROSS-REFERENCE                                                       PAGE    1

SYMBOL     LEN   VALUE  DEFN      REFERENCES                                                                06/23/76

ANS        00004 00003E 00032    0010  0011  0012  0013  0014
CON1       00004 00002A 00027    0010
CON2       00004 00002E 00028    0011
CCN3       00004 000032 00029    0012
CON4       00004 000036 00030    0013
FIRST      00004 000000 00007    0033
RESULT     00004 00003A 00031    0014

NO STATEMENTS FLAGGED IN THIS ASSEMBLY

// EXEC LNKEDT

JOB  BURIAN    06/23/76   DISK LINKAGE EDITOR DIAGNOSTIC OF INPUT

ACTION TAKEN  MAP
LIST   ENTRY

06/23/76   PHASE   XFR-AC  LOCORE  HICORE  DSK-AD   ESD TYPE  LABEL     LOADED  REL-FR

       PHASE***   004000  004000  004041  5B 13 1  CSECT               004000  004000

// EXEC

0S03I PROGRAM CHECK INTERRUPTION - HEX LOCATION C04006 - CONDITION CODE 0 - DATA EXCEPTION
0S00I JOB BURIAN   CANCELED
```

(4) Address instruction in error: $00400C_{16}$
load address: 004000_{16}
Relative address instruction in error: $00000C_{16}$

(1) Address and cause of error

Figure 7-21 (Continued)

```
         BURIAN           06/23/76                                                         00.06.52             PAGE   1

GR 0-7   00004000 00004000 0001F7FF 00004000   0001F784 FFFFFF7C 00004000 00003F98   (2) General purpose registers
GR 8-F   00005B0A 0A0407F1 00004010 00004010   40004006 00005FD8 000002D0 0000007B
FP REG   00000000 00000000 00000000 00000000   00000000 00000000 00000000 00000000
COMREG   BG ACCR IS 0002D0
(3) Storage printout
000000   00000000 00000000 00000000 00000000   00000000 000002D0 FF050000 00000000   ................  ................
000020   FF050007 40003B66 FF150007 C000400C   5B5BC2C5 D6D1F440 FF05000E 80004C28   .... .......... .  $$BEOJ4 ......).
000040   00003C88 08000000 00003C78 00000000   FD0B6F00 00FEF029 00040000 0F001EEA   ................  ......0.........
000060   00040000 000003FE 00040000 00001EAA   00000000 00000E1C 00040000 000003A4   ................  ................
000080   00000000 00000000 00000000 00000003   00050003 06B006B0 06B041BB 00734570   ................  ................
0000A0   0168940F BEAB41A0 CF1C4570 0DEA18A8   419001A8 92FFB583 458000EA 9200B583   ................  ................
0000C0   47F0BCC0 06B006B0 06B006B0 06B006B0   06B006B0 06B006B0 06B041BB 001741BB   .0..............  ................
0000E0   00504570 01684180 01A89640 A0019120   A00C4710 00FA9260 A0019604 A00F95E2   .&.......... ....  .......-.......S
000100   A0024780 B0EC95C1 A0024780 B0EC9561   A0024780 01229104 A0004780 01229203   .......A......./  ................
000120   008F9281 A0004BA0 032A487A CE0C49A0   036C41AA CF0C0778 94F9703B D7017058   ................  .........9..P...
000140   70589283 A00095FF B5829200 B5820788   9680A001 440004FC 4780BBA0 947FA001   ................  ................
000160   92F0BBBD 47F0BBA0 42B000F7 58B002B8   9180A000 07175890 A0044880 02445000   .0...0.....7....  ..............&.
000180   902C6000 90586020 90606040 90686060   9070D21B 90100298 D2079008 80009680   ..-...-..-- ..--  ..K.....K.......
0001A0   A00007F7 45700170 D20EB562 B57258E0   02C4DC0E B562CF0C 1BAADD0F B562000C   ...7....K.......  .D..............
0001C0   43A10010 42A0036F 4AA0C34C D20002FF   A00D5AA0 03644400 A0045890 A0044220   ...........)K...  ................
0001E0   A0009140 A0014710 CB96D207 02989008   9560036F 47200270 68009058 68209060   ... ......K.....  .-.............-
000200   68409068 68609070 4BA0032A 41AACE0C   D2010016 A0009898 90108200 02984400   . ...-..........  K...............
000220   A0049500 A0014780 02364400 04FC4780   023647F0 01A45890 A0049818 9030989F   ................  ...0............
000240   02988200 00389284 CF6CD207 0298B698   9890B6A0 82000298 9680A000 41100030   ...........K....  ................
000260   47F0BAF0 96030039 96010038 82000038   92FF0298 96050299 440004FC 478001F8   .0.0............  ...............8
000280   03000299 02FF47F0 01F8615C 40615040   44F00000 00000000 FF050007 40003B66   L.......0.8/* /&  .0.......... ...
0002A0   00001000 00002000 00003000 00004000   000038B0 8000197A 00001000 00002000   .............. .  ................
0002C0   00003000 00004000 30420000 00C00000   F0F661F2 F361F7F6 40004000 00000000   ...... .........  06/23/76 . .....
0002E0   00000000 00000000 C2E4D9C9 C1D54040   0001F7FF 00004041 00004041 00000010   ..........BURIAN  ..7... ... .....
000300   0003FFFF FC777CD0 A8A07CD0 0097319D   31A43295 32963310 34403444 344838F0   ......'...'.....  ......... .....0
000320   F6F2F3F7 F6F1F7F5 00002F0C 0000001E   139014CA 157C15F4 15FC0010 31240010   62376175........  .....'.4........
000340   5B5BC2D6 0007000A 020016E0 2E0C0000   00000000 02D00080 0000035C 00000000   $$BO............  ............*...
000360   0000357C 00000100 00001614 00100010   0000317E 00001572 00000000 00000000   ...'............  ................
000380   00000000 00000000 00000000 00000000   00000000 00000000 00003028 00003C78   ................  ................
0003A0   000037D4 92380245 909F0298 98BE02B8   41900A14 48A0036E 4AA0032A 9180A000   ...M............  ................
0003C0   47100302 58B0A004 9018B030 98BE02B8   07F99601 A00098BE 02B895FF A00F0789   ...K............  .9..............
0003E0   5000B6BC 48E00244 D207B698 E00058E0   02C494FD B699D21B B6A00298 07F9909F   &.......K.......  .D....K......9..
000400   02989220 02454590 03844190 021E9500   00234780 04E89535 002347B0 00CE4860   ................  .....Y........,-
000420   00221A66 487002C8 48667000 07F6181F   1B664121 000F4570 B2304860 B4D81B22   .......H.....6..  ...........-.Q..
000440   43201007 4130003D 1B234740 04584130   003D1B23 47B0045A 1A234220 05F54320   ........... ....  .............5..
000460   1007950B 10074780 049847F0 055E4720   00DA4230 05F54320 036E4322 CE0F1A23   ............0...  .....5..........
000480   950B1007 47800490 950B1007 47F0055A   487002FE 47F0049E 1B774370 BA648870   .............0..  .....0..........
0004A0   00031177 4337CE0C 47F0056A 472000D8   96801002 960C1004 07F91858 41430002   .........0.....Q  ..........9.....
0004C0   43540000 41455000 1A444A40 B4D095FF   40004770 04C04284 000007F9 95FF05B7   ......&.... ....  ...........9....
0004E0   07891B00 5000B6BC 95FF05B7 4780BBEA   4860036E 9560036F 4780042E D502A005   ....&...........  .-...-......N...
000500   03494770 05144111 00004910 B2AE47B0   05141B66 4121000F 4570B230 D5021009   ................  ............N...
000520   030147B0 00D64400 06145870 039CD502   70010301 47B000D6 1B334330 10079501   .....0........N.  .......0........
000540   10064770 046E92FF 05F5D200 0553A00D   4123000B D5001007 A00E47B0 00DA4182   ..........5K....  ....N...........
000560   20004870 031C4338 7000D403 1002CF78   4930B2AC 47B004AC 89300003 4A300310   ..........M.....  ................
000580   91F03004 4780C070 D5010022 C5CC4780   C356D501 B4C8B4D6 472005B4 4930B4F0   .O......N...E...  C.N..H.O.......0
0005A0   477005B4 950F0023 4780C5B4 91103006   4780BBEA 41800001 41488000 1A444A40   ................  ................
0005C0   B4D01858 4A50033C D20005B7 40005010   400092FF 40004220 50004260 505A4260   .....&..K... .&.   ... ...&..-&..-
0005E0   501E91F0 501E4780 05F44A60 034CD200   501E600D 9203503C 91F03004 4780C090   &..O&....4.-.)K.  &.-...&..O......
```

Figure 7-21 (Continued)

```
         BURIAN              0C/23/76                                                                                      PAGE    9

0036C0   00003754 00000000 F0F661F2 F361F7F6   400040CC 00000000 00000000 00000000    .........06/23/76   . ..............
0036E0   D5D640D5 C1D4C540 0003FFFF 00003F10   00003F10 00000030 0003FFFF FC777CD0    NO NAME .........   ...............'.
003700   80007C50 00973190 31A43295 32963310   34403444 344838F0 F6F2F3F7 F6F1F7F5    ..'&.............   . .....062376175
003720   00002F0C 0000001E 145014CA 157C15F4   15FC0010 31240030 00000000 00000000    ..........&...'.4   ................
003740   00000000 2E0C0000 00000000 02D00080   00003794 00000000 0000357C 00000100    ................    ............'....
003760   00001614 00200020 0000317E 00001572   00000000 00000000 00000000 00000000    ................    ................
003780   00000000 00000000 00000000 00000000   00003031 00000000 0000357C 00000100    ................    ............'....
0037A0   00001614 00300030 0000317E 00001572   00000000 00000000 00000000 00000000    ................    ................
0037C0   00000000 00000000 00C00000 00000000   0000303A 00000700 FF000001 00FF0000    ................    ................
0037E0   0000FF00 000000FF 00C00000 FF000000   00FF0000 0000FF00 000000FF 00000000    ................    ................
003800   FF000000 00FF0000 0000FF00 000000FF   00000000 FF000000 00FF0000 0000FF00    ................    ................
003820   000000FF FF000000 00C00000 00000000   00000000 00000000 00000000 00000000    ................    ................
003840   00000000 --SAME--                                                            ....
0038A0   00000000 00000000 00000000 00000000                                          ................

LBLTYP   HEX LENGTF IS 0000
--BG--
003F80                     D5D64CD5 C1D4C540   FF150007 C000400C 0A0407F1 00004010             NO NAME    ...... ....1.. .
003FA0   00004010 40004006 00005FD8 000002D0   0000007B 00004000 00004000 0001F7FF    .. . . ....Q....    ...... ... ...7.
003FC0   00004000 0001F784 FFFFFF7C 00004000   00003F98 00005B0A 00000000 00019E01    .. ...7....'.. .    ......$.........
003FE0   00000000 --SAME--                                                            ....
004000   90ECD00C 05C0FA33 C038C024 FA33C038   C028FA33 C038C02C FA33C038 C030F333    ................    ..............3.
004020   C034C038 98ECD00C 07FE0000 010C0000   020C0000 030C0000 040C0000 00000000    ................    ................
004040   00000000 --SAME--                                                            ....
005FE0   00000000 000002D0 0000007B 00004000   00004000 0001F7FF 00004000 0001F784    ............... .   .. ...7... ...7.
006000   FFFFFF7C 00004000 00003F98 00005B0A   0A0407F1 00004010 00004010 00004FD8    ...'.. ........$.   ...1.. ... ....Q
006020   00000000 --SAME--                                                            ....
01F7E0   00000000 00000000 00000000 00000000   00000000 00000000 00000000 00000000    ................    ................
```

⑥ ANS in storage

Figure 7-21 (*Concluded*)

DOS/370 Storage Dump. The DOS/370 storage dump (Figure 7-21) does not contain as many operating system messages as the OS/370 listing. We do, however, find the cause of the error, and the address of the instruction causing the error (1). The dump gives us the contents of the registers (2), and a printout of main storage (3). The printout of storage is similar to the OS/370 dump.

We must know the *load address* (entry address) of our program before we can determine the instruction in error. We find that the program is loaded at location 004000_{16}. The instruction causing the error resides at location $00400C_{16}$. We subtract the load address from the address of the instruction in error to determine the relative location of the instruction in error. We find that the relative address of the instruction in error is $00000C_{16}$. (4). We now can locate this instruction in the source listing (5). We find that the AP instruction is in error. A data exception occurs if one or both operands in an arithmetic operation do not contain packed data. The AP instruction references two fields ANS and PKFLD. We initialize PKFLD when we pack CON1. The field in error is ANS. We did not intialize ANS to packed data.

We can locate ANS in storage. To determine the storage address of ANS, we add the entry address to the relative address of ANS (6). We find that ANS resides at location $00403E_{16}$. We locate ANS in storage. We find that ANS appears as

00	00	00	00

The field does not contain packed data. A data exception occurred.

Debugging Procedure

When a language error causes the computer to stop processing, we must determine the reason. We first determine the address of the instruction in error and the cause of the error. The operating system dump gives us this information. We then must determine the instruction in error. We subtract the load address of our program from the address of the instruction in error. This gives us the relative address of the instruction in error. We use this address to locate the instruction in the source listing.

Sometimes we can determine the cause of the error by examining the source code. Often, however, we must examine the data as it appears in storage. To locate data in storage, we *add* the relative address of the data to the load address of the program.

PROBLEMS 7.1 The ED instruction converts packed to zoned data, inserting punctuation and suppressing leading zeros according to the edit mask. The contents of seven storage locations are given below. Give the contents of the first operand field after each of the following instructions is executed.

storage location	contents	instruction
DATA1	0000123C	ED MASK1(7),DATA1
DATA2	1234567C	ED MASK2(10),DATA2
DATA3	1234567D	ED MASK3(10),DATA3
MASK1	4020202020202020	ED MASK4(13),DATA3
MASK2	4020206B2020204B2020	ED MASK4(13),DATA4
MASK3	5B20206B2020204B2020	ED MASK4(13),DATA1
MASK4	5B20206B2021204B20204060	ED MASK2(10),DATA1
		ED MASK3(10),DATA1

7.2 Program 6 involves a first-time situation. We can use a *switch* to program a first-time condition. A switch is an indicator whose value directs the path of program execution. Figure 7-22 gives a segment of a program flowchart using a first-time

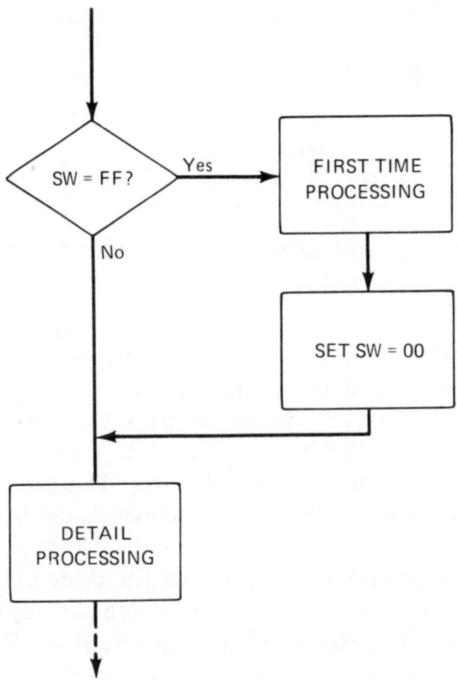

Figure 7-22 First-time switch.

switch. Code this segment using the CLI instruction to test the switch, and the MVI instruction to change the switch. You must define the switch and assign an initial value to it. Let switch be a 1-byte area of storage. If the switch is on, it will contain FF_{16}. If the switch is off, it will contain 00_{16}.

7.3 Code Program 6 using a first-time switch. You may define and set the switch in any manner you wish.

7.4 Write a program to find the average number of dependents of the employees within each department. Use the I/O specifications given on page 154. Punch the average number of dependents of each department in positions 4–6 of the output record. The number of dependents is found in positions 49–50 of each record.

7.5 Appendix C contains problem statements expanding the ideas presented in Program 6. Develop solutions to the following problems, using the HSKPING, GET, and PUT statements to handle the read and write operations.

a. Program 6d
b. Program 6e
c. Program 6f
d. Program 6g
e. Program 6h

7.6 Examine the following code for errors.

```
              .
              .
              .
INIT      MVC    CTR,ONE
          MVI    CTR,ZERO
BODY      AP     ANS,CTR
TEST      CP     CTR,LIMIT
          BE     EXIT
          AP     CTR,ONE
          BR     BODY
EXIT      UNPK   RESULT,ANS(1)
              .
              .
              .
LIMIT     DS     PL1'5'
ONE       DC     ZL1'1'
ZERO      DC     PL2'0'
ANS       DS     CL1
CTR       DS     CL2
RESULT    DS     CL2
          END
```

Indicate if an error would be expected to show at assembly or at execution time. What is the reason for each error?

8

A Binary Subset

This chapter is concerned with binary data. We will learn how to define binary constants, how to move binary data, and how to perform arithmetic and compare operations on binary data.

DEFINING BINARY DATA

One storage bit is used to represent a single binary digit. For example, the number 1111_2 requires four bits for proper representation in storage. In order to understand how binary data is represented in storage, we must review some basic concepts concerning binary numbers.

Halfword and Fullword Constants

Binary numbers are often referred to as fixed-length data. Binary numbers are represented as halfword constants (two bytes) or fullword constants (four bytes). The number fifteen is represented as the binary number 1111_2. It appears that we need only four bits of computer storage to represent this binary number, but actually we need sixteen bits! The computer requires that we represent binary data as either halfword or fullword constants. The number fifteen appears in storage as the halfword constant 0000000000001111_2. Sixteen bits—or one halfword.

We also could represent the number fifteen as a fullword binary constant using 32 bits. The number appears in storage as

$$00000000000000000000000000001111_2.$$

The representation of binary numbers becomes confusing when we examine each bit. For example, the binary number 0000000001111100_2 represents the decimal number 124. We find it easier to represent binary notation using hexadecimal numbers. We represent the binary constant for the number 124 as $007C_{16}$. Each hexadecimal digit represents four bits (binary digits). We will use

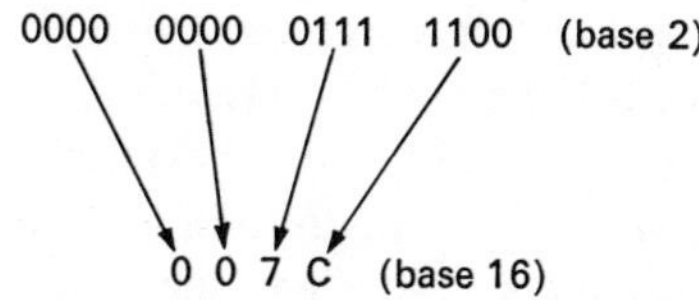

this hexadecimal notation in our discussion of binary instructions unless a specific example is made easier by the use of binary notation.

Representing Positive and Negative Numbers

The first bit of a binary number determines the sign of the number. Positive numbers have a 0 in the high-order position. Positive numbers are in true form—that is, the value of the binary number is the value of the number represented. For example, the fullword constant $0000001F_{16}$ is a positive number. We know this by examining the high-order bit (Figure 8-1). The number is represented using hexadecimal notation. We must examine the first hexadecimal digit to determine the sign of the number. The first hexadecimal digit is zero—0000 in binary. And the first *bit* is zero. We are representing a positive number. The decimal equivalent of $1F_{16}$ is 31. The fullword constant $0000001F_{16}$ represents the decimal number 31.

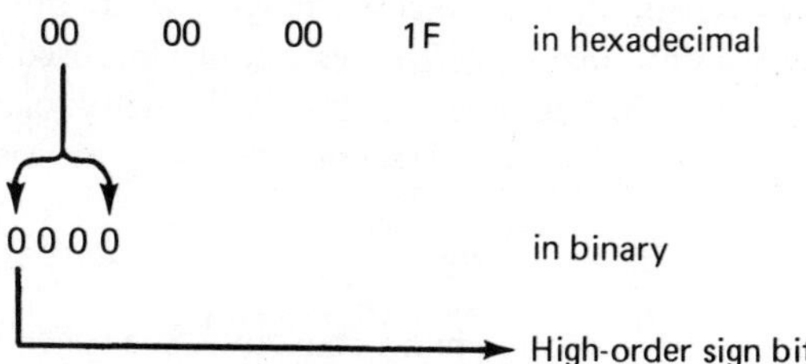

Figure 8-1 Sign control in binary numbers.

Negative numbers have a 1 in the high-order sign position. Negative numbers are carried in complement form. Let's consider the number −31. We must complement this number before we express it as a fullword binary constant. First we express the number as a binary constant

$$00000000000000000000000000011111_2$$

To complement a binary number we reverse the digits

$$11111111111111111111111111100000_2$$

and add one

$$11111111111111111111111111100001_2$$

We can represent this number using the hexadecimal notation FFFFFFE1_{16}.

Table 8-1 shows the representation of some decimal numbers as halfword and fullword constants, using hexadecimal notation. Remember, positive numbers have a 0 in the high-order sign position and are carried in true form. Negative numbers have a 1 in the sign position and are carried in complement form.

Table 8-1 Representing Positive and Negative Binary Numbers

number	type	hex representation
+10	H	000A
−10	H	FFF6
+20	F	00000014
−20	F	FFFFFFEC
+65,536	H	doesn't fit
+65,536	F	00010000
−65,536	F	FFFF0000

At this point the student may wonder why binary numbers are fixed length. After all, decimal numbers are variable length; we do not have halfword and fullword operands in decimal data. The restrictions imposed on binary data are related to the design of the computer hardware. We will explain this concept in more detail when we examine the instructions used to process binary data.

The DC Instruction

We use the DC instruction to define binary constants. We specify the name and value of the constant. For example, the instruction

```
BIN1   DC   H'10'
```

instructs the computer to generate a halfword binary constant with a value of ten. The generated constant appears as $000A_{16}$. Remember, we are using hexadecimal notation. Each hexadecimal digit represents four binary digits or bits. The number $000A_{16}$ represents the binary number 0000000000001010_2. A total of sixteen binary bits—and a value of ten. Notice that the first bit is zero. We are representing a positive number.

We also can ask the computer to generate a negative binary constant. For example, the instruction

```
CON1NEG  DC  H'-10'
```

tells the computer to generate a halfword binary constant with a value of *minus* ten. The constant generated appears as $FFF6_{16}$. This constant is a negative number and appears in complement form. Let's expand the hexadecimal notation to binary and complement the number.

The number $FFF6_{16}$ expands to 1111111111110110_2. The first bit is 1 so we know we are dealing with a negative number. To determine the value of the number we must recomplement. We reverse the digits

$$0000000000001001_2$$

and add one

$$0000000000001010_2$$

Just what we expected! The number ten in binary.

Format of the DC Statement. The format of the DC instruction is given in Figure 8-2. The type attribute specifies either a halfword or fullword constant. We specify a halfword constant using the letter H. For example

```
BIN2  DC  H'123'
```

We specify a fullword constant using the letter F.

```
BIN3  DC  F'456'
```

name	operation	operands
Optional name	DC	One or more operand fields
		D T M 'constant'

D T M 'constant'
- 'constant' → Value of constant, required
- M → Modifiers, optional
- T → Type of data, required
- D → Duplication factor, optional

Figure 8-2 Format of the DC statement.

The modifiers are optional. We will omit them at this point. And finally, the value of the constant itself, enclosed in quotes. We specify a *decimal* value within quotes—the computer generates the binary equivalent.

We also may use the duplication factor when we define binary constants. For example, the statement

```
BIN4  DC  2H'10'
```

generates $000A000A_{16}$.

Table 8-2 shows the use of the DC statement to define fullword and halfword constants, both positive and negative. The generated value of the constant is given on the left. This is the hexadecimal representation of the data as it will later appear in storage. Remember, constants are a special type of data. They are not *read* into main storage, but are placed in storage as part of the program itself.

Table 8-2 Use of the DC Instruction

generated constant	description constant		
0000000A	WORD1	DC	F'10'
00000014	WORD2	DC	F'20'
000007B8	WORD3	DC	F'1976'
FFFFFFF6	WORD4	DC	F'-10'
00000000	WORD5	DC	F'0'
FFFFF848	WORD6	DC	F'-1976'
000A	WORD7	DC	H'10'
0014	WORD8	DC	H'20'
07B8	WORD9	DC	H'1976'
FFF6	WORD10	DC	H'-10'
0000	WORD11	DC	H'0'
F848	WORD12	DC	H'-1976'

Since binary data may be represented as fullword or halfword operands, it follows that we must tell the computer the type of data with which we are working. We do not code the length of the operand (halfword or fullword) as part of the instruction, but code a separate instruction for each type of data. For example, the instruction

```
AH  4,HALF1
```

tells the computer to add the halfword of data at storage location HALF1 to the contents of register 4.* The instruction

*Registers are introduced and discussed in Chapter 3.

```
A    4,FULL1
```

tells the computer to add the fullword of data at FULL1 to register 4. This chapter presents only those instructions concerned with fullword operands. We will examine the instructions that move fullword operands between storage and the registers, those that add and subtract fullword operands, and those that compare fullword operands. We will examine the move instructions first. These instructions are a prerequisite to all arithmetic instructions as binary arithmetic operations require that at least one operand be in a register. We must learn to move data between registers and storage before we can perform any arithmetic operations.

BINARY MOVE INSTRUCTIONS

The L (Load) instruction loads a fullword of data from a main storage location (the second operand) into a register (the first operand). The contents of the storage location are unchanged. For example, the instruction

```
L    3,FLDA
```

places the fullword of data at location FLDA into register 3.

The ST (STore) instruction stores the contents of a register (the first operand) into main storage (the second operand). The contents of the first operand register remain unchanged.

The use of the L and ST instructions is shown in Figure 8-3.

Boundary Requirements

The instructions we code are symbolic instructions. The label FULL1 is a symbolic label for a storage location. If the address of FULL1 is location $00207C_{16}$, the base and displacement in the machine instruction generated by the assembler will address this location. Location $00207C_{16}$ is the effective or *actual* storage address of FULL1.

Third generation IBM computers require that all fullword operands reside on fullword boundaries. For example, the instruction

```
ST   3,FULL1
```

stores the fullword of data in register 3 into FULL1. The effective address of FULL1 must be on a fullword boundary. Remember, a fullword boundary is any storage address that is divisable by 4. When we consider the halfword instructions in Chapter 10, we will learn that each halfword operand residing in storage must be on a halfword boundary.

The IBM S/370 does not have this requirement. Binary data does not have to be aligned on halfword or fullword boundaries. But the programmer should be aware of boundary requirements—necessary when using an S/360 computer.

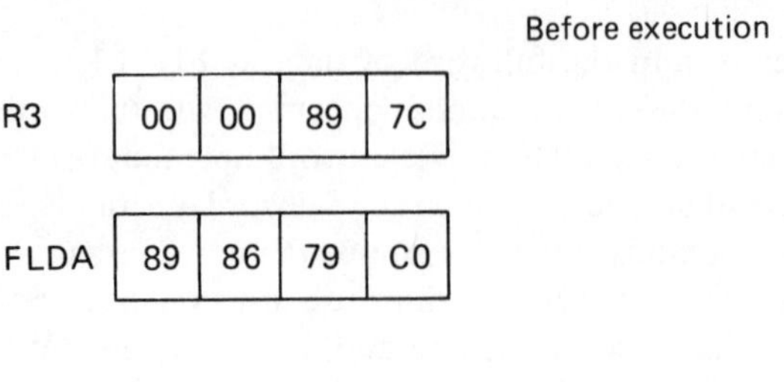

L 3, FLDA

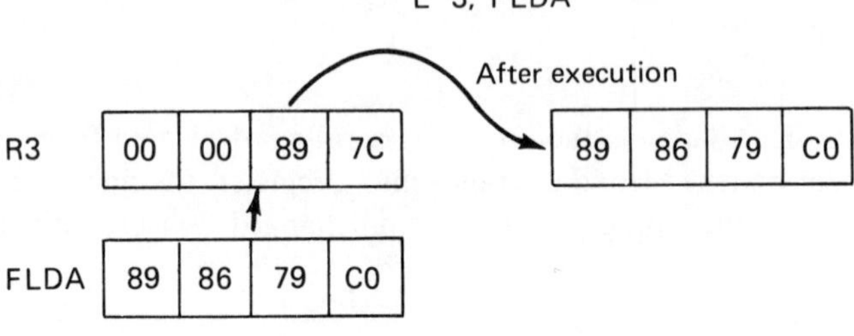

ST 3, FLDA

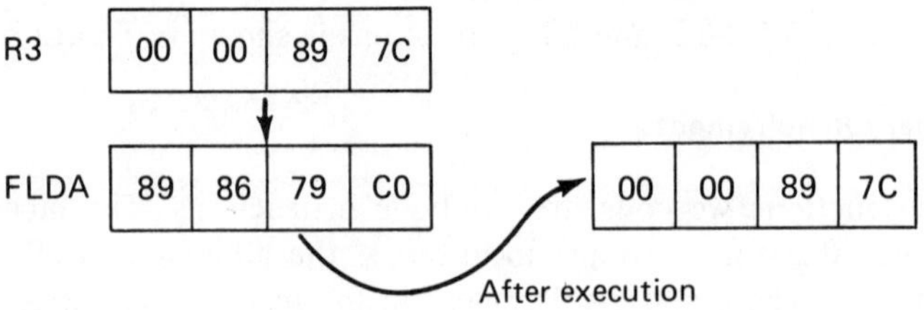

Figure 8-3 L and ST instructions.

BINARY ARITHMETIC

Whenever we talk about arithmetic operations, we are considering *two* operands. We add two numbers, we subtract one number from another.

The assembly language does not give us the facility to perform arithmetic operations on more than two numbers in a single instruction—we must execute two or more arithmetic instructions.

Binary arithmetic is concerned with two operands. At least one of these operands must be in a register. The second operand may be in a register, or may be a main storage location. In all cases, the first operand is always a register and the result of the operation is placed in the first operand register.

Let's consider an example. The instruction

```
A    4,FULL1
```

adds the contents of the fullword of data at a location labeled FULL1 to the fullword of data in register 4. The result of the addition is placed in register 4.

Register 4 is the first operand register. The result of the operation is placed in the first operand register. FULL1 is the second operand location. The contents of FULL1 are unchanged.

Addition and Subtraction

We will introduce the binary arithmetic instructions using the add and subtract instructions which operate on fullword operands with the second operand residing in storage.

The A Instruction. The A (Add fullword) instruction adds the contents of the second operand storage location to the contents of the first operand register. If the result does not fit into the first operand register, an error called an *overflow* occurs. The addition is performed on signed integers—the sign of a binary number is determined by the high-order bit of the number. The sign of the answer is determined by the rules of algebra.

Let's consider some examples of the A instruction. Table 8-3 illustrates the use of the A instruction in situations resulting in positive and negative results, and in an overflow situation.

Table 8-3 Examples of the A Instruction

location		instruction	first operand after execution
R2:	00000001	A 2,FULL1	R2: 0000000B
R4:	FFFFFFFA	A 4,FULL2	R4: FFFFFFED
R10:	FFFFFF9C	A 10,FULL1	R10: FFFFFFA6
R12:	00000064	A 12,FULL1	R12: 0000006E
R13:	7FFFFFFF	A 10,FULL2	R10: FFFFFF8F
FULL1:	0000000A	A 13,FULL3	R13: overflow
FULL2:	FFFFFFF3		
FULL3:	7FFFFFFF		

An overflow occurs when the result is too large for the receiving location (first operand). A fixed-point or binary overflow occurs when there is a carry into without a carry out, or a carry out without a carry into the sign position. Let's examine this concept further.

To make our discussion easier, we will consider binary operands of only four bits. The high-order bit still represents the sign of the number. Consider the addition of the following positive numbers.

```
0011₂  (+3 carried in true form)
0001₂  (+1 carried in true form)
-----
0100₂  (+4 carried in true form)
```

There is no overflow. No bits are carried into the sign position and no bits are carried out. The answer is positive—sign bit set to zero—and is carried in true form.

In the example

```
0100₂  (+4 carried in true form)
1101₂  (−3 carried in complement form)
-----
0001₂  (+1 carried in true form)
```

the addition results in a carry into *and* a carry out of the sign position. No overflow has occurred.

Finally, two additions resulting in an overflow situation.

```
0111₂  (+7 carried in true form)
0111₂  (+7 carried in true form)
-----
1110₂  overflow—carry into without a carry out of the sign
       position
```

Inspection tells us that the answer should be fourteen. We cannot represent the number fourteen in three bits and one sign bit. The answer is invalid!

In the example

```
1001₂  (−7 carried in complement form)
1011₂  (−5 carried in complement form)
-----
0100₂  overflow—carry out of the sign position without a carry
       into the sign position
```

an overflow occurs as a bit is carried out of the sign position without a carry into the sign position. The correct answer—a negative twelve—cannot be expressed in three bits and a sign bit.

The S Instruction. The S (Subtract fullword) instruction is similar to the A instruction. The contents of the second operand storage location are subtracted from the contents of the first operand register. The result is placed in the first operand register. If the result does not fit into the first operand register an overflow occurs.

The sign of the result is determined by the rules of algebra as shown in Table 8-4. An overflow is determined by the difference between a carry into and a carry out of the sign position.

Table 8-4 Examples of the S Instruction

location	instruction	first operand after execution
R2: 0000001D	S 2,FULL1	R2: 0000001C
R3: 00000001	S 2,FULL2	R2: 00000027
R4: FFFFFFF6	S 4,FULL3	R4: FFFFFFF7
FULL1: 00000001	S 4,FULL2	R4: 00000000
FULL2: FFFFFFF6	S 3,FULL3	R3: 00000002
FULL3: FFFFFFFF	S 4,FULL4	overflow
FULL4: 80000000		

A Sample Program

Let's see how binary arithmetic is used in a sample program. Program 2 finds the sum of four fullword constants in storage.*

First we must describe our data. This program does not involve files. The data are defined within the program itself. We begin by defining the four constants.

```
CON1   DC   F'10'
CON2   DC   F'20'
CON3   DC   F'30'
CON4   DC   F'40'
```

We also must define the area for our answer. We will place the answer in an area of storage called RESULT. Let's assume that the sum does not exceed a fullword. We can reserve a fullword of storage using the DS statement

```
RESULT  DS  F
```

This statement reserves a fullword or four bytes of storage for RESULT. We are saying that the type attribute of this storage area is F—a fullword. The assembler not only reserves four bytes for RESULT, but makes certain that RESULT resides on a fullword boundary. Remember the boundary requirements of the IBM S/360.

The DS statement does not assign an initial value to RESULT. We can make no assumptions about the data in these four bytes. We are merely reserving this area for future use.

Now that we have defined the data and reserved space for the answer, we can begin the processing statements.

Before we can perform any arithmetic operation on binary data, we must have at least one operand in a register. All the constants used in this program

*The problem statements for all the programs used in the text are found in Appendix C.

reside in main storage. We must move the data from storage to a register. The load instruction does this for us.

```
L  5,CON1
```

Now that we have the first constant in a register, we can use the add instruction to add the next constant from storage.

```
A  5,CON2
```

We now repeat this procedure for the remaining two constants.

```
A  5,CON3
A  5,CON4
```

The sum of the four constants is now in register 5. We must move the result back into main storage. We use the store instruction to accomplish this.

```
ST  5,RESULT
```

The complete solution to Program 2 is given in Figure 8-4. Let's review the required statements which all our programs contain.* The PRINT statement is used to simplify the listing, eliminating certain required instructions from the source listing. We use the HSKPING statement to perform certain initialization functions. We then code the processing instructions. The RETURN statement tells the operating system that this program is complete. The final coding consists of the data descriptions. The listing includes the constants generated by the assembler. Remember, we express the value of the constants in decimal, but the assembler generates binary data. These binary data are represented in hexadecimal notation on the source listing.

Our brief introduction to binary programming has included the load (L), store (ST), add (A), and subtract (S) instructions. We have seen these instructions used in programs involving sequential instruction execution. Now let's consider nonsequential instruction execution and, of course, the compare instructions.

THE COMPARE INSTRUCTION

The compare instruction compares the arithmetic value of two operands. The compare is algebraic—the result of the compare is affected by the sign of the operand. The C (Compare) instruction compares a fullword operand in a register (first operand) with a fullword operand in main storage (second operand). The operands are treated as signed binary integers. Remember, the sign of a binary number is determined by the high-order sign bit.

Assume that register 10 contains $00000064_{16}(+100)$ and FULL1 contains

*The format which our programs follow is introduced and discussed in Chapter 5.

```
*
* PROGRAM 2
* SUM OF FOUR FULLWORD BINARY CONSTANTS
*
          PRINT NOGEN
FIRST     HSKPING
*         *
*         *         SOME
*         *         HOUSEKEEPING
*         *         STATEMENTS
*         *         ARE
*         *         OMITTED
*         *         HERE
*         *
          L         5,CON1                         LOAD FIRST CONSTANT
          A         5,CON2                         ADD SECOND CONSTANT
          A         5,CON3                         ADD THIRD CONSTANT
          A         5,CON4                         AND LAST CONSTANT
          ST        5,RESULT                       STORE RESULT
*         *
*         *         THE PROGRAM IS COMPLETE
*         *         THE RETURN STATEMENT
*         *         SIGNIFIES END-OF-JOB
*         *
          RETURN (14,12)                           RETURN TO OPERATING SYSTEM
*
* DATA AREAS
*
CON1      DC        F'10'                          * DEFINE
CON2      DC        F'20'                          * FOUR
CON3      DC        F'30'                          * FULLWORD
CON4      DC        F'40'                          * CONSTANTS
RESULT    DS        F
          END       FIRST
```

Generated constants

```
0000000A
00000014
0000001E
00000028
```

Figure 8-4 Program 2—solution.

$0000000A_{16}(+10)$. The instruction

```
C 10,FULL1
```

compares the fullword of data in register 10 with the fullword of data at FULL1. We are comparing a decimal 100 with a decimal 10—the first operand is greater than the second operand.

We also must consider the sign of each operand. Assume that register 10 contains $FFFFFF9C_{16}(-100)$ and FULL1 contains $FFFFFFF6_{16}(-10)$. Now execution of the instruction

```
C 10,FULL1
```

results in the indicator showing that the first operand is less than the second operand. That is, a −100 is less than a −10. We see examples of the C instruction using both positive and negative operands in Table 8-5.

Table 8-5 Examples of the C Instruction

location		instruction	result
FULL1:	0000001C	C 3,FULL3	OP1 < OP2
FULL2:	FFFFFF60	C 5,FULL3	OP1 < OP2
FULL3:	00000013	C 4,FULL3	OP1 > OP2
R3:	0000000E	C 5,FULL1	OP1 < OP2
R4:	000000A3	C 4,FULL1	OP1 > OP2
R5:	FFFFFF60	C 5,FULL2	OP1 = OP2
		C 5,FULL3	OP1 < OP2

Usually the result of the compare alters the sequence in which the instructions in our program are executed. We must have a means of testing this result and determining if a change in instruction sequence—a branch—is to occur.

Compare instructions are usually followed by a conditional branch instruction.* Assume that we want to branch to the code at HIGH if the first operand in a compare operation is greater than the second operand. Otherwise, we want to branch to NEXT. The instructions

```
C  10,FULL1
BH HIGH
B  NEXT
```

accomplish this. The instruction BH (Branch High) is a conditional branch instruction. The other conditional branch instructions are BL (Branch Low)

*The conditional branch instructions are introduced and discussed in Chapter 6.

and BE (Branch Equal). The instruction B (Branch) is an unconditional branch instruction. The branch occurs regardless of the result of the compare.

One last consideration before we examine the use of the compare instruction in a program. The compare instructions, like the binary arithmetic instructions, involve fullword storage operands. IBM S/360 computers require that these operands reside on integral fullword storage boundaries. If storage operands are not properly aligned, an error called a specification exception occurs.

A Sample Program

We now can code the solution to Program 5—finding the sum of the numbers from 1 to 5—using the add and compare instructions. (See Figure 8-5.)

First, we must define the data. We need a counter, an area to store the result, the limit itself, and an increment to change the value of the counter. We

```
*
* PROGRAM 5
* SUM OF NUMBERS  FROM 1 - 5
* BINARY ARITHMETIC
*
         PRINT NOGEN
SUM      HSKPING
*        *
*        *        SOME
*        *        HOUSEKEEPING
*        *        STATEMENTS
*        *        ARE
*        *        OMITTED
*        *        HERE
*        *
INIT     L        6,ZERO                INITIALIZE R6 TO ZERO
BODY     A        6,CTR                 ADD TO ACCUMULATOR
TEST     L        5,CTR                 LOAD CTR INTO R5
         C        5,LIMIT               AND COMPARE TO LIMIT
         BE       EXIT                  BRANCH IF EQUAL
         A        5,ONE                 ELSE INCREMENT CTR IN R5
         ST       5,CTR                 STORE CTR IN STORAGE
         B        BODY                  AND LOOP BACK TO BODY
EXIT     ST       6,RESULT              STORE RESULT
*        *
*        *        THE PROGRAM IS COMPLETE
*        *        THE RETURN STATEMENT
*        *        SIGNIFIES END-OF-JOB
         RETURN (14,12)                 AND RETURN
*        *
*
* DATA AREAS
*
CTR      DC       F'1'                  DEFINE AND SET COUNTER
RESULT   DS       F                     RESERVE SPACE FOR SUM
LIMIT    DC       F'5'                  DEFINE LIMIT
ONE      DC       F'1'                  DEFINE INCREMENT
ZERO     DC       F'0'                  INITIAL VALUE ACCUMULATOR
         END      SUM
```

Figure 8-5 Program 5—binary arithmetic.

also must define a constant which is used to initialize the accumulator to zero.*

```
CTR      DC  F'1'
RESULT   DS  F
LIMIT    DC  F'5'
ZERO     DC  F'0'
```

We accumulate the sum in register 6. First, we must initialize the accumulator.

```
INIT     L  6,ZERO
```

The body of the loop consists of incrementing the accumulator (register 6) by the contents of the counter.

```
BODY     A  6,CTR
```

We now code the instructions to compare the contents of the counter with the limit.

```
         L  5,CTR
         C  5,LIMIT
```

We place the contents of the counter in register 5, then compare the contents of register 5 with the contents of a fullword constant in storage. We are effectively comparing the contents of the counter with the limit. If these values are equal, we exit from the loop.

```
         BE  EXIT
```

Otherwise, we increment the counter and branch unconditionally back to the body of the loop.

```
         A  5,ONE
         B  BODY
```

The instructions at EXIT store the sum accumulated in register 6 in RESULT.

```
EXIT     ST 6,RESULT
```

The reader should follow the instructions in the program developing the sum in register 6. We call this process *desk checking*. If the program is followed exactly, register 6 contains fifteen when the branch to EXIT is taken.

CONVERSIONS We have seen that data exist in many different forms. We may record data on external media such as cards or tape using one type of code. When these data are read into storage, they are represented in the EBCDIC

*The flowchart and logic involved in the solution to this program are discussed in Chapters 2 and 5.

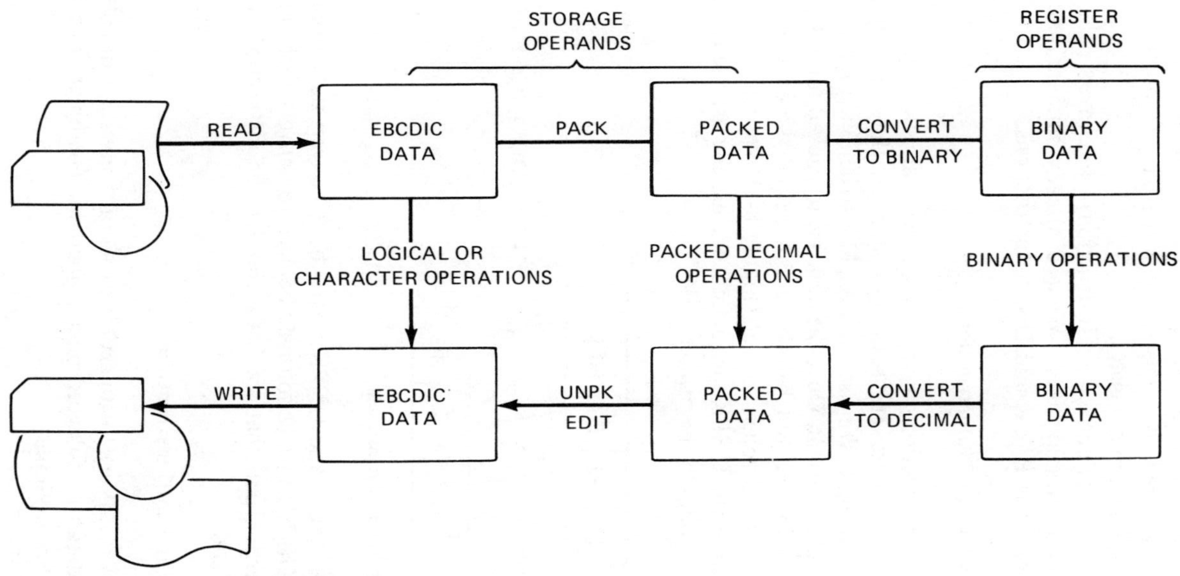

Figure 8-6 Data conversion summary.

code. We must convert these data to packed format before we can perform decimal arithmetic operations. (See Figure 8-6.)

If we are going to perform binary operations on the data, a further conversion is required. We must convert the data to binary form, and place at least one operand in a register.

The need for conversion instructions—to convert data from one form to another—becomes apparent. We are already familiar with two conversion instructions—the PACK and UNPK instructions.

The PACK and UNPK Instructions

The PACK instruction converts zoned decimal data to packed decimal format. When numeric data are read into storage, they are represented in zoned (EBCDIC) format. We use the PACK instruction (Figure 8-7) to convert the data to packed format. Once the data are in packed format, decimal arithmetic may be performed. But before we can output the data, we must convert the packed results to zoned format (Figure 8-8). We may do this using the EDit instruction or the UNPK instruction. We usually use the EDit instruction when the data is going to the printer.

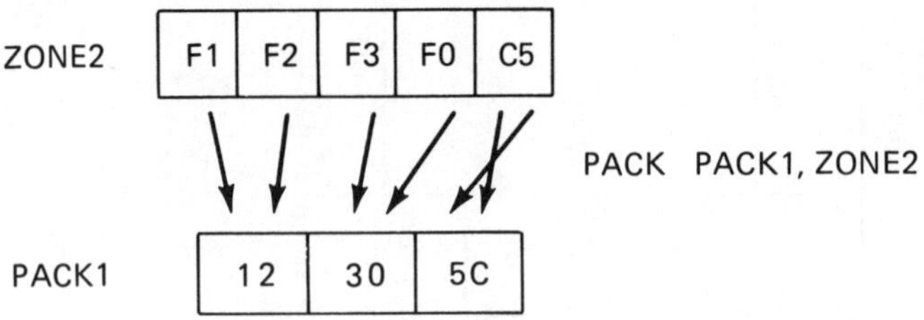

Figure 8-7 The PACK instruction.

The PACK and UNPK instructions convert data from zoned to packed format. The ED instruction may be used to convert packed data to zoned format, inserting punctuation. Let's examine the instructions to convert data to binary form.

The CVB and CVD Instructions

The CVB (ConVert to Binary) instruction converts a double word of packed decimal data to a fullword binary operand. The binary operand is placed in a register. For example

```
       CVB  4,DOUBLE
        .     .
        .     .
        .     .
DOUBLE DC   PL8'10'
```

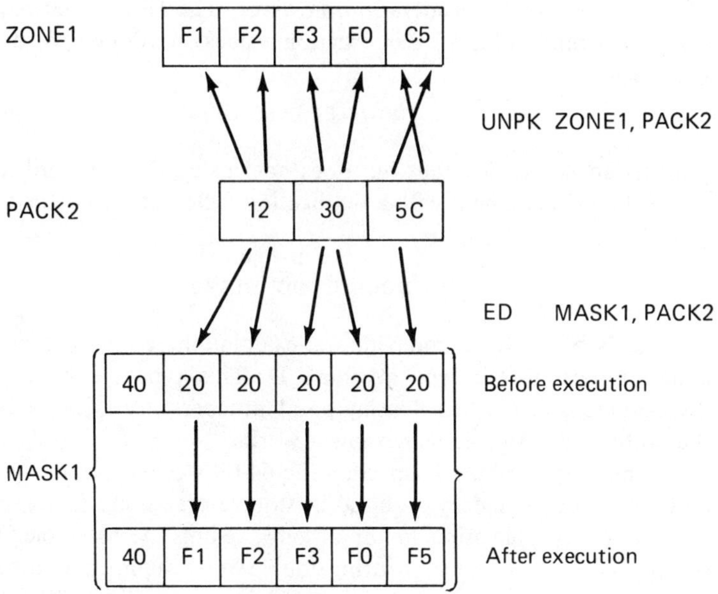

Figure 8-8 Converting packed data to zoned format.

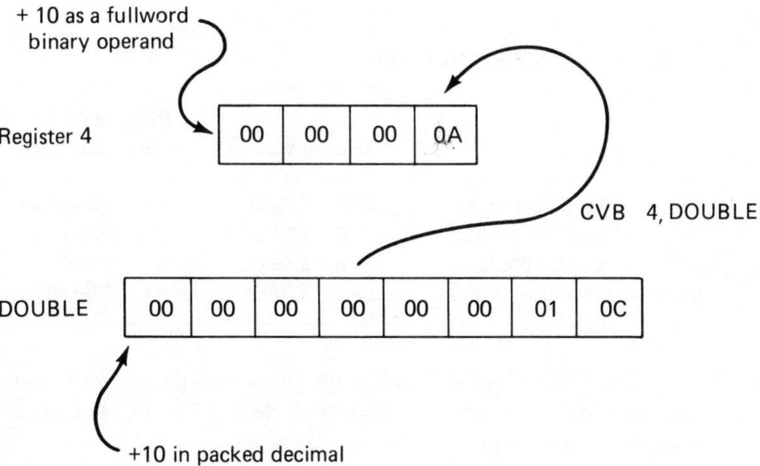

Figure 8-9 The CVB instruction.

The CVB instruction (Figure 8-9) converts the 8-byte packed constant at DOUBLE to binary and places the result in register 4.

When we convert the packed constant $0000010C_{16}$ to binary, we place the value $0000000A_{16}$ in register 4. A packed $0000010C_{16}(+10)$ is equivalent to a binary $0000000A_{16}(+10)$.

We have one consideration, however. The IBM S/360 requires that the storage operand in the CVB instruction resides on a double word boundary. The statement

```
DOUBLE  DC  PL8'10'
```

gives us an 8-byte constant but does not ensure double word alignment. The use of the DS statement with a duplication factor of zero helps us out.

```
        DS  0D
DOUBLE  DC  PL8'10'
```

Let's pause for a moment and examine these instructions. We are using a new notation—the type attribute D. This type attribute is reserved for double-precision (64-bit) floating-point numbers. Certainly a long way from the problem at hand. Let's see how it works.

The type attribute D specifies the 64-bit storage area properly aligned on a double word boundary required by double-precision floating-point numbers. We specify a duplication factor of zero, telling the assembler not to reserve storage ($O \times D = 0$), but ensuring double word alignment of the next data item.

We see more examples of the CVB instruction in Table 8-6. Some of the data are negative. When we convert a negative packed number to binary, the result is expressed in complement form.

Table 8-6 The CVB Instruction

location	instruction	first operand after execution
DBL1: 000000000000020C	CVB 3,DBL1	R3: 00000014
DBL2: 000000000000100C	CVB 3,DBL2	R3: 00000064
DBL3: 000000000000020D	CVB 3,DBL3	R3: FFFFFFEC
DBL4: 000000000000100D	CVB 3,DBL4	R3: FFFFFF9C

The CVD (ConVert-to-Decimal) instruction converts a fullword of binary data residing in a register to packed decimal form. The result is placed in a double word location in storage. The code

```
        CVD  4,DOUBLE
         .
         .
         .
DOUBLE  DS   D
```

converts the fullword of binary data in register 4 to packed format and places the result in the double word storage location DOUBLE. Again, the IBM S/360 requires that the storage operand reside on a double word boundary.

If register 4 contains FFFFFFF6(−10), the instruction

```
CVD   4,DOUBLE
```

places the number $000000000000010D_{16}$(−10) in storage location DOUBLE. Table 8-7 gives more examples of the CVD instruction.

Table 8-7 The CVD Instruction

location	instruction	second operand after execution
register 3: 00000019	CVD 3,DBL	DBL: 000000000000025C
register 4: 0000003E	CVD 4,DBL	DBL: 000000000000062C
register 5: FFFFFFE7	CVD 5,DBL	DBL: 000000000000025D
register 6: FFFFFFC2	CVD 6,DBL	DBL: 000000000000062D

A Sample Program

Program 5 asks us to find the sum of a series of numbers. We have solved this problem to find the sum of the numbers from 1 to 5, defining the limit as a constant in storage. We can, however, make this program more general if we introduce the limit of the series as data on a punched card. If we allow a 4-position field to specify the limit, we can find the sum of any series of numbers up to 9999. Let's examine the solution to this problem.

We first must define the data used in the program. The limit is to be read as data on a punched card. We must reserve space for the input record.

```
INWORK   DS  0CL80
LIMITIN  DS  CL4
         DS  CL76
```

Remember, the use of zero as a duplication factor in the DS statement tells the assembler not to reserve space for this constant, but to associate a length attribute—80 in this case—and a name (INWORK) with this storage area. The subsequent DS statements format INWORK.

The data card is read into an area of storage called INWORK. The first four bytes of this data card constitute the limit. These four bytes are contained in the area of storage associated with the label LIMITIN. We must convert the limit to packed decimal and then to a binary operand in a register. We must define an area into which we can pack LIMITIN.

```
LIMIT  DS  D
```

Now let's discuss the solution to Program 5 as given in Figure 8-10.

```
*
* PROGRAM 5
* SUM OF A SERIES OF NUMBERS
* LIMIT ON A CARD
* BINARY ARITHMETIC
*
         PRINT NOGEN
         START 0
SUM      HSKPING CARDID=INCARD          NAME INPUT FILE
*        *
*        *        SOME
*        *        HOUSEKEEPING
*        *        STATEMENTS
*        *        ARE
*        *        OMITTED
*        *        HERE
*        *
READRT   GET      INCARD,INWORK         READ LIMIT
INIT     L        6,ZERO                CLEAR ACCUMULATOR
         PACK     LIMIT,LIMITIN         PACK LIMIT
         CVB      7,LIMIT               CONVERT TO BINARY IN R7
BODY     A        6,CTR                 ADD TO ACCUMULATOR
TEST     C        7,CTR                 COMPARE WITH LIMIT
         BE       EXIT                  EXIT IF EQUAL
         L        5,CTR                 ELSE LOAD CTR IN R5
         A        5,ONE                 INCREMENT R5
         ST       5,CTR                 STORE R5
         B        BODY                  AND LOOP TO BODY
EXIT     ST       6,RESULT              STORE RESULT AND
         B        READRT                GET NEXT CARD IF ANY
*        *
*        *        AFTER ALL INPUT CARDS
*        *        HAVE BEEN READ AND PROCESSED
*        *        THE PROGRAM IS COMPLETE
*        *
*
* DATA AREAS
*
CTR      DC       F'1'
ZERO     DC       F'0'
LIMIT    DS       D
ONE      DC       F'1'
INWORK   DS       0CL80
LIMITIN  DS       CL4
         DS       CL76
RESULT   DS       F
         END      SUM
```

Figure 8-10 Program 5—solution.

The first statements in the program are familiar. These are the housekeeping statements required to establish addressability and define the files, the program will reference. Yes, this program has files—we are reading an input data card, a 1-card file.

The next statement

READRT GET INCARD,INWORK

reads a single data card into an area of storage called INWORK. The first four positions of this card contain the limit. If the first four positions of the data card contain the number 0005, we will find the sum of the numbers from 1 to 5. This program allows us to find the sum of any series of numbers with the limit varying from 1 to 9999.

We now must initialize the work areas and convert the limit to a binary operand. We first pack the limit and then issue the CVB instruction.

```
INIT  L     6,ZERO
      PACK  LIMIT,LIMITIN
      CVB   7,LIMIT
```

We now enter the body of the loop The instruction

```
BODY  A  6,CTR
```

adds the contents of CTR to register 6 (used to accumulate the sum). We then test the counter

```
TEST  C   7,CTR
      BE  EXIT
      L   5,CTR
      A   5,ONE
      ST  5,CTR
      B   BODY
```

We compare the limit in register 7 to the value of CTR. We exit when the operands are equal. Otherwise, we increment the counter and return to the body of the loop.

When the contents of the counter are equal to the limit in register 7, we branch to the code at EXIT.

```
EXIT  ST  6,RESULT
      B   READRT
```

We store the sum in RESULT and return to read the next card, if any.

We could, of course, output the result.

```
EXIT      CVD   6,DBL               CONVERT TO DECIMAL
          UNPK  RESULT(8),DBL       UNPACK, TRUNCATING HIGH-
          PUT   PRINT,PRINTBLD      ORDER BYTES, AND PRINT
          .
          .
          .
PRINTBLD  DS    0CL120
RESULT    DS    CL8
          DC    112CL1' '
DBL       DS    D
```

In this example, we purposely truncate the high-order digits when we unpack DBL into RESULT. We know that the sum of the numbers from 1 to

9999 will not exceed eight digits. It is not necessary for us to print the extra digits acquired when we convert the binary sum to a double word of packed data in storage.

We also could eliminate the leading zeros using the ED instruction. For example

```
EXIT        CVD  6,DBL
            MVC  RESULT(9),MASK
            ED   RESULT(9),DBL
            PUT  PRINT,PRINTBLD
            .
            .
            .
PRINTBLD    DS   0CL120
RESULT      DS   CL9
            DC   111CL1' '
MASK        DC   X''402020202020202020'
DBL         DS   D
```

In this manner, leading zeros are replaced by the fill character, a 40_{16} (a blank).

PROBLEMS 8.1 The DC instruction is used to define binary data. Write the instructions to define the following constants and give the assembled value of the constant in hexadecimal.

1. a fullword constant with a value of 10
2. a halfword constant with a value of 5
3. a fullword constant with a value of 256
4. a halfword constant with a value of 0
5. a fullword constant with a value of −256
6. a halfword constant with a value of −782

8.2 The contents of five storage locations and two registers are given below. Give the contents of the receiving location after the execution of each of the following instructions.

location	contents	instruction
FULL1	00000003	L 3,FULL1
FULL2	0000703C	L 4,FULL2
FULL3	0000C098	L 3,FULL3
FULL4	0234CD09	L 3,FULL4
FULL5	807E0001	ST 4,FULL5
register 3	0000709E	ST 3,FULL1
register 4	0087805F	ST 3,FULL3

8.3 The contents of five storage locations and two registers are given below. Give the contents of the first operand location after each of the following instructions is executed.

location	contents	instruction
FULL1	00000034	A 6,FULL1
FULL2	000080EC	A 8,FULL2
FULL3	70EC908D	A 6,FULL3
FULL4	C0980001	A 6,FULL4
FULL5	FFFFFFFA	A 8,FULL1
register 6	00008093	A 8,FULL5
register 8	80930000	S 8,FULL1
		S 6,FULL2
		S 6,FULL5
		S 8,FULL5
		S 6,FULL4

8.4 Write a program to find the sum of the numbers from 1 to 5. Use binary constants and the binary arithmetic instructions. Do not code a loop. Use repetitive add instructions.

8.5 The contents of four storage locations and two registers are given in the following table. Give the result of the compare for each of the instructions in the table.

location	contents	instruction
FULL1	0000000A	C 3,FULL1
FULL2	FFFFFFF0	C 3,FULL2
FULL3	8000000A	C 3,FULL3
FULL4	0000FFFF	C 3,FULL4
FULL5	7000809C	C 3,FULL5
register 3	0000000A	C 12,FULL1
register 12	FFFF000A	C 12,FULL2
		C 12,FULL3
		C 12,FULL4
		C 12,FULL5

8.6 The contents of two registers and four storage locations are supplied. Give the contents of the second operand location after each of the following instructions is executed.

location	contents	instruction
DATA1	000000000000010C	PACK DATA1,DATA3
DATA2	000000000000100D	PACK DATA4,DATA3

location	contents	instruction
DATA3	F1F9F0D3	PACK DATA3,DATA4
DATA4	0000009C	PACK DATA2,DATA4
register 2	0000000C	UNPK DATA3,DATA4
register 3	FFFFFFAB	UNPK DATA1,DATA3
		CVB 2,DATA1
		CVB 3,DATA2
		CVD 2,DATA1
		CVD 3,DATA2

8.7 Negative numbers may be represented on a punched card. How would you represent the number −5 in *one* column of a punched card? How would this number appear in storage?

8.8 Sometimes we need to call attention to (*flag*) certain records within a file. Perhaps we want to flag overdue accounts in an accounts receivable file or certain employees in a payroll master file. An eleven overpunch (11-punch) over the last position of a numeric field is often used to flag a field. Can you see why?

Using the data for Program 6, assume that those employees approaching retirement are flagged with an 11-punch over the last position of the gross pay field. Write a program to list employee number, name, and gross pay. Flag those employees approaching retirement with an asterisk (*) following the gross pay field. For example

```
000245  JOHN CHARLES  $  536.89*
```

How would the output appear if we did not edit the gross pay field?

Note: Use the macros HSKPING, GET, and PUT in your solution. The use of these macros is described in detail in Chapters 5, 6, and 7.

8.9a Given the code

```
                .
                .
                .
                GET     INFILE,INWORK
FIRST           PACK    PKFLD,DATA
                AP      PKFLD,CTR
                CVB     7,PKFLD
                A       7,BIN
                CVD     7,PKFLD
                MVC     OUT,MASK
LAST            ED      OUT,PKFLD+5
                PUT     PRINT,PRINTBLD
                .
                .
                .
```

```
INWORK    DS    0CL80
DATA      DS    CL5
          DS    CL75
PRINTBLD  DS    0CL120
OUT       DS    CL8
          DC    CL122' '
PKFLD     DS    D
CTR       DC    PL2'10'
BIN       DC    F'-20'
MASK      DC    X'402020204B202060'
          END
```

give the contents of the first operand (PKFLD in the CVD instruction) location after each of the instructions from FIRST to LAST is executed assuming that the first five positions of the data card contain

a. 12345
b. 00123
c. 123
d. 1206L
e. 1238B
f. 00005
g. 0000E

b Give the value in DATA after the GET statement is issued. Show the appearance of the data on the printed report after the PUT statement is executed. Do this for each data card in Problem 8.9a.

9

Establishing Addressability

BACKGROUND AND REVIEW Our discussion thus far has involved symbolic instructions with no mention of the generated machine code. But we know that each symbolic instruction is translated into a machine language instruction. For example, the instruction

```
AR   3,4
```

is a symbolic instruction. The assembler translates this instruction into a machine language instruction. The generated machine language instruction is an RR-type instruction. It appears as 1A34 in hexadecimal (Figure 9-1). 1A is the op-code (operation code). The first operand is register 3 and the second operand is register 4.

Most machine language instructions contain an operation code and the address of the operands. The operands may reside in registers or in main storage. Operands residing in registers are addressed by the register number. The instruction

```
AR   3,4
```

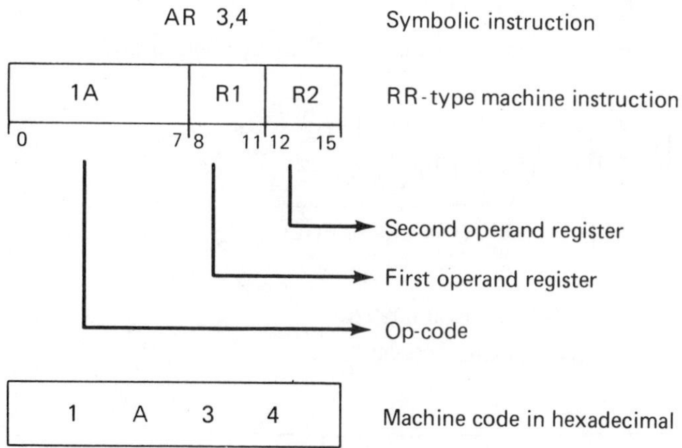

Figure 9-1 Symbolic and machine instructions.

tells the computer to add the operand in register 4 to the operand in register 3 and to place the result in register 3.

Operands residing in main storage are not addressed by the actual storage address. The effective address is determined by adding the contents of a base register, in some instances the contents of an index register, to a 12-bit displacement.

We have been addressing storage operands by a symbolic name rather than by specifying actual registers and displacement. The assembler has been generating the registers and displacement. Until now we have avoided a discussion of how the assembler generates a base register, index register if required, and displacement assignment for a given symbolic name.

Let's develop this concept further. The instruction

```
A 4,FULL
```

instructs the computer to add the fullword of data at a storage location called FULL to the fullword of data in register 4. This, however, is the *symbolic* instruction. The assembler must generate the correct machine instruction following the RX-type format. Let's assume that FULL resides at location $00903C_{16}$. Assume the assembler uses register 12 as the base register and is told that register 12 contains 009000_{16}. The assembler will generate the machine language instruction illustrated in Figure 9-2.

We can find the effective address of the storage operand by adding the contents of the base register 12 (009000_{16}) to the value of the displacement ($03C_{16}$). But what about the index register—register 0? When register 0 is used as a base register or as an index register it is ignored. We treat register 0 as if it contained 00000000_{16}. The effective address of the storage operand becomes $00903C_{16}$.

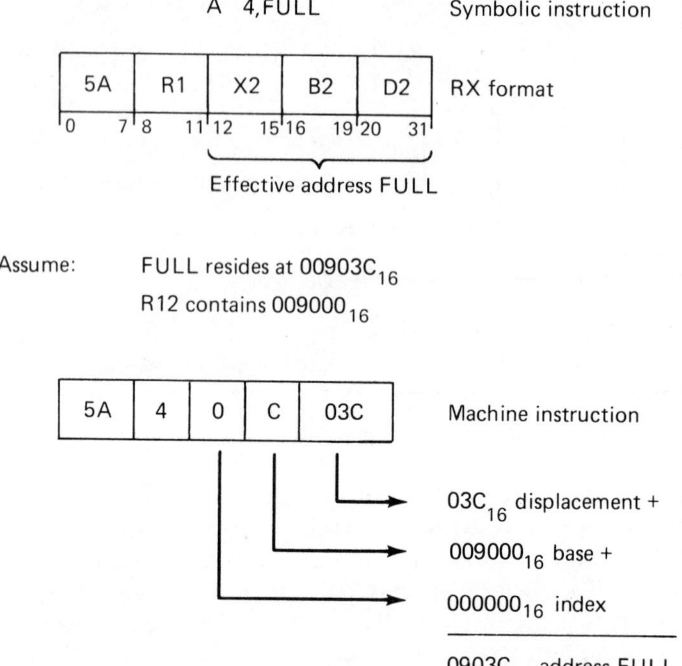

Figure 9-2 Determining an effective address.

We must tell the assembler exactly which base register to use and what value that register will contain. Given this information, the assembler generates the machine instruction, calculating the correct displacement. Let's see how this is done.

Address Generation—An Example

We'll use Program 2—finding the sum of four consecutive constants in storage—as an example.

```
         .
         .
         .
         L    5,CON1
         A    5,CON2
         A    5,CON3
         A    5,CON4
         ST   5,RESULT
         .
         .
         .
```

```
CON1    DC  F'10'
CON2    DC  F'20'
CON3    DC  F'30'
CON4    DC  F'40'
RESULT  DS  F
```

We will attempt to generate the correct machine code from these symbolic instructions. In other words—play assembler. The first symbolic instruction is

```
L  5,CON1
```

We know that this instruction is an RX-type instruction. The format for this instruction is given in Figure 9-3. The first eight bits contain the op-code, 58_{16}.

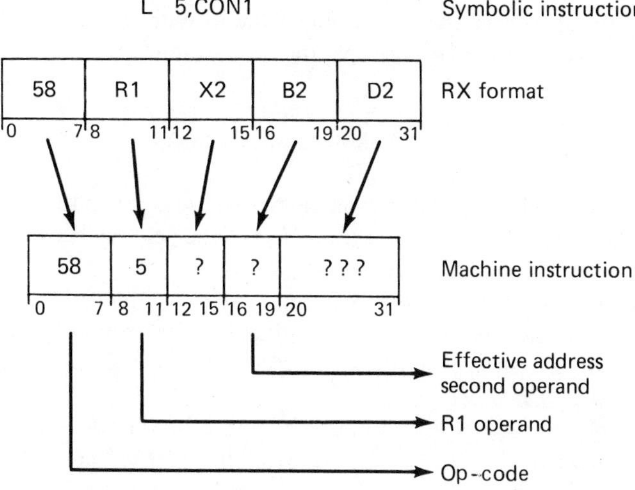

Figure 9-3 Instruction generation.

The first operand register is 5. The first operand address appears in bits 8–11 of the generated instruction.

We must now generate the address of the second operand. The second operand resides in main storage. The RX-type instruction addresses storage operands using a base register an index register and a displacement. We—or the assembler—must assign these registers and a displacement. When the program is executed, the effective address of the second operand must be the address of CON1.

The problem is somewhat simplified if register 0 is used as the index register. Its contents are ignored in determining the storage address and the effective address becomes dependent on the base register and displacement as shown in Figure 9-2. The problem is that we do not know which base registers to use. And if we did know which base register to use, we would not know the correct displacement to address CON1.

The assembler must be told which base register to use and also must be given enough information to *calculate* the correct displacement for each symbolic label. Without this information, the assembler only can generate part of the machine code.

ASSEMBLY STATEMENTS

Now let's examine the statements which provide the assembler with this information.

The USING Statement

The USING statement tells the assembler which base register to use and provides a point of reference from which the assembler can calculate the correct displacement for each storage operand. For example

```
         USING FIRST,12
FIRST    L     5,CON1
```

The USING statement tells the assembler to use register 12 as the base register. It also tells the assembler that the *address* of the next instruction, the instruction labeled FIRST, will be in register 12.

It is important to note that the USING statement *does not generate* a machine language instruction. This statement *provides information* for the assembler, but it does not generate an instruction. We call this assembler-directing statement a *pseudo operation.*

Table 9-1 shows Program 2 with the USING statement. The generated code is shown at the left. Let's assume that the instruction labeled FIRST resides at location 008002_{16}. The numbers in the rightmost column represent the storage address of each instruction and constant. We have told the assembler that the address of FIRST will be in register 12. Using this information, the assembler generates the correct machine code for each symbolic instruction.

Let's examine the first instruction. The machine code addresses a storage location using register 12 as the base register, register 0 as the index register, and a displacement of 016_{16}. Register 12 contains 008002_{16}, the address of FIRST. The effective address of the storage operand in the first instruction is 008018_{16} ($008002_{16} + 016_{16}$) . . . the address of CON1!

The USING statement is really a promise to the assembler. We tell the assembler to use register 12 as the base register and *promise* that register 12 will contain the address of FIRST. For our discussion, we assume that FIRST resides at 008002_{16} and therefore register 12 contains 008002_{16}.

The USING statement is an assembly time instruction. At execution time—when the program is loaded into computer storage an executed—we must keep

Table 9-1 Program 2 with the USING Statement

generated code	symbolic instruction			hexadecimal storage address
		.[†]		
		.		
		.		
		USING	FIRST,12	
5850C016	FIRST	L	5,CON1	008002
5A50C01A		A	5,CON2	008006
5A50C01E		A	5,CON3	00800A
5A50C022		A	5,CON4	00800E
5050C026		ST	5,RESULT	008012
		.		
		.		
		.		
0000000A	CON1	DC	F'10'	008018
00000014	CON2	DC	F'20'	00801C
0000001E	CON3	DC	F'30'	008020
00000028	CON4	DC	F'40'	008024
	RESULT	DS	F	008028
		.		
		.		
		.		

[†]Dots indicate that statements are omitted.

our assembly time promise. We must make certain that register 12 *does* contain the address of FIRST. To do this, we need a new assembly language instruction which will put the address of FIRST into register 12.

The BAL and BALR Instructions

At this point we will digress from our discussion of addressability and introduce a new branching instruction. We will then see how this new instruction may be used to load the base register in a program.

The BAL Instruction. The BAL (Branch and Link) instruction is a special type of unconditional branch instruction. Let's consider an example. The instruction

```
BAL   10,LOOPRT
```

effects a branch to LOOPRT. In addition, *the address* of the next sequential instruction—the instruction following the BAL instruction—is placed in register 10.

Table 9-2 The BAL Instruction

symbolic instruction			hexadecimal storage address	
	.			
	.			
	.			
	BAL	10,LOOPRT	009000	RX-type
	L	5,ANYDATA	009004†	RX-type
	.		.	
	.		.	
	.		.	
LOOPRT	L	5,ANYLABEL	00900C	RX-type
	.		009010	
	.			
	.			

†This address is placed in register 10 by the BAL instruction.

The numbers to the right of the code represent the storage addresses of the instructions. The BAL instruction resides at location 009000_{16}. This instruction is an RX-type instruction requiring four bytes of main storage. The address of the next instruction, the L instruction, is 009004_{16}. When the BAL instruction is executed, a branch to the instruction labeled LOOPRT ($00900C_{16}$) is effected and the address of the instruction following the BAL instruction is placed in register 10. After execution of the BAL instruction register 10 contains 009004_{16}.

The BALR Instruction. The BALR (Branch and Link Register) instruction is an RR-type instruction. The second operand also identifies the branch address. But in this instance, the branch address is contained in a register. For example, the instruction

```
BALR 10,11
```

tells the computer to branch to the instruction whose address is contained in register 11 and to place the address of the *next sequential instruction* in register 10. Perhaps Table 9-3 can clarify this concept.

Assume register 11 contains the address of LOOPRT, $00900C_{16}$. The BALR instruction causes a branch to the instruction at location $00900C_{16}$, and the address of the next instruction, 009006_{16}, is placed in register 10.

The BAL and BALR Instructions—A Summary. The BAL and BALR are unconditional branch instructions. The second operand identifies the branch address. When either instruction is executed, the address of the next instruction is placed in the first operand register.

Table 9-3 The BALR Instruction

symbol	instruction		hexadecimal storage address	
	BALR	10,11	009004	RR-type
	.		009006†	
	.			
	.			
LOOPRT	L	5,ANYPLC	00900C	

†This address is placed in register 10 by the BALR instruction.

Why did we introduce these instructions at this point? Remember, we are discussing a method of loading the base register with the address of the first instruction in our program. A special form of the BALR instruction accomplishes this.

The BALR/USING Pair

We can use the BALR instruction to load the address of the next sequential instruction *without* effecting a branch. For example, the instruction

```
BALR   10,0
```

loads the address of the next instruction into register 10 but a branch does *not* occur! You expect a branch to the address contained in register 0 to occur. But register 0 is a somewhat special register. We saw that when register 0 is used as a base or index register, its contents are ignored. And when register 0 is used as the second operand in the BALR instruction, a branch does not take place—regardless of the contents of register 0.

Just how does this form of the BALR instruction help us in establishing addressability? Consider the program in Table 9-4. Again the figures to the right indicate the storage address of each instruction in the program. The USING statement still promises that the address of FIRST will be in register 12. Let's see how this is accomplished.

The first instruction in the program is the BALR instruction. This instruction resides at 008000_{16}. The BALR instruction is an RR-type instruction requiring two bytes of storage. The next instruction

```
L   5,CON1
```

resides at 008002_{16}. (Remember that the USING statement only supplies information to the assembler—it does not take up storage). When the BALR instruction is executed, a branch does not occur. The second operand is register 0. But the address of the next sequential instruction *is* placed in register 12. After

Table 9-4 Program 2—BALR/USING Pair

generated code		symbolic code		hexadecimal storage address
		.		
		.		
		.		
05C0	GO	BALR	12,0	008000
—		USING	FIRST,12	—
5850C016	FIRST	L	5,CON1	008002
5A50C01A		A	5,CON2	008006
5A50C01E		A	5,CON3	00800A
5A50C022		A	5,CON4	00800E
5050C026		ST	5,RESULT	008012
		.		
		.		
		.		
0000000A	CON1	DC	F'10'	008018
00000014	CON2	DC	F'20'	00801C
0000001E	CON3	DC	F'30'	008020
00000028	CON4	DC	F'40'	008024
	RESULT	DS	F	008028
		END	GO	

execution of the BALR instruction register 12 contains 008002_{16}. We have kept the assembly time promise made in the USING statement. Register 12 contains the address of FIRST!

When the second instruction, the L instruction, is executed, CON1 is addressed. The L instruction tells the computer to take the fullword of data at an area of storage addressed by register 12 as the base, register 0 as the index, and a displacement of 016_{16}. Register 12 contains 008002_{16}—courtesy of the BALR instruction. The effective address of the second operand is 008018_{16}—the address of CON1.

Notice that the base register is loaded only once within the program. The assembler uses this register to address all the storage operands and expects to find the value in the register unchanged. The programmer must be careful not to issue an instruction which alters the contents of the base register.

Summary

We have shown that the assembler must be told which base register to use, and must be provided some reference point from which to calculate displacements. The USING statement provides the base register and the point of reference, promising that a certain address will be in the base register at execution time. The BALR instruction keeps this promise. We use the BALR instruction to load the base register at execution time.

A COMPLETE PROGRAM

We will now examine the listing produced when Program 2 is assembled. We will see how the assembler determines the relative postitions of the instructions and constants within the program, and we will examine the generated instructions in detail.

The Source Listing

The assembly process produces both a printed output and an object program. The printed output contains the source listing and a list of errors, if there are any. We will discuss the source listing here and save our examination of the error listing until later.

Figure 9-4 gives the source listing for Program 2. The listing contains the source statements exactly as punched into the source cards (1). The comments to the right also are punched into the source cards.

The assembler numbers each source statement (2). These statement numbers make it easier to reference individual instructions. Notice that statements 8 and 9 are missing. These instructions are part of the SAVE instruction and are not printed on this listing. More on this later.

The *location counter* gives the relative position of each instruction or constant within the program (3). The location counter usually starts at 000000_{16}, although the programmer may assign some other initial value. The location counter is changed every time an instruction or constant requires space in storage. The amount of space required depends upon the type of instruction, or the size of the constant.

The object code (4) gives the generated machine code in hexadecimal.

The two remaining fields (5) give the relative address of each operand within the source program. Notice the ADDR2 field for statement 12. This field tells us that the second operand has a relative address of 00020_{16}. If we go to location 00020_{16}—using the location counter value—we find the constant labeled CON1. Statement 12 references CON1 as the second operand. There are no addresses in the ADDR1 field. Can you explain why?

Housekeeping Statements

There are several statements in Figure 9-4 which appear in all assembly programs. We often refer to these statements as housekeeping statements—they keep the program neat and orderly, and must always be performed.

The PRINT Statement. The PRINT statement, with the NOGEN option, tells the assembler not to print all the instructions abbreviated by the macro statements. We use the PRINT statement for simplicity. For example, the PRINT statement causes statements 8 and 9 to be omitted from the listings. These are the instructions abbreviated by the SAVE macro.

```
                                                                                    PAGE    1
 (3)      (4)          (5)        (2)         (1)
 LOC  OBJECT CODE   ADDR1 ADDR2  STMT   SOURCE STATEMENT                          F04MAR74   6/17/76

                                    1 *
                                    2 * PROGRAM 2
                                    3 * SUM OF FOUR FULLWORD BINARY CONSTANTS
                                    4 *
                                    5           PRINT NOGEN
000000                              6           START 0
                                    7 GO        SAVE  (14,12)       SAVE REGISTERS
000004 05C0                        10           BALR  12,0          LOAD BASE
000006                             11           USING *,12          ESTABLISH ADDRESSABILITY
000006 5850 C01A         00020     12 FIRST     L     5,CON1        LOAD FIRST CONSTANT
00000A 5A50 C01E         00024     13           A     5,CON2        ADD SECOND CONSTANT
00000E 5A50 C022         00028     14           A     5,CON3        ADD THIRD CONSTANT
000012 5A50 C026         0002C     15           A     5,CON4        AND LAST CONSTANT
000016 5050 C02A         00030     16           ST    5,RESULT      STORE RESULT
                                   17           RETURN (14,12)      RETURN TO OPERATING SYSTEM
                                   18 *
                                   19 * DATA AREAS
                                   20 *
00002C 0000000A                    21 CON1      DC    F'10'         * DEFINE
000024 00000014                    22 CON2      DC    F'20'         * FOUR
000028 0000001E                    23 CON3      DC    F'30'         * FULLWORD
00002C 00000028                    24 CON4      DC    F'40'         * CONSTANTS
000030                             25 RESULT    DS    F
000000                             26           END   GO
```

Figure 9-4 Program 2—computer listing.

The START Statement. The START statement sets the initial value of the location counter. If this statement is omitted, the location counter is set to 000000_{16}. The START statement is also used to mark the beginning of the program.

The SAVE and RETURN Statements. The SAVE and RETURN statements are concerned with linking our program to the operating system. We will not become involved with the purpose of these statements until we discuss linkage conventions. At this point we must accept the fact that these statements appear in all our programs.

Notice that the HSKPING macro can now be omitted. The functions of the HSKPING statement are now handled by the SAVE, BALR, and USING statements.

The END Statement. The END statement must be the last statement in the assembly program. The END statement may be coded without an operand, or it may have an entry in the operand field as shown. The label GO in the operand field tells the assembler that the first instruction to be executed is the instruction at GO.

The Assembly Process

Let's examine the steps the assembler takes in generating the object program and the source listing. The assembler examines the source statements in two steps. The first step or *pass* determines the relative position—the location counter setting—of each instruction and constant within the program. In addition, the assembler develops a table containing information about each symbol in the symbolic program. We call this *the symbol table.*

The assembler generates the correct machine language instructions and constants during the second pass, assigning base, index, and displacement to address storage operands, and producing the assembler listing.

The First Pass. The assembler examines each instruction in the source program. Some instructions, such as the PRINT and START statements do not generate machine code. The START statement does, however, tell the assembler to set the location counter to 000000_{16}. As each instruction is examined, the assembler increments the location counter by the proper value. For example, an RR-type instruction increments the location counter by two bytes an SS-type instruction increments the location counter by six bytes. The location counter is also incremented by the length of each constant defined, or by the amount of storage requested by a DS statement.

Each time the assembler encounters a symbolic label it is entered in the symbol table with the length(LEN) associated with that label, the location counter value(VALUE), the statement where the label is defined(DEFN), and the statements which reference it(REFERENCES). This information is printed during the second pass in the *Cross Reference* listing. Remember, the location counter does not reflect the actual storage address of an instruction or a constant. The value of the location counter is a *relative* address.

CROSS-REFERENCE

SYMBOL	LEN	VALUE	DEFN	REFERENCES
CON1	000004	000020	00021	0012
CON2	000004	000024	00022	0013
CON3	000004	000028	00023	0014
CON4	000004	00002C	00024	0015
FIRST	000004	000006	00012	
GO	000004	000000	00007	0026
RESULT	000004	000030	00025	0016

The Second Pass. The assembler now must generate the correct machine instruction for each symbolic instruction, and produce the assembler listing. It is at this point that the importance of the USING instruction becomes apparent.

The USING statement provides the reference point from which the assembler calculates the displacement. The USING statement in Figure 9-4 is slightly different from previous examples. The notation

```
      USING *,12
FIRST L     5,CON1
```

is identical to the statement

```
      USING FIRST,12
FIRST L     5,CON1
```

The asterisk (*) in the first example *implies* the use of the next statement, rather than specifying the label FIRST. The first notation is preferred and we will use it exclusively. We introduced the statement

```
      USING FIRST,12
```

for simplicity in explaining the function of the USING statement.

The assembler knows that the address of the first load instruction resides in register 12. All displacements are calculated relative to this point. The correct displacement to address CON1 is $01A_{16}$. The assembler arrives at this number by examining the location counter setting at the USING statement, and the location counter setting for CON1. This information was stored in the symbol table during the first pass.

000020_{16}	location counter setting for CON1
-000006_{16}	location counter setting for USING
$00001A_{16}$	displacement to address CON1

The assembler uses this displacement to complete the machine instruction for the first load instruction. The remaining instructions are assembled in the same manner.

The assembler also generates the hexadecimal value for each constant defined in the program. Notice the fullword (8 hexadecimal digits) of data generated for CON1, CON2, CON3, and CON4.

At Execution Time

The process we have just discussed—that of assembling the source program and producing the machine language object program—must occur prior to the execution of the program. The student must remember that there are two distinct phases—compile or assembly time, and object or execution time.

The object program produced at assembly time does not have to be executed immediately. It may be stored on punched cards. We refer to this punched program as the *object deck*. The object program also may be be stored on tape or disk. Usually, the operating system governs the form in which the object program is generated. The programmer is not concerned with this function.

At some point, however, the operating system loads the object program into the computer for execution. The object program consists of both instructions *and* constants. The generated object code must correctly address the constants no matter where the program is loaded. Let's see if the program given in Figure 9-4 is valid for any load address.

Let's assume that the program is loaded at 009014_{16}. The BALR instruction resides at 009018_{16}. The first load instruction resides at $00901A_{16}$. and CON1 resides at 009034_{16}.

Table 9-5 Program 2—A Different Load Address

generated code	symbolic instruction			hexadecimal storage addresses
		PRINT	NOGEN	
		START	0	
	GO	SAVE	(14,12)	009014
05C0		BALR	12,0	009018
		USING	*,12	
5850C01A	FIRST	L	5,CON1	00901A
.		.		.
.		.		.
.		.		.
0000000A	CON1	DC	F'10'	009034
.		.		
.		.		
.		.		
		END	GO	

When the BALR instruction is executed, the number $00901A_{16}$ is placed in register 12. The load instruction is the next instruction executed. The effective address of the second operand is 009034_{16} (contents of register 12 plus a displacement of $01A_{16}$). This the correct address for CON1, assuming a load address of 009014_{16}.

Using Multiple Base Registers

Occasionally a program becomes so large that a single base register cannot address the entire program. For example

```
LOC            SOURCE STATEMENT
                 .
                 .
                 .
000004           BALR        12,0
000006           USING       *,12
000006           L           4,DATA
                 .
                 .
                 .
0010F0   DATA    DC          F'10'
                 .
                 .
                 .
```

The constant DATA has a location counter value of $0010F0_{16}$. When the assembler calculates the displacement based on the information supplied in the USING statement

$0010F0_{16}$	location counter setting for DATA
-000006_{16}	location counter setting for USING
$0010EA_{16}$	displacement to address DATA

we find a 4-digit displacement is required. But the machine language format allows only three hexadecimal digits (a 12-bit displacement). We must provide the assembler with a second base register. The statement

```
USING   FIRST,12,11
```

tells the assembler to use register 12 to address the first 4096 bytes of the program, and register 11 to address the next 4096 bytes of the program. We must, of course, load the second base register

```
        BALR    12,0
        USING   FIRST,12,11
FIRST   LR      11,12
        A       11,FULL
        .
        .
        .
FULL    DC      F'4096'
```

In this example, we load register 12 first, then place the address in register 12 into register 11 and increment the contents of register 11 by 4096.

A more sophisticated approach involves the use of a special type of constant called the *address constant.*

```
        BALR   12,0
        USING  FIRST,12,11
FIRST   L      11,BASE
        .
        .
        .
BASE    DC     A(FIRST+4096)
        .
        .
        .
```

We are asking the assembler to define a constant called BASE whose value is the address of FIRST plus 4096. We initialize the second base register by loading this fullword constant into register 11.

The address constant is described using the DC statement. Remember, we use the DC statement to define constants used in our program. All our examples have used data introduced either as input on a data card, or as a constant defined within the program using the DC statement. The *literal* provides us with yet another way of introducing data into the program.

Literals—A New Approach to Data

A literal is data coded as part of the symbolic instruction. Do not confuse literals with immediate operands. Immediate operands are associated with SI-type instructions and consist of only one byte of data contained within the *machine* instruction. A literal is part of the *symbolic* instruction.

The literal is a shorthand convenience for referring to a storage location that contains a constant without having to devise a name. For example, the instruction

```
      A   4,FULL
      .
      .
      .
FULL  DC  F'100'
```

adds the contents of a fullword storage location labeled FULL to the contents of register 4. We devised a label (FULL) to name this storage location, and initialized FULL to 100.

Let's see how the use of the literal accomplishes the same thing.

```
A  4,=F'100'
```

We are defining the second operand within the symbolic instruction, specifying a constant with a value of 100, but not defining a label. We are asking the assembler to generate the correct constant.

```
                                                                                                    PAGE    1
  LOC  OBJECT CODE     ADDR1 ADDR2  STMT    SOURCE STATEMENT                                  F04MAR74   6/19/76

                                       1          PRINT  NOGEN
                                       2 LITERALS SAVE   (14,12)
000004 05C0                            5          BALR   12,0                      LOAD BASE
000006                                 6          USING  *,12                      ADDRESSABILITY
000006 5A40 C032             00038     7          A      4,=F'10'                  INCREMENT R4 BY 10
00000A 4B40 C036             0003C     8          SH     4,=H'-10'                 DECREMENT R4 BY 10
00000E 4B40 C032             00038     9          SH     4,=F'10'                  VALUE R4 UNCHANGED - SEE WHY?
000012 FA00 C030 C038 00036 0003E     10          AP     CTR(1),=PL1'1'            INCREMENT CTR BY 10
000018 D200 C030 C039 00036 0003F     11          MVC    CTR(1),=X'0C'             INITIALIZE CTR TO PACKED ZEROS
00001E D200 C030 C03A 00036 00040     12          MVC    CTR(1),=X'40'             INITIALIZE CTR TO SPACES
000024 D200 C031 C03B 00037 00041     13          MVC    SW,=B'00000001'           INITIALIZE SW
00002A D500 C031 C03B 00037 00041     14          CLC    SW,=B'00000001'           COMPARE SW TO BINARY CONSTANT
                                      15          RETURN (14,12)                   RESTORE REGISTERS
000036 0C                             18 CTR      DC     PL1'0'
000037                                19 SW       DS     CL1
000000                                20          END    LITERALS
000038 0000000A                       21                 =F'10'
00003C FFF6                           22                 =H'-10'
00003E 1C                             23                 =PL1'1'
00003F 0C                             24                 =X'0C'
000040 40                             25                 =X'40'
000041 01                             26                 =B'00000001'
```

Index, base and displacement to address = F'10'

Assembler generates correct literal

Literal pool is placed after the END statement

Literals are assigned relative locations and are addressable

Figure 9-5 Examples of literals.

The assembler must translate this symbolic instruction into machine code, generating an RX type instruction. The assembler generates the correct value foı the literal, and then determines the correct base, index, and displacement to address this data. (See Figure 9-5.)

We may use literals whenever the symbolic instruction specifies an operand residing in storage, with the restriction that an instruction may contain only one literal. The assembler places all the literals together into a group called the *literal pool.* The literal pool is placed at the end of the program unless we specify another location. We will examine the LTORG statement in a moment and see how this statement is used to change the location of the literal pool.

ASSEMBLY STATEMENTS

The programs we have examined contain both instructions and statements. *Assembly instructions* generate machine language instructions. The assembly language instruction

```
AR   4,5
```

generates the machine language instruction 1A45. These instructions direct the compuıer at *execution* time.

Assembly statements, often called *pseudo-instructions,* do not generate machine language code. Some assembly statements, however, do reserve storage and define constants. We know the use of the DS and DC statements. The DS and DC statements are assembly statements which direct the assembler at *assembly* time. Let's look at other assembly statements.

Symbol Definition Instruction

The EQU (EQUate) statement is used to equate a value or an expression to a symbol. The EQU statement often is used for documentation. In the code

```
CTR    EQU  4
        .
        .
        .
       A     CTR,FULL
        .
        .
        .
FULL   DC    F'3'
```

the EQU statement is used to equate the symbol CTR with the value 4. The programmer now can reference register 4 using the symbol CTR, making the purpose of the instruction easier to understand.

The use of a symbol rather than the register number has a further use. Should the programmer find that he has already used register 4, he need not recode his program. Every reference to register 4 is changed by changing the EQU statement. For example

```
CTR   EQU  5
```

Register 5 now is used to replace the symbol CTR in the symbolic instruction.

A common use of the EQU statement involves the use of the asterisk (*) in the operand field. For example

```
                .
                .
                .
                B      INSTR5
                .
                .
                .
       INSTR5   EQU    *
                GET    CARDIN,WORK
                .
                .
                .
```

Here we are equating the label INSTR5 with a location within the program. Since the EQU statement does not generate code, we are essentially equating the label INSTR5 with the next instruction—the GET statement.

Listing Control Statements

The listing control statements provide the programmer with a means of identifying the printed and punched output of the assembly process.

The TITLE Statement. The TITLE statement allows the programmer to name the assembly listing and to identify any punched output. For example, the statement

```
ASM1    TITLE    'LISTING ASM1'
```

provides a heading for each page of the assembler output, and an identifier which appears in columns 73–76 of the punched output. The heading LISTING ASM1 will appear at the top of each page of the listing. The identifier ASM1 will appear in columns 73–76 of the object deck. More than one TITLE statement may appear in the assembly program, but only the first statement may contain a name in the label field. For example

```
        TITLE    'ASM1 DATA DESCRIPTIONS'
```

causes the subsequent output to start on a new page, with the heading ASM1 DATA DESCRIPTIONS.

Any subsequent TITLE statements cause a skip to a new page, and a change in the heading. The identifier punched in columns 73-76 of the output deck, however, is unchanged.

The EJECT Statement. The EJECT statement causes the assembly listing to skip to a new page. The EJECT statement is convenient if the programmer wishes to space sections of the program.

The SPACE Statement. The SPACE statement is used to space one or more lines in the listing. For example

```
SPACE 2
```

causes the listing to skip two lines. This is another convenient means of spacing the sections of a program.

The PRINT Statement. The PRINT statement controls the information printed on the assembly listing. We use the PRINT NOGEN statement to suppress the code generated in the HSKPING macro. The PRINT statement may, however, be used with other operands.

ON —a listing is printed
OFF —no listing is printed

GEN —all statements generated by a macro statement are printed
NOGEN —none of the statements generated by a macro statement are printed, although the macro itself appears

DATA —the entire constant is printed in the listing
NODATA—only the leftmost eight bytes of the generated constant are printed

Program Control Statements

The program control statements are used to:

1. specify changes in source card format
2. punch or reproduce source data
3. set and change the value of the location counter and literal pool
4. in the case of the CNOP and CALL instructions, insert required code

The PUNCH Statement. The PUNCH statement causes from 1 to 80 characters in the operand field to be punched as assembly output. The statement

```
PUNCH 'ASM1 OBJECT DECK'
```

might be used to identify the resulting object deck.

The ORG Statement. The ORG statement is used to change the value of the location counter.

The LTORG Statement. Normally, literals are assembled at the end of the assembly program. The LTORG statement is used to change the location of the literal pool.

The CNOP Instruction. The CNOP instruction is used to align instructions. The format of the instruction is

name	operation	operand
label	CNOP	b,w

The operands specify which byte (b = 0, 2, 4, or 6) of the word (w = 4 or 8) the instruction is to be aligned at. The instruction

```
CNOP  0,8
BALR  12,0
```

tells the assembler to align the BALR instruction at the beginning of the next double word. The values of b and w are given below.

b,w	specifies
0,4	beginning of a word
2,4	middle of a word
0,8	beginning of a double word
2,8	second halfword of a double word
4,8	third halfword of a double word
6,8	fourth halfword of a double word

The CNOP statement generates the required number of no-operation instructions to ensure alignment. For example, the code

```
CNOP  2,8
BALR  12,0
  .
  .
  .
```

states that the BALR instruction is to reside on the second halfword of a double word in storage. The code generated depends upon the current setting of the location counter. Assume the location counter is set at 000008_{16}, a double word boundary. The CNOP instruction generates a single BCR instruction

```
CNOP  2,8
BCR   0,0    RR INSTRUCTION ALTERS
             LOCATION COUNTER BY 2
BALR  12,0
```

```
PGM6  PROGRAM6 - ILLUSTRATING ASSEMBLY COMMANDS                                        PAGE   1

LOC   OBJECT CODE    ADDR1 ADDR2  STMT   SOURCE STATEMENT                    F04MAR74   6/17/76

                                     2 *
                                     3 * CALCULATE THE SUM OF A SERIES
                                     4 * LIMIT ON A CARD
                                     5 * DECIMAL ARITHMETIC
                                     6 *

                                     8          PRINT NOGEN               SUPPRESS MACRO GENERATION
000000                               9          START
000003                              10 THREE    EQU   3
                                    11 *        SAVE  (14,12)             GENERATED IN HSKP MACRO
                                    12 *        BALR  12,0                GENERATED IN HSKP MACRO
                                    13 *        USING *,12                GENERATED IN HSKP MACRO
                                    14 SUM      HSKPING CARDID=INCARD,PRINTID=PRINT
                                   158          GET   INCARD,INWORK       GET DATA CARD
```

From operand field in TITLE statement
From name field in TITLE statement-this label also appears in punched output
Caused by SPACE 3 instruction
Suppress macro generation
START statement marks beginning of program and starts location counter at 000000
EQU statement associates name THREE with number 3
Skip to next page caused by EJECT statement

Figure 9-6.

```
PGM6   PROGRAM6 - ILLUSTRATING ASSEMBLY COMMANDS                                     PAGE    2

  LOC    OBJECT CODE      ADDR1 ADDR2   STMT   SOURCE STATEMENT                                  F04MAR74   6/17/76

000016A D202 C716 C1B2 0071C 001B8      164 INIT      MVC   CTR(THREE),=PL3'1'       SET CTR TO 1
0000170 D206 C70F C1B5 00715 001BB      165           MVC   ANS,=PL7'0'              CLEAR ANS
0000176 F223 C70C C6BC 00712 006C2      166           PACK  LIMIT(THREE),LIMITIN     PACK LIMIT
000017C FA62 C70F C716 00715 0071C      167 BODY      AP    ANS,CTR                  ADD TO ANS
0000182 F922 C716 C70C 0071C 00712      168 TEST      CP    CTR(THREE),LIMIT         TEST
0000188 4780 C194            0019A      169           BE    EXIT                     EXIT IF EQUAL
000018C 0700C7C0                        170           CNOP  0,8                      ALIGN ON DOUBLE WORD
0000190 FA22 C716 C1B2 0071C 001B8      171           AP    CTR(THREE),=PL3'1'       ELSE INCREMENT COUNTER
0000196 47F0 C176            0017C      172           B     BODY                     AND LOOP TO BODY


000019A F356 C719 C70F 0071F 00715      174 EXIT      UNPK  RESULT,ANS               UNPACK ANS TO RESULT
                                        175           PUT   PRINT,PRINTBLD
00001AE 58DD C004            00004      180           L     13,4(13)                 RESTORE SAVEAREA POINTER
                                        181           PRINT GEN                      START MACRO GENERATION
                                        182 EOJ       RETURN (14,12)                 END OF JOB
00001B2                                 183+EOJ       DS    0H
00001B2 98EC D00C            0000C      184+          LM    14,12,12(13) RESTORE THE REGISTERS
00001B6 07FE                            185+          BR    14 RETURN
```

- Information from TITLE statement appears on second page
- Equivalent to number 3 by virtue of EQU statement
- Caused by SPACE 3 statement
- Generate code
- CNOP statement generates BCR 0,0 instructions to allign next instruction on a double word boundary

Figure 9-6 (Continued)

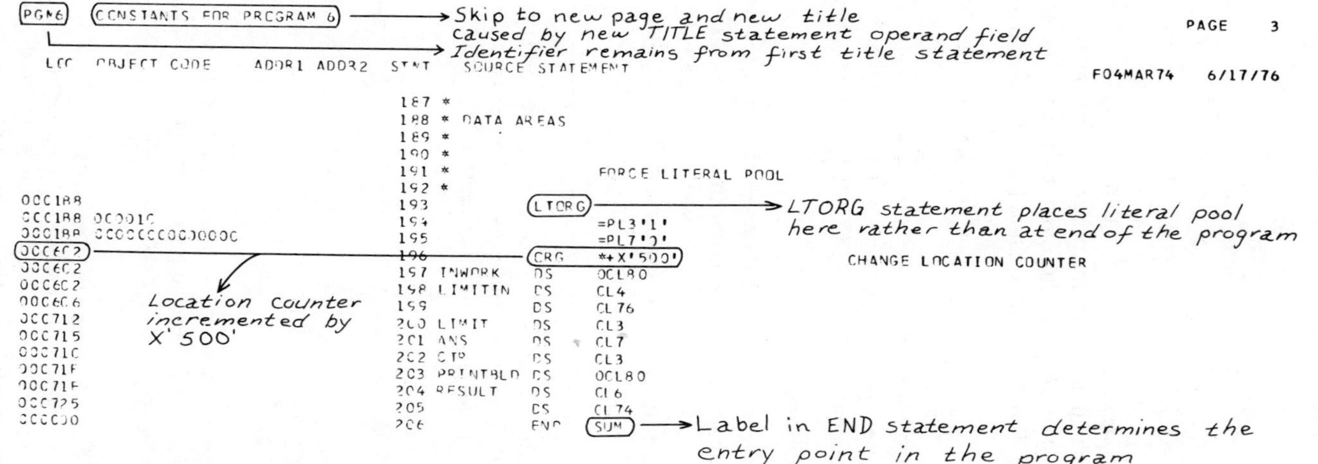

```
PGM6  CONSTANTS FOR PROGRAM 6                                              PAGE    3

LOC    OBJECT CODE      ADDR1 ADDR2  STMT   SOURCE STATEMENT                       F04MAR74   6/17/76

                                      187 *
                                      188 * DATA AREAS
                                      189 *
                                      190 *
                                      191 *                            FORCE LITERAL POOL
                                      192 *
000188                                193               LTORG
000188 00001C                         194                      =PL3'1'
00018B 0000000000000C                 195                      =PL7'0'
0006C2                                196               ORG    *+X'500'          CHANGE LOCATION COUNTER
0006C2                                197 INWORK        DS     0CL80
0006C2                                198 LIMITIN       DS     CL4
0006C6                                199               DS     CL76
000712                                200 LIMIT         DS     CL3
000715                                201 ANS           DS     CL7
00071C                                202 CTR           DS     CL3
00071F                                203 PRINTBLD      DS     0CL80
00071F                                204 RESULT        DS     CL6
000725                                205               DS     CL74
000000                                206               END    SUM
```

Skip to new page and new title caused by new TITLE statement operand field
Identifier remains from first title statement
Location counter incremented by X'500'
LTORG statement places literal pool here rather than at end of the program
Label in END statement determines the entry point in the program

Figure 9-6 (Continued)

If, however, we request alignment on the fourth halfword of a double word, the CNOP instruction generates three no-operation instructions.

```
CNOP  6,8
BCR   0,0
BCR   0,0
BCR   0,0
BALR  12,0
```

The COPY Statement. The COPY statement allows the programmer to include pre-coded *source* statements in the program. Frequently-used routines often are coded and placed in an operating system library. The programmer may reference this library during assembly time. For example, the statement

```
COPY  'CODE1'
```

references a set of instructions named CODE1. This code is a member of a partitioned data set in OS/370, or a book in the DOS Source Statement Library.* The source statements comprising CODE1 are assembled with the user's program.

The END Statement. The END statement is the last statement in the assembly program. The label in the END statement is optional. This label names the first statement to be executed we call this statement the entry point.

Some of the statements discussed are illustrated in Figure 9-6.

PROBLEMS

9.1 Give the effective address of the storage operand(s) for each of the following instructions. You may assume that register 12 contains 009070_{16}. Why do you not need to know the contents of register 0?

a. 5A50C01B
b. 5060C00A
c. 9067C02C
d. F331C012C080
e. 95FFC012
f. 4130C12C

9.2 The solution to Program 3—finding the average of four binary constants—is given in Figure 9-7. Develop a Cross Reference listing for this program.

9.3 Give the generated code for each instruction and constant in Figure 9-7†. Then

*These concepts are discussed in Chapter 17.

†The solution contains two unfamiliar instructions (SR, D). This should present no problem if you use the information in Appendix A. In this problem we are only concerned with *generating* the instruction, not what occurs during execution.

```
*
* PROGRAM 3
* AVERAGE OF FOUR FULLWORD BINARY CONSTANTS
*
         PRINT NOGEN
FIRST    SAVE  (14,12)              SAVE REGISTERS
         BALR  12,0                 LOAD BASE
         USING *,12                 ESTABLISH ADDRESSABILITY
         L     5,CON1               LOAD FIRST CONSTANT
         A     5,CON2               ADD SECOND CONSTANT
         A     5,CON3               ADD THIRD CONSTANT
         A     5,CON4               AND LAST CONSTANT
         SR    4,4                  CLEAR R4
         D     4,FOUR               DIVIDE EVEN-ODD PAIR
         ST    5,RESULT             STORE QUOTIENT
*                                   REMAINDER IN R4
*        *
*        *     THE PROGRAM IS COMPLETE
*        *     THE RETURN STATEMENT
*        *     SIGNIFIES END-OF-JOB
*        *
         RETURN (14,12)             RETURN TO OPERATING SYSTEM
*
* DATA AREAS
*
FOUR     DC    F'4'                 DEFINE DIVISOR
CON1     DC    F'10'                * DEFINE
CON2     DC    F'20'                * FOUR
CON3     DC    F'30'                * FULLWORD
CON4     DC    F'40'                * CONSTANTS
RESULT   DS    F
         END   FIRST
```

Figure 9-7 Program 3—binary arithmetic.

assume a load address of 009000_{16} and verify that your code addresses the correct storage operand. What is the relation between the storage address of a given instruction and its location counter setting?

9.4 Use the Cross Reference listing to answer the following questions.

SYMBOL	LEN	VALUE	DEFN	REFERENCES	
FIRST	000001	000000	000000		
GROSSIN	000008	00008C	000012	0010	
HALF	000002	000013	000020	0006	0008
MONEY	000007	000071	000019	0020	
NEXT	000006	000012	000009		
PACKIT	000006	000018	000010	0018	
RESULT	000004	000090	000013		

1. Could the field RESULT be a halfword constant? Why?
2. If the label PACKIT names a machine instruction, to which of the five instruction types does PACKIT belong?
3. Is it possible for PACKIT to name an instruction even though it is referenced in the operand field of another instruction?

4. HALF has a length of two bytes. Is it a valid halfword binary constant? Why?

9.5 The solution to Program 3 using decimal arithmetic is given in Figure 9-8. Develop a Cross Reference listing for this program. Remember, decimal instructions usually require six bytes of main storage (SS-type instructions).

```
*
* PROGRAM 3
* AVERAGE FOUR DECIMAL CONSTANTS
*
         PRINT NOGEN
FIRST    HSKPING
*        *
*        *        SOME
*        *        HOUSEKEEPING
*        *        STATEMENTS
*        *        ARE
*        *        OMITTED
*        *        HERE
*        *
         AP       ANS,CON1                   ADD FIRST CONSTANT
         AP       ANS,CON2                   ADD SECOND CONSTANT
         AP       ANS,CON3                   ADD THIRD CONSTANT
         AP       ANS,CON4                   ADD FOURTH CONSTANT
         DP       ANS,FOUR                   AND FIND AVERAGE
         UNPK     RESULT,ANS(3)              UNPACK QUOTIENT - IGNORE REMAINDER
*        *
*        *        THE PROGRAM IS COMPLETE
*        *        THE RETURN STATEMENT
*        *        SIGNIFIES END-OF-JOB
*        *
         RETURN (14,12)                      RETURN
*
* DATA AREAS
*
FOUR     DC       PL1'4'
PKFLD    DS       CL3
CON1     DC       PL4'10'                    * FOUR
CON2     DC       PL4'20'                    * PACKED
CON3     DC       PL4'30'                    * DECIMAL
CON4     DC       PL4'40'                    * CONSTANTS
ANS      DC       PL4'0'
RESULT   DS       CL4
         END      FIRST
```

Figure 9-8 Program 3—decimal arithmetic.

9.6 Give the generated code for each instruction and constant in Figure 9-8. Assume a load address of 009000_{16} and verify that your code addresses the correct storage operands.

Hint! SS-type instructions do not use an index register. They also require a length attribute for each operand. The generated length attribute is *one less* than the coded length. For example, the instruction

AP FLDA(3),FLDB(2)

generates a hexadecimal FA21 in bits 0–15 of the machine instruction. Bits 8–11 represent the length attribute of the first operand. A 2_{16} is coded—0010_2—one less than the length attribute in the symbolic instruction.

9.7 Assume that your program requires three base registers. Show how you would code the USING statement for such a program, and how you would load the base registers.

9.8 What is the effective address of the second operand in the instruction

```
        A       4,CON2
```

in the following section of code.

```
        .
        .
        .
        BALR    12,0
        USING   *,12
INIT    SR      12,12
        .
        .
        .
BODY    A       4,CON2
        .
        .
        .
```

Give a reason for your answer.

Note: The SR (Subtract Register) instruction subtracts the contents of the second operand register from the contents of the first operand register.

9.9 What would happen when the program loads the second base register in the following segment of code?

```
LOC              SOURCE   STATEMENT

000004           BALR     12,0
000006           USING    FIRST,12,11
000006     FIRST L        11,BASE
                 .
                 .
                 .
00100C     BASE  DC       A(FIRST+4096)
                 .
                 .
                 .
```

Give a reason for your answer.

9.10 Recode each of the following instructions replacing the second operand with the correct literal, if appropriate.

```
         .
         .
         .
         A     7,FULL
         LA    6,HALF
         MVI   DATA,C' A'
         AP    DATA,DEC1
         A     7,BIN
         .
         .
         .
HALF     DC    H' 10'
FULL     DC    F' 10'
DATA     DC    P' 123'
DEC      DC    PL1' 1'
BIN      DC    F' 1'
         END
```

section three

Understanding the Assembly Language

10

Binary Instructions

We have developed a subset of the binary instructions using the fullword move, add, subtract, and compare instructions. We will now expand these concepts into a complete binary instruction set.

BINARY MOVE INSTRUCTIONS

The binary move instructions move data between storage and the registers, and from one register to another. The load instructions move binary data into a register. The RR form of the load instruction moves data from one register to another. The RX form of the load instruction moves data from main storage to a register.

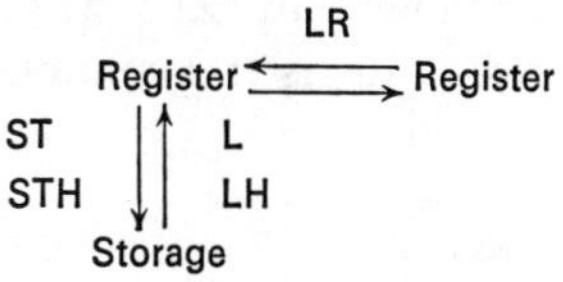

```
              LR
     Register<====> Register
ST     | ^    L
STH    v |    LH
     Storage
```

The store instructions move data from a register to a location in storage. The store instructions are RX-type instructions.

Register-to-Register Instruction

The LR (Load Register) instruction moves a fullword of binary data from the second operand register to the first operand register. The contents of the second operand register remain unchanged. The instruction

```
LR   3,4
```

takes the fullword of data in register 4 and places or loads that data into register 3. The data in register 4 are unchanged. For example

```
R3:  0000087C    before execution
R4:  FC00898D
R3:  FC00898D    after execution
R4:  FC00898D
```

The LR instruction is an RR-type instruction. The instruction contains an operation code and two operands. The operands are the numbers of the registers involved.

Register-to-Storage Instructions

The register-to-storage instructions may involve either halfword or fullword operands. The load instructions move data from main storage to a register. The store instructions move data from a register to a main storage location. We introduced the L and ST instructions in Chapter 8. Now let's examine the instructions which load and store halfword operands.

Halfword Instructions. The LH (Load Halfword) instruction and STH (STore Halfword) instruction move halfword operands between registers and main storage.

The LH instruction moves a halfword of data from the second operand (main storage) location and places it in the first operand register. But we have an additional consideration here. If we are placing a *halfword* of data into a *fullword* register, just where does the data go? The LH instruction places the data in the low-order (rightmost) halfword of the register.

In addition, the sign bit of the data is propagated through the high-order bits of the register. In loading a halfword of data into a register, we are essentially converting a halfword operand to a fullword operand! Let's see how this works.

Storage location CON1 contains $000A_{16}$. Register 3 contains $0234F90F_{16}$. After execution of the instruction

```
LH   3,CON1
```

register 3 contains $0000000A_{16}$. Now let's assume that CON1 contains $FFF6_{16}$ (−10). After execution of the same instruction register 3 contains $FFFFFFF6_{16}$. Figure 10-1 helps illustrate this concept.

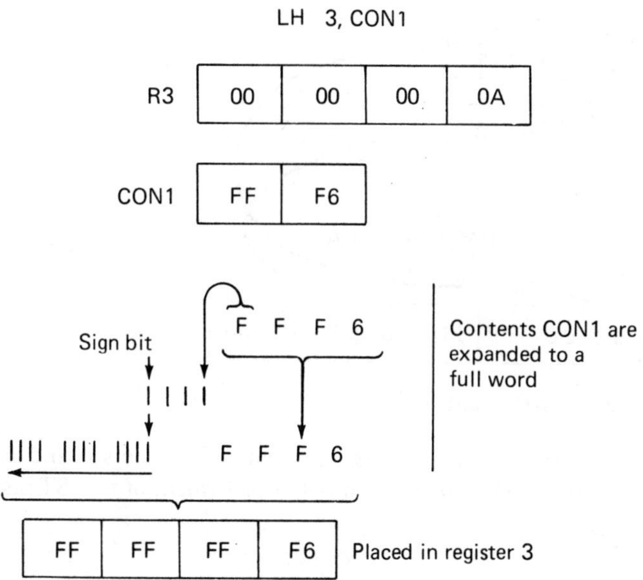

Figure 10-1 The LH instruction.

The STH instruction places the low-order halfword of the first operand register into the second operand location. The contents of the register remain unchanged.

Table 10-1 LH and STH Instructions

location	instruction	receiving field after execution
R3: 0000897C	LH 3,H2	R3: 0000707C
R4: 0000108D	LH 4,H1	R4: FFFF809F
H1: 809F	STH 3,H1	H1: 897C
H2: 707C	STH 4,H2	H2: 108D

The LM and STM Instructions. We have discussed the instructions which move data between registers and main storage. Those instructions move a halfword or fullword of data.

Two additional instructions move data between registers and main storage. These instructions do not move a single halfword or fullword. Rather, they involve the movement of one or more fullwords of data.

The STM (STore Multiple) instruction places the data from consecutive registers into main storage. The instruction

```
STM 4,5,LOCA
```

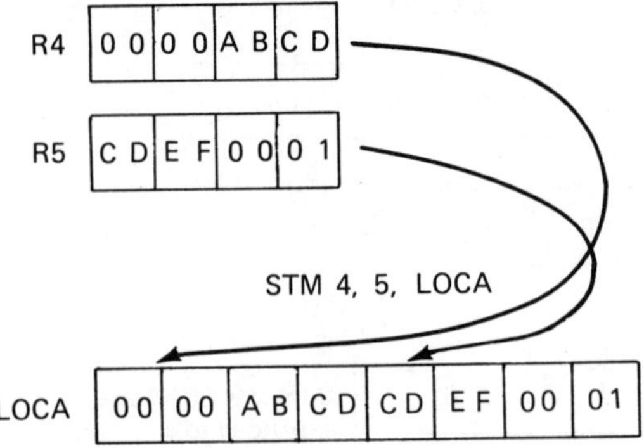

Figure 10-2 The STM instruction.

stores two fullwords of data—the contents of registers 4 and 5—into LOCA (see Figure 10-2). This instruction is the equivalent of two ST instructions. For example

```
ST   4,LOCA
ST   5,LOCA+4
```

The notation LOCA+4 is called relative addressing. We are addressing an area of storage four bytes beyond LOCA.

The LM (Load Multiple) instruction is used to load data from consecutive storage locations into adjacent registers. The instruction

```
LM   5,7,FLDB
```

loads registers 5 through 7 with the adjacent fullwords of data starting at FLDB.

```
        R5 [  ]   R6 [  ]   R7 [  ]
FLDB    00076312  001FEC9A  873D9E00
        3 CONSECUTIVE FULLWORDS
```

Register 5 will contain the fullword of data residing at FLDB, register 6 will contain the fullword of data residing at FLDB+4, and so forth.

Both the LM and STM instructions are RS-type instructions. In these instructions, the second operand is addressed by only a base register and a displacement. No index register is used. We use symbolic labels to address the storage location. It is the assembler's responsibility to assign a base and displacement when the program is assembled.

BINARY ARITHMETIC

We have developed the basic concepts of binary arithmetic using the A and S instructions. Now let's expand these concepts to include multiplication and division, RR-type fullword instructions, and RX-type instructions involving halfword operands. We will take this opportunity to review the fullword instructions discussed in Chapter 8.

Addition and Subtraction

We have said that at least one operand must reside in a register. In the A and S instructions, the second operand is a fullword operand residing in storage. The second storage operand also may be a halfword of data (AH,SH), or it may be a fullword of data residing in register.

Table 10-2 Add and Subtract Instructions

operation	second operand	instruction
AR	FULLWORD	Add Register
A	FULLWORD	Add (fullword)
AH	HALFWORD	Add Halfword
SR	FULLWORD	Subtract Register
S	FULLWORD	Subtract (fullword)
SH	HALFWORD	Subtract Halfword

These instructions are all quite similar. In all cases, the contents of the second operand location are added to or subtracted from the contents of the first operand register. The storage operand must reside on a halfword (AH,SH) or fullword (A,S) boundary if the IBM S/360 is used. The result is placed in the first operand register. The contents of the second operand location remain the same. If the result of the operation does not fit into the first operand location, an overflow occurs.

Register-to-Register Instructions. The AR (Add Register) instruction adds the contents of the second operand register to the contents of the first operand register.

Table 10-3 AR Instruction

location	instruction	first operand after execution
R2: 00000013	AR 3,2	R3: 0000833F
R3: 0000832C	AR 4,2	R4: 100FF9A0
R4: 100FF98D	AR 2,6	R2: 00000012
R5: 800FFFF3	AR 5,4	R5: 901FF980
R6: FFFFFFFF	AR 6,6	R6: FFFFFFFE
R7: 7FFFFFF3	AR 7,7	OVERFLOW

The SR (Subtract Register) instruction subtracts the contents of the second operand register from the contents of the first operand register.

Table 10-4 SR Instruction

location	instruction	first operand after execution
R2: 0000001D	SR 2,3	R2: 0000001C
R3: 00000001	SR 2,4	R2: 00000027
R4: FFFFFFF6	SR 4,5	R4: FFFFFFF7
R5: FFFFFFFF	SR 4,4	R4: 00000000
	SR 3,5	R3: 00000002

Register-to-Storage Instructions. We examined the fullword RX-type instructions in Chapter 8. To review, the fullword of data in the second operand storage location is added to or subtracted from the fullword of data in the first operand register. The result is placed in the first operand register.

The halfword instructions involve the addition or subtraction of a halfword of data in main storage to or from a fullword of data in the register (Figure 10-3).

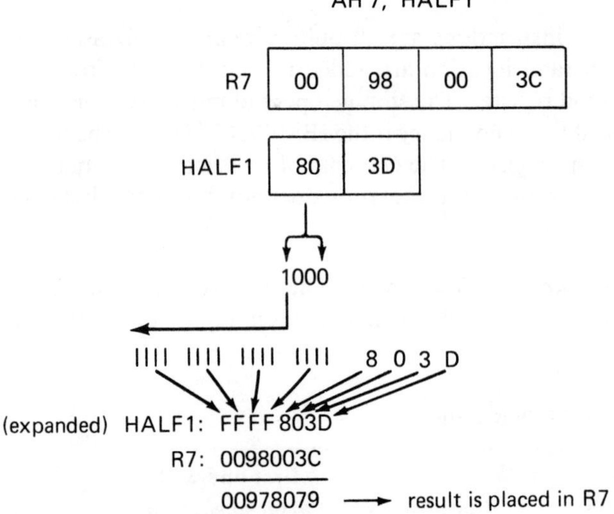

Figure 10-3 The AH instruction.

Again, we are faced with the difference in operand lengths. Does the instruction add the halfword operand to the low-order or high-order part of the register? The answer is neither. The halfword of data is expanded into a fullword and then the specified operation takes place. The high-order bit—the sign bit—of the second operand is propagated sixteen positions to the left. The halfword of data is expanded to a fullword. But the value of the data is unchanged! And the sign of the number is the same!

Table 10-5 shows some examples of the AH and SH instructions. Remember, these operations are determined by the rules of algebra. You must consider the sign of each operand as you perform the specified operation.

Table 10-5 AH and SH Instructions

location	instruction	first operand after execution
R5: 80000011	AH 6,H1	R6: 00000086
R6: 0000007C	AH 6,H2	R6: 00000072
R7: FFFFFFFA	SH 7,H1	R7: FFFFFFF0
H1: 000A	AH 7,H3	R7: FFFF9086
H2: FFF6	SH 7,H2	R7: 00000004
H3: 908C	AH 5,H3	OVERFLOW

Multiplication and Division

The instructions to accomplish multiplication and division follow the same general pattern as the instructions for addition and subtraction. At least one operand must be in a register. The second operand may be in another register (MR and DR instructions) or in a main storage location (M, MH, D instructions). The second operand in the RX-type multiply instruction (M,MH) may be a halfword or a fullword of data. The RX form of the divide instruction (D) handles only a fullword of data.

In all cases, the contents of the second operand—whether in a register or in main storage—are multiplied by or divided into the contents of the first operand register. Again, the storage operand must reside on a halfword (MH) or fullword (M,D) boundary if the IBM S/360 is used.

There is no overflow condition in binary multiplication. The rules for this operation ensure that no overflow can occur. We will see just why in the next section. There is, however, the possibility of an overflow during binary division. If the first operand register cannot hold the result (called the quotient) an error called a *fixed-point divide exception* occurs. This error may cause the computer to stop processing the program.

Register-to-Register Instructions. The MR (Multiply Register) and DR (Divide Register) instructions involve fullword operands residing in registers.

Let's consider the MR instruction first. Our main concern is with the size of the answer (product). When two fullwords (32-bit operands) are multiplied, the product requires 64 bits. Certainly the product cannot fit into the first operand register!

The MR instruction solves this problem by placing the product not in a single register, but in a register pair! For example, the instruction

```
MR 4,7
```

appears to multiply the contents of register 4 by the contents of register 7, placing the product in register 4. Assuming, of course, that the product fits into register 4!

In the MR instruction, the first operand addresses a register pair. The first operand is actually registers 4 *and* 5, treated as a pair! The instruction multiplies the contents of *register 5* by the contents of register 7 and places the 64-bit product in registers 4 *and* 5. In other words, the first operand is contained in the higher register of the pair. The assembly language requires that the register pair be an even–odd pair. Registers 2 and 3, 4 and 5, and so forth. The first operand is always contained in the *odd* register of the even–odd register pair. The value in the even (low) reqister is not used. Remember, the reason for this seemingly awkward arrangement is to accommodate the 64-bit product generated by the multiplication of two fullwords of data.

Let's illustrate these concepts with a specific example. Register 4 contains $0000000A_{16}$, register 5 contains 00000006_{16}, and register 7 contains 00000008_{16}. The instruction

```
MR 4,7
```

causes the contents of *register 5* to be multiplied by the contents of register 7. The product, although it does in this case fit into a single register, is placed in registers 4 and 5. After execution of this instruction, register 4 contains 00000000_{16} and register 5 contains 00000030_{16}.

You might think of the operation as follows:

$$
\begin{array}{rl}
00000008_{16} & (8_{10}) \\
\times 00000006_{16} & (6_{10}) \\
\hline
\underbrace{00000000}_{\text{register 4}}\underbrace{00000030}_{\text{register 5}}{}_{16} & (48_{10})
\end{array}
$$

The low-order fullword of the product is placed in register 5. The high-order fullword of the product is placed in register 4.

Binary multiplication is performed on signed integers. The sign of the product is determined by the rules of algebra. Table 10-6 gives examples of the MR instruction.

The DR instruction also involves fullword operands. Our problem here is that division results in both a quotient and a remainder. We must accommodate both.

The DR instruction uses an even–odd register to contain the quotient and remainder. For example, the instruction

```
DR 4,7
```

Table 10-6 The MR Instruction

location		instruction	first operand register pair
R2: FFFFFFFE	(−2)	MR 2,4	R2–R3: 0000000000000018
R3: 00000002	(+2)	MR 4,3	R4–R5: 000000000000000A
R4: 0000000C	(+12)	MR 4,2	R4–R5: FFFFFFFFFFFFFFF6
R5: 00000005	(+5)	MR 6,2	R6–R7: 00000000000000C8
R6: FFFFFFFA	(−6)		
R7: FFFFFF9C	(−100)		

divides the double word contents of registers 4 and 5 (the dividend) by the contents of register 7 (the divisor). The quotient is placed in register 5 (the odd register). The remainder is placed in register 4 (the even register).

Assume register 4 contains 00000000_{16} and register 5 contains 00000064_{16}. The double word 0000000000000064_{16} is the dividend in this example. And let's assume register 7 contains $0000000D_{16}$. Register 7 contains the divisor. Figure 10-4 shows how the instruction works.

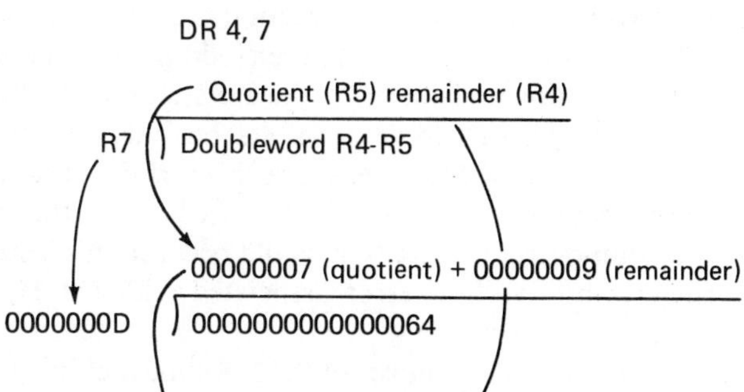

Figure 10-4 The DR instruction.

In the example just discussed, both operands are positive. The quotient and remainder are both positive. Binary division does, however, follow the rules of algebra. Dividing numbers of the same sign results in a positive quotient. Dividing numbers of different signs results in a negative quotient, and the remainder takes the sign of the dividend. Table 10-7 gives examples of the DR instruction, using the letter *r* to represent the remainder and the letter *q* to represent the quotient.

Table 10-7 The DR Instruction

location	instruction	first operand register pair	
R4: 00000000	DR 4,8	R4: 00000001	($r = +1$)
R5: 00000015 (+21)		R5: 0000000A	($q = +10$)
R6: FFFFFFFF	DR 4,9	R4: 00000001	($r = +1$)
R7: FFFFFFEB (−21)		R5: FFFFFFF6	($q = -10$)
R8: 00000002 (+2)	DR 6,8	R6: FFFFFFFF	($r = -1$)
R9: FFFFFFFE (−2)		R7: FFFFFFF6	($q = -10$)
	DR 6,9	R6 FFFFFFFF	($r = -1$)
		R7: 0000000A	($q = +10$)

Register-to-Storage Instructions. There are two RX-type instructions for binary multiplication. The M (Multiply) instruction multiplies the contents of a register (first operand) by the contents of a fullword in main storage. The product is placed in the even–odd register pair specified by the first operand. For example, the instruction

```
M    4,MPLIER
```

multiplies the contents of *register 5* by the contents of the fullword at MPLIER. The 64-bit product is placed in registers 4 and 5.

The MH (Multiply Halfword) instruction multiplies the fullword contents of a register (we are not concerned with even–odd pairs in the MH instruction) by the contents of a halfword in storage. We are multiplying a 32-bit operand by a 16-bit operand. The product contains 48 bits, but only the low-order 32 bits of the product are stored in the first operand register. If the product requires more than 31 bits and a sign bit, the high-order bits are lost and the answer is invalid. You might think an overflow condition would occur in this instance. This is not the case. There is no overflow error associated with the M, MR, and MH instructions.

Table 10-8 gives some examples of the RX-type multiply instructions.

Table 10-8 RX Multiply Instructions

location	instruction	first operand after execution
R4: 0000000A (+10)	MH 6,H1	R6: 00000014 (+20)
R5: 00000014 (+20)	MH 6,H2	R6: FFFFFFEC (−20)
R6: 0000000A (+10)	MH 7,H1	R7: FFFFFFD8 (−40)
R7: FFFFFFEC (−20)	MH 7,H2	R7: 00000028 (+40)
H1: 0002 (+2)	M 4,F1	R4–R5: 000000000000003C (+60)
H2: FFFE (−2)	M 4,F2	R4–R5: FFFFFFFFFFFFFFC4 (−60)
F1: 00000003 (+3)	M 6,F1	R6–R7: FFFFFFFFFFFFFFC4 (−60)
F2: FFFFFFFD (−3)	M 6,F2	R6–R7: 000000000000003C (+60)

The D (Divide) instruction divides the double word contents of an even–odd register pair by the contents of a fullword in main storage. The quotient is placed in the odd register. The remainder is placed in the even register. If the quotient does not fit in the even register, an error called a fixed-point divide occurs.

Let's assume that register 4 contains 00000000_{16}, register 5 contains $0000002C_{16}$, and DIVSOR contains $0000000E_{16}$. The instruction

```
D   4,DIVSOR
```

is essentially dividing the double word $000000000000002C_{16}$ (44_{10}) by the fullword $0000000E_{16}$ (14_{10}). The quotient is 3; the remainder is 2. After execution of the instruction, register 5 contains the quotient and register 4 contains the remainder. Register 5 contains 00000003_{16}. Register 4 contains 00000002_{16}. Table 10-9 gives additional examples of the divide instruction. Remember, the sign of the quotient is determined by the rules of algebra. The sign of the remainder is the sign of the dividend.

Table 10-9 The D Instruction

location	instruction	first operand after execution
R2: 00000000	D 2,FULL1	R2: 00000004 ($r = +4$)
R3: 00000064 (+100)		R3: 00000010 ($q = +16$)
R4: FFFFFFFF	D 2,FULL2	R2: 00000004 ($r = +4$)
R5: FFFFFF9C (−100)		R3: FFFFFFF0 ($q = -16$)
FULL1: 00000006 (+6)	D 4,FULL1	R4: FFFFFFFC ($r = -4$)
FULL2: FFFFFFFA (−6)		R5: FFFFFFF0 ($q = -16$)
	D 4,FULL2	R4: FFFFFFFC ($r = -4$)
		R5: 00000010 ($q = +16$)

Two Sample Programs

Program 3 Program 3 finds the average of four constants and stores the quotient in RESULT (Figure 10-5). The student should be familiar with the initial steps in solving this problem. We first must define the data used in the program and reserve space for RESULT.

```
CON1    DC  F'10'
CON2    DC  F'20'
CON3    DC  F'30'
CON4    DC  F'40'
RESULT  DS  F'
```

The program asks for the average of four constants. We must find the sum of the

```
*
* PROGRAM 3
* AVERAGE OF FOUR FULLWORD BINARY CONSTANTS
*
         PRINT NOGEN
FIRST    SAVE  (14,12)                    SAVE REGISTERS
         BALR  12,0                       LOAD BASE
         USING *,12                       ESTABLISH ADDRESSABILITY
         L     5,CON1                     LOAD FIRST CONSTANT
         A     5,CON2                     ADD SECOND CONSTANT
         A     5,CON3                     ADD THIRD CONSTANT
         A     5,CON4                     AND LAST CONSTANT
         SR    4,4                        CLEAR R4
         D     4,FOUR                     DIVIDE EVEN-ODD PAIR
         ST    5,RESULT                   STORE QUOTIENT
*                                         REMAINDER IN R4
*        *
*        *     THE PROGRAM IS COMPLETE
*        *     THE RETURN STATEMENT
*        *     SIGNIFIES END-OF-JOB
*        *
         RETURN (14,12)                   RETURN TO OPERATING SYSTEM
*
* DATA AREAS
*
FOUR     DC    F'4'                       DEFINE DIVISOR
CON1     DC    F'10'                      * DEFINE
CON2     DC    F'20'                      * FOUR
CON3     DC    F'30'                      * FULLWORD
CON4     DC    F'40'                      * CONSTANTS
RESULT   DS    F
         END   FIRST
```

Figure 10-5 Program 3—solution.

constants and divide by 4. We must define an additional constant whose value is four.

```
FOUR  DC  F'4'
```

The processing instructions find the sum of the four constants and then divide the sum by the constant FOUR. (We developed the sum of four constants in Program 2.)

```
L  5,CON1
A  5,CON2
A  5,CON3
A  5,CON4
```

The sum of the four constants is now in register 5. We want to divide the contents of register 5 by the fullword constant at FOUR. But the divide instruction requires the use of an even–odd register pair. We must treat the double word in registers 4 and 5 as the dividend. The dividend is now in register 5. We must clear register 4 to zeros (we are assuming that the dividend is positive)

```
SR   4,4
```

and then code the divide instruction.

```
D    4,FOUR
```

The quotient is now in register 5. We can store the quotient in RESULT.

```
ST   5,RESULT
```

The remainder in register 4 is ignored.

Program 4 Program 4 finds the volume of a sphere using the equation

$$V = (4/3)\pi R^3$$

We assume the value of π is 3, and the value of the radius is 10.

We begin the solution (see Figure 10-6) by defining the constants and reserving space for the answer.

```
FOUR     DC   F'4'
THREE    DC   F'3'
RADIUS   DC   F'10'
PI       DC   H'3'
RESULT   DS   F
```

The processing instructions begin by finding the cube of RADIUS.

```
L    5,RADIUS
M    4,RADIUS
M    4,RADIUS
```

The value of RADIUS is loaded into register 5. We want to multiply the contents of register 5 by RADIUS. We are using a fullword RX-type instruction so we must address register 5 using an even–odd pair.

```
M    4,RADIUS
```

The square of RADIUS is now in register 5. We repeat this instruction to cube the radius. We now multiply* by PI

```
MH   5,PI
```

*The choice of halfword or fullword instructions is arbitrary in this example. Both are included to show the reader examples of each instruction.

```
*
* PROGRAM 4
* VOLUME OF A SPHERE
* VOLUME=(4/3)PI(R**3)
* BINARY INTEGER ARITHMETIC
* SOLUTION BY JUDY ADCOCK
*
         PRINT NOGEN
BEGIN    SAVE  (14,12)                   SAVE REGISTERS
         BALR  12,0                      LOAD BASE
         USING *,12                      ESTABLISH ADDRESSABILITY
         L     5,RADIUS                  LOAD RADIUS INTO R5
         M     4,RADIUS                  SQUARE RADIUS
         M     4,RADIUS                  CUBE RADIUS
         MH    5,PI                      MULTIPLY BY PI
         MH    5,FOUR                    MULTIPLY BY 4
         D     4,THREE                   DIVIDE BY 3
         ST    5,RESULT                  AND STORE RESULT
*
*        *
*        *     THE PROGRAM IS COMPLETE
*        *     THE RETURN STATEMENT
*        *     SIGNIFIES END-OF-JOB
*        *
         RETURN (14,12)                  RETURN
*
* DATA AREAS
*
FOUR     DC    H'4'                      DEFINE CONSTANT FOUR

THREE    DC    F'3'                      DEFINE CONSTANT THREE
RADIUS   DC    F'10'                     DEFINE RADIUS AS TEN
PI       DC    H'3'                      DEFINE PI
RESULT   DS    F                         RESERVE STORAGE FOR RESULT
         END   BEGIN
```

Figure 10-6 Program 4—solution.

and multiply by 4

```
MH 5,FOUR
```

Finally, we must divide the double word in registers 4 and 5 by 3.

```
D 4,THREE
```

The quotient is in register 5. We now store the quotient in RESULT.

```
ST 5,RESULT
```

BINARY COMPARE INSTRUCTIONS

The binary compare instructions operate on fullword and halfword *signed* binary integers. At least one operand must be in a register. The second operand may be in a register (RR-type compare) or in main storage (RX-type compare). The storage operand may be a halfword or a fullword. These instructions are algebraic—the result of the compare is affected by the sign of the operands.

RR-type Compare Instruction

The CR (Compare Register) instruction compares two fullword operands contained in registers. The operands are treated as signed binary integers. The sign of a binary number is determined by the high-order sign bit.

Assume register 4 contains $0000000A_{16}$ (+10) and register 8 contains 00000014_{16} (+20). The instruction

```
CR  4,8
```

compares the fullword integer in register 4 (first operand) with the fullword integer in register 8 (second operand). In this case we are comparing a positive 10 with a positive 20. The first operand is less than the second operand ($+10 < +20$). An indicator within the CPU is set to show that the first operand is less than the second operand.

We always must consider the sign of each operand. Assume that register 4 contains $0000000A_{16}$ (+10) and register 8 contains $FFFFFFEC_{16}$ (−20). When the instruction

```
CR  4,8
```

is executed, the indicator is set to show that the first operand is greater than the second operand ($+10 > -20$). However, when the instruction

```
CR  8,4
```

is executed, the indicator shows that the first operand is less than the second operand ($-20 < +10$).

Table 10-10 The CR Instruction

location	instruction	result
R3: 0000000A	CR 3,4	$Op_1 < Op_2$
R4: 0000003D	CR 4,3	$Op_1 > Op_2$
R5: FFFFFFF5	CR 4,4	$Op_1 = Op_2$
R6: FFFFFF60	CR 4,5	$Op_1 > Op_2$
	CR 5,4	$Op_1 < Op_2$
	CR 5,6	$Op_1 > Op_2$
	CR 6,5	$Op_1 < Op_2$

RX-type Compare Instruction

The C (Compare) instruction, described in Chapter 8, compares a fullword operand in a register (first operand) with a fullword operand in storage. The CH (Compare Halfword) instruction compares a fullword operand in the first operand register with a halfword operand in storage. The halfword operand is expanded to a fullword before the compare takes place.

The instruction

```
CH    10,HALF
```

compares the data in register 10 with the halfword of data at HALF. Assume that register 10 contains 00000064_{16} and HALF contains $000A_{16}$. The contents of HALF are expanded to $0000000A_{16}$ and compared to the contents of register 10. An indicator is set to show that the first operand is greater than the second operand ($+100 > +10$).

Now assume that HALF contains $FFF3_{16}$. The contents of HALF are expanded to $FFFFFFF3_{16}$. Remember, we expand a halfword by propagating the sign bit sixteen positions to the left. The compare is executed. The indicator is set to show that the first operand (+100) is greater than the second operand (−13).

Table 10-11 The C and CH Instructions

location	instruction	result
R3: 0000000E	CH 3,HALF	Op1 < Op2
R4: 000000A3	CH 5,HALF	Op1 < Op2
R5: FFFFFF60	CH 4,HALF	Op1 > Op2
FULL1: 0000001C	CH 5,FULL1	Op1 < Op2†
FULL2: FFFFFF60	C 4,FULL1	Op1 > Op2
HALF: 0013	C 5,FULL2	Op1 = Op2
	C 5,FULL1	Op1 < Op2

†The instruction expands the first 2 bytes of FULL1 to a fullword and then executes the compare.

The Logical Instructions

The CR, C, and CH instructions are arithmetic compare instructions. The sign of each operand affects the result of the compare. The CL (Compare Logical) and CLR (Compare Logical Register) instructions are logical compare instructions, performed on 32-bit operands. The sign of the operands does not affect the result of the compare.

The CLR and CL instructions compare fullwords of data. The first operand must be in a register, the second operand may be in a register (CLR) or in main storage (CL).

One last consideration—the RX-type compare instructions involve fullword and halfword operands. IBM S/360 computers require these operands to reside on integral storage boundaries. If halfword and fullword operands are not properly aligned, an error called a specification exception occurs.

Table 10-12 The CL and CLR Instructions

location	instruction	results
R3: 0000001C (+28)	CLR 3,4	$O_{P1} < O_{P2}$
R4: 0000003C (+60)	CLR 3,5	$O_{P1} < O_{P2}$
R5: FFFFFF60 (−160)	CLR 5,3	$O_{P1} > O_{P2}$
FULL1: 0000003F (+53)	CL 3,FULL1	$O_{P1} < O_{P2}$
FULL2: FFFFFFCF (−49)	CL 3,FULL2	$O_{P1} < O_{P2}$
	CL 5,FULL1	$O_{P1} > O_{P2}$
	CL 5,FULL2	$O_{P1} < O_{P2}$

IMPLICIT AND EXPLICIT ADDRESSING

Our programs to this point have used an addressing technique called implied or *implicit* addressing. For example, the statement

```
L  4,CON1
```

used in our solutions *implies* the use of register 12 to address CON1. Why register 12? We specify the use of register 12 in the USING statement

```
USING  *,12
```

There is another form of addressing called *explicit* addressing. We use explicit addressing when we state *explicitly* which base register the assembler is to use in an instruction. For example

```
L  4,0(0,3)
```

This instruction loads a fullword of data from the second operand location into register 4. The difference is the means by which we address the second operand location. The effective address of the second operand location is determined using register 3 as the base register, register 0 as the index register, and the number 000_{16} as the displacement (Figure 10-7).

In this example, the effective address of the second operand is determined solely by the contents of register 3. We could have used register 12, or any register other than register 0 as the base.

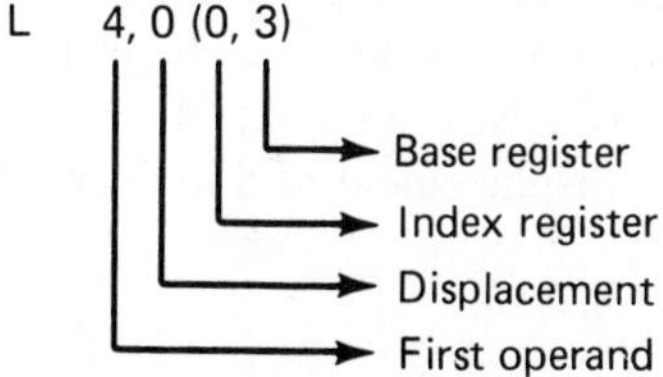

Figure 10-7 Explicit addressing.

Let's examine this new address concept using Program 2, now quite familiar to the reader, as an example. The solution to Program 2 using explicit addressing follows.

```
        .
        .
        .
        L    4,0(0,3)
        A    4,4(0,3)
        A    4,8(0,3)
        A    4,12(0,3)
        ST   4,16(0,3)
        .
        .
        .
CON1    DC   F'10'              RESIDES AT 008000
CON2    DC   F'20'              RESIDES AT 008004
CON3    DC   F'30'              RESIDES AT 008008
CON4    DC   F'40'              RESIDES AT 00800C
RESULT  DS   F                  RESIDES AT 008010
        .
        .
        .
```

The first instruction

```
L   4,0(0,3)
```

loads a fullword of data from the second operand location into register 4. Let's assume that CON1 resides at 008000_{16}. We want the effective address of the second operand to equal 008000_{16}. This means that register 3 must contain the address of CON1, the number 008000_{61}. Let's assume for a moment that register 3 *does* contain 008000_{16}. Then we load the fullword of data residing at 008000_{16} into register 4.

The next instruction

```
A   4,4(0,3)
```

is an add instruction. The computer is instructed to add the fullword of data residing at the second operand location to register 4. The effective address of the second operand is determined by the contents of register 3 (the base register) and the displacement 004_{16}. The index register, register 0, is ignored. The effective address of the second operand becomes 008004_{16}. The instruction adds the fullword of data residing at 008004_{16} (CON2) to register 4.

The next instruction specifies a displacement of 8 in decimal.

```
A   4,8(0,3)
```

An important point here! The symbolic explicit instruction is coded in decimal.

We use decimal operands to specify the base and index registers, and the displacement. The assembler generates the binary equivalents of these operands in the RX-form machine instruction.

The effective address of the second operand in the instruction shown above becomes 008008_{16}. Remember, we are assuming that register 3 contains 008000_{16}.

The last add instruction

```
A  4,12(0,3)
```

adds the fullword of data residing at $00800C_{16}$ to register 4. Again, the displacement is coded in decimal. The generated code and effective address are binary numbers, usually expressed using the hexadecimal notation.

The program now is complete. The sum developed in register 4 is stored in location 008010_{16} by the instruction

```
ST  4,16(0,3)
```

The logic of this solution is based upon the assumption that register 3 contains the address of CON1, in this instance the number 008000_{16}. We now must add the instruction which will always place the address of CON1 in register 3, regardless of the load address of the program.

The LA Instruction

The LA (Load Address) instruction is an RX-type instruction. The effective address of the second operand is placed in the first operand register. For example, the instruction

```
LA  3,CON1
```

places the *address* of CON1 in register 3. Another form of the same instruction

```
LA  3,0(0,8)
```

places the effective address of the second operand in register 3. We must know the contents of the base register, in orders to determine the effective address of the second operand. Let's assume that register 8 contains $00801C_{16}$. Then the instruction

```
LA  3,0(0,8)
```

places the number $00801C_{16}$ in register 3. Similarly, the instruction

```
LA  3,4(0,8)
```

places the number 008020_{16} in register 3.

Only a 24-bit address is used in this instruction. The first eight bits of the first operand register are cleared to zeros. Assume that register 8 contains

$8800801C_{16}$ (Figure 10-8). When the instruction

```
LA  3,0(0,8)
```

is executed, the contents of register 3 are changed to $0000801C_{16}$.

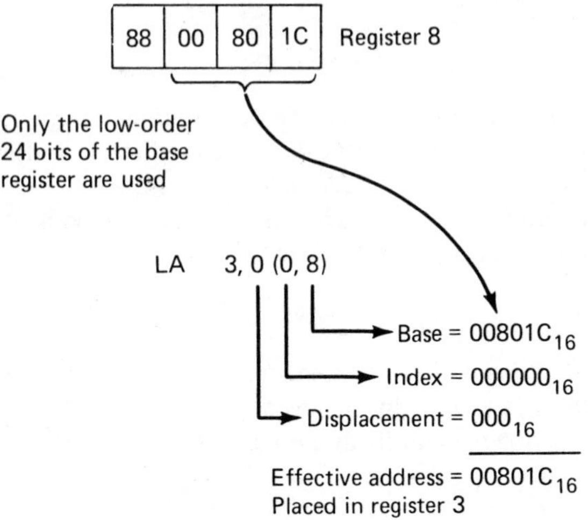

Figure 10-8 The LA instruction.

The LA instruction may be used to place a small number in a register. For example, the instruction

```
LA  12,4(0,0)
```

places the number four (000004_{16}) into register 12 (Figure 10-9). We might code this same instruction in a different way,

```
LA  12,4
```

In this example, we have omitted the base and index registers. The assembler must, however, provide for a base and index register in the RX-form of the generated instruction. The assembler uses register 0 as both base and index register. Effectively then, the address of the second operand becomes 000004_{16}.

The LA instruction may also be used to increment a register (Figure 10-10). Consider the instruction

```
LA  3,7(0,3)
```

The address of the second operand is placed in the first operand register. Assume register 3 contains $00703D_{16}$. The effective address of the second operand

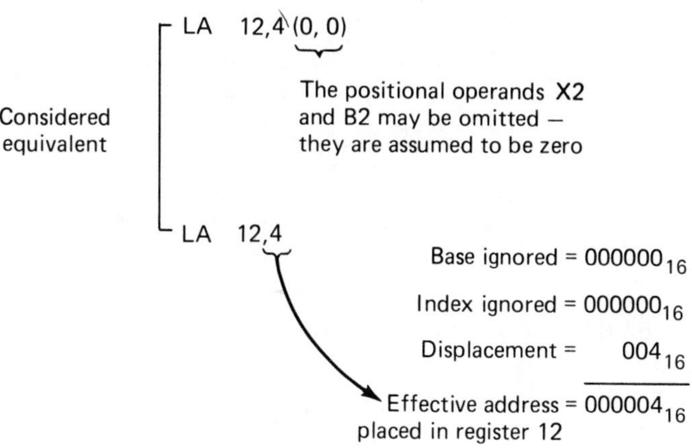

Figure 10-9 Use of the LA instruction.

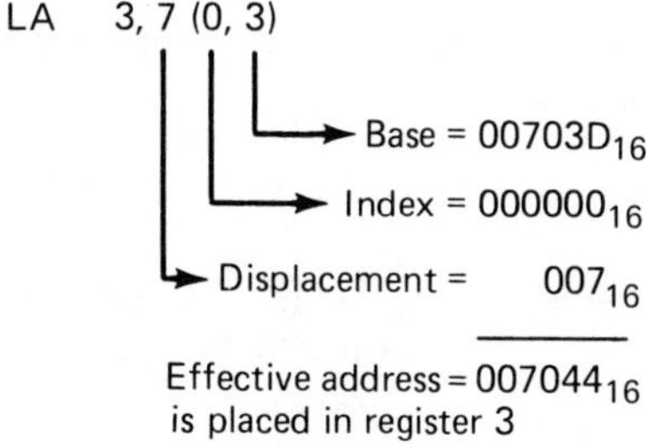

Figure 10-10 Use of the LA instruction to increment a register.

becomes 007044_{16}. This number is placed in the 24 low-order bits of register 3. The 8 high-order bits are cleared to zero. We have incremented register 3 by the value of the displacement. By how much does the instruction

```
LA 3,12(0,3)
```

increment register 3?

The LA instruction is one of the more versatile instructions within the S/370 instruction set. We see examples of the use of the instruction in Table 10-13.

Let's see how the LA instruction may be used to help solve Program 2 using explicit addressing. The solution developed on page 256 is based on the

Table 10-13 Use of the LA Instruction

location	instruction	first operand register after execution
R3: 00003000	LA 7,0(0,3)	R7: 00003000
R4: 00004000	LA 6,0(3,4)	R6: 00007000
R5: FF005000	LA 7,4(5,6)	R7: 0000D004
R6: 80008000	LA 7,0	R7: 00000000
R7: 0000FFFF	LA 6,4	R6: 00000004
	LA 6,6(6)	R6: 00008006

assumption that register 3 contains the address of CON1. We now can use the instruction

```
LA   3,CON1
```

to place the address of CON1 in register 3. The complete solution to the program is given in Figure 10-11.

Let's assume that the program is loaded at location 009100_{16}. We now can discuss the solution referring to the actual addresses involved.

The first statements perform the required housekeeping functions and establish addressability. The instruction

```
LA   3,CON1
```

places the address of CON1 (009124_{16}) in register 3. Let's pause for a moment and see just how this is accomplished. The LA instruction generates the machine code

```
4130C01E
```

The effective address of the second operand takes the sum of the contents of register 12 (the base register), and the displacement $01E_{16}$. The contents of register 0 (the index register) are ignored. Register 12 contains 00009106_{16}. The BALR instruction loaded this number. The effective address of the second operand becomes 009124_{16}(009106_{16} + $01E_{16}$)—the address of CON1! This address is placed in register 3.

The next instruction

```
L   4,0(0,3)
```

loads the fullword at 009124_{16} into register 4. The reader should verify that the effective address of the second operand is indeed 009124_{16}, remembering that register 3 contains 00009124_{16}.

```
                                                                                                    PAGE    1
                        Address assuming program is loaded at 009100₁₆
  LOC  OBJECT CODE     ADDR1 ADDR2  STMT   SOURCE STATEMENT                                     F04MAR74   6/17/76

                                       1 *
                                       2 * PROGRAM 2
                                       3 * SUM OF FOUR BINARY CONSTANTS
                                       4 * USING EXPLICIT ADDRESSING
                                       5 *
                                       6            PRINT  NOGEN
000000                                 7            START
                       009100          8 FIRST      SAVE   (14,12)              SAVE REGISTERS
000004 05C0            009104         11            BALR   12,0                 LOAD BASE
000006                                12            USING  *,12                 ADDRESSABILITY
000006 4130 C01E       009106 00024   13            LA     3,CON1               LOAD ADDRESS CON1 INTO R3
00000A 5840 3000       00910A 00000   14            L      4,0(0,3)             LOAD FIRST CONSTANT
00000E 5A40 3004       00910E 00004   15            A      4,4(0,3)             ADD SECOND CONSTANT
000012 5A40 3008       009112 00008   16            A      4,8(0,3)             ADD THIRD CONSTANT
000016 5A40 300C       009116 0000C   17            A      4,12(0,3)            ADD LAST CONSTANT
00001A 5040 3010       00911A 00010   18            ST     4,16(0,3)            STORE RESULT
                                      19            RETURN (14,12)              AND RETURN
                                      22 *
                                      23 * DATA AREAS
                                      24 *
000024 0000000A        009124         25 CON1       DC     F'10'                * DEFINE
000028 00000014        009128         26 CON2       DC     F'20'                * FOUR
00002C 0000001E        00912C         27 CON3       DC     F'30'                * FULLWORD
000030 00000028        009130         28 CON4       DC     F'40'                * CONSTANTS
000034                 009134         29 RESULT     DS     F
000000                                30            END    FIRST
```

Figure 10-11 Program 2—explicit addressing.

Now we continue with the program until the contents of the remaining three constants have been added to register 4. The result is then stored using the instruction

```
ST 4,16(0,3)
```

The effective address of the second operand becomes 009134_{16}, the address of RESULT. The program is complete and the RETURN statement terminates processing.

We have introduced explicit addressing at this point to provide a second means of addressing. The choice of addressing technique—implied or explicit—is dependent upon the program involved. The beginning programmer feels more comfortable with implied addressing. The sophisticated programmer often prefers explicit addressing—a technique we will examine further in Chapter 12.

PROBLEMS

10.1 The contents of five consecutive storage locations and two registers are given below. Give the contents of the receiving location after the execution of each of the following instructions.

location	contents	instruction
HALF1	0003	LH 3,HALF1
HALF2	703C	LH 4,HALF2
HALF3	C098	LH 3,HALF3
FULL1	0234CD09	LH 3,FULL1
FULL2	807E0001	L 3,FULL1
register 3	0000709E	LH 4,FULL1
register 4	0076805F	ST 3,FULL2
		ST 4,FULL1
		STH 4,HALF2
		LH 4,FULL1 + 4
		LM 3,4,HALF1
		LM 3,4,FULL1
		STM 3,4,FULL1

10.2 The contents of five storage locations and two registers are given below. Give the contents of the first operand location after each of the following instructions is executed.

location	contents	instruction
HALFA	0034	AH 6,HALFA
HALFB	80EC	AH 8,HALFB
FULLC	70EC908D	AH 6,FULLC

location	contents	instruction
FULLD	C0980001	A 6,FULLC
FULLE	FFFFFFFA	AR 6,8
register 6	00008093	AR 8,8
register 8	80930000	AR 8,6
		SH 6,HALFA
		SH 6,HALFB
		SH 8,HALFA
		SH 8,HALFB
		S 6,FULLE
		S 6,HALFA
		S 6,FULLD
		SR 6,8
		SR 6,6
		SR 8,6

10.3 Binary arithmetic instructions operate on both fullword and halfword operands, yet the instructions do not contain a length attribute. Explain why.

10.4 The contents of four storage locations and four registers are given below. Give the contents of the first operand location after each of the following instructions is executed.

location	contents	instruction
HALFPOS	000A	MH 3,HALFPOS
HALFNEG	FF9C	MH 3,HALFNEG
FULLPOS	0000001A	MH 5,HALFPOS
FULLNEG	FFFFFFEC	MH 5,HALFNEG
register 2	00000000	M 2,FULLPOS
register 3	00000064	M 2,FULLNEG
register 4	FFFFFFFF	M 4,FULLPOS
register 5	FFFFFF9C	M 4,FULLNEG
		D 2,FULLPOS
		D 3,FULLPOS
		D 4,FULLNEG
		MR 3,3
		MR 3,5
		DR 5,3

10.5 Write a program to find the sum of the numbers from 1–5. Use binary constants and the binary arithmetic instructions. Do not code a loop. Use repetitive add instructions.

10.6 Write a program to calculate the value of the following expression

$$X = \frac{(A + B) - C}{(D + E)}$$

Use the following constants in your program.

```
A  DC  F'123'
B  DC  F'1'
C  DC  F'3'
D  DC  H'2'
E  DC  H'3'
```

10.7 The contents of four storage locations and two registers are given below. Give the result of the compare for each of the following instructions.

location	contents	instruction
HALFA	000A	CH 3,HALFA
HALFB	FFF7	CH 4,HALFA
FULLA	00000010	CH 3,HALFB
FULLB	FFFFFFF7	CH 4,HALFB
register 3	00000010	CH 3,FULLA
register 4	FFFFFFFA	CH 4,FULLB
		C 3,FULLA
		C 4,FULLB
		CR 3,4
		CR 4,3

10.8 The logical compare instructions do not consider the sign of the operands involved. Using the data in Problem 10.7, give the result of each of the following compares.

a. CL 3,FULLA
b. CL 4,FULLA
c. CL 3,FULLB
d. CL 4,FULLB
e. CLR 3,4
f. CLR 4,3

10.9 Write a program to find the value of any constant NUM raised to a power EXP. Develop your own specifications for the size of NUM and EXP. What considerations are critical as you design your input format and set up work areas?

10.10 The following program segment multiplies the fullword in register 5 by 1.

```
         .
         .
         .
         M    4,ONE
         .
         .
         .
ONE      DC   F'1'
```

If register 4 contains $0000000A_{16}$ and register 5 contains $0000000B_{16}$, what will be in register 4 and in register 5 after execution of the multiply instruction? What will be in register 4 and register 5 if register 5 contains $FFFFFFF5_{16}$? How can multiplying the contents of an odd register by 1 help prepare for binary division, and what are the advantages over clearing the even register to zero using the SR instruction?

10.11 Binary arithmetic performs operations on integers and provides no facilities for placing decimal (or should we say binary) points and rounding. This becomes the programmer's responsibility. When we round a number we add 5 to the last digit we wish to drop and divide by the appropriate power of ten. Develop the instructions to round the following numbers as shown.

a. BIN1 DC F'123.456' round to one decimal place
b. BIN2 DC F'123.456' round to two decimal places
c. BIN3 DC F'1.23456' round to three decimal places

Note: Although the decimal point is shown in the constant, the constants are assembled as integers.

10.12 Write a program to determine if the fullword at RESULT is odd or even. If the data is odd, move the fullword to an area of storage called ODD; if the data is even, move the fullword to EVEN.

10.13 Solve any of the variations of Program 6 (Appendix C) using binary arithmetic.

10.14 Program 5 asks us to find the sum of a series of numbers. The limit of the series may be entered as data on a punched card. Now let's use this number in another way. Find the *factorial* value of the number punched in columns 1–4. The factorial value of a number is the number itself multiplied by the number one less than itself, and then multiplied by the number two less than itself, and so on, until we multiply the number by 1. For example, 5 factorial (expressed as 5!) is represented as

$$5! = 5 \times 4 \times 3 \times 2 \times 1$$

10.15 The contents of five registers are shown here. Give the contents of the first operand register after each of the following instructions is executed.

register	contents	instruction
register 3	00009030	LA 3,0(0,3)
register 4	0000803C	LA 3,0(4,3)
register 5	FF001030	LA 3,5(4,3)
register 6	00000000	LA 4,0(0,5)
register 7	00FF9000	LA 4,0(5,5)
		LA 5,1(0,5)
		LA 5,1(5,5)
		LA 5,5(5,5)
		LA 5,0
		LA 5,4
		LA 6,4(6)
		LA 6,7(6)

Hint! Only the low-order 24 bits of the base and index register are used in determining effective addresses.

10.16 Assume that register 3 contains 00009040_{16}. What will be in register 3 after each of the following instructions is executed? Give a reason for your answer.

a. LA 3,1(0,3)
b. LA 3,1(,3)
c. LA 3,1(3)

10.17 Give the generated code for each of the following symbolic instructions.

1. AH 3,0(0,4)
2. CLI 10(9),X'FF'
3. A 4,10(3,9)
4. ST 5,20(6,8)
5. AP 0(2,12),2(4,12)
6. AP 20(12,3),42(12,4)

10.18 Develop the solution to Program 3 (using binary arithmetic) using explicit addressing.

Hint! You must use the LA instruction to load the base register you select in your explicit instructions. *Question?* Do you need a BALR/USING pair and why?

11

Sequence Control

We have learned that there are two types of branching instructions—conditional and unconditional. We also have learned that the branching instructions direct the order in which the instructions within a program are executed. We have developed the concept of a loop—executing a series of instructions over and over until some condition is reached. We have learned that we need to control the execution of a loop. We need a counter to keep track of the number of times we executed the loop, a means of incrementing the counter, a means of testing the counter, and a branch instruction to return us to the loop, or to exit from the loop.

We know the assembly language instructions to control branching; the compare instructions, the conditional branching instructions, and the unconditional branching instructions. The branching instructions (B, BE, BH, BL) are all different forms of the same machine instruction. This chapter examines these instructions in more detail, and then introduces four new instructions used in controlling the sequence of instruction execution.

THE PROGRAM STATUS WORD

Certain assembly instructions cause an indicator in the CPU to be set. When a compare instruction is executed, this indicator is set to show the result of the compare. The operands may be equal, the first operand may be greater than the second operand, or the first operand may be less than the second operand.

The arithmetic instructions set this indicator to show whether the result of an arithmetic operation is equal to zero, greater than zero, or less than zero. The indicator also is set if an overflow occurs.

The indicator we reference is part of a special double word called the PSW (Program Status Word). The PSW, residing in the control section of the CPU, reflects the status of the computer and controls program execution. There are many fields within the PSW (Figure 11-1). We are only interested in one field—the condition code. The condition code is a 2-bit field (bits 34–35) which may have one of four possible settings: 00_2, 01_2, 10_2, 11_2.

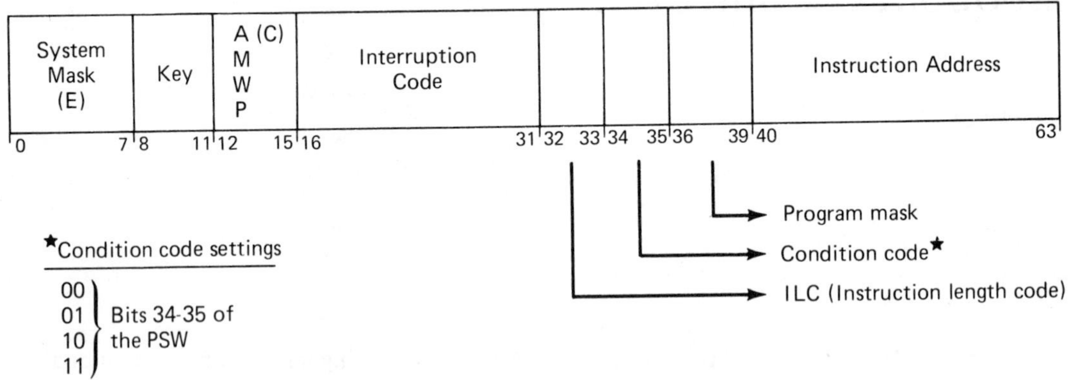

Figure 11-1 The program status word.

When an arithmetic or compare instruction is executed, the result of the operation is recorded in the PSW. Where in the PSW? In the condition code—bits 34–35. For example, let's assume that register 3 contains $0000000A_{16}$ and register 4 contains $0000100C_{16}$. When the instruction

```
AR   3,4
```

is executed, the result (00001016_{16}) is placed in register 3. The condition code is set to 10_2 to show the result of the add operation is positive. The condition code settings for the arithmetic and compare instructions are given in Table 11-1.

Let's consider a compare instruction. Register 3 contains $FFFFFFFE_{16}$ and FULL contains $0000000C_{16}$. The instruction

```
C   3,FULL
```

compares the negative number $FFFFFFFE_{16}$ with the positive number

Table 11-1 Condition Code Settings

instruction	condition code setting			
	00_2	01_2	10_2	11_2
ADD H/F (AR,A,AH)	ZERO	< ZERO	> ZERO	OVERFLOW
SUBTRACT H/F (SR,S,SH)	ZERO	< ZERO	> ZERO	OVERFLOW
ADD DECIMAL (AP)	ZERO	< ZERO	> ZERO	OVERFLOW
SUBTRACT DECIMAL (SP)	ZERO	< ZERO	> ZERO	OVERFLOW
COMPARE H/F (CR,C,CH) A:B	EQUAL	A LOW	A HIGH	
COMPARE DECIMAL (CP) A:B	EQUAL	A LOW	A HIGH	

$0000000C_{16}$. The first operand is less than the second operand. The condition code is set to 01_2.

A conditional branch instruction often follows an arithmetic or compare instruction. The branch instruction determines the next instruction to be executed, based upon the result of the previous operation. For example

```
C    3,FULL
BH   HIGHRT
```

compares the contents of two fullwords. If the contents of register 3 are greater than the contents of FULL, a branch to HIGHRT is effected.

The C instruction sets the condition code in the PSW. The BH instruction is a conditional branch to HIGHRT—*only* if the condition code is 10_2, The conditional branch instructions are tied to the value in the condition code. The value of the condition code determines whether or not a branch occurs. We might recode the above example as

```
C    3,FULL
BC   cc = 10,HIGHRT
```

where the mnemonic BC stands for Branch on Condition. The notation, $cc = 10_2$ is not valid in assembly language, but it clarifies the fact that the conditional branch instruction must relate to the value of the condition code. More on this later.

THE CONDITIONAL INSTRUCTIONS

The branching instructions BH, BL, BE, and B are all forms of one conditional branching instruction, the BC (Branch on Condition) instruction. The BC instruction tests the condition code in the PSW. The value of the condition code determines whether a branch occurs.

We cannot, however, use the notation $cc = 01_2$ or $cc = 11_2$ in the BC instruction. The instruction

```
BC   cc = 10,HIGHRT
```

is conceptually correct—we want to branch to HIGHRT if the value in the condition code is 10_2—but the assembly language does not provide for this notation. Instead, we use a 4-bit binary code to represent the desired condition.

desired condition	mask: binary code	mask: decimal value
cc = 00_2	1000	8
cc = 01_2	0100	4
cc = 10_2	0010	2
cc = 11_2	0001	1

We refer to the binary code as a mask. There is no relation between the value of the condition code and the corresponding mask code.

The hypothetical instruction

```
BC   cc = 10,HIGHRT
```

implies that we wish to branch to HIGHRT if the condition code equals 10_2. Let's use the binary mask in the same instruction.

```
BC   0010,HIGHRT
```

This looks more like a valid assembly instruction. Almost—but not quite! The *decimal* equivalent of the *binary* mask is used in the symbolic instruction.

```
BC   2,HIGHRT
```

The decimal value 2 is associated with the binary mask 0010_2, and a mask of 0010_2 is associated with a condition code setting of 10_2.

This certainly appears to be a roundabout way of coding an instruction. The programmer must remember which mask is associated with which condition code setting. There is, however, a reason for this approach which will soon become apparent.

Format of the BC and BCR Instructions

There are two conditional branching instructions available to the assembly language programmer. The RX form of the instruction supplies the branch address as the effective address of the second operand (BC—Branch on Condition). The RR form of the instruction supplies the branch address in a register (BCR—Branch on Condition Register). In both instructions, the first operand represents a 4-bit binary mask used to test the condition code. The format of the BC and BCR instructions is given in Figure 11-2.

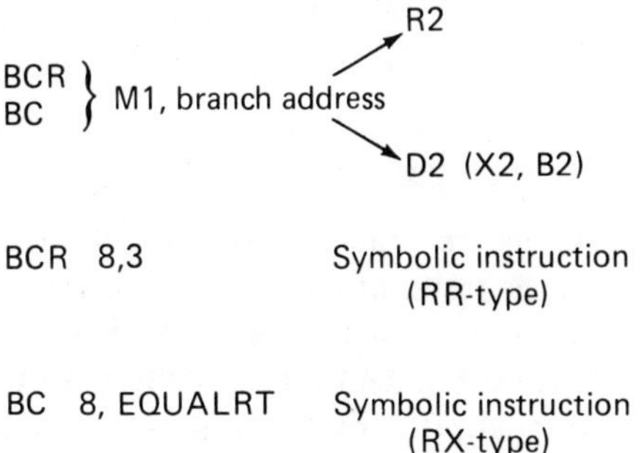

Figure 11-2 Format of the BC and BCR instructions.

Testing Multiple Conditions

Figure 11-3 gives a segment of a program flowchart. The result of the add operations determines the next instruction executed. If the result is positive, the

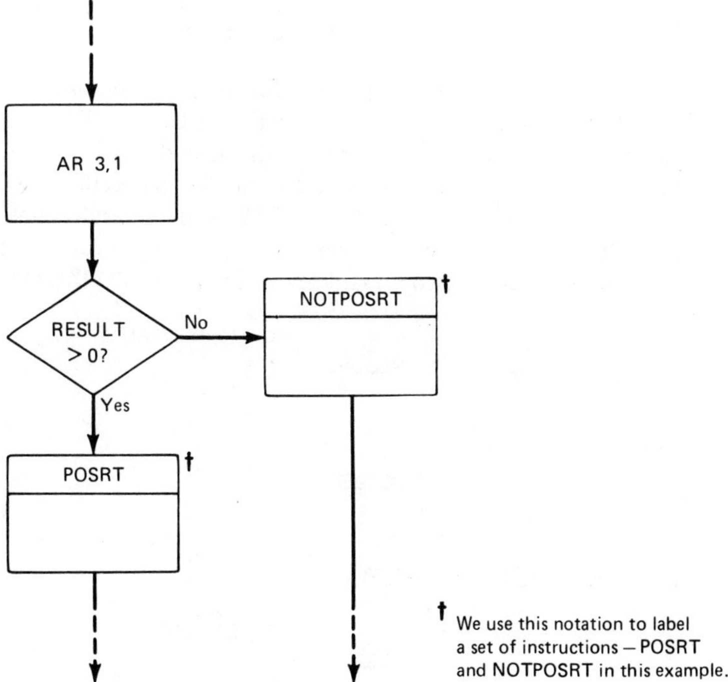

Figure 11-3 Flowchart showing a conditional branch.

instruction at POSRT is executed. If the result is not positive, the instruction at NOTPOSRT is executed. We might code this as

```
         AR   3,1
         BC   2,POSRT
         .
         .
         .
```

The decimal mask of 2 tells us we branch if the condition code is 10_2. The condition code is set to 10_2 if the result of the operation is greater than zero. On the other hand, we could code a branch to NOTPOSRT if the result is not greater than zero. This means we branch to NOTPOSRT if the condition code following the add operation is 00_2, 01_2, or 11_2. But how do we code this? The hypothetical instruction

```
BC   8,4, or 1,NOTPOSRT
```

clearly states what we want. We branch to NOTPOSRT using a mask of 8, 4 or 1. We branch to NOTPOSRT if the condition code is 00_2, 01_2 or 11_2. Logically correct—but the code is not valid assembly programming.

The correct notation is

```
         BC   13,NOTPOSRT
```

We have *added* the three mask values for the three condition codes. We branch to NOTPOSRT on a condition code setting of 00_2 (mask is 8), a condition code setting of 01_2 (mask is 4), and on a condition code setting of 11_2 (mask is 1). In other words, we branch if the result of the AR instruction is *not* postive.

Suppose we wish to branch to POSZERO if the result is positive or zero, and to NEGOFLO if the result is negative or an overflow occurs. We can code these instructions in one of two ways. We can branch to POSZERO

```
         BC   10,POSZERO
NEGOFLO  .
         .
         .
         .
POSZERO  .
         .
         .
```

or we can branch to NEGOFLO.

```
         BC   5,NEGOFLO
POSZERO  .
         .
         .
         .
         .
```

```
NEGOFLO  .
         .
         .
         .
         .
```

In both cases, if the branch is not taken, we continue executing the instructions in the order coded. We say that we *fall through* to the next instruction. In the first example, we either branch to POSZERO or fall through to NEGOFLO. In the second example, we either branch to NEGOFLO or fall through to POSZERO.

It is possible that the alternative routine does not immediately follow the BC instruction. In this case, we might code an unconditional branch instruction

```
         BC   10,POSZERO
         B    NEGOFLO
         .
         .
         .
         .
POSZERO  .
         .
         .
NEGOFLO  .
         .
         .
```

The unconditional branch instruction

```
         B    NEGOFLO
```

is a special form of the BC instruction. We call the B operation an *extended mnemonic*. We could code the unconditional branch instruction as

```
         BC   15,NEGOFLO
```

Can you see why a mask of 15 effects an unconditional branch? We are saying that no matter what the value of the condition code—00_2, 01_2, 10_2, 11_2 (mask values of 8, 4, 2, 1 respectively) we will branch to NEGOFLO.

There is another form of the BC instruction that is so commonly used it deserves discussion here. The instruction

```
         BC   0,FIRSTRT
NEXTRT   .
         .
         .
         .
```

does *not* effect a branch. A mask of zero says we will not branch regardless of the value of the condition code. We refer to this type of a statement as a NOP (No OPeration) instruction. The extended mnemonic for the RX form of the NOP instruction is

```
          NOP   FIRSTRT
NEXTRT    .
          .
          .
          .
```

A branch does not occur in either of the two preceding examples. The next instruction executed is the instruction labeled NEXTRT.

The Extended Mnemonics

The instructions B, BH, BL, BE and NOP are called extended mnemonics. Extended mnemonics are different forms of the BC or BCR instructions. We use extended mnemonics for clarity. It is much easier to understand the instruction

```
          BE    RTA
```

than the instruction

```
          BC    8,RTA
```

The use of the BC instruction requires the programmer to remember which mask is associated with which condition code and just what that condition code indicates in a given situation. The problem becomes more complex when we use multiple conditions. For example

```
          BC    13,RTB
```

In this example we branch if the result is zero, negative, or an overflow occurs. In other words, if the result is not positive. The use of the extended mnemonic BNP (Branch Not Positive) clarifies this code

```
          BNP   RTB
```

All the extended mnemonics generate either a BC or BCR instruction (Figure 11-4). The binary value of the decimal mask appears in bits 8–11 of the generated instruction. The second operand supplies the branch address. The RR form of the instruction gives the branch address in a register (BCR instruction). The RX form of the instruction derives the branch address from the sum of the base register, index register, and displacement (BC instruction).

We have not discussed all the extended mnemonics available. The reader should review the instructions given in Table 11-2 and use them as he sees fit. We will use both the extended mnemonics and the BC instructions in our programming examples.

A Sample Program

Let's see how the BC instruction is used in an assembly program. Figure 11-5 gives the solution to Program 5 using the BC instruction. We have replaced the

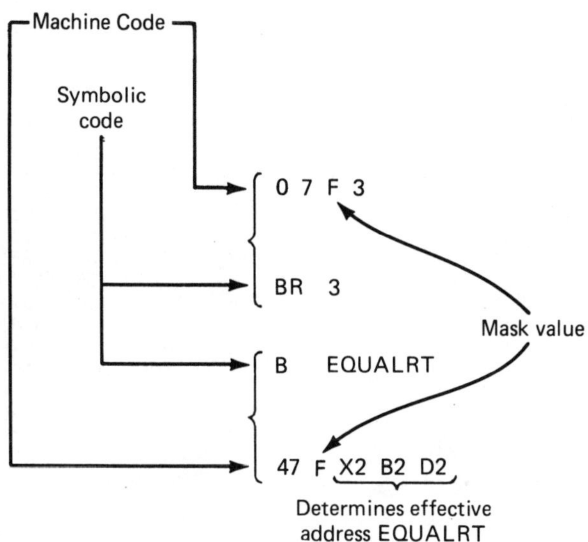

Figure 11-4 The extended mnemonics—generated code.

Table 11-2 The Extended Mnemonics

	extended code	machine instruction	meaning
general	B	BC 15,	BRANCH UNCONDITIONALLY
↓	BR	BCR 15,	BRANCH UNCONDITIONALLY (RR)
	NOP	BC 0,	NO OPERATION
	NOPR	BCR 0,	NO OPERATION (RR)
after	BH	BC 2,	BRANCH A HIGH
compare	BL	BC 4,	BRANCH A LOW
instructions	BE	BC 8,	BRANCH A EQUAL B
↓	BNH	BC 13,	BRANCH A NOT HIGH
	BNL	BC 11,	BRANCH A NOT LOW
	BNE	BC 7,	BRANCH A NOT EQUAL
after	BO	BC 1,	BRANCH ON OVERFLOW
arithmetic	BP	BC 2,	BRANCH POSITIVE
instructions	BM	BC 4,	BRANCH MINUS
↓	BZ	BC 8,	BRANCH ZERO
	BNP	BC 13,	BRANCH NOT PLUS
	BNM	BC 11,	BRANCH NOT MINUS
	BNZ	BC 7,	BRANCH NOT ZERO

BE and B instructions used in previous examples with the BC instruction. The machine instructions generated from the BE and BC 8, instructions are identical! Bits 8–11 of the generated instruction contain the *same* binary mask. The only difference between the instruction

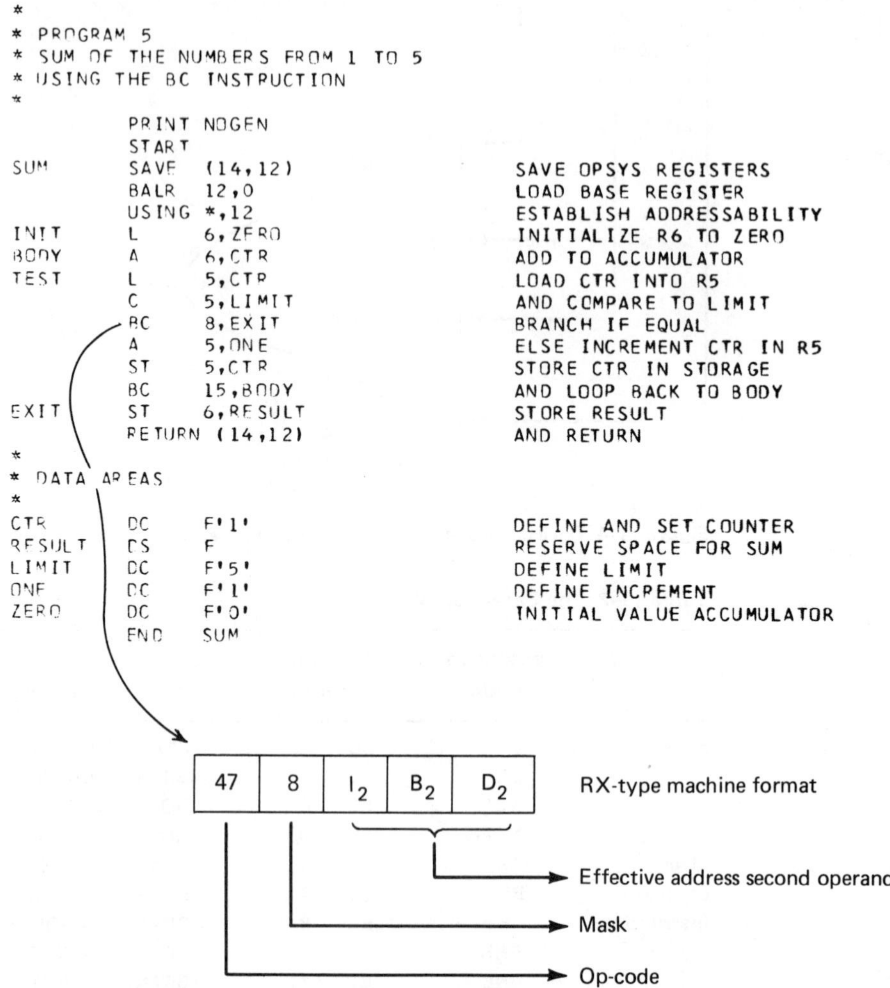

```
*
* PROGRAM 5
* SUM OF THE NUMBERS FROM 1 TO 5
* USING THE BC INSTRUCTION
*
         PRINT NOGEN
         START
SUM      SAVE  (14,12)           SAVE OPSYS REGISTERS
         BALR  12,0              LOAD BASE REGISTER
         USING *,12              ESTABLISH ADDRESSABILITY
INIT     L     6,ZERO            INITIALIZE R6 TO ZERO
BODY     A     6,CTR             ADD TO ACCUMULATOR
TEST     L     5,CTR             LOAD CTR INTO R5
         C     5,LIMIT           AND COMPARE TO LIMIT
         BC    8,EXIT            BRANCH IF EQUAL
         A     5,ONE             ELSE INCREMENT CTR IN R5
         ST    5,CTR             STORE CTR IN STORAGE
         BC    15,BODY           AND LOOP BACK TO BODY
EXIT     ST    6,RESULT          STORE RESULT
         RETURN (14,12)          AND RETURN
*
* DATA AREAS
*
CTR      DC    F'1'              DEFINE AND SET COUNTER
RESULT   DS    F                 RESERVE SPACE FOR SUM
LIMIT    DC    F'5'              DEFINE LIMIT
ONE      DC    F'1'              DEFINE INCREMENT
ZERO     DC    F'0'              INITIAL VALUE ACCUMULATOR
         END   SUM
```


Figure 11-5 Program 5—using the BC instruction.

BE EXIT

and the instruction

BC 8,EXIT

is the notation used in the *symbolic* statements. The generated machine instructions are the same.

Program 5 has been used to illustrate the basic principles involved in looping. All program loops contain four basic phases—the initialization phase, the body of the loop, the testing phase, and the exit phase. We see these four components illustrated in Figure 11-6.

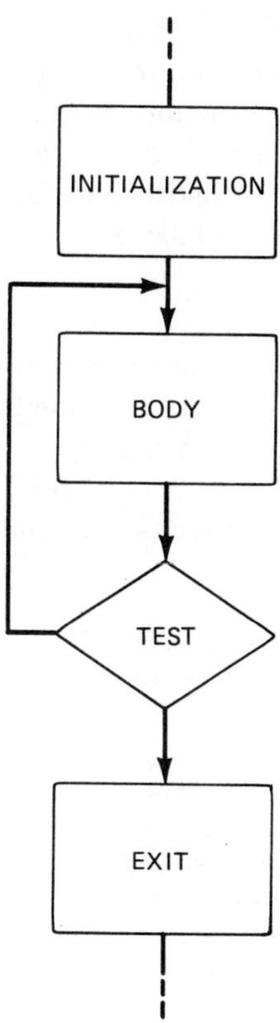

Figure 11-6 Four components of the loop.

The programmer must control the number of times he (or she) executes the instructions comprising the body of the loop. He usually establishes a counter, increments the counter each time he executes the loop, and tests the counter against a limit to determine when he should exit from the loop. Most loops involve this type of control—an instruction which tests the counter against a limit, a conditional branch instruction, and a means of incrementing or changing the counter. In our solution to Program 5, the counter is in the area of storage called CTR. The limit is the number five. We increment CTR each time we execute the loop until the value in CTR equals the value of the limit.

Three separate instructions are required to control the loop! Obviously, a more efficient method is the use of a single instruction which accomplishes the same objectives—testing, incrementing, and branching.

LOOP CONTROL INSTRUCTIONS

There are two types of loop control instructions (which increment or decrement, test *and* branch in a single operation). The BXH (Branch on indeX High) and BXLE (Branch on indeX Low or Equal) instructions increment a counter by a value contained in a register, test the counter against a specified limit, and branch accordingly. The BCT (Branch on Count) and BCTR (Branch on Count Register) instructions decrement a register by 1, and branch if the result is non-zero. The BXLE and BXH instructions give us more flexibility. We can increment *or* decrement by any amount, and compare against any limit. The BCT and BCTR instructions are easier to understand, but we can only alter the indicator by 1 and compare against the number zero.

The BCT and BCTR Instructions

The BCT and BCTR instructions follow the same general pattern. The contents of the first operand register are decremented by 1. The number in the first operand register is then examined. If the number in the first operand register (as decremented) is non-zero, a branch to the second operand address is effected. If the number in the first operand register (as decremented) is zero, branching does not occur.

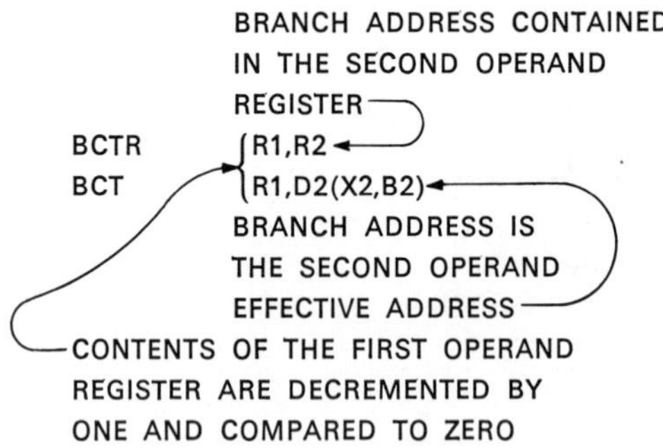
BRANCH ADDRESS CONTAINED IN THE SECOND OPERAND REGISTER
BCTR R1,R2
BCT R1,D2(X2,B2)
BRANCH ADDRESS IS THE SECOND OPERAND EFFECTIVE ADDRESS
CONTENTS OF THE FIRST OPERAND REGISTER ARE DECREMENTED BY ONE AND COMPARED TO ZERO

The BCT and BCTR instructions differ in the way the branch address is provided. The BCTR (RR-form) instruction branches to the *address* contained in the second operand register. The BCT (RX-form) instruction specifies the branch address in terms of a base register, index register, and displacement. For example, the instructions

```
LA    3,FIRSTRT
BCTR  4,3
```

serve the same purpose as the instruction

```
BCT   4,FIRSTRT
```

In the first example, the address of the desired routine is placed in register 3 and the RR-form of the instruction is coded. In the second example, the effective address of FIRSTRT (the second operand) becomes the branch address.

Does a branch occur when either of the above instructions is executed? To determine if a branch occurs, we must know the contents of the first operand register. Assume register 4 contains $0000000A_{16}$. When the instruction

```
BCT   4,FIRSTRT
```

is executed, the contents of register 4 are first decremented by 1. The contents of register 4 are changed from $0000000A_{16}$ to 00000009_{16}. This number, as decremented, is not equal to zero. A branch to FIRSTRT is effected. The same result is obtained using the LA and BCTR instructions.

If, however, register 4 contains 00000001_{16}, the results are quite different. When we execute the BCT instruction, the contents of register 4 are decremented to 00000000_{16}. The result in the first operand register is zero. A branch does not occur and the next sequential instruction is executed.

Table 11-3 gives additional examples of the BCT and BCTR instructions. As you examine these instructions, remember that when you decrement a negative number the result is still negative.

Table 11-3 Examples of the BCT and BCTR Instructions

location	instruction		result
R3: 0000000A	BCTR	3,7	BRANCH TO INSTRUCTION AT $00900C_{16}$
R4: 00000001	BCTR	4,7	NO BRANCH
R5: 00000000	BCTR	5,7	BRANCH TO INSTRUCTION AT $00900C_{16}$
R6: FFFFFFFF	BCT	3,0(0,7)	BRANCH TO INSTRUCTION AT $00900C_{16}$
R7: 0000900C	BCT	6,4(4,7)	BRANCH TO INSTRUCTION AT 009011_{16}
	BCT	6,NEXTRT	BRANCH TO INSTRUCTION AT NEXTRT

A Sample Program

Let's see how the BCT instruction may be used to solve Program 5. We should be able to combine three instructions into a single BCT instruction. The code

```
TEST  C   5,LIMIT
      BE  EXIT
      A   5,ONE
      B   BODY
```

will be replaced by the instruction

```
TEST  BCT  11,BODY
```

We must, of course, properly initialize register 11 in the initialization phase of our loop.

Figure 11-7 gives the solution to Program 5 using the BCT instruction. We are using register 5 as the counter in this example. We must initialize register 5. The instruction

```
LA  5,5
```

places the number 00000005_{16} in register 5. We initialize register 6 to zero using the instruction

```
SR  6,6
```

```
*
* PROGRAM 5
* SUM OF THE NUMBERS FROM 1 TO 5
* USING THE BCT INSTRUCTION
*
         PRINT  NOGEN
         START
SUM      SAVE   (14,12)            SAVE REGISTERS
         BALR   12,0               LOAD BASE
         USING  *,12               ESTABLISH ADDRESSABILITY
INIT     LA     5,5                LOAD LIMIT INTO R1 OPERAND
         SR     6,6                CLEAR ACCUMULATOR
BODY     AR     6,5                INCREMENT ACCUMULATOR
TEST     BCT    5,BODY             DECREMENT
*                                  TEST AND BRANCH IF
*                                  REGISTER 5 IS NON-ZERO
EXIT     ST     6,RESULT           ELSE STORE SUM
         RETURN (14,12)            AND RETURN
*
* DATA AREAS
*
RESULT   DS     F                  RESERVE SPACE FOR RESULT
         END    SUM
```

Figure 11-7 Program 5—solution using the BCT instruction.

The body of the loop,

```
BODY AR 6,5
```

adds the contents of register 5 to register 6. The next instruction is the BCT instruction. The instruction

```
TEST BCT 5,BODY
```

decrements register 5 by 1. If the result is non-zero, a branch to BODY is effected. Otherwise, we fall through to the code at EXIT. We add to register 6 each time we execute the loop. First the number five, then the number four until, finally, we add the number one. At this point, register 5 contains 00000001_{16}. When we execute the BCT instruction, we decrement register 5. The result is zero and we do not branch. We exit from the loop. We store the result from register 6 and the program is complete.

It is sometimes difficult for the student to understand all the operations accomplished by a single instruction. But once the BCT and BCTR instructions are understood, they become powerful and effective means of controlling the number of times the code comprising a loop is executed.

The BXH and BXLE Instructions

The BXH and BXLE instructions, like the BCT and BCTR instructions, increment, test, and branch in a single operation. But these instructions are more flexible than the BCT and BCTR instructions. The BXH and BXLE instructions allow us to increment a counter by any value (within the restrictions of the numbers that can be represented in a single register), and compare that counter to any limit. The BCT and BCTR instructions only allow us to decrement a register by 1, and to compare against a limit of zero.

Before we present the format of the complex BXH and BXLE instructions, let's look at an example in an effort to understand the instruction. Assume register 4 contains 00000010_{16}, register 6 contains $0000000A_{16}$, and register 7 contains $000001A0_{16}$. Why register 7? We will see how register 7 is used in a moment.

The instruction

```
BXLE  4,6,FIRST
```

executes as illustrated in Figure 11-8. The contents of the first operand register (register 4) are incremented by the contents of the second operand register (register 6). That is, the contents of register 4 are changed from 00000010_{16} to $0000001A_{16}$. The contents of register 4 are then compared to the contents of *register 7*. Register 4 is the index in this problem. If the contents of the index register are *less than* or *equal to* the contents of the limit (register 7), a branch occurs. Otherwise, the next sequential instruction is executed. Again, we compare the contents of register 4 *as incremented* ($0000001A_{16}$) to the contents of register 7 ($000001A0_{16}$). The contents of the index register are less than the contents of the limit. A branch to FIRST occurs.

A tremendous amount of action is taking place! We are incrementing, testing, and branching in one operation. This instruction requires a counter, an increment, a limit, and a branch address. We use the contents of registers as the counter, increment, and limit. But even the complex RS-type instruction allows

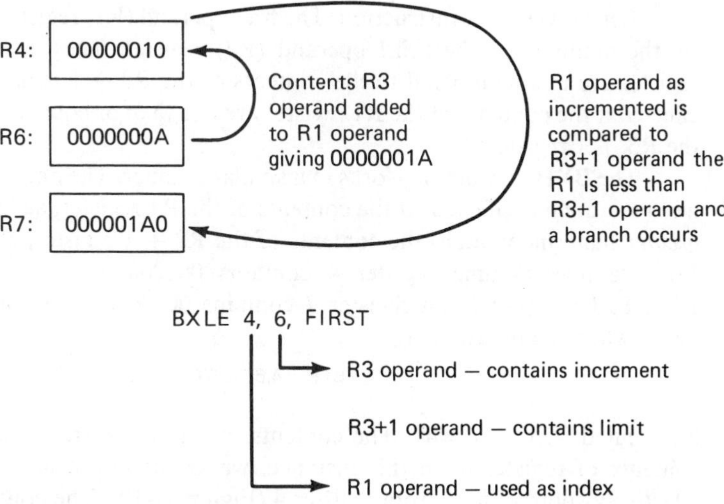

Figure 11-8 The BXLE instruction.

for only two register operands. The third operand is provided by the use of a register pair (Figure 11-9). The R3 operand is not a single register but an even–odd register pair! The R3 register contains the increment. The R3 + 1 register (the odd register of the pair) contains the limit. The first operand register contains the index or counter, and the effective address of the second operand (base plus displacement) is the branch address. If the R3 operand specifies an odd register, this register contains both increment and limit.

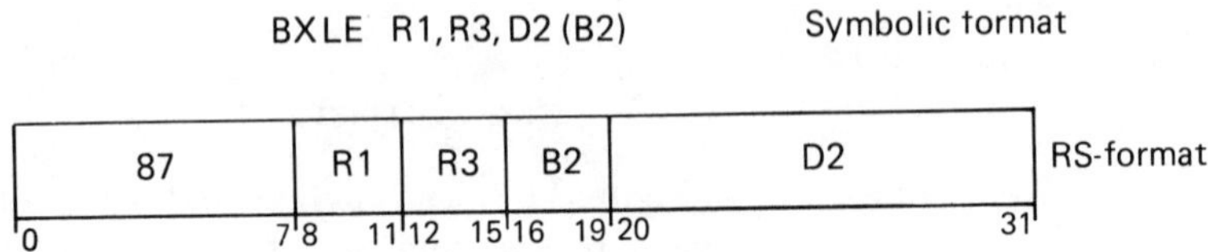

A branch occurs if the R1 operand is less than or equal to the R3+1 operand

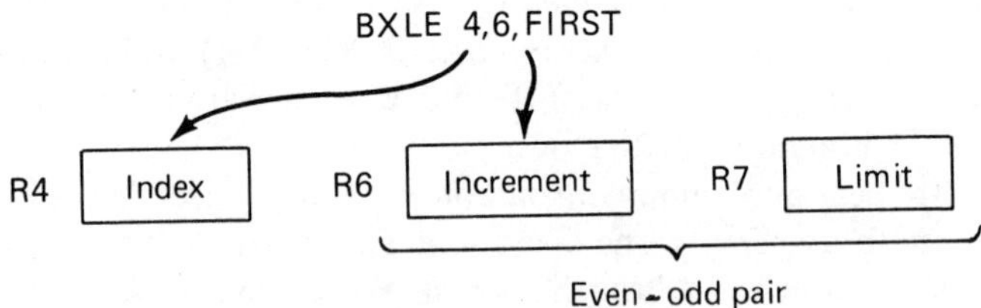

Figure 11-9 Use of the even-odd pair in the BXLE instruction.

Let's review this instruction. The first operand (R1) register is incremented by the contents of the third operand (R3) register. The contents of the R1 register are then compared to the contents of the R3 + 1 register. A branch is effected if the contents of the R1 register are less than or equal to the contents of the R3 + 1 register.

The BXH instruction works in a similar manner. The only difference lies in *when* a branch is effected. If the contents of the R1 register, as incremented, are *greater than* (index high) the contents of the R3 + 1 register, a branch occurs. For example, assume register 4 contains $0000000A_{16}$, register 6 contains $FFFFFFFF_{16}$ (−1), and register 7 contains 00000009_{16}. A branch does not occur when the instruction

```
BXH    4,6,FIRST
```

is executed. Let's see why. The contents of register 4 are incremented by the contents of register 6. In this instance, we are adding a negative number or effectively subtracting 1 from register 4 (Figure 11-10). The contents of register 4 are changed from $0000000A_{16}$ to 00000009_{16}. The contents of register 4 are

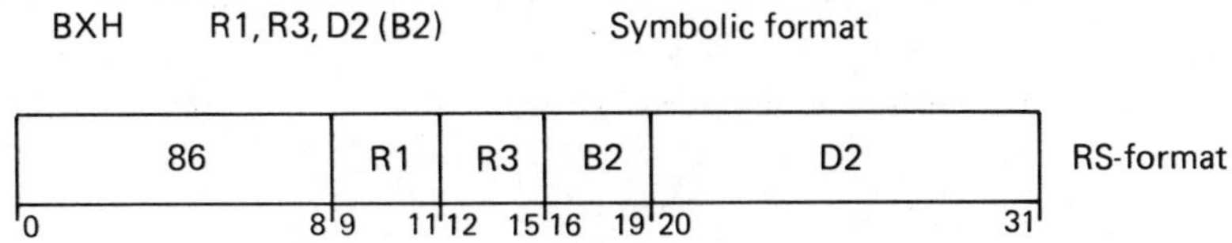

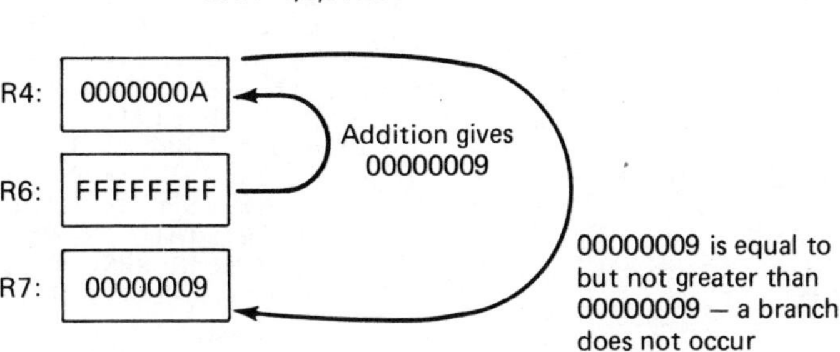

Figure 11-10 The BXH instructions.

then compared to the contents of register 7, the R3 + 1 register. The computer compares the number 00000009_{16} to the number 00000009_{16}. The numbers are equal. A branch does *not* occur! The index is *not greater than* the limit.

Table 11-4 gives some additional examples of the BXH and BXLE instructions. Remember, these instructions may be used either to increment or decrement the contents of the first operand register, depending upon the sign of the number in the third operand (R3) register. If the sign of the R3 operand is

Table 11-4 Examples of the BXLE and BXH Instructions

location	instruction	result
R2: FFFFFFFF	BXLE 3,4,RTA	index equal-branch
R3: 00000000	BXLE 2,4,RTA	index low-branch
R4: 0000000A	BXLE 6,4,RTA	index high-no branch
R5: 0000000A	BXH 6,2,RTA	index high-branch
R6: 00000006	BXH 3,4,RTA	index equal-no branch
	BXH 2,4,RTA	index low-no branch
	BXH 6,4,RTA	index high-branch
	BXLE 3,5,RTA	index equal-branch

positive, the index is incremented. If the sign of the R3 operand is negative, the index is decremented.

The BXLE and BXH instructions may be used in the solution to Program 5. Figure 11-11 gives the solution using the BXLE instruction.

```
*
* PROGRAM 5
* FIND THE SUM OF THE NUMBERS FROM 1 TO 5
* USING THE BXLE INSTRUCTION
*
         PRINT NOGEN
         START 0
SUM      SAVE  (14,12)                 SAVE REGISTERS
         BALR  12,0                    LOAD BASE
         USING *,12                    ESTABLISH ADDRESSABILITY
INIT     SR    6,6                     CLEAR ACCUMULATOR
         LA    7,1                     INITIALIZE INDEX
         LA    8,1                     INITIALIZE INCREMENT
         LA    9,5                     INITIALIZE LIMIT
BODY     AR    6,7                     ADD TO ACCUMULATOR
TEST     BXLE  7,8,BODY                INCREMENT,TEST AND BRANCH
*                                      IF INDEX IS LESS THAN OR
*                                      EQUAL TO LIMIT IN R9
EXIT     ST    6,RESULT                STORE SUM IN RESULT
         RETURN (14,12)                RETURN TO OPERATING SYSTEM
*
* DATA AREAS
*
RESULT   DS    F                       DEFINE SPACE FOR SUM
         END   SUM
```

Figure 11-11 Program 5—solution using the BXLE instruction.

Our program consists of the four phases common to all loops—initialization, body, test, and exit. We use register 7 as the index, register 8 to contain the increment, register 9 to contain the limit, and register 6 to accumulate the sum. The initialization phase sets the value in each of these registers.

```
INIT SR 6,6
     LA 7,1
     LA 8,1
     LA 9,5
```

We clear register 6 to zeros. We initialize the index, register 7, to a value of 1. We place the number one in register 8. Register 8 contains the increment. Each time we execute the loop, we increment register 7 by the contents of register 8. Register 9 contains the limit. In our program, the limit is the number five.

The body of the program contains only the add statement.

```
BODY AR 6,7
```

We add the contents of the index, register 7, to the accumulator. The contents of register 7 vary from 1 to 5 as the program progresses.

The BXLE instruction comprises the test phase.

```
TEST   BXLE   7,8,BODY
```

This instruction increments the contents of register 7 by the contents of register 8. The result in register 7 is compared to the contents of register 9 (the odd member of the even–odd pair). If the contents of register 7 are less than or equal to the contents of register 9, the program loops back to BODY. This occurs four times. The fifth time we execute the loop register 7 contains the number five. We increment register 7 by 1 and compare the result to the contents of register 9. The result is high. A branch does not occur, and we fall through to the exit phase

```
EXIT   ST   6,RESULT
```

The sum in register 6 is stored in an area of storage called RESULT. The program is complete.

PROBLEMS

11.1 The BC (Branch on Condition) instruction tests the condition code in the PSW. The condition code is set after arithmetic and compare instructions. Give the condition code setting in binary after each of the following instructions is executed.

location	contents	instruction
register 3	0000000A	CR 3,4
register 4	FFFFFFF6	CR 4,3
register 5	00000001	AR 3,4
register 6	FFFFFFFF	AR 4,3
		SR 6,6
		CR 3,3
		AR 6,4

11.2 Using the data in Problem 11.1, indicate whether a branch occurs after each of the following BC instructions is executed.

a. CR 3,4
BC 4,LABEL

b. CR 4,3
BC 8,LABEL

c. AR 3,6
BC 15,LABEL

d. AR 4,5
BC 12,LABEL

e. AR 6,5
BC 0,LABEL

11.3 The extended mnemonics allow us to code the BC instruction without coding a mask value. Give the extended mnemonics for each of the following BC instructions. Indicate if there is no extended mnemonic available.

a. BC 8,LABEL
b. BC 2,LABEL
c. BC 6,LABEL
d. BC 15,LABEL
e. BCR 0,8
f. BC 0,LABEL
g. BCR 0,12
h. BC 1,LABEL
i. BC 3,LABEL

11.4 The BCT and BCTR allow the programmer to decrement a register, test the register against zero, and branch accordingly. Indicate if a branch occurs after each of the following instructions is executed.

location	contents	instruction
register 3	00000001	BCT 3,LABEL
register 4	FFFFFFFF	BCT 4,LABEL
register 5	00000010	BCT 5,LABEL
register 6	FFFFFF66	BCT 6,LABEL
		BCTR 6,5

11.5 Code the solution to Program 5—finding the sum of the numbers from 1 to 5—using the BCTR instruction.

11.6 The BXH and BXLE instructions allow the programmer to increment an index (R1 operand), test the index against a limit (R3+1) operand) and branch accordingly. Indicate if a branch occurs after each of the following instructions is executed.

location	contents	instruction
register 2	00002FFF	BXLE 3,4,LABEL1
register 3	00003000	BXLE 2,4,LABEL2
register 4	00000001	BXH 3,6,LABEL3
register 5	00003000	BXH 2,4,LABEL4
register 6	0000000A	BXLE 2,6,LABEL5
register 7	00007000	BXH 3,6,LABEL6
register 11	00009000	BXLE 11,12,LABEL7
register 12	FFFFFFFF	BXH 11,12,LABEL8
register 13	00008FFF	BXLE 2,3,LABEL8

11.7 Code the solution to Program 5 using the BXH instruction.

11.8 Write a program to find the value of any constant NUM raised to a power EXP using the BCT(R) instruction. Use either binary or decimal arithmetic in your solution.

12

Address Modification and Arrays

Often we arrange related items in groups called tables or arrays. Conceptually a table appears as

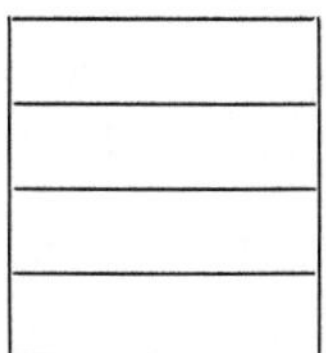

We can give the table a symbolic name which lets us reference the information within the table.

TBL
TBL + 4
TBL + 8
TBL + 12

Each piece of information within a table is called an element. The data handled in Program 2—finding the sum of four constants— is a table containing four elements.

Table 12-1 Program 2—Data Arranged in a Table

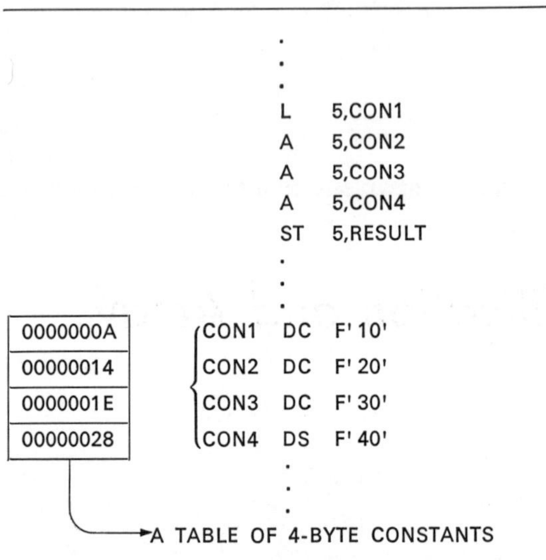

```
           .
           .
           .
           L     5,CON1
           A     5,CON2
           A     5,CON3
           A     5,CON4
           ST    5,RESULT
           .
           .
           .
0000000A   CON1  DC    F'10'
00000014   CON2  DC    F'20'
0000001E   CON3  DC    F'30'
00000028   CON4  DS    F'40'
           .
           .
           .
```


We are able to find the sum of these four elements by adding each element to a register. Let's increase the number of elements to thirty. This approach to the solution becomes unwieldy.

```
.
.
.
A   3,CON1
A   3,CON2
.
.
.
A   3,CON30
.
.
.
```

ADDRESSING DATA IN A TABLE

We find that the techniques used to address single data items in storage become awkward when applied to data in arrays. We must develop new programming techniques.

A Sample Program

Let's use Program 7 as an example.

Program 7 ***Problem Statement.*** Find the sum of a variable number of constants. The first constant does not contain data. The first constant contains the number of constants in the table as illustrated in Figure 12-1.

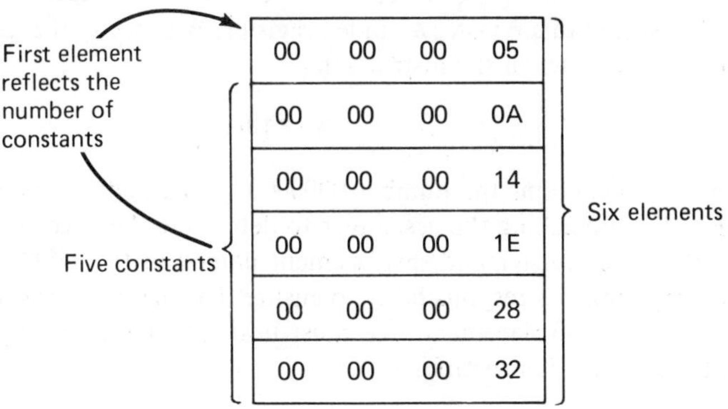

Figure 12-1 Program 7—a variable length table.

Solution. Let's develop the solution to Program 7 using binary constants. We must define a table containing fullword binary constants. We will use the data given in Figure 12-1.

```
TBL  DC  F'5'
     DC  F'10'
     DC  F'20'
     DC  F'30'
     DC  F'40'
     DC  F'50'
```

We now must develop the instructions to add each constant to a register. We call this register an accumulator—an area used to accumulate a sum. We cannot code these instructions using symbolic labels. That is, we cannot say

```
A  6,CON2
A  6,CON3
A  6,CON4
.
.
.
```

First, we did not label each constant within the table. Second, we want to program a loop—to use a single add instruction and repeat it. We must find a new means to address the entries in TBL.

We can address the first byte of table using the label TBL, and we can address relative entries within TBL using relative addressing. For example

```
A  6,TBL + 4
A  6,TBL + 8
A  6,TBL + 12
A  6,TBL + 16
```

We are using the relative displacement to address or index the correct element in TBL. But again, we are coding repetitive add instructions. We need a single add instruction which may be used to address the successive elements in TBL.

We can use a register to contain the relative displacement of an element in TBL. We call this register an index register. We specify the use of register 10 as the index register in the instruction

```
A   6,TBL(10)
```

If register 10 contains the number 00000004_{16}, we address the second element in TBL. We are asking the assembler to determine the correct address of TBL using the base register and displacement named in the USING statement. It is the programmer's responsibility to ensure that the index register contains the correct relative displacement. We must initialize the index register before we issue the first add instruction.

```
LA   10,4
```

and increment the index register each time we issue the add instruction

```
AH   10, = H'4'
```

Our program now evolves as

```
      .
      .
      .
INIT  LA   10,4
      .
      .
      .
BODY  A    6,TBL(10)
      .
      .
      .
      AH   4, = H'4'
      .
      .
      .
TBL   DC   F'5'
      DC   F'1'
      DC   F'2'
      .
      .
      .
      DC   F'5'
```

Done! We have added the first constant (second element in TBL) to register 6. We now must determine whether to exit from the loop (all the constants have been processed) or whether to return to BODY and process the next constant. We must compare the number of times we execute the add instruction to the number of constants in the table. We exit from the loop when we have executed the add instruction 5 times. We can use a register—register 4 in this example—to count the number of times we execute the add instruction. Register 4 is the counter. We add to (increment) the counter each time we execute the add instruction,

```
AH   4, = H'1'
```

and compare the counter to the number (limit) contained in the first entry in the table

```
C   4,TBL
```

We exit from the loop on an equal condition

```
BE   EXIT
```

The complete solution to Program 7 is given in Figure 12-2. The first statements are housekeeping statements. They should be familiar by now. The next instructions are initialization instructions. They are executed only once. We say

```
*
* PROGRAM 7
* SUM OF A VARIABLE NUMBER OF CONSTANTS
*
         PRINT NOGEN
         START
FIRST    SAVE  (14,12)              SAVE REGISTERS
         BALR  12,0                 LOAD BASE REGISTER
         USING *,12                 ESTABLISH ADDRESSABILITY
INIT     LA    10,4                 LOAD INDEX TO BYPASS FIRST ENTRY
         LA    4,1                  INITIALIZE COUNTER
         SR    6,6                  AND CLEAR ACCUMULATOR
BODY     A     6,TBL(10)            ADD FROM TABLE INDEXED BY R10
TEST     C     4,TBL                COMPARE CTR TO LIMIT AT TBL
         BE    EXIT                 EXIT IF EQUAL
         AH    10,=H'4'             ELSE INCREMENT INDEX REGISTER
         AH    4,=H'1'              AND COUNTER
         B     BODY                 AND LOOP TO BODY
EXIT     ST    6,RESULT             STORE THE SUM IN RESULT
         RETURN (14,12)             AND RETURN
*
* DATA AREAS
*
TBL      DC    F'5'                 * NUMBER OF CONSTANTS
         DC    F'1'                 * TABLE
         DC    F'2'                 * OF
         DC    F'3'                 * FULLWORD
         DC    F'4'                 * CONSTANTS
         DC    F'5'                 *
RESULT   DS    F
         END   FIRST
               =H'4'
               =H'1'
```

Figure 12-2 Program 7—solution.

these instructions are *outside* the loop. The instruction

```
LA  10,4
```

places the relative displacement of the second element in TBL in register 10. We then initialize register 4, the counter, by

```
LA  4,1
```

and register 6 by

```
SR  6,6
```

Register 6 is used as the accumulator. We must set it to zero before we start the program. We now enter the main program loop.

The instruction

```
BODY  A  6,TBL(10)
```

adds from the table to register 6 using register 10 to index the correct element.

We now enter the test routine. The instruction

```
TEST  C  4,TBL
```

compares the contents of register 4 with the limit at TBL. Register 4 contains the number 00000001_{16}, representing the number of times we have executed the add instruction. The constant at TBL contains 00000005_{16}, the number of constants in TBL. The operands are not equal. We fall through the branch instruction

```
BE  EXIT
```

and execute the instruction

```
AH  10,=H'4'
```

This instruction adds four to register 10. We now increment the counter

```
AH  4,=H'1'
```

The final instruction within the loop

```
B  BODY
```

is an unconditional branch back to BODY. When we execute the instruction

```
BODY  A  6,TBL(10)
```

we add the *next* fullword of data to register 6.

We continue the loop until register 4 contains 00000005_{16} at which point the compare instruction finds an equal condition. We then branch out of the loop to the instruction at EXIT.

The instructions

```
EXIT  ST        6,RESULT
      RETURN    (14,12)
```

store the contents of register 6 at RESULT and the program is complete. The RETURN statement tells the operating system that this program is finished.

Program 7 ***Using the BCT Instruction.*** We can use the BCT instruction in another approach to the solution of Program 7. Remember, the BCT instruction allows us to decrement, test, and branch in one operation. Figure 12-3 gives the solution to Program 7 using the BCT instruction.

We use register 3 to point to the correct entry in TBL. Each time we execute the loop, we increment the contents of register 3, decrement register 4, and branch accordingly.

```
*
* PROGRAM 7
* SUM OF A VARIABLE NUMBER OF CONSTANTS
*
         PRINT NOGEN
         START
FIRST    SAVE  (14,12)              SAVE REGISTERS
         BALR  12,0                 LOAD BASE REGISTER
         USING *,12                 ESTABLISH ADDRESSABILITY
INIT     LA    10,0                 LOAD INDEX
         L     4,TBL                INITIALIZE LIMIT
         SR    6,6                  AND CLEAR ACCUMULATOR
BODY     AH    10,=H'4'             INCREMENT INDEX REGISTER
         A     6,TBL(10)            ADD FROM TABLE INDEXED BY R10
TEST     BCT   4, BODY              DECREMENT LIMIT AND BRANCH
EXIT     ST    6,RESULT             STORE THE SUM IN RESULT
         RETURN (14,12)             AND RETURN
*
* DATA AREAS
*
TBL      DC    F'5'                 * NUMBER OF CONSTANTS
         DC    F'1'                 * TABLE
         DC    F'2'                 * OF
         DC    F'3'                 * FULLWORD
         DC    F'4'                 * CONSTANTS
         DC    F'5'                 *
RESULT   DS    F
         END   FIRST
               =H'4'
               =H'1'
```

Figure 12-3 Program 2—using the BCT instruction.

The initialization instructions are executed only once. The instruction

```
INIT  LA  10,0
```

initializes the index register with the displacement of the first element in TBL. *Not an error*—we will see why in a moment. The SR instruction clears the accumulator. The instruction

```
L  4,TBL
```

places the limit in register 4. Each time we execute the loop, we decrement register 4 by 1.

We now bypass the first entry in TBL,

```
AH  10, = H'4'
```

and execute the add instruction

```
A  6,TBL(10)
```

The first time we execute this instruction, we add the contents of the second entry to register 6. The instruction

```
BCT  4,BODY
```

decrements register 4 by 1. If the contents of register 4 are non-zero, a branch to BODY is effected. When we have executed the add instruction five times—and decremented register 4 five times—register 4 contains 00000000_{16}. A branch does not occur and we fall through to the code at EXIT. The result is stored and the RETURN statement tells the operating system that the program is finished.

Program 7 ***Decimal Data.*** Suppose that we now solve Program 7 using decimal data. We define a table of packed constants

```
TBL  DC  PL4'5'
     DC  PL4'10'
     DC  PL4'20'
     DC  PL4'30'
     DC  PL4'40'
```

we must use decimal arithmetic and compare instructions. We must define a packed decimal field to accumulate the sum.

```
ANS  DC  PL4'0'
```

A problem arises when we attempt to code the AP instruction to add from TBL to ANS. The AP instruction is an SS-type instruction—there is no provision for an index register!

We can index the elements in TBL only by modifying the contents of the base register. But we must be very careful. We cannot change the contents of the base register named in the USING statement. We must tell the assembler to use another register to address the elements in TBL, and then increment this register. We use the concept of *explicit addressing*.

When we use explicit addressing, we name the base register in the symbolic instruction. The instruction

```
AP  ANS,0(4,3)
```

explicitly states that register 3 is to be used as the base register in the machine instruction. The length of the second operand is 4. Let's assume that register 3 contains the address of the second entry in TBL (remember, we must bypass the first entry in the table). We then can use the explicit instruction shown in Figure 12-4 to add the contents of the second element to register 6. If, somehow, we

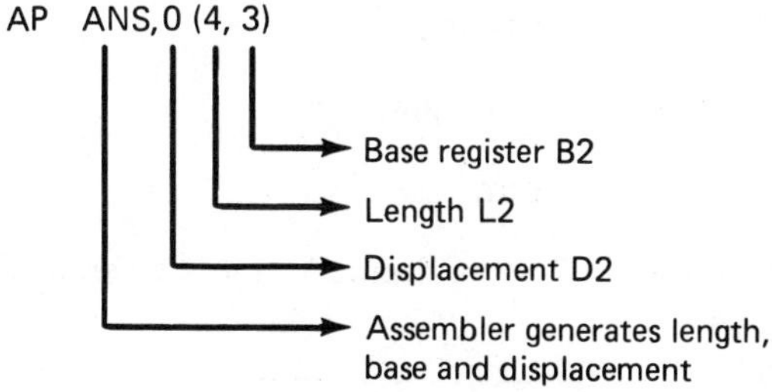

Figure 12-4 Using explicit addressing.

could change the value in register 3 to address the next element in TBL, we then could loop back to the same add instruction. (See Figure 12-5.)

We must initialize register 3 to point to the second entry in TBL.

```
LA  3,TBL + 4
```

We are using relative addressing. We specify a symbolic address *relative* to a label in our program. This statement initializes register 3 to address the second element in TBL.

Our program appears as

```
          .
          .
          .
INIT      LA   3,TBL + 4
          .
          .
          .
BODY      AP   ANS,0(4,3)
          .
          .
          .
```

```
TBL   DC  PL4'5'
      DC  PL4'10'
      DC  PL4'20'
      DC  PL4'30'
      DC  PL4'40'
      DC  PL4'50'
```

Now we must develop the instructions to control the number of times we execute the instructions comprising the body of the loop. We can define a counter,

```
CTR  DC  PL2'1'
```

increment the counter each time we execute the AP instruction,

```
AP  CTR,=PL1'1'
```

test the counter against the limit

```
CP  CTR,TBL
```

and exit when the counter equals the limit

```
BE  EXIT.
```

The solution to Program 7 using decimal data is given in Figure 12-6.

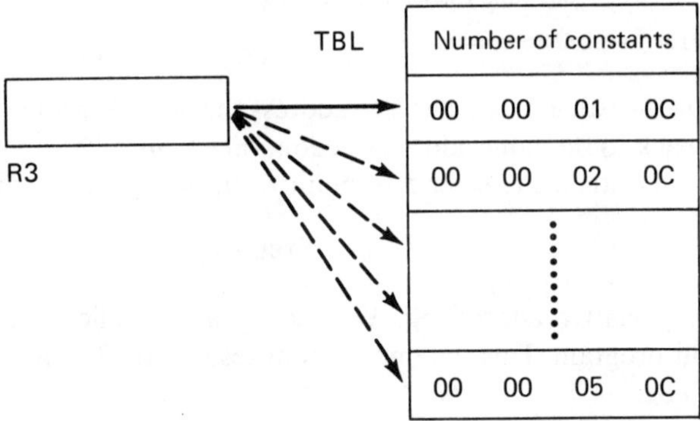

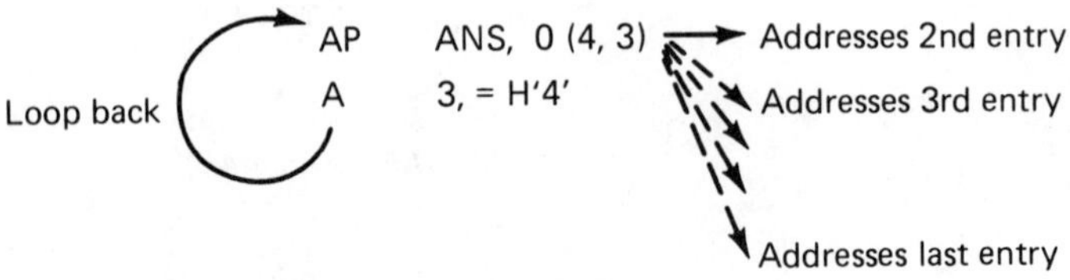

Figure 12-5 Use of register 3 to address entries in TBL.

```
*
* PROGRAM 7
* SUM OF A VARIABLE NUMBER OF CONSTANTS
* EXPLICIT ADDRESSING - DECIMAL DATA
*
         PRINT NOGEN
         START
FIRST    SAVE  (14,12)             SAVE REGISTERS
         BALR  12,0                LOAD BASE
         USING *,12                ESTABLISH ADDRESSABILITY
INIT     LA    3,TBL+4             LOAD ADDRESS FIRST CONSTANT
*                                  BYPASSING FIRST ENTRY IN THE TBL
BODY     AP    ANS,0(4,3)          ADD FROM TABLE - R3 ADDRESSES
*                                  CORRECT ENTRY
         CP    CTR,TBL             COMPARE COUNTER TO LIMIT AT TBL
         BE    EXIT                EXIT IF EQUAL
         AH    3,=H'4'             ELSE INCREMENT BASE
         AP    CTR,=PL1'1'         AND COUNTER
         B     BODY                AND LOOP TO BODY
EXIT     RETURN (14,12)            AND RETURN
*
*        DATA AREAS
*
TBL      DC    PL4'5'              * NUMBER OF CONSTANTS IN THE TBL
         DC    PL4'10'             * TABLE
         DC    PL4'20'             * OF
         DC    PL4'30'             * DECIMAL
         DC    PL4'40'             * CONSTANTS
         DC    PL4'50'             *
ANS      DC    PL4'0'
CTR      DC    PL2'1'
         END   FIRST
               =H'4'
               =PL1'1'
```

Figure 12-6 Program 7—solution using decimal arithmetic.

Search Reference and Direct Reference Tables

Now that we have developed the techniques of indexing and explicit addressing to processs data arranged in a table, let's use these techniques to locate a specific element within a table.

Search Reference Tables. Each element within a search reference table has two components. We call these components the *argument* and the *function.* Let's consider the following table.

argument	function
001001	JOHN DOE
001003	HENRY LEE
001937	JANE CHRISTIAN
002002	MARILYN EIWEB
032009	JACK RUDE
032197	PAM GEORGE

Each element within the table has an employee number—the argument—and an employee name—the function. We can use the information in this table to find the name of an employee, providing we know the employee number. We use the employee number to search the table.

We call the employee number the *search argument*. Let's assume that we have read a card containing the employee number into an area of storage called INWORK. We address the employee number using the label NUMIN. We now want to find the entry in the table with the corresponding employee number and move the function—the employee name—to a field called NAMEOUT in an output area called PRINTBLD.

For example, if we read a card which has the number 001937 in columns 1–6, we want to search the table until we find the element whose argument is 001937. We find a match on the third element, and move the function JANE CHRISTIAN to the output area. We can represent these processes in a flowchart (Figure 12-7). Now let's develop the code to solve this problem. We must first define the table.

```
TBL  DC  C'001001'
     DC  CL20'JOHN DOE'
     DC  C'001003'
     DC  CL20'HENRY LEE'
     .
     .
     .
     DC  C'032197'
     DC  CL20'PAM GEORGE'
```

Each element in the table contains a 6-position argument and a 20-position function. Let's assume that there are six entries in the table.

```
        .
        .
        .
INIT    LA   3,TBL                 R3 ADDRESSES TBL
BODY    CLC  NUMIN(6),0(3)         COMPARE SEARCH ARG WITH TBL
        BE   FOUND                 ARG AND BRANCH IF EQUAL
        AH   3,=H'26'              ELSE INCREMENT R3 BY LENGTH
        .                          OF THE ELEMENT
        .
        .
        B    BODY                  AND BRANCH TO BODY
FOUND   MVC  NAMEOUT(20),6(3)      MOVE CORRECT FUNCTION
        .
        .
        .
INWORK  DS   0CL80
NUMIN   DS   CL6
        .
        .
        .
```

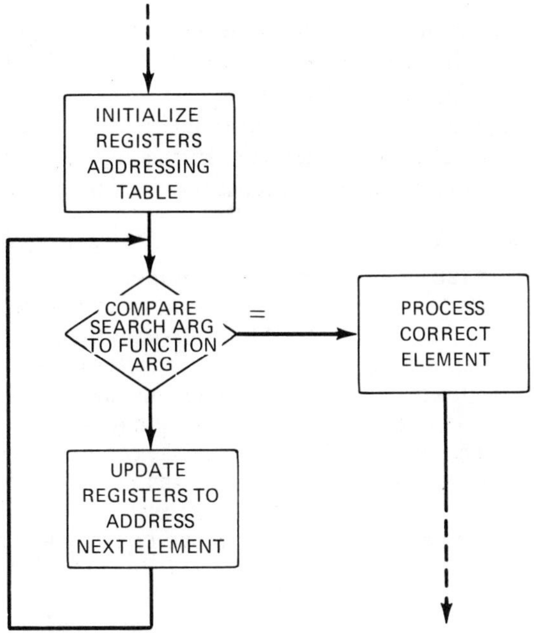

Figure 12-7 Searching a direct entry table.

```
PRINTBLD  DS   0CL120
          DC   CL26' '
NAMEOUT   DS   CL20
          DS   CL74' '
TBL       DC   C'001001'
               .
               .
               .
```

The load address instruction at INIT places the address of the first element in TBL in register 3. We are using register 3 to address the table. The instruction

```
BODY  CLC  NUMIN(6),0(3)
```

compares the 6-position at NUMIN—the search argument read from the input card—with the 6-position field in storage addressed by register 3 as a base and a displacement of 0. Remember the format of the explicit instruction. The parameter outside parenthesis gives the displacement of the second operand, the parameter within parenthesis gives the base register. We are comparing the input search argument with the argument of the first element in TBL. If these arguments are equal, we exit from the loop. If they are not, register 3 is incremented by 26 to point to the next element and a branch back to the compare instruction at BODY is effected.

When a match occurs, the instruction

```
FOUND  MVC  NAMEOUT(20),6(3)
```

is executed. We are moving the 20 positions from an area of storage addressed by register 3 and a displacement of 6 to NAMEOUT. We are moving the function portion of the correct element.

We must, however, anticipate the possibility that an input card might not have a corresponding element in the table. In this instance, we search all six elements without finding a match. We must provide for this possibility in our program.

```
INIT      LA   3,TBL              R3 ADDRESSES TBL
          LA   4,6                INITIALIZE CTR TO NUMBER OF
*                                 ELEMENTS IN TBL
BODY      CLC  NUMIN(6),0(3)      COMPARE SEARCH ARG WITH TBL
          BE   FOUND              ARG AND BRANCH IF EQUAL
          AH   3,=H'26'           ELSE INCREMENT R3
          BCT  4,BODY             DECREMENT CTR AND LOOP BACK
          B    NOMATCH            UNLESS ALL ELEMENTS HAVE BEEN
*                                 EXAMINED
FOUND     MVC  NAMEOUT(20),6(3)   MOVE CORRECT FUNCTION
          .
          .
          .
NOMATCH   .
          .
          .
INWORK    DS   0CL80
NUMIN     DS   CL6
          .
          .
          .
PRINTBLD  DS   0CL120
          DC   CL26' '
NAMEOUT   DS   CL20
          .
          .
          .
TBL       DC   C'001001'
          .
          .
          .
```

We are using the BCT instruction to control the number of times we execute the loop. We place the number of elements in the table in register 4,

```
          LA   4,6
```

and decrement the contents of register 4 each time we execute the loop.

```
          BCT  4,BODY
```

When we have executed the loop six times and still have not found a match, the contents of register 4 as decremented are zero. A branch to BODY does not occur and we exit through the instruction

```
B   NOMATCH
```

Direct Reference Tables. A direct reference table does not contain an argument. In this type of table the position of the element in the table must be related to a *search key*. Let's assume that a direct reference table reflects the percentage of income withheld for taxes in each pay period.

2000
3005
4250
5275
6925
7500

A code on the input payroll card (ICODE) reflects the income bracket of an employee.

code	income bracket
1	below $20,000
2	$20,001–$28,000
3	$28,001–$32,000
4	$32,001–$45,000
5	$45,001–$99,000
6	over $99,000

Each income bracket has a corresponding element in the direct reference table. For example, on employee with a code of 2 has 30.05 percent of his earnings withheld.

We can use this table to calculate the percentage of gross income withheld for taxes. Let's assume we have read the payroll card into storage. We address the income code using the label ICODE. We use the argument ICODE to go directly to the correct element in the table. We then can use this element to calculate taxes withheld.

First we must define the direct reference table.

```
TBL   DC   PL4'2000'
      DC   PL4'3005'
      DC   PL4'4250'
      DC   PL4'5275'
      DC   PL4'6925'
      DC   PL4'7500'
```

We define the elements in TBL as packed constants. This saves space and allows us to use the data in subsequent arithmetic operations without issuing the PACK instruction.

The instructions to locate an element in a direct reference table follow.

```
         .
         .
         .
         LA    3,TBL                  REGISTER 3 ADDRESSES TBL
         .
         .
         .
         PACK  PCODE,ICODE            PACK SEARCH ARGUMENT AND
         CVB   5,PCODE                CONVERT TO BINARY
         S     5, = H'1'              DECREMENT SEARCH ARGUMENT BY 1
         M     4, = F'4'              AND MULTIPLY BY 4 TO FIND
         AR    3,5                    RELATIVE DISPLACEMENT—ADD TO R3
         MVC   PERCENT,0(4,3)         MOVE CORRECT ELEMENT FROM
         .                            TBL TO PERCENT
         .
         .
TBL      DC    PL4'002000'
         .
         .
         .
PCODE    DS    D
PERCENT  DS    PL4
INWORK   DS    0CL80
         .
         .
         .
ICODE    DS    CL1
         .
         .
         .
```

We use register 3 to address the elements in TBL. The instruction

```
LA 3,TBL
```

places the address of the first element in TBL in register 3. We must increment register 3 to point to the correct element. A code of 6, for example, tells us to address the sixth element in TBL. The sixth element is 20 bytes from the beginning of TBL. The code

```
PACK  PCODE,ICODE
CVB   5,PCODE
.
.
.
S     5, = H'1'
M     4, = F'4'
.
.
.
```

converts the search argument ICODE to the relative displacement needed to address the correct element in TBL. We now add this displacement to register 3,

```
AR   3,5
```

and move the correct percentage to PERCENT.

```
MVC   PERCENT(4),0(3)
```

We now can use this value to calculate the correct tax deductions.

We have one remaining responsibility. We must ensure that the search argument is valid. ICODE must be numeric and less than seven.

```
.
.
.
CLC   ICODE, = X'F1'          IF CODE IS LESS THAN
BL    ERROR                   X'F1' OR IF CODE IS
CLC   ICODE, = X'F6'          GREATER THAN X'F6'
BH    ERROR                   IT IS AN ERROR
.
.
.
```

PROBLEMS **12.1** Give the generated code (instructions and constants) for each instruction and constant in the following program segment.

```
 LOC   OBJECT CODE     ADDR1 ADDR2  STMT    SOURCE STATEMENT

000000                                 1            BALR   10,0
000002                                 2            USING  *,10
000002                        0001C    3            L      5,TABLE
000006                        0001C    4            LA     5,TABLE
00000A                        00020    5            L      5,TABLE+4
00000E                        00020    6            LA     5,TABLE+4
000012                        0002C    7            LA     5,LAST
                                       8            RETURN (14,12)
000016                        0000C    9+           LM     14,12,12(13) RESTORE REGISTERS
00001A                                10+           BR     14 RETURN
00001C                                11 TABLE      DC     F'4'
000020                                12            DC     F'100'
000024                                13            DC     F'200'
000028                                14            DC     F'300'
00002C                                15 LAST       DC     F'400'
                                      16             END
```

12.2 Assume the program segment in Problem 12.1 loads at location 006000_{16}—ie., the address of the BALR instruction is 006000_{16}. Give the contents of register 5 after each of the following instructions is executed.

a. L 5,TABLE
b. LA 5,TABLE
c. L 5,TABLE+4

d. LA 5,TABLE+4
e. LA 5,LAST
f. L 5,LAST

12.3 Given the following code

```
              .
              .
              .
TABLE   DS   F
        DC   F'10'
        DC   F'20'
LAST    DC   F'30'
```

How can we place the address of LAST in the first entry in TBL?

12.4 The solution to Program 7 developed in this chapter assumed that the first entry in the table represented the number of constants contained in the table. Now assume that the first entry in the table contains the *address* of the last entry. For example

```
TBL     DC   A(LAST)
        DC   F'10'
        DC   F'20'
        DC   F'30'
        DC   F'40'
LAST    DC   F'50'
```

Develop a solution to Program 7 using

1. an index register and implied base
2. explicit addressing

12.5 Write a program to read the employee master file and build a table reflecting employee number and gross salary. The data specifications follow. Use the macros HSKP, GET, and PUT to handle the I/O coding in your solution.

input positions	field	position in TBL
1–6	Employee Number	1–6
51–58	Gross Salary	7–14

The first entry in TBL contains the number of entries in the table in zoned format, and an employee number of 999999.

12.6 Write a program to update the employee master file. Changes in salary are reflected in a search reference table. The argument in each table element contains a 6-position employee number. The function contains a change in gross salary. Search the table to find an element corresponding to the input record.

If there is a match, punch a new employee record reflecting the new salary. If there is no match, reproduce the record with no changes. Use the following I/O specifications.

input positions	field	output positions
1–6	Employee Number	1–6
51–58	Gross Salary	51–58 (updated if necessary)

1. Assume that the employee cards are nonsequential.
2. Assume that the employee cards are arranged in ascending employee number sequence.

12.7 Write a program to print the employee number, employee name, gross salary, and percentage at which the salary is taxed.

input positions	field	output positions
1–6	Employee Number	10–16
7–26	Employee Name	27–46
47	Income Code	
	1 – 20.00%	
	2 – 30.05%	
	3 – 42.40%	
	4 – 52.75%	
	5 – 69.25%	
	6 – 75.00%	
51–58	Gross Salary	50–63 ($d,ddd,ddd.dd)
	Percentage Withheld	70–74 (dd.dd)
	Amount Withheld (optional)	80–89 ($dd,ddd.dd)

The tax rate is contained in a direct entry table where each element in the table is related to an income code in the input record. Assume that the income code varies from 1 to 6. For extra credit calculate the dollar amount withheld.

12.8 Direct entry tables are often used to tabulate information. Using the input specifications in Problem 12.7, determine the number of employees in each income bracket. Develop your solution using

1. binary arithmetic
2. decimal arithmetic

Hint: Use the income code to address one of the nine elements in the table. An income bracket of 2 should increment the second element in the table by 1, an income bracket of 9 should increment the ninth element in the table. When all the cards have been read, each element reflects the number of employees in that income bracket.

If you wish, you may print a report reflecting the number of employees in each bracket. Remember, the data in the table must be converted to the correct form for output.

12.9 The time required to locate the correct element in a search-reference table may be reduced if we can avoid examining each element in the table. Suppose we examine the search argument against the table argument located in the middle of the table. If the search argument is less than the table argument, we know the correct element is in the first half of the table, otherwise the correct element is in the last half of the table. We can continue this procedure, cutting the number of elements to be searched in half each time, until a match is found. We call this procedure a *binary search.*

Develop a flowchart and program to seach a table (TBL) consisting of N (assume ten elements in the table) elements, each of which is L (assume a length of 20) bytes long. The first four bytes of each element comprise the argument. When a match is found, move the entire element to DATAFLD. You must also provide for the possibility that there is no element for a given search argument. Use either binary or decimal instructions.

12.10 Write a program to find the element with the highest argument in a table. The arguments are *not* arranged in sequence. Move the entire element to an area called HIGH. There are ten elements in the table, each element consisting of a 4-byte argument and a 10-byte function. Use either binary or decimal instructions.

12.11 Write a program to sort the elements in the table described in Problem 12.10 into ascending sequence by argument.

13

Bit and Byte Manipulation

This chapter introduces the instructions which work with one or more bits of data, and discusses instructions which handle a single byte of information.

BIT MANIPULATION

We have seen the binary concept play an important part in computer arithmetic and design. The binary concept also extends into computer programming. We often are faced with two choices—a yes or no situation. We can represent this situation in a segment of a flowchart. Figure 13-1 shows the use of a program decision to direct the flow of logic. If the person whose record is being processed is under twenty-one, the record is processed in one way. If, however, he or she is twenty-one years old or over, the record is processed in a different way.

The program must determine the age of the person whose record is being processed. We are not interested in the person's actual age—only whether he is over twenty-one. We are faced with a yes or no situation. There are only two possibilities—the person is over twenty-one or he is not.

We might designate a single bit in the person's employee record to indicate his age. If the bit is on, he is over 21. Within a single byte of the employee record we have 8 bits. We have the potential of recording eight characteristics about

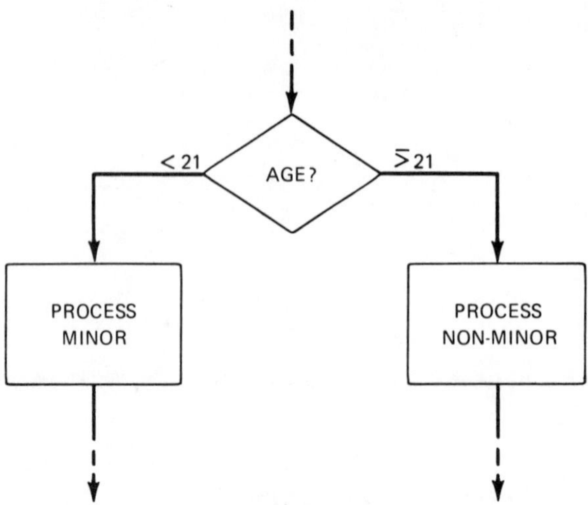

Figure 13-1 Flowcharting a decision.

the employee. We might refer to these characteristics as an *employee profile.* Figure 13-2 shows the employee profile included in the employee record we have been using in our programs. The last bit, bit seven, is used to indicate the age of the employee.

The flowchart presented in Figure 13-1 requires us to distinguish between employees. We must examine the bits comprising the profile and determine whether bit seven is on or off. Until this point we have been using assembly language instructions which work with one or more *bytes.* We must now introduce a new instruction to examine a particular bit. We must be able to determine whether that bit is on or off.

The TM Instruction

The TM (Test under Mask) instruction allows us to examine one or more bits. Let's see how the instruction is used in our problem, and then examine other uses of the instruction.

The following code shows the use of the TM instruction to determine the relative age of an employee, and to branch to the appropriate code.

```
TM   PROFILE,X'01'     TEST BIT 7
BC   1,OVER21          BRANCH TO OVER21 IF BIT 7 ON
B    UNDER21           ELSE BRANCH TO UNDER21
```

The instruction examines one byte of the record, specifically the PROFILE byte. The mask tells us which *bit* we are examining. In this example, it is the seventh or last bit. Remember, the mask is in hexadecimal. The binary represen-

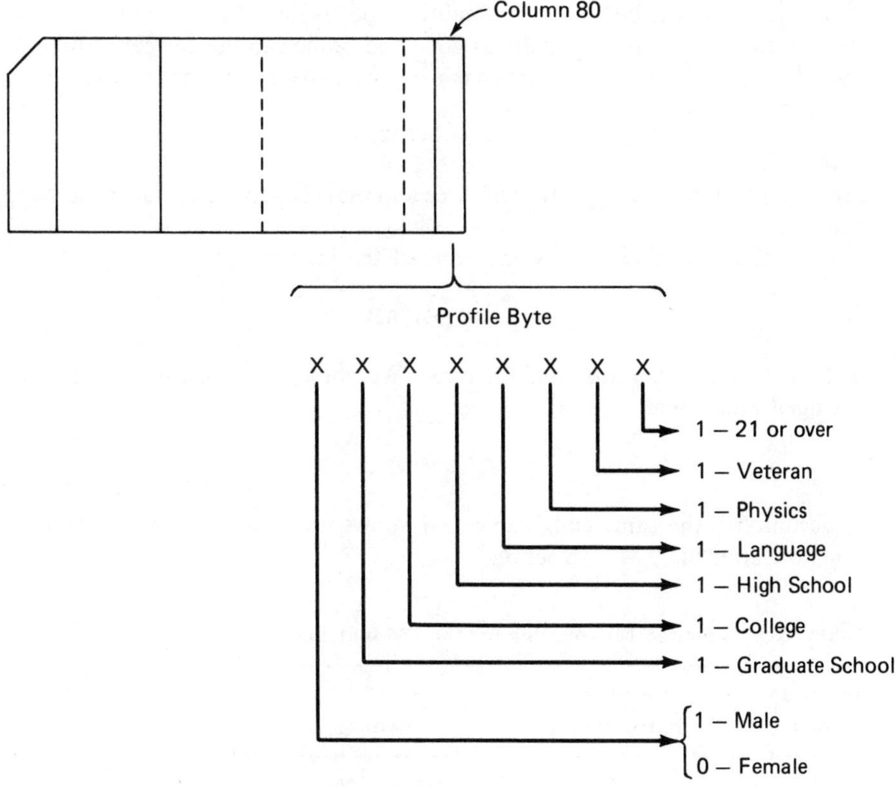

Figure 13-2 Format of the profile byte.

tation is 00000001_2. The last bit of the mask is on. This means the instruction examines the last bit of the PROFILE byte.

```
PROFILE: xxxxxxxx      xxxxxxxx
BITS:    01234567      01234567
MASK:    X'01'         X'80'
         00000001      10000000
                ↑      ↑
         BIT 7 selected BIT 0 selected
```

If we wished to examine the first bit (bit zero) of the field PROFILE, the correct mask would be 80_{16}. The instruction would read

```
TM    PROFILE,X'80'
```

In our example there are two possibilities. The selected bit may be *on* or it may be *off*. If the selected bit (bit seven in this example) is on, the condition code is set to three. If the bit is off, the condition code is set to zero. We must use the BC instruction to test the condition code and branch to the correct routine. If the selected bit is on, the employee is over twenty-one. The instruction

```
BC  1,OVER21
```

tests for a condition code setting of three and branches to the correct processing routine.

In the preceding discussion, we used the instruction

```
BC  1,OVER21
```

to branch if the condition code is three. We could, however, have coded the extended mnemonic

```
BO  OVER21
```

to accomplish the same end. Table 13-1 shows the four extended mnemonics available after the TM instruction.

Table 13-1 Extended Mnemonics for the TM Instruction

extended code	machine instruction	meaning
BO	BC 1,	Branch if Ones
BM	BC 4,	Branch if Mixed
BZ	BC 8,	Branch if Zero
BNO	BC 14,	Branch if Not Ones

The TM is an SI-type instruction. The instruction tests one byte of main storage against a mask. The mask determines which bits are to be tested. The condition code is set to indicate one of three possibilities:

condition code	result TM instruction
00_2	selected bits are all zeros
01_2	selected bits are mixed—zeros and ones
11_2	selected bits are all ones

The following examples show the condition code setting following execution of the TM instruction.

0 1 0 1 0 1 0 1	PROFILE byte
TM PROFILE,X' 55'	cc = 11_2
TM PROFILE,X' AA'	cc = 00_2
TM PROFILE,X' A1'	cc = 01_2

The examples given show that the TM instruction may be used to test more than one bit. We could, for example, use the TM instruction to select employees having qualifications other than the correct age.

A Sample Program

Now let's see how the TM instruction is used in a program.

Program 8 ***Problem Statement.*** Use the TM instruction to select male employees who are college graduates with a second language. List employees with any of these characteristics. Use an asterisk to flag employees with *all* the specified characteristics. The input and output specifications follow.

input positions	field	output positions
1–6	Employee Number	11–16
7–26	Employee Name	21–40
	Flag	42
80	Profile	
↓ *Bit*		
0	1—male, 0—female	
1	1—graduate school	
2	1—college	
3	1—high school	
4	1—language	
5	1—physics	
6	1—veteran	
7	1—21 or over	

The program is looking for men with college degrees and a second language. Bits 0, 2 and 4 of the profile byte determine these characteristics. A mask of X′ A8′ examines these bits. If an employee has none of these characteristics, his record is bypassed. If an employee has one or more of the desired characteristics, his name and employee number are printed. If he possesses all the desired characteristics, his name is flagged with an asterisk.

Solution. The program (Figure 13-3) reads the employee card. The TM instruction is used to examine the profile field. If the employee has none of the desired

```
*
* PROGRAM 8
* ILLUSTRATING THE TM INSTRUCTION
*
         START 0
         PRINT NOGEN
*        SAVE  (14,12)                  CODED IN HSKP MACRO
*        BALR  12,0                     CODED IN HSKP MACRO
*        USING *,12                     CODED IN HSKP MACRO
PROG8    HSKPING CARDID=INCARD,PRINTID=PRINT
*        *
*        *     SOME
*        *     HOUSEKEEPING
*        *     STATEMENTS
*        *     ARE
*        *     OMITTED
*        *     HERE
*        *
READRT   GET   INCARD,INWORK            READ A RECORD
TESTRT   TM    PROFILE,X'A8'            TEST PROFILE
         BZ    READRT                   BYPASS RECORD IF ALL BITS ZERO
         BO    ASTERIK                  BRANCH TO INSERT ASTERISK
BLDRT    MVC   NUMOUT(6),NUMIN          MOVE NUMBER
         MVC   NAMEOUT(20),NAMEIN       AND NAME
         PUT   PRINT,PRINTBLD           WRITE FROM PRINTBLD
         B     READRT                   AND LOOP TO NEXT READ
ASTERIK  MVI   CODE,C'*'                MOVE CODE
         B     BLDRT                    AND BRANCH TO BLDRT
*        *
*        *     AFTER ALL CARDS HAVE BEEN
*        *     READ AND PROCESSED
*        *     THE PROGRAM IS COMPLETE
*        *
*
* DATA AREAS
*
INWORK   DS    0CL80                    INPUT AREA
NUMIN    DS    CL6                      *
NAMEIN   DS    CL20                     *
         DS    CL53                     *
PROFILE  DS    CL1                      *
PRINTBLD DS    0CL120                   OUTPUT AREA
         DC    10CL1' '                 *
NUMOUT   DS    CL6                      *
         DC    4CL1' '                  *
NAMEOUT  DS    CL20                     *
         DC    CL1' '                   *
CODE     DS    CL1                      *
         DC    78CL1' '                 *
         END   PROG8
```

Figure 13-3 Program 8—solution.

characteristics, he is bypassed and the next card is read

```
TM  PROFILE,X' A8'
BZ  READRT
```

The extended mnemonic BZ is used in place of the instruction

```
BC  8,READRT
```

If the employee is not rejected, his profile is then examined to see if he has all of the desired qualifications.

```
BO ASTERISK
```

Employees having all the desired qualifications are flagged with an asterisk

```
ASTERISK MVI CODE,C'*'
```

The print line PRINTBLD is completed and is printed using the statement

```
PUT PRINT,PRINTBLD
```

and the program loops back to read the next record

```
B READRT
```

The Logical Operations

We have seen how the TM instruction may be used to test a single bit or several bits. In addition to testing, we may find the need to turn a bit on or off. If a bit is being used as a program switch—to direct the flow of logic to one of two possible paths—we must provide a way of setting the bit to the correct value.

There are three instructions used to manipulate bits in assembly language. These instructions are closely related to a branch of logical mathematics known as Boolean algebra. Boolean algebra is not concerned with arithmetic as we know it, but with a new concept—the *logical* operation.

The three logical operations are the AND operation, the OR operation, and the XOR (eXclusive OR) operation.

The AND Operation. The AND operation performs a logical operation on two binary numbers. There is no relation between the AND function and binary arithmetic. When two numbers are 'ANDed' together, the result is totally different from binary addition or subtraction. Let's consider an example:

$$\begin{array}{r} 0011_2 \\ \text{AND } \underline{0101_2} \\ 0001_2 \end{array}$$

The AND operation requires both bits to be on for the resulting bit to be set to one. Only in the low-order position do we find both bits on, and the resulting bit set to 1. All other resulting bits are set to zero. Note that when both bits are zero (high-order position in the example given) the resulting bit is set to 0.

The AND operation may be used to set a bit to zero. Let's assume that we have a 1-byte field labeled SWITCH. The logic of a program requires us to set the last bit, bit 7, to zero. We use the NI (aNd Immediate) instruction to accomplish this. For example

```
NI SWITCH,X'FE'
```

Assume SWITCH has a value of 11110011_2. When we perform the AND operation,

```
     11110011₂  SWITCH
AND  11111110₂  immediate operand
     ---------
     11110010₂  value of SWITCH after
                the operation
```

we find that the low-order bit is set to zero. If we wished to set the high-order bit to zero, the instruction would read

```
NI   SWITCH,X'7F'
```

If we wished to set all bits to zero, the instruction would read

```
NI   SWITCH,X'00'
```

The OR Operation. The OR instruction performs a different logical operation. When two numbers are 'ORed', the resulting bit is set to 1 if either or both of the operand bits are on. For example

```
    1010₂
OR  1011₂
    -----
    1011₂
```

Both high-order bits are on. The resulting bit is on. In the next position, both bits are off; the resulting bit is off. In the third position, both bits are on, and the resulting bit is on. In the low-order position, only one bit is on, but the resulting bit is on.

The OR instruction may be used to turn a bit on. Assume we want to turn on the low-order bit of a 1-byte field called SWITCH. We would use the OI (Or Immediate) instruction.

```
OI   SWITCH,X'01'
```

If SWITCH has the value 00110100_2, the operation proceeds as

```
    00110100₂  SWITCH
OR  00000001₂  value of immediate operand
    ---------
    00110101₂  value of SWITCH after
               the operation
```

The OR instruction is used to turn the low-order bit in the first operand field to 1.

The XOR (eXclusive OR) Instruction. The OR instruction is often referred to as an inclusive OR. If either bit *or both* bits are on, the resulting bit is set to 1. The XOR requires that either *but not both* bits are on for the resulting bit to be set to one. For example

$$
\begin{array}{rl}
 & 1010_2 \\
\text{XOR} & \underline{1011_2} \\
 & 0001_2
\end{array}
$$

Both of the high-order bits are on. The resulting bit is off. Proceeding from left to right, in the next position both bits are off and the resulting bit is off. Next, both bits are on and the resulting bit is off. But in the low-order position, only one bit is on, *the resulting bit is on.*

The XOR instructions may be used to *flip* a bit. If the bit is on, we want to turn it off. If the bit is off, we want to turn it on. We can use the XOR instruction to flip the last bit in a 1-byte field called SWITCH.

```
XI   SWITCH,X'01'
```

If SWITCH has a value of 00000000_2, the instruction turns the last bit on.

$$
\begin{array}{rll}
 & 00000000_2 & \text{SWITCH} \\
\text{XOR} & \underline{00000001_2} & \text{immediate operand} \\
 & 00000001_2 & \text{value of SWITCH after the operation}
\end{array}
$$

If SWITCH has a value of 00001111, the instruction turns the last bit off.

$$
\begin{array}{rll}
 & 00001111_2 & \text{SWITCH} \\
\text{XOR} & \underline{00000001_2} & \text{immediate operand} \\
 & 00001110_2 & \text{value of SWITCH after the operation}
\end{array}
$$

Format of the Logical Instructions. The logical instructions may be RR, RX, SI, or SS instructions. The length of the operands may vary from 1 byte in the SI form of the instructions to 16 bytes in the SS form of the instruction. The logical instructions are summarized in Table 13-2.

Table 13-2 Logical Instructions

type instruction	mnemonic AND,OR,XOR	operand location	operand length
RR	NR,OR,XOR	register-register	fullword
RX	N,O,X	register-storage	fullword
SI	NI,OI,XI	storage-immediate	1 byte
SS	NC,OC,XC	storage-storage	1–16 bytes

Use of the Logical Instructions. We have introduced the TM instruction and the logical instructions. We use the TM instruction to test a bit. We use the logical instructions to turn bits on or off. Let's see how these new concepts may be applied in a program segment. We will examine a concept referred to as the *first-time* switch. Often we want to execute a section of code only once in a program. For example, we want to open our files only once. When we enter the same set of code a second time, we want to bypass the open routine. Figure 13-4 represents this concept in a flowchart.

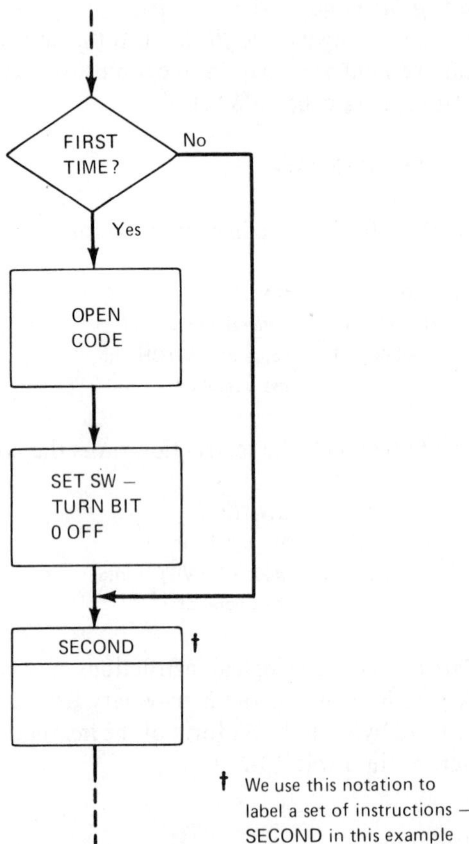

Figure 13-4 Flowchart of a first-time SW.

We use a switch to determine when we enter the code for the first time. We define a 1-byte area of storage called SW. The first bit of SW is set to 1. We test the switch when we enter the program. If the bit is 1, we know we are entering the code for the first time. We open the files, and *turn the bit off.* The next time through we bypass the open routine.

```
              .
              .
              .
              TM      SW,X'80'      TEST BIT 0
              BZ      SECOND        BYPASS OPEN IF OFF
FIRST         OPEN    ...           ELSE OPEN FILES
              NI      SW,X'7F'      AND TURN BIT OFF
              .
              .
              .
SECOND        .
              .
              .
SW            DC      X'80'         DEFINE SW AS 10000000
              .
              .
              .
```

The logical instructions may also be used to change the sign of packed decimal data. If the result of the operation

```
UNPK  ANS(3),CTR
```

is positive, the low-order zone bits of ANS will contain 1100_2. If the result is negative, the low-order zone bits will contain 1101_2. The instruction

```
OI  ANS + 2,X'F0'
```

sets these bits to 1111_2, ensuring that a number will be printed in the last position of ANS.

ROUNDING AND SHIFTING BINARY NUMBERS

Let's examine what happens when we round the number 26.689. We may round the number to two decimal places (26.69) or to one decimal place (26.7). We are adding five to the digit we wish to drop,

```
26.689     26.689
  .005       .050
------     ------
26.694     26.739
     \         \_/
      \_________\____→ dropped
```

and dropping one or two digits. When we drop one digit, we are dividing by ten. When we drop two digits, we are dividing by one hundred.

Rounding Binary Numbers

We round binary numbers using the same approach. We first must add five (we use the term *half-adjust*) to the number, and then divide by the correct power of ten. Let's consider the example we just examined—rounding the number

26.689 to one or two decimal places. The following code rounds a positive number to two decimal places.

```
              .
              .
              .
              L    5,NUM         LOAD NUM IN R5
              AH   5,RND1        HALF-ADJUST NUM
              SR   4,4           CLEAR HIGH-ORDER REGISTER
              D    4,CON         DIVIDE BY TEN
              ST   5,ANS         STORE RESULT
              .
              .
              .
       NUM    DC   F'26689'
       RND1   DC   H'00005'
       CON    DC   F'10'
       ANS    DS   F
```

We define NUM as a fullword constant with a value of 26689. We do not code the decimal place, but must remember where it belongs. The program segment loads NUM into register 5, and then half-adjusts the number by adding the constant RND1 to the contents of register 5. We now must divide by ten, dropping the low-order digit. The divide instruction requires the use of an even–odd register pair. The dividend is in register 5. We clear register 4 using the SR instruction, and then divide the even–odd register pair by the fullword CON. The result (the number 2669 expressed in binary) is stored in the fullword location ANS.

To round the same number to one decimal place, we change the value of RND1 and CON.

```
              .
              .
              .
              L    5,NUM         LOAD NUM IN R5
              AH   5,RND2        HALF-ADJUST
              SR   4,4           CLEAR HIGH-ORDER REGISTER
              DR   4,CON         DIVIDE BY 100
              ST   5,ANS         STORE RESULT
              .
              .
              .
       NUM    DC   F'26689'
       RND2   DC   F'00050'
       CON    DC   F'100'
       ANS    DS   F
```

A Sample Problem. Figure 13-5 shows the solution to Program 4 using fractional numbers and binary arithmetic.

```
*
* PROGRAM 4
* VOLUME OF A SPHERE
* VOLUME=(4/3)PI(R**3)
* BINARY ARITHMETIC WITH ROUNDING
* SOLUTION BY JUDY ADCOCK
*
         PRINT NOGEN
         START 0
BEGIN    SAVE  (14,12)              SAVE REGISTERS
         BALR  12,0                 LOAD BASE
         USING *,12                 ESTABLISH ADDRESSABILITY
         L     5,RADIUS             LOAD RADIUS INTO R5
         M     4,RADIUS             SQUARE RADIUS
         AH    5,=H'50'             ROUND
         D     4,=F'100'            DROP THE TWO EXTRA DIGITS
         M     4,RADIUS             CUBE RADIUS
         AH    5,=H'50'             ROUND
         D     4,=F'100'            AND DROP THE EXTRA TWO DIGITS
         M     4,PI                 MULTIPLY BY PI
         AH    5,=H'50'             ROUND
         D     4,=F'100'            AND DROP THE EXTRA TWO DIGITS
         M     4,=F'4'              MULTIPLY BY FOUR
         D     4,=F'3'              DIVIDE BY 3
         ST    5,RESULT             STORE RESULT
         RETURN (14,12)             AND RETURN
*
* DATA AREAS
*
RADIUS   DC    F'1012'              RADIUS = 10.12
PI       DC    F'314'               PI = 3.14
RESULT   DS    F                    STORAGE AREA FOR THE RESULT
         END   BEGIN
               =F'100'
               =F'4'
               =F'3'
               =H'50'
```

Figure 13-5 Program 4—binary arithmetic with rounding.

In rounding numbers, we drop the correct number of digits by dividing by a power of ten. We also can think of dropping digits as a *shift* of one or more positions to the right. Each time we shift one digit to the right, we divide by ten. Why not use a shift instruction to round binary numbers? The answer lies in the representation of numbers. We divide a decimal number by ten by shifting one place to the right. We divide a binary number by *two* when we shift one place to the right. Can we divide a binary number by ten using this approach? If we shift three places to the right, we divide the numder by eight, If we shift four places to the right we divide the number by sixteen. We cannot divide a binary number by a power of ten using the shifting concept.

We have been considering binary numbers as integers. We can, however, express fractional numbers in binary form. The number 26.689 may be defined as a factional binary number. For example

```
NUM    DC    FS7'26.689'
```

The modifier S is a new term. The S is referred to as a *scaling factor*. We are asking the computer to define a constant whose value is 26.689. There are to be 7 *binary* digits to the right of the *binary point*. Since we are discussing binary numbers, we use the term binary point rather than decimal point.

The computer develops a fullword constant with a hexadecimal value of $000D58_{16}$. The low-order twelve bits represent the number 26.689. This number

11010.1011000

is not an exact equivalent of the decimal fraction. Conversion of decimal fractions to binary numbers is not exact. We can increase the accuracy of the binary fraction, however, by increasing the number of digits to the right of the binary point.

Now that we can express a fraction as a binary number, we can consider the use of shift instructions to drop superfluous digits.

Binary Shift Instructions

The binary shift instructions operate on binary numbers in registers. Data may be shifted to the left or to the right within the register. Shifting may involve from 1 to 63 bits, and may involve one or two adjacent registers. The first operand specifies the register (or register pair) involved in the operation. The effective address of the second operand specifies the number of bits to be shifted. Only the low-order six bits of the second operand address are used in determining the number of bits to be shifted. For example, the instruction

```
SRL  4,1
```

shifts the contents of register 4 one bit to the right (the effective address of the second operand is 000001_{16}). The SRL (Shift Right Logical) instruction shifts the contents of a single register to the right. The high-order position(s) are filled with binary zeros.

Shift operations may be to the left or to the right. The shift instructions may involve one or two registers. There is still another consideration. Shift instructions may be arithmetic or logical. Arithmetic shift instructions do not involve the sign (high-order) bit. Logical shift instructions involve all the bits in the register, regardless of sign. The eight possible shift instructions are given in Table 13-3.

Let's examine the action of these instructions assuming that registers 4 and 5 contain $A1B2C3D4_{16}$ and $0A0B0C0D'_{16}$ respectively. Table 13-4 gives the contents of these registers after each shift instruction is executed. Notice that the logical shift instructions involve the sign bit. In some instances, a shift changes the sign of the number.

The arithmetic shift instructions do not involve the sign of the number. In shifts to the left the sign bit is not disturbed. In shifts to the right, the sign bit

Table 13-3 The Shift Instructions

instruction	operation
SLL	Shift Left Logical 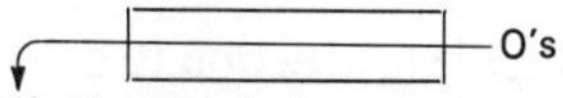
SRL	Shift Right Logical 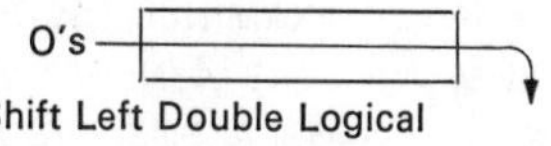
SLDL	Shift Left Double Logical 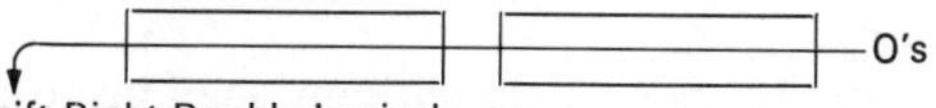
SRDL	Shift Right Double Logical 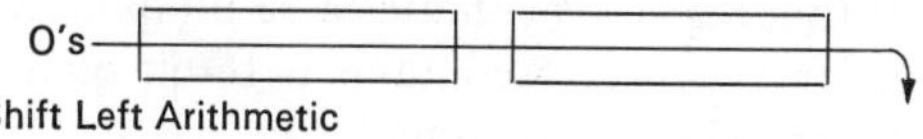
SLA	Shift Left Arithmetic 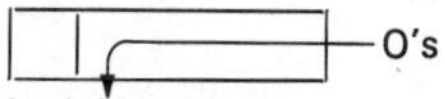
SRA	Shift Right Arithmetic 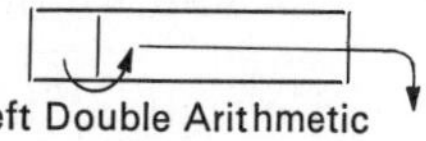
SLDA	Shift Left Double Arithmetic 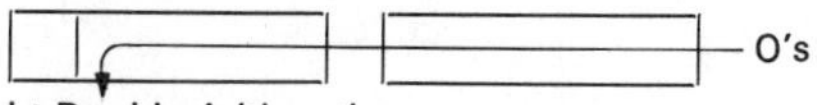
SRDA	Shift Right Double Arithmetic 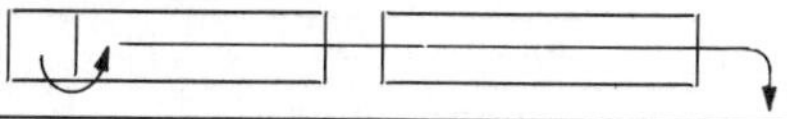

Table 13-4 The Shift Instructions

location	instruction		first operand after execution		
R4: A1B2C3D4	SLL	4,4	R4:	1B2C3D40	
R5: 0A0B0C0D	SRL	5,4(0)	R5:	00A0B0C0	
	SLDL	4,16	R4–R5:	C3D40A0B	0C0D0000
	SRDL	4,16	R4–R5:	0000A1B2	C3D40A0B
	SLA	5,4	R5:	20B0C0D0	
	SRA	4,4	R4:	FA1B2C3D	
	SLDA	4,0(0)	R4–R5:	A1B2C3D4	0A0B0C0D
	SRDA	4,4	R4–R5:	FA1B2C3D	40A0B0C0

is moved to fill the correct number of positions. We say that the sign bit is *propagated* to the right.

It is possible to use the binary shift instructions to round binary fractions defined by using the scaling modifier. The more direct approach, however, involves half-adjusting and dividing by the correct power of ten. The fractional number also may be represented as a floating-point number and floating-point arithmetic may be performed.

The shift instructions often are used to isolate bits. Suppose we want to examine the sign of the binary number in register 5. We could use the instructions

```
SR      4,4     CLEAR REGISTER 4
SLDL    4,1     AND SHIFT SIGN BIT FROM REGISTER 5
```

We now can use a compare instruction to determine if the shifted bit was 0 or 1.

```
CH   4,=H'1'    EXAMINE LOW-ORDER BIT
BE   NEGNUM     IT IS A NEGATIVE NUMBER
B    POSNUM     OR A POSITIVE NUMBER
```

We also can use the shift instructions to squeeze data into a single register. Assume that register 4 contains a 16-bit quantity (A) in the low-order half of the register, and register 5 contains a 16-bit quantity (B) in the low-order half of the register. The instructions

```
SLL     5,16    B IN HIGH-ORDER HALF OF R5
SLDL    4,16    A AND B NOW IN R4
```

squeeze these two halfword quantities into register 4.

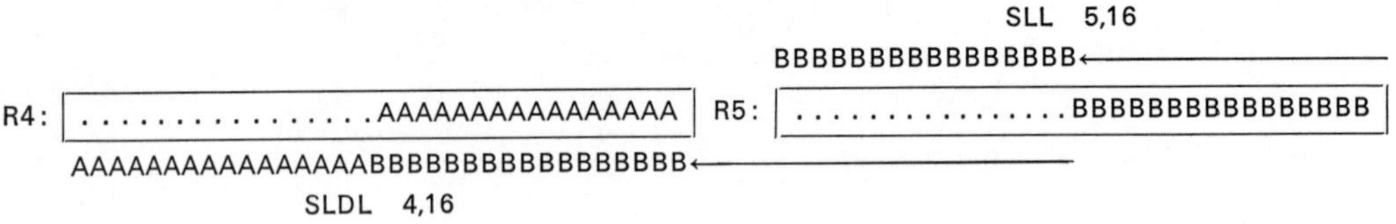

```
                                                        SLL   5,16
                                          BBBBBBBBBBBBBBBB←————————————————
R4: | ................AAAAAAAAAAAAAAAA | R5: | ................BBBBBBBBBBBBBBBB |
AAAAAAAAAAAAAAAABBBBBBBBBBBBBBBB←——————————————————————
              SLDL  4,16
```

Now we can store these data in FULL.

```
ST   4,FULL
```

BYTE MANIPULATION AND LOGICAL ARITHMETIC

The TM and binary shift instructions are concerned with *bits* of data. We will now examine the instructions available to manipulate a single byte of data and then examine the instructions which perform unsigned or logical arithmetic.

Byte Manipulation

The IC (Insert Characters) and STC (STore Characters) instructions may be used to insert or store a single byte of data. In addition, the S/370 provides three new instructions which insert, store, and compare selected bytes of data.

The STC and IC Instructions. The STC instruction (Figure 13-6) stores the low-order eight bits of the first operand register in the second operand storage location. The condition code is not affected by this operation.

The IC instruction (Figure 13-7) inserts the byte at the second operand storage location in the low-order byte of the first operand register. Again, the condition code is not affected.

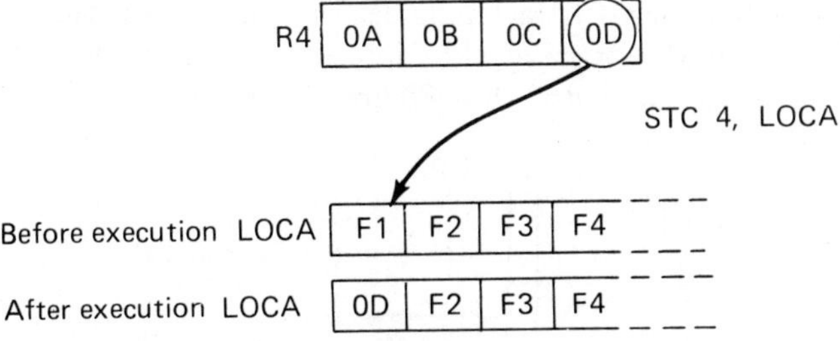

Figure 13-6 Execution of the STC instruction.

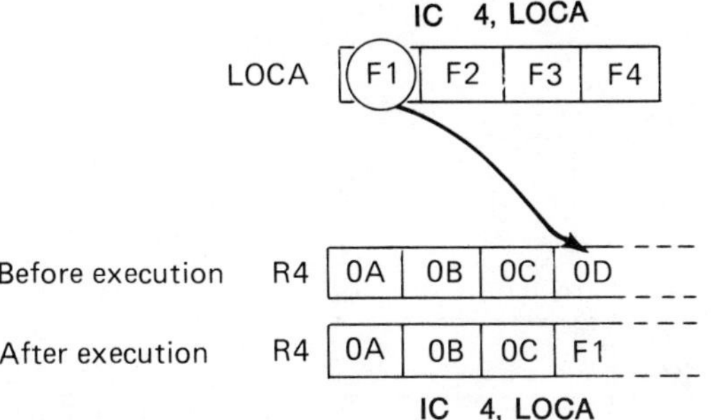

Figure 13-7 Execution of the IC instruction.

The STCM and ICM Instructions. The S/370 provides two additional instructions for storing or inserting one or more bytes of data. Both instructions are RS-type instructions. The R3 operand is replaced by a 4-bit mask.

The STCM (STore Characters under Mask) stores the bytes of the first operand register selected by the mask in consecutive bytes in the second operand storage location. (See Figure 13-8.)

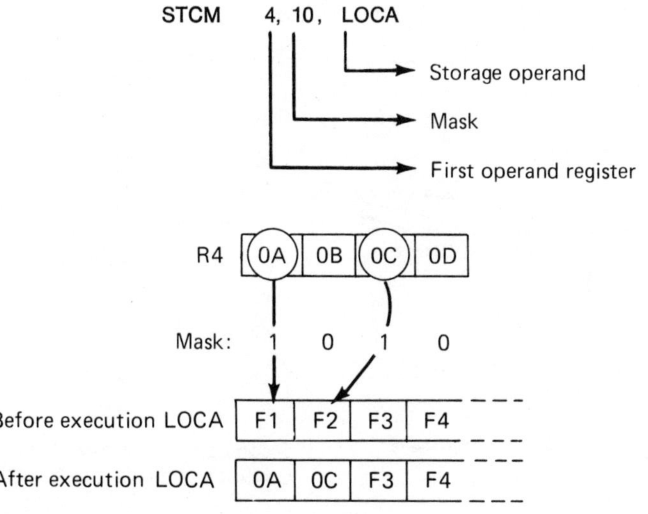

Figure 13-8 Execution of the STCM instruction.

The ICM (Insert Characters under Mask) inserts consecutive bytes from the second operand storage location into the first operand register in the positions indicated by the mask. (See Figure 13-9.)

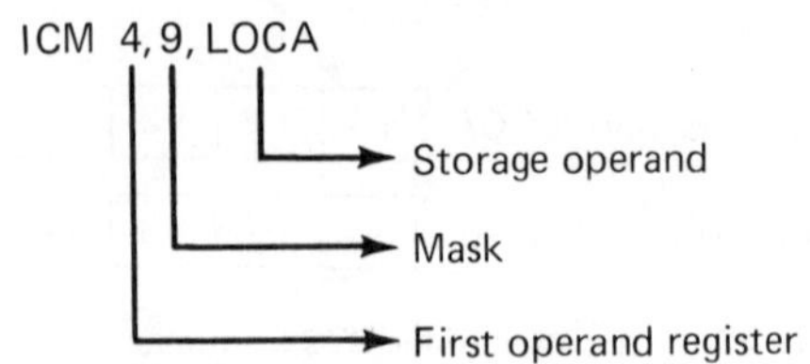

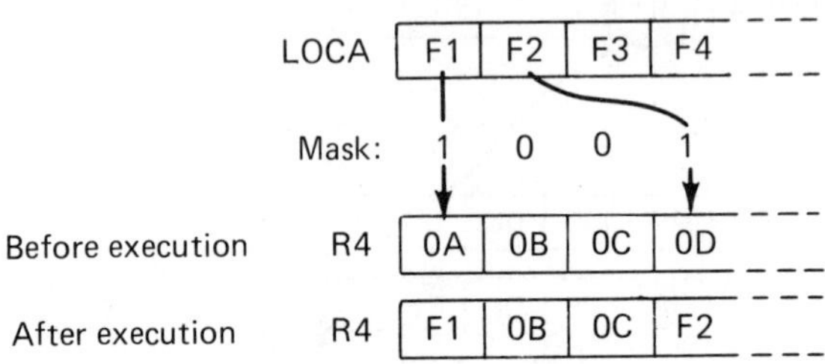

Figure 13-9 Execution of the ICM instruction.

The CLM Instruction. The CLM (Compare Logical under Mask) instruction (Figure 13-10) compares the bytes in the first operand register selected by the

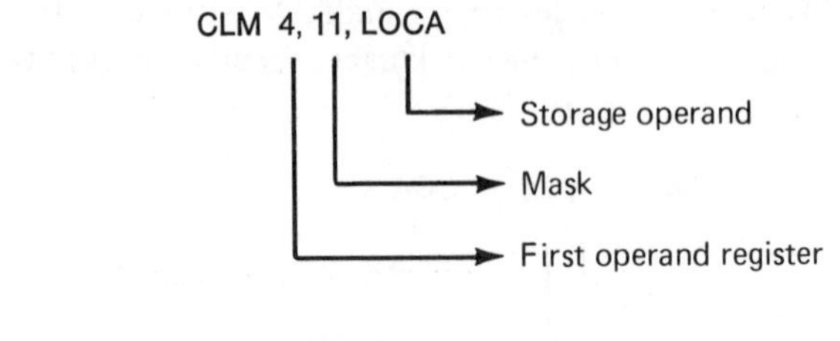

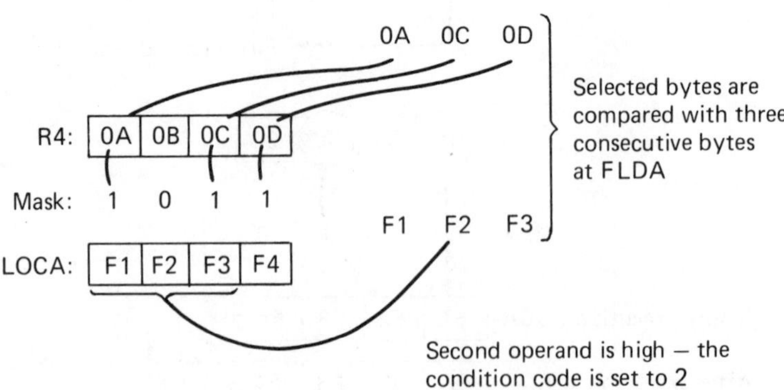

Figure 13-10 The CLM instruction.

mask with consecutive bytes in the second operand storage location. The condition code is set as a result of the operation.

condition code	result
00_2	selected bytes are equal or the mask is zero
01_2	first operand is low
10_2	first operand is high
11_2	not used

Logical Arithmetic

We have seen the concept of logical and arithmetic instructions developed throughout the text. Arithmetic operations are performed on signed operands. Logical operations are performed on unsigned operands. For example, arithmetic compare operations consider the sign of each operand. The compare is algebraic. Logical compare operations do not consider the sign of the operands.

Just as we have signed and unsigned compare instructions, we have signed and unsigned arithmetic operations. We refer to unsigned arithmetic as logical arithmetic.

Logical arithmetic is performed on fullword operands. The operands may both be in registers, or the second operand may be in main storage. There are two types of logical arithmetic operations, addition and subtraction. The logical arithmetic instructions are given in Table 13-5.

Table 13-5 The Logical Instructions

instruction	operation
AL	Add Logical (RX)
SL	Subtract Logical (RX)
ALR	Add Logical Register (RR)
SLR	Subtract Logical Register (RR)

The logical add and subtract instructions place the result in the first operand register. If the result cannot be contained in the register, a carry occurs. This logical carry is not the same as the fixed-point overflow we discussed earlier. The logical carry does not cause an interrupt. It does, however, affect the setting of the condition code.

result of logical operation	condition code setting
zero, no carry	0
non-zero, no carry	1
zero, carry	2
non-zero, carry	3

Table 13-6 Logical Arithmetic

location	instruction	first operand after execution	condition code
R3: 00000000	ALR 4,5	R4: 80000014	CC = 01
R4: 0000000A	SLR 4,4	R4: 00000000	CC = 10†
R5: 8000000A	SLR 3,3	R3: 00000000	CC = 00
OP1: 00000013	AL 5,OP2	R5: 80000000	CC = 11
OP2: FFFFFFF6	AL 4,OP1	R4: 0000001D	CC = 01
	AL 4,OP2	R4: 00000000	CC = 10

†Carry occurs because the operation is essentially the addition $0000000A_{16}$ + $FFFFFFF6_{16}$—we add the complement of the second operand

Examples of the logical arithmetic instructions are given in Table13-6. The condition code settings resulting from these operations are indicated.

A Sample Problem. Binary integer arithmetic is limited to numbers which may be expressed in 31 bits (one bit must be reserved for the sign). Larger numbers usually are handled by floating-point arithmetic, but we can solve some problems involving larger numbers using logical arithmetic.

Program 2 finds the sum of four constants. We have solved this problem using decimal data and binary data. Now we will solve the problem using four 8-byte binary constants. Our solution uses the AL instruction. First, let's define the four double word constants.

```
CON1    DC    F'10'
        DC    F'20'
CON2    DC    F'30'
        DC    F'40'
CON3    DC    F'50'
        DC    F,-60'
CON4    DC    F'70'
        DC    F'-80,
```

The hexadecimal representation of these constants would be:

CON1	0000000A00000014
CON2	0000001E00000028
CON3	00000032FFFFFFC4
CON4	00000046FFFFFFB0

We must clear a register pair for use as an accumulator. Remember, we are working with 8-byte constants—we cannot use a single register. The solution works with registers 4 and 5. We clear the accumulators.

```
          SR   4,4
          SR   5,5
```

We now add the *low-order* portion of CON1 to register 5.

```
          AL   5,CON1 + 4
```

It is possible that this addition results in an overflow. If an overflow occurs, we must add the overflow bit to the low-order position of register 4. We can then proceed to add the four high-order bytes of CON1 to register 4. Our code becomes

```
          AL   5,CON1 + 4         ADD LOW-ORDER WORD OF CONSTANT
          BC   12,NOCARRY         TEST IF CARRY
          AH   4, = H'1'          !NCREMENT IF CARRY
NOCARRY   AL   4,CON1             ADD HIGH-ORDER WORD OF DATA
```

This code adds the contents of CON1 to registers 4 and 5. (See Figure 13-11.) We must repeat this code for the remaining constants. The solution becomes easier if we treat our data as a table and use a register to index the table. For example

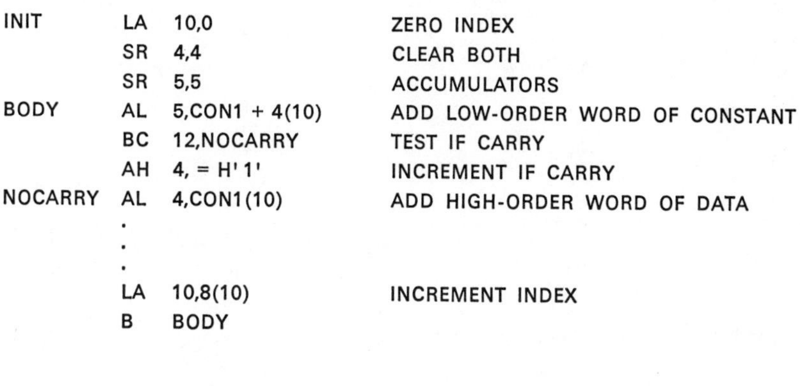

```
INIT      LA   10,0               ZERO INDEX
          SR   4,4                CLEAR BOTH
          SR   5,5                ACCUMULATORS
BODY      AL   5,CON1 + 4(10)     ADD LOW-ORDER WORD OF CONSTANT
          BC   12,NOCARRY         TEST IF CARRY
          AH   4, = H'1'          INCREMENT IF CARRY
NOCARRY   AL   4,CON1(10)         ADD HIGH-ORDER WORD OF DATA
          .
          .
          .
          LA   10,8(10)           INCREMENT INDEX
          B    BODY
```

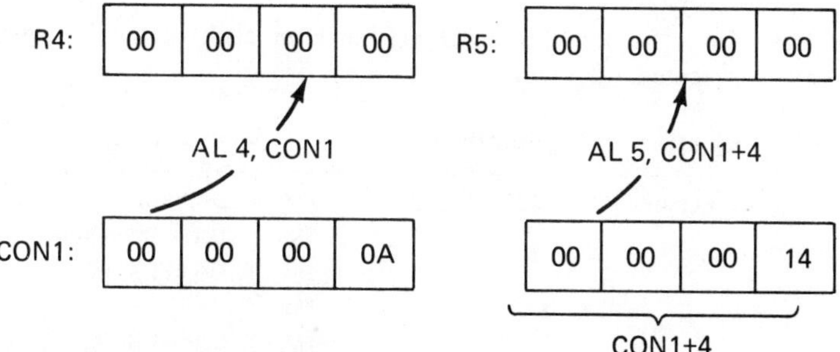

Figure 13-11 Program 2—logical ADD.

All that remains is to code the loop control statement, and to test for overflow in the second AL instruction. The complete solution to Program 2 using 8-byte constants and logical arithmetic is given in Figure 13-12.

```
*
* PROGRAM 2
* SUM OF FOUR 8-BYTE BINARY CONSTANTS
*
         PRINT NOGEN
         START
FIRST    SAVE  (14,12)               SAVE REGISTERS
         BALR  12,0                  LOAD BASE
         USING *,12                  ADDRESSABILITY
INIT     LA    10,0                  ZERO INDEX
         SR    4,4                   ZERO BOTH
         SR    5,5                   ACCUMULATORS
BODY     AL    5,CON1+4(10)          ADD LOW ORDER WORD OF CONSTANT
         BC    12,NOCARRY            TEST IF CARRY
         AH    4,=H'1'               INCEMENT IF CARRY
NOCARRY  AL    4,CON1(10)            ADD HIGH ORDER WORD OF DATA
         BC    3,EXIT                EXIT IF OVERFLOW
         C     10,LIMIT              TEST EXIT
         BE    EXIT                  EXIT OR
         LA    10,8(10)              INCREMENT R10
         B     BODY                  AND LOOP
EXIT     STM   4,5,RESULT            STORE SUM
         RETURN (14,12)              AND RETURN
*
* DATA AREAS
*
LIMIT    DC    F'24'                 DEFINE LIMIT
CON1     DC    F'10'                 *
         DC    F'20'                 *
CON2     DC    F'30'                 * DEFINE
         DC    F'40'                 * FOUR
CON3     DC    F'50'                 * 8-BYTE
         DC    F'-60'                * CONSTANTS
CON4     DC    F'70'                 *
         DC    F'-80'                *
RESULT   DS    D                     RESERVE SPACE FOR RESULT
         END   FIRST
               =H'1'
```

Figure 13-12 Program 2—logical arithmetic.

PROBLEMS **13.1** Give the condition code setting after each of the following instructions is executed.

location	contents	instruction
FLDA	00F100C2	TM FLDA,X' 00'
		TM FLDA,B' 00000000'
		TM FLDA + 1,X' FF'
		TM FLDA + 1,C' 1'
		TM FLDA + 2,X' 00'
		TM FLDA + 3,C' 2'
		TM FLDA + 3,C' B'

13.2 Write a program to create the file used in Program 8. The data specifications are:

input positions	field	output positions
1–6	Employee Number	1–6
7–26	Employee Name	7–26
27–34	Profile	80

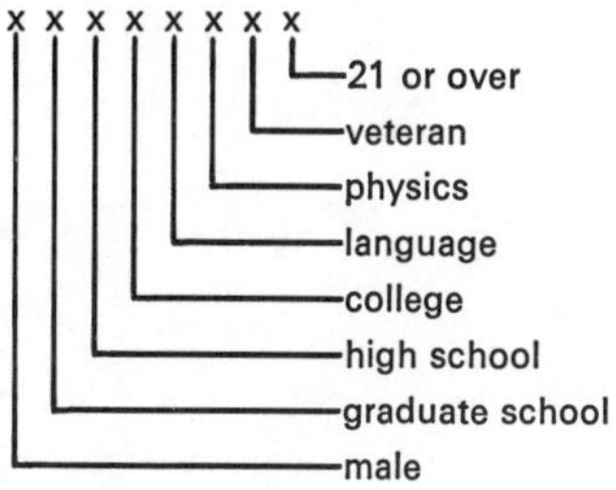

```
x x x x x x x x
| | | | | | | └─21 or over
| | | | | | └───veteran
| | | | | └─────physics
| | | | └───────language
| | | └─────────college
| | └───────────high school
| └─────────────graduate school
└───────────────male
```

For example, an input record with a 1-punch in columns 27 and 34 would result in a profile byte of 10000001_{16}. This byte is then punched in column 80 of the output record. Use the entry

```
PUNCHID = CARDOUT
```

in the HSKPING statement, and the instruction

```
PUT   CARDOUT,PUNCHBLD
```

to punch each record.

13.3 Solve Program 8 giving a detail listing of the employees meeting any of the specified qualifications. The data specifications are:

input position	field	output positions
1–6	Employee Number	11–16
7–26	Employee Name	21–40
80	Profile	
	MALE	61 (X in)
	FEMALE	71 (X in)
	COLLEGE	81 (X in)
	LANGUAGE	91 (X in)
	ALL	101 (X in)

You may develop a total of the number of employees in each category. As a special challenge, you may want to maintain totals in a direct reference table. You then must relate 1-bit in the profile byte to an element in the table.

13.4 Give the contents of the first operand location after each of the following instructions is executed.

location	contents	instruction
Register 4	000000AA	NR 4,5
Register 5	FFFFFF0A	OR 4,5
Register 6	00000012	XR 4,5
LOCA	F1F2F3F4	XR 4,4
		N 4,LOCA
		O 5,LOCA
		X 6,LOCA
		NC LOCA(1),LOCA + 1
		OC LOCA(2),LOCA + 1
		XC LOCA + 2(2),LOCA
		NI LOCA,X' F1'
		OI LOCA + 1,X' 0F'
		XI LOCA + 3,X' F4'

13.5 The XOR instruction may be used to exchange the contents of two locations:

```
XC   FLDA,FLDB
XC   FLDB,FLDA
XC   FLDA,FLDB
```

a. Show how this exchange is accomplished if FLDA contains 11110001_2 and FLDB contains 00011111_2.
b. Code the program segment to exchange the contents of registers 9 and 10.

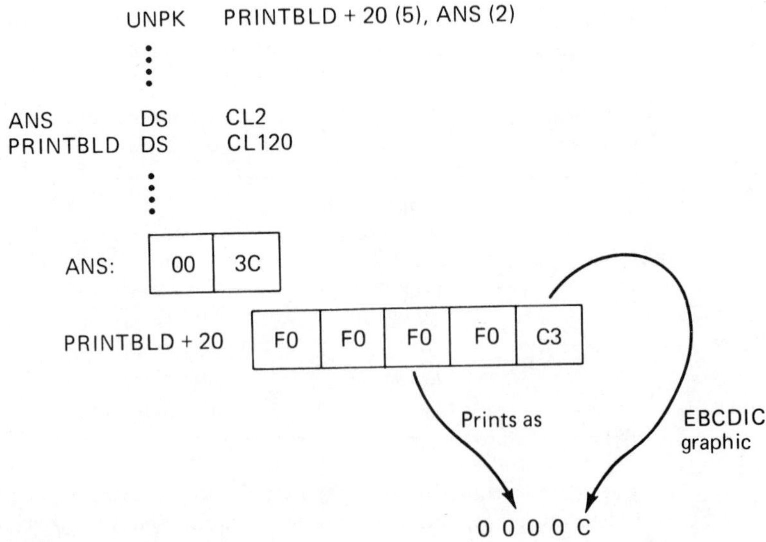

Figure 13-13.

13.6 When numeric data is unpacked, the low-order sign appears in the zone position of the last digit (Figure 13-13). Show how the OR instruction may be used to convert this zone to 1111_2 for printing. Code the instructions to place a plus sign (+) before the data if the field is positive, and a minus sign (−) before the data if the field is negative. Could one of the decimal instructions be used for the same purpose? How?

13.7 Write an assembly program to calculate the value of the expression

$$X = \frac{(A + B) - C}{(D + E)}$$

Use the following data values in the program.

$$A = 12.3$$
$$B = 0.01$$
$$C = 3.00$$
$$D = 2.020$$
$$E = 3.030$$

Round the answer to two decimal places using binary arithmetic.

13.8 Give the contents of the first operand register(s) after execution of each of the following instructions.

location	data	instruction
Register 4	000000B9	SRL 4,3
Register 5	FFFFFF1A	SRL 5,8
Register 6	00000018	SRA 5,8
		SLL 6,12
		SRDL 4,16
		SLDA 4,16

13.9 The binary shift instructions may be used to reverse the bits in a data string. Consider the simple example

1011_2 reverses to 1101_2

This process may be represented as

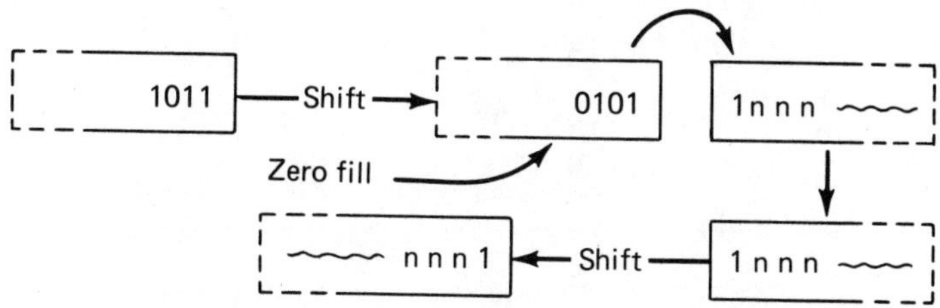

and repeated for each of the four bits. Write a program to reverse all 32 bits in register 4.

13.10 In the divide instructions, the dividend is an even–odd register pair. Usually we place the dividend in the odd register. The sign bit of the dividend must be extended to the even register. Show how the shift instructions may be used to accomplish this.

13.11 The SL or SLR instructions never give a zero result without a carry. But does the subtraction of zero from zero yield a carry? Why?

13.12 How many bits will be shifted in the instruction

```
SRL  4,64
```

Why?

13.13 Use the logical shift instructions to squeeze A (an 8-bit field in the low-order bits of register 4), B (a 12-bit field in the low-order bits of register 5), and C (a 12-bit field in the low-order bits of register 6) into a single word D in storage.

```
Register 4:  . . . . . . . . . . . . AAAAAAAA
Register 5:  . . . . . . . . BBBBBBBBBBBB
Register 6:  . . . . . . . : . CCCCCCCCCCCC
Location D:  AAAAAAAABBBBBBBBBBBBCCCCCCCCCCCC
```

13.14 Write a program to add two 12-byte fields. The high-order bit of each field contains the sign. Place the sum in three consecutive fullwords at RESULT.

13.15 Give the contents of the affected operand after each of the following instructions is executed.

location	contents	instruction	
Register 4	F1F2F3F4	IC	4,LOCA
Register 5	00000A0B	STC	5,LOCB
Register 6	010204C4	IC	6,LOCA + 1
LOCA	C1C2C3C4	STC	6,LOCA + 3
LOCB	0123456C	ICM	6,12,LOCA
		STCM	5,8,LOCB
		STCM	6,15,LOCC

13.16 Using the data in Problem 13.15, give the condition code after each of the following instructions is executed.

a. CLM 4,15,LOCA
b. CLM 5,8,LOCB
c. CLM 6,9,LOCB+1
d. CLM 5,6,LOCB
e. CLM 4,4,LOCA

14

An Expanded Business Subset

This chapter expands the decimal concepts introduced in section two, including instructions to perform decimal shift operations, rounding, and more complex editing operations. We then introduce the instructions to handle strings of data containing special characters as delimiters, and the instructions to handle conversions from one code to another. Finally, we examine two new instructions which perform logical move and compare operations on character strings of more than 256 bytes.

SHIFTING AND ROUNDING DECIMAL NUMBERS

The Decimal Move Instructions. The MVN (MoVe Numerics) instruction and the MVZ (MoVe Zones) instruction involve the movement of four bits(!) from the second operand to the first operand. The MVN instruction moves the four low-order bits of each byte of the second operand to the corresponding positions in the first operand. For example

```
         MVN  FIRST(3),SECOND
          .
          .
          .
FIRST    DC   XL3'12ABC0'
SECOND   DC   XL3'197C6D'
```

The contents of the second operand (SECOND) remain unchanged. After execution of the instruction, FIRST contains a hexadecimal $19ACCD_{16}$ (Figure 14-1).

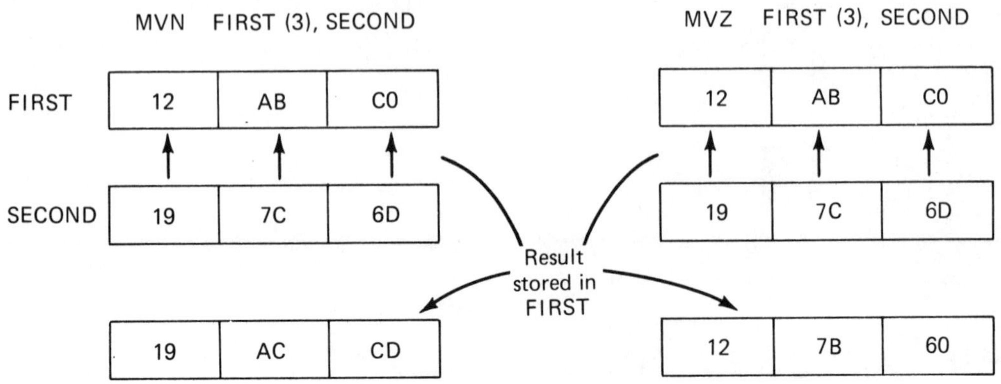

Figure 14-1 The MVN and MVZ instructions.

The MVZ instruction moves the four high-order bits of each byte in the second operand to the corresponding positions in the first operand.

```
         MVZ   FIRST(3),SECOND
          .
          .
          .
FIRST    DC    XL3'12ABC0'
SECOND   DC    XL3'197C6D'
```

As before, the contents of the second operand location remain unchanged. After execution of the instruction, FIRST contain $127B60_{16}$.

The last of the decimal move instructions is the most complex. Figure 14-2 illustrates the MVO (MoVe with Offset) instruction.

The four low-order bits of the rightmost byte of the second operand replace the four high-order bits of the rightmost byte of the first operand. Replacement continues from right to left. If the second operand is greater than the first operand, high-order digits in the second operand are lost. If the second operand is less than the first operand, zeros are filled in the result. There is no checking for valid decimal (packed) data. The condition code is not affected by the MVO instruction.

Shifting Decimal Numbers

There are no special instructions designed to shift decimal numbers to the left (multiplying by powers of ten) or to the right (dividing by powers of ten). But we can use combinations of the decimal move instructions to effect shifting.

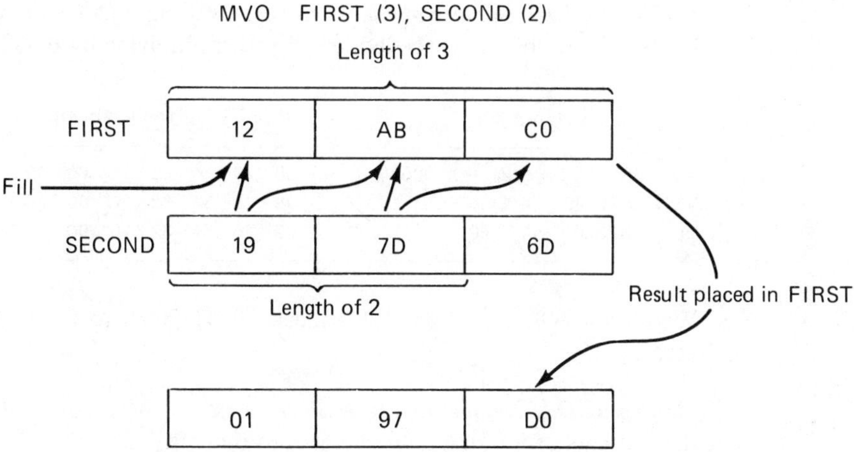

Figure 14-2 The MVO instruction.

Shifting an Even Number of Places to the Right. Let's assume that we want to shift a field called RESULT two positions to the right. Actually, we are dividing the contents of RESULT by 100. Assume that RESULT contains

98	76	54	32	1C

We use the MVN instruction to move the sign, effectively dropping the last two digits.

instruction	RESULT after execution
MVN RESULT + 3(1),RESULT + 4	98 76 54 3C 1C

We now reference RESULT using a length of three. For example

```
MVC  EDFLD(3), RESULT
ED   MASK, EDFLD
```

Shifting an Odd Number of Places to the Right. We can use the MVO instruction to shift an odd number of places. Assume that we want to shift the contents of RESULT three places to the right, dividing by 1000.

instruction	RESULT after execution
MVO RESULT(5),RESULT(3)	00 09 87 65 4C

Shifting an Even Number of Places to the Left. Now let's shift the contents of RESULT four places to the left, effectively multiplying by 10,000.

instruction		RESULT after execution
MVC	RESULT + 5(2), = X' 0000'	98 76 54 32 1C 00 00
MVN	RESULT + 6(1),RESULT + 4	98 76 54 32 1C 00 0C
NI	RESULT + 4,X' F0'	98 76 54 32 10 00 0C

We use the NI instruction with a mask of 11110000_2 to set the old sign bits to zeros.

Shifting an Odd Number of Places to the Left. As a last example, we will shift the contents of RESULT three places to the left.

instruction		RESULT after execution
MVC	RESULT + 5(2), = X' 0000'	98 76 54 32 1C 00 00
MVN	RESULT + 6(1),RESULT + 4	98 76 54 32 1C 00 0C
NI	RESULT + 4,X' F0'	98 76 54 32 10 00 0C
MVO	RESULT(6),RESULT(5)	09 87 65 43 21 00 0C

Rounding Decimal Numbers

Now let's review the concept of rounding before we discuss fractional decimal numbers. In the simple addition

$$\begin{array}{r} 12.986 \\ 13.703 \\ \hline 26.689 \end{array}$$

the result is expressed in three decimal places. The answer also may be rounded to two decimal places giving us the number 26.69. How did we round the number 26.689 to 26.29? We added .005 to the answer and dropped the rightmost digit.

$$\begin{array}{r} 26.689 \\ .005 \\ \hline 26.69\downarrow \\ 4 \end{array} \textit{ dropped}$$

To round the number 26.689 to one decimal place we add the number .050 and drop the last two digits. We use the term half-adjust to describe the addition of .005 and .05 to the number we are rounding.

Now let's develop the instructions to accomplish these processes, using the number 26.689. First we will round to one decimal place. We do not code the decimal point when we express 26.689 as a packed number. We must remember the location of the implied decimal as we code the rounding operation.

```
         AP    NUM(3),RND1            HALF-ADJUST
         MVN   NUM + 1(1),NUM + 2     MOVE SIGN
         MVC   ANS(2),NUM             MOVE RESULT
         .
         .
         .
NUM      DC    XL3'26689C'
RND1     DC    XL3'00050C'
ANS      DS    CL2
```

The logic of this program segment works only if NUM is positive. If NUM is negative, we must subtract RND1, *or*—convert the sign of RND1 to the sign of NUM and add! If we do not know the sign of NUM, the following code solves our problem.

```
         MVN   RND1 + 2(1),NUM + 2    MOVE SIGN
         AP    NUM(3),RND1            HALF-ADJUST
         MVN   NUM + 1(1),NUM + 2     MOVE SIGN
         MVC   ANS(2),NUM             MOVE RESULT
         .
         .
         .
NUM      DC    XL3'26689C'
RND1     DC    XL3'00050C'
ANS      DS    CL2
```

The rounding operation is shown in Figure 14-3.

Let's round the number 26.689 to two decimal places. To do this, we must use the MVO instruction (Figure 14-4).

```
         MVN   RND2 + 2(1),NUM + 2    MOVE SIGN
         AP    NUM(3),RND2            HALF-ADJUST
         MVO   ANS(3),NUM(2)          MOVE AND DROP DIGIT
         MVN   ANS + 2(1),NUM + 2     MOVE SIGN
         .
         .
         .
NUM      DC    XL3'26689C'
RND2     DC    XL3'00005C
ANS      DS    CL3
```

A Sample Program

Let's use Program 4—finding the volume of a sphere—to show how the rounding concepts are handled. We use fractional values in our solution, rounding after

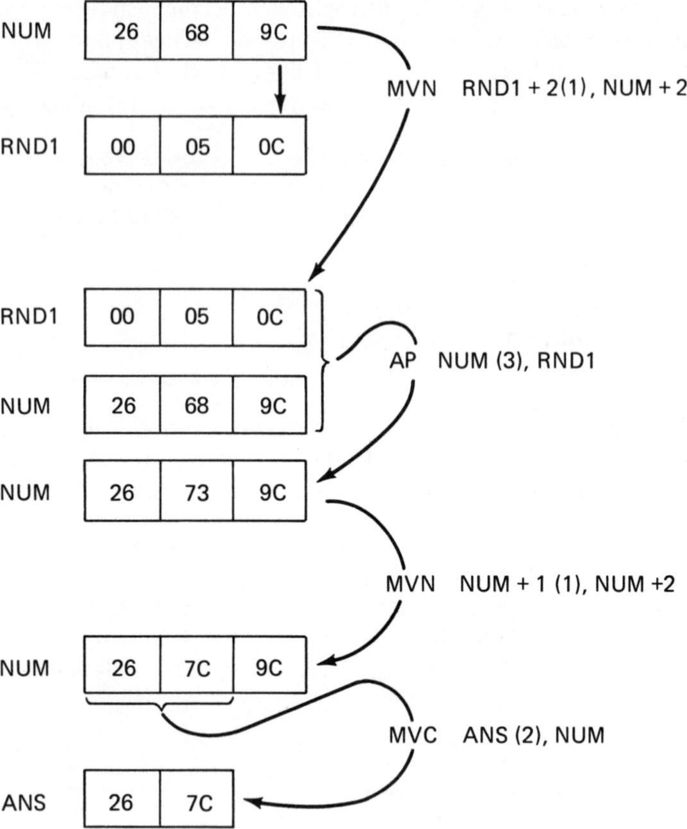

Figure 14-3 Decimal rounding.

each computation. The value of PI is taken as 3.14. The value of the radius is taken as 10.12. Figure 14-5 shows the solution to Program 4 using fractional values.

The SRP Instruction

The S/370 provides a single instruction to perform both the shifting and rounding operations we have been discussing. The SRP (Shift and Round Packed) instruction shifts the contents of the first operand either to the left or to the right for a specified number of digits. Rounding is performed when a right shift is specified. (See Figure 14-6.)

The SRP instruction is an SS-type instruction. The second operand address does not, however, contain data. Bits 26–31 (low-order 6 bits) of the address are taken as a signed binary number indicating the direction and number of digits to

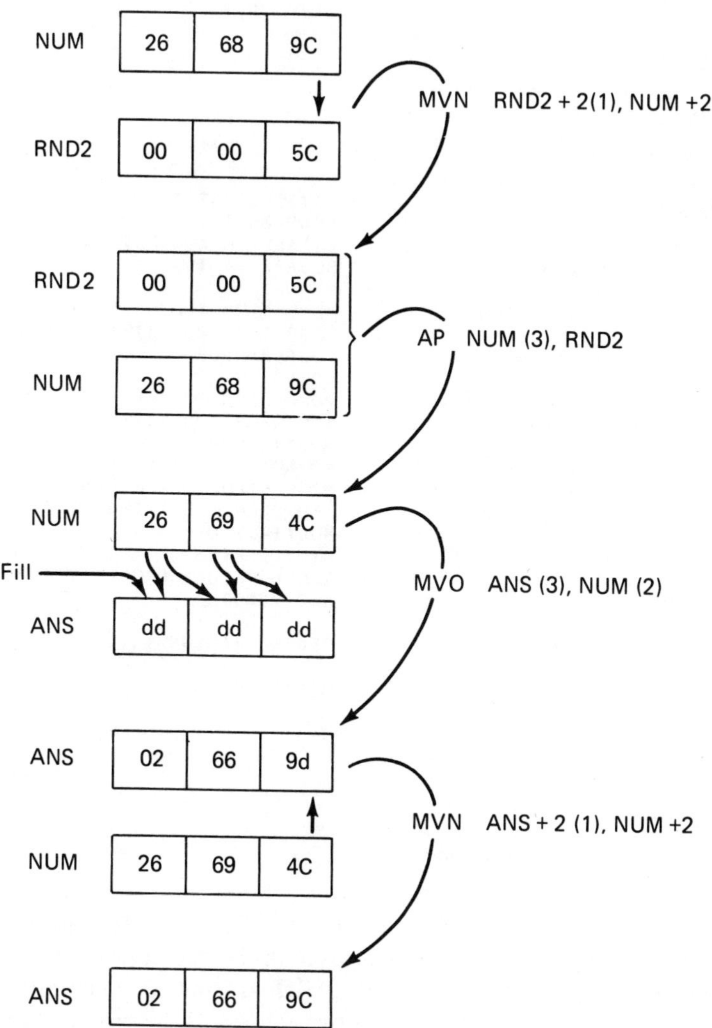

Figure 14-4 Decimal rounding.

be shifted. A zero in bit 26 specifies a left shift. The number in bits 27–31 specifies the number of digits shifted. A 1 in bit 26 specifies a right shift—the number expressed in bits 27–31 in *complement form* determines the number of digits shifted. Rounding occurs during a right shift. The rounding digit (I3 operand) is added to the last digit shifted and a carry is propagated into the next digit if necessary.

For example, the instructions

```
SRP   RESULT,0(3),5
```

```
*
* PROGRAM 4
* VOLUME OF A SPHERE
* VOLUME=(4/3)PI(R**3)
* DECIMAL ARITHMETIC WITH ROUNDING
* SOLUTION BY JUDY ADCOCK
*
         PRINT NOGEN
         START 0
BEGIN    SAVE  (14,12)                  SAVE REGISTERS
         BALR  12,0                     LOAD BASE
         USING *,12                     ESTABLISH ADDRESSABILITY
         MP    RCUBE,RADIUS             SQUARE RADIUS
         AP    RCUBE,=P'50'             ROUND
         MVN   RCUBE+4(1),RCUBE+5       MOVE SIGN TO THE LEFT
         ZAP   RCUBE,RCUBE(5)           DROP THE TWO EXTRA DIGITS
         MP    RCUBE,RADIUS             CUBE RADIUS
         AP    RCUBE,=P'50'             ROUND
         MVN   RCUBE+4(1),RCUBE+5       MOVE SIGN TO THE LEFT
         ZAP   RCUBE,RCUBE(5)           AND DROP TWO EXTRA DIGITS
         MP    RCUBE,PI                 MULTIPLY BY PI
         AP    RCUBE,=P'50'             ROUND
         MVN   RCUBE+4(1),RCUBE+5       MOVE SIGN TO THE LEFT
         ZAP   RCUBE,RCUBE(5)           AND DROP TWO EXTRA DIGITS
         MP    RCUBE,=P'4'              MULTIPLY BY 4
         DP    RCUBE,=P'3'              DIVIDE BY 3
         MVC   RESULT(5),RCUBE          STORE RESULT DROPPING REMAINDER
         RETURN (14,12)                 AND RETURN
*
RADIUS   DC    PL3'1012'                DEFINE RADIUS=10.12
RCUBE    DC    PL6'1012'
PI       DC    P'314'                   DEFINE PI=3.14
RESULT   DS    PL5
         END   BEGIN
               =P'50'
               =P'4'
               =P'3'
```

Figure 14-5 Program 4—rounding decimal arithmetic.

shift the contents in a packed field called RESULT. The direction of the shift is determined by the effective address of the second operand. If register 3 contains 00000004_{16}, the contents of RESULT are shifted four positions to the left. Remember, if bit 26 of the effective address of the second operand is positive, the shift is to the left.

If, however, register 3 contains $FFFFFFFC_{16}$, the contents of RESULT are shifted four positions to the right. The last digit shifted is rounded by adding the rounding factor 5, specified in the I3 operand. What would be the direction and magnitude of the shift if register 3 contains $FFFFFFFC_{16}$ in the instruction?

```
SRP   RESULT,10(3),5
```

A data exception occurs if the first operand does not contain packed data, and a decimal overflow occurs if significant high-order digits are lost. The condition code is set as a result of the operation.

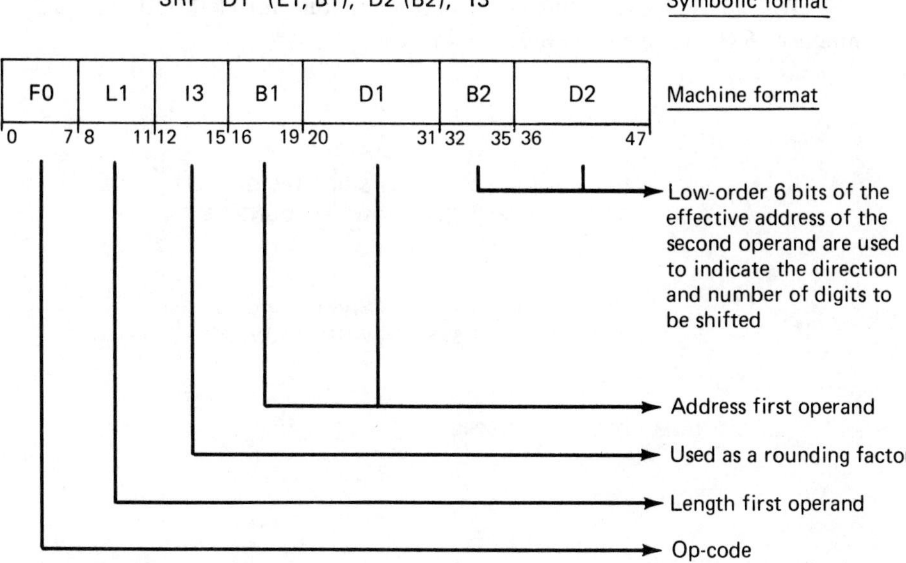

Figure 14-6 The SRP instruction.

condition code	result
00_2	Result is zero
01_2	Result is less than zero
10_2	Result is greater than zero
11_2	Overflow

Let's see how we can use this instruction to accomplish the results obtained using the decimal move instructions. Assume that RESULT contains

00	00	76	54	32	1C

shift	instruction	RESULT after execution
right—2 places	LA 3, = F' − 2'	
	SRP RESULT,0(3),0	00 00 00 76 54 3C
right—3 places	LA 3, = F' − 3'	
	SRP RESULT,0(3),0	00 00 00 07 65 4C
left—4 places	LA 3, = F' 4'	
	SRP RESULT,0(3),0	76 54 32 10 00 0C
left—3 places	LA 3, = F' 3'	
	SRP RESULT,0(3),0	07 65 43 21 00 0C

We can use the rounding factor in conjunction with a left shift to round the number 26.689 to one or two decimal places.

```
           .
           .
           .
           LA    3, = F' - 1'        SHIFT 1 DIGIT LEFT
           SRP   NUM(3),0(3),5       WITH ROUNDING
           .
           .
           .
           LA    3, = F' - 2'        SHIFT 2 DIGITS LEFT
           SRP   NUM(3),0(3),5       WITH ROUNDING
           .
           .
           .
     NUM   DC    XL3' 26689C'
           .
           .
           .
```

The EDMK Instruction

The EDMK instruction is used to edit packed data. The EDMK instruction is similiar to the ED instruction, but provides the programmer with the address of the first non-zero byte. The EDMK instruction may be used to place the dollar sign to the left of the first significant digit.

Until this point, we used the MVI or MVC instruction to place the dollar sign in the first position of the edited result, overlaying the fill character. This technique is satisfactory when all digits in the edited result are significant ($12,345.67). If the numeric data contains leading zeros the result might appear as $00,005.67. To avoid this undesirable format, we used the fill character to replace leading zeros. We could replace leading zeros with a blank ($ 5.67), or with a check-protection character such as the asterisk ($*****5.67). The most desirable technique, however, is to *float* the dollar sign to the left of the first significant digit. The edited result then appears as $5.67.

The ED instruction does not tell us where the first significant digit is encountered. The EDMK instruction does. The EDMK instruction places the address of the first significant digit in register 1. The instructions are identical in all other respects.

Our problem is to place the dollar sign to the left of the first significant digit. Let's use the solution to Program 1 (Figure 14-7) as our example. We replace the ED instruction with the EDMK instruction

```
EDMK   GROSSOUT(13),GROSSPK
```

Register 1 now contains the address of the first significant digit in GROSSOUT. We want to move the dollar sign to the *left* of this digit. We must decrement

```
*
* PROGRAM 1
* CARD TO PRINT
* USE OF THE EDMK INSTRUCTION
*
         PRINT NOGEN
         START
FIRST    HSKPING CARDID=INCARD,PRINTID=PRINT       NAME FILES
*        *
*        *       SOME
*        *       HOUSEKEEPING
*        *       STATEMENTS
*        *       ARE
*        *       OMITTED
*        *       HERE
*        *
READRT   GET     INCARD,INWORK                     GET RECORD INTO INWORK
         MVC     NUMOUT(6),NUMIN                   MOVE EMP NUMBER
         MVC     NAMEOUT(20),NAMEIN                AND EMP NAME
         PACK    GROSSPK(5),GROSSIN                PACK GROSS
         MVC     GROSSOUT(13),GROSSMSK             MOVE MASK
         LA      1,GROSSOUT+9                      ESTABLISH SIGNIFICANCE
         EDMK    GROSSOUT(13),GROSSPK              EDIT PACKED DATA
         SH      1,=H'1'                           BACKSPACE 1 THEN
         MVI     0(1),C'$'                         MOVE DOLLAR
         PUT     PRINT,PRINTBLD                    WRITE RECORD THEN
         B       READRT                            LOOP BACK
*        *
*        *       AFTER ALL INPUT CARDS
*        *       HAVE BEEN READ AND PROCESSED
*        *       THE PROGRAM IS COMPLETE
*        *
*
* DATA AREAS
*
INWORK   DS      0CL80                             INPUT AREA
NUMIN    DS      CL6                               *
NAMEIN   DS      CL20                              *
         DS      CL24                              *
GROSSIN  DS      CL8                               *
         DS      CL22                              *
PRINTBLD DS      0CL120                            OUTPUT AREA
         DC      10CL1' '                          *
NUMOUT   DS      CL6                               *
         DC      10CL1' '                          *
NAMEOUT  DS      CL20                              *
         DC      10CL1' '                          *
GROSSOUT DS      CL13                              *
         DC      51CL1' '                          *
GROSSPK  DS      CL5                               PACK DATA BEFORE EDIT
GROSSMSK DC      XL13'40206B2020206B2021204B2020'  EDIT MASK
         END     FIRST
                 =H'1'
```

Figure 14-7 Program 1—solution using the EDMK instruction.

register 1, and then use register 1 to address the correct position in GROSSOUT explicitly. For example

```
SH    1,=H'1'
MVI   0(1),C'$'
```

Or, using the BCTR instruction*

```
BCTR 1,0
MVI  0(1),C'$'
```

The new segment of code now appears as

```
EDMK  GROSSOUT(13),GROSSPK
BCTR  1,0
MVI   0(1),C'$'
```

Suppose, however, that no significant digits are encountered before the significance starter. In this case, the contents of register 1 remain unchanged. The code shown above is incorrect. We must place the address of the significance starter in register 1 before we start the edit operation. If significance is not encountered, register 1 contains the correct address for the dollar sign. If significance is encountered before the significance indicator is examined, the EDMK instruction changes the contents of register 1 accordingly. The correct code becomes

```
LA    1,GROSSOUT + 9
EDMK  GROSSOUT(13),GROSSPK
BCTR  1,0
MVI   0(1),C'$'
```

THE TRT, EX, AND TR INSTRUCTIONS

The TRT (Translate and Test) instruction searches for certain characters within a data field. We can use this instruction to search for the delimiters in a table containing variable length entries.

The EX (EXecute) instruction allows us to modify bits 8–15 of a machine instruction before executing the instruction. We can use the execute instructions to move fields which do not contain the same number of bytes.

The TR instruction is used to convert a data field from one computer code to another.

The TRT Instruction

The TRT instruction examines each byte within a string of characters (*the argument*) against a corresponding byte within a table (*the function*). For example, the instruction

```
TRT  ARG(20),FUNCTION
```

examines each byte within the 20-byte field called ARG against a 256-byte field called FUNCTION. The instruction requires that the function table contains 256 bytes. We will see why in a moment.

*When the second operand register is register 0, a branch does not occur regardless of the contents of the first operand register.

Let's assume that FUNCTION contains binary zeros in every byte except one (Figure 14-8). The sixty-fifth byte in FUNCTION contains a 40_{16}. And ARG contains three sets of numbers, separated by blanks.

The instruction

```
TRT   ARG(20),FUNCTION
```

examines each byte in ARG against the corresponding byte in FUNCTION. For example, the first byte in ARG contains $F1_{16}$. The byte at FUNCTION + $F1_{16}$

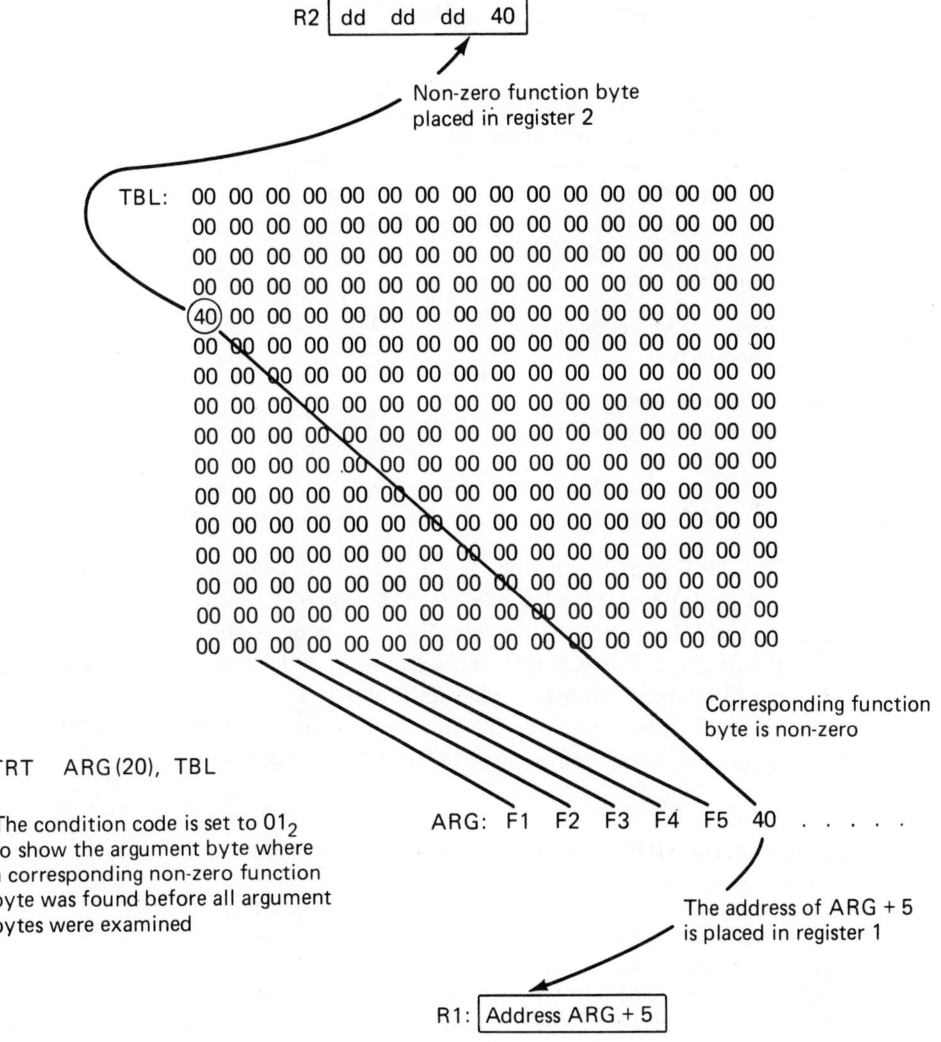
R2 dd dd dd 40
Non-zero function byte placed in register 2
TBL:
40
Corresponding function byte is non-zero
TRT ARG(20), TBL
The condition code is set to 01₂ to show the argument byte where a corresponding non-zero function byte was found before all argument bytes were examined
ARG: F1 F2 F3 F4 F5 40 . . . . .
The address of ARG + 5 is placed in register 1
R1: Address ARG + 5

Figure 14-8 The TRT instruction.

is examined. This byte, the 242nd byte in FUNCTION is zero. The scan continues. The next byte in ARG, $F2_{16}$, is examined against the byte at FUNCTION + $F2_{16}$. This byte is also zero. The scan continues until the sixth argument byte is examined. This byte is examined against the byte at FUNCTION + 40_{16}, the sixty-fifth byte in FUNCTION. This byte is non-zero. It contains 40_{16}. The scan of ARG stops at this point. The address of the *argument* byte whose corresponding function byte was found to be non-zero is placed in register 1. In our example, the address of ARG + 5 is placed in register 1. The non-zero function byte is placed in the eight low-order bits of register 2. And, finally, the condition code is set to 01 to show that a non-zero function byte was found before all twenty bytes in ARG had been examined.

Table 14-1 Condition Code Settings after the TRT Instruction Is Executed

condition	CC setting
All argument bytes have corresponding zero function bytes	00
Last argument byte has corresponding non-zero function byte	10
Argument byte with corresponding non-zero function byte found before end of argument string	01

The TRT instruction does a great deal. It examines each byte in the argument field (proceeding from left to right) against a function table. The scan proceeds until the corresponding function byte is non-zero. The condition code is set, the function byte is placed in the eight low-order bits of register 2, and the address of the argument byte is placed in register 1.

Table 14-2 illustrates the TRanslate and Test instructions for three different argument fields, using the data for TBL in Figure 14-8.

Table 14-2 The TRT Instruction Condition Code Settings

location	instruction	result
ARG1: C1 C2 40	TRT ARG1(3),TBL	CC = 10
ARG2: F1 F2 40 F3 F4	TRT ARG2(5),TBL	CC = 01
ARG3: F1 F2 F3 F4 F5	TRT ARG3(5),TBL	CC = 00
TBL: See Figure 14-8.		

We find a non-zero byte in TBL at TBL + 40_{16}. The instruction scans a 3-byte argument field called ARG. In the first example, the instruction examines the first byte of ARG. The corresponding function byte at TBL + $C1_{16}$ is zero. The scan continues with the second argument byte, ARG + 1. The corresponding function byte (TBL + $C2_{16}$) is zero. The scan moves to the last argument byte ARG+2. The corresponding function byte (TBL + 40_{16}) is non-zero. The condition code is set to 10_2. The non-zero function byte corresponds to the last argument byte. There are no more argument bytes to be examined. The non-zero function (40_{16}) is placed in register 2. The address of the argument byte (ARG+2) is placed in register 1.

In the second example, the non-zero function byte is not the last byte in the argument field. The condition code is set of 01_2. There are still more argument bytes to be examined. The value of the non-zero function byte is placed in register 2. The address of the argument byte (ARG+1) is placed in register 1.

In the last example, all corresponding function bytes are non-zero. The condition code is set to 00_2. The contents of registers 1 and 2 remain unchanged.

A Sample Program

The most common use of the TRT instruction involves searching for special characters. Let's consider the use of this instruction in locating delimiters.

Program 9 ***Problem Statement.*** A table of employee names and addresses resides in storage (Table 14-3). A FF_{16} marks the end of the table. The entries within the table are separated by colons. The fields within each entry are separated by semicolons. The maximum length of any field is twenty bytes. Use the information in this table to print name and address labels.

Table 14-3 Program 9—Data Table

assembly code			table
DATATBL	DC	CL17' PRISCILLA STRONG;'	PRISCILLA STRONG;
		CL18' 128 EAST 6 STREET;'	128 EAST 6 STREET;
		CL14' NEW YORK, NY:'	NEW YORK, NY:
		CL13' MARY MICHAEL;'	MARY MICHAEL;
		CL14' 883 HUGO RD;'	883 HUGO RD;
		CL13' CHICAGO,ILL:'	CHICAGO, ILL:
		.	.
		.	.
		.	.
		X' FF'	X FF

Solution. The logic for Program 9 is given in Figure 14-9. We must search the argument table for one of three delimiters. A semicolon marks the end of a field.

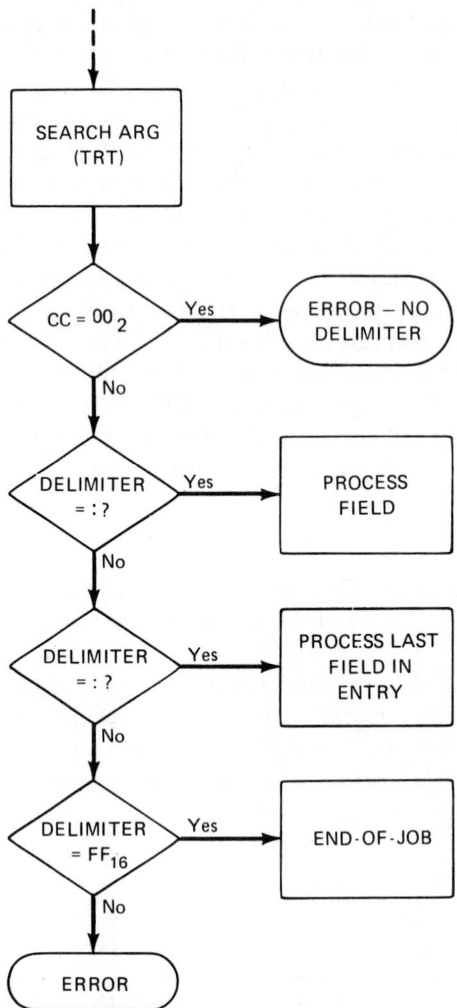

Figure 14-9 Program 9—flowchart.

We must move each field to the print line, and print a line. The colon marks the end of an entry. We must move the last field to the print line, write a line, and skip to the next label. FF_{16} marks the end of the table. We now proceed to the end-of-job routine.

We use the TRT instruction to locate the delimiters. We translate the argument field against a function table (TRTTBL). TRTTBL is established with non-zero function bytes at TRTTBL+$5E_{16}$, TRTTBL+$7A_{16}$, and TRTTBL +FF_{16}. The relative displacements within TRTTBL are the hexadecimal codes for a semicolon, colon, and FF_{16} respectively. We shall see why in a moment.

The following code is used to initialize TRTTBL:

```
         MVI   TRTTBL + X'5E',C';'
         MVI   TRTTBL + X'7A',C':'
         MVI   TRTTBL + X'FF',X'FF'
          .
          .
          .
TRTTBL   DC    256X'00'
```

Notice that the non-zero function bytes coded in TRTTBL represent the codes of our delimiters. The reason for this becomes apparent shortly.

Now that we have initialized TRTTBL, we can proceed with our program. We now must code the TRT instruction. Since the maximum size of each field is twenty bytes, we code the TRT instruction specifying a length of twenty

```
TRT   DATATBL(20),TRTTBL
```

We use the label DATATBL to reference the name and address table. Let's assume DATATBL contains the data shown in Table 14-3. The first delimiter in DATATBL is a semicolon. The TRT instruction scans DATATBL until the semicolon is encountered (corresponding non-zero function byte in TRTTBL is non-zero). The scan stops. The condition code is set to 01_2—a non-zero function byte is encountered before the end of the 20-byte argument. The address of the non-zero argument byte (DATATBL+16) is placed in register 1. The non-zero function byte found at TRTTBL+$5E_{16}$ is placed in register 2.

The program now must examine register 2 to determine which delimiter stopped the search. We initialized TRTTBL to help us solve this problem. The non-zero function bytes in TRTTBL represent the delimiters for which we are searching. A semicolon is the first delimiter found (Figure 14-10). The hexadecimal configuration for the semicolon was placed in TRTTBL+$5E_{16}$. This hexadecimal code is now placed in the eight low-order bits of register 2.

We cannot examine the low-order bits of a register. We must move these eight bits to a main storage location. The STC (STore Character) instruction stores the eight low-order bits of a register into a main storage location. We can store the delimiter code as follows:

```
STC   2,TESTFLD
```

The non-zero function byte is now in TESTFLD. We now examine the contents of TESTFLD,

```
CLI   TESTFLD,C';'
BE    SEMICOL
CLI   TESTFLD,C':'
BE    COLON
CLI   TESTFLD,X'FF'
BE    EOJRT
B     ERROR
```

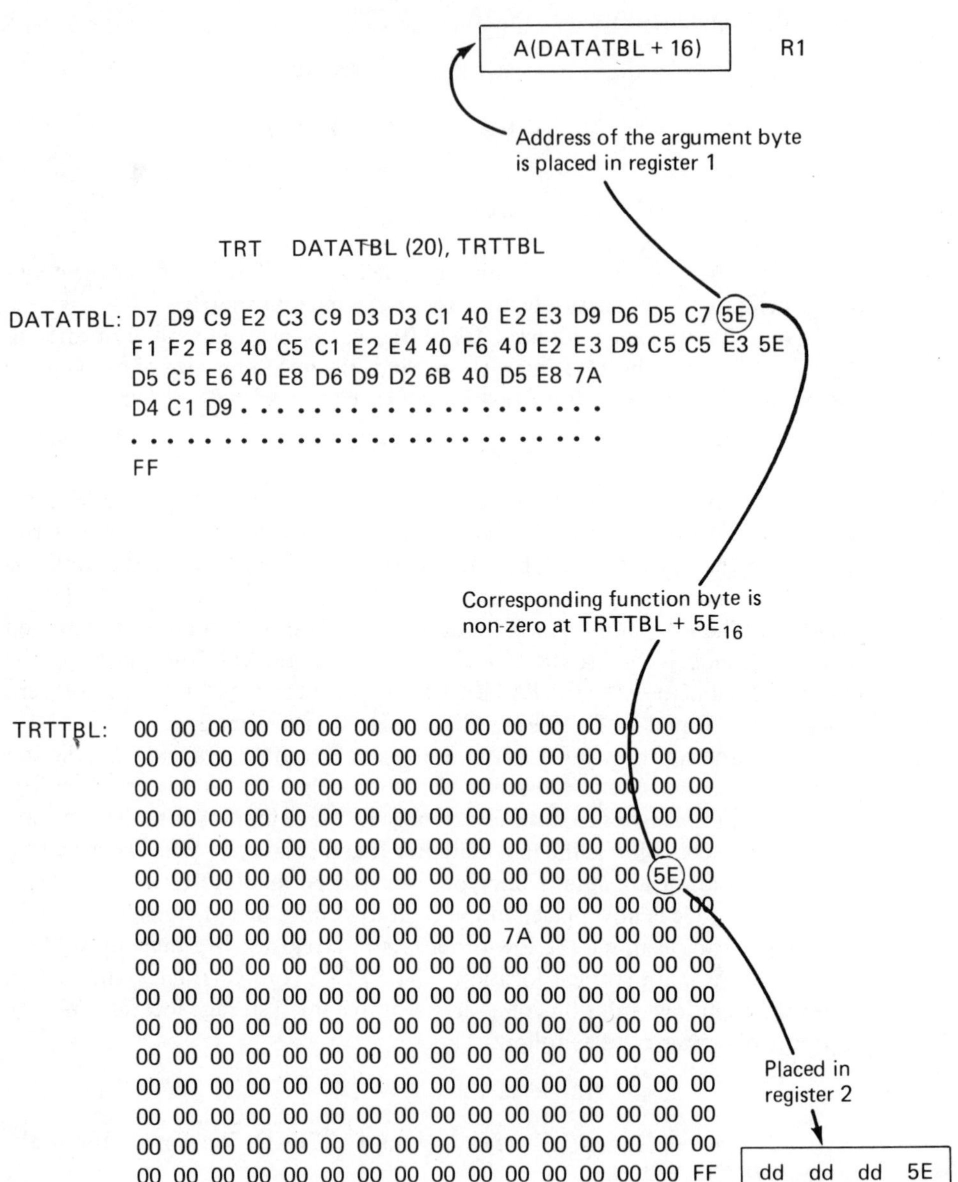

Figure 14-10 Program 9—the TRT instruction.

and branch to the routine called SEMICOL. The flowchart (Figure 14-9) tells us we must move the first field to the output line. We will use the MVC instruction to move the data to the output line. But wait a moment! We do not know how many bytes to move. We must somehow determine the length of the argument field and *modify* bits 8–15 (the length field) of the MVC instruction.

The EXecute Instruction. The EX (EXecute) instruction allows us to modify bits 8–15 of *another* instruction, and then execute the modified instruction. The EX instruction OR's bits 8–15 of the specified instruction against the low-order byte of a register. Let's consider the instruction

```
MVCINSTR  MVC  OUT(20),IN
```

which moves twenty bytes of data from a field called IN to a field called OUT. Suppose, during the course of our program, we wish to move only ten bytes from IN to OUT. Examine the following code.

```
          LA   4,9
          EX   4,MVCINSTR
          .
          .
          .
MVCINSTR  MVC  OUT(0),IN
```

The LA instruction places the number nine in register 4. We then execute the instruction labeled MVCINSTR. Bits 8–15 of MVCINSTR are OR'd against the low-order byte of register 4. Register 4 contains the binary number nine. When the EX instruction is excuted, bits 8–15 of MVCINSTR are OR'ed as follows:

```
      1001    REGISTER 4
OR    0000    BITS 8–11 OF MVCINSTR
      ----
      1001    RESULT IN BITS 8–11
```

We move *ten* bytes of data. Remember, the binary number contained in bits 8–15 of the MVC machine instruction is *one less* than the number of bytes actually moved.

Let's return to our problem. First we must determine the length of the argument field; that is, the length of the data we wish to move to the output line. We know the address of the first delimiter. The TRT instruction placed this address in register 1. We also can determine the address of the first character in DATATBL. The difference between these two addresses gives us the length of the argument field less 1.

```
          LA   3,DATATBL             LOAD ADDRESS ARG
          TRT  DATATBL(20),TRTTBL    FIND DELIMITER
          LR   4,1                   SAVE DELIMITER ADDRESS
          SR   4,3                   GET LENGTH ARGUMENT LESS ONE
          BCTR 4,0                   DROP DELIMITER
          EX   4,MVCINSTR            MOVE DATA TO PRINTBLD
          .
          .
          .
MVCINSTR  MVC  PRINTBLD,DATATBL
```

The LA instruction places the address of the first byte in DATATBL in register 3. The TRT instruction places the address of the first delimiter in register

1. We save the address of the delimiter in register 4. The difference between register 4 and register 3 gives us the length of the first argument field—less one—in register 4. We must decrement register 4 by 1 to drop the delimiter. We use register 4 in the EX instruction to move the correct number of bytes to the print line and print the first line of the label

```
         PUT   PRINT.PRINTBLD
```

Now we must return to the argument field and search for the next delimiter. We cannot use the instruction

```
         TRT   DATATBL(20),TRTTBL
```

at this point. We do not want to start the search at the beginning of DATATBL. We want to start the search at the position *following* the first argument byte. Since we know that the address of the first argument byte is contained in register 1, we can use explicit addressing to code the solution.

```
         LA    3,DATATBL            LOAD ADDRESS ARG
TRTLOOP  TRT   0(20,3),TRTTBL       FIND DELIMITER
         LR    4,1                  SAVE DELIMITER ADDRESS
         SR    4,3                  GET LENGTH ARGUMENT LESS ONE
         BCTR  4,0                  DROP DELIMITER
         .
         .
         .
         EX    4,MVCINSTR           MOVE DATA TO PRINTBLD
         LA    1,1(1)               INCREMENT REGISTER 1
         LR    3,1                  POINT TO NEXT ARG BYTE
         PUT   PRINT,PRINTBLD       WRITE A LINE
         B     TRTLOOP              BRANCH BACK
         .
         .
         .
MVCINSTR MVC   PRINTBLD(0),0(3)     MOVE DATA FROM DATATBL
```

The complete solution to Program 9 is given in Figure 14-11.

The housekeeping instructions at INIT establish the non-zero function bytes in TRTTBL and load the address of the first byte in DATATBL in register 3.

The main loop at TRTLOOP scans the argument field DATATBL against the function field TRTTBL. If the first twenty bytes of the argument do not have a corresponding non-zero function byte, an error is recognized. A condition code of zero (mask of 8 in the BC instruction) indicates that no corresponding non-zero function bytes were found. The instruction

```
         BC  8,ERROR
```

branches us to the error code in this instance.

```
*
* PROGRAM 9
* ILLUSTRATING THE TRT AND EX INSTRUCTIONS
*
         START
         PRINT NOGEN
*        SAVE  (14,12)                        CODED IN HSKP MACRO
*        BALR  12,0                           CODED IN HSKP MACRO
*        USING *,12                           CODED IN HSKP MACRO
PROG9    HSKPING PRINTID=PRINT                NAME OUTPUT FILE
*        *
*        *      SOME
*        *      HOUSEKEEPING
*        *      STATEMENTS
*        *      ARE
*        *      OMITTED
*        *      HERE
*        *
INIT     MVI   TRTTBL+X'5E',C';'              MOVE DELIMITER
         MVI   TRTTBL+X'7A',C':'              MOVE DELIMITER
         MVI   TRTTBL+X'FF',X'FF'             MOVE DELIMITER
         LA    3,DATATBL                      LOAD ADDRESS ARG
TRTLOOP  TRT   0(20,3),TRTTBL                 FIND DELIMITER
         BC    8,ERROR                        ERROR IF NOT FOUND
         STC   2,TESTFLD                      SAVE DELIMITER
         CLI   TESTFLD,C';'                   IS IT A ;?
         BE    SEMICOL                        THEN BRANCH TO MOVE
         CLI   TESTFLD,C':'                   IS IT A :?
         BE    COLON                          THEN BRANCH TO MOVE
         CLI   TESTFLD,X'FF'                  IS IT A X'FF'?
         BE    EOJRT                          THEN BRANCH TO EOJRT
         B     ERROR                          ELSE ERROR
COLON    EQU   *
SEMICOL  LR    4,1                            SAVE DELIMITER ADDRESS
         SR    4,3                            GET LENGTH ARGUMENT
         SH    4,=H'1'                        DROP DELIMITER
         MVI   PRINTBLD,X'40'                 MOVE BLANK
         MVC   PRINTBLD+1(119),PRINTBLD CLEAR PRINTAREA
         EX    4,MVCINSTR                     MOVE DATA TO PRINTBLD
         LA    1,1(1)                         INCREMENT REGISTER 1
         LR    3,1                            POINT TO NEXT ARG BYTE
         PUT   PRINT,PRINTBLD                 WRITE A LINE
         CLI   TESTFLD,C':'                   TEST DELIMITER
         BNE   TRTLOOP                        RETURN IF NOT A :
         CNTRL PRINT,SK,1                     ELSE SKIP TO NEXT LABEL
         B     TRTLOOP                        AND RETURN
MVCINSTR MVC   PRINTBLD(0),0(3)               MOVE DATA FROM DATATBL TO
*                                             PRINTBLD - LENGTH IN R4
ERROR    EQU   *                              ABNORMAL END-OF-JOB
EOJRT    EQU   *
         L     13,4(13)                       REQUIRED BY HSKPING
         RETURN (14,12)
*
* DATA AREAS
*
TRTTBL   DC    256XL1'00'
DATATBL  DC    CL17'PRISCILLA STRONG;'
         DC    CL18'128 EAST 6 STREET;'
         DC    CL14'NEW YORK, NY:'
         DC    CL13'MARY MICHAEL;'
         DC    CL14'993 HUGO ROAD;'
         DC    CL13'CHICAGO, ILL:'
         DC    X'FF'
TESTFLD  DS    CL1
PRINTBLD DS    CL120
         END   PROG9
               =H'1'
```

Figure 14-11 Program 9—solution.

Otherwise, we store the non-zero function byte in TESTFLD,

```
STC   2,TESTFLD
```

and use the CLI instructions to examine the contents of TESTFLD.

If the non-zero function byte is a semicolon or colon, we branch to the instructions which move the data string from DATATBL to the output print area PRINTBLD. If the non-zero function byte is FF_{16} we branch to the end-of-job code.

The code at SEMICOL calculates the length of the data field in register 4 and then executes the MVC instruction at MVCINSTR. The length of the data field moved depends on the contents of register 4. The data string is moved to PRINTBLD and is printed using the PUT instruction. The instructions

```
CLI    TESTFLD,C':'  TEST IF COLON
BNE    TRTLOOP       RETURN IF NOT A:
CNTRL  PRINT,SK,1    ELSE SKIP TO NEXT LABEL
```

test the value of TESTFLD. If the delimiter is not a colon, a conditional branch to TRTLOOP is effected. If the delimiter is a colon, signifying the end of a table entry, the CNTRL statement causes the printer to skip to the next label.

The code at EOJRT is entered when the TRT instruction locates FF_{16}. The print file is closed and the program is finished.

This example concludes our discussion of the TRT and EX instructions. There is, however, one additional instruction which is often examined in conjunction with these two statements, the TR instruction.

The TR Instruction

Some data processing applications involve data conversion. Second generation IBM computers used the BCD code. Third and fourth generation IBM computers use the EBCDIC code. Let's assume that a deck of cards mistakenly was punched on a keypunch using the BCD code. The cards should have been punched using the EBCDIC code. We must convert this deck from BCD to EBCDIC.

The relation between selected BCD and EBCDIC codes is given in Table 14-4. For example, the card contains a 6-8 punch. The fourth generation computer interprets this punch code as an equal (=) sign. But the operator keyed a greater-than (>) sign. We want the card to contain the code that the fourth generation computer interprets as a greater-than sign. We want to change the code from BCD to EBCDIC. Figure 14-12 represents our problem.

We must read each card. We must convert the BCD code to the appropriate EBCDIC code. In the example shown, we must convert the bit configuration 01111110_2 ($7E_{16}$—the internal code generated from a 6-8 punch) to bit configuration 01101110_2 ($6E_{16}$—the EBCDIC code for the greater-than sign).

Table 14-4 Relation between BCD and EBCDIC Graphics

desired graphic	BCD punch	internal code	EBCDIC interpretation	correct code
>	6–8	X'7E'	=	X'6E'
<	12–6–8	X'4E'	+	X'4C'
(	0–4–8	X'6C'	%	X'4D'
=	3–8	X'7B'	#	X'7E'

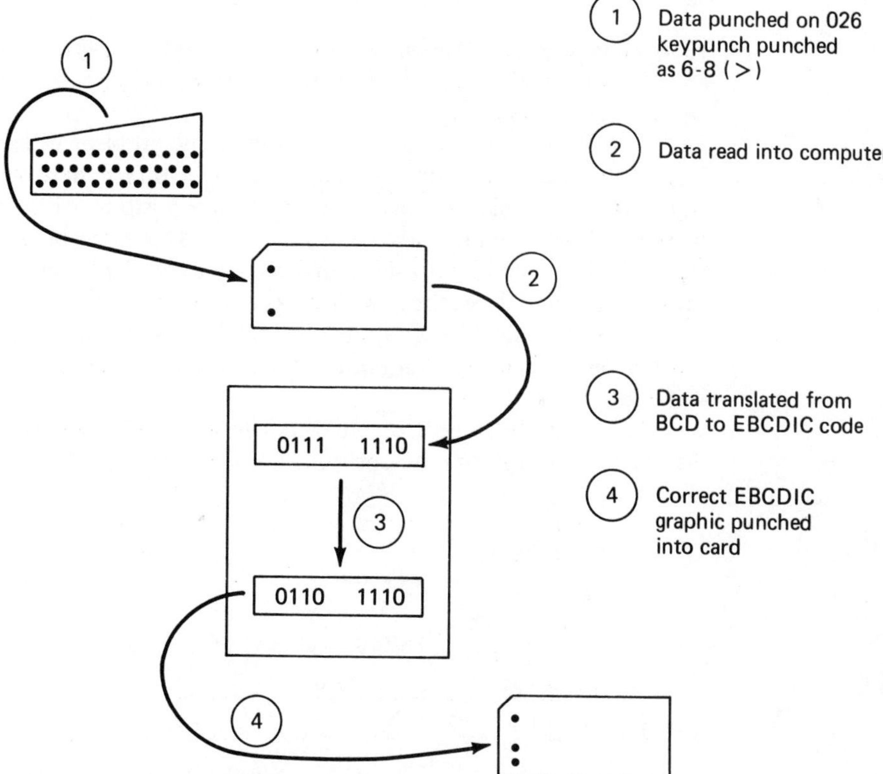

Figure 14-12 Program 10–graphic representation.

We must convert the BCD codes to the correct EBCDIC code. Numbers and letters do not need to be converted. When we punch an A on an 026 keypunch (a keypunch which punches the BCD code), we punch a 12-1 punch. When this code is read into storage, it is interpreted as an A (bit configuration 11000001_2). Our problem is mainly with the special characters.

We could use a compare instruction to determine if conversion is necessary. For example

```
                  .
                  .
                  .
          CLI   INPUT,C' = '     IF CHARACTER IS NOT AN = SIGN
          BNE   NEXTCOMP         EXAMINE NEXT CHARACTER
          MVI   INPUT,C' > '     ELSE REPLACE WITH > SIGN
NEXTCOMP  CLI   INPUT,C' + '     IF CHARACTER . . .
                  .
                  .
                  .
```

We must code a separate compare for each character we wish to convert, and we must loop through this routine for each position in the card. That is, we must repeat the code 80 times.

The TR (TRanslate) instruction solves our problem with one statement. The TR instruction examines each position within a data field (called the argument) and replaces the character in each position with the appropriate character from a table (called the function). This concept is represented in Figure 14-13. For example, if the first character in INPUT is an A ($C1_{16}$), the TR instruction replaces the A with the character at TABLE+$C1_{16}$.

Each table must be set up for the specific problem. Our table must be 256 bytes in length—one byte for each of the possible hexadecimal combinations in an 8-bit byte.

The table developed for our problem will have the correct replacement character in the appropriate position. For example, we want to replace the bit

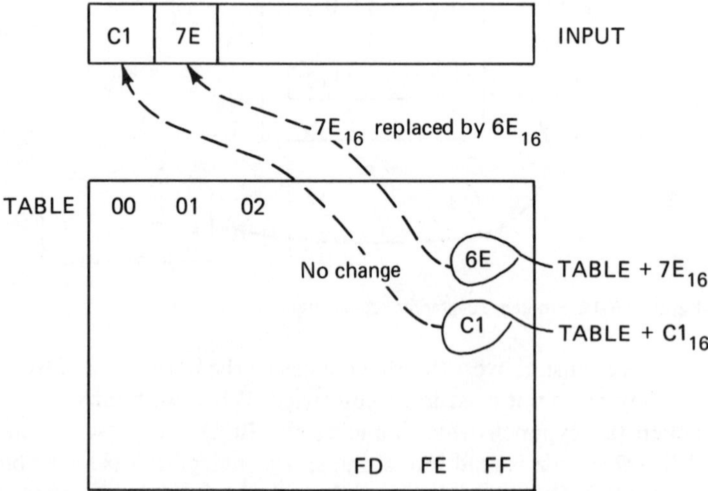

Figure 14-13 Use of the TR instruction.

configuration 01111110_2 ($7E_{16}$) with the bit configuration 01101110_2 ($6E_{16}$). At TABLE+$7E_{16}$ we find the code 01101110_2. Figure 14-14 shows how the TR instruction gives the replacement we want.

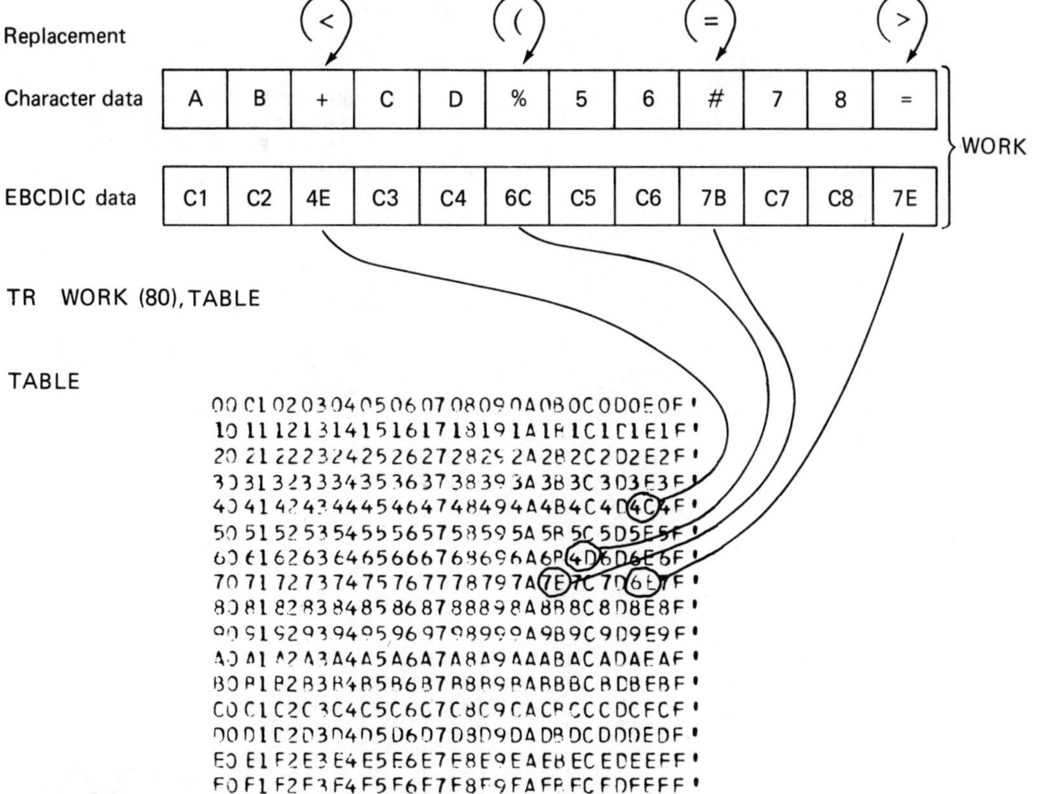

Figure 14-14 Program 10–use of the TR instruction.

The instruction examines the data field INPUT one byte at a time. The first byte of INPUT is A. The TR instruction goes to TABLE+$C1_{16}$. The instruction replaces the first byte of INPUT with the byte found in TABLE +$C1_{16}$. In this case, the argument byte is replaced by 11000001_2. The data is not changed.

The next argument byte contains a $7E_{16}$. When the corresponding function byte is located at TABLE+$7E_{16}$, we find a $6E_{16}$. This byte replaces the second byte in INPUT. This replacement continues until all 80 bytes of INPUT are examined.

Figure 14-15 shows the complete program to convert a deck of cards punched in the BCD code to the EBCDIC code. The TR instruction converts all 80 bytes of the input area WORK in one statement.

```
*
* PROGRAM 10
* BCD TO EBCDIC CONVERSION
* USING TR INSTRUCTION
* SOLUTION BY FU-SHIH CHENG, SPRING 1974
*
          START 0
          PRINT NOGEN
*         SAVE  (14,12)                    GENERATED IN HSKP MACRO
*         BALR  12,0                       GENERATED IN HSKP MACRO
*         USING *,12                       GENERATED IN HSKP MACRO
FIRST     HSKPING CARDID=INCARD,PUNCHID=OUTCARD
*         *
*         *     SOME
*         *     HOUSEKEEPING
*         *     STATEMENTS
*         *     OMITTED
*         *     HERE
*         *
LOOP      GET   INCARD,WORK                READ DATA TO BE CONVERTED
          TR    WORK(80),TABLE             TRANSLATE ALL 80 COLUMNS
          PUT   OUTCARD,WORK               WRITE TRANSLATED CARD
          B     LOOP                       AND LOOP BACK
*         *
*         *     AFTER ALL INPUT CARDS
*         *     HAVE BEEN READ AND PROCESSED
*         *     THE PROGRAM IS COMPLETE
*         *
*         *
*
* DATA AREAS
*
WORK      DC    CL80' '
TABLE     DC    X'000102030405060708090A0B0C0D0E0F'
          DC    X'101112131415161718191A1B1C1D1E1F'
          DC    X'202122232425262728292A2B2C2D2E2F'
          DC    X'303132333435363738393A3B3C3D3E3F'
          DC    X'404142434445464748494A4B4C4D404F'   —Replaces X'
          DC    X'505152535455565758595A5B5C5D5E5F'   —Replaces X'
          DC    X'606162636465666768696A6B4D6D6E6F'   —Replaces X'
          DC    X'707172737475767778797A7E7C7D6E7F'   —Replaces X'
          DC    X'808182838485868788898A8B8C8D8E8F'
          DC    X'909192939495969798999A9B9C9D9E9F'
          DC    X'A0A1A2A3A4A5A6A7A8A9AAABACADAEAF'
          DC    X'B0B1B2B3B4B5B6B7B8B9BABBBCBDBEBF'
          DC    X'C0C1C2C3C4C5C6C7C8C9CACBCCCDCECF'
          DC    X'D0D1D2D3D4D5D6D7D8D9DADBDCDDDEDF'
          DC    X'E0E1E2E3E4E5E6E7E8E9EAEBECEDEEEF'
          DC    X'F0F1F2F3F4F5F6F7F8F9FAFBFCFDFEFF'
          END   FIRST
```

Figure 14-15 Program 10—solution.

S/370 MOVE AND COMPARE INSTRUCTIONS

Our programs have used the MVC and CLC instructions to perform logical compare operations on operands containing from 1 to 256 bytes. Two new instructions, available only on the S/370, provide the capability of moving and comparing fields of more than 256 bytes.

The MVCL Instruction

The MVCL (MoVe Characters Long) instruction moves data from one storage location to another. The address and length of each operand is kept in a register, thus the MVCL instruction is one of the few RR-type instructions which references data in storage.

For example, the instruction

```
MVCL 4,8
```

tells the computer to move the string of bytes starting at the address contained in register 8, to the storage address contained in register 4. The length of the second operand (sending field) is contained in register 9 (the R2+1 register). The length of the receiving field is contained in register 5 (the R1+1 register). Movement is from left to right. If the first operand location is larger than the second operand location, the receiving field is padded with the character contained in the high-order byte of the R2+1 register.

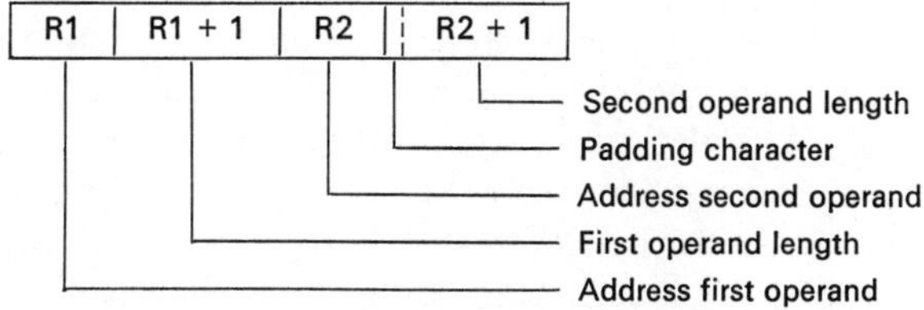

After execution of the MVCL instruction, the contents of the R1 register are incremented by the length specified in the R1+1 register. The contents of the R1+1 register are decremented by the length of the receiving field. The contents of the R2 register are incremented by the number of bytes moved, and the contents of the R2+1 register are decremented by the number of bytes moved.

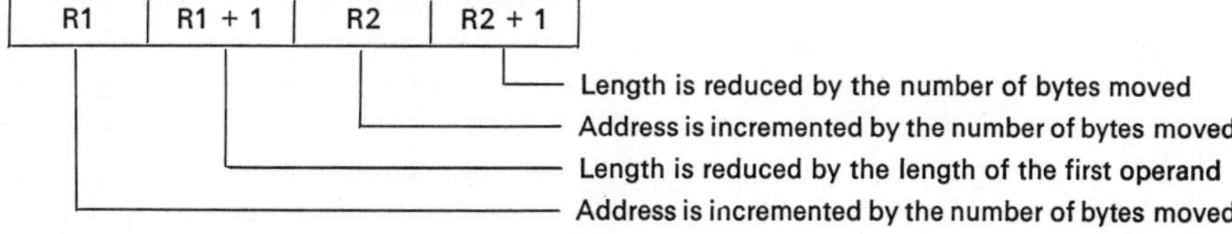

The condition code is set as follows:

condition code	result
00_2	first and second operand lengths are equal
01_2	first operand length is low
10_2	first operand length is high
11_2	no data is moved because of destructive overlap

Let's consider an example of the MVCL instruction.

Table 14-5 Execution of the MVCL Instruction

location	instruction	registers after execution
Register 4: 00008000	MVCL 4,8	Register 4: 00008101
Register 5: 00000101		Register 5: 00000000
Register 8: 0000923B		Register 8: 0000933C
Register 9: 40000101		Register 9: 40000000

This instruction moves 257 (101_{16}) bytes from location $00923B_{16}$ to the field at location 008000_{16}. The low-order bytes of the receiving field are padded with blanks. The padding character is specified in the high-order byte of register 9. The condition code is set to 00_2.

The CLCL Instruction

The CLCL (Compare Logical Characters Long) instruction compares the contents of the second operand location to the contents of the first operand location. The CLCL is also an RR-type instruction. The uses of the even–odd register pairs is the same as for the MVCL instruction. The padding character contained in the high-order byte of the R2+1 register is inserted if an inequality is not realized before the shorter string of bytes is exhausted.

The operands are compared from left to right. The compare stops when an inequality is realized. The R1 and R2 operand registers contain the addresses of the unequal bytes. The R1+1 and R2+1 registers contain the relative location of the unequal bytes in each field.

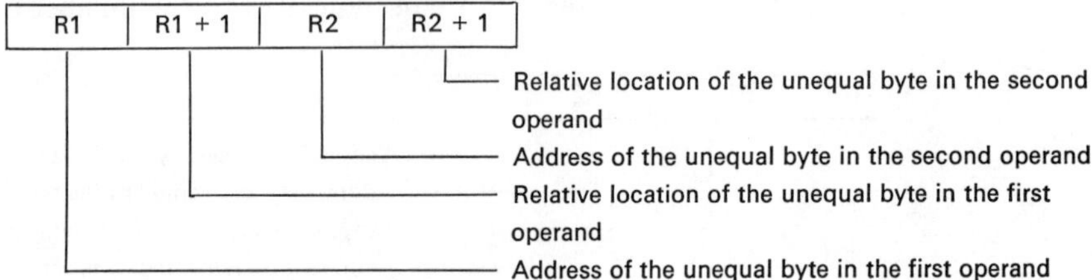

The condition code is set as follows:

condition code	result
00_2	operands are equal or both operands have a length of zero
01_2	first operand is low
10_2	first operand is high
11_2	not used

Let's consider an example of the CICL instruction.

Table 14-6 Execution of the CLCL Instruction

location	instruction	registers after execution
Register 4: 00008000	CLCL 4,6	Register 4: 00008001
Register 5: 00000004		Register 5: 00000003
Register 8: 0000923B		Register 8: 0000923C
Register 9: 40000003		Register 9: 00000002
Location 008000: F1F3F3F4		
Location 00923B: F1F2F3		

We are comparing the 4-byte field at location 008000_{16} with the 3-byte field at location $00923B_{16}$. An inequality is found when the second bytes in each field are compared. The condition code is set to 10_2—an $F3_{16}$ is greater than an $F2_{16}$. The counts in registers 5 and 9 are decremented by the number of bytes examined.

PROBLEMS

14.1 Give the contents of the first operand location after each of the following instructions is executed.

storage location	contents	intruction
FLDA	F1F2F3F4F5F6	MVZ FLDA(5),FLDB
FLDB	C7C0C8C0C9C0	MVN FLDA(5),FLDB
FLDC	001234567C	MVN FLDA + 1(1),FLDA + 5
		MVZ FLDA + 2(3),FLDB
		MVN FLDA + 1(3),FLDB + 1
		MVO FLDA(6),FLDA(3)
		MVO FLDB(4),FLDB(3)
		MVO FLDC(5),FLDC(2)

14.2 Code the move instructions to accomplish the following:

1. Multiply the number 00123C by 100.
2. Multiply the number 00123C by 100,000.
3. Divide the number 1234567C by 10,000.
4. Divide the number 1234567C by 10.

14.3 Code the add and move instructions to round the following numbers:

a. 27,623 to two decimal places
b. 456.98761 to three decimal places

c. 1.234 to one decimal place
d. 1905.78023 to one decimal place

14.4 Write a program to calculate the value of the expression

$$X = \frac{(A + B) - C}{(D + E)}$$

Use the following data values in the program.

$$A = 12.3$$
$$B = .001$$
$$C = 3.00$$
$$D = 2.020$$
$$E = 3.030$$

Use the decimal add and move instructions in your solution.

14.5 Give the contents of the first operand location after each of the following instructions is executed.

location	contents	instruction
Register 3	00000002	SRP DATA,0(3),5
Register 4	FFFFFFFE	SRP DATA,0(4),0
Register 5	00000003	SRP DATA,0(4),5
Register 6	FFFFFFFD	SRP DATA,0(5),5
DATA	0006780C	SRP DATA,1(3),0
		SRP DATA,3(4),0
		SRP DATA,4(6),5

14.6 Answer Problems 14.2, 14.3, and 14.4 using the SRP instruction.

14.7 Using the TRT instruction, write a program segment that could be used to verify that the data in a 4-byte field called NUMIN contains numeric data. The field was read from a card.

14.8 What will be the condition code after each of the following EX instructions is executed? Explain why.

location	contents	instruction
Register 3	000000C1	EX 3,INSTR1
Register 4	F1000040	EX 3,INSTR2
FIELD	F1C10040	EX 4,INSTR1
INSTR1	CLI FIELD,X'00'	EX 4,INSTR2
INSTR2	CLI FIELD+1,X'00'	EX 3,INSTR3
INSTR3	CLI FIELD+2,X'00'	EX 4,INSTR3
INSTR4	CLI FIELD+3,X'00'	EX 3,INSTR4
		EX 4,INSTR4

14.9 How many bytes are moved when the following instructions are executed? Explain why.

```
                  LA    3,80
                  EX    3,MVCINSTR
                  .
                  .
                  .
MVCINSTR          MVC   PRINTBLD(20),DATA
```

14.10 The EBCDIC code is not the only internal computer code available on the S/360 and S/370. Data also may be represented using the ASCII code (Appendix A). Write a program to convert a 120 character string called DATA from BBCDIC code to ASCII code. Use the information in appendix A to determine the correct ASCII configuration. The TR instruction provides a direct solution to this problem. Can you see another approach using an instruction which manipulates bits?

14.11 Write a program to convert the character data in a card file to lower-case characters. Is there another instruction besides the TR instruction that you might use?

14.12 Write a program to print the data in a card file. The program should print the words using both upper and lower case letters. For example, a card containing the data

```
THE CAT IS BLACK. THE DOG IS WHITE.
```

should be printed as

The cat is black. The dog is white.

14.13 The information on 80-column punched cards is to be written to the printer. Write a program to align or justify the right margin on the output page. You may assume a length of 120 characters. The end of a paragraph is marked by a FF_{16}. You do not have to justify the last line in the paragraph.

Hint: You must determine the number of characters in the line, and then calculate the number of spaces which must be inserted.

14.14 Write a program to create a table reflecting employee number, employee name and gross salary. The data specifications are given below. Notice the delimiter appearing after the name field on the input card.

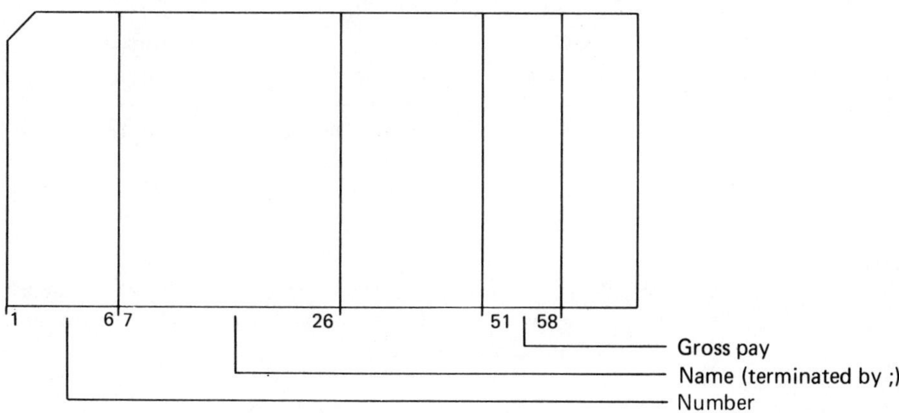

input positions	field	position in table
1–6	Employee Number	1–6
7–26	Employee Name (a semicolon follows the last letter of the employee name)	7–*n*
51–58	Gross Salary Pay (a colon follows each entry in TBL)	*n* + 1 – *y*

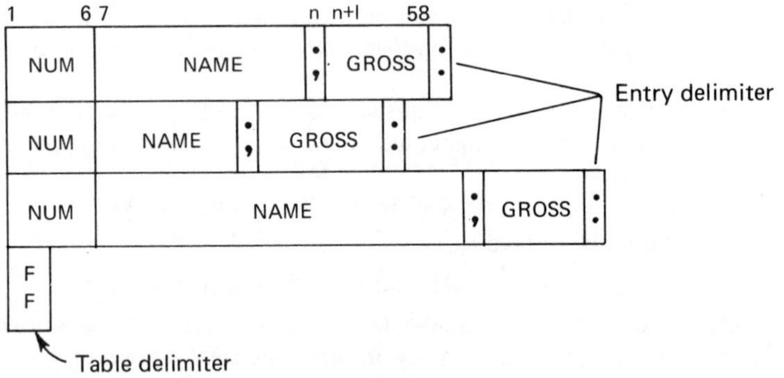

Code the solution assuming:

1. The employee name consists only of the last name.
2. The employee name consists of a first and last name separated by a blank.

14.15 Write a program to print the table created in Problem 14.14. The data follows.

TBL positions	field	output positions
1–6	Employee Number	11–16
7–*n*	Employee Name	21–40
n + 1 – *y*	Gross Salary	51–58

14.16 Write a program to create a table reflecting employee number, employee name, and gross salary. The name and salary fields are variable length and are terminated by a semicolon.

input positions	field	position in table
1–6	Employee Number	1–6
7–n	Employee Name	7–n
$n + 1$	Delimiter (;)	$n + 1$
$n + 2 - m$	Gross Salary	$n + 2 - m$
$m + 1 - x$	Delimiter (;)	$m + 1 - x$

14.17 Write a program to print the table created in Problem 14.14. Use the EDMK instruction to move the dollar sign in front of the first significant digit in the salary field. Use the output specifications given in Problem 14.15.

14.18 The employee master deck is mispunched. Leading zeros are punched as blanks. Write a program to convert any blanks appearing in numeric data fields to zeros.

input positions	field	output positions
1–50	Miscellaneous	1–50
51–58	Gross Salary	51–58 (converted)
59–65	FICA	59–65 (converted)
66–72	Federal Taxes	66–72 (converted)
73–79	State Taxes	73–79 (converted)
80	Miscellaneous	80

14.19 Develop a solution to Program 9 (Appendix C) using the MVCL instruction.

section four

Operating System Concepts

15

Input/Output Macros

INTRODUCTION Most of the instructions discussed thus far have dealt only with the processing of data; not with the transfer of data to and from main storage. Special instructions are required to effect these input/output or I/O operations. We have been using two of these special instructions: GET and PUT.

These statements, and many others, fall into a new category. They are called *macros*. A single macro replaces many machine instructions. We say that a macro is assembled. This means that the assembler generates the required machine language statements to replace the coded macro instruction.

Why bother with macros at all? Couldn't the programmer code the statements necessary to transfer data into the computer? Yes. But many assembly instructions are required, and the programmer would need a detailed knowledge of the particular reader or tape drive involved, as well as a knowledge of the operating system. The macro allows the programmer to specify the operation, such as GET or PUT, and to let the assembler generate the correct code to effect the transfer of data.

The transfer of data between device and computer storage is controlled by the operating system, thus I/O macros differ from one operating system to another. In spite of these differences, many aspects of file handling are common to most operating systems. We use the terms *record* and *block size*, *physical* and *logical record*, and *buffering* regardless of the operating system involved. Before we can understand the macros used to handle data, we must understand some of these basic concepts.

Data-Handling Concepts

The term record size refers to the number of characters in a record. Punched card files have 80-character records. Tape and disk files may have longer record sizes.

When we record data on tape, we leave a space between each record. We call this space the interrecord gap (IRG). Often we group or block records on tape. We block records to save space and to enable us to process more records in a single I/O operation (Figure 15-1).

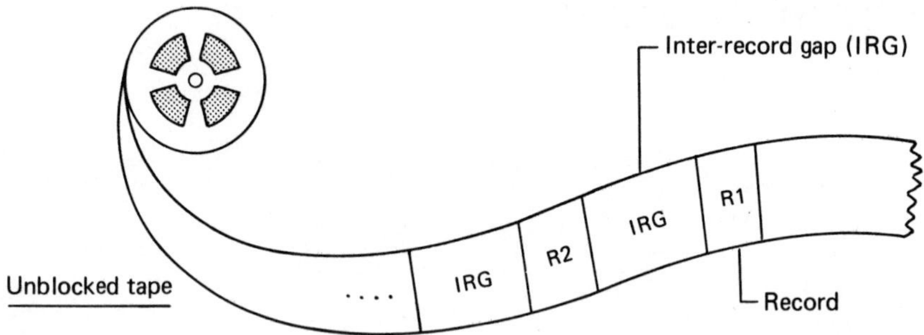

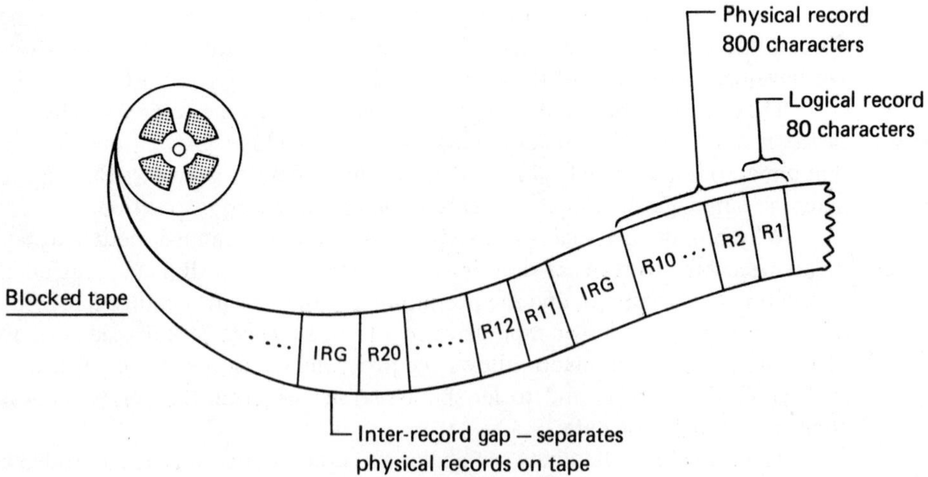

Figure 15-1 The relation between physical and logical records.

Each group of records is called a *block* of data. We often refer to a block as the *physical* record. Each record within the block is called the *logical* record. Physical records are separated by interrecord gaps. The length of each logical record is called the logical record length, the length of each physical record is called the physical record length or *block size*.

Most computer installations require additional records containing information about the file—name of the file, date of creation, format, and so forth. We call these identifying records *labels*. The operating system examines the information in the labels before processing the file, and usually again at completion of the program, to ensure that we are processing the correct file and the correct number of records.

Before data can be processed, we must read the data into storage. Remember the basic data processing pattern. No instructions are processed until the input operation is complete. Valuable computer time is wasted during each input operation.

The concept of buffering allows us to overlap processing with I/O operations. Figure 15-2 shows the use of two areas of storage. While the instructions process the record in one area of storage, the next record is read into another area. We call these areas of storage *buffer areas*.

Figure 15-2 represents two buffer areas. The next logical record may be in

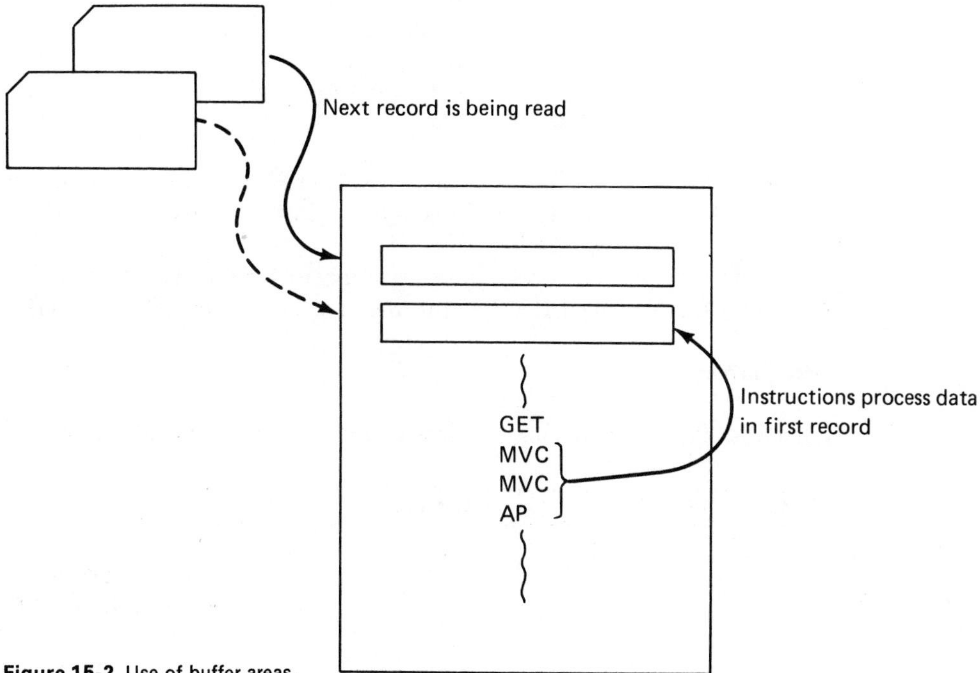

Figure 15-2 Use of buffer areas.

either area. As programmers, we are not concerned with *which* area—this is the operating system's responsibility—but we need some means of identifying *where* the next record is. We can ask the operating system to move the record to another area of storage called a work area. We define the work area in our program. We call this concept *move mode.*

Or, we can process the record in the buffer area itself. But the operating system must locate the record for us—a concept called *locate mode.* We will examine both modes of operation.

Types of Macros

There are two types of macros, *declarative* and *imperative.* Declarative macros are passive. They do not cause an event to occur. Quite often they are used to define files. The DCB macro is a declarative macro used to define a file.

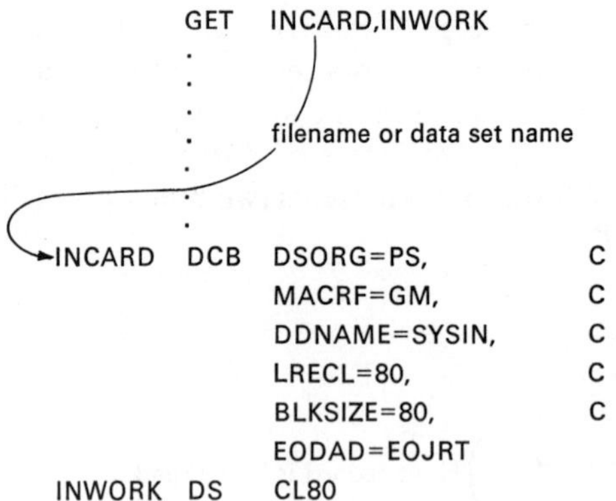

GET INCARD,INWORK
filename or data set name
INCARD DCB DSORG=PS, C
MACRF=GM, C
DDNAME=SYSIN, C
LRECL=80, C
BLKSIZE=80, C
EODAD=EOJRT
INWORK DS CL80

Imperative macros effect an action. GET and PUT are imperative macros used to transfer data to and from the computer. These macros reference the file defined by a declarative macro.

In the example shown, the imperative macro GET is used to transfer a record from the file called INCARD to the area of storage called INWORK.

Macro Format

All macros, like assembly language instructions, follow a general format.

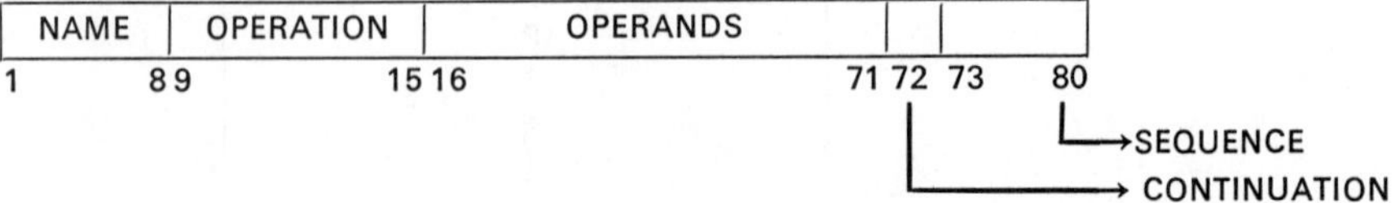

Name Field. The name or symbol field is optional. Remember, not all assembly language instructions are required to have labels.

Operation Field. The operation field specifies exactly which operation occurs. An imperative macro might specify a GET or PUT operation. A declarative macro might have an operation field of DCB or DTFCD.

Operand Field. The operand field further clarifies the function of the macro. The operand field might contain information about the file defined in a declarative macro, or it might specify the name of the file referenced in an imperative macro.

There are two types of operands, *keyword* and *positional.* The operands shown in the previous example are keyword operands. The entry

```
BLKSIZE = 80,
```

is a keyword operand. The keyword is BLKSIZE. The number associated with this entry is 80. The assembler now knows that each block associated with the file INCARD has a length of 80. Keyword operands may be coded in any order, each operand deriving its meaning from the keyword associated with it.

Keyword operands are associated with declarative macros. Similarly, positional operands are associated with imperative macros. The statement

```
GET   INCARD,INWORK
```

causes a record from the file INCARD to be placed in an area of storage called INWORK. How do we know that a record from the file INWORK is not to be placed in an area of storage called INCARD? Because of the *position* of each operand. The first operand of the GET macro specifies the file name, the second operand specifies the name of an area of storage into which the record is placed.

All operands, whether positional or keyword, must be coded consecutively, followed by commas, with no spaces between operands (Figure 15-3). The only exception to this rule occurs when the macro is to be continued.

Continuation. Any punch in column 72 of the source statement signfies that the macro is to be continued. The programmer may code the operand field through and including column 71, or may break the macro at the end of an operand. The latter is sometimes preferred because the operands are easier to read.

Program Structure

Most programs, regardless of operating system or file organization, follow the same pattern.

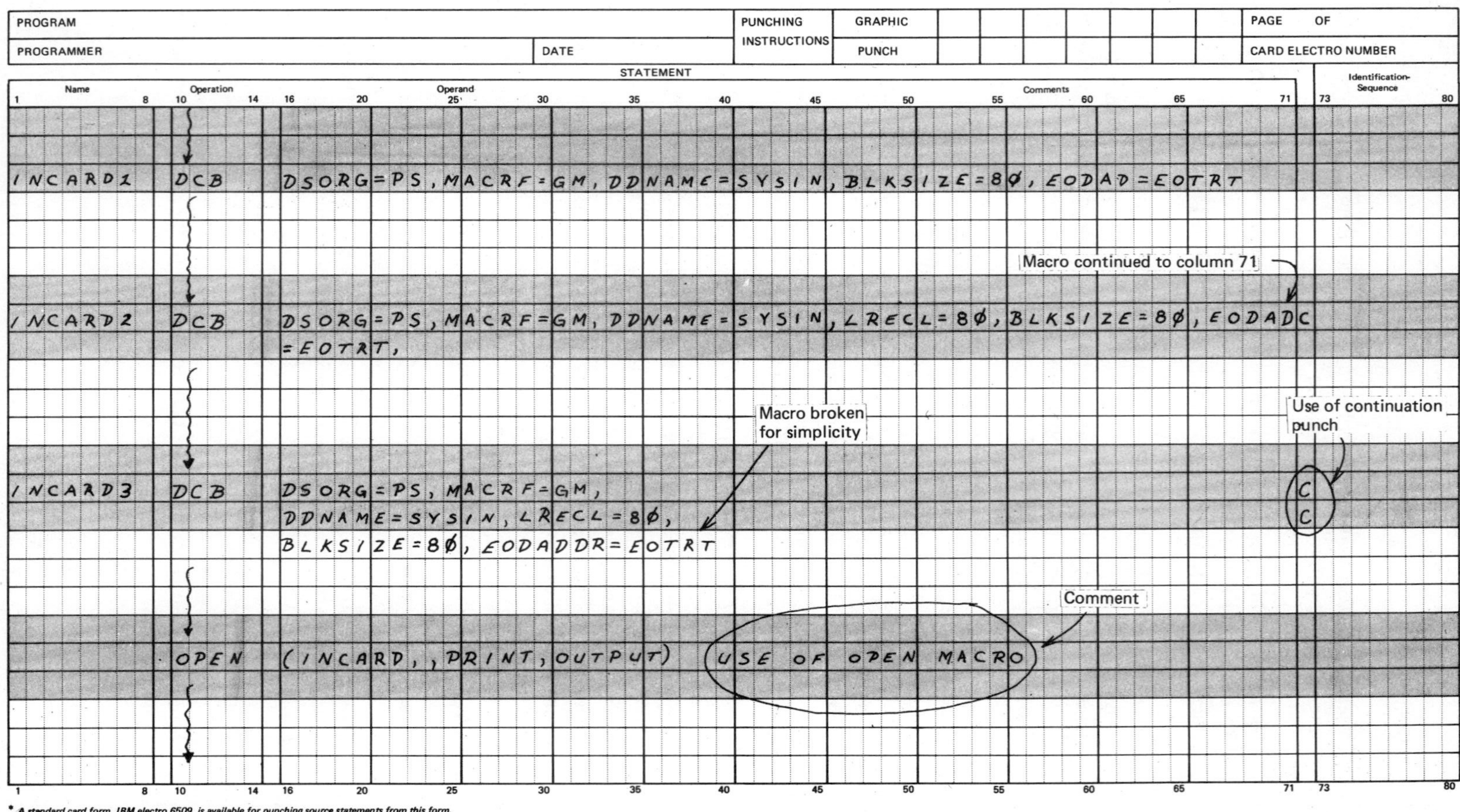

IBM

IBM System/360 Assembler Coding Form

GX28-6509-6 U/M 050*
Printed in U.S.A.

PROGRAM		PUNCHING INSTRUCTIONS	GRAPHIC	PAGE OF
PROGRAMMER	DATE		PUNCH	CARD ELECTRO NUMBER

STATEMENT

Name (1–8)	Operation (10–14)	Operand (16–) / Comments	72	Identification-Sequence (73–80)
INCARD1	DCB	DSORG=PS,MACRF=GM,DDNAME=SYSIN,BLKSIZE=8Ø,EODAD=EOTRT		
INCARD2	DCB	DSORG=PS,MACRF=GM,DDNAME=SYSIN,LRECL=8Ø,BLKSIZE=8Ø,EODAD	C	
		=EOTRT,		
INCARD3	DCB	DSORG=PS,MACRF=GM,	C	
		DDNAME=SYSIN,LRECL=8Ø,	C	
		BLKSIZE=8Ø,EODADDR=EOTRT		
	OPEN	(INCARD,,PRINT,OUTPUT) USE OF OPEN MACRO		

* A standard card form, IBM electro 6509, is available for punching source statements from this form. Instructions for using this form are in any IBM System/360 assembler language reference manual. Address comments concerning this form to IBM Nordic Laboratory, Publications Development, Box 962, S-181 09 Lidingö 9, Sweden.

*No of forms per pad may vary slightly.

Figure 15-3 Use of continuation and comments in macros.

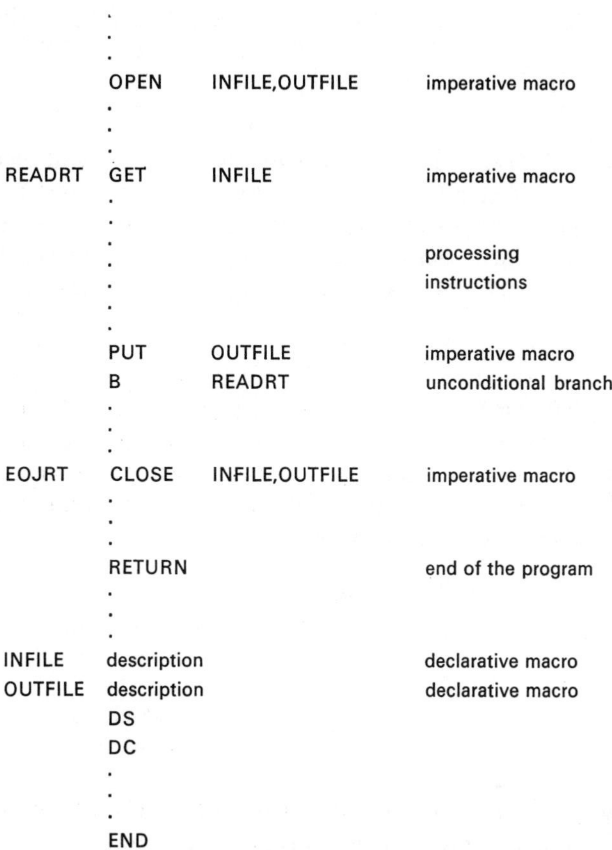

```
                .
                .
                .
                .
         OPEN   INFILE,OUTFILE         imperative macro
                .
                .
                .
READRT   GET    INFILE                 imperative macro
                .
                .
                .                      processing
                .                      instructions
                .
                .
                .
         PUT    OUTFILE                imperative macro
         B      READRT                 unconditional branch
                .
                .
                .
EOJRT    CLOSE  INFILE,OUTFILE         imperative macro
                .
                .
                .
         RETURN                        end of the program
                .
                .
                .
INFILE   description                   declarative macro
OUTFILE  description                   declarative macro
         DS
         DC
                .
                .
                .
         END
```

A file must be opened before it is processed. Labels are checked at this time. We use the imperative macro OPEN to open each file in the program.

The main program loop inputs data using the GET macro. The GET macro specifies the name of the file; in this segment the label INFILE. INFILE is subsequently described in a declarative macro.

The processing instructions follow, and then the data are output using the imperative macro PUT. The program then branches to READRT to read, process, and write the next record.

When all the records have been processed, the instructions at EOJRT are executed. The operating system determines when all records are processed. We call this condition the end-of-file or end-of-data condition. Most operating systems require that all files are closed. We use the imperative macro CLOSE, and the program is complete.

The file descriptions appear after the RETURN statement—usually grouped with the DC and DS statements. Notice that each imperative macro references a file described in a declarative macro statement.

We now will examine the use of macros in sample programs. First we will consider the macros used in Operating System/370 (OS/370), and then the macros used in the Disk Operating System (DOS/370). The macros introduced are also valid for S/360 operating systems.

OS MACROS

There are two types of OS macros. The declarative macros are used to define files. The imperative macros are used to effect an action against a file. The term *data set* is often used instead of the term file. Often we refer to files when we are referencing DOS macros, and to data sets when we are coding OS macros. We will use the term data set in this section.

Declarative Macros

The DCB (Data Control Block) macro tells the assembler the characteristics of the data set with which we are working. We must tell the assembler how the data set is organized, its logical and physical record size, the mode (move or locate) of processing involved, and so on. We also must tell the computer on what device the data set resides.

```
INCARD  DCB  DSORG=PS,          C
             MACRF=GM,          C
             DDNAME=SYSIN,      C
             LRECL=80,          C
             BLKSIZE=80,        C
             EODAD=EOJRT
```

We name the data set INCARD. The operation is the macro itself, DCB. The keyword parameters supply the characteristics of the data set.

The DSORG (Data Set ORGanization) keyword specifies the type of data set we are processing. The entry

```
DSORG = PS
```

tells us that we are processing a sequential (PS–Physical Sequential) data set. Other types of data set organization include direct and indexed sequential. We associate these parameters with direct access devices.

The MACRF entry specifies the type of imperative macro issued against this data set. The first letter of the entry specifies whether a GET (G) or PUT (P) macro is issued. The second letter indicates the mode of operation. The entry

```
MACRF = GM
```

tells the assembler that we will issue a GET macro and process the data set using move mode.

The DDNAME entry tells us the logical name of the data set. This name will subsequently appear on a job control card which tells the operating system to which device the data set is assigned.

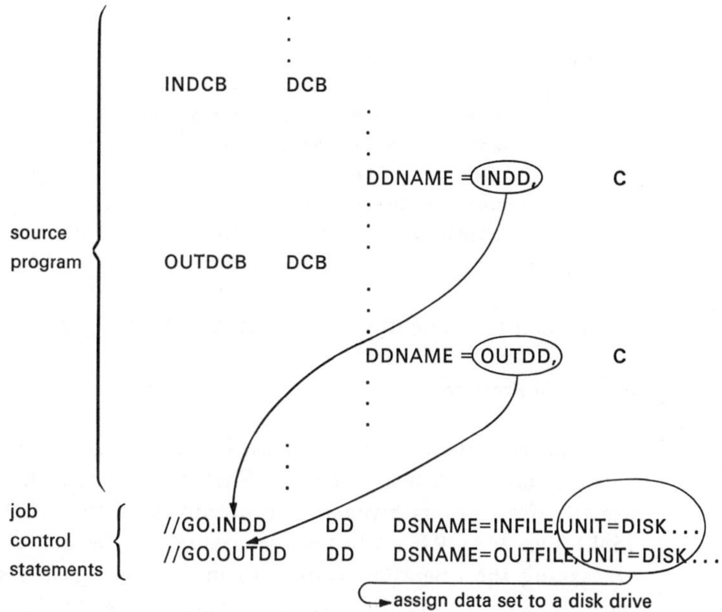

The LRECL entry specifies the size of the logical record. The BLKSIZE parameter specifies the length of the physical record. The size of the logical and physical records is the same in unit-record data sets.

The EODAD parameter names the end-of-data routine. The label coded in this entry appears in the program, usually associated with the CLOSE macro.

The DCB for an output data set is similar to the DCB for an input data set.

```
OUTCARD  DCB  DSORG=PS,          C
              MACRF=PM,          C
              DDNAME=SYSPRINT    C
              LRECL=80,          C
              BLKSIZE=80
```

The data set name and the DDNAME entry are changed to reflect a different device. Notice too, that the keyword EODAD is omitted. We are creating an output data set. The data set is complete when all records are written and we close the data set. This condition usually occurs when an end-of-data condition occurs on the *input* data set. The keyword EODAD only is associated with input data sets.

Our discussion of the DCB macro has not included all the parameters or all the possible options. The reader is referred to Appendix D for a summary of all OS macros, including all parameters and options available.

Imperative Macros

There are four imperative macros available.

macro	function
OPEN	makes the data set available for processing and checks any labeled data sets
GET	transfers a record into storage
PUT	transfers a record from storage
CLOSE	all processing of a data set is complete

The format for these macros is given in Appendix D.

A Sample Program

Let's see how these macros are used in the solution to Program 1—listing a deck of cards with field selection. First, we must define the data sets. We will use the descriptions given in the examples of the DCB macro. (See Figure 15-4.) The MACRF entry tells the assembler we are using move mode. We are asking the operating system to move the logical record from the input buffer area to a work area. We must define both input and output work areas.

Now let's examine the complete program. We perform the initial housekeeping functions and establish addressability. We no longer need the HSKPING macro. We are coding the data set description in the program. We must however, adhere to a convention involving register 13. The purpose of the statements

```
ST  13,SAVEAREA+4
LA  13,SAVEAREA
.
.
.
L   13,SAVEAREA+4
RETURN  (14,12)
```

becomes apparent in Chapter 16. Until then, we must accept the fact that these statements appear in all our programs.

We open the data sets, and clear PRINTBLD to spaces. We then issue a GET statement using move mode. We ask the operating system to move the record to an area of storage called INWORK. We now can reference the fields within INWORK.

```
MVC  NUMOUT(6),NUMIN
MVC  NAMEOUT(20),NAMEIN
MVC  GROSSOUT(8),GROSSIN
```

```
*
* PROGRAM 1
* USE OF IMPERATIVE AND DECLARATIVE MACROS
*
         PRINT NOGEN
         START
FIRST    SAVE  (14,12)                SAVE REGISTERS
         BALR  12,0                   LOAD BASE
         USING *,12                   ADDRESSABILITY
         ST    13,SAVEAREA+4          FOLLOW R13 CONVENTIONS
         LA    13,SAVEAREA            FOLLOW R13 CONVENTIONS
         OPEN  (INCARD,,PRINT,OUTPUT) OPEN FILES
READRT   GET   INCARD,INWORK          GET RECORD THEN
         MVC   NUMOUT(6),NUMIN        MOVE NUMBER
         MVC   NAMEOUT(20),NAMEIN     NAME
         MVC   GROSSOUT(8),GROSSIN    AND GROSS
         PUT   PRINT,PRINTBLD         WRITE A RECORD
         B     READRT                 AND LOOP BACK
EOJRT    CLOSE (INCARD,,PRINT)        CLOSE FILES
         L     13,SAVEAREA+4          RESTORE R13 POINTER
         RETURN (14,12)               AND RETURN
*
* DATA AREAS
*
INCARD   DCB   DSORG=PS,                                               C
               MACRF=GM,                                               C
               DDNAME=SYSIN,                                           C
               BLKSIZE=80,                                             C
               LRECL=80,                                               C
               EODAD=EOJRT
PRINT    DCB   DSORG=PS,                                               C
               MACRF=PM,                                               C
               DDNAME=SYSPRINT,                                        C
               BLKSIZE=120,                                            C
               LRECL=120
INWORK   DS    0CL80                  INPUT AREA
NUMIN    DS    CL6                    *
NAMEIN   DS    CL20                   *
         DS    CL24                   *
GROSSIN  DS    CL8                    *
         DS    CL22                   *
PRINTBLD DS    0CL120                 OUTPUT WORK AREA
         DC    10CL1' '               *
NUMOUT   DS    CL6                    *
         DC    10CL1' '               *
NAMEOUT  DS    CL20                   *
         DC    10CL1' '               *
GROSSOUT DS    CL8                    *
         DC    56CL1' '               *
SAVEAREA DS    18F
         END   FIRST
```

Figure 15-4 Program 1—solution using OS macros.

We build the output record in PRINTBLD. We now use move mode to PUT the record to a data set called PRINT and loop back to the GET statement. When all the cards are processed, we execute the code at EOJRT and the program is complete.

DOS MACROS There are two types of DOS macros. The declarative macros are used to define files and generate I/O routines called *logic modules*. The declarative macros contain keyword operands. DOS imperative macros specify the action to be taken against a file. The imperative macros contain positional operands.

Macros for Card Processing

There is one declarative macro and four imperative macros associated with card processing. The DTFCD (Define The File for CarD) macro tells the assembler the characteristics of the file. We must tell the assembler the device on which the file resides, the type of record we are processing, the size of the record, the name of the input or output area, etc.

name	operation	operands	continuation
INCARD	DTFCD	DEVADDR=SYS004,	C
		IOAREA1=AREA1,	C
		BLKSIZE=80,	C
		DEVICE=2540,	C
		EOFADDR=EOJRT,	C
		RECFORM=FIXUNB,	C
		TYPEFLE=INPUT	

We name the file INCARD. The operation is the macro itself, DTFCD. The keyword parameters supply the characteristics of the file.

The DEVADDR entry tells us the logical unit of the file. This name will appear on a job control card which tells the operating system the address of the device on which the file resides. The relation between logical unit and job control statement is illustrated in Table 15-1.

Table 15-1 Relation between DEVADDR and JCL Card

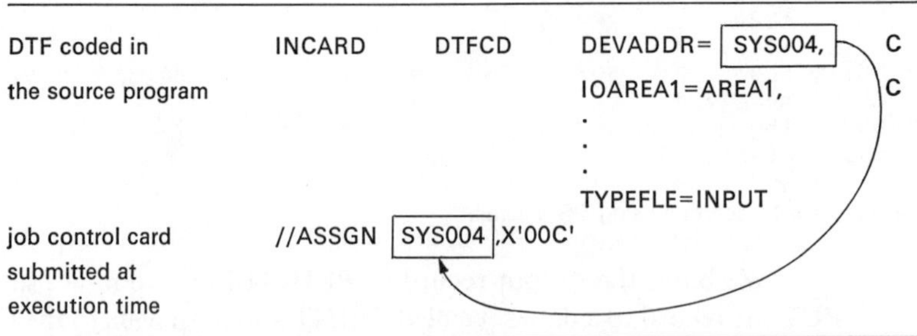

DTF coded in the source program	INCARD	DTFCD	DEVADDR= SYS004,	C
			IOAREA1=AREA1,	C
			.	
			.	
			.	
			TYPEFLE=INPUT	
job control card submitted at execution time	//ASSGN SYS004,X'00C'			

The IOAREA1 entry names the storage location where the input record is placed. We must define AREA1 in a DS or DC statement.

The BLKSIZE entry tells us the size of the physical record. The physical and logical record sizes are the same with unit record files. We do not block unit record files.

The DEVICE entry tells us the physical device where the files reside. The IBM 2540 is a reader/punch.

The EOFADDR entry tells us the name of the end-of-file routine. This is the routine we branch to when all the records in the file are processed.

The RECFORM entry tells us the format of the data. The statement

```
RECFORM=FIXUNB,
```

tells us that we are working with fixed-length unblocked records.

The TYPEFLE entry specifies whether the file is input or output.

The example on page 380 describes an input card file. We may use the DTFCD macro to describe punch (output) files as well.

name	operation	operands	continuation
OUTCARD	DTFCD	DEVADDR=SYS005,	C
		IOAREA1=OUT1,	C
		BLKSIZE=80,	C
		DEVICE=2540	C
		RECFORM=FIXUNB,	C
		TYPEFLE=OUTPUT	

Imperative Macros for Card Processing. There are four imperative macros available for card processing. (Refer to Appendix D for the format of the imperative macros.)

macro	function
OPEN	makes the file available for processing
GET	transfers a record into storage
PUT	transfers a record from storage to the punch
CLOSE	all processing against the file is complete

A Sample Program

Let's see how the DOS declarative and imperative macros are used in a simple program to reproduce a deck of cards. In order to reproduce a deck of cards, we read a record into storage. We call this area the input buffer area. We move this record to the output buffer area and punch the record. We repeat this procedure for each of the remaining records. (See Figure 15-5.)

First, we must define the files (we will use the DTFCD macros previously illustrated). We also must reserve space for the input buffer area and the output buffer area.

```
                .
                .
                .
                OPEN     INCARD,OUTCARD
        LOOP    GET      INCARD
                MVC      OUT1(80),AREA1
                PUT      OUTCARD,
                B        LOOP
        EOJRT   CLOSE    INCARD,OUTCARD
                EOJ      END OF JOB
        *
        * DATA  AREAS
        *
        INCARD  DTFCD    DEVADDR=SYS004,                      C
                         IOAREA1=AREA1,                       C
                         BLKSIZE=80,                          C
                         DEVICE=2540                          C
                         EOFADDR=EOJRT,                       C
                         RECFORM=FIXUNB,                      C
                         TYPEFLE=INPUT
        OUTCARD DTFCD    DEVADDR=SYS005,                      C
                         IOAREA1=OUT1,                        C
                         DEVICE=2540                          C
                         TYPEFLE=OUTPUT                       C
                         BLKSIZE=80,                          C
                         RECFORM=FIXUNB
        AREA1   DS       CL80
        OUT1    DS       CL80
                END
```

First, we open both the input file, INCARD, and the output file, OUTCARD. We then read the first record. The statement

```
GET   INCARD
```

places the first record in AREA1. Remember, AREA1 is specified as the input area in the DTFCD macro. We use the MVC instruction to move this record from AREA1 to OUT1.

```
MVC   OUT1(80),AREA1
```

We then use the PUT statement to punch the record. The unconditional branch statement

```
B   LOOP
```

completes the main loop in the program. We continue executing the loop until all the records have been processed. The operating system knows when the last card is processed. The code at EOJRT, the name specified in the EOFADDR

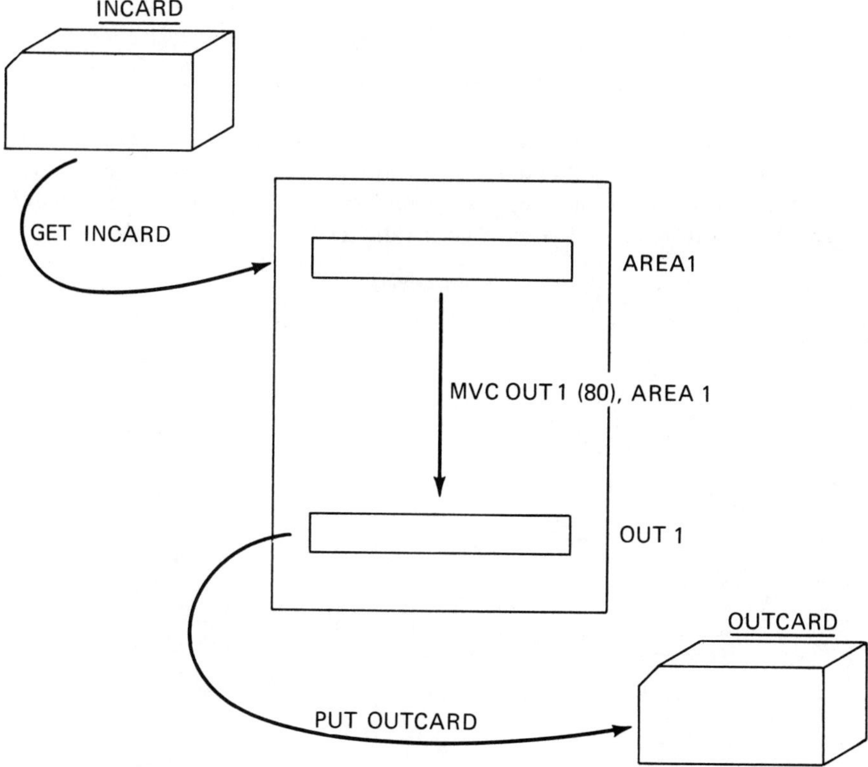

Figure 15-5 Memory map to reproduce a deck of cards.

entry, is executed. We close the files,

```
CLOSE   INCARD,OUTCARD
```

and the program is complete. The EOJ statement, also a macro, returns control to the operating system. The EOJ statement is often used to replace the RETURN statement in DOS programs.

Sometimes we use two buffer areas for each file. We specify a second buffer area using the keyword IOAREA2. We must, of course, reserve space for the second buffer area.

```
INCARD   DTFCD   DEVADDR=SYS004,        C
                 IOAREA1=AREA1,         C
                 IOAREA2=AREA2,         C
                 .
                 .
                 .
AREA1    DS      CL80
AREA2    DS      CL80
                 .
                 .
                 .
```

Now let's consider what happens when we issue the imperative macro

```
GET   INCARD
```

The operating system reads a record and places it in one of two available buffer areas. We do not know which buffer area to reference in the MVC instruction.

We code an additional keyword parameter to tell the operating system to move the record to a work area. The parameter

```
WORKA=YES
```

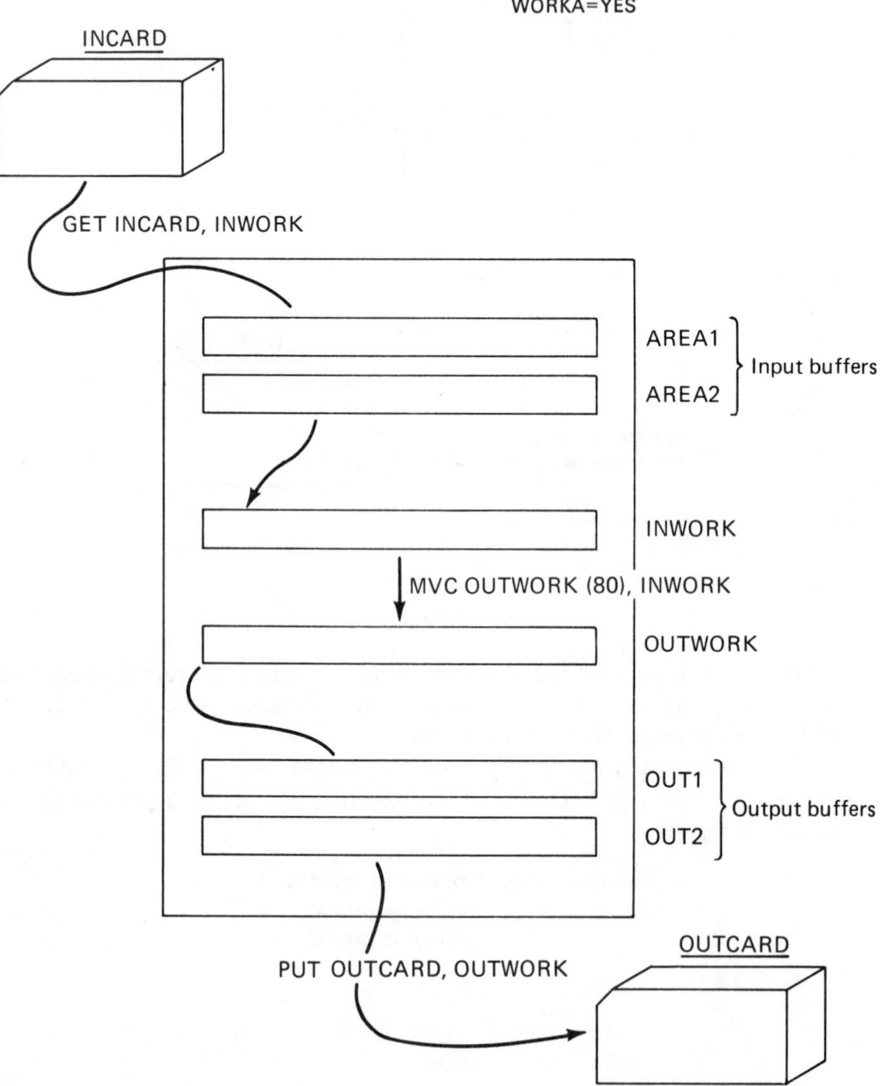

Figure 15-6 Use of a work area to reproduce a deck of cards.

specifies move mode. We also must code a different form of the GET macro. The second operand in the GET macro specifies the name of the programmer's work area.

```
GET   INCARD,INWORK
```

We must define INWORK.

```
INWORK  DS  CL80
```

Let's see how we can use these concepts (Figure 15-6) to reproduce a deck of cards.

```
                .
                .
                .
         OPEN   INCARD,OUTCARD
LOOP     GET    INCARD,INWORK
         MVC    OUTWORK(80),INWORK
         PUT    OUTCARD,OUTWORK
         B      LOOP
EOJRT    CLOSE  INCARD,OUTCARD
         EOJ    END OF JOB
*
* DATA   AREAS
*
INCARD   DTFCD  DEVADDR=SYS004,            C
                IOAREA1=AREA1,             C
                IOAREA2=AREA2,             C
                BLKSIZE=80,                C
                DEVICE=2540,               C
                EOFADDR=EOJRT,             C
                RECFORM=FIXUNB,            C
                TYPEFLE=INPUT,             C
                WORKA=YES
OUTCARD DTFCD   DEVADDR=SYS005,            C
                IOAREA1=OUT1,              C
                IOAREA2=OUT2,              C
                BLKSIZE=80,                C
                DEVICE=2540,               C
                RECFORM=FIXUNB,            C
                TYPEFLE=OUTPUT,            C
                WORKA=YES
AREA1    DS     CL80
AREA2    DS     CL80
OUT1     DS     CL80
OUT2     DS     CL80
INWORK   DS     CL80
OUTWORK  DS     CL80
         END
```

We specify move mode for both files using the parameter

```
WORKA = YES
```

We also must specify the name of the work area in both the GET and PUT macros.

First, we open the files. The statement

```
GET   INCARD,INWORK
```

reads the first record into one of the two available buffer areas. The operating system moves the record to INWORK. The programmer's next statement moves the record from the input work area to the output work area,

```
MVC   OUTWORK(80),INWORK
```

and uses the work area option of the PUT macro to write the record.

```
PUT   OUTCARD,OUTWORK
```

This instruction moves the record from OUTWORK to one of the available output areas (OUT1, OUT2) and writes the record. The branch instruction completes the loop. When all the records are processed the code at EOJRT is executed and the program is complete.

Macros for Printer Output

We use the DTFPR macro to describe printer files. Many of the DTFCD entries are repeated in the DTFPR macro.

Table 15-2 DOS Declarative Macro Operands

operand	applicable for DTFCD	applicable for DTFPR
BLKSIZE=	opt	opt
DEVADDR=	req	req
EOFADDR=	opt	
IOAREA1=	req	req
IOAREA2=	opt	opt
RECFORM=	opt	opt
TYPEFLE=	opt	
WORKA=	(1)	(1)

(1) Required if using two I/O areas and move mode

The imperative macros for handling printer files are similar to the macros for handling output card files.

Table 15-3 DOS Imperative Macros

imperative macro	applicable for card	printer
OPEN	x	x
CLOSE	x	x
GET	x	
PUT	x	x

Let's see how these macros are used in Program 1 (Figure 15-7). Program 1 asks us to list a deck of cards with field selection. We perform the initial housekeeping functions and establish addressability. We no longer need the HSKPING macro. We are coding the file descriptions in our program.

We open the files. We then issue a GET statement using move mode. We ask the operating system to move the record to an area of storage called INWORK. We now reference fields within INWORK.

```
MVC  NUMOUT(6),NUMIN
MVC  NAMEOUT(20),NAMEIN
MVC  GROSSOUT(8),GROSSIN
```

We build the output record in PRINTBLD. Our description of PRINTBLD ensures that the spaces between our data fields contain blanks. We now use move mode to PUT the record to a file called PRINT from an area of storage called PRINTBLD,

```
PUT  PRINT,PRINTBLD
```

and loop back to the read statement

```
B  READRT
```

When all the cards are processed, we execute the code at EOJRT and the program is complete.

PRINTER CONTROL

We have developed both OS and DOS programs to list a deck of cards, single spaced. There are no headings or page numbers. Most business programs cannot accept this simple output format. Business applications require headings, spacing of total and detail lines, and in general, formatting of output data. The assembly language provides two macros for handling spacing and forms control.

The CNTRL Macro

The CNTRL macro allows the programmer to space one, two, or three lines on the printed report, and to skip to the top of the page when required.

```
*
* PROGRAM 1
* USE OF IMPERATIVE AND DECLARATIVE MACROS
*
         PRINT NOGEN
         START
FIRST    BALR  12,0                            LOAD BASE
         USING *,12                            ADDRESSABILITY
         OPEN  INCARD,PRINT                    OPEN FILES
         MVI   PRINTBLD,X'40'                  MOVE BLANK
         MVC   PRINTBLD+1(119),PRINTBLD        PROPAGATE THRU PRINTBLD
READRT   GET   INCARD,INWORK                   GET RECORD
         MVC   NUMOUT(6),NUMIN                 MOVE NUMBER
         MVC   NAMEOUT(20),NAMEIN              MOVE EMP NAME
         MVC   GROSSOUT(8),GROSSIN             MOVE GROSS
         PUT   PRINT,PRINTBLD                  WRITE RECORD
         B     READRT                          LOOP BACK
EOJRT    CLOSE INCARD,PRINT                    CLOSE FILES
         EOJ                                   END OF JOB
*
* DATA AREAS
*
INCARD   DTFCD DEVADDR=SYS004,                                         C
               IOAREA1=AREA1,                                          C
               BLKSIZE=80,                                             C
               DEVICE=2540,                                            C
               EOFADDR=EOJRT,                                          C
               RECFORM=FIXUNB,                                         C
               WORKA=YES,                                              C
               TYPEFLE=INPUT
PRINT    DTFPR DEVADDR=SYS005,                                         C
               IOAREA1=OUT1,                                           C
               BLKSIZE=120,                                            C
               WORKA=YES,                                              C
               RECFORM=FIXUNB,                                         C
               DEVICE=1403
AREA1    DS    CL80                            INPUT BUFFER
OUT1     DS    CL120                           OUTPUT BUFFER
INWORK   DS    0CL80                           INPUT WORK AREA
NUMIN    DS    CL6                             *
NAMEIN   DS    CL20                            *
         DS    CL24                            *
GROSSIN  DS    CL8                             *
         DS    CL22                            *
PRINTBLD DS    0CL120                          OUTPUT WORK AREA
         DS    CL10                            *
NUMOUT   DS    CL6                             *
         DS    CL10                            *
NAMEOUT  DS    CL20                            *
         DS    CL10                            *
GROSSOUT DS    CL8                             *
         DS    CL56                            *
         END   FIRST
               =C'$$BOPEN '
               =C'$$BCLOSE'
               =A(PRINT)
               =A(INCARD)
               =A(INWORK)
               =A(PRINTBLD)
```

Figure 15-7 Program 1—solution using DOS macros.

The CNTRL macro may specify either a spacing (SP) option or a skip (SK) option. The integer coded for *n* specifies the number of lines spaced. For example, the macro

```
CNTRL   PRINT,SP,2
```

tells the computer to space two lines after writing a record to the file named PRINT.

The CNTRL macro allows us to space one, two, or three lines before or after printing. We also may use the CNTRL macro to skip to a specific position on the printed form. Forms positioning is controlled by a carriage control tape (Figure 15-8). Punches in the carriage control tape mark the beginning and end of the page. By convention, a channel 1 punch marks the top of the page. The last line on the page corresponds to a channel 9 or channel 12 punch on the carriage control tape. We position the form by telling the printer to skip to a certain control punch. For example

```
CNTRL   PRINT,SK,1
```

tells the computer to skip to channel 1 after writing a line to the file called PRINT. A skip to channel 1 means a skip to the top of the page.

We can use the CNTRL macro to space or to position the report. We must, however, code an additional entry in the declarative macro. OS programmers must code the entry

```
MACRF=PMC,
```

in the DCB macro. DOS programmers must code the entry

```
CONTROL=YES,
```

in the file description (DTFPR).

The PRTOV Macro

We issue the CNTRL macro when we are at the end of a page in the printed reports. We want to skip to the next page and continue printing. We must, however, determine when we are at the end of the page. The PRTOV macro tests the printer for an end-of-page condition. For example, the macro

```
PRTOV   PRINT,12
```

tells the computer to skip to the top of the next page when a channel 12 punch is sensed on the printer. Remember, a channel 9 or a channel 12 punch in the carriage control tape marks the end of the page.

Sometimes the programmer wishes to print headings, update a page counter, or build page totals. In this instance he or she must enter a separate

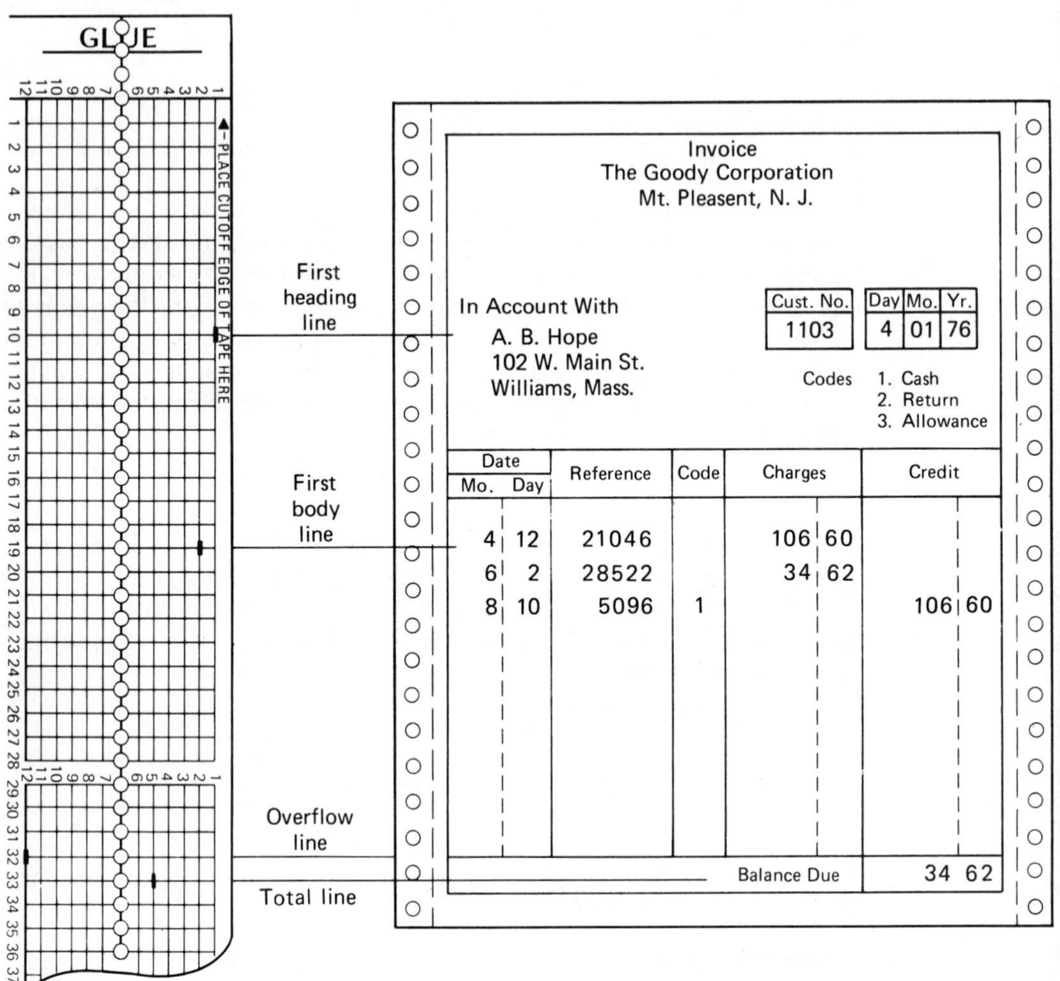

Figure 15-8.

routine at each end-of-page condition. If the programmer codes the name of this routine as part of the PRTOV macro, the operating system branches to the specified code at each end-of-page condition. For example

```
PRTOV   PRINT,9,OFLO
```

When a channel 9 punch is sensed, the operating system branches to a routine called OFLO, and places the address of the next sequential instruction in register 14. The programmer uses this address to return to the main program. The following segment of code illustrates these concepts.

```
* USE OF PRTOV MACRO TO
* SKIP TO NEXT PAGE
*
         .
         .
         .
         PUT     PRINT,PRINTBLD       WRITE FROM PRINTBLD
         PRTOV   PRINT,12             SKP TO CHANNEL 1 ON 12 PUNCH
         .
         .
         .
*
* USE OF PRTOV MACRO TO
* BRANCH TO SUBROUTINE
*
         .
         .
         .
         PUT     PRINT,PRINTBLD       WRITE FROM PRINTBLD
         PRTOV   PRINT,9,OFLO         BRANCH TO OFLO ON 9 PUNCH
NEXT     B       ...                  ELSE LOOP BACK
         .
         .
         .
OFLO     SAVE    (14,12)              SAVE REGS—R14 POINTS
*                                     TO RETURN POINT
         CNTRL   PRINT,SK,1           SKIP—I/O ROUTINE USES R14
         RETURN  (14,12)              RESTORE REGS AND BR14
*                                     WHICH SENDS US BACK TO NEXT
```

Whenever the PRTOV macro is issued, an additional parameter must be coded in the DOS declarative macro DTFPR. We must code the entry

```
PRINTOV=YES,
```

if we plan to issue the PRTOV macro against this file. Let's see how these concepts work in a sample program.

A Sample Program—OS Macros

Figure 15-9 shows the use of the PRTOV and CNTRL macros in Program 1. The simplest form of the PRTOV macro is used. The operating system causes the printer to skip to the next page whenever a channel 12 punch is sensed. Notice that the MACRF keyword in the PRINT DCB macro is changed. The letter C is added, specifying that the CNTRL macro is issued against this data set.

A Sample Program—DOS Macros

Figure 15-10 shows the use of the PRTOV and CNTRL macros in a DOS environment. The DTFPR macro for PRINT contains the two new entries

```
CONTROL = YES,
PRINTOV = YES,
```

specifying that both the CNTRL and PRTOV macros are issued.

```
*
* PROGRAM 1
* USE OF PRTOV AND  CNTRL MACROS
*
         PRINT NOGEN
         START
FIRST    SAVE  (14,12)                        SAVE REGISTERS
         BALR  12,0                           LOAD BASE
         USING *,12                           ESTABLISH ADDRESSABILITY
         ST    13,SAVEAREA+4                  FOLLOW R13 CONVENTIONS
         LA    13,SAVEAREA                    DISCUSSED IN CH 16
         OPEN  (INCARD,,PRINT,OUTPUT)         OPEN FILES
         CNTRL PRINT,SK,1                     SKIP TO TOP OF PAGE
         MVI   PRINTBLD,X'40'                 CLEAR PRINTBLD
         MVC   PRINTBLD+1(119),PRINTBLD       PROPAGATING A BLANK
READRT   GET   INCARD,INWORK                  GET RECORD INTO INWORK
         MVC   NUMOUT(6),NUMIN                MOVE NUMBER
         MVC   NAMEOUT(20),NAMEIN             MOVE EMP NAME
         MVC   GROSSOUT(8),GROSSIN            MOVE GROSS
         PUT   PRINT,PRINTBLD                 WRITE RECORD
         CNTRL PRINT,SP,2                     SPACE TWO
         PRTOV PRINT,12                       TEST FOR END OF PAGE
         B     READRT                         LOOP BACK
EOJRT    CLOSE (INCARD,,PRINT)                CLOSE FILES
         L     13,SAVEAREA+4                  SEE CHAPTER 16
         RETURN (14,12)                       RETURN
*
* DATA AREAS
*
INCARD   DCB   DSORG=PS,                                               C
               MACRF=GM,                                               C
               DDNAME=SYSIN,                                           C
               BLKSIZE=80,                                             C
               LRECL=80,                                               C
               EODAD=EOJRT
PRINT    DCB   DSORG=PS,                                               C
               MACRF=PMC,                                              C
               DDNAME=SYSOUT,                                          C
               BLKSIZE=120,                                            C
               LRECL=120
INWORK   DS    0CL80                          INPUT WORK AREA
NUMIN    DS    CL6                            *
NAMEIN   DS    CL20                           *
         DS    CL24                           *
GROSSIN  DS    CL8                            *
         DS    CL22                           *
PRINTBLD DS    0CL120                         OUTPUT WORK AREA
         DS    CL10                           *
NUMOUT   DS    CL6                            *
         DS    CL10                           *
NAMEOUT  DS    CL20                           *
         DS    CL10                           *
GROSSOUT DS    CL8                            *
         DS    CL56                           *
SAVEAREA DS    18F
         END   FIRST
```

Figure 15-9 Program 1—solution using PRTOV and CNTRL OS macros.

```
*
*  PROGRAM 1
*  USE OF PRTOV AND  CNTRL MACROS
*
         PRINT NOGEN
         START
FIRST    BALR  12,0                               LOAD BASE
         USING *,12                               ESTABLISH ADDRESSABILITY
         OPEN  INCARD,PRINT                       OPEN FILES
         CNTRL PRINT,SK,1                         SKIP TO TOP OF PAGE
         MVI   PRINTBLD,X'40'                     CLEAR PRINTBLD
         MVC   PRINTBLD+1(119),PRINTBLD           PROPAGATING A BLANK
READRT   GET   INCARD,INWORK                      GET RECORD INTO INWORK
         MVC   NUMOUT(6),NUMIN                    MOVE NUMBER
         MVC   NAMEOUT(20),NAMEIN                 MOVE EMP NAME
         MVC   GROSSOUT(8),GROSSIN                MOVE GROSS
         PUT   PRINT,PRINTBLD                     WRITE RECORD
         CNTRL PRINT,SP,2                         SPACE TWO
         PRTOV PRINT,12                           TEST FOR END OF PAGE
         B     READRT                             LOOP BACK
EOJRT    CLOSE INCARD,PRINT                       CLOSE FILES
         EOJ                                      END OF JOB
*
* DATA AREAS
*
INCARD   DTFCD DEVADDR=SYS004,                                         C
               IOAREA1=AREA1,                                          C
               BLKSIZE=80,                                             C
               DEVICE=2540,                                            C
               EOFADDR=EOJRT,                                          C
               RECFORM=FIXUNB,                                         C
               WORKA=YES,                                              C
               TYPEFLE=INPUT
PRINT    DTFPR DEVADDR=SYS005,                                         C
               IOAREA1=OUT1,                                           C
               BLKSIZE=120,                                            C
               CONTROL=YES,                                            C
               PRINTOV=YES,                                            C
               WORKA=YES,                                              C
               RECFORM=FIXUNB,                                         C
               DEVICE=1403
AREA1    DS    CL80                              INPUT  BUFFER
OUT1     DS    CL120                             OUTPUT BUFFER
INWORK   DS    0CL80                             INPUT WORK AREA
NUMIN    DS    CL6                               *
NAMEIN   DS    CL20                              *
         DS    CL24                              *
GROSSIN  DS    CL8                               *
         DS    CL22                              *
PRINTBLD DS    0CL120                            OUTPUT WORK AREA
         DS    CL10                              *
NUMOUT   DS    CL6                               *
         DS    CL10                              *
NAMEOUT  DS    CL20                              *
         DS    CL10                              *
GROSSOUT DS    CL8                               *
         DS    CL56                              *
         END   FIRST
               =C'$$BOPEN '
               =C'$$BCLOSE'
               =A(PRINT)
               =A(INCARD)
               =A(INWORK)
               =A(PRINTBLD)
```

Figure 15-10 Program 1—solution using PRTOV and CNTRL DOS macros.

Use of the Line Counter

In the preceding examples, we used the PRTOV macro to indicate the end-of-page condition. This technique is valid only if the data is going directly to the printer. In today's multiprogramming environment, printed data is often stored temporarily on tape or disk, and is sent to the printer at a later time. If the data does not go directly to the printer, the operating system never senses a channel 9 or channel 12 punch, and the overflow routine is never entered. When the data finally reach the printer, they appear as a continuous stream of lines with no headings.

In this instance, the programmer must set up a line counter. He or she must increment this counter each time a line is written, and test it to determine when the bottom of the page is reached. He must then branch to an overflow routine.

```
              .
              .
              .
FIRST
              BALR
              USING
              OPEN
              MVC     PRINTBLD(120),PRINTBLD—1      CLEAR PRINTBLD
              CNTRL   PRINT,SK,1                    SKIP TO NEW PAGE
              PUT     PRINT,HEAD                    WRITE HEADING
              CNTRL   PRINT,SP,2                    AND SPACE 2
              MVC     LINECTR, = PL2'3'             SET LINE COUNTER
READ          .
              .
              .
PROCESS       .
              .
              .
WRITE         PUT     PRINT,PRINTBLD                WRITE RECORD
              CNTRL   PRINT,SP,1                    SKIP A LINE
              AP      LINECTR, = PL1'2'             INCREMENT LINECTR
              CP      LINECTR, = PL2'55'            TEST AD
              BL      READ                          LOOP BACK IF LOW
              CNTRL   PRINT,SK,1                    ELSE SKIP TO NEW PAGE
              PUT     PRINT,HEAD                    PRINT HEADING
              CNTRL   PRINT,SP,2                    AND SPACE 2
              MVC     LINECTR, = PL2'3'             RESET LINE COUNTER
              B       READ                          AND LOOP BACK
              .
              .
              .
PRINT                                               file description
              .
              .
              .
```

```
         DC     X'40'
PRINTBLD DS     OCL120
         .
         .
         .
LINECTR  DS     CL2
HEAD     DC
         .
         .
         .
         END    FIRST
```

In this example, the line counter is set up as a packed field. A compare against a constant of 55 determines the end-of-page condition. Some programmers prefer another technique—the use of the BCT or BCTR instructions. The number of lines per page is loaded into a register. The register is decremented using the BCT(R) instruction each time a line is written.

TAPE AND DISK PROCESSING

Processing data on tape or sequential disk is similar to processing unit-record files. We must, however, consider the concept of blocking when we reference tape and disk units.

A Sample Program—OS Macros

Figure 15-11 is an example of a data set program which may be used to duplicate an existing sequential data set.

The name selected for the input data set is INDCB. The program does not specify the devices involved. At execution time the label specified in the DDNAME entry is assigned to a physical device. This assignment is a function of the job control language. For example, the job control statement

```
//INDD   DD   UNIT=TAPE
```

assigns the input data set to a tape drive.

We know, however, that INDCB is not a unit-record data set. The DCB entry

```
RECFM=FB,
```

specifies that this data set contains fixed-length blocked records. Unit-record data sets cannot contain blocked records.

We see that the blocking factor for this data set is 10. The logical record length is 80 (LRECL=80) and the physical record length is 800 (BLKSIZE=800).

We are using move mode in this program. Each GET statement makes the next logical record available to the programmer in the area of storage called WORK. Notice that WORK is 80 characters, just the size of the logical record.

```
*
* FILE-TO-FILE PROGRAM
*
         PRINT NOGEN
         START
FIRST    SAVE  (14,12)                                    SAVE REGISTERS
         BALR  12,0                                       LOAD BASE
         USING *,12                                       ADDRESSABILITY
         ST    13,SAVEAREA+4                              FOLLOW R13 CONVENTIONS
         LA    13,SAVEAREA                                DISCUSSED IN CH 16
         OPEN  (INDCB,,OUTDCB,OUTPUT)                     OPEN FILES
READRT   GET   INDCB,WORK                                 GET RECORD
         PUT   OUTDCB,WORK                                WRITE RECORD
         B     READRT                                     LOOP TO READRT
EOJRT    CLOSE (INDCB,,OUTDCB)                            CLOSE FILES
         L     13,SAVEAREA+4                              SEE CHAPTER 16
         RETURN (14,12)                                   RETURN
*
* DATA AREAS
*
INDCB    DCB   DSORG=PS,                                              C
               MACRF=GM,                                              C
               DDNAME=INDD,                                           C
               LRECL=80,                                              C
               BLKSIZE=800,                                           C
               RECFM=FB,                                              C
               EODAD=EOJRT
OUTDCB   DCB   DSORG=PS,                                              C
               DDNAME=OUTDD,                                          C
               LRECL=80,                                              C
               BLKSIZE=800,                                           C
               RECFM=FB,                                              C
               MACRF=PM
WORK     DS    CL80                                      WORK AREA STORAGE
SAVEAREA DS    18F                                       SAVEAREA STORAGE
         END   FIRST
```

Figure 15-11 File-to-file utility program.

Let's assume that INDCB is assigned to a tape drive at execution time. The first GET issued causes the first block of data to be transferred to storage. The data is held in the operating system's buffer area. The first logical record within this block is moved to the programmer's work area. When the second GET is issued, no transfer of data occurs. The second logical record already is in storage. It is in the operating system's buffer area. The record is moved to the programmer's work area. No transfer of data occurs until the eleventh GET is issued. At this time the entire second block of data is read into storage.

Similarly, no transfer of data is effected to the output device until ten PUT statements have been issued. At this time, an entire block of data has been built in the output buffer area. This entire block of data now is written to the device assigned to OUTDCB.

A Sample Program—DOS Macros

We use the DTFMT macro to describe files residing on tape. Many of the entries in the DTFMT macro printer files are identical to the entries for card and printer files.

Table 15-4 DOS Declarative Macro Operands

operand	applicable for DTFCD	DTFPR	DTFMT
BLKSIZE=	opt	opt	req
CONTROL=	opt	opt	
DEVADDR=	req	req	
DEVICE=	opt	opt	
EOFADDR=	opt		opt
IOAREA1=	req	req	req
IOAREA2=	opt	opt	opt
PRINTOV=		opt	
TYPEFLE=	opt		opt
WORKA=	(1)	(1)	(1, 2)

(1) Required if using two I/O areas and move mode
(2) Required if processing blocked records or using two I/O areas and move mode

We must consider two additional concepts when discussing tape files. Tape files may be labeled. We use the entry

```
        {STD }
FILABL= {NSTD}
        {NO  }
```

to describe the type of labeling on the file. The programmer must make a choice of the options in brackets. The labels may be standard (STD)—processed by the operating system—nonstandard (NSTD)—the programmer must process the labels himself—or the tape may be unlabeled (NO). If the FILABL entry is omitted, the operating system assumes that the tape is unlabeled.

We also must consider blocking. We specify the size of the physical record using the BLKSIZE parameter, and the size of the logical record using the RECSIZE parameter. Figure 15-12 shows how these entries are used in a program.

Figure 15-12 is an example of a tape-to-tape program. We name the input file TAPEIN. We specify a physical record length of 800,

```
BLKSIZE=800,
```

and a logical record length of 80

```
RECSIZE=80
```

We name the output file TAPEOUT. This file also has a physical record length of 800 and a logical record length of 80.

```
*
* TAPE-TO-TAPE UTILITY PROGRAM
*
         PRINT NOGEN
         START
FIRST    BALR  12,0                              LOAD BASE
         USING *,12                              ADDRESSABILITY
         OPEN  TAPEIN,TAPEOUT                    OPEN FILES
READRT   GET   TAPEIN,WORK                       GET RECORD - MOVE TO WORK
         PUT   TAPEIN,WORK                       WRITE RECORD FROM WORK
         B     READRT                            LOOP TO READRT
EOJRT    CLOSE TAPEIN,WORK                       CLOSE FILES
         EOJ                                     END OF JOB
*
* DATA AREAS
*
TAPEIN   DTFMT DEVADDR=SYS004,                                         C
               BLKSIZE=800,                                            C
               EOFADDR=EOJRT,                                          C
               FILABL=STD,                                             C
               IOAREA1=AREA1,                                          C
               RECFORM=FIXBLK,                                         C
               RECSIZE=80,                                             C
               WORKA=YES,                                              C
               TYPEFLE=INPUT
TAPEOUT  DTFMT DEVADDR=SYS005,                                         C
               BLKSIZE=800,                                            C
               FILABL=STD,                                             C
               IOAREA1=OUT1,                                           C
               RECFORM=FIXBLK,                                         C
               RECSIZE=80,                                             C
               WORKA=YES,                                              C
               TYPEFLE=OUTPUT
WORK     DS    CL80                              WORK AREA STORAGE
AREA1    DS    CL800                             INPUT  BUFFER
OUT1     DS    CL800                             OUTPUT BUFFER
         END   FIRST
               =C'$$BOPEN '
               =C'$$BCLOSE'
               =A(TAPEIN)
               =A(WORK)
```

Figure 15-12 Tape-to-tape utility program.

When we reserve space for the input and output buffer areas, we reserve enough space for the physical record length.

```
AREA1   DS   CL800
OUT1    DS   CL800
```

When we reserve space for the work area, we reserve enough space for the logical record.

```
WORK   DS   CL80
```

The first statements perform the required housekeeping functions, establishing addressability and opening the files. We then read a record,

```
GET   TAPEIN,WORK
```

It is DOS's responsibility to transfer each block of data into the I/O area, and place the next logical record in WORK. We use the PUT statement to write this record from WORK and loop back to the GET statement. The operating system determines the end-of-file condition, and the code at EOJRT is executed.

The imperative macros issued against the tape files are the same macros we have used for card and printer programs. We now can summarize the declarative and imperative macros available for card, printer, and tape files.

device	imperative macros	declarative macros
card	OPEN,CLOSE,GET,PUT	DTFCD
printer	OPEN,CLOSE,GET,PUT, CNTRL,PRTOV	DTFPR
tape	OPEN,CLOSE,GET,PUT	DTFMT

The entries within each DTF also are similar. Table 15-5 summarizes these entries for card, printer, and tape files. We have not discussed all the possible DTF entries. The reader should refer to Appendix E for a complete description of the DTF entries.

Table 15-5 DOS Declarative Macro Operands

		applicable for	
operand	**DTFCD**	**DTFPR**	**DTFMT**
BLKSIZE=	opt	opt	req
CONTROL=		opt	
DEVADDR=	req	req	req
DEVICE=	opt	opt	
EOFADDR=	opt		opt
FILABL=			opt
IOAREA1=	req	req	req
IOAREA2=	opt	opt	opt
PRINTOV=		opt	
RECFORM=	opt	opt	opt
RECSIZE=	opt	opt	opt
TYPEFLE=	opt		opt
WORKA=	(1)	(1)	(2)

(1) Required if using two I/O areas move mode
(2) Required if processing blocked records or using two I/O areas and move mode

LOCATE MODE Sometimes the programmer doesn't want the logical record moved to a work area. Perhaps he (or she) doesn't have the storage required for the work area. Or, perhaps, he would just rather process the data in the operating system's buffer area. Before he can do this, he must know where the buffer area is located. He must have a way of knowing where the operating system put the next record. In the case of blocked records, he must have a way of locating the correct logical record within the block of physical records in the buffer area. The programmer can ask the operating system to locate the record for him. We call this concept *locate mode*.

Locate Mode—OS Macros

The OS programmer specifies locate mode in the MACRF keyword entry, and uses the locate-mode form of the GET or PUT macro.

```
         GET    INCARD
          .
          .
          .
INCARD   DCB    MACRF=GL,
          .
          .
          .
```

Let's see how these new concepts are used in Program 1 (Figure 15-13).

The first instructions establish addressability and perform the necessary housekeeping functions. The first GET issued reads a record into storage and places the address of this record in register 1. The programmer now saves this address in register 9.

```
LR    9,1
```

Before he or she can move the data to the output buffer, the programmer must get the address of the next available buffer area from the operating system. He does this by issuing a PUT command. It may seem illogical to issue this command before moving the data to the output atea. This initial PUT, however, does not cause the output of data, but loads the address of the next buffer area into register 1. The programmer now saves this address in register 8.

```
LR  8,1
```

He now uses register 9 to address the input buffer, and register 8 to address the output buffer.

```
MVI   0(8),X'40'
MVC   1(119,8),0(8)
MVC   10(6,8),0(9)
MVC   26(20,8),6(9)
MVC   56(8,8),50(9)
```

These instructions clear the buffer area by propagating a blank through the output area addressed by register 8, and then move the three desired fields

```
*
* PROGRAM 1
* USE OF OS MACROS USING LOCATE MODE
* NO PRINTER CONTROL OR EDITING
*
         PRINT NOGEN
         START
FIRST    SAVE  (14,12)                     SAVE REGISTERS
         BALR  12,0                        LOAD BASE
         USING *,12                        ADDRESSABILITY
         ST    13,SAVEAREA+4               FOLLOW R13 CONVENTIONS
         LA    13,SAVEAREA                 DISCUSSED IN CH 16
         OPEN  (INCARD,,PRINT,OUTPUT)      OPEN FILES
READRT   GET   INCARD                      GET DATA - REGISTER 1
*                                          POINTS TO BUFFER AREA
         LR    9,1                         SAVE BUFFER ADDRESS
         PUT   PRINT                       GET ADDRESS NEXT
*                                          OUTPUT BUFFER
         LR    8,1                         SAVE ADDRESS IN R8
         MVI   0(8),X'40'                  MOVE SPACE
         MVC   1(119,8),0(8)               CLEAR OUTPUT BUFFER
         MVC   10(6,8),0(9)                MOVE NUMBER
         MVC   26(20,8),6(9)               MOVE NAME
         MVC   56(8,8),50(9)               MOVE GROSS
         B     READRT                      LOOP BACK
EOJRT    CLOSE (INCARD,,PRINT)             CLOSE FILES
         L     13,SAVEAREA+4               SEE CHAPTER 16
         RETURN (14,12)                    RETURN
INCARD   DCB   DSORG=PS,                                   C
               MACRF=GL,                                   C
               DDNAME=SYSIN,                               C
               EODAD=EOJRT,                                C
               BLKSIZE=80,                                 C
               LRECL=80
PRINT    DCB   DSORG=PS,                                   C
               MACRF=PL,                                   C
               DDNAME=SYSOUT,                              C
               BLKSIZE=120,                                C
               LRECL=120
SAVEAREA DS    18F                       RESERVE SAVEAREA
         END   FIRST
```

Figure 15-13 Program 1—solution using locate mode OS macros.

from the input area to the output area. Once the data is moved to the output area, the program loops back to the next GET. Data is transferred. The PUT statement is issued. The first record is written and the address of the next buffer area is given in register 1.

Locate Mode—DOS Macros

To use locate mode, the DOS programmer must supply an additional parameter in the DTF for the file, and use the locate mode form of the GET or PUT macro. The entry

```
IOREG=n
```

specifies the register the operating system uses to give us the address of the next record.

```
                 GET      INCARD
                 .
                 .
                 .
        INCARD   DTFCD    IOREG=9,
                 .
                 .
                 .
```

In this instance the operating system reads the record and places the address of the buffer area in register 9.

Let's see how these same concepts are used in Program 1 (Figure 15-14). We define each file specifying two I/O areas. The entry

```
IOREG=9,          C
```

tells the operating system that register 9 is used to address the correct input buffer area. The entry

```
IOREG=8,          C
```

tells the operating system that register 8 is used to address the correct output buffer area.

The first instructions establish addressability and perform the necessary housekeeping functions. The statement

```
GET   INCARD,
```

reads the first logical record into one of the two available buffer areas. The address of the record is placed in register 9. The next instructions clear the output buffer area and move the appropriate fields from the input buffer area to the output buffer area.

```
MVI    0(8),X'40'
MVC    1(119,8),0(8)
MVC    10(6,8),0(9)
MVC    26(20,8),6(9)
MVC    56(8,8),50(9)
```

We are using register 8 to address the output buffer area. The statement

```
PUT   PRINT
```

writes a record from the buffer area to the printer. The branch statement

```
B   READRT
```

loops back to read the next card.

```
*
* PROGRAM 1
* USE OF DOS MACROS USING LOCATE MODE
* NO PRINTER CONTROL OR EDITING
*
         PRINT NOGEN
         START
FIRST    BALR  12,0                          LOAD BASE
         USING *,12                          ADDRESSABILITY
         OPEN  INCARD,PRINT                  OPEN FILES
READRT   GET   INCARD                        R9 POINTS TO RECORD
         MVI   0(8),X'40'                    MOVE SPACE
         MVC   1(119,8),0(8)                 CLEAR OUTPUT BUFFER
         MVC   10(6,8),0(9)                  MOVE NUMBER
         MVC   26(20,8),6(9)                 MOVE NAME
         MVC   55(8,8),50(9)                 MOVE GROSS
         PUT   PRINT                         R8 POINTS TO RECORD
*                                            OUTPUT BUFFER
         B     READRT                        LOOP BACK
EOJRT    CLOSE INCARD,PRINT                  CLOSE FILES
         EOJ                                 END OF JOB
INCARD   DTFCD DEVADDR=SYS004,                                    C
               IOAREA1=AREA1,                                     C
               IOAREA2=AREA2,                                     C
               IOREG=9,                                           C
               BLKSIZE=80,                                        C
               DEVICE=2540,                                       C
               EOFADDR=EOJRT,                                     C
               RECFORM=FIXUNB,                                    C
               TYPEFLE=INPUT
PRINT    DTFPR DEVADDR=SYS005,                                    C
               IOAREA1=OUT1,                                      C
               IOAREA2=OUT2,                                      C
               IOREG=8,                                           C
               BLKSIZE=120,                                       C
               CONTROL=YES,                                       C
               PRINTOV=YES,                                       C
               RECFORM=FIXUNB,                                    C
               DEVICE=1403
AREA2    DS    CL80
AREA1    DS    CL80
OUT1     DS    CL120
OUT2     DS    CL120
         END   FIRST
               =C'$$BOPEN '
               =C'$$BCLOSE'
               =A(INCARD)
               =A(PRINT)
```

Figure 15-14 Program 1—solution using locate mode DOS macros.

The explicit notation used in these programs is difficult to follow. It is possible to use symbolic addressing with locate mode if the DSECT is used.

Use of the DSECT

The DSECT does not reserve storage but equates the labels within the DSECT with a displacement.

relative displacement	assembly statement		
000000	INWORK	DSECT	
000000	NUMIN	DS	CL6
000006	NAMEIN	DS	CL20
00001A		DS	CL24
000032	GROSSIN	DS	CL8
00003A		DS	CL22
000000	OUTBLD	DSECT	
000000		DS	CL10
00000A	NUMOUT	DS	CL6
000010		DS	CL10
00001A	NAMEOUT	DS	CL20
00002E		DS	CL10
000038	GROSSOUT	DS	CL8
000040		DS	CL56

The programmer must tell the assembler which register to use when these labels are referenced. This is done with the USING statement.

```
USING   INWORK,9
USING   OUTBLD,8
```

Now, when the programmer codes the statement

```
MVC   NUMOUT(6),NUMIN
```

the assembler uses register 9 to address NUMIN, and register 8 to address NUMOUT. Let's examine the machine instruction generated from this statement.

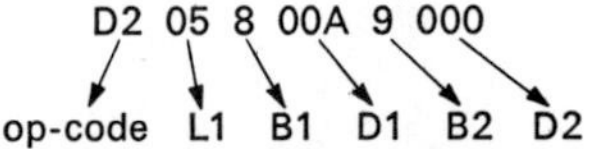

The second operand is addressed by the contents of register 9 plus a displacement of zero. Let's assume register 9 contains the address of the input buffer area. This instruction addresses the first six positions of the buffer area—specifically the field NUMIN—and moves it to the area of storage addressed by register 8 and a displacement of 10. If register 8 points to the output buffer area, we are moving the first six positions of the input buffer area to positions 11–16 of the output buffer area.

Now let's see how we ensure that the correct register is pointing to the correct buffer area. The programmer tells the operating system how to address the labels within the DSECT with the statements

```
USING  INWORK,9
USING  OUTBLD,8
```

These USING statements are no different from the USING statement which determines addressability for the entire program. The USING statement is an assembly-time promise that a specified address will be in the register at execution time. We load the base register for the program with the BALR instruction. How are the registers which address the DSECTs loaded?

The DSECT in an OS Program. OS loads register 1 with the address of the next available buffer. (See Figure 15-15 on page 406.) The statement

```
USING  INWORK,9
```

promises the assembler that register 9 will contain the address of INWORK. After we issue the GET statement, the address of the buffer area is in register 1. We now load this address into register 9.

```
LR  9,1
```

The same procedure is followed for the output buffer.

The DSECT in a DOS Program. DOS loads registers 8 and 9 as part of the I/O routine. The IOREG entry tells DOS which register to use to locate the next record. The IOREG entry specifies the registers named in the USING statement. (See Figure 15-16 on page 407.)

PROBLEMS **15.1** Write the declarative macro descriptions for each of the following files. Use either the DTF or DCB macros.

1. An input card file called CARDRD, assigned to the 2540, to be processed in move mode. Two buffer areas are associated with the file. Use the external name SYS004.
2. A printer file called PRINTOUT, assigned to the 1403, to be processed in locate mode. One buffer area is associated with the file. Both the PRTOV and CNTRL macros are issued against the file. Use the external name SYS005.
3. An input tape file called TAPEIN, assigned to the 2400 tape drive, to be processed in move mode. The logical record length is 100, blocked 50. One buffer area is associated with the file. Use the external name SYS004.

```
*
* PROGRAM 1
* USE OF DSECT AND LOCATE MODE
* NO PRINTER CONTROL OR EDITING
*
         PRINT NOGEN
         START
FIRST    SAVE  (14,12)                        SAVE REGISTERS
         BALR  12,0                           LOAD BASE
         USING INWORK,9                       ADDRESS INWORK
         USING OUTBLD,8                       ADDRESS OUTBLD
         USING *,12                           ADDRESSABILITY FOR PROGRAM
         ST    13,SAVEAREA+4                  FOLLOW R13 CONVENTIONS
         LA    13,SAVEAREA                    DISCUSSED IN CH 15
         OPEN  (INCARD,,PRINT,OUTPUT)
READRT   GET   INCARD                         GET DATA - REGISTER 1
*                                             POINTS TO BUFFER AREA
         LR    9,1                            SAVE BUFFER ADDRESS
         PUT   PRINT                          GET ADDRESS NEXT
*                                             OUTPUT BUFFER
         LR    8,1                            SAVE ADDRESS IN R8
         MVI   OUTBLD,X'40'                   MOVE SPACE
         MVC   OUTBLD+1(119),OUTBLD           CLEAR BUFFER
         MVC   NUMOUT(6),NUMIN                MOVE NUMBER
         MVC   NAMEOUT(20),NAMEIN             MOVE NAME
         MVC   GROSSOUT(8),GROSSIN            MOVE GROSS
         B     READRT                         LOOP BACK
EOJRT    CLOSE (INCARD,,PRINT)                CLOSE FILES
         L     13,SAVEAREA+4                  SEE CHAPTER 15
         RETURN (14,12)                       RETURN
INCARD   DCB   DSORG=PS,                                               C
               MACRF=GL,                                               C
               DDNAME=SYSIN,                                           C
               EODAD=EOJRT,                                            C
               BLKSIZE=80,                                             C
               LRECL=80
PRINT    DCB   DSORG=PS,                                               C
               MACRF=PL,                                               C
               DDNAME=SYSOUT,                                          C
               BLKSIZE=120,                                            C
               LRECL=120
SAVEAREA DS    18F                            RESERVE SAVEAREA
INWORK   DSECT                                DSECT
NUMIN    DS    CL6                            FORMATS
NAMEIN   DS    CL20                           INPUT
         DS    CL24                           RECORD
GROSSIN  DS    CL8                            *
         DS    CL22                           *
OUTBLD   DSECT                                DSECT
         DS    CL10                           FORMATS
NUMOUT   DS    CL6                            OUTPUT
         DS    CL10                           RECORD
NAMEOUT  DS    CL20                           *
         DS    CL10                           *
GROSSOUT DS    CL8                            *
         DS    CL56                           *
         END   FIRST
```

Figure 15-15 Program 1—solution using DSECT and locate mode OS macros.

```
*
* PROGRAM 1
* USE OF DSECT AND LOCATE MODE
* NO PRINTER CONTROL OR EDITING
*
         PRINT NOGEN
         START
FIRST    BALR  12,0                          LOAD BASE
         USING INWORK,9                      ADDRESS INWORK
         USING OUTBLD,8                      ADDRESS OUTBLD
         USING *,12                          ADDRESSABILITY FOR PROGRAM
         OPEN  INCARD,PRINT                  OPEN FILES
READRT   GET   INCARD                        GET DATA - REGISTER 9
*                                            POINTS TO BUFFER AREA
         MVI   OUTBLD,X'40'                  MOVE SPACE
         MVC   OUTBLD+1(119),OUTBLD          CLEAR BUFFER
         MVC   NUMOUT(6),NUMIN               MOVE NUMBER
         MVC   NAMEOUT(20),NAMEIN            MOVE NAME
         MVC   GROSSOUT(8),GROSSIN           MOVE GROSS
         B     READRT                        LOOP BACK
         PUT   PRINT                         GET ADDRESS NEXT
EOJRT    CLOSE INCARD,PRINT                  CLOSE FILES
         EOJ                                 END OF JOB
INCARD   DTFCD DEVADDR=SYS004,                                         C
               IOAREA1=AREA1,                                          C
               BLKSIZE=80,                                             C
               DEVICE=2540,                                            C
               EOFADDR=EOJRT,                                          C
               IOAREA2=AREA2,                                          C
               IOREG=9,                                                C
               RECFORM=FIXUNB,                                         C
               TYPEFLE=INPUT
PRINT    DTFPR DEVADDR=SYS005,                                         C
               IOAREA1=OUT1,                                           C
               IOAREA2=OUT2,                                           C
               IOREG=8,                                                C
               BLKSIZE=120,                                            C
               CONTROL=YES,                                            C
               PRINTOV=YES,                                            C
               RECFORM=FIXUNB,                                         C
               DEVICE=1403
OUT1     DS    CL120                       DEFINE 2
OUT2     DS    CL120                       OUTPUT BUFFERS
AREA1    DS    CL80                        DEFINE 2
AREA2    DS    CL80                        INPUT BUFFERS
INWORK   DSECT                             DSECT FORMATS
NUMIN    DS    CL6                         INPUT RECORD
NAMEIN   DS    CL20                        *
         DS    CL24                        *
GROSSIN  DS    CL8                         *
         DS    CL22                        *
OUTBLD   DSECT                             DSECT FORMATS
         DS    CL10                        OUTPUT RECORD
NUMOUT   DS    CL6
         DS    CL10
NAMEOUT  DS    CL20
         DS    CL10
GROSSOUT DS    CL8
         DS    CL56
         END   FIRST
```

Figure 15-16 Program 1—solution using DSECT and locate mode DOS macros.

15.2 Give the imperative macros for each of the following operations. Use either the OS or DOS form of the macro.

1. Open an input file called CARDRD, an output file called PRINT, and an output file called REPORT.
2. Read a record from a file called INFILE into an area of storage called WORK. Use move mode.
3. Read a record from a file called INFILE. Use locate mode. Move the logical record to WORK. Use whatever register notation is required.
4. Write a record to a file called OUTFILE from an area of storage called WORK. Use move mode.
5. Close an input file called CARDRD, an output file called PRINT, and an output file called REPORT.

15.3 Code any of the problems in Program 6 (Appendix C) using the appropriate I/O macros. Use either move or locate mode. Develop headings when appropriate.

16

Subroutines and Linkages

INTRODUCTION The programs discussed in this text are not long or complex. Yet even in these simple illustrativè programs it is sometimes necessary to repeat sections of code. The code necessary to skip to the top of the next page and print headings must be entered at the beginning of each program, and upon each overflow or end-of-page condition. This repetition means coding the same instructions twice—a waste of time on the part of the programmer, and the use of unnecessary storage. If we could somehow code our overflow routine *once*, and branch to it whenever necessary, we could save coding time and expensive computer storage.

We refer to the heading routine as a *subroutine* (Figure 16-1). We enter this subroutine from two distinct parts of the main or calling program: at beginning of job housekeeping, and on each overflow condition. The concept of the subroutine saves storage.

Need for the Subroutine

One purpose of the subroutine is to eliminate repetition of code. The heading routine is one example. Another common subroutine is the data conversion routine. If our program involves complex mathematical calculations, most

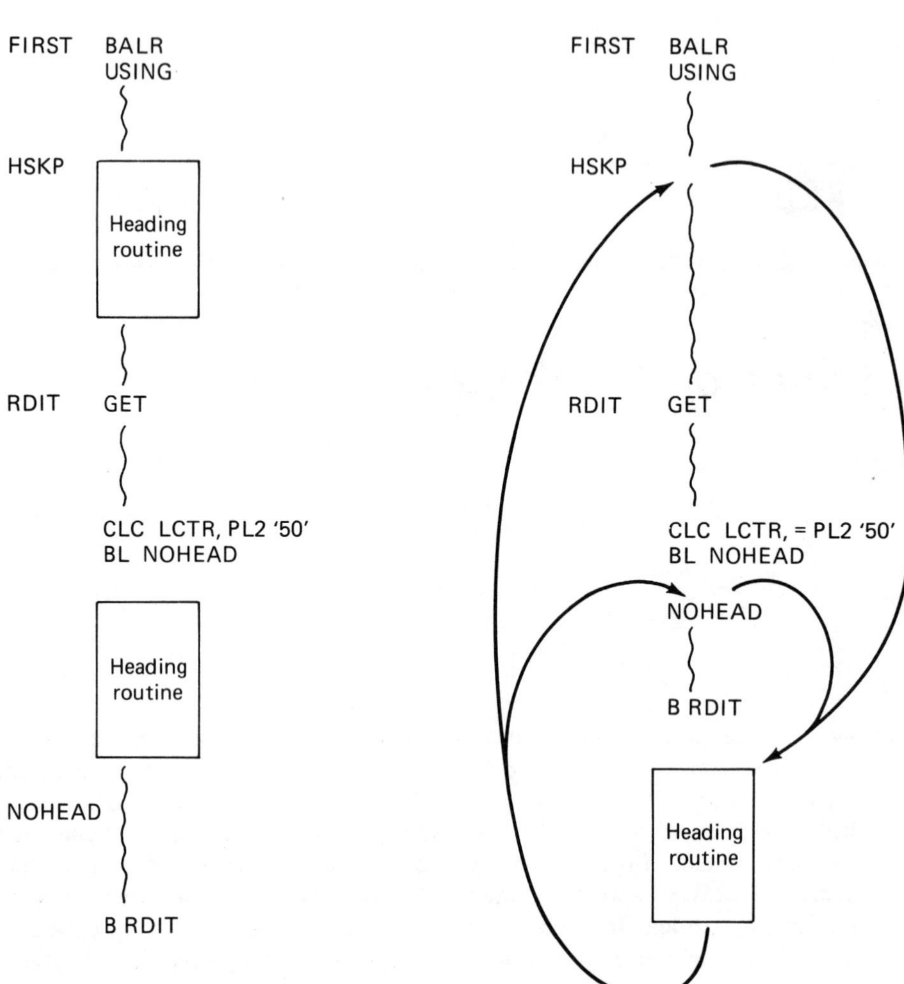

Figure 16-1 Concept of a subroutine.

probably we will use floating-point instructions to solve the problem. Each piece of data referenced in our program must be converted to floating-point notation. Rather than continually repeat this code, we code the conversion instructions as a subroutine and execute the code whenever we find it necessary to convert data to floating-point.

Perhaps our program calls for the calculation of the logarithm of each data item entering the program. Again, this mathematical routine could be coded as a subroutine and entered whenever necessary.

The use of subroutines is so common that certain conventions have been established to aid in the flowcharting and coding of programs using subroutines. Figure 16-2 represents the flowchart for a program containing the heading routine coded as a subroutine. The subroutine may be entered from two points in the main (calling) program: at the beginning of job housekeeping, or on an overflow condition. In each case, the subroutine is referenced by name.

Internal and External Subroutines

There are two types of subroutines—internal and external. *Internal subroutines* are coded and assembled as part of the main program. If the programmer codes HEADRT and assembles it with the main program, it becomes an internal subroutine. If, however, HEADRT is assembled separately from the main program, it becomes an *external subroutine.* In this latter case an operating system program called the *linkage editor* links or ties the subroutine to the main program.

We use the term *control section* to refer to these independent blocks of code. We often use the assembler pseudo-instruction CSECT (Control SECTion) to identify the beginning of a control section.

Some programs are so large and complex that they are broken into several smaller programs or control sections, each of which is worked on by a single programmer. At some point, each of these program segments must be linked together into one complete program module. Because all the control sections (subroutines) are directed at solving one data processing problem, they must be interrelated. Data must be passed from one control section to another. Certain conventions are followed to ensure that the data is passed correctly.

When several programmers work on the routines comprising a large program, the routines are usually separately assembled and linked together by the *linkage editor* (Figure 16-3).

Notice that each program segment is coded and assembled independently of the other segments. The resulting object modules are then linked into one program. Although each object module is comprised of machine language instructions, the original source modules do not have to be coded in the same language. The mathematical subroutines may be coded in FORTRAN, the I/O routines in assembly language, and the main processing coded in COBOL. No matter which high-level language is used, the resulting object modules are in machine language.

INTERNAL SUBROUTINES

First we shall discuss internal subroutines. We are concerned with branching to or entering the subroutine, and most especially, returning to the correct place in the calling program. We use Program 1 as our example, and code the headings as an internal subroutine. Figure 16-2 gives the flowchart for the solution.

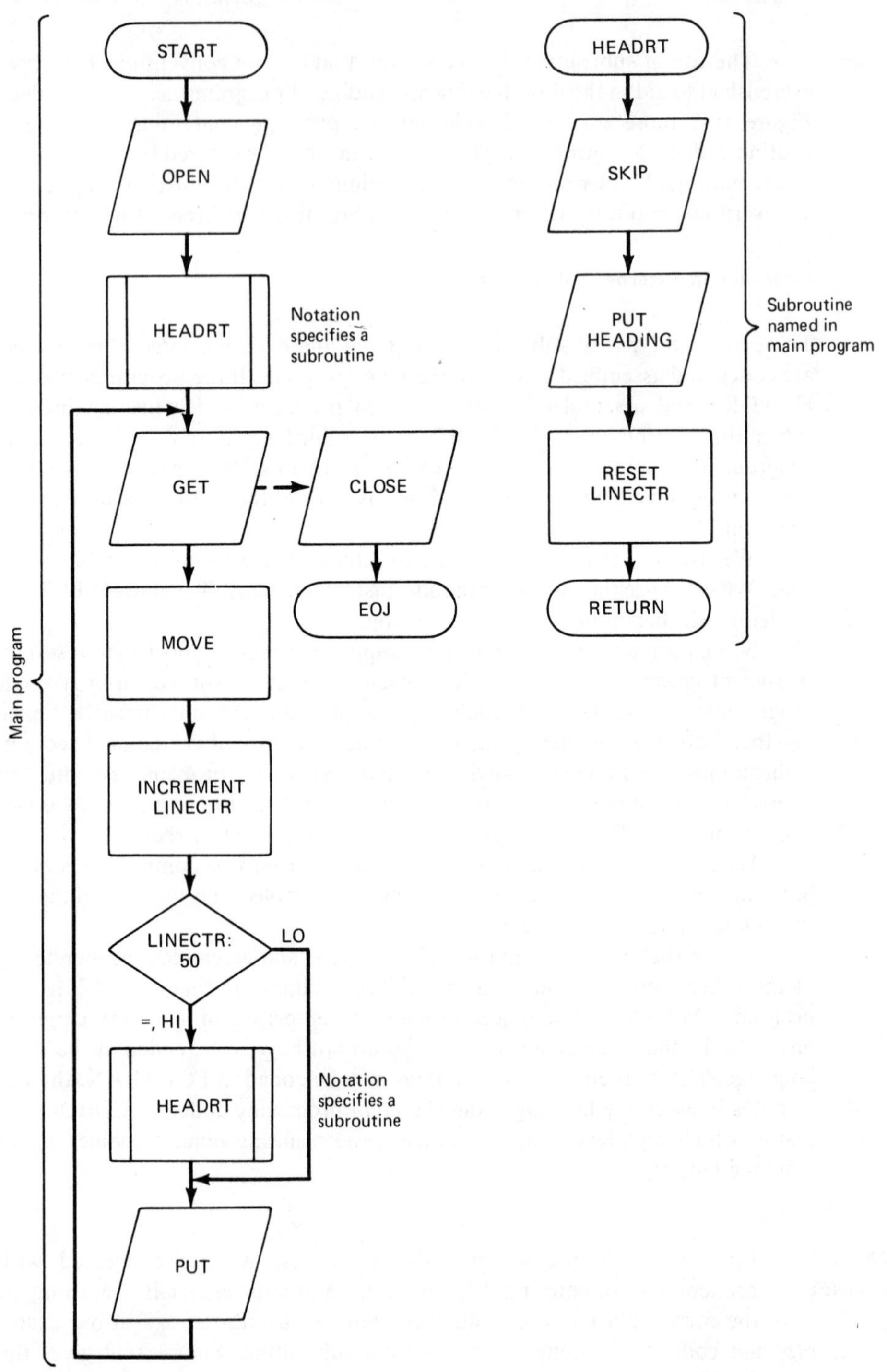

Figure 16-2 Flowchart for a subroutine.

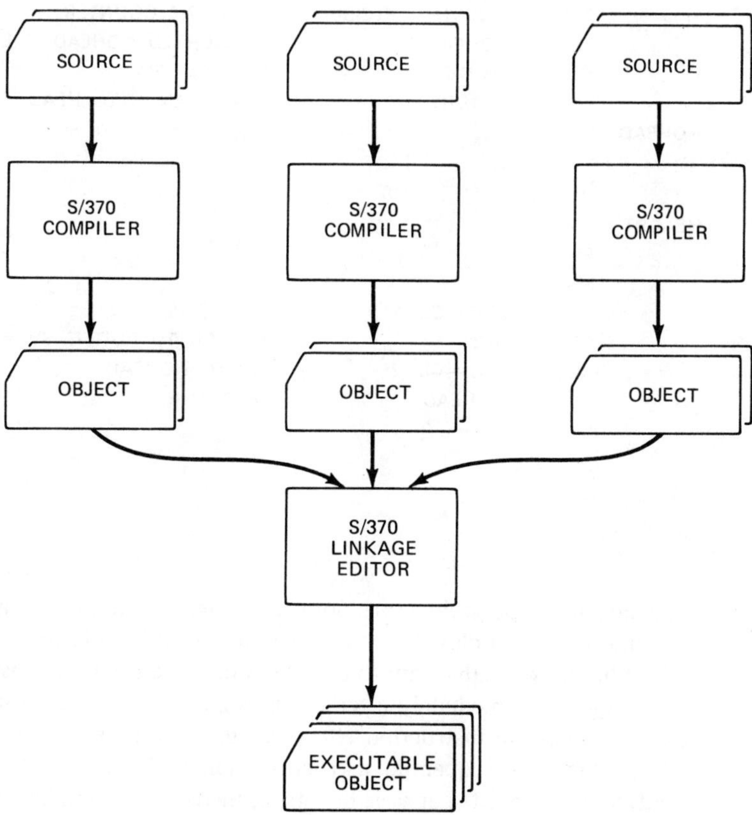

Figure 16-3 Linkage of separately compiled modules.

Use of BAL and BALR

Our first problem is entering the subroutine. If we use an unconditional branch instruction to enter the subroutine, we do not know whether to return to the GET statement, or to the PUT statement. We could use a switch to direct us back to the correct statement in the calling program. Our code might appear as follows:

```
FIRST   SAVE
        BALR
        USING
          .
          .
          .
HSKP    MVI     SW,C'1'                 SET SW TO SHOW FIRST TIME
        B       HEADRT                  AND BRANCH TO HEADRT
RDIT    GET
          .
          .
          .
```

```
         CLC    LINECTR, = PL2'50'    TEST LINE COUNTER
         BL     NOHEAD                BRANCH TO NOHEAD IF LESS THAN 50
         MVI    SW,C'2'               ELSE SET SW
         B      HEADRT                AND BRANCH TO HEADRT
NOHEAD   PUT
         .
         .
         .
HEADRT   CNTRL
         PUT
         MVC
         CLC    SW, = CL1'1'          TEST SW
         BE     RDIT                  RETURN TO RDIT IF SW = 1
         CLC    SW, = CL1'2'          OR TO NOHEAD
         BE     NOHEAD                IF SW = 2
         .
         .
         .
SW       DS     CL1
         .
         .
         .
```

If we have many possible return points, the logic of the subroutine exit becomes more and more complex. We must arrive at a simpler solution.

What do we really want to do? We want to return to the instruction in our main program immediately after the unconditional branch instruction. What assembly language instruction effects an unconditional branch *and* saves the address of the next sequential instruction? The BALR and BAL instructions are exactly what we need! Let's see how these instructions simplify the solution.

```
FIRST    SAVE
         BALR
         USING
         .
         .
         .
HSKP     BAL    10,HEADRT
RDIT     GET
         .
         .
         .
         CLC    LINECTR, = PL2'50'
         BL     NOHEAD
         BAL    10,HEADRT
NOHEAD   PUT
         .
         .
         .
HEADRT   CNTRL
         PUT
         MVC
         BR     10
```

We use the BAL instruction to enter the subroutine. The address of the next sequential instruction is saved in register 10. When we return from the subroutine, we need only branch to the address contained in register 10.

```
BR   10
```

We return either to the GET statement, or to the PUT statement, depending upon the contents of register 10.

Figure 16-4 shows the complete coding for this problem.* We enter the heading routine from two places in the program. The use of the BAL instruction ensures that we return to the correct instruction in the main program.

Use of the ADCON

In our example, we use the label HEADRT to name the first instruction in our subroutine. We call this, instruction the *entry point,* and reference the entry point in the BAL instruction. We could, however, use the RR format, the BALR instruction, if we load the address of HEADRT into a register. For example, the code

```
LA     11,HEADRT
BALR   10,11
```

gives us the same results as the instruction

```
BAL    10,HEADRT
```

The LA instruction puts the effective address of HEADRT in register 11. We achieve the same results using a special type of constant called the ADCON (ADdress CONstant). For example

```
         L      11,ADDHEAD
         BALR   10,11
         .
         .
         .
ADDHEAD  DC     A(HEADRT)
```

The constant ADDHEAD is a 4-byte constant which, when the computer executes the program, contains the address of HEADRT. The L instruction loads a fullword of data from the storage location called ADDHEAD. This fullword of data contains the *address* of the subroutine to which we are branching. The ADCON helps us branch to the correct entry point in *external* subroutines.

*The solution in Figure 16-4 uses OS macros. Only the macros differ between operating systems—the logic of each linkage is unchanged.

```
*
* PROGRAM 1
* HEADINGS AS AN INTERNAL SUBROUTINE
*
         PRINT NOGEN
         START
FIRST    SAVE  (14,12)                             SAVE REGISTERS
         BALR  12,0                                LOAD BASE
         USING *,12                                ADDRESSABILITY
         ST    13,SAVEAREA+4                       FOLLOW R13 CONVENTIONS
         LA    13,SAVEAREA                         DISCUSSED IN CH 16
         OPEN  (INCARD,,PRINT,OUTPUT)              OPEN FILES
         BAL   10,HEADRT                           AND BRANCH TO PRINT
READRT   GET   INCARD,INWORK                       GET RECORD
         MVC   NUMOUT(6),NUMIN                     MOVE NUMBER
         MVC   NAMEOUT(20),NAMEIN                  MOVE EMP NAME
         MVC   GROSSOUT(8),GROSSIN                 MOVE GROSS
         AP    LINECTR(2),=PL1'1'                  INCREMENT LINECTR
         CP    LINECTR(2),=PL2'50'                 TEST FOR OVERFLOW
         BL    NOHEAD                              BYPASS HEADINGS IF LOW
         BAL   10,HEADRT                           LINK TO HEADRT
NOHEAD   EQU   *                                   ELSE
         PUT   PRINT,PRINTBLD                      WRITE RECORD AND
         B     READRT                              LOOP BACK
HEADRT   CNTRL PRINT,SK,1                          SKIP TO NEXT PAGE
         PUT   PRINT,HEAD1                         WRITE FIRST HEADING
         PUT   PRINT,HEAD2                         WRITE SECOND HEADING
         CNTRL PRINT,SP,2                          THEN SPACE 2
         MVC   LINECTR(2),=PL2'4'                  RESET LINECTR AND
         BR    10                                  RETURN TO MAINLINE
EOJRT    CLOSE (INCARD,,PRINT)                     CLOSE FILES
         L     13,SAVEAREA+4                       FOLLOW R13 CONVENTIONS
         RETURN (14,12)                            AND RETURN
*
* DATA AREAS
*
HEAD1    DC    CL9' '                              FORMAT FIRST HEADING
         DC    CL8'EMPLOYEE'                       *
         DC    CL15' '                             *
         DC    CL8'EMPLOYEE'                       *
         DC    CL16' '                             *
         DC    CL12'YEAR-TO-DATE'                  *
         DC    CL52' '                             *
HEAD2    DC    CL10' '                             FORMAT SECOND HEADING
         DC    CL6'NUMBER'                         *
         DC    CL18' '                             *
         DC    CL4'NAME'                           *
         DC    CL22' '                             *
         DC    CL5'GROSS'                          *
         DC    CL55' '                             *
LINECTR  DC    CL2'0'
INCARD   DCB   DSORG=PS,
               MACRF=GM,
               DDNAME=SYSIN,
               BLKSIZE=80,
               LRECL=80,                                                C
               EODAD=EOJRT
PRINT    DCB   DSORG=PS,                                                C
               MACRF=PMC,                                               C
               DDNAME=SYSOUT,                                           C
               BLKSIZE=120,                                             C
               LRECL=120
INWORK   DS    0CL80                               INPUT WORK AREA
NUMIN    DS    CL6                                 *
NAMEIN   DS    CL20                                *
         DS    CL24                                *
GROSSIN  DS    CL8                                 *
         DS    CL22                                *
PRINTBLD DS    0CL120                              OUTPUT WORK AREA
         DC    10CL1' '                            *
NUMOUT   DS    CL6                                 *
         DC    10CL1' '                            *
NAMEOUT  DS    CL20                                *
         DC    10CL1' '                            *
GROSSOUT DS    CL8                                 *
         DS    56CL1' '                            *
SAVEAREA DS    18F                                 RESERVE SAVEAREA
         END   FIRST
               =PL2'50'
               =PL2'4'
               =PL1'1'
```

Figure 16-4 Program 1—using headings as an internal subroutine.

EXTERNAL SUBROUTINES

External subroutines are not compiled with the main program. Because they are separately compiled, they may be coded in a different source language (Figure 16-3).

We face the same considerations in coding external subroutines as we do in coding internal subroutines. We must enter the subroutine at the correct place, and we must return to the calling program at the correct place. In addition, we must be able to reference data in the subroutine that may have been defined in the main program. We also may need to pass information from one subroutine to another. And most important, we must make certain that the subroutine does not destroy information the main program is using—most especially the general purpose registers.

Subroutine Linkages

Determining the Entry Point. We use a branch instruction to enter the subroutine from the main routine. But now we face a new problem. When we use the BAL instruction in Program 1 (Figure 16-4) the assembler generates the correct base and displacement for HEADRT based on the coded USING statement. The label HEADRT is an integral part of the program, and as such is addressable by register 12.

If however, we assemble HEADRT separately, the label is not present in the main program. The instruction

```
         BAL   10,HEADRT
```

results in an error.*

The use of the ADCON does not solve our problem either. In the code

```
         L     11,ADDHEAD
         BALR  10,11
         .
         .
         .
ADDHEAD  DC    A(HEADRT)
```

the assembler must address the label HEADRT. We still have an error.

Somehow we must tell the assembler not to worry about the label HEADRT—this is a special label that does not appear in the program. If our program is to work at execution time, however, we must get the address of HEADRT into the fullword storage location ADDHEAD.

The linkage editor resolves the problem. Remember, the linkage editor ties together (links) all the separately compiled object modules into one executable program. The linkage editor knows where HEADRT is in relation to the

*Assembly-time errors are discussed in Chapter 18.

main or calling program. The linkage editor is responsible for placing the correct value into the area of storage called ADDHEAD.

At this point we must introduce a new assembly language statement, the EXTRN statement. This statement tells the assembler that a label used in the source program does not appear in this segment of code, but is EXTeRNal to the program. The EXTRN statement also supplies information to the linkage editor. It tells the linkage editor to locate a label and relate it to the main program.

Figure 16-5 summarizes the possible ways to code a branch to a subroutine. LINKA and LINKB branch to an internal subroutine called LABEL1. In LINKA the assembler develops the address of LABEL1 based on the USING statement. Register 12 is used to address LABEL1. In LINKB the address of LABEL1 is defined as an address constant. At compile time the assembler locates LABEL1 in the program and generates the relative location, that is, the location counter setting, of LABEL1 for the constant ADDRLAB1. The value of ADDRLAB1 is completed when the linkage editor determines where the program is loaded. If the program is loaded at 002000_{16}, the value in ADDRLAB1 becomes 002024_{16}, (the original location counter setting incremented by 002000_{16}).

LINKC illustrates a branch to an external subroutine. The address of the entry point, LABEL2, is external to our program. We inform the assembler of this using the EXTRN statement. Notice the value generated for ADDRLAB2. The assembler has no way of addressing LABEL2 and generates a fullword constant containing binary zeros. At execution time ADDRLAB2 must contain the absolute address of LABEL2. This is the linkage editor's responsibility.

LINKD introduces a new type of constant—the V-type address constant. The label in a V-type constant is assumed to be external. It is not necessary to code an EXTRN statement.

LINKE and LINKF show the use of the literal. In this case, the assembler generates the constant in the literal pool at the end of the program.

The EXTRN statement constitutes only one part of the linkage. The linkage editor may be linking many modules; it must know which module contains the entry point. The ENTRY statement, which appears in the subroutine, helps the linkage editor locate the label. The following code shows the relation between the EXTRN and ENTRY statements.

```
* MAIN OR CALLING PROGRAM
              EXTRN   SUB
MAIN          STM
              BALR
              USING
              .
              .
              .
              L       15,ADDRSUB
              BALR    14,15
```

```
LOC    OBJECT CODE    ADDR1 ADDR2  STMT   SOURCE STATEMENT                                                  F04MAR74   6/17/76

                                     1 *
                                     2.* PROGRAM SEGMENT ILLUSTRATING LINKAGE BRANCHING TECHNIQUES
                                     3 *
                                     4            EXTRN LABEL2,LABEL4
0C0C00 05C0                          5 LINKAGES BALR  12,0
000002                               6            USING *,12
                                     7 *          *
                                     8 *          *
000002 45A0 CC22          00024      9 LINKA      BAL   10,LABEL1
                                    10 *          *
                                    11 *          *
00C006 58B0 C022          00024     12 LINKB      L     11,ADDRLAB1
03C00A 05AB                         13            BALR  10,11
                                    14 *          *
                                    15 *          *
00CC0C 58B0 C026          00028     16 LINKC      L     11,ACDRLAB2
00CC10 05AB                         17            BALR  10,11
                                    18 *          *
                                    19 *          *
000012 58B0 C02A          0002C     20 LINKD      L     11,ACDRLAB3
030C16 05AB                         21            BALR  10,11
                                    22 *          *
                                    23 *          *
000C18 58B0 C02E          00030     24 LINKE      L     11,=A(LABEL4)
000C1C 05AB                         25            BALR  10,11
                                    26 *          *
                                    27 *          *
00C01E 58B0 C032          00034     28 LINKF      L     11,=V(LABEL5)
00CC22 05AB                         29            BALR  10,11
                                    30 *          *
                                    31 *          *
00CC24                              32 LABEL1     EQU   *
                                    33 *
                                    34 * SUBROUTINE CODING HERE
                                    35 *
                                    36 *          DATA AREAS
                                    37 *
000024 0C00C024                     38 ADDRLAB1 DC    A(LABEL1)
00CC28 0C000000                     39 ADDRLAB2 DC    A(LABEL2)
00002C 0C0CC000                     40 ADDRLAB3 DC    V(LABEL3)
0C0000                              41            END   LINKAGES
00CC30 0CCCC000                     42                  =A(LABEL4)
00CC34 0CCCC000                     43                  =V(LABEL5)
```

Figure 16-5 Use of linkages.

```
          .
          .
          .
ADDRSUB   DC      A(SUB)
          END     MAIN
* SUBROUTINE OR CALLED PROGRAM
* SEPARATELY COMPILED
*
          ENTRY   SUB
SUB       STM
          .
          .
          .
          END
```

Determining the Return Point. We determine the return point in external subroutines in the same manner as we did in internal subroutines—through the branch and link instructions.

Passing Data

Often it is necessary to pass data to the subroutine. Let's consider Program 2—finding the sum of four fullword constants in storage. We assume the constants are defined in the main program, and that the add instructions are coded in an external subroutine. How will the subroutine reference the constants? We must pass the data to the subroutine. Since the general purpose registers are accessable to both the main program and subroutine, we could load each constant into a register, and let the subroutine reference the data using the RR-type instructions.

```
* MAIN OR CALLING PROGRAM
          EXTRN   SUB
MAIN      SAVE    (14,12)            SAVE REGISTERS
          BALR    12,0               LOAD BASE
          USING   12,0               ADDRESSABILITY
          LM      1,4,CON1           LOAD DATA
          L       15,ADDRSUB         AND ENTRY POINT
          BALR    14,15              AND BRANCH—R14 IS RETURN
          ST      5,RESULT           STORE SUM UPON RETURN
          RETURN  (14,12)            AND RETURN TO OPERATING SYSTEM
ADDRSUB   DC      A(SUB)
CON1      DC      F'10'
          DC      F'20'
          DC      F'30'
          DC      F'40'
RESULT    DS      F
          END     MAIN
```

```
* SUBROUTINE—SEPARATELY COMPILED
         ENTRY   SUB
SUB      LR      5,1              LOAD CON1
         AR      5,2              ADD SECOND CONSTANT
         AR      5,3              AND THIRD
         AR      5,4              AND LAST
         BR      14               AND RETURN TO MAIN PROGRAM
```

This solution works well when we have only a few constants. If, however, we are asked to find the sum of twenty constants, we cannot use this technique. We do not have twenty registers available.

Often the subroutine must reference many items in the main program. In this case, we define a list of addresses—called an *argument list*.

```
* MAIN PROGRAM
         EXTRN   SUB
MAIN     .
         .
         .
         LA      1,ARGLIST        POINT TO ARGLIST
         L       15,ADDRSUB       POINT TO ENTRY
         BALR    14,15            LINK
         .
         .
         .
ADDRSUB  DC      A(SUB)
ARGLIST  DC      A(CON1)
         DC      A(RESULT)
CON1     DC      F'10'
         .
         .
         .
RESULT   DC      F
         END     MAIN

* SUBROUTINE SEPARATELY COMPILED
SUB      L       3,0(1)           POINT TO CON1
         L       5,0(3)           LOAD DATA AT CON1 TO R5
         .
         .
         .
         L       4,4(1)           POINT TO RESULT
         ST      5,0(4)           STORE R5 IN RESULT
         BR      14               RETURN
```

We use register 1 to pass the address of the argument list to the subroutine. The subroutine must reference the first entry in the list to get the address of CON1. The subroutine uses register 1 to address the argument list.

```
L   3,0(1)
```

This instruction places the *address* of CON1, the *first* fullword in the list addressed by register 1, in register 3. The subroutine now uses register 3 to address the *data* at the location CON1. For example, the instruction

```
L 5,0(3)
```

loads the data at CON1, addressed by register 3, into register 5.

The subroutine must reference the *second* item in the argument list to get the address RESULT. For example

```
L 4,4(1)
```

The *address* of RESULT is now in register 4. The subroutine uses register 4 to address RESULT. (See Figure 16-6.)

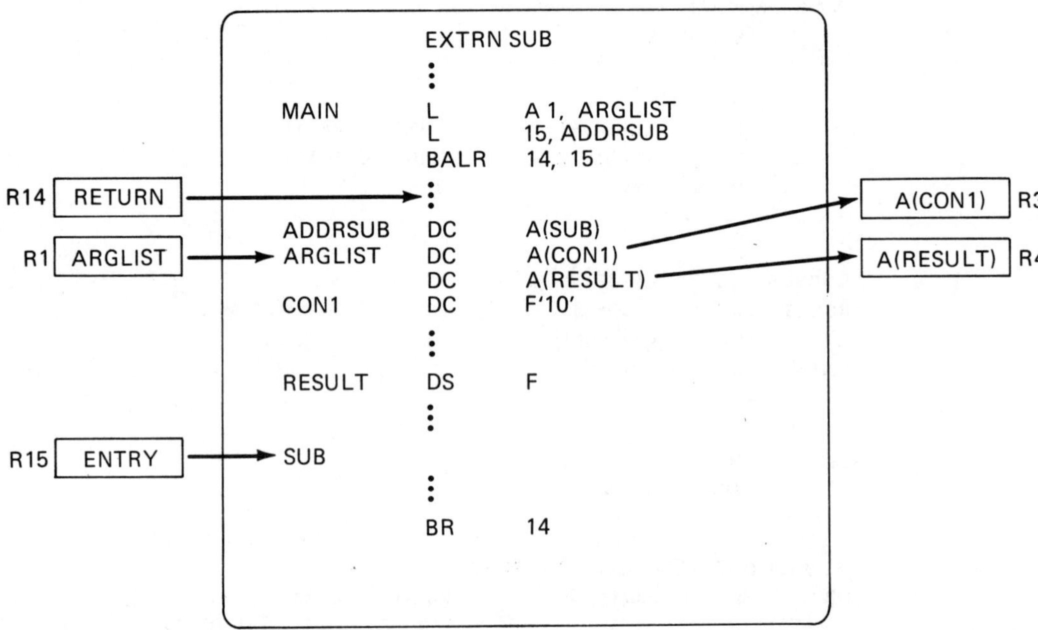

Figure 16-6 Use of the argument list.

Saving the Registers of the Calling Program

Each subroutine is a complete program in itself. Each has its own base register, and probably uses registers during processing. They are the same registers used by the calling program, but the calling program expects to find these registers unchanged. It is the responsibility of the subroutine (*called* program) to save the registers of the calling program.

The STM instruction can be used to save all the registers. For example

```
STM 0,15,SAVEAREA
```

stores all sixteen registers in an area of storage called SAVEAREA. The location SAVEAREA is located in the subroutine.

By convention, another technique is used. The registers are saved, not in the subroutine, but back in the calling or main program. The label SAVEAREA is defined in the main program. But the subroutine cannot reference the label SAVEAREA. The main program must pass the *address* of SAVEAREA to the subroutine. The address of the calling program's save area is passed in register 13.

Figure 16-7 illustrates this convention. The calling program places the address of its own save area in register 13 *before* branching to the subroutine. The first statement in the subroutine stores all the registers *except* register 13 back in the calling program. Where in the calling program?—in the area of storage addressed by register 13!

Notice that the registers are stored twelve bytes from the beginning of the save area. The first three words of the save area are reserved for other uses. (See Figure 16-8.)

When the subroutine is ready to return to the main program, it must restore the main program's registers before returning.

It is possible that the subroutine in turn calls another program. In this case, the subroutine must establish its own save area and pass the address to the subroutine. Again, register 13 is used. But wait, register 13 is already being used. It points to the save area of the main program. Its contents must be stored first. We store the address in register 13—the address of the *calling* program's save area—in the second fullword of the *called* program's save area. We must follow these conventions in all our programs. This is because our program becomes a subroutine of the operating system itself. The instructions used to effect this convention, and the graphic representation of the linkage established is given in Figure 16-9.

Use of the SAVE and RETURN Macros

Some programmers prefer to use the SAVE and RETURN macros. The instructions

```
             .
             .
             .
BEGIN   STM      14,12,12(13)
        BALR     12,0
        USING    *,12
        ST       13,SAVEAREA + 4
        LA       13,SAVEAREA
             .
             .
             .
EOJRT   L        13,SAVEAREA + 4
        LM       14,12,12(13)
        BR       14
```

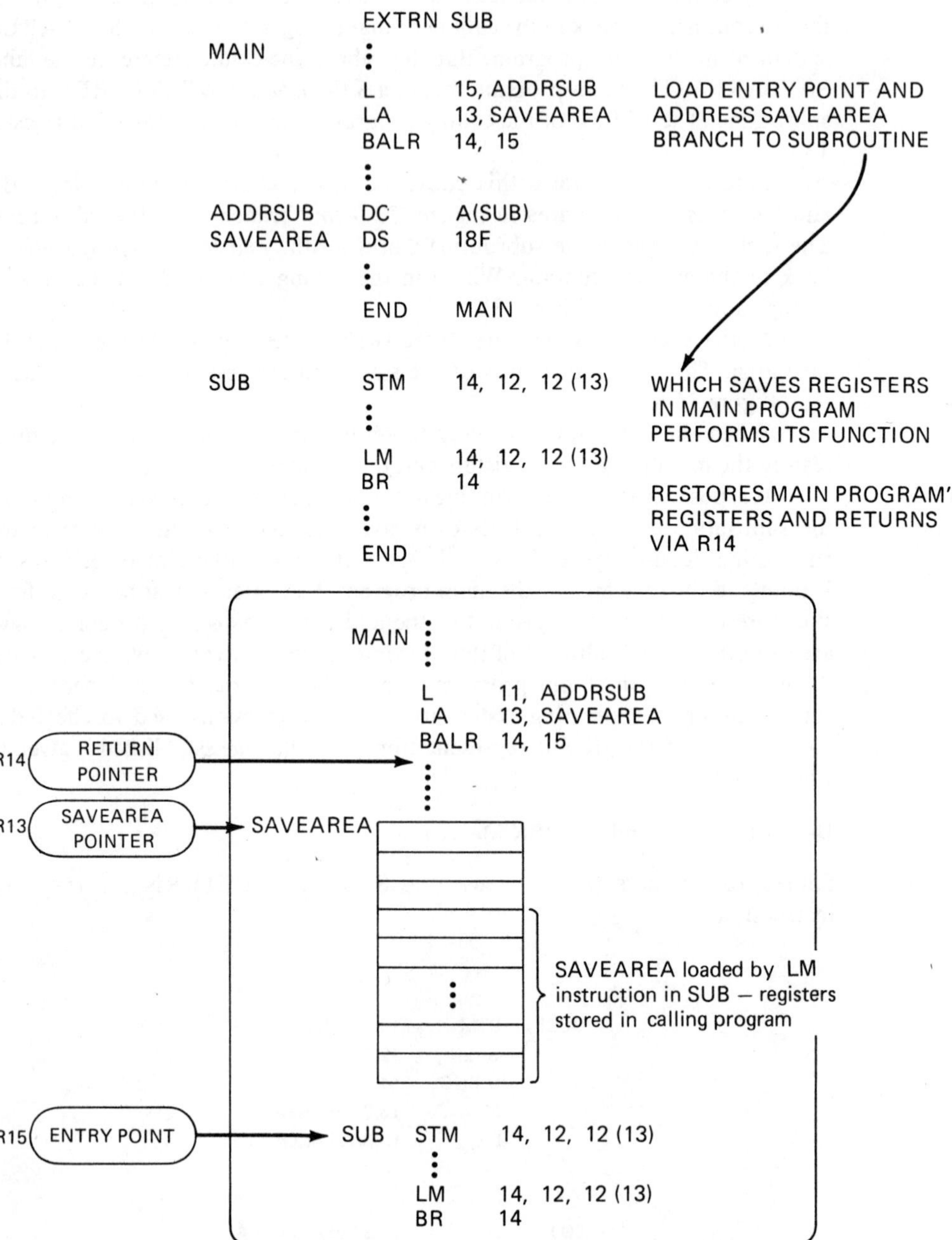

EXTRN SUB
MAIN
L 15, ADDRSUB
LA 13, SAVEAREA
BALR 14, 15
LOAD ENTRY POINT AND
ADDRESS SAVE AREA
BRANCH TO SUBROUTINE
ADDRSUB DC A(SUB)
SAVEAREA DS 18F
END MAIN
SUB STM 14, 12, 12 (13)
LM 14, 12, 12 (13)
BR 14
END
WHICH SAVES REGISTERS
IN MAIN PROGRAM
PERFORMS ITS FUNCTION
RESTORES MAIN PROGRAM'S
REGISTERS AND RETURNS
VIA R14
MAIN
L 11, ADDRSUB
LA 13, SAVEAREA
BALR 14, 15
R14
RETURN
POINTER
R13
SAVEAREA
POINTER
SAVEAREA
SAVEAREA loaded by LM
instruction in SUB — registers
stored in calling program
R15
ENTRY POINT
SUB STM 14, 12, 12 (13)
LM 14, 12, 12 (13)
BR 14

Figure 16-7 Use of the savearea.

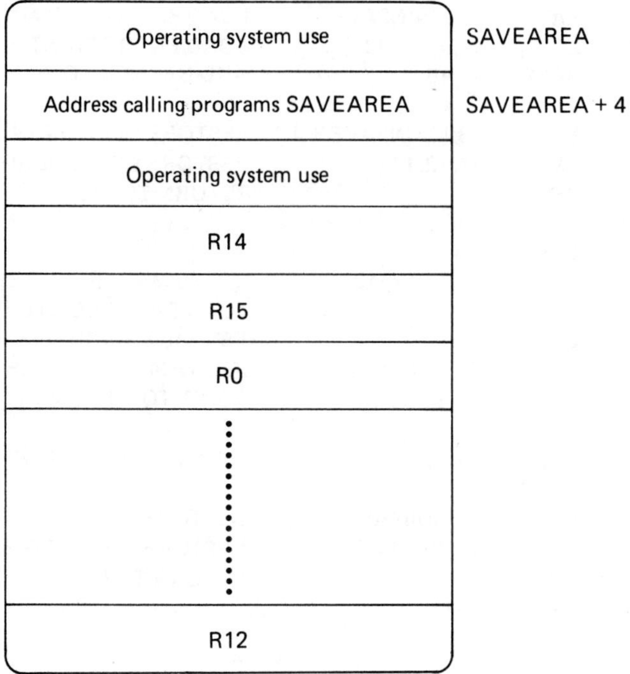

Figure 16-8 Format of the savearea.

may be coded using the SAVE and RETURN macros as

```
             .
             .
             .
BEGIN  SAVE      (14,12)
       BALR      12,0
       USING     *,12
       ST        13,SAVEAREA + 4
       LA        13,SAVEAREA
             .
             .
             .
EOJRT  L         13,SAVEAREA + 4
       RETURN    (14,12)
```

The SAVE macro replaces the STM instruction. The RETURN macro replaces the instructions

```
       LM        14,12,12(13)
       BR        14
```

We use these same macros in all our programs regardless of whether we are using subroutines. This is because our program is treated as a subroutine of

```
Main routine
MAIN      STM   14,12,12 (13)    STORE OPSYS REGISTERS
          BALR                   LOAD BASE REGISTER
          USING                  ESTABLISH ADDRESSABILITY
          ST    13,MAINSAVE + 4  SAVE OPSYS POINTER
          LA    13,MAINSAVE      LOAD POINTER TO MAINSAVE
          L     15, = A(SUB)     LOAD ENTRY POINT
          BALR  14,15            ADD BRANCH TO SUB
          :
          L     13,MAINSAVE + 4  RESTORE OPSYS POINTER
          LM    14,12,12 (13)    RESTORE OPSYS REGISTERS
          BR    14               RETURN TO OPSYS
MAINSAVE  DS    18F
          END   MAIN
Subroutine
SUB       STM   14,12,12 (13)    STORE MAIN REGISTERS IN MAINSAVE
          BALR                   LOAD BASE REGISTER
          USING                  ESTABLISH ADDRESSABILITY
          ST    13,SUBSAVE + 4   STORE MAIN POINTER
          LA    13,SUBSAVE       POINT TO SUBSAVE

          BALR  14,15            EXIT TO SUBROUTINE

          L     13,SUBSAVE + 4   RESTORE MAIN POINTER
          LM    14,12,12 (13)    RESTORE MAIN REGISTERS
          BR    14               RETURN TO MAIN
SUBSAVE   DS    18F
          END
```

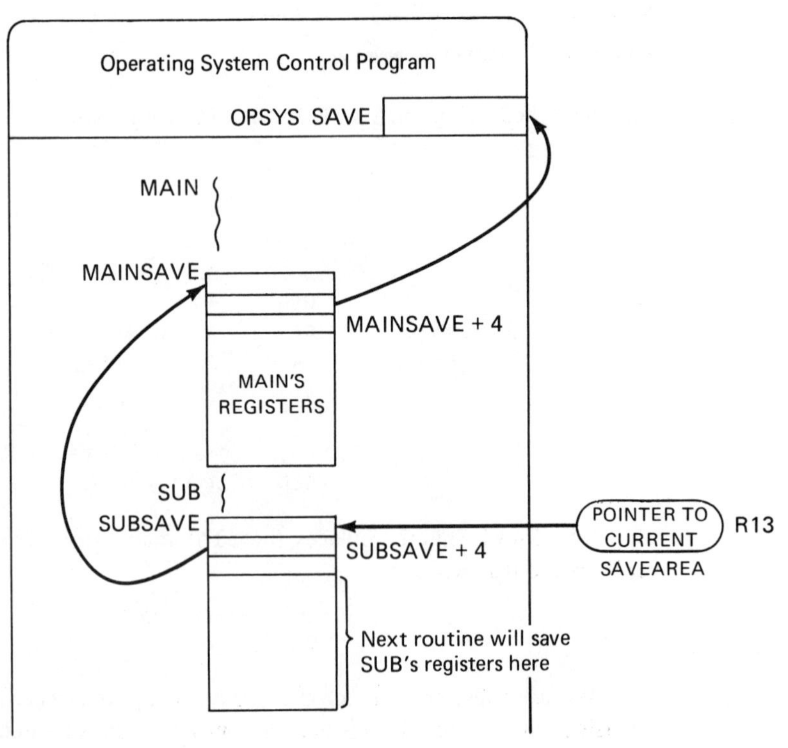

Figure 16-9 Savearea conventions.

the operating system. We must save the operating system's registers at the beginning of our program, and restore these registers at the end of the program.

```
       .
       .
       .
BEGIN  SAVE     (14,12)
       .
       .
       .
       RETURN   (14,12)
```

The SAVE macro saves the operating system's registers in the operating system's save area. The RETURN macro restores these registers and branches back to the calling program—the operating system.

A Sample Program—Linkage Conventions

We have discussed entering and returning from a subroutine, the passing of data, and the conventions for establishing a save area linkage. The branch and link instructions are used to enter the subroutine and to save the return address. We usually use register 15 to point to the entry point in the subroutine, and register 14 to point to the return point. We use register 1 to point to the argument list and register 13 to point to the save area.

Figure 16-10 shows the use of these linkage conventions in Program 2. The table is defined in the main or calling program. The address of the table, and the address of RESULT comprise the argument list. The address of this list, ARGLIST, is placed in register 1. Before branching to the subroutine, the main program must first establish the save area linkage. Let's examine this code.

The main program is a subroutine of the operating system. The instruction

```
BEGIN  STM  14,12,12(13)
```

stores the registers in an area of the operating system. When we enter the program at BEGIN, register 13 points to the operating system's save area.

The next instruction establishes addressability. The instruction

```
ST   13,SAVEAREA + 4
```

saves the pointer to the operating system's save area in the second word in SAVEAREA. Finally, the address of SAVEAREA is placed in register 13.

```
LA   13,SAVEAREA
```

The L and BALR instructions branch to SUBRT. The first statement in SUBRT saves the calling program's registers in SAVEAREA (remember, register 13 points to SAVEAREA in the main program). Processing continues.

```
*
* PROGRAM 2
* SUM OF FOUR CONSTANTS
* CALCULATIONS AS A SUBROUTINE
*
         START
BEGIN    STM   14,12,12(13)   SAVE OPSYS REGISTERS
         BALR  12,0           LOAD BASE
         USING *,12           ESTABLISH ADDRESSABILITY
         ST    13,SAVEAREA+4  SAVE OPSYS POINTER
         LA    13,SAVEAREA    POINT TO MAIN SAVEAREA
         LA    1,ARGLIST      POINT TO ARGLIST
         L     15,ENTRY       LOAD ENTRY
         BALR  14,15          AND BRANCH TO SUBROUTINE
         L     13,SAVEAREA+4  POINT TO OPSYS SAVEAREA
         LM    14,12,12(13)   RESTORE OPSYS REGS
         BR    14             AND RETURN TO OPSYS
*
* DATA AREAS
*
ARGLIST  DC    A(CON1)        TWO ENTRIES ARE
         DC    A(RESULT)      IN THE ARGUMENT LIST
ENTRY    DC    V(SUBRT)       DEFINE EXTERNAL LABEL
CON1     DC    F'10'          * FOUR
CON2     DC    F'20'          * FULLWORD
CON3     DC    F'30'          * BINARY
CON4     DC    F'40'          * CONSTANTS
SAVEAREA DS    18F            RESERVE SAVEAREA
RESULT   DS    F              SPACE OF SUM
         END BEGIN
```

```
*
* SUBROUTINE CALCULATES SUM OF CONSTANT IN MAIN PROGRAM
*
         ENTRY SUBRT
         USING *,15           ESTABLISH ADDRESSABILITY
SUBRT    STM   14,12,12(13)   SAVE MAIN PROGRAM'S REGISTERS
INIT     L     3,0(1)         LOAD ADDRESS CON1 FROM FIRST
*                             ENTRY IN ARGLIST
         SR    5,5            CLEAR R5
BODY     A     5,0(3)         ADD CON1
         A     5,4(3)         ADD CON2
         A     5,8(3)         ADD CON3
         A     5,12(3)        ADD CON4
         L     4,4(1)         LOAD ADDRESS RESULT FROM SECOND
*                             ENTRY IN ARGLIST
         ST    5,0(4)         STORE SUM IN RESULT
         LM    14,12,12(13)   RESTORE REGISTERS
         BR    14             AND RETURN TO CALLING PROGRAM
         END
```

Figure 16-10 Program 2—illustrating linkage conventions.

Before returning to the calling program, the subroutine restores the calling program's registers.

```
LM   14,12,12(13)
BR   14
```

The calling program in turn restores the pointer to the operating system's save area

```
L 13, SAVEAREA +4
```

and returns to the operating system

```
LM   14,12,12(13)
BR   14
```

Now let's examine how the information contained in register 1 is handled. Register 1 contains the address of ARGLIST. We might say that register 1 contains the *address* of a list of addresses. The first entry is the address of CON1. We want to load this value into register 3. We load register 3 from an area of storage addressed by register 1 with a displacement of 0.

```
L  3,0(1)
```

We are loading register 3 from the first entry in ARGLIST. Register 3 now contains the address of CON1.

The subroutine develops the sum in register 5. The contents of register 5 must be stored in an area called RESULT. Again, RESULT is in the calling program. Somehow we must obtain the address of RESULT. But the address of RESULT also is in the calling program; it is the second entry in ARGLIST. We know how to reference ARGLIST. Register 1 points to it. We can obtain the address of RESULT from the second entry in ARGLIST. The statement

```
L  4,4(1)
```

loads the address of RESULT into register 4. The subroutine now stores the contents of register 5 in RESULT (in the calling program) using the instruction

```
ST  5,0(4)
```

The last code in SUBRT restores the calling program's registers and returns to the calling program using the address in register 14.

I/O Coding as an External Subroutine

The programmer may want to code the I/O macro instructions as a subroutine. There are several reasons for this. First, the macro coding is usually straightforward and once coded needs little or no debugging. Since the macros take a long time to assemble, it would reduce assembly time if they could be assembled once and linked to the main program by the linkage editor.

Another reason for coding the macros separately relates to the operating systems. There are differences in the macros, depending upon the operating system used. If the macros are coded as part of the main program, the entire program must be reassembled and tested if a change in operating system is made. If, however, the macros are coded as a subroutine, only the subroutine must be recoded.

Figure 16-11 is a flowchart for Program 1. Notice that although the end-of-file condition is detected in the subroutine, the end-of-job exit to the operating system is coded in the main routine. We must not return to the operating system from the subroutine or the STM instruction would restore the wrong set of registers. We must go from *subroutine* to *calling program* to *operating system.*

It is necessary to test a switch after returning from the GET routine. The

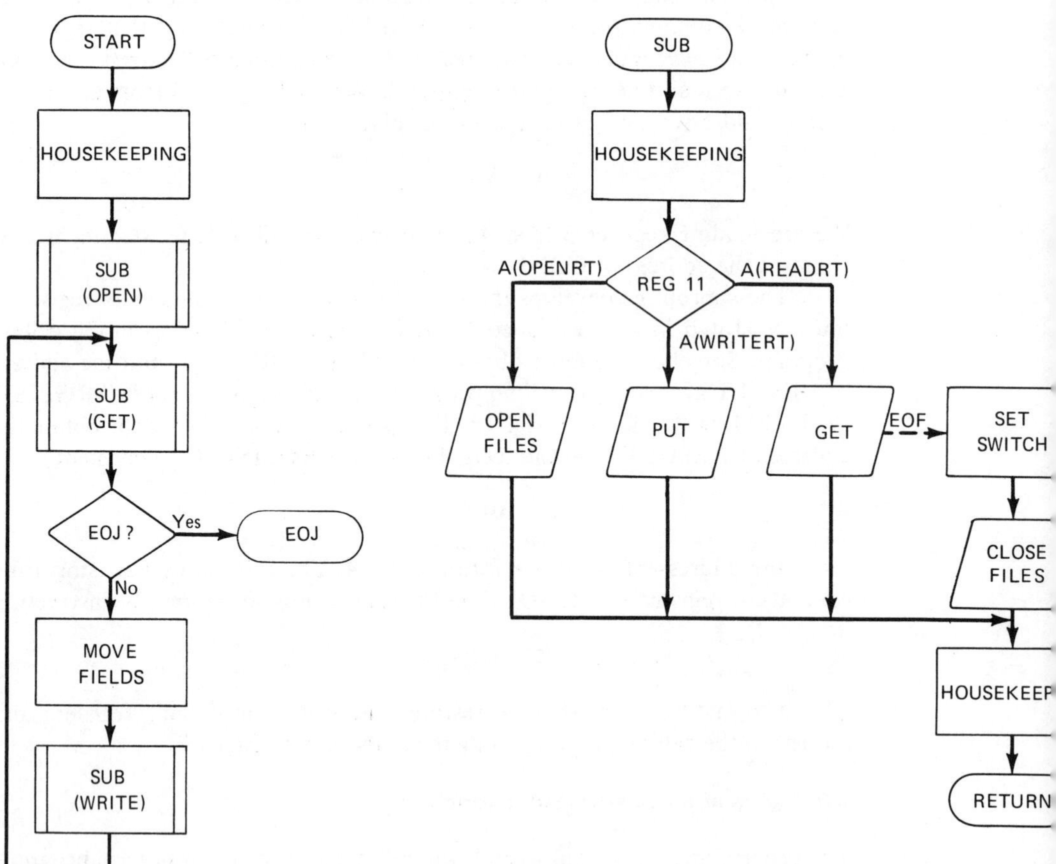

Figure 16-11 I/O coding as a subroutine.

switch indicates whether the last GET issued transferred a record—in which case we continue with the move instructions—or whether an end-of-file condition was encountered—in which case we enter our end-of-job coding.

Figure 16-12 shows Program 1 coded with the I/O macros as an external subroutine. Both the imperative and declarative macros are in the subroutine. Notice that the main routine contains only assembly language statements. There are no macro statements. The main program is operating system independent.

The macros shown in the subroutine are operating system macros. Although the macros are different from DOS macros, the logic involved is the same.

We enter the subroutine under three separate conditions: at OPEN time, when we issue a GET statement, and when we issue a PUT statement (the close routine is entered as a condition of the GET statement). The linkage editor must supply the addresses of three labels to the main routine; the address of OPENRT, READRT, and WRITERT.

```
AOPENRT   DC  A(OPENRT)
AREADRT   DC  A(READRT)
AWRITERT  DC  A(WRITERT)
```

The buffer areas are associated with the subroutine, but the work areas are defined in the calling program. The argument list contains the address of the input work area INWORK, and the output work area PRINTBLD.

Let us follow the code, starting at the label BEGIN in the calling program. The save area linkages are established and the base register is loaded.

```
BEGIN  STM    14,12,12(13)
       BALR   12,0
       USING  *,12
       ST     13,SAVEAREA + 4
       LA     13,SAVEAREA
```

We place the address of OPENRT in register 11, and the entry address in register 15.

```
L  11,AOPENRT
L  15,ASUB
```

The use of register 11 is not a linkage convention. It is used in this program as an example of one technique for handling multiple entry points.

The statement

```
BALR  14,15
```

branches us to SUB. We follow the save area linkage conventions. The address of the subroutine's save area is loaded into register 13.

```
*
* PROGRAM 1
* I/O CODING AS AN EXTERNAL SUBROUTINE
*
         EXTRN OPENRT,READRT,WRITERT,SUB
         START 0
         PRINT NOGEN
BEGIN    STM   14,12,12(13)              SAVE OPSYS REGISTERS
FIRST    BALR  12,0                      LOAD BASE
         USING *,12                      ADDRESSABILITY
         ST    13,SAVEAREA+4             STORE R13 POINTER
         LA    13,SAVEAREA               POINT TO SAVEAREA
         L     11,AOPENRT                LOAD ADDRESS OPENRT
         L     15,ASUB                   LOAD ADDRESS SUB
         BALR  14,15                     BRANCH TO SUBROUTINE
READIT   LA    1,ARGLIST                 LOAD ARGLIST PTR
         L     11,AREADRT                LOAD ENTRY POINT
         L     15,ASUB                   LOAD BRANCH ADDRESS
         BALR  14,15                     BRANCH TO SUBROUTINE
         TM    SW,X'FF'                  TEST SW
         BO    EOJRT                     BRANCH ONES TO EOJRT
         MVC   NUMOUT(6),NUMIN           MOVE NUMBER
         MVC   NAMEOUT(20),NAMEIN        MOVE EMP NAME
         MVC   GROSSOUT(8),GROSSIN       MOVE GROSS
         L     11,AWRITERT               LOAD ENTRY POINT
         LA    1,ARGLIST                 LOAD ARGLIST PTR
         L     15,ASUB                   LOAD BRANCH ADDRESS
         BALR  14,15                     BRANCH TO SUBROUTINE
         B     READIT                    LOOP BACK
EOJRT    L     13,SAVEAREA+4             RESTORE R13 POINTER
         LM    14,12,12(13)              RESTORE OPSYS REGS
         BR    14                        RETURN TO OPSYS
*
* DATA AREAS
*
SAVEAREA DS    18F                       DEFINE SAVEAREA
INWORK   DS    0CL80                     INPUT WORK AREA
NUMIN    DS    CL6                       *
NAMEIN   DS    CL20                      *
         DS    CL24                      *
GROSSIN  DS    CL8                       *
         DS    CL22                      *
PRINTBLD DS    0CL120                    OUTPUT WORK AREA
         DC    10CL1' '                  *
NUMOUT   DS    CL6                       *
         DC    10CL1' '                  *
NAMEOUT  DS    CL20                      *
         DC    10CL1' '                  *
GROSSOUT DS    CL8                       *
         DC    56CL1' '                  *
         DS    CL56                      *
ASUB     DC    A(SUB)                    SUB ENTRY POINTS
AOPENRT  DC    A(OPENRT)                 *
AREADRT  DC    A(READRT)                 *
AWRITERT DC    A(WRITERT)                *
ARGLIST  DC    A(INWORK)                 ARGUMENT LIST
         DC    A(PRINTBLD)               *
         DC    A(SW)                     *
SW       DC    XL1'00'                   DEFINE SW
         END   BEGIN
```

Figure 16-12 Program 1—solution using I/O coding as a subroutine.

```
*
* SUBROUTINE CONTAINING I/O CODING
*
         PRINT NOGEN
         ENTRY OPENRT,READRT,WRITERT,SUB
         USING *,12                         ADDRESSABILITY
SUB      STM   14,12,12(13)                 SAVE MAIN PROGR REGS
         LR    12,15                        LOAD BASE
         ST    13,SAVESUB+4                 STORE R13 POINTER
         LA    13,SAVESUB                   AND POINT TO SAVEAREA
         LR    10,1                         SAVE ARGLIST PTR
         BR    11                           BRANCH TO ENTRY POINT
OPENRT   OPEN  (INCARD,,PRINT,OUTPUT)       OPEN FILES AND
         B     EXIT                         GO TO EXIT
READRT   L     0,0(10)                      GET ADDRESS INWORK
         GET   INCARD,(0)                   GET RECORD INTO
*                                           MAIN PROGRAM AREA
         B     EXIT                         GO TO EXIT
WRITERT  L     0,4(10)                      GET ADDRESS OUTWORK
         PUT   PRINT,(0)                    WRITE FROM MAIN
*                                           PROGRAM AREA
         B     EXIT                         GO TO EXIT
EOFRT    L     9,8(10)                      GET ADDRESS SW
         MVI   0(9),X'FF'                   SET EOF SW
         CLOSE (INCARD,,PRINT)              CLOSE FILES
EXIT     L     13,SAVESUB+4                 RESTORE REG13
         LM    14,12,12(13)                 RESTORE CALLING REGS
         BR    14                           RETURN TO CALLING
*                                           PROGRAM
SAVESUB  DS    18F
INCARD   DCB   DSORG=PS,                                              C
               MACRF=GM,                                              C
               DDNAME=SYSIN,                                          C
               BLKSIZE=80,                                            C
               LRECL=80,                                              C
               EODAD=EOFRT
PRINT    DCB   DSORG=PS,                                              C
               MACRF=PMC,                                             C
               DDNAME=SYSOUT,                                         C
               BLKSIZE=120,                                           C
               LRECL=120
         END
```

Figure 16-12 (Continued)

We always enter SUB at the same point, and perform the same initial housekeeping functions.

```
SUB   STM   14,12,12(13)
      LR    12,15
      ST    13,SAVESUB + 4
      LA    13,SAVESUB
```

We save the pointer to ARGLIST in register 10

```
LR  10,1
```

This is because the contents of register 1 are changed by the I/O subroutines. Then we branch to the correct routine within SUB.

```
BR   11
```

We always exit SUB using the same code.

```
EXIT   L    13,SAVESUB + 4
       LM   14,12,12(13)
       BR   14
```

The first time we enter SUB we perform the OPEN routine (remember the address of OPENRT is in register 11), and return to the main program. The statement

```
BR   14
```

returns us to the statement *following* the BALR instruction which caused the branch.

The code

```
LA      1,ARGLIST
L       11,AREADRT
BALR    14,15
```

effects the branch to the GET routine in SUB. The code at READRT places a logical record in the area of storage called INWORK. Can you see why?

The statement

```
GET   INCARD,(0)
```

places the next record in the area of storage addressed by register 0. This is a new form of the GET statement. In this instance, the second operand contains the number of a register. Register 0 contains the address of the work area. The statement

```
L  0,0(10)
```

is executed before the GET statement. This statement loads register 0 from an area of storage addressed by register 10. Register 10 contains the address of the argument list, and the first entry in ARGLIST is the address of INWORK. The GET statement places the data in the main program. We exit from the subroutine and return to the main program where we move the data to PRINTBLD.

```
MVC   NUMOUT(6),NUMIN
MVC   NAMEOUT(20),NAMEIN
MVC   GROSSOUT(8),GROSSIN
```

We now enter the subroutine to write the record.

```
         L     11,AWRITERT
         LA    1,ARGLIST
         L     15,ASUB
         BALR  14,15
```

When we return from writing this record, we loop back to the instructions to read the next record.

```
         B   READIT
```

We want to exit from this loop when all the records have been read—an end-of-file condition. This condition occurs in the subroutine. When the end-of-file condition is reached, the operating system branches to EOFRT. The instructions at EOFRT set a switch to indicate that an end-of-file condition has occurred,

```
EOFRT    L     9,8(10)
         MVI   0(9),X'FF'
```

close the files and return to the main program.

The instruction

```
         TM   SW,X'FF'
```

tests the value of SW. A branch to EOJRT will occur in this instance and control is returned to the operating system.

PROBLEMS **16.1** The following segment of code is found in the main or calling program.

```
              .
              .
              .
              LA    1,LIST
              LA    13,SAVEAREA
              L     15,ENTRY
              BALR  14,15
              .
              .
              .
A             DC    F
B             DC    F
C             DC    F
LIST          DC    A(A)
              DC    A(B)
              DC    A(C)
SAVEAREA      DC    18F
ENTRY         DC    V(SUB1)
```

Answer the following questions with reference to this segment of code.

a. Which of the following statements could be used in place of the instruction LA 1,LIST?

```
1. L    1,LIST
2. L    1, = V(LIST)
3. L    1,A(LIST)
4. LA   1, = A(LIST)
5. L    1, = A(LIST)
```

b. Is an EXTRN statement required for the label SUB1? Why?

c. Assume that the BALR instruction resides at location $0090C0_{16}$. What is the return address contained in register 14?

d. Which of the following instructions could be used in place of the instruction L 15,ENTRY?

```
1. LA   15,SUB1
2. LA   15, = V(SUB1)
3. L    15, = V(SUB1)
4. LA   15, = A(SUB1) with EXTRN statement required
```

e. Code the L (Load) instruction that could be used in place of the statement LA 13,SAVEAREA.

f. Code the subroutine which could be used to find the sum of the constants A and B. Place the result in the fullword C. Use the code segment in Problem 16.1 as the calling or main program.

16.2 Distinguish between V-type and A-type address constants. How do the EXTRN and ENTRY statements affect the use of these address constants?

16.3 Program 7 finds the sum of a variable number of constants in storage (Appendix C). Code this program in two segments. Define the data in the main program. Code the processing instructions as a subroutine. Use the conventions discussed in this chapter in your solution. *Note:* use an argument list to pass the address of each constant in the subroutine.

16.4 Code the variations of Program 6 using subroutines. You may want a subroutine for headings, and for each total break. Develop a flowchart for each program.

Hint: You must determine the presence of a break in the main program and then enter the subroutine to write a total card.

16.5 Code the programs in Program 6 (Appendix C) in two segments. Code the I/O macros as a subroutine. The main program consists of the processing statements and the data areas.

17

Job Control Language

INTRODUCTION Job control statements provide the programmer with a means of communicating with the operating system. Let's review our concept of an operating system before we begin our discussion of job control.

An operating system is a collection of programs. These programs are usually supplied by the vendor (Honeywell, IBM, Control Data, etc.) to enable the customer to use his computer efficiently. Operating systems provide programs which help the programmer, the operations staff, and the management of the installation.

The compilers, assembler, and linkage editor are programs which assist the programmer. The compilers and the assembler translate source language statements into machine language. If these programmer aids were not available, the user would have to code all programs in machine language. The linkage editor links program segments into one complete program.

Data management programs help both the programmer and the operations staff. Data management programs supply the I/O macros and subroutines used by the programmer, and also contain routines which locate files the programmer needs. These programs also issue messages to the computer operator when a file is needed, or allow the operating system to go from one job to the next without the intervention of an operator. We refer to this concept as job-to-job transition. Locating data files and job-to-job transition are examples of aids to the operator provided by an operating system.

Data processing management also benefits from the operating system. Accounting routines are provided to keep track of machine utilization. Management can analyze the use of the computer and allocate computer costs accordingly. If several customers are using a single computer, billing is based on the information maintained by the operating system's accounting routines.

An operating system is comprised of many large and complex programs. These programs are not stored in main storage. They would take too much space. Operating system programs are stored on tape or disk and are called into computer storage as they are needed.

One operating system program is always in storage. We call this program the *supervisor*. When another program, such as a compiler, is needed, the supervisor loads the program into storage. The supervisor must know which of the many programs available was requested. Does the programmer want the COBOL compiler or the assembler? The programmer uses job control statements to tell the operating system the name of the program he or she needs for a specific job.

The programmer uses a language to communicate with the operating system. We call this language *job control language* (JCL). Each operating system has its own job control language. We shall examine the job control language used in OS/370 and then the language used in DOS.

OS/370 JOB CONTROL LANGUAGE

All OS job control statements follow the same format (Figure 17-1). Job control statements contain a double slash (//) in columns 1 and 2. The name field follows. There are no spaces between the // and the name field.

The name field is optional. The operation field is required. It must be separated from the name field by a least one space. The operation field specifies the type of job control statement.

The operand field supplies the operating system with additional information. Operands may be either keyword or positional (see Chapter 15).

Figure 17-1 gives an example of a job control statement. The slashes in

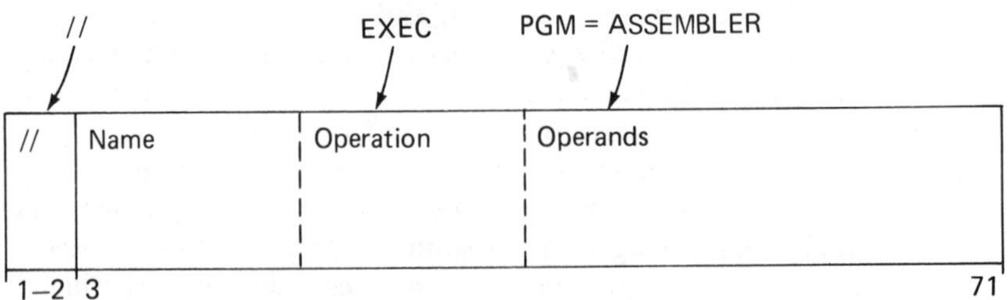

Figure 17-1 Format of the job control statement.

columns 1 and 2 identify this statement as a job control statement. The name field is omitted, but one space is used before the operation, EXEC. The operand field contains one keyword parameter.

Types of Job Control Statements

There are three major types of job control statements, the job statement (JOB), the execute statement (EXEC), and the data definition statement (DD). Not all job control statements fall into the three major categories. There are also a number of special purpose job control statements. The discussion which follows describes the major types of job control statements and the special purpose statements.

The Job Statement. Each job submitted to the operating system must have a job statement. The job statement names the job and supplies information to the operating system (see Table 17-1).

The two slashes in columns 1 and 2 are required. The *jobname* also is required and immediately follows, starting in column 3. The programmer supplies the jobname. The jobname may be from 1 to 8 alphanumeric (A–Z, 0–9) characters. Three special characters called *national* characters are allowed. The national characters are #, @, and $. The jobname must begin with an alphabetic or national character.

The jobname must be followed by at least one blank. The next field is the operation field, containing the word JOB, followed by at least one blank.

The operand field contains both keyword and positional operands. Although the format statement indicates that these operands are optional (square brackets indicate optional), they may be required in a given installation.

The first two positional operands contain accounting information. The type of information supplied is determined by the installation. If both positional parameters are coded, they must be enclosed in parenthesis as shown in Table 17-1. If the first positional parameter is omitted, a comma must replace it.

The accounting information is followed by the programmer's name. This is the last positional parameter. The remaining parameters are keyword parameters. The CLASS= parameter is a keyword parameter which directs the program to the proper storage area. Let's see how.

Table 17-1 Format of the JOB Statement

name	operation	operands
//jobname	JOB	[([acct#][, acctg information])] [, programmer's name] [, CLASS = jobclass] [, additional parameters]

When more than one program is in computer storage we are operating in a multiprogramming environment. Computer storage is divided into areas called partitions.* The class parameter directs the program to the correct partition (Figure 17-2).

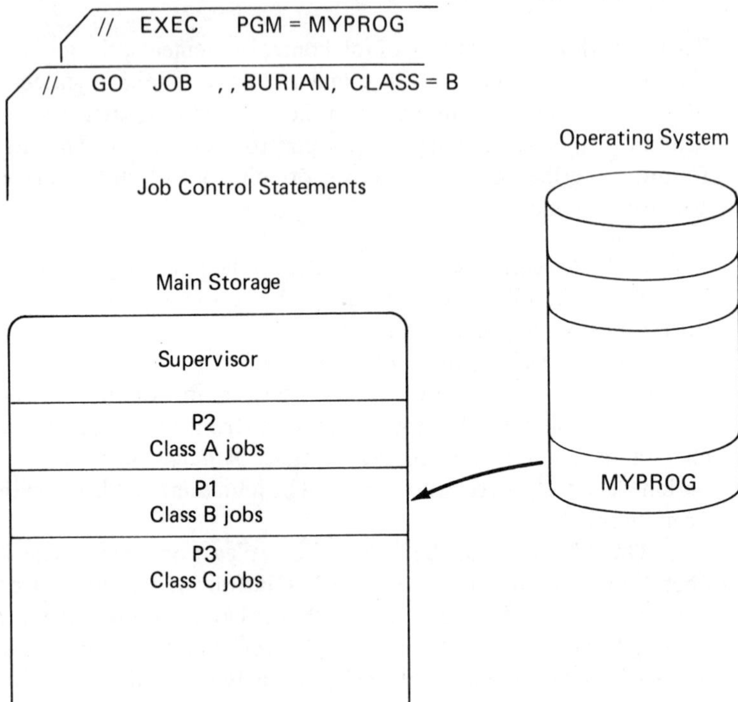

Figure 17-2 Use of the class parameter.

Following are examples of job cards using the parameters we have discussed. There are additional keyword parameters available which are summarized in Appendix E.

```
//JOB1  JOB  (123,ABC),BURIAN,CLASS = C
//JOB2  JOB  (,ABC),BURIAN,CLASS = C
//JOB3  JOB  123,BURIAN,CLASS = C
//JOB4  JOB  ,BURIAN,CLASS = C
//JOB5  JOB  ,,CLASS = C
//JOB6  JOB  (123,ABC),BURIAN
```

The Execute Statement. The EXEC (EXECute) statement names the program or procedure to be executed. The format of the execute statement is given in Table 17-2.

*OS/MFT uses the term partition; OS/MVT uses the term region.

Table 17-2 Format of the EXEC Statement

name	operation	operands
//[stepname]	EXEC	{[PROC =] procedure name / PGM = program name} [,additional parameters]

The two slashes in columns 1 and 2 are required. The name field is optional. We refer to the name coded in the EXEC statement as the *stepname*. The stepname is provided by the programmer and follows the rules described for selecting the jobname.

The operation EXEC is separated from the stepname by the least one blank.

The operands must be separated from the operation by at least one blank. Braces ({ }) show that a choice must be made between two keyword operands. The keyword operand tells the operating system to execute either a program (consisting of machine-language instructions) or a procedure (consisting of job control statements). The keyword entry

PGM = IEUASM,

tells the operating system to execute a program. IEUASM is the name of the assembler. The keyword entry

PROC = ASMFC,

tells the operating system to execute a procedure. ASMFC is the name of the procedure to assemble a source program. If the keyword is omitted, the operating system assumes that we are requesting a procedure. Table 17-3 gives examples of the use of the execute statement. Again, there are additional parameters available to the user. The reader can reference Appendix E for a summary of the execute options.

Table 17-3 Examples of the EXEC Statement

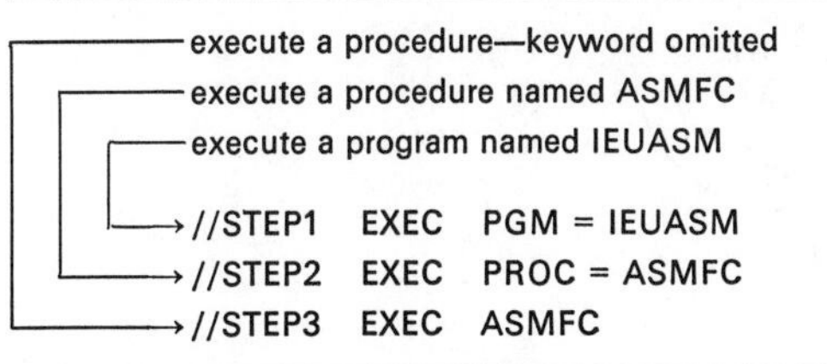
execute a procedure—keyword omitted
execute a procedure named ASMFC
execute a program named IEUASM
//STEP1 EXEC PGM = IEUASM
//STEP2 EXEC PROC = ASMFC
//STEP3 EXEC ASMFC

The Data Definition Statement. The DD (Data Definition) statement is used to tell the operating system the name and characteristics of the data sets required by the program. We need a DD statement for each data set referenced. We must tell the operating system whether the data set resides on disk, tape, or unit-record device. We must name the data set and give the operating system sufficient information to locate the data set on a disk or tape *volume* (the term volume is used to refer to a single reel of magnetic tape or one magnetic disk pack).

Table 17-4 gives the format of the DD statement. We cannot discuss all the parameters available at this point (the reader should reference Appendix E). The best way to introduce the DD statement is by example.

Table 17-4 Format of the DD Statement

name	operation	operands
//[ddname]	DD	[DSNAME = dsname / DSN = dsname] [,UNIT = {unit-address / device-type / group-name}] [,DISP = ([status][,disposition])] [,VOL = SER = nnnnnn] [,additional parameters]

The DD statements required to execute Program 1 (a card-to-printer program) are shown in the following example. We use the DCB macro to define the data sets in the program. We associate a DDNAME parameter with each data set, SYSIN with the input card data set, and SYSOUT with the data set going to the printer. The DDNAME defined in the DCB macro must appear in the ddname field on the DD statement.

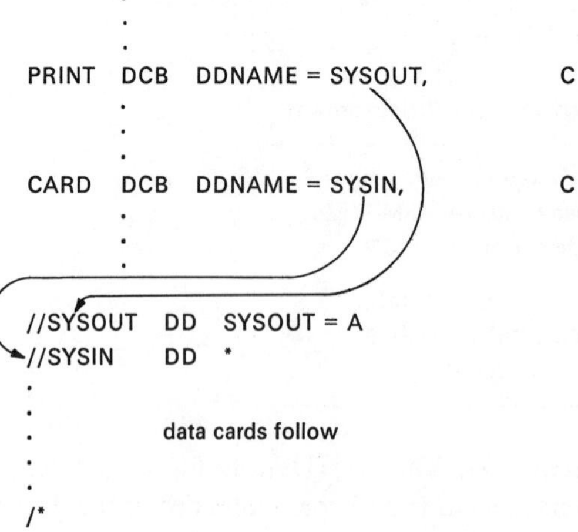

```
        .
        .
        .
PRINT   DCB   DDNAME = SYSOUT,          C
        .
        .
        .
CARD    DCB   DDNAME = SYSIN,           C
        .
        .
        .
//SYSOUT    DD   SYSOUT = A
//SYSIN     DD   *
.
.
.           data cards follow
.
.
/*
```

The first DD statement describes the output data set going to the printer. The entry SYSOUT=A directs the data set to a specific output device. We say the data set is going to a certain class device—in this example, a class A device. There is no relation between this Class A and the CLASS= keyword on the job card.

In most installations Class A output goes to the printer. If we want the output to go to the punch, we would code the entry

SYSOUT = B

The second DD statement describes the input card data set. This is a special DD statement. The asterisk (*) in the operand field tells the operating system that the input data set follows immediately. The programmer places the sample data following the DD * card.

Special Purpose Statements. There are four job control statements that do not fall into the categories we have discussed.

The delimiter statement (/*) is used to indicate an end-of-data condition. The DD * statement is used to mark the beginning of data. The use of these statements is given in Table 17-5.

The null statement (//) is sometimes used to mark the end of a job. Remember that the job statement marks the beginning of the job.

The DD DATA card is another special purpose statement. The DD DATA statement also is used to mark the beginning of data. But the data itself will contain job control statements.

Table 17-5 Control Cards for Program 1

Job Card	//JOBGO	JOB	(123,ABC),BURIAN,CLASS = A
Exec Card	//STEP1	EXEC	PGM = PROG1
DD Cards	//SYSOUT	DD	SYSOUT = A
	//SYSIN	DD	*
	.		
	.	data cards inserted here	
	.		
Deiimiter	/*		
Null Card	//		

The Testing Environment

When we write a program in assembly language, we are using a symbolic language. The source program must be translated to machine language. The assembler accomplishes this translation. The assembler accepts a source deck as input, produces an object module of machine language statements, and a printed listing. The assembler needs work space to accomplish this task. This work space is referred to as work files. If macro statements are to be assembled, the assembler also requires access to the macro library. Figure 17-3 represents the assembly process.

The assembler is a program requiring a number of data sets to assemble a source program. Each data set must have a complex DD statement defining it. Many job control cards are required to assemble even a very simple program.

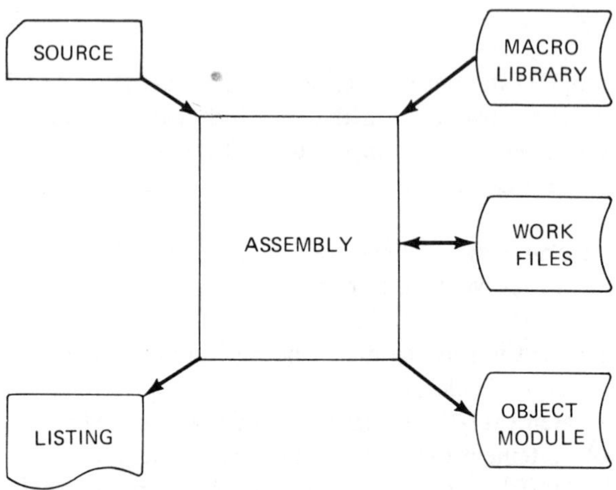

Figure 17-3 The assembly process.

Catalogued Procedures. IBM supplies the job control statements to assemble a program. We refer to this set of job control statements as a procedure. IBM also supplies procedures for other frequently required jobs. These procedures are stored on the operating system disk. The operating system consists of many groupings of programs and procedures. We call these groupings *libraries.* Procedures are stored in the procedure library. We say the procedures are catalogued—thus the name catalogued procedures.

Each procedure is given a name when it is placed in the procedure library. The programmer references this name in the EXEC statement. We shall discuss two procedures in this section.

Assemble Only. The programmer may encounter errors in syntax the first time he or she assembles a new program. These assembly-time errors must be corrected before the program can be tested. We refer to this procedure as an *edit* assembly. The programmer uses a procedure which only assembles the program; a different procedure is used when the program is ready to be tested.

The procedure to assemble only is called ASMFC. All the necessary job control cards are included in the procedure, with one exception. The programmer must include the DD statement to define the input data set. The input data, comprised of the source program, immediately follows the job control statements. We use the DD * card to indicate that the source deck immediately follows the job control statements

```
//ASM.SYSIN   DD   *
```

The ddname ASM.SYSIN is a special name—called a *qualified* name. We will see why in a moment.

The following cards are needed to assemble a source program.

```
//ASMSRCE     JOB    (123,ABC),BURIAN,CLASS = A
//            EXEC   ASMFC
//ASM.SYSIN   DD     *
.
.
.             source statements inserted here
.
.
/*
//
```

The assembler program has many options available. It may produce an object deck, or pass the object module to another program for testing. It may or may not produce a listing. The assembler assumes the following options:

DECK—punch a deck
LIST—produce a source listing
XREF—produce a cross reference listing
NOTEST—suppress TESTRAN option
ALGN—give alignment messages
NORENT—do not flag nonreentrant code
LINECT = 55—55 lines to a page

The programmer may want to change one of the assembler options. He may, for example, want to suppress the DECK option. The programmer is able to change assembler options using the PARM entry on the EXEC statement. To suppress a deck, the programmer would code

```
PARM.ASM = 'NODECK'
```

The following code uses the PARM parameter to suppress the DECK and XREF listing.

```
//ASMSRCE     JOB    (123,ABC),BURIAN,CLASS = A
//STEP1       EXEC   ASMFC,PARM.ASM = 'NODECK,NOXREF'
//ASM.SYSIN   DD     *
.
.
.             source statements inserted here
.
.
/*
//
```

Assemble, Link, and Go. When the programmer has eliminated all syntax errors, the program is ready to be tested. The object module produced by the assembler cannot be executed immediately. It first must be link-edited. The program which link-edits one or more object modules into a single executable program (called the load module) is the linkage editor.

Testing a program consists of three distinct operations; assembling, link-editing, and testing. We refer to this process as an *assemble, link, and go* (or test). The programmer may use a procedure called ASMFCLG to test his programs.

Each operation—assembling, link-editing and testing—is called a job step. The three steps constitute a single job. A job is determined by a job card. A job step is determined by an *execute* card. A job may consist of one or more job steps as shown in Table 17-6.

Table 17-6 Jobs and Job Steps

		//JOB1	JOB	(123,ABC),BURIAN,CLASS = A
a		//STEP1	EXEC	PGM = PROG1
one	STEP1	//DS1	DD	
step		//DS2	DD	
job		/*		
		//		
a		//JOB2	JOB	(123,ABC),BURIAN,CLASS = C
two	STEP1	//STEP1	EXEC	PGM = EDIT
step		/*		
job		//STEP2	EXEC	PGM = GOWITH
		//DD1	DD	
	STEP2	//DD2	DD	
		/*		
		//		

The ASMFCLG procedure (Figure 17-4) consists of three steps. The first step (ASM step) assembles the program, producing an object module. The second step (LKED step) link-edits the object module producing the load module. The load module is then executed (GO step). Data sets may be required to test the load module.

We can now understand the use of the qualified name ASM.SYSIN. We are adding a card to the procedure ASMFC. But to which of the three steps in the procedure? To the first step, the ASM step. The qualified name supplies both the ddname and the step name.

Each data set used in the GO step must be defined by a DD statement. The job control statements to assemble, link, and test Program 1 are:

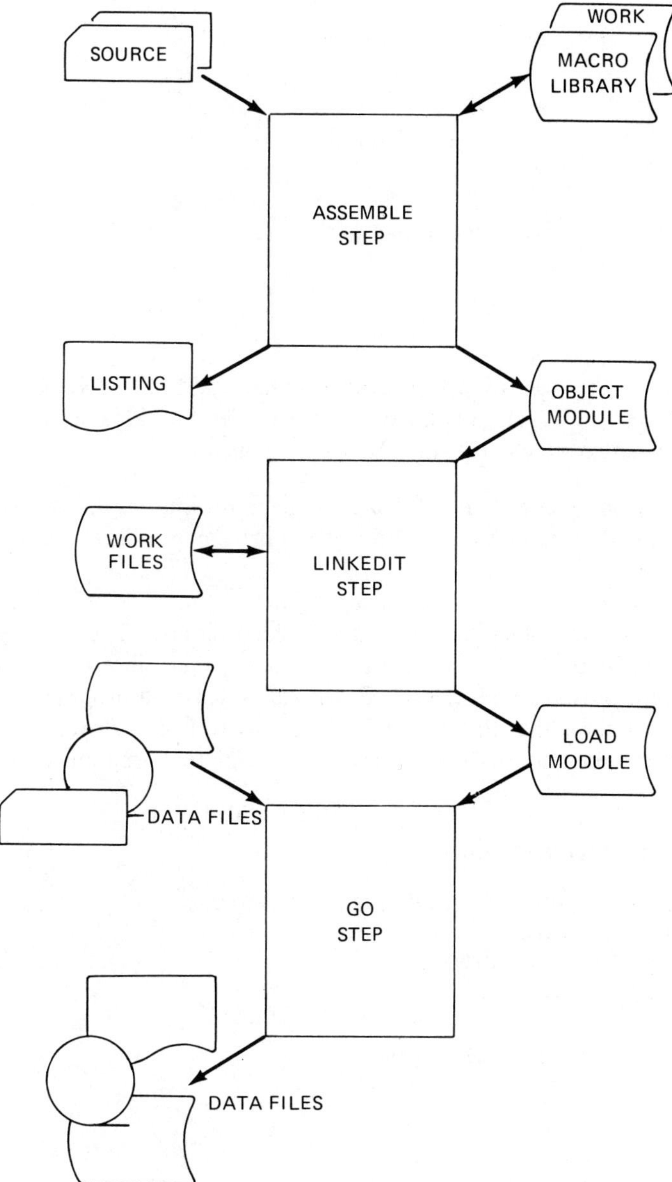

Figure 17-4 ASMFCLG procedure.

```
//GOPROG1     JOB    (123,ABC),BURIAN,CLASS = A
//STEP1       EXEC   ASMFCLG
//ASM.SYSIN   DD     *
.
.
.             source statements inserted here
.
.
/*
//GO.SYSOUT   DD     SYSOUT = A
//GO.SYSIN    DD     *
.
.
.             data cards inserted here
.
.
/*
//
```

Notice the use of the qualified names ASM.SYSIN, GO. SYSIN, and GO.SYSOUT. The qualified name provides the ddname of the data set and specifies to which step this DD card belongs.

Executing from a System Library. When a program is thoroughly tested, it may be stored in either a system library or a private user library, to be executed when required.

In order to be executed, a program first must be link-edited (Figure 17-4). We call the link-edited program the load module. The load module might be stored in SYS1.LINKLIB, an operating system library. When we execute a program from SYS1.LINKLIB, we are executing a program, not a procedure. Let's assume that Program 1 has been tested and is stored in SYS1.LINKLIB under the name PROG1. In order to execute this program we use the entry

```
PGM = PROG1
```

on the execute statement.

```
//TESTP1      JOB    (123,ABC),BURIAN,CLASS = A
//TESTSTEP    EXEC   PGM = PROG1
//SYSOUT      DD     SYSOUT = A
//SYSIN       DD     *
.
.
.             data cards inserted here
.
.
/*
//
```

Symbolic Device Assignment

Let's continue our discussion of job control language using a more complex program. Figure 17-5 gives the system flowchart for a payroll program. The

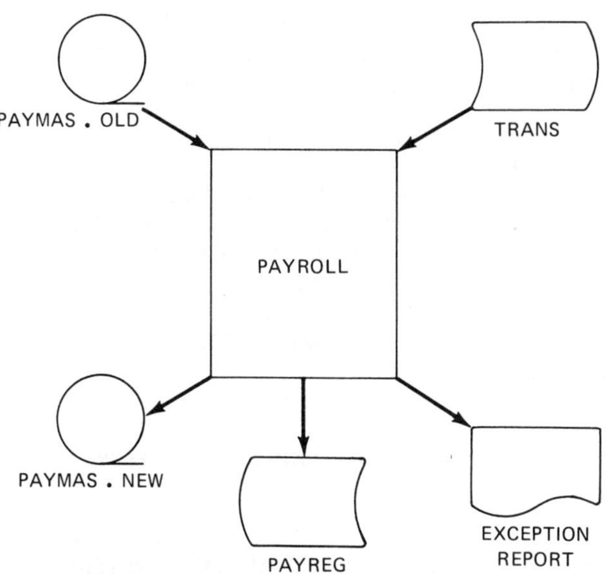

Figure 17-5 Payroll program.

payroll master data set is on tape. The edited transactions are on magnetic disk. The program produces a new payroll data set on tape and the payroll register on disk. An exception report also is printed. The program requires five data sets, thus five data definition cards are needed. Let's first see how these data sets are defined in the source program, and then examine the required DD statements.

Table 17-7 shows a segment of the source program for the payroll problem.

Table 17-7 DD Cards for Payroll

source program			job control cards	
PAYRT	DCB	DDNAME = PAYREGDD, . . .	//PAYREGDD	DD .....
EXCPT	DCB	DDNAME = EXCEPTDD, . . .	//EXCEPTDD	DD .....
MASOUT	DCB	DDNAME = NEWMASDD, . . .	//NEWMASDD	DD .....
TRNS	DCB	DDNAME = TRANSDD, . . .	//TRANSDD	DD .....
MASIN	DCB	DDNAME = OLDMASDD,	//OLDMASDD	DD .....

There are five DCB macros—one for each data set. Each DCB macro contains a DDNAME entry. This ddname must appear in a DD job control card. The job control cards to execute the payroll program follow:

```
//PAYROLL     JOB   (123,ABC),BURIAN,CLASS = A
//STEP1       EXEC  PGM = PAYROLL
//OLDMASDD    DD    UNIT = TAPE,VOL = SER = 123455,
//                  DSNAME = PAYMAS.OLD,DISP = (OLD,KEEP)
//TRANSDD     DD    UNIT = DISK,VOL = SER = 003212,
//                  DSNAME = TRANS,DISP = (OLD,KEEP)
//NEWMASDD    DD    UNIT = TAPE,VOL = SER = 098765,
//                  DSNAME = PAYMAS.NEW,DISP = (NEW,KEEP)
//EXCEPTDD    DD    SYSOUT = A
//PAYREGDD    DD    UNIT = DISK,DISP = (NEW,KEEP),
//                  DCB = (BLKSIZE = 120,LRECL = 120),
//                  VOL = SER = ABC123,DSNAME = PAYREG,
//                  SPACE = (TRK,200)
//
```

We need additional parameters in the DD statement to describe data sets which reside on tape or disk. The UNIT parameter tells the operating system whether the data set is to be assigned to tape or disk. The UNIT parameter may specify a particular device type such as TAPE or DISK, or it may specify a device number. We could code the unit parameter

UNIT = 3330,

or perhaps,

UNIT = 2400.

These numbers refer to IBM devices. The 3330 is a disk drive, the 2400 is a tape drive.

The DISP parameter tells the operating system the disposition of the data set. The first entry in parenthesis states the disposition of the data set at the beginning of the job. The disposition on the input payroll master is

DISP = (OLD,KEEP)

This means that the data set existed at the beginning of the job—it is an *old* data set—and the operating system is to *keep* the data set at end of job. This allows us to reference the data set in a subsequent run. If we code the parameter

DISP = (OLD,DELETE),

we cannot reference the data set again.

The payroll program creates a new payroll master data set. The disposition parameter associated with this data set is

DISP = (NEW,KEEP)

which tells the operating system that the data set is to be created in this job and is to be kept at normal end of job.

A third parameter is available in the disposition entry. This parameter tells the operating system the disposition of the data set at abnormal end of job. If an error occurs while we are creating the new master, we probably want to delete the data set. It is of no use to us. We would code the disposition parameter

```
DISP = (NEW,KEEP,DELETE),
```

The data set is new at the beginning of the job. We will keep it if we go to normal end-of-job. We will delete it if we abnormally terminate the run.

The DD statement also must tell the operating system which tape or disk volume the data set resides on. Tape and disk volumes are identified by a label containing up to a 6-position number. The label, the volume label, is the first record on a reel of tape and the third record on a disk pack (Figure 17-6). The entry

```
VOL = SER = nnnnnn
```

is used to request a specific volume. We tell the operating system that we want the

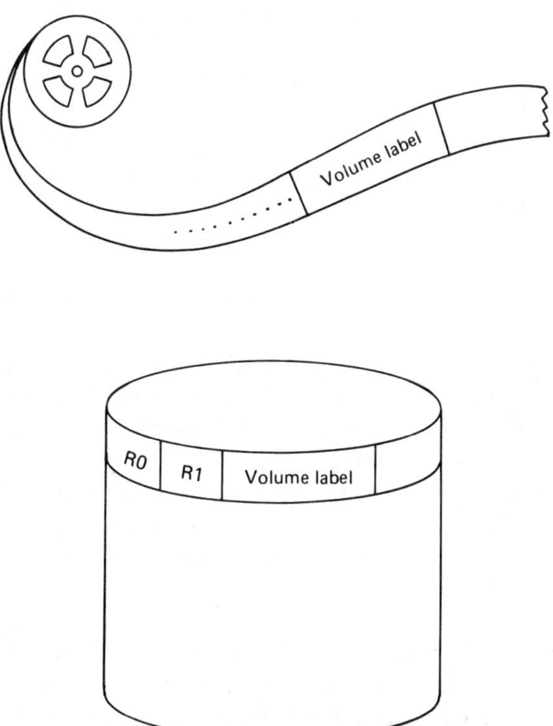

Figure 17-6 Volume labels on disk and tape.

data set residing on tape volume 123456 using the entries

```
UNIT = TAPE,
VOL = SER = 123456,
```

The DSNAME entry gives the name of the data set. This name is associated with the data set when it is created using the DISP=(NEW,KEEP) parameter. When the data set is referenced in a subsequent job, the programmer must provide the operating system with the data set name. Each DD card must contain the DSNAME entry.

The operating system requires three entries to locate a data set: the UNIT parameter, the VOL=SER parameter, and the DSNAME parameter. The programmer can omit the first two entries if he asks the operating system to *catalogue* the data set. He specifies CATLG in the disposition entry. For example

```
DSNAME = NEWDS,
UNIT = DISK,
VOL = SER = 098765,
DISP = (NEW,CATLG)
```

These entries create a new data set on disk volume 098765. The operating system catalogues the unit and volume number. The programmer need only supply the DSNAME parameter in subsequent runs.

The SPACE parameter is associated with data sets which are being created. The space parameter tells the operating system how much direct access space is required. The SPACE parameter does not apply to tape or unit-record data sets. The entry

```
SPACE = (TRK,200)
```

tells the operating system that the data set PAYREG requires 200 tracks on a disk volume.

The last entry we shall discuss is the DCB parameter. This entry relates to the *data control block* defined in the source program. In Chapter 15 we discussed the DCB macro. This entry reserves space for a table of information about the data set called the data control block.

The data control block must contain all the information about a data set before it can be read or written. Information may be entered to the data control block from three sources: the DCB macro, job control statements, and the label on the data set itself.

Table 17-8 shows the use of the DCB entry to supply information about the data set PAYREG. The programmer did not code the BLKSIZE and LRECL entries in the DCB macro. He now supplies the block size and logical record length in the DD statement defining the data set. If the programmer did not supply these entries in the DD statement, the operating system would not be able to OPEN the data set. The data control block would be incomplete—missing the block size and logical record length.

Table 17-8 Use of Job Control Statements to Complete the DCB

Source Program	.			
	.			
	.			
	PAYREG	DCB	DSORG = PS,	C
			MACRF = GM,	C
			EODAD = EOJRT,	C
			DDNAME = PAYREGDD	
Job Control Statements	//PAYREG	DD	UNIT = DISK,DISP = (NEW,KEEP),	
	//		DCB = (BLKSIZE = 120,LRECL = 120)	

If PAYREG were an input data set, the operating system might find the missing information on the data set label. But we are creating PAYREG in our program; it does not yet have a label. The label is written when the data set is created. The data control block table must be built with information supplied in the DCB macro or in the DD statement.

Our discussion has involved only a few of the possible entries on the data definition statement. There are many additional parameters available in the entries we did discuss. The reader is referred to the tables in Appendex E.

DOS/370 JOB CONTROL LANGUAGE

All DOS job control statements follow the same general format (Figure 17-7). Job control statements contain a double slash (//) in columns 1 and 2, followed by a space. The operation field follows, starting in column 4.

The operation field is required. The operation field specifies the type of job control statement. If this statement names the job, the operation field is coded as JOB. If this statement tells the operating system the name of the program to be executed, the operation field is coded as EXEC. We shall discuss these and other types of job control statements in the next section.

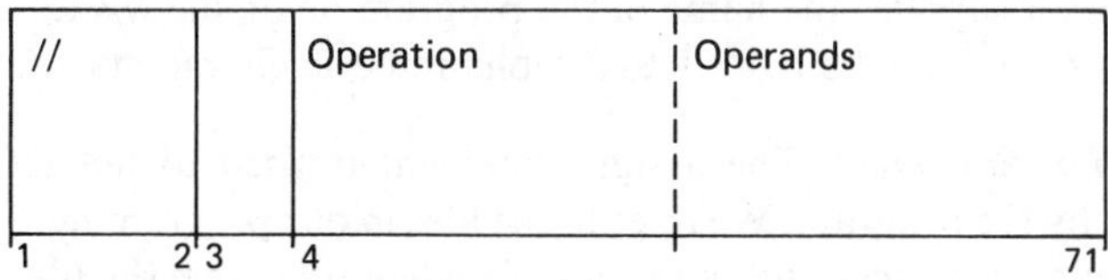

Figure 17-7 Format of DOS job control cards.

The operand field supplies the operating system with additional information. Operands may be either keyword or positional. The reader should reference Chapter 15 for a discussion of keyword and positional operands.

Types of Job Control Statements

We shall discuss four types of job control statements. The job statement names the job to be executed. The execute statement gives the name of the program to be executed. The assign statement supplies information about the files used in the program. And the option card specifies parameters for the job.

The Job Statement. Each job submitted to DOS must have a job statement naming the job. The format of the job statement is

operation	operand
// JOB	jobname

The programmer supplies the jobname. The jobname may be from 1 to 8 alphanumeric characters. For example

```
// JOB ASSEMBLY
```

Comments may follow the jobname, separated by at least one blank.

```
// JOB ASSEMBLY  FIRST ASSEMBLY ON PAYROLL
```

The statement

```
FIRST ASSEMBLY ON PAYROLL
```

is treated as a comment. The jobname is ASSEMBLY.

The Execute Statement. The execute statement tells DOS the name of the program to be executed. The format of the execute statement is

operation	operand
// EXEC	program name

The two slashes in columns 1 and 2 are required. The operation is EXEC. The programmer supplies the name of the program he or she wishes to execute. The program name may be from 1 to 8 alphanumeric characters.

The Assign Statement. The assign statement is used to tell DOS the devices required by the program. We refer to the files in our program by symbolic names. We associate a logical unit with each file when we define the file.

```
DEVADDR = SYS004
```

SYS004 is the logical unit. The assign statement equates this logical unit with a physical device such as disk or tape. The format of the assign statement is

operation	operand
// ASSGN	SYSxxx,X'cuu'

The slashes in columns 1 and 2 are required. The operation is ASSGN. The first positional operand specifies the logical unit. The second operand specifies the device. The device is addressed by channel, control unit, and device. (See Figure 17-8.) In this example we are addressing the tape drive to channel 1 (C=1), control unit eight (U=8), and the *third* (U=2) drive on the control unit. Why third and not second? The first drive is adressed as 180, the second as 181, and so on.

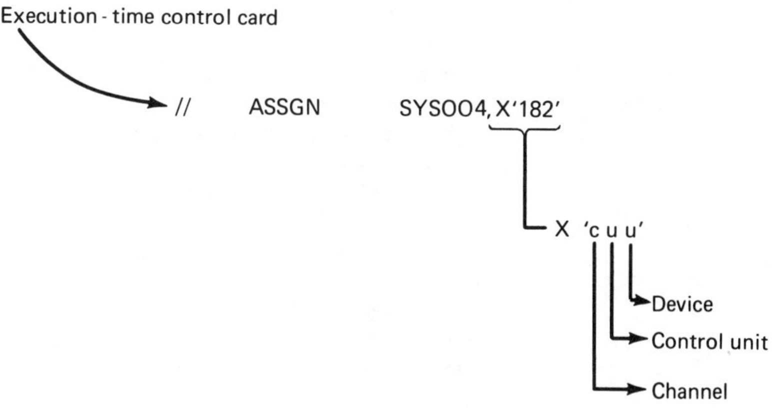

Figure 17-8 The ASSGN card.

When we define the file, TAPEIN, we specify a logical unit of SYS004.

```
TAPEIN   DTFMT   DEVADDR = SYS004,        C
```

At execution time we must equate this device to a specific tape drive.

```
// ASSGN SYS004,X'182'
```

We are assigning the file TAPEIN to drive 182.

The Option Statement. The option statement allows the programmer to specify the parameters to be followed for the job. The format of the option statement is

operation	operand
// OPTION	one or more operands

The slashes in columns 1 and 2 are required. The operation is OPTION. The operands specify the desired options. *Default options* are assigned when the system is generated. If the programmer does not include an option card, DOS assumes the default options which vary from one installation to another.

Table 17-9 Available Options

option	description
LOG	Log control statements on SYSLST
NOLOG	Suppress LOG option
DUMP	Dump registers and main storage on SYSLST in case of abnormal end-of-job
NODUMP	Suppress DUMP option
LINK	Write output of language translator on SYSLNK for linkage editing
NOLINK	Suppress LINK option
DECK	Output object module on SYSPCH
NODECK	Suppress deck option
LIST	Output listing of source module on SYSLST
NOLIST	Suppress LIST option
LISTX	Output listing of object module on SYSLST
NOLISTX	Suppress LISTX option
SYM	Punch symbol deck on SYSPCH
NOSYM	Suppress SYM option
XREF	Output symbolic cross-reference on SYSLST
NOXREF	Suppress XREF option
ERRS	Output listing of all errors on SYSLST
NOERRS	Suppress ERRS option
CATAL	Catalogue program into core image library (CIL)
STDLABEL	Causes all sequential disk or tape labels to be written on the standard label track
USRLABEL	Causes all sequential disk or tape labels to be written on the user label track
48C	48-character set
60C	60-character set

Special Purpose Cards. There are three special purpose cards. The /* card is a delimiter card. This card follows input card files. The /* card marks the end of a card file.

The /& card is the end-of-job delimiter. This card is the last card in a job deck.

The programmer may insert comment cards in his job. The comment card has an * in column 1, followed by at least one blank. The remainder of the card is treated as a comment.

```
* THIS IS THE PAYROLL JOB
```

In this example the comment THIS IS THE PAYROLL JOB is printed on the console, and upon the printed listing.

The Testing Environment

When we write a program in assembly language, we are using a symbolic language. The assembler translates the source program to machine language. The assembler accepts a source deck as input, produces an object module of machine statements and gives us a listing. The assembler needs work space to accomplish its tasks—we refer to this work space as work files. And, finally, the assembler requires access to the macro library if macro definitions are to be assembled. Figure 17-9 represents the assembly process.

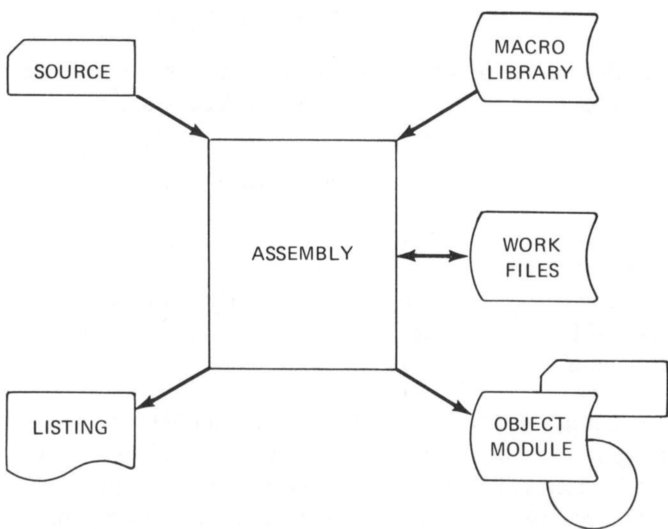

Figure 17-9 The assembly process.

The assembler is a program requiring a number of files to assemble a source program. Each file used by the assembler must have an ASSGN statement. These standard assignments are stored on the operating system disk (SYSRES volume). DOS knows which files the assembler uses. The programmer need only submit a few job control cards.

Assemble Only. The programmer may encounter syntax errors the first time he or she assembles a new program. These errors must be corrected before the program can be tested. We refer to this assembly as an edit assembly. We are editing the source program for errors.

```
//  JOB ASSEMBLE
*   EDIT ASSEMBLY
//  OPTION LIST,NODECK  LISTING BUT NO DECK
//  EXEC ASSEMBLY
.
.
.   source statements inserted here
.
.
/*  END OF SOURCE
/&  END OF JOB
```

The job name is ASSEMBLE. The next card

```
* EDIT ASSEMBLY
```

is a comment card. The programmer is *documenting* the job. The option statement

```
// OPTION LIST,NODECK
```

tells DOS that the programmer wants a listing but not an object deck. If the program contains syntax errors, an object deck is useless.

The execute statement

```
// EXEC ASSEMBLY
```

tells the DOS supervisor to execute the program called ASSEMBLY. This is the name of the assembler.

The assembly source program immediately follows the execute statement. The end of the source statement is marked by a /* card, and the end of the job by a /& card.

Assemble, Link, and Go. When the programmer has eliminated all syntax errors, the program is ready to be tested. The object module produced by the assembler cannot be executed. It must be link-edited first. The program which link-edits one or more object modules into a single executable program (called a program *phase*) is the linkage editor.

Three distinct operations are required in order to test a program; assembling, link-editing, and testing. We refer to this process as an assemble, link, and go (or test). Each operation—assembling, link-editing and testing is called a job step. The three steps constitute a single job. A job is determined by a job card. A job step is determined by an execute card. A job may consist of one or more job steps (see Table 17-10).

The testing procedure consists of three steps (see Figure 17-10). The first step assembles the program, producing an object module. The second step link-edits the object module, producing the program phase. The program phase is then executed. Files may be required to test the program phase. Each file used in the test step must be defined by an assign statement. The job control statements to assemble, link, and test Program 1 (card-to-printer with field selection) are given in Table 17-11.

Table 17-10 Jobs and Job Steps

```
a                      // JOB ONE
one        step 1      // ASSGN SYS001 .....
step                   // ASSGN SYS002 .....
job                    // EXEC PROG1
                       /*
                       /&
a                      // JOB TWO
two        step 1      // ASSGN SYS001 .....
step                   // ASSGN SYS002 .....
job                    // EXEC  EDIT
                       .
                       .
                       .  data cards are inserted here
                       .
                       .
                       /*
                       // ASSGN SYS001 .....
                       // ASSGN SYS002 .....
                       // EXEC PAYROLL
                       .
           step 2      .
                       .  data cards are inserted here
                       .
                       .
                       /*
                       /&
```

Table 17-11 Assemble, Link, and Go—Program 1

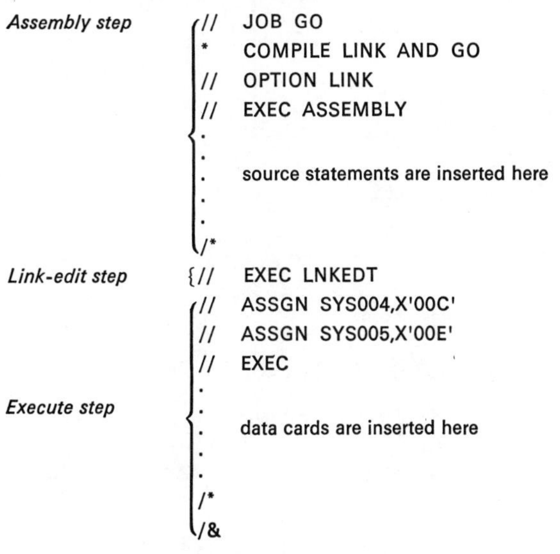

```
Assembly step      // JOB GO
                   *  COMPILE LINK AND GO
                   // OPTION LINK
                   // EXEC ASSEMBLY
                   .
                   .
                   .  source statements are inserted here
                   .
                   .
                   /*
Link-edit step     // EXEC LNKEDT
                   // ASSGN SYS004,X'00C'
                   // ASSGN SYS005,X'00E'
                   // EXEC
                   .
Execute step       .
                   .  data cards are inserted here
                   .
                   .
                   /*
                   /&
```

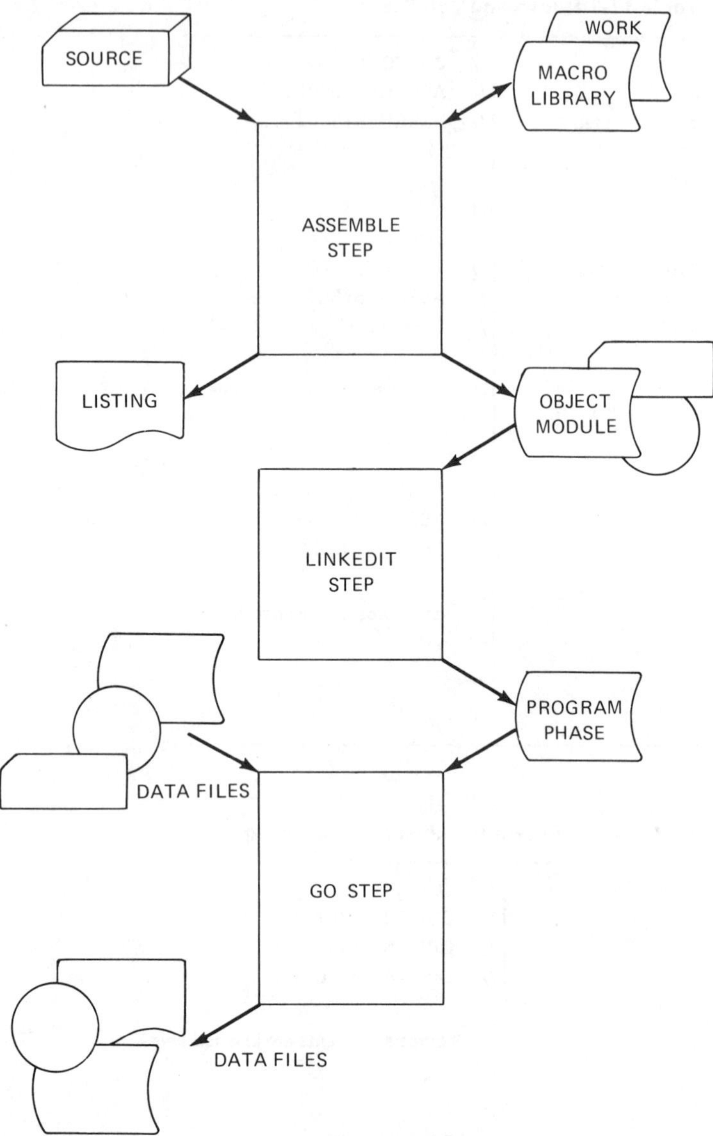

Figure 17-10 An assemble link-and-go.

The name of this job is GO. The comments card

```
* COMPILE LINK AND GO
```

tells us the purpose of the program. The next card, the option statement

```
// OPTION LINK
```

tells the operating system that this is not only an assembly—the object module produced by the assembly step is to be link-edited and executed.

The execute statement

```
// EXEC ASSEMBLY
```

tells the supervisor to load the assembler. The source cards—input to the assembler—immediately follow the execute statement. The /* card marks the end of the source deck.

The next step—the execute card determines a job step—is the link-edit step. The card

```
// EXEC LNKEDT
```

tells the supervisor to load the linkage editor. The linkage editor links the object module with any required subroutines and DOS I/O routines, producing the executable program phase.

The last step is the GO or test step. The assign statements

```
// ASSGN SYS004,X'00C'
// ASSGN SYS005,X'00E'
```

are to the reader and printer respectively. The address of the reader is X'OOC'. The address of the printer is X'OOE'. Most installations follow this convention.

The statement

```
// EXEC
```

is a special form of the execute statement. There is no operand. In this case, the supervisor knows that the program just link-edited is to be executed. The data cards for this program immediately follow the execute card. The /* card marks the end of the input card file, and the /& card marks the end of job.

The testing procedure involves three steps. The assembly step produces the object module. This module is then link-edited with subroutines and DOS subroutines into an executable program phase. This program phase is then tested.

How are these modules passed from one step to another? Where does the assembler put the object module? How does the linkage editor know where to place the program phase? To answer these questions, we must know a little about DOS itself.

System Libraries. DOS is a collection of programs. These programs are stored on a disk pack (see Figure 17-11). Programs are grouped together in libraries.

All executable program phases are placed in *core image library* (CIL). The supervisor executes programs from core image library. Core image library contains all the programs comprising the operating system, and all user programs. The output of the linkage editor is placed in core image library.

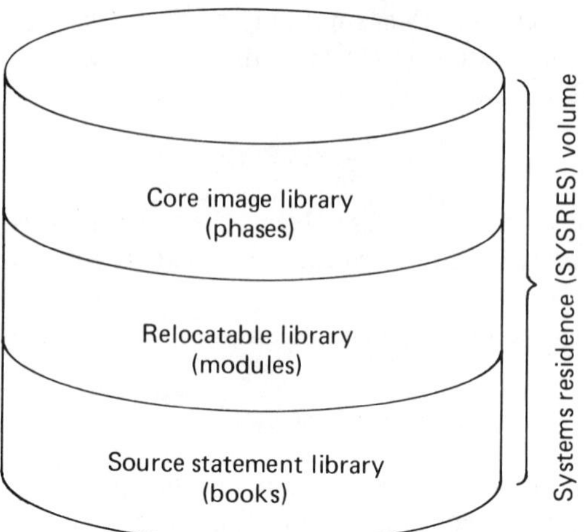

Figure 17-11 DOS libraries.

Object modules—the output of a compiler or the assembler—may be placed in *relocatable* library. These modules are not executable. They have not been link-edited. Relocatable library contains subroutines and I/O routines. These must be link-edited into core image library prior to execution.

Macro definitions—the statements the assembler references to assemble a macro—are stored on *source statement* library. The user may store his own programs—in source form—in source statement library. Entries in source statement library are called books.

In an assemble-link-and-go procedure, we must tell the operating system whether the output of the linkage editor, the program phase, is to be a temporary or permanent entry in core image library. The statement

```
// OPTION LINK
```

tells the operating system that the entry is a temporary entry in the library. After the phase is tested, it is to be deleted. Can you see the need for temporary entries in core image library? If all the preliminary versions of our program were catalogued into the library, we would soon run out of space.

However, once we have tested the program and are satisfied with the results, we may want to catalogue the output of the linkage editor permanently into core image library. We also must name the entry. We specify a permanent entry in core image library using the option card

```
// OPTION CATAL
```

and name the entry using the phase card

```
PHASE PROG1,*
```

The phase card names the program and tells the operating system where the program is to be loaded. The asterisk (*) tells the supervisor to load the program in the next available storage location.

The job cards to assemble, link, and catalogue Program 1 are as follows:

```
//   JOB CATALOG
//   OPTION CATAL
     PHASE PROG1,*
//   EXEC ASSEMBLY
.
.
.    source statements are inserted here
.
.
/*
//   EXEC LNKEDT
/*
/&
```

Programs residing in core image library do not have to be assembled. They are in executable form. We can execute program phases from core image library in one job step.

```
//   JOB   PROG1   SAMPLE CONTROL CARDS
//   ASSGN   SYS004,X'00C'
//   ASSGN   SYS005,X'00E'
//   EXEC   PROG1
.
.
.    data cards are inserted here
.
.
/*
/&
```

We need only supply the assign cards for the job, and tell the operating system the name of the program phase. The name in the execute card

```
// EXEC PROG1
```

is the name by which the program is catalogued into core image library. We catalogued the program in a previous job

```
// OPTION CATAL
   PHASE PROG1,*
```

Link-Editing Several Modules. Often a program is so large that it must be coded in sections. Let's see how four sections of a single program may be linked and tested as a single phase. One section of the program has been assembled and catalogued into relocatable library using the name SUB1. Another section has been assembled and is in object form—a card deck. The two remaining sections must be assembled.

The job SUM consists of four job steps. The first step assembles the first section of the program. The object module is stored temporarily on a work file. The next step assembles the second section of the program, storing the object module on a work file. The link-edit step is next. The linkage editor must link four modules—two of which are stored on a work file. The statement

```
INCLUDE SUB1
```

tells the linkage editor to locate the module SUB1 on relocatable library and to link it. The statement

```
INCLUDE
```

Table 17-12 Assemble, Link, and Go—Four Modules

Assemble first module		// JOB SUM
	temporary entry	// OPTION LINK
		// EXEC ASSEMBLY
		.
		.
		. source cards are inserted here
		.
		.
Assemble second module		/*
		// EXEC ASSEMBLY
		.
		.
		. source cards are inserted here
		.
		.
		/*
Link-edit four modules		INCLUDE SUB1
	include module from RLB	INCLUDE
		.
	include object deck	.
		. insert object module here
		.
		.
		/*
		// EXEC LNKEDT
Test complete program		// ASSGN
		// ASSGN
		// EXEC
		.
		.
		. data cards are inserted here
		.
		.
		/*
		/&

tells the linkage-editor to include the object deck which follows. All four modules are linked into one phase and stored temporarily in core image library by the statement

```
// OPTION LINK
```

The last step

```
// EXEC
```

executes the phase which was just link-edited.

PROBLEMS

17.1 Give the job control statements for each of the following jobs. Give the purpose of each card. Use either OS or DOS statements.

1. Compile an assembly program—get a source listing, an error listing, but no deck.
2. Compile, link-edit and execute an assembly program—a card file and a printer file are required for execution.
3. Execute a program from the operating system's library—the program's name is PROG1 and it requires an input card file and an output punch file.

17.2 Code the job control cards to compile and execute a program called MASTER1. The following files are required.

name[1]	unit	file[2] name	volume label
SYS004	tape	INMAS	123001
SYS005	tape	OUTMAS	123002
SYS006	card		
SYS007	printer		

[1]DDNAME in OS, DEVADDR in DOS
[2]DSNAME in OS, filename in DOS

17.3 Give the name of each of the following DOS libraries.

a. Library containing executable program phases
b. Library containing object modules
c. Library containing macro definitions

17.4 Give the DOS control statements for each of the following jobs.

1. Compile, link-edit and catalogue a program called PROG2 into core image library.
2. Execute the program PROG2 from core image library. No files are required.
3. Compile an assembly program and punch an object deck
4. Compile, link-edit and test a program. Create a temporary entry in core image library.

18

Testing and Debugging

INTRODUCTION When the programmer finishes coding his (or her) program, he enters a new phase of program development—that of testing. There are three levels of testing. *Program testing* consists of executing the program with sample test data to determine if it functions correctly. *Volume testing* includes larger files, often testing the communication between the analyst and programmer, and *systems testing* checks out many programs and their relation to each other. We are concerned with program testing in this chapter.

Assembly Time Errors

Figure 18-1 shows an assembly language listing with several different types of assembly time errors.* Errors are flagged in the source listing. For example, an error occurs in statement 14. This error is described in the assembler diagnostic listing (1). The diagnostic listing gives the statement number (2), an error code (3), and the error message (4).

*The output given is an OS/370 listing. The macros are different but the concepts apply to both OS and DOS.

```
LOC    OBJECT CODE     ADDR1 ADDR2  STMT   SOURCE STATEMENT                                         F04MAR74   6/17/76

                                       1 * PROGRAM 5 WITH ERRORS
000000                                 2           START 0
                                       3 BEGIN     SAVE  (14,12)                                   SAVE REGISTERS
000000                                 4+BEGIN     DS    0H
000000 90EC D00C             0000C     5+          STM   14,12,12(13) SAVE REGISTERS
000004 05C0                            6           BALR  12,0                                      ESTABLISH BASE
000006                                 7           USING *,12                                      ADDRESSABILITY
000006 50D0 C17A             00180     8           ST    13,SAVEAREA+4                             FOLLOW R13 CONVENTIONS
00000A 41D0 C176             0017C     9           LA    13,SAVEAREA                               DISCUSSED IN CH 14
                                      10           OPEN  (INCARD,,PRINT,OUTPUT)                    OPEN FILES
00000E 0700                           11+          CNOP  0,4 ALIGN LIST TO FULLWORD
000010 4510 C016             0001C    12+          BAL   1,*+12 LOAD REG1 W/LIST ADDR.
000014 00                             13+          DC    AL1(0) OPTION BYTE
000015 000000                         14+          DC    AL3(INCARD) DCB ADDRESS ———— Macro INCARD in error
          *** ERROR ***
000018 8F                             15+          DC    AL1(143) OPTION BYTE
000019 000078                         16+          DC    AL3(PRINT) DCB ADDRESS
00001C 0A13                           17+          SVC   19 ISSUE OPEN SVC
                                      18 READRT    GET   INCARD,INWORK                             READ INTO INWORK
00001E 0000 0000             00000    19+READRT    LA    1,INCARD LOAD PARAMETER REG 1 ———— Macro in error
          *** ERROR ***
000022 4100 C0D2             000D8    20+          LA    0,INWORK LOAD PARAMETER REG 0
000026 58F0 1030             00030    21+          L     15,48(0,1) LOAD GET ROUTINE ADDR.
00002A 05FF                           22+          BALR  14,15 LINK TO GET ROUTINE
00002C D204 C159 C0D2 0015F 000D8     23           MVC   LIMOUT,LIM                                SET UP PRINT LINE
000032 F224 C122 C0D2 00128 000D8     24           PACK  LIMP(3),LIM                               PACK LIMIT
000038 FA52 C125 C12B 0012B 00131     25 LOOP      AP    ANSP,CTR                                  ADD CTR TO ANSP
00003E F922 C12B C122 00131 00128     26           CP    CTR,LIMP                                  COMPARE
000044 0000 0000             00000    27           BE    (EXIT)                                    EXIT IF EQUAL
          *** ERROR ***
000048 0000 0000 0000 00000 00000     28           AP    CTR,(PL1'1')                              INCREMENT CTR ———— Should be a literal
          *** ERROR ***
00004E 47F0 C032             00038    29           B     LOOP                                      ELSE CONTINUE LOOP
000052 D211 C163 C12E 00169 00134     30 [EXI]     MVC   ANSOUT,MASK                               MOVE MASK
000058 DE11 C163 C125 00169 0012B     31           ED    ANSOUT,ANSP                               EDIT ANSWER
                                      32           PUT   PRINT,PRINTBLD                            WRITE
00005E 4110 C072             00078    33+          LA    1,PRINT LOAD PARAMETER REG 1
000062 4100 C140             00146    34+          LA    0,PRINTBLD LOAD PARAMETER REG 0
000066 58F0 1030             00030    35+          L     15,48(0,1) LOAD PUT ROUTINE ADDR.
00006A 05FF                           36+          BALR  14,15 LINK TO PUT ROUTINE
00006C 0000                           37           (BR)  READRT                                    FORCE EOF CONDITION ———— Should be B
          *** ERROR ***
                                      38 EOJRT     CLOSE (INCARD,,PRINT ———— Macro in error
          *** ERROR ***
00006E 58D0 C17A             00180    39           L     13,SAVEAREA+4                             SEE CHAPTER 14
                                      40           RETURN (14,12)                                  RETURN
000072 98EC D00C             0000C    41+          LM    14,12,12(13) RESTORE THE REGISTERS
000076 07FE                           42+          BR    14 RETURN
                                      43 *
                                      44 * DATA AREAS
                                      45 *
                                      46 INCARD    DCB   DSORG=PS,                                                  C
                                                         DDNAME=SYSIN,                                              C
                                                         MACRF=GM,                                                  C
                                                         BLKSIZE=80,                                                C
```

Figure 18-1.

```
                                                                                          PAGE    2

LOC  OBJECT CODE    ADDR1 ADDR2  STMT   SOURCE STATEMENT                            F04MAR74   6/17/76

                                                    LREC=80,                                  C
                                                    EODAD=EOJRT
      *** ERROR ***
                                  47 PRINT    DCB   DSORG=PS,                                 C
                                                    DDNAME=SYSOUT,                            C
                                                    MACRF=PM,                                 C
                                                    BLKSIZE=80,                               C
                                                    LRECL=80

                                  49+*                     DATA CONTROL BLOCK
                                  50+*
000C78                            51+PRINT    DC    0F'0' ORIGIN ON WORD BOUNDARY

                                  53+*                     DIRECT ACCESS DEVICE INTERFACE

000C78 0000000000000000           55+         DC    BL16'0' FDAD,DVTBL
000C88 00000000                   56+         DC    A(0) KEYLE,DEVT,TRBAL

                                  58+*                     COMMON ACCESS METHOD INTERFACE

000C8C 00                         60+         DC    AL1(0) BUFNO
000C8D 000001                     61+         DC    AL3(1) BUFCB
000C90 0000                       62+         DC    AL2(0) BUFL
000C92 4000                       63+         DC    BL2'0100000000000000' DSORG
000C94 00000001                   64+         DC    A(1) IOBAD

                                  66+*                     FOUNDATION EXTENSION

000C98 00                         68+         DC    BL1'00000000' BFTEK,BFLN,HIARCHY
000C99 000001                     69+         DC    AL3(1) EODAD
000C9C 00                         70+         DC    BL1'00000000' RECFM
000C9D 000000                     71+         DC    AL3(0) EXLST

                                  73+*                     FOUNDATION BLOCK

000CA0 E2E8E2D6E4E34040           75+         DC    CL8'SYSOUT' DDNAME
000CA8 02                         76+         DC    BL1'00000010' OFLGS
000CA9 00                         77+         DC    BL1'00000000' IFLG
000CAA 0C50                       78+         DC    BL2'0000000001010000' MACR

                                  80+*                     BSAM-BPAM-QSAM INTERFACE

000CAC 00                         82+         DC    BL1'00000000' RER1
000CAD 000001                     83+         DC    AL3(1) CHECK, GERR, PERR
000CB0 00000001                   84+         DC    A(1) SYNAD
000CB4 0000                       85+         DC    H'0' CIND1, CIND2
000CB6 0C50                       86+         DC    AL2(80) BLKSIZE
000CB8 00000000                   87+         DC    F'0' WCPO, WCPL, OFFSR, OFFSW
000CBC 00000001                   88+         DC    A(1) IOBA
000CC0 00                         89+         DC    AL1(0) NCP
000CC1 000001                     90+         DC    AL3(1) EOBR, EOBAD

                                  92+*                     QSAM INTERFACE
```

Invalid parameter causes macro to be flagged as an error

Figure 18-1 (*Continued*)

```
                                                                                      PAGE    3

  LOC  OBJECT CODE     ADDR1 ADDR2  STMT    SOURCE STATEMENT                        F04MAR74  6/17/76

0000C4 00000001                      94+            DC    A(1) RECAD
0000C8 0000                          95+            DC    H'0' QSWS
0000CA 0050                          96+            DC    AL2(80) LRECL
0000CC 00                            97+            DC    BL1'00000000' EROPT
0000CD 000001                        98+            DC    AL3(1) CNTRL
0000D0 00000000                      99+            DC    F'0' PRECL
0000D4 00000001                     100+            DC    A(1) EOB
0000D8                              101 INWORK      DS    0CL80
0000D8                              102 LIM         DS    CL5
0000DD                              103             DS    CL75
000128                              104 LIMP        DS    CL3
000128 00000000000C                 105 ANSP        DC    PL6'0'
000131 00001C                       106 CTR         DC    PL3'1'
000134 4020482020204B20             107 MASK        DC    X'40204B2020204B2020204B2020204B202120'
000146 E2E4D440D6C640D5             108 PRINTFLD    DC    CL25'SUM OF NUMBERS FROM 1 TO '
00015F                              109 LIMOUT      DS    CL5
000164                              110             DS    CL5
000169                              111 ANSOUT      DS    CL18
00017C                              112 SAVEAREA    DS    18F
000000                              113             END   BEGIN

  (2)    (3)          (4)                  (1)       DIAGNOSTICS                              PAGE    1

STMT  ERROR CODE   MESSAGE                                                                     6/17/76

   14  IEU024      NEAR OPERAND COLUMN    5--UNDEFINED SYMBOL
   19  IEU024      NEAR OPERAND COLUMN    3--UNDEFINED SYMBOL
   27  IEU024      NEAR OPERAND COLUMN    1--UNDEFINED SYMBOL
   28  IEU024      NEAR OPERAND COLUMN    5--UNDEFINED SYMBOL
   28  IEU085      NEAR OPERAND COLUMN    8--INVALID SYNTAX IN EXPRESSION
   37  IEU010      NEAR OPERAND COLUMN    7--INCORRECT SPECIFICATION OF REGISTER OR MASK FIELD
   38  IEU039      INVALID DELIMITER
   46  IEU066      UNDEFINED OR DUPLICATE KEYWORD OPERAND


    7 STATEMENTS FLAGGED IN THIS ASSEMBLY
   12 WAS HIGHEST SEVERITY CODE
*STATISTICS*     SOURCE RECORDS (SYSIN) =     50      SOURCE RECORDS (SYSLIB) =  2997
*OPTIONS IN EFFECT*   LIST, NODECK, LOAD, NORENT, XREF, NOTEST, ALGN, OS, NOTERM, LINECNT =  55
  164 PRINTED LINES



PRINT REPEATED   BY OPERATOR
```

Figure 18-1 (*Concluded*)

The statement number (2) refers to the statement number in the source listing. The error code may be found in the Assembly Language reference manual published by IBM. It is usually not necessary to reference this publication, the message itself tells the programmer what is wrong.

The message referencing statement 14 tells us that the symbol INCARD is not defined. The programmer may be confused when he examines this message because statement 14 is not one of the instructions in his program. Statement 14 is generated from the OPEN macro.

There is nothing wrong with the OPEN macro. The error is in the declarative macro describing INCARD (statement 46). The message in the diagnostic listing tells us that we have specified an undefined or duplicate keyword operand. The operand in error is the incorrectly spelled (and therefore undefined to the assembler which expects keyword operands to be spelled as specified) LRECL parameter. This error results in an error for the entire macro. And every reference (OPEN, GET, CLOSE) to this macro causes an error! When the LRECL entry is corrected, these macros will assemble correctly.

The message referencing statement 27 tells us that the label EXIT is undefined. The program defines EXIT in statement 30, but spells it differently. The statement

```
BE   EXIT
```

is not in error. The label in statement 30 must be corrected.

The next message tells us that we are using invalid syntax in statement 28. The instruction

```
AP   CTR,PL1'1'
```

should read

```
AP   CTR, = PL1'1'
```

Finally, the error in statement 37 occurs because the second operand specifies the *label* READRT, rather than the *address* of a register. The BR instruction is the extended mnemonic for the instruction

```
BCR   15,R2
```

an RR-type instruction. The second operand should specify a register, or we must code the RX-form of the BC instruction, using the extended mnemonic

```
B   READRT
```

Execution Time Errors

Two types of errors may be encountered during execution—logic errors and language errors. We discussed these errors in Chapter 7. Some of these errors are so severe that the program cannot continue executing. Processing stops and the programmer is given information about the status of the program at the time the error occurs. We say that an *interrupt* has occurred. The execution of the instructions has been interrupted. We will examine the interrupt system, and then see how we determine the reason for a particular interrupt.

The Interrupt System

We must reference the PSW (Program Status Word) to understand the concept of an interrupt. The PSW is a double word residing in the control section of the CPU. The format of the PSW is shown in Figure 18-2. The PSW controls program execution, the fields within the PSW giving the status of the program being executed.

Program Status Word

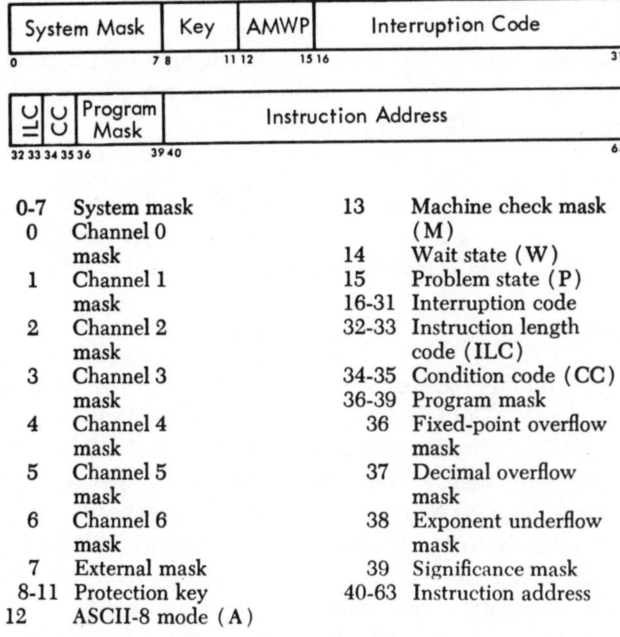

0-7	System mask	13	Machine check mask (M)
0	Channel 0 mask	14	Wait state (W)
1	Channel 1 mask	15	Problem state (P)
2	Channel 2 mask	16-31	Interruption code
3	Channel 3 mask	32-33	Instruction length code (ILC)
4	Channel 4 mask	34-35	Condition code (CC)
5	Channel 5 mask	36-39	Program mask
6	Channel 6 mask	36	Fixed-point overflow mask
7	External mask	37	Decimal overflow mask
8-11	Protection key	38	Exponent underflow mask
12	ASCII-8 mode (A)	39	Significance mask
		40-63	Instruction address

Figure 18-2.

The address portion of the PSW points to the next instruction to be executed. This address changes each time an instruction is fetched from main storage to the control section. We also can change the instruction address by changing the entire PSW. That is what happens when an interrupt occurs.

There are five types of interrupts. We are interested in the *program check interrupt*. A program check interrupt is caused by an error. The programmer has

Table 18-1 Five Classes of Interrupts

interrupt	cause
Supervisor Call	issuing an SVC instruction
I/O	completion of an I/O operation by the channel
External	external interrupt caused by the operator
Program Check	error in program
Machine Check	machine malfunction

made a mistake and the computer cannot continue processing the program. An interrupt occurs. The PSW controlling the execution of the problem program—our program—is replaced by a new PSW. This new PSW tells the control section to execute the instructions in a supervisor program. The supervisor (operating system program) analyzes the information in the problem program PSW (called the old PSW) and gives this information to the programmer. The operating system then goes on to the next program.

LOCATING ERRORS

In the case of a program check interrupt, the interrupt handling routine in the supervisor will print out or *dump* computer storage, giving the programmer all the information necessary to locate the cause of the interrupt.

Analyzing the Interrupt

When the programmer receives a storage dump, he (or she) first must locate the instruction in error. The PSW helps in this, The instruction address points to the instruction *after* the instruction causing the error. We use this address to locate the machine language instruction causing the interrupt. We then must locate the corresponding symbolic language instruction in our program, and find the reason for the interrupt. Was our data too big? Perhaps it was not in the correct format. Did we try to reference data outside main storage? We might have tried to move data into another programmer's area of storage. Many kinds of errors cause a program check interrupt.

Program Check Interrupts

There are fifteen types of program check interrupts. The cause of the interrupt appears in the interrupt code in the PSW (bits 16–31). Table 18-2 summarizes the interrupt codes resulting from a program check interrupt.

Operation Exception. An operation exception occurs when the instruction fetched by the control section contains an invalid op-code. If the programmer

Table 18-2 Interrupt Codes

interruption code	program interruption cause
1 00000001	Operation
2 00000010	Privileged operation
3 00000011	Execute
4 00000100	Protection
5 00000101	Addressing
6 00000110	Specification
7 00000111	Data
8 00001000	Fixed-point overflow
9 00001001	Fixed-point divide
10 00001010	Decimal overflow
11 00001011	Decimal divide
12 00001100	Exponent overflow
13 00001101	Exponent underflow
14 00001110	Significance
15 00001111	Floating-point divide

has coded his problem correctly, this should not occur. However, misplaced constants would force an operation exception. For example

```
        .
        .
        .
        L     3,FLDA
        L     4,FLDB
FLDA    DC    F'1'
FLDB    DC    F'2'
        AR    3,4
        .
        .
        .
```

The computer executes the two load instructions. The PSW points to the next sequential 'instruction'. The 'instruction' fetched actually would be FLDA, the fullword 00000001_{16}. The first 8 bytes should represent the op-code, but 00 is an invalid op-code. A program check interruption, operation exception, occurs.

Privileged Operations. Some assembly language instructions affect the PSW itself. It is possible to alter fields within the PSW. If the average programmer had access to these instructions, he might inadvertently alter the computer programming system. Thus certain instructions are said to be *privileged.* They may be executed only in the supervisory (bit 15 of the PSW set to 1) state. Our programs operate in the problem state (bit 15 of the PSW set to 0). An attempt to execute one of the privileged instructions from the problem state causes a program check interrupt, privileged operation.

Execute Exception. An attempt to execute another EX instruction causes an interrupt. The interrupt code of the PSW indicates that an execute exception has occurred.

Protection Exception. An attempt to move data into another programmer's partition of storage, or into the supervisor, results in a protection exception. Each program residing in main storage is protected by a code called a *protection key* (bits 8–11) in the PSW. The supervisor is protected by a key of zero or 0000_2. The key of the user program is assigned by the operating system. Let's assume that our program is operating in an area of storage protected by a key of twelve. Bits 8–11 of the PSW are set to 1100_2. This key will not change as the instruction address is incremented during normal program execution.

Let's examine an instruction which might cause a protection exception.

```
ST   3,0(0,4)
```

If register 4 contains the number 00000000_{16}, the effective address of the second operand is 000000_{16}. The instruction is attempting to store data from register 3 into the supervisor. But our program is protected by a key of 1100_2. The supervisor is protected by a key of 0000_2. A program check interruption, protection exception, occurs.

Addressing Exception. An addressing exception is caused when the effective address of a storage operand is outside the limits of the computer. Let's assume that the highest address available is $65{,}535_{10}$. Consider the same store instruction,

```
ST   3,0(0,4)
```

Let's assume that register 4 now contains 40404040_{16}. The effective address of the second operand is 404040_{16}, a number greater than $65{,}535_{10}$. The instruction is attempting to store data outside main storage. An addressing exception occurs.

Specification Exception. The failure to address data properly is the most common cause of the specification exception. A specification exception occurs in the instruction

```
DR   3,4
```

because the R1 operand does not specify an even–odd pair.

A specification exception occurs when the instruction

```
A   3,FULL
```

is executed if the storage operand FULL is not on a fullword boundary. This limitation applies only to the S/360.

Data Exception. The data exception is a common interrupt encountered by beginning programmers. In the code shown below, the programmer specifies the wrong data for FLDB. Notice that the last byte, a 40_{16}

```
            .
            .
            .
            PACK  FLDAP,FLDA
            PACK  FLDBP,FLDB
            AP    FLDAP,FLDBP
            .
            .
            .
     FLDA   DC    X'F1F2F3F4'
     FLDB   DC    X'F5F6F740'
```

is not a valid zoned constant. When FIDB is packed,

```
           F 5 F 6 F 7 4 0
fill ────►0 5 6 7 0 4
```

the result does not contain valid packed decimal data. There is no low-order zone.

The PACK instruction proceeds without interrupt. But the attempt to add packed non-numeric data causes a program check, data exception.

Fixed-Point Overflow. A fixed-point overflow occurs when the result of a binary addition or subtraction does not fit into 31 bits (the high-order bit of the register is reserved for the sign). A fixed-point overflow is determined by the difference between a carry into and a carry out of the sign position.

In the instruction,

```
AR    3,4
```

a fixed-point overflow occurs if register 3 contains $7FFFFFFF_{16}$ and register 4 contains $7FFFFFFF_{16}$. Consider the addition in binary

$$\begin{array}{r} 01111111\ \ 11111111\ \ 11111111\ \ 11111111_2 \\ 01111111\ \ 11111111\ \ 11111111\ \ 11111111_2 \\ \hline 11111111\ \ 11111111\ \ 11111111\ \ 11111110_2 \end{array}$$

carry into the sign position
no carry out of the sign position

An interrupt occurs only if bit 36 of the PSW is set to 1. This bit is called the fixed-point overflow mask. The programmer can control the setting of the bit. To suppress a program check on a fixed-point overflow, he must set the bit to 0. If he wishes an interrupt to occur on a fixed-point overflow, he must set the bit to 1. The following code ensures an overflow:

```
         BALR   12,0
         USING  *,12
         OR     12,MASK
         SPM    12,0
         .
         .
         .
MASK     DC     X'08000000'
```

The BALR instruction actually loads bits 32–63 of the PSW into the R1 operand. We are interested in bit 36. The OR instruction turns this bit on.

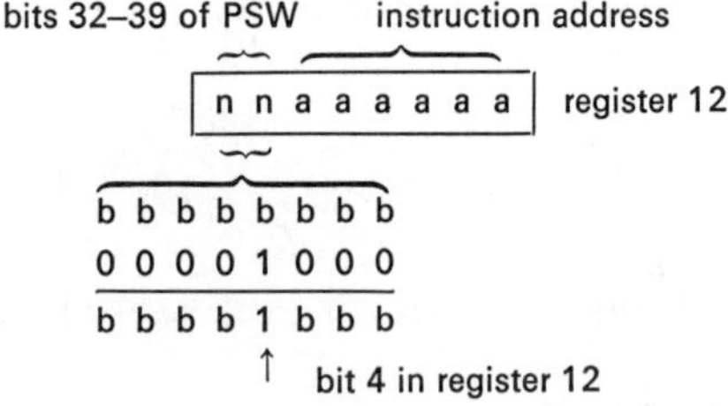

The Set Program Mask instruction (SPM) is one of the few nonprivileged instructions that can be used to alter the current PSW. The instruction stores bits 2–7 of the R1 operand into positions 34–39 of the PSW. The second operand is ignored.

We have set bit 4 in register 12 to 1. When we execute the SPM instruction, bits 2–7 of register 12 are stored in bits 34–39 of the PSW.

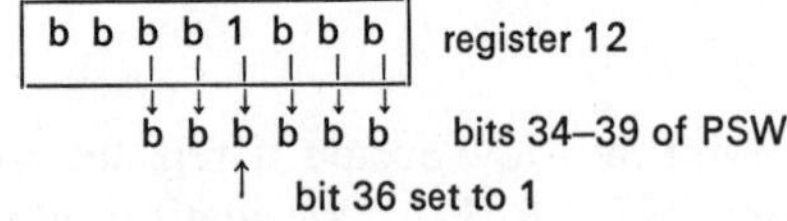

The PSW is now masked to give an interrupt when a fixed-point overflow occurs.

Fixed-Point Divide. A fixed-point divide occurs when the quotient resulting from a binary division is too large to be expressed in the R1 operand. The CVB instruction also generates a fixed-point divide exception if the binary result cannot be expressed in a register.

Decimal Overflow. A decimal overflow occurs when the result of a decimal AP or SP instruction does not fit in the S1 location. For example

```
generated
code
                          .
                          .
                          .
                          AP   FLDAP,FLDBP
                          .
                          .
                          .
999C          FLDAP   DC   PL2'999'
999C          FLDBP   DC   PL2'999'
```

The result of this arithmetic operation is $01998C_{16}$. The answer does not fit into a 2-byte field (FLDAP is the first operand and has a length attribute of 2 bytes). A decimal overflow occurs. *Note*: the programmer can use bit 37 of the PSW to prevent a decimal overflow.

Decimal Divide. A decimal divide exception occurs when the quotient in the DP instruction is too large to be placed in the first operand.

Additional Interrupts. The remaining interrupts involve floating-point operations and will not be discussed here.

ANALYZING STORAGE LISTINGS

We have discussed the causes of the program check interrupt. We now shall examine the computer output produced when the interrupt occurs. Figure 18-3 shows the complete OS/370 and DOS listings obtained from a program check interruption.

Discussion of the Listing

The listing returned to the programmer contains job control statements, operating system messages, the source listing, information from the linkage editor, and a printout (dump) of computer storage.

The source listing contains both the user-submitted source code, and the generated machine code. We are most interested in the generated machine code, and how to locate the instruction causing the interrupt.

Analyzing the Dump. The supervisor supplies the programmer with the contents of the registers at the time of the interrupt, and a dump of main storage. The information contained in the PSW points us to the instruction causing the interrupt. But before we locate the instruction in storage, let's examine the format of the printout.

```
//CH16AOKK JOB (GG38,4637,,,,3),'BB',CLASS=F                                        JOB 263
// EXEC ASMFCLG
XXASM      EXEC  PGM=IEUASM,PARM='LOAD,NODECK',REGION=50K,ROLL=(NO,YES)
XXSYSLIB DD      DSNAME=SYS1.MACLIB,DISP=SHR                                  IEUD  00040016
XXSYSUT1   DD    DSNAME=&SYSUT1,UNIT=SYSSQ,SPACE=(1700,(400,50))
XXSYSUT2   DD    DSNAME=&SYSUT2,UNIT=SYSSQ,SPACE=(1700,(400,50))
XXSYSUT3   DD    DSNAME=&SYSUT3,SPACE=(1700,(400,50)),UNIT=SYSSQ
XXSYSPRINT DD    SYSOUT=A
XXSYSGO    DD    DSNAME=&LOADSET,UNIT=SYSSQ,SPACE=(80,(200,50)),
XX               DISP=(MOD,PASS)
//ASM.SYSIN DD *
IEF236I ALLOC. FOR CH16AOKK ASM
IEF237I 154   ALLOCATED TO SYSLIB
IEF237I 150   ALLOCATED TO SYSUT1
IEF237I 151   ALLOCATED TO SYSUT2
IEF237I 150   ALLOCATED TO SYSUT3
IEF237I 434   ALLOCATED TO SYSPRINT
IEF237I 151   ALLOCATED TO SYSGO
IEF237I 501   ALLOCATED TO SYSIN
IEF142I - STEP WAS EXECUTED - COND CODE 0000
IEF285I   SYS1.MACLIB                                     KEPT
IEF285I   VOL SER NOS= SYSRES.
IEF285I   SYS76169.T170717.RV000.CH16AOKK.SYSUT1          DELETED
IEF285I   VOL SER NOS= ACC002.
IEF285I   SYS76169.T170717.RV000.CH16AOKK.SYSUT2          DELETED
IEF285I   VOL SER NOS= ACC003.
IEF285I   SYS76169.T170717.RV000.CH16AOKK.SYSUT3          DELETED
IEF285I   VOL SER NOS= ACC002.
IEF285I   SYS76169.T170717.RV000.CH16AOKK.LOADSET         PASSED
IEF285I   VOL SER NOS= ACC003.
IEF373I STEP /ASM     / START 76169.1738
IEF374I STEP /ASM     / STOP  76169.1739 CPU    0MIN 04.24SEC MAIN 150K LCS    OK
IEFACTAI -                                            1.82 RESIDENT MIN          RC =      0 <-----<<
IEFACTBI - I/O UTILIZATION FOR STEP ASM       WAS -
IEFACTCI -         -DEVICE TYPE-    -EXCP COUNT-
IEFACTDI -          DASD                   122
IEFACTDI -          TAPE                     0
IEFACTDI -          UNIT RECORD             61
IEFACTDI -          OTHER                    0
IEFACTDI -          -----------    -----------
IEFACTDI -          TOTAL                  183
XXLKED     EXEC  PGM=IEWL,PARM='LIST,LET',COND=(9,LT,ASM),REGION=150K,
XX               ROLL=(NO,YES)
XXSYSLIN   DD    DSNAME=&LOADSET,DISP=(OLD,DELETE)
XX         DD    DDNAME=SYSIN
XXSYSLMOD  DD    DSNAME=&GOSET(GO),UNIT=SYSDA,
XX               SPACE=(1024,(50,20,1)),DISP=(MOD,PASS)
XXSYSUT1   DD    DSNAME=&SYSUT1,UNIT=SYSDA,SPACE=(1024,(50,20))
XXSYSPRINT DD    SYSOUT=A
IEF236I ALLOC. FOR CH16AOKK LKED
IEF237I 151   ALLOCATED TO SYSLIN
IEF237I 150   ALLOCATED TO SYSLMOD
IEF237I 150   ALLOCATED TO SYSUT1
IEF237I 434   ALLOCATED TO SYSPRINT
IEF142I - STEP WAS EXECUTED - COND CODE 0000
IEF285I   SYS76169.T170717.RV000.CH16AOKK.LOADSET         DELETED
IEF285I   VOL SER NOS= ACC003.
IEF285I   SYS76169.T170717.RV000.CH16AOKK.GOSET           PASSED
IEF285I   VOL SER NOS= ACC002.
IEF285I   SYS76169.T170717.RV000.CH16AOKK.SYSUT1          DELETED
IEF285I   VOL SER NOS= ACC002.
```

Job control statements

Job control listing

Figure 18-3.

```
IEF373I STEP /LKED     / START 76169.1739
IEF374I STEP /LKED     / STOP  76169.1740 CPU    0MIN 00.77SEC MAIN 136K LCS    OK
IEFACTAI -                                               0.60 RESIDENT MIN         RC =      0  <-----<<
IEFACTBI - I/O UTILIZATION FOR STEP LKED      WAS -
IEFACTCI -         -DEVICE TYPE-    -EXCP COUNT-
IEFACTDI -          DASD                      11
IEFACTDI -          TAPE                       0
IEFACTDI -          UNIT RECORD                5
IEFACTDI -          OTHER                      0
IEFACTDI -          -----------    -----------
IEFACTDI -          TOTAL                     16
XXGO         EXEC  PGM=*.LKED.SYSLMOD,COND=((8,LT,ASM),(4,LT,LKED)),
XX           ROLL=(NO,YES)
//GO.SYSUDUMP DD SYSOUT=A
//
IEF236I ALLOC. FOR CH16AOKK GO
IEF237I 150    ALLOCATED TO PGM=*.DD
IEF237I 436    ALLOCATED TO SYSUDUMP
COMPLETION CODE - SYSTEM=0C8  USER=0000
IEF285I    SYS76169.T170717.RV000.CH16AOKK.GOSET          PASSED
IEF285I    VOL SER NOS= ACC002.
IEF373I STEP /GO       / START 76169.1740
IEF374I STEP /GO       / STOP  76169.1741 CPU    0MIN 01.76SEC MAIN   8K LCS    OK
IEFACTAI -                                               0.77 RESIDENT MIN         RC = ABEND  <-----<<
IEFACTBI - I/O UTILIZATION FOR STEP GO        WAS -
IEFACTCI -         -DEVICE TYPE-    -EXCP COUNT-
IEFACTDI -          DASD                       0
IEFACTDI -          TAPE                       0
IEFACTDI -          UNIT RECORD              232
IEFACTDI -          OTHER                      0
IEFACTDI -          -----------    -----------
IEFACTDI -          TOTAL                    232
IEF285I    SYS76169.T170717.RV000.CH16AOKK.GOSET          DELETED
IEF285I    VOL SER NOS= ACC002.
IEF375I   JOB /CH16AOKK/ START 76169.1738
IEF376I   JOB /CH16AOKK/ STOP  76169.1741 CPU    0MIN 06.77SEC
IEFACTBI - I/O UTILIZATION FOR THE JOB CH16AOKK WAS -
IEFACTCI -         -DEVICE TYPE-    -EXCP COUNT-
IEFACTDI -          DASD                     133
IEFACTDI -          TAPE                       0
IEFACTDI -          UNIT RECORD              298
IEFACTDI -          OTHER                      0
IEFACTDI -          -----------    -----------
IEFACTDI -          TOTAL                    431

IEFACTFI - ACCOUNT GG384637 HAS USED      $4.25 TO DATE, AND HAS     $20.75 REMAINING  $ $ $ $
```

Indicates fixed-point overflow (9)

Figure 18-3 (*Continued*)

Assembler listing

```
                                                                              PAGE    1
  LOC  OBJECT CODE    ADDR1 ADDR2  STMT   SOURCE STATEMENT                F04MAR74   6/17/76

                                     1 * FIXED POINT OVERFLOW ON AR
000000                               2          START 0
                                     3          PRINT NOGEN
                                     4 BEGIN    SAVE  (14,12)               SAVE REGISTERS
000004 05C0                          7          BALR  12,0                  LOAD BASE
000006                               8          USING *,12                  ADDRESSABILITY
000006 56C0 C016          0001C      9          O     12,MASK               SET OFLO BITS ON
00000A 04C0                         10          SPM   12                    SET MASK IN PSW TO
                                    11 *                                    ALLOW INTERRUPT
00000C 5830 C01A          00020     12          L     3,DATA3               LOAD DATA
000010 5840 C01E          00024     13          L     4,DATA4               LOAD DATA
000014 1A34                         14          AR    3,4                   ADD REGISTERS
                                    15          RETURN (14,12)              RETURN
                                    18 *
                                    19 * DATA AREAS
                                    20 *
00001C                              21          DS    0F                    ALIGN AT FULLWORD
00001C 0C000000                     22 MASK     DC    XL4'0C000000'
000020 7FFFFFFF                     23 DATA3    DC    XL4'7FFFFFFF'
000024 7FFFFFFF                     24 DATA4    DC    XL4'7FFFFFFF'
000000                              25          END   BEGIN
```

Figure 18-3 (*Continued*)

```
JOB CH16AOKK          STEP GO           TIME 174050   DATE 76169    Sysodump listing                PAGE 0001

COMPLETION CODE       SYSTEM = 0CB ——— From interrupt code in PSW - fixed overflow (9)

PSW AT ENTRY TO ABEND  FF85000D 7C1AE7EE ——— Address of instruction after instruction in error

TCB  02AF38  RBP   000142D0  PIE     CC000000  DEB  0002B134  TIO 0002B190  CMP    800C8000  TRN  00000000
             MSS   02031218  PK-FLG  80852400  FLG  00007F7B  LLS 00018CD0  JLB    00000000  JPQ  00016B08
             FSA   011D2F68  TCB     C0000000  TME  00000000  JST 0002AF38  NTC    00000000  OTC  0002D0A0
             LTC   CC000000  IQE     00C00000  ECB  0002AAB4  TSF 20000000  D-PQE  000313D0  SQS  0002A3B0
             NSTAE C0000000  TCT     8002ADE0  USEP 00000000  DAR 00000000  RESV   00000000  JSCB 8702E758
             RESV  00000000  IOB     CCC00000

ACTIVE RBS

PRB  015870  RESV    00000000   APSW   7C1AE7EE   WC-SZ-STAB 0C040082   FL-CDE 00016FD0   PSW FF85000D 7C1AE7EE
             C/TTR   00000000   WT-LNK 0002AF38

SVRB 0145A0  TAB-LN  00380220   APSW   F9F0F1C3   WC-SZ-STAB 0012D002   TQN    00000000   PSW 00040033 500089BA
             Q/TTR   00005212   WT-LNK 00015870
             RG 0-7   FD000008   001D2FF8   0002CC90   FFFFFFFE   7FFFFFFF   0002D0A0   0002B1D4   0002D6A0
             RG 8-15  0002AA90   0002ADE0   0002AAB8   00000000   4C1AE7DE   001D2F68   00010BDA   011AE7D8
             EXTSA    000021BE   8F1D2F10   C0000000   00000000   FF030000   0001461C   00014624   E2E8E2C9
                      C5C1F0F1   C9C5C138   C1C2C5D5   C4F90C80

SVRB 0142D0  TAB-LN  007803D8   APSW   F1F0F5C1   WC-SZ-STAB 0012D002   TQN    00000000   PSW FF04000C 401D27A6
             C/TTR   00005321   WT-LNK 000145A0
             RG 0-7   001058B0   00014600   800088D2   0000AA50   0002AF38   000145A0   0402AF38   000145A0
             RG 8-15  0002AF38   4000881A   0002AF38   8F1D2F10   0002B1C0   00014624   400085DC   00000000
             EXTSA    E2E8E2C9   C5C1F0F1   C0204770   C0161301   00000001   C0181801   4110C022   0A2207FE
                      000CE2E3   C1C54040   40404040   404007FE

LOAD LIST

        NE 00018C98   RSP-CDE 02016B08      NE 00018CF8   RSP-CDE 01015E00      NE 00018CE8   RSP-CDE 01015E18
        NE C0018C70   RSP-CDE 01015D88      NE 00000000   RSP-CDE 01015DA0

CDE                                                                         (8)

     016FD0      ATR1 0B   NCDE 000000   ROC-RB 00015870   NM GO         USE 01   EPA 1AE7D8   ATR2 20   XL/MJ 017DF0
     016B08      ATR1 30   NCDE 016FD0   ROC-RB 00000000   NM IGC0A05A   USE 02   EPA 1D2058   ATR2 28   XL/MJ 017D90
     015E00      ATR1 B0   NCDE 015DE8   ROC-RB 00000000   NM IGG019CF   USE 02   EPA 27C3F0   ATR2 20   XL/MJ 017470   OS Control
     015E18      ATR1 B0   NCDE 015E00   ROC-RB 00000000   NM IGG019CL   USE 02   EPA 27E818   ATR2 20   XL/MJ 017480   Blocks
     015D88      ATR1 B1   NCDE 015D70   ROC-RB 00000000   NM IGG019BA   USE 02   EPA 27D018   ATR2 28   XL/MJ 017420
     015DA0      ATR1 B0   NCDE 015D88   ROC-RB 00000000   NM IGG019BB   USE 02   EPA 27C988   ATR2 20   XL/MJ 017430

XL                                               LN         ADR        LN         ADR        LN         ADR

     017DF0   SZ C0000010   NO 0C000001      80000028   001AE7D8
     017D90   SZ C0000010   NO 00000001      800007A8   001D2058
```

Figure 18-3 *(Continued)*

```
              R1   001D2FF8    R2   0002CC90    R3   5C02AAB8    R4   0002CE38    R5   0002D0A0    R6   0002B1D4
              R7   0002D6A0    R8   0002AA90    R9   0002ADE0    R10  0002AAB8    R11  00000000    R12  4027DBD2

INTERRUPT AT 1AE7EE

PROCEEDING BACK VIA REG 13

GO        WAS ENTERED VIA LINK

SA    1D2F68  WD1  CC000000   HSA  00000000   LSA  00000000   RET  00010BDA   EPA  011AE7D8   R0   FD000008
              R1   001D2FF8   R2   0002CC90   R3   5C02AAB8   R4   0002CE38   R5   0002D0A0   R6   0002B1D4
              R7   0002D6A0   R8   0002AA90   R9   0002ADE0   R10  0002AAB8   R11  00000000   R12  4027DBD2

REGS AT ENTRY TO ABEND

     FLTR 0-6       404040404040007E        0C69F00000177061               1A3660E09976169F      0000000000000000

     REGS 0-7       FD000008   001D2FF8   0002CC90   FFFFFFFE              7FFFFFFF   0002D0A0   0002B1D4   0002D6A0
     REGS 8-15      0002AA90   0002ADE0   0002AAB8   00000000              4C1AE7DE   001D2F68   00010BDA   011AE7D8

LOAD MODULE    GO

1AE7C0                                                               90ECD00C 05C056C0   *.......... F.....D.............*
1AE7E0     C01604C0 5830C01A 5840C01F 1A3498EC      D000C07FE 0C000000 7FFFFFFF 7FFFFFFF   *........ ....................*

LOAD MODULE    IGC0A05A

1C2040                                                               4180D099 18114313   *...............................*
1D2060     00001A81 41330001 95FF3000 47806068      1BEE1BFF 18001B11 43E30000 43030001   *......................T......*
1D2C8C     8CFCC004 88F0001C 8C000004 8810001C      1A2044F0 60701A1E 41818001 44F06076   *.....0....................0..*
1C20A0     F384D069 0069DC07 D06962C6 41FFF001      44F0607C 47F066F8 413E3003 47F06010   *3..........F..0..0....0.8.....0..*
1D20C0     41330001 47F060E2 D2008000 30020200      D0692000 D2008000 D0695050 D08C5000   *......0.SK.....K.....K.........*
1C20F0     D12094FC D1235800 D1201A10 5800D120      41110003 5010D064 94FCD067 D703D06C   *J...J...J......J.............P...*
1C2100     D06C1810 54006290 19014780 6CBC1B10      4010D06C 5810D064 4A10D06C 1B005D00   *...............................*
1D2120     668C4000 D06A1211 4770611C 4810D06A      12114770 60E85850 D08C5860 D12407F5   *.. ...............Y.......J..5*
1C2140     4120D121 45B06236 5820D120 413062C4      48A0D06A 48A0D06C 88A00002 45B0623E   *...J........J....D..............*
1D2160     46AC61C4 9640D112 455062DA 94BFD112      47F060DE 18A15810 D1204B10 D06C5010   *..... J........J...0.......J.......*
1D2180     D0704120 DC714580 62364810 DC6C8810      00011A31 5820D120 45B0623E 5020D120   *.......................J.......J.*
1C21A0     9640D112 455062DA 94BFD112 4810D06C      12114770 61984700 615E4110 0001191A   *. J........J.....................*
1D21C0     47B061A6 18125B10 6680051F 1C002000      477061A6 4810D06E 41110001 4010D06E   *...........N.....................*
1C21E0     41220020 5020D120 46A0615E 47F061B0      1B114010 D06C46A0 611E47F0 60D44810   *.........J.......0..........0.M..*
1C2200     D06E1211 4780619E 5810D120 4800D06E      89C00005 18105010 D0704120 D0714810   *...........J.....................*
1C2220     D06EC610 12114770 62020203 D09F629D      41306294 45B0623E D20DD0AA 62A29640   *..........K...............K...... *
1D2240     D1124550 62DA948F D1120701 DC6ED06E      12A44780 60D447F0 619ED204 D09F629D   *J.......J.P...........M.0..K.....*
1C2260     41306297 45B0623E 9260D0A8 5810D120      58106680 5010D070 4120D071 4130629A   *...........J.....................*
1C2280     45B0623E D20DD082 62A247F0 61E64130      62B047F0 65744180 D09995FF 30004780   *....K.......0.W.....0...........*
1C22A0     627C1800 43030000 18114313 0C011480      44106284 F3840070 D070DC07 D07062C6   *....................3...........F*
1C22C0     41111001 4410628A 41330002 41220004      47F0623E 41330001 07FBD078 D200D070   *..K...............0.........K....*
1C22E0     20C0D200 8C00D070 FFFFFFE0 0BC2FF0C      02FF1302 FFD3C9D5 C5E240E2 C1D4C540   *..K.................LINES SAME *
1D2300     C1E240C1 C2D6E5C5 0002FF09 0312031B      03240330 03390342 034B03FF 0903FF12   *AS ABOVE.........................*
1C2320     03FF1B03 FF2403FF 3003FF39 03FF4203      FFC098E0 D08012EE 47806310 D27CF000   *..............................K.0.*
1D2340     DC9441FF 007D50F0 D084411F 0C7D1910      47D06332 13FF40F0 D090D203 E000D090   *........0................ 0..K.....*
```


Figure 18-3 (*Continued*)

```
// JOB A                                                          00.21.44
// OPTION LINK
// EXEC ASSEMBLY
```

Listing of DOS job control

```
                                      EXTERNAL SYMBOL DICTIONARY                                   PAGE    1

SYMBOL    TYPE ID  ADDR  LENGTH LD ID

          PC  01 000000 000028
```

ESD table produced by assembler

```
                                                                                                   PAGE    1

LOC   OBJECT CODE    ADDR1 ADDR2  STMT   SOURCE STATEMENT                                FDOS CL3-9 06/04/74

                                     1 * FIXED POINT OVERFLOW ON AR
                                     2          PRINT NOGEN
000000                               3          START 0
                                     4 BEGIN    SAVE (14,12)                         SAVE REGISTERS
000004 05C0                          7          BALR 12,0                            LOAD BASE
000006                               8          USING *,12                           ADDRESSABILITY
000006 56C0 C016          0001C      9          O     12,MASK                        SET OFLO BITS ON
00000A 04C0                         10          SPM   12                             SET MASK IN PSW TO
                                    11 *                                             ALLOW INTERRUPT
00000C 5830 C01E          00024     12          L     3,DATA3                        LOAD DATA
000010 5840 C01A          00020     13          L     4,DATA4                        LOAD DATA
000014 1A34                         14          AR    3,4                            ADD REGISTERS
                                    15          RETURN (14,12)                       RETURN
                                    19 *
                                    20 * DATA AREAS
                                    21 *
00001C                              22          DS    0F                             ALIGN AT FULLWORD
00001C 0C000000                     23 MASK     DC    XL4'0C000000'
000020 7FFFFFFF                     24 DATA4    DC    XL4'7FFFFFFF'
000024 7FFFFFFF                     25 DATA3    DC    XL4'7FFFFFFF'
000000                              26          END   BEGIN
```

Source statement listing

```
                                      CROSS-REFERENCE                                              PAGE    1

SYMBOL    LEN   VALUE   DEFN     REFERENCES                                                     06/04/74

BEGIN    00004 000000 00006    0026
DATA3    00004 000024 00025    0012
DATA4    00004 000020 00024    0013
MASK     00004 00001C 00023    0009


NO STATEMENTS FLAGGED IN THIS ASSEMBLY
```

Cross reference table

Figure 18-3 *(Continued)*

```
// EXEC LNKEDT
```

Job control card

```
JOB  A        06/04/74   DISK LINKAGE EDITOR DIAGNOSTIC OF INPUT

ACTION TAKEN  MAP
LIST   ENTRY
```

Linkage editor listing

```
06/04/74   PHASE    XFR-AD  LOCORE  HICORE  DSK-AD   ESD TYPE  LABEL    LCADED  REL-FR

           PHASE***  004000  004000  004027  56 11 2  CSECT              004000  004000
```

(8) Load address or relocation-factor

Linkage editor listing

```
// EXEC
```

Job control card

```
0S03I PROGRAM CHECK INTERRUPTION - HEX LOCATION 004014 - CONDITION CODE 3 - FIXEC-POINT OVERFLOW EXCEPTION
0S00I JOB A       CANCELED
```

(9)

(7) Address of instruction causing error

Figure 18-3 (*Continued*)

```
        A                  06/04/74          Invalid result in R3           00.22.43            PAGE   1

GR 0-7   00004000 00004000 0001F7FF FFFFFFFE   7FFFFFFF FFFFFF7C 00004000 00003F98  (2) General registers
GR 8-F   00005B0A 0A0407F1 00004010 00004010   4C004006 00005FD8 000002D0 0000007B
FP REG   00000000 00000000 00000000 00000000   00000000 00000000 00000000 00000000  (1) Floating-point registers
COMREG   BG ADDR IS 0002D0

000000   00000000 00000000 00000000 00000000   00000000 000002D0 FF050000 00000000   ................ ................
000020   FF050007 40003B66 FF150008 7C004016   5B5BC2C5 D6D1F440 FF05000E 80004C28   .... .......'. . $$BEOJ4 ......).
000040   00003C88 08000000 00003C78 00000000   F8A71400 00FEE624 00040000 0F001EEA   ................ 8.....W.........
000060   00040000 000003FE 00040000 00001EAA   00000000 00000E1C 00040000 000003A4   ................ ................
000080   00000000 00000000 00000000 00000003   00050003 06B006B0 06B041BB 00734570   ................ ................
0000A0   0168940F BEAB41A0 CF1C4570 0DEA18A8   419001A8 92FFB583 458000EA 9200B583   ................ ................
0000C0   47F0BCC0 06B006B0 06B006B0 06B006B0   06B006B0 06B006B0 06B041BB 001741BB   .0.............. ................
0000E0   00504570 01684180 01A89640 A0019120   A00C4710 00FA9260 A0019604 A00F95E2   .&......... .... ......-........S
000100   A0024780 B0EC95C1 A0024780 B0EC9561   A0024780 01229104 A0004780 01229203   .......A......./ ................
000120   008F9281 A0004BA0 032A487A CE0C49A0   036C41AA CF0C0778 94F9703B D7017058   ................ ..........9..P...
000140   70589283 A00095FF B5829200 B5820788   9680A001 440004FC 4780BBA0 947FA001   ................ ................
000160   92F0BBBD 47F0BBA0 42B000F7 58B002B8   9180A000 07175890 A0044880 02445000   .0...0.....7.... ...............&.
000180   902C6000 90586020 90606040 90686060   9070D21B 90100298 D2079008 80009680   ..-....-..-- ..-- ..K.....K.......
0001A0   A00007F7 45700170 D20EB562 B57258E0   02C4DC0E B562CF0C 1BAADD0F B562000C   ...7.....K...... .D..............
0001C0   43A10010 42A0036F 4AA0034C D20002FF   A00D5AA0 03644400 A0045890 A0044220   ............)K..... ................
0001E0   A0009140 A0014710 CB96D207 02989008   9560036F 47200270 68009058 68209060   ... .......K..... .-..............-
000200   68409068 68609070 4BA0032A 41AACE0C   D2010016 A0009898 90108200 02984400   . ...-........... K...............
000220   A0049500 A0014780 02364400 04FC4780   023647F0 01A45890 A0049818 9030989F   ................ ...0............
000240   02988200 00389284 CF6CD207 0298B698   9890B6A0 82000298 9680A000 41100030   ...........K.... ................
000260   47F0BAF0 96030039 96010038 82000038   92FF0298 96050299 440004FC 478001F8   .0.0............ ................8
000280   D3000299 02FF47F0 01F8615C 40615040   44F00000 00000000 FF050007 40003B66   L......0.8/* /& .0.......... ...
0002A0   00001000 00002000 00003000 00004000   000038B0 8000197A 00001000 00002000   ............... . ................
0002C0   00003000 00004000 30420000 00000000   F0F661F0 F461F7F4 40004000 00000000   ...... ......... 06/04/74 . .....
0002E0   00000000 00000000 C1404040 40404040   0001F7FF 00004027 00004027 00000010   ........A....... ..7... ... .....
000300   0003FFFF FC777CD0 A8A07CD0 0097319D   31A43295 32963310 34403444 344838F0   ......'...'..... ........ ......0
000320   F6F0F4F7 F4F1F5F5 00002F0C 0000001E   139014CA 157C15F4 15FC0010 31240010   60474155........ .....'.4........
000340   5B5BC2D6 0007000A 020016E0 2E0C0000   00000000 02D00080 0000035C 00000000   $$BO............ ...........*....
000360   0000357C 00000100 00001614 00100010   0000317E 00001572 00000000 00000000   ...'............ ................
000380   00000000 00000000 00000000 00000000   00000000 00000000 00003028 00003C78   ................ ................
0003A0   000037D4 92380245 909F0298 98BE02B8   41900A14 48A0036E 4AA0032A 9180A000   ...M............ ................
0003C0   471003D2 58B0A004 9018B030 98BE02B8   07F99601 A00098BE 02B895FF A00F0789   ...K............ .9..............
0003E0   5000B6BC 48E00244 D207B698 E00058E0   02C494FD B699D21B B6A00298 07F9909F   &.......K....... .D....K.......9..
000400   02989220 02454590 03B44190 021E9500   00234780 04E89535 002347B0 00CE4860   ................ .....Y..........-
000420   00221A66 487002C8 48667000 07F6181F   1B664121 000F4570 B2304860 B4D81B22   .......H.....6.. ...........-.Q..
000440   43201007 4130003D 1B234740 04584130   003D1B23 47B0045A 1A234220 05F54320   ........... .... ............5..
000460   1007950B 10074780 049847F0 055E4720   00DA4230 05F54320 036E4322 CE0F1A23   ...........0.... .....5..........
000480   95081007 47800490 950B1007 47F0055A   487002FE 47F0049E 1B774370 BA648870   ..............0... .....0..........
0004A0   00031177 4337CE0C 47F0056A 472000D8   96801002 960C1004 07F91858 41430002   ..............0.....Q ..........9.......
0004C0   43540000 41455000 1A444A40 B4D095FF   40004770 04C04284 000007F9 95FF05B7   .......&...... .... ..........9......
0004E0   07891B00 5000B6BC 95FF05B7 4780BBEA   4860036E 9560036F 4780042E D502A005   ....&............ .-...-........N...
000500   03494770 05144111 00004910 B2AE47B0   05141B66 4121000F 4570B230 D5021009   ................ ...............N...
000520   03014780 00D64400 06145870 039CD502   70010301 47B00D6 1B334330 10079501   .....0.........N. ........0.........
000540   10064770 046E92FF 05F5D200 0553A00D   4123000B D5001007 A00E47B0 00DA4182   ..........5K..... ....N...........
000560   20004870 031C4338 7000D403 1002CF78   4930B2AC 47B004AC 89300003 4A300310   ..........M..... ................
000580   91F03004 4780C070 D5010022 C5CC4780   C356D501 B4C8B4D6 472005B4 4930B4F0   .0.......N...E... C.N..H.O........0
0005A0   477005B4 950F0023 478005B4 91103006   4780BBEA 41800000 41488000 1A444A40   ................ ...............
0005C0   B4D01858 4A50033C D20005B7 40005010   400092FF 40004220 50004260 505A4260   .....&..K....&. ... ...&..-&..-
0005E0   501E91F0 501E4780 05F44A60 034CD200   501E600D 9203503C 91F03004 4780C090   &..0&.....4.-.)K. &.-....&..0......
```

(3) Hexadecimal dump of storage

(4) Address

(5) Data in storage - one hexadecimal digit represents four bits

(6) Interpretation of storage

Figure 18-3 (*Continued*)

```
        A                 06/04/74                                                                                    PAGE   9

0036E0  D5D640D5 C1D4C540 0003FFFF 00003F10   00003F10 00000030 0003FFFF FC777CD0     NO NAME .........  ...............'.
003700  80007C50 0097319D 31A43295 32963310   34403444 344838F0 F6F0F4F7 F4F1F5F5     ..'&.............  . .....060474155
003720  00002F0C 0000001E 145014CA 157C15F4   15FC0010 31240030 00000000 00000000     ..........&...'.4  ................
003740  00000000 2E0C0000 00000000 02D00080   00003794 00000000 0000357C 00000100     ................   ...........'....
003760  00001614 00200020 0000317E 00001572   00000000 00000000 00000000 00000000     ................   ................
003780  00000000 00000000 00000000 00000000   00003031 00000000 0000357C 00000100     ................   ...........'....
0037A0  00001614 00300030 0000317E 00001572   00000000 00000000 00000000 00000000     ................   ................
0037C0  00000000 00000000 00000000 00000000   0000303A 00000200 FF000000 00FF0000     ................   ................
0037E0  0000FF00 000000FF 00000000 FF000000   00FF0000 0000FF00 000000FF 00000000     ................   ................
003800  FF000000 00FF0000 0000FF00 000000FF   00000000 FF000000 00FF0000 0000FF00     ................   ................
003820  000000FF FF000000 00000000 00000000   00000000 00000000 00000000 00000000     ................   ................
003840  00000000 --SAME--                                                             ....
0038A0  00000000 00000000 00000000 00000000                                           ................

LBLTYP  HEX LENGTH IS 0000
--BG--
003F80                    D5D640D5 C1D4C540   FF150008 7C004016 0A0407F1 00004010             NO NAME    ....'. ....1.. .
003FA0  00004010 4C004006 00005FD8 000002D0   0000007B 00004000 00004000 0001F7FF     .. .). ....Q.....  ...... ... ...7.
003FC0  FFFFFFFE 7FFFFFFF FFFFFF7C 00004000   00003F98 00005B0A 00000000 0005F929     ............'.. .  .......$.......9.
003FE0  00000000 --SAME--                                                             ....
004000  90ECD00C 05C056C0 C01604C0 5830C01E   5840C01A 1A3498EC D00C07FE 0C000000     ................   . ..............
004020  7FFFFFFF 7FFFFFFF 00000000 00000000   00000000 00000000 00000000 00000000     ................   ................
004040  00000000 --SAME--                                                             ....
005FE0  00000000 000002D0 0000007B 00004000   00004000 0001F7FF 00004000 0001F784     ............... .  .. ...7... ...7.
006000  FFFFFF7C 00004000 00003F98 00005B0A   0A0407F1 00004010 00004010 00004FD8     ...'.. ........$.  ...1.. ... ....Q
006020  00000000 --SAME--                                                             ....
01F7E0  00000000 00000000 00000000 00000000   00000000 00000000 00000000 00000000     ................   ................
```

Data 4   Data 3

⑦ Instruction in error at 004014

Figure 18-3 (*Concluded*)

We are given the contents of the four double word floating-point registers (1), the sixteen general purpose registers (2), and a hexadecimal listing of the contents of main storage (3). The leftmost column (4) represents main storage addresses. The data (5) is presented in hexadecimal—each grouping represents a fullword of data (8 hexadecimal digits in a word). The information to the right is an attempt to interpret the storage dump (6). That is, to print the contents of storage. Since much of main storage contains machine language instructions, an attempt to interpret fails and the hexadecimal digits are replaced by a period (.). Any valid graphic is printed—notice the letters P and J in the OS/370 listing. Can you locate the hexadecimal representation of these letters in storage? The letter P appeared at location $1D2CFC_{16}$ and the letter J at location $1D213C_{16}$. Remember that the addresses are given in hexadecimal. Now look at the DOS listing. The code at location 000030_{16} is interpreted as $$BEOJ4. This is the name of one of the routines used by DOS to terminate a job.

Now let's see what information this listing can supply us regarding the cause of the program check. The address in the PSW points to the instruction *after* our problem. The instruction following the error is found at location $1AE7EE_{16}$ in the OS listing. Now we must find the address of the *previous* instruction. S/370 instructions are one, two, or three halfwords in length. Bits 32–33 of the PSW provide the instruction length code (ILC). Bits 32–33 are contained in the second half of the PSW. We find bits 32–33 contain 01_2. To determine this we look at the first byte in the second half of the PSW

```
01110000
└→bits 32–33
```

The ILC of 01_2 tells us that the instruction in error contained one halfword. We back up 2 bytes of storage to find the instruction in error at location $1AE7EC_{16}$(7).

The DOS supervisor performs this calculation for us and provides the address of the instruction in error at location 004014_{16}. That instruction appears in storage as

```
1A34
```

This is the machine language code generated from the statement

```
AR 3,4
```

Let's see how we can locate this instruction in the source program.

Our program is loaded in storage by the linkage editor. We must find this address, called the load point or entry point. The DOS linkage editor supplies this address(8). The DOS program is loaded at location 004000_{16}. The OS/370 supervisor treats our program as a subroutine of the operating system. As such register 15 often contains the entry point. The operating system also tells us the entry point—it is labelled USE 01 in the OS/370 listing (8)

If we subtract the entry point from the address of the instruction causing the program check we will have the relative address of the invalid statement,

DOS/370	OS/370	
004014_{16}	$IAE7EC_{16}$	(error address)
-004000_{16}	$-IAE7D8_{16}$	(entry point)
000014_{16}	000014_{16}	(location counter value)

The relative address, or location counter value, is 000014_{16}. The instruction causing the program check is

```
AR 3,4
```

Why does the execution of this instruction result in a program check? Let's examine the contents of register 3 and register 4. Register 3 is loaded from an area of storage called DATA3. We must calculate the address of DATA3 by adding the location counter value to the entry point

DOS/370	OS/370	
004000_{16}	$1AE7D8_{16}$	(entry point)
000024_{16}	000020_{16}	(value location counter at DATA3)
004024_{16}	$1AE7F8_{16}$	(storage address)

And register 4 was loaded from location $1AE7FC_{16}$ in the OS/370 listing, location 004020_{16} in the DOS listing. The reader should verify the address of DATA4. Thus the instruction

```
AR 3,4
```

is effectively adding the contents of DATA4 to DATA3. The addition would appear as

$$
\begin{array}{r}
01111111111111111111111111111111_2 \\
01111111111111111111111111111111_2 \\
\hline
11111111111111111111111111111110_2
\end{array}
$$

with a carry into the sign position but no carry out of the sign position. A fixed-point overflow condition.

And this is exactly what occurs! Register 4 still contains the constant DATA4. Register 3 contains the result of the addition. But the result is invalid—the sign indicates that the result is a negative number. This is impossible. The result of the addition is so large that it could not be expressed in 31 bits. The answer needs the sign bit.

When the program check interruption occurs, the cause of the problem is stored in the PSW. The interrupt handling routine analyzes the PSW and presents the information in the Interrupt Code (IC) to the user (9). An OS/370 system completion code of OC8 indicates that a fixed-point overflow has occurred. DOS interprets the interrupt code for us (9). Note that this error does not result in a program check if we do not set the fixed-point overflow mask (bit 36) to one. In this case the programmer must detect the overflow by testing the condition code using the BC instruction.

```
  LOC  OBJECT CODE    ADDR1 ADDR2  STMT   SOURCE STATEMENT                                          F04MAR74   6/17/76

                                      1 * PROGRAM 5 ILLUSTRATING PROGRAM CHECK INTERTUPTION
000000                                2          START 0
                                      3          PRINT NOGEN
                                      4 BEGIN    SAVE  (14,12)                                  SAVE REGISTERS
000004 05C0                           7          BALR  12,0                                     ESTABLISH BASE
000006                                8          USING *,12                                     ADDRESSABILITY
000006 50D0 C1FE           00204      9          ST    13,SAVEAREA+4                            FOLLOW R13 CONVENTIONS
00000A 41D0 C1FA           00200     10          LA    13,SAVEAREA                              DISCUSSED IN CH 16
                                     11          OPEN  (INCARD,,PRINT,OUTPUT)                   OPEN FILES
                                     19 READRT   GET   INCARD,INWORK                            READ INTO INWORK
00002C D204 C1C6 C142 001CC 00148    24          MVC   LIMOUT,LIM                               SET UP PRINT LINE
000032 F224 C192 C142 00198 00148    25          PACK  LIMP(3),LIM                              PACK LIMIT
000038 FA52 C195 C198 0019B 001A1    26 LOOP     AP    ANSP,CTR                                 ADD CTR TO ANSP
00003E F922 C19B C192 001A1 00198    27          CP    CTR,LIMP                                 COMPARE
000044 4780 C04C           00052     28          BE    EXIT                                     EXIT IF EQUAL
000048 FA20 C19B C242 001A1 00248    29          AP    CTR,=PL1'1'                              INCREMENT CTR
00004E 47F0 C032           00038     30          B     LOOP                                     ELSE CONTINUE LOOP
000052 D20E C1CC C19E 001D2 001A4    31 EXIT     MVC   ANSOUT,MASK                              MOVE MASK
000058 DF0E C1CC C195 001D2 0019B    32          ED    ANSOUT,ANSP                              EDIT ANSWER
                                     33          PUT   PRINT,PRINTBLD                           WRITE
00006C 47F0 C018           0001E     38          B     READRT                                   FORCE EOF CONDITION
                                     39 EOJRT    CLOSE (INCARD,,PRINT)                          CLOSE FILES
00007E 58D0 C1FE           00204     47          L     13,SAVEAREA+4                            RESTORE R13 POINTER
                                     48          RETURN (14,12)                                 RETURN
                                     51 *
                                     52 * DATA AREAS
                                     53 *
                                     54 INCARD   DCB   DSORG=PS,                                                      C
                                                       DDNAME=SYSIN,                                                  C
                                                       MACRF=GM,                                                      C
                                                       BLKSIZE=80,                                                    C
                                                       LRECL=80,                                                      C
                                                       EODAD=EOJRT
                                    108 PRINT    DCB   DSORG=PS,                                                      C
                                                       DDNAME=SYSOUT,                                                 C
                                                       MACRF=PM,                                                      C
                                                       BLKSIZE=80,                                                    C
                                                       LRECL=80
000148                              162 INWORK   DS    0CL80
000148                              163 LIM      DS    CL5
00014D                              164          DS    CL75
000198                              165 LIMP     DS    CL3
00019B 00000000000C                 166 ANSP     DC    PL6'0'
0001A1 00001C                       167 CTR      DC    PL3'1'
0001A4 4020205B2020205B             168 MASK     DC    XL15'4020205B2020205B2020205B202120'
0001B3 E2E4D440D6C640D5             169 PRINTBLD DC    CL25'SUM OF NUMBERS FROM 1 TO '
0001CC                              170 LIMOUT   DS    CL5
0001D1 7A                           171          DC    CL1':'
0001D2                              172 ANSOUT   DS    CL15
0001E1 4040404040404040             173          DC    CL29' '
000200                              174 SAVEAREA DS    18F
000000                              175          END   BEGIN
000248 1C                           176                =PL1'1'
```

Instruction in error (2)

Figure 18-4.

```
JOB CH16GOKK          STEP GO               TIME 174634   DATE 76169                                  PAGE 0001

COMPLETION CODE       SYSTEM = 0C7

PSW AT ENTRY TO ABEND   FF75000D E01D3DF4

TCB  02AFE8  RBP    00014510  PIE      CC000000  DEB  0002A9BC  TIO  00028188  CMP    800C7000  TRN  00000000
             MSS    02030FB0  PK-FLG   70852400  FLG  00007F78  LLS  00018BD8  JLB    00000000  JPQ  000170D8
             FSA    011F8768  TCB      0002A300  TME  00000000  JST  0002AFE8  NTC    00000000  OTC  0002C850
             LTC    00000000  IQE      0C000000  ECB  0002B7A4  TSF  20000000  D-PQE  000313D0  SQS  0002A848
             NSTAE  00000000  TCT      8002AF18  USER 00000000  DAR  00000000  RESV   00000000  JSCB 8702E758
             RESV   00000000  IOB      00000000

ACTIVE RBS

PRB  015930  RESV    00000000  APSW    E01D3DF4   WC-SZ-STAB 00040082   FL-CDE 00016C40   PSW FF75000D E01D3DF4
             C/TTR   00000000  WT-LNK  0C02AFE8

SVRB 014360  TAB-LN  00380220  APSW    F9F0F1C3   WC-SZ-STAB 0012D002   TQN    00000000   PSW 00040033 5000898A
             C/TTR   00005212  WT-LNK  C0015930
             RG 0-7   0C00000A   001D3EF8   0002B6F8   5C02B7A8   0002BF88   0002C850   0002B1F4   0002D670
             RG 8-15  0002B780   0C02AF13   0002B7A8   00000000   401D3DB6   001D3FB0   401D3DDC   00000000
             EXTSA    000021BE   8F1F84F0   00000000   00000000   FF030000   000143DC   000143E4   E2E8E2C9
                      C5C1F0F1   C9C5C1E8   C1C2C5D5   C4F90C70

SVRB 014510  TAB-LN  007803D8  APSW    F1F0F5C1   WC-SZ-STAB 0012D002   TQN    00000000   PSW FF04000C 401F7FA6
             C/TTR   00005321  WT-LNK  00014360
             RG 0-7   001058B0   0C0143C0   800088D2   000CAA50   0002AFE8   00014360   0402AFE8   00014360
             RG 8-15  0002AFE8   4000881A   C002AFE8   8F1F84F0   0002B1CC   000143E4   400085DC   00000000
             EXTSA    E2E8E2C9   C5C1F0F1   081D33E8   00013BD8   001D37B8   001B3848   001D37E0   0002B5B0
                      00001BE0   801B7BF0   00000000   0026AF52

LOAD LIST

        NE 00018AF0   RSP-CDE 020170D8      NE 00018CE8   RSP-CDE 01015F00      NE 00018C78   RSP-CDE 01015E18
        NE C0C18B80   RSP-CDE 01015D88      NE 00018B88   RSP-CDE 01015DA0      NE 00018B70   RSP-CDE 01015DE8
        NE 00C18BD0   RSP-CDE 01015E18      NE 00018D10   RSP-CDE 01015D28      NE 00018BC0   RSP-CDE 01015D58
        NE C0C18C08   RSP-CDE 01015CC8      NE 00018B78   RSP-CDE 01015CF8      NE 00018BF8   RSP-CDE 01015FF8
        NE CCC00000   RSP-CDE 01015CF0

CDE

     016C40      ATR1 0B   NCDE 000000   ROC-RB 00015930   NM GO         USE 01   EPA 1D3DB0   ATR2 20   XL/MJ 017DD0
     0170D8      ATR1 30   NCDE 016C40   ROC-RB 00000000   NM IGC0A05A   USE 02   EPA 1F7858   ATR2 28   XL/MJ 017E40
     C15E00      ATR1 B0   NCDE 015DE8   ROC-RB 00000000   NM IGG019CF   USE 02   EPA 27C3F0   ATR2 20   XL/MJ 017470
     015E18      ATR1 B0   NCDE 015EC0   ROC-RB 00000000   NM IGG019CL   USE 02   EPA 27E818   ATR2 20   XL/MJ 017480
     015D88      ATR1 B1   NCDE 015D70   ROC-RB 00000000   NM IGG019BA   USE 02   EPA 27D018   ATR2 28   XL/MJ 017420
     015DA0      ATR1 B0   NCDE 015D88   ROC-RB 00000000   NM IGG019BB   USE 02   EPA 27C988   ATR2 20   XL/MJ 017430
     015DE8      ATR1 B0   NCDE 015DD0   ROC-RB 00000000   NM IGG019CE   USE 02   EPA 27C660   ATR2 20   XL/MJ 017460
     015D28      ATR1 B0   NCDE 015D10   ROC-RB 00000000   NM IGG019CC   USE 02   EPA 27D228   ATR2 20   XL/MJ 0173E0
     015D58      ATR1 B1   NCDE 015D40   ROC-RB 00000000   NM IGG019CI   USE 02   EPA 27CD90   ATR2 28   XL/MJ 017400
```

Handwritten annotations:

Address instruction *after* error (pointing to 1D3DF4 in the PSW)

② 1D3DEE Address instruction in error
1D3DB0 Entry point
00003E Relative address instruction in error

Entry point (pointing to USE 01 EPA 1D3DB0)

Figure 18-4 *(Continued)*

```
   R7  0002D670   R8  0002B780   R9  0002AE18   R10 0002B7A8   R11 00000000   R12 4027DBD2

REGS AT ENTRY TO ABEND

     FLTR 0-6      4040404040400095     1269F00000177061          97FA6130DA76169F   0000000000000000

     REGS 0-7      C000000A  001D3EF8  0002B6F8  5C02B7A8         0002BE88  0002C850  0002B1F4  0002D670
     REGS 8-15     0002B780  0002AE18  0002B7A8  00000000         401D3DB6  001D3FB0  401D3DDC  00000000

LOAD MODULE     GO
```

Instruction causing error ①

```
1D3DA0                                            90ECD00C 05C050D0 C1FE41D0 C1FA0700   *..............B.........A...A...*
1D3DC0   4510C016 001D3E38 8F1D3E98 0A134110     C0824100 C14258F0 103005EF D204C1C6   *.....................A..O....K.AF*
1D3DE0   C142F224 C192C142 FA52C195 C19BF922     C19BC192 4780C04C FA20C19B C24247F0   *A.2.A.A...A.A.9.A.A.......A.B..0*
1D3E00   C032020E C1CCC19E DE0FC1CC C1954110     C0F24100 C1AD58F0 103005EF 47F0C018   *..K.A.A...A.A....S..A..0.....0..*
1D3E20   4510C076 001D3E38 801D3E98 0A1458D0     C1FE98EC D00C07FF 00000000 00000000   *..................A.............*
1D3E40   CCCCCCCC 00000000 00410000 021F86C0     00004000 00000001 041D3E20 90000000   *................ ...............*
1D3E60   CC545000 0002AC54 12276098 0C27E160     06C00001 00090050 28022828 001F85E8   *...............................Y*
1D3E80   001F8768 001F8768 00000050 0C000001     00000000 0027D228 00000000 00000000   *.......................K........*
1D3EA0   CCCCCCCC 00000000 00480000 021F3618     00004000 00000001 04000001 00000000   *................ ...............*
1D3EC0   002C0050 0002AB04 9227E2D8 0C27F050     07000001 00090050 28022828 421F8548   *.......M..SQ....................*
1D3EE0   0C1F8670 001F8620 00000050 CC000001     00000000 0027C660 F5404040 40404040   *.....................F.5        *
1D3F00   40404040 40404040 40404040 40404040     40404040 40404040 40404040 40404040   *                                *
     LINE 1D3F20  SAME AS ABOVE
1D3F40   40404040 40404040 50000400 00000000     1C00001C 4020205B 2020205B 2020205B   *        ........... ...........*
1D3F60   202120E2 E4D440D6 C640D5F4 D4C2C5D9     F240C6D9 D6D440F1 40E3D640 F5404040   *...SUM OF NUMBERS FROM 1 TO 5   *
1D3F80   407AC000 C0000C00 0C000000 0C000000     00404040 40404040 40404040 40404040   * ...............                *
1D3FA0   40404040 40404040 40404040 404C0000     00000000 001F8768 00000000 00000000   *                ................*
1D3FC0   CCCC0000 401D3CDC 12276098 0C1D3EF8     001D3F38 0002B6F8 5C02B7A8 0002BF88   *.... ..........8.......8........*
1D3FE0   0002C850 CC02B1F4 0002D670 0002B780     402761AC 0027E160 1C000000 00000000   *..H....4..0..... ...............*
```

INWORK (LIM) ③

LIMP - data causing error ④

CTR - contains valid packed data

```
LOAD MODULE     IGC0A05A

1F7840                                                              4180D099 1B114313   *................................*
1F7860   00001A81 41330001 95FF3000 47806068     1BEE1BFF 1B001B11 43E30000 43030001   *.........................T......*
1F7880   8CE0C004 38F0001C 8C000004 881C001C     1A2C44E0 60701A1E 41818001 44F06076   *.....0......................0..*
1F78A0   F3840069 0069DC07 D06562C6 41FFF001     44F0607C 47F066F8 413E3003 47F06010   *3.........F..0..0...0.8.....0..*
1F78C0   4133C0C1 47F060E2 D2008000 3C02D200     DC692000 D2008000 D0695050 D08C5000   *.....0.SK.....K.....K..........*
1F78E0   D12094FC D12358D0 D1201A10 5800D120     41110003 5010D064 94FCD067 D703D06C   *J...J...J.....J.............P...*
1F7900   D06C1810 54006290 19014780 60BC1810     4010D06C 5810D064 4A10D06C 1B005D00   *............... ...............*
1F7920   668C4000 DC6A1211 4770611C 4810D06A     12114770 60E85850 D08C5860 D12407F5   *.. ...................Y......J..5*
1F7940   4120D121 45806236 5820D120 413062C4     48A0D06A 48A0D06C 88A00002 45B0623E   *..J.......J....D................*
1F7960   46A061C4 9640D112 455062DA 94BFD112     47F060DE 18A15810 D1204B10 D06C5010   *..... J.......J..0......J.......*
1F7980   D0704120 D07145B0 62364810 D06C8810     00011A31 58200120 45B0623E 5020D120   *.........................J......J.*
1F79A0   9640D112 455062DA 94BFD112 4810D06C     12114770 61984700 615E4110 0001191A   *. J.......J.....................*
1F79C0   47B061A6 18125810 6680D51F 1CCC2000     47706146 4810D06E 41110001 4010D06E   *..........N................. ...*
1F79E0   41220020 5020D120 46A0615E 47F06130     1B114010 D06C46A0 611E47F0 60D44810   *......J.......0.... .........0.M..*
1F7A00   DC6E1211 4780619F 5810D120 4800D06E     89C00005 1B105010 D0704120 D0714810   *..........J.....................*
1F7A20   D06EC610 12114770 6202D203 D09F629D     41306294 45B0623E D20DD0AA 62A29640   *..........K.............K...... *
1F7A40   D1124550 620A943F D112D701 D06ED06E     12AA4780 600447F0 619ED204 D09F629D   *J.......J.P..........M.0..K.....*
1F7A60   41306297 45B0623F 9260D0AB 58100120     5B1C6680 5010D070 4120D071 4130629A   *.............J..................*
1F7A80   45B0623E D20DD0B2 62A247F0 61F64130     62B047F0 65744180 D09995FF 30004780   *....K......0.W.....0.............*
1F7AA0   627C1800 43030000 1B114313 0C011A80     44106284 F384D070 D070DC07 D07062C6   *.........................3..........F*
1F7AC0   41111001 4410628A 41330002 41220004     47F0623E 41330001 07FBD078 D2000070   *....................0.........K...*
```

Figure 18-4 (*Continued*)

```
  LOC  OBJECT CODE    ADDR1 ADDR2  STMT   SOURCE STATEMENT                                        FDOS CL3-9 06/01/74

                                      1 * PROGRAM 5 ILLUSTRATING PROGRAM CHECK INTERUPTION
000000                                2           START 0
                                      3           PRINT NOGEN
000000 05C0                           4 BEGIN     BALR  12,0                                 ESTABLISH BASE
000002                                5           USING *,12                                 ADDRESSABILITY
                                      6           OPEN  INCARD,PRINT
                                     15 READRT    GET   INCARD,INWORK                        READ INTO INWORK
000026 D204 C232 C1AE 00234 001B0    21           MVC   LIMOUT,LIM                           SET UP PRINT LINE
00002C F224 C1FE C1AE 00200 001B0    22           PACK  LIMP(3),LIM                          PACK LIMIT
000032 FA52 C201 C207 00203 00209    23 LOOP      AP    ANSP,CTR                             ADD CTR TO ANSP
000038 F922 C207 C1FE 00209 00200    24           CP    CTR,LIMP  (2) Instruction causing error  COMPARE
00003E 4780 C04A            0004C    25           BE    EXIT                                 EXIT IF EQUAL
000042 FA20 C207 C286 00209 00288    26           AP    CTR,=PL1'1'                          INCREMENT CTR
000048 47F0 C030            00032    27           B     LOOP                                 ELSE CONTINUE LOOP
00004C D20E C238 C20A 0023A 0020C    28 EXIT      MVC   ANSOUT,MASK                          MOVE MASK
000052 DE0E C238 C201 0023A 00203    29           ED    ANSOUT,ANSP                          EDIT ANSWER
                                     30           PUT   PRINT,PRINTBLD                       WRITE
000068 47F0 C014            00016    36           B     READRT                               FORCE EOF CONDITION
                                     37 EOJRT     CLOSE INCARD,PRINT
                                     46           EOJ                              END OF JOB
                                     49 *
                                     50 * DATA AREAS
                                     51 *
                                     52 INCARD    DTFCD DEVADDR=SYS004,                                          C
                                                        IOAREA1=AREA1,                                           C
                                                        BLKSIZE=80,                                              C
                                                        DEVICE=2540,                                             C
                                                        EOFADDR=EOJRT,                                           C
                                                        RECFORM=FIXUNB,                                          C
                                                        WORKA=YES,                                               C
                                                        TYPEFLE=INPUT
                                     72 PRINT     DTFPR DEVADDR=SYS005,                                          C
                                                        IOAREA1=OUT1,                                            C
                                                        BLKSIZE=120,                                             C
                                                        CONTROL=YES,                                             C
                                                        PRINTOV=YES,                                             C
                                                        WORKA=YES,                                               C
                                                        DEVICE=1403                                              C
                                                        RECFORM=FIXUNB
0000E8                               93 AREA1     DS    CL80
000138                               94 OUT1      DS    CL120
000180                               95 INWORK    DS    0CL80
000180                               96 LIM       DS    CL5
0001B5                               97           DS    CL75
000200                               98 LIMP      DS    CL3
000203 00000000000C                  99 ANSP      DC    PL6'0'
000209 00001C                       100 CTR       DC    PL3'1'
00020C 4020205B2020205B             101 MASK      DC    XL15'4020205B2020205B2020205B202120'
00021B E2E4D440D6C640D5             102 PRINTBLD  DC    CL25'SUM OF NUMBERS FROM 1 TO '
000234                              103 LIMOUT    DS    CL5
000239 7A                           104           DC    CL1' '
```

Figure 18-4 *(Continued)*

```
                                                                                              PAGE    2

  LOC  OBJECT CODE     ADDR1 ADDR2  STMT    SOURCE  STATEMENT                           FDOS CL3-9 06/01/74

00023A                              105 ANSOUT    DS     CL15
000249 404040404040404040           106           DC     CL29' '
000000                              107           END BEGIN
000268 5B5BC2D6D7C5D540             108                  =C'$$BOPEN '
000270 5B5BC2C3D3D6E2C5             109                  =C'$$BCLOSE'
000278 00000080                     110                  =A(INCARD)
00027C 000001B0                     111                  =A(INWORK)
000280 00000088                     112                  =A(PRINT)
000284 0000021B                     113                  =A(PRINTBLD)
000288 1C                           114                  =PL1'1'
```

```
                                  RELOCATION DICTIONARY                              PAGE    1

POS.ID   REL.ID   FLAGS   ADDRESS                                                    06/01/74

  01       01      0C     00000C
  01       01      0C     000010
  01       01      0C     000074
  01       01      0C     000078
  01       01      0C     000088
  01       02      18     000091
  01       01      0C     000093
  01       01      0C     00009C
  01       01      08     0000A1
  01       01      0C     0000C0
  01       03      18     0000C9
  01       01      0C     0000D0
  01       01      08     0000E1
  01       01      0C     000278
  01       01      0C     00027C
  01       01      0C     000280
  01       01      0C     000284
```

Figure 18-4 *(Continued)*

```
                                                  CROSS-REFERENCE                                                  PAGE    1

SYMBOL     LEN  VALUE  DEFN      REFERENCES                                                                         06/01/74

ANSOUT    00015 00023A 00105    0028  0029
ANSP      00006 000203 00099    0023  0029
AREA1     00080 0000E8 00093    0066  0068
BEGIN     00002 000000 00004    0107
CTR       00003 000209 00100    0023  0024  0026
EOJRT     00004 00006C 00040    0067
EXIT      00006 00004C 00028    0025
IJCX0006  00008 0000A0 00068    0058
IJJC0004  00004 000070 00042
IJJ00001  00004 000008 00011
IJJZ0006  00001 0000B2 00071
IJJZ0007  00001 0000E6 00092
INCARD    00006 000060 00055    0012  0017  0043  0110
INWORK    00080 0001B0 00095    0018  0111
LIM       00005 0001B0 00096    0021  0022
LIMOUT    00005 000234 00103    0021
LIMP      00003 000200 00098    0022  0024
LOOP      00006 000032 00023    0027
MASK      00015 00020C 00101    0028
OUT1      00120 000138 00094    0080  0091
PRINT     00006 0000B6 00075    0013  0032  0044  0112
PRINTBLD  00025 000218 00102    0053  0113
READRT    00004 000016 00017    0036


NO STATEMENTS FLAGGED IN THIS ASSEMBLY
```

```
// EXEC LNKEDT
```

```
JOB  PROG       06/01/74   DISK LINKAGE EDITOR DIAGNOSTIC OF INPUT

ACTION TAKEN  MAP
LIST   AUTOLINK   IJCFZIW0
LIST   AUTOLINK   IJDFCPZW
LIST   ENTRY
```

Figure 18-4 *(Continued)*

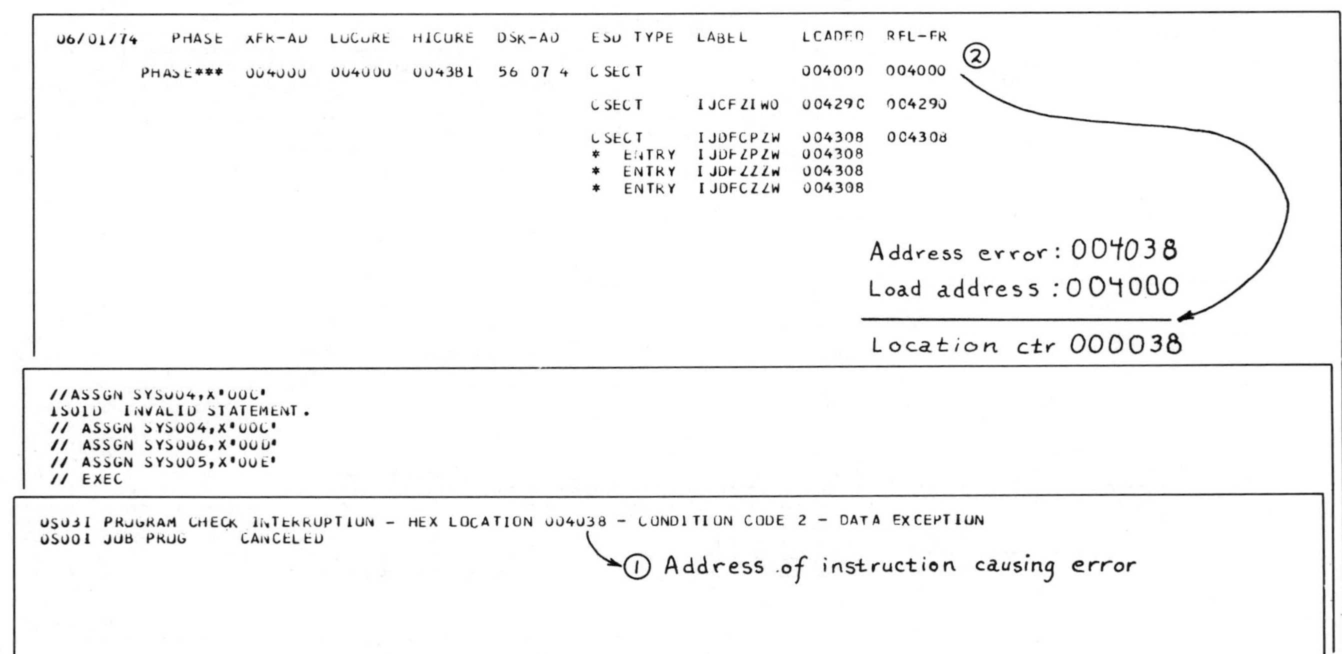

```
06/01/74   PHASE    XFR-AD   LOCORE   HICORE   DSK-AD    ESD TYPE   LABEL      LOADED   REL-FR

        PHASE***    004000   004000   0043B1   56 07 4   CSECT                 004000   004000

                                                         CSECT      IJCFZIW0   00429C   004290

                                                         CSECT      IJDFCPZW   004308   004308
                                                         *  ENTRY   IJDFZPZW   004308
                                                         *  ENTRY   IJDFZZZW   004308
                                                         *  ENTRY   IJDFCZZW   004308
```

```
//ASSGN SYS004,X'00C'
1S01D  INVALID STATEMENT.
// ASSGN SYS004,X'00C'
// ASSGN SYS006,X'00D'
// ASSGN SYS005,X'00E'
// EXEC
```

```
0S03I PROGRAM CHECK INTERRUPTION - HEX LOCATION 004038 - CONDITION CODE 2 - DATA EXCEPTION
0S00I JOB PROG      CANCELED
```


Figure 18-4 (*Continued*)

```
        PROG                06/01/74                                                             00.13.32                      PAGE   1

GR 0-7  000041B0 00004080 0001F7FF 00004000   0001F784 FFFFFF7C 00004000 00003F98
GR 8-F  00005B0A 0A0407F1 00004010 00004010   40004002 00005FD8 80004026 00004290
FP REG  45186A00 00000000 45186A00 00000000   00000000 00000000 4FDE0B6B 3A763FE0
COMREG  BG ADDR IS 000200

000000  00000000 00000000 00000000 00000000   00000000 00000200 FF050000 0000000C   ................  ................
000020  FF050007 40003B66 FF150007 E000403E   5B5BC2C5 D6D1F440 FF05000E 80004C28   .... ......... .  $$BEOJ4 ......).
000040  00003C88 08000000 00003C78 00000000   FB315000 00FEEAE3 00040000 0F001EEA   ................  ..&....T........
000060  00040000 000003FE 00040000 00001EAA   00000000 00000E1C 00040000 000003A4   ................  ................
000080  00000000 00000000 00000000 00000003   00050003 06B006B0 06B041BB 00734570   ................  ................
0000A0  0168940F BEAB41A0 CF1C4570 0DEA18A8   419001A8 92FFB563 458000EA 9200B583   ................  ................
0000C0  47F0BCC0 06B006B0 06B006B0 06B006B0   06B006B0 06B006B0 06B041BB 001741BB   .0..............  ................
0000E0  00504570 01684180 01A89640 A0019120   A00C4710 00FA9260 A0019604 A00F95E2   .&.......... ....  .......-.......S
000100  A0024780 B0EC95C1 A0024780 B0EC9561   A0024780 01229104 A0004780 01229203   .......A......./  ................
000120  008F9281 A0004BA0 032A487A CF0C49A0   036C41AA CF0C0778 94F9703B D7017058   ................  .........9..P...
000140  70589283 A00095FF B5829200 B5820788   9680A001 44J004FC 478088A0 947FA001   ................  ................
000160  92F0BBBD 47F0BBA0 42B000F7 58B002B8   918CA000 07175890 A0044880 02445000   .0...0.....7....  ...............&.
000180  902C6000 90586020 90606040 90686060   9070D21B 90100298 D2079008 80009680   ..-...-.-- ..--  ..K.....K.......
0001A0  A00007F7 45700170 D20EB562 B57258E0   02C4DC0E B562CF0C 1BAAD00F B562000C   ...7....K.......  .D..............
0001C0  43A10010 42A0036F 4AA0034C D20002FF   A00D5AA0 03644400 A0045890 A0044220   ..........)K....  ................
0001E0  A0009140 A0014710 CB96D207 02989008   9560036F 47200270 68009058 68209060   ... ......K.....  .-.............-
000200  68409068 68609070 48A0032A 41AACE0C   02010016 A0009898 90108200 02984400   . ...-..........  K...............
000220  A0049500 A0014780 02364400 04FC4780   023647F0 01A45890 A0049818 9030989F   ................  ...0............
000240  02988200 00389264 CF6CD207 0298B698   9890B6A0 82000293 9680A000 41100030   ..........K.....  ................
000260  47F0BAF0 96030039 96010038 82000038   92FF0298 96050299 440004FC 478001F8   .0.0............  ...............8
000280  D3000299 02FF47F0 01F8615C 40615040   44F00000 00000000 FF050007 40003B66   L.......0.8/* /&  .0.......... ...
0002A0  00001000 00002000 00003000 00004000   00003880 8000197A 00001000 00002000   ........ ....... .  ................
0002C0  00003000 00004000 30420000 00000000   F0F661F0 F161F7F4 40004000 00000000   ...... ........  06/01/74 . .....
0002E0  00000000 00000000 D7D9D6C7 40404040   0001F7FF 000043B1 000043B1 0000001C   ........PROG      ..7.............
000300  0003FFFF FC777CD0 A8A07CD0 0097319D   31A43295 32963310 34403444 344838F0   .........'..'.....  .......... .....0
000320  F6F0F1F7 F4F1F5F2 00002F0C 0000001E   139014CA 157C15F4 15FC0010 31240010   60174152........  .....'.4........
000340  5B5BC2D6 0007000A 020016E0 2E0C0000   00000000 02000080 0000035C 00000000   $$BO............  ...........*....
000360  0000357C 00000100 00001614 00100010   0000317E 00001572 00000000 00000000   ...'............  ................
000380  00000000 00000000 00000000 00000000   00000000 00000000 00003028 00003C78   ................  ................
0003A0  000037D4 92380245 909F0298 98BE02B8   41900A14 48A0036E 4AA0032A 9180A000   ...M............  ................
0003C0  47100302 58B0A004 9018B030 98BE02B8   C7F99601 A00098BE 028895FF A00F0789   ...K............  .9..............
0003E0  5000B6BC 48E00244 D207B698 E000C58E0   020494FD 3699D21B B6A00298 C7F9909F   &.......K.......  .D....K......9..
000400  02939220 02454590 03B44190 021E9500   00234780 04E89535 002347B0 00CF4860   ................  .....Y.........-
000420  00221A88 487002C8 48607000 07F6181F   18664121 000F4570 B2304860 B4D81B22   ........H.....6..  .............-.Q..
000440  43201007 4130003D 18234740 04584130   00301823 4780045A 1A234220 05F54320   ................  ...............5..
000460  10079508 10074780 049847F0 055E4720   00DA4230 05F54320 036E4322 CE0F1A23   .............0..  .....5..........
000480  95081007 47800490 95061007 47F0055A   487002FE 47F0049E 1B774370 BA648870   ..............0..  .....0..........
0004A0  00031177 4337CE0C 47F0056A 472000D8   96801002 960C1004 07F91858 41430002   .........0.....Q  ..........9.....
0004C0  43540000 41450000 1A444A40 B4D095FF   40004770 04C04284 000007F9 95FF05B7   ......&.... ....  ...........9....
0004E0  07891B00 5000B6BC 95FF0387 4780BBEA   4360036E 9560036F 4780042E D502A005   ......&.........  .-..-.......N...
000500  03494770 05144111 00004910 B2AE4780   C5141B66 4121000F 45708230 D5021009   ................  .............N...
000520  03014780 00D64400 00145870 039CD502   70010301 47600006 18334330 10079501   .....0.........N.  ........J.......
000540  10004770 046E92FF 05F5D200 0553A00D   41230003 05001007 A00E47B0 00D44182   ............5K.....  ....N...........
000560  20004870 031C4338 7000D403 1002CF78   4930B2AC 476004AC 89300003 4A30031C   ............M.....  ................
000580  91F03004 4780C070 D5010022 C5CC4780   C3560501 B4C3B4D6 472005B4 4930B4FC   .0.......E....  C.N..H.U.......0
0005A0  477005B4 950F0023 478005B4 91103006   478088EA 41300001 41488000 1A444A40   ................  ................
0005C0  B4D01850 4A50033C D2000587 40005010   400092FF 40004220 50004260 505A4260   ......&..K... .&..  ... ....&..-&..-
0005E0  501E91F0 501E4730 05F44A80 034CD200   501E6000 9200303C 91F03004 4780C090   &..0&.....4.-.)K.  &.-...&..0......
```

Figure 18-4 *(Continued)*

```
0036E0   D5D640D5 C1D4C540 0003FFFF 00003F10   00003F10 00000030 0003FFFF FC777CDC   NO NAME ........ ...............'.
003700   80007C50 0097319D 31A43295 32963310   34403444 344838F0 F6F0F1F7 F4F1F5F2   ..'&............ . ......060174152
003720   00002F0C 0000001E 145014CA 157C15F4   15FC0010 31240030 00000000 00000000   .........&...'.4 ................
003740   00000000 2E0C0000 00000000 02D00080   00003794 00000000 0000357C 00000100   ................ ...........'....
003760   00001614 00200020 0000317E 00001572   00000000 00000000 00000000 00000000   ................ ................
003780   00000000 00000000 00000000 00000000   00003031 00000000 0000357C 00000100   ................ ...........'....
0037A0   00001614 00300030 0000317E 00001572   00000000 00000000 00000000 00000000   ................ ................
0037C0   00000000 00000000 00000000 00000000   0000303A 00000700 FF000000 00FF0000   ................ ................
0037E0   0000FF00 000000FF 00000000 FF000000   00FF0000 0000FF00 000000FF 00000000   ................ ................
003800   FF000000 00FF0000 0000FF00 000000FF   00000000 FF000000 00FF0000 0000FF00   ................ ................
003820   000000FF FF000000 00000000 00000000   00000000 00000000 00000000 00000000   ................ ................
003840   00000000 --SAME--                                                             ....
0038A0   00000000 00000000 00000000 00000000                                           ................

LBLTYP   HEX LENGTH IS 0000
--BG--
003F80                     D5D640D5 C1D4C540   FF150007 E000403E 0A0407F1 00004010       NO NAME   ...... ....1.. .
003FA0   00004010 40004002 00005FD8 80004026   0000C4290 000041B0 00004080 0001F7FF   .. . . ....Q.. . .......... ...7.
003FC0   00004000 0001F784 FFFFFF7C 00004000   00003F98 00005B0A 00000000 00033C43   .. ...7....'.. . ......$.........
003FE0   45186A00 00000000 45186A00 00000000   00000000 00000000 4FDE0B6B 3A763FE0   ................ ................
004000   05C00700 4110C266 4500C012 00004080   000040B8 0A025810 C2765800 C27A58F1   ......B....... . .. .....B...B..1
004020   001045EF 0008D204 C232C1AE F224C1FE   C1AEFA52 C201C207 F922C207 C1FE4780   ......K.B.A.2.A. A...B.B.9.B.A...
004040   C04AFA20 C207C286 47F0C030 020EC238   C2CADE0E C238C201 5810C27E 5800C282   ....B.B..0..K.B. B...B.B...B...B.
004060   58F10010 45EF000C 47F0C014 4110C26E   4500C07A 00004080 000040B8 0A020A0E   .1.......0....B. ...... ... .....
004080   00008000 08000104 000040A0 000040A8   00004290 02810202 000040E8 0000406C   .......... ... . .......... Y.. .
0040A0   020040E8 20000050 47000000 D24FD000   E0000000 00000000 00008400 0C000105   .. Y...&....K... ................
0040C0   000040E0 00003AD8 00004308 08920909   00004138 00000000 07004700 00000000   .. ....Q........ ................
0040E0   09004138 20000078 F5404040 40404040   40404040 40404040 40404040 40404040   ........5
004100   40404040 --SAME--
004120   40404040 40404040 40404040 40404040   40404040 40404040 5810C456 5800C466                    ..D...D.
004140   58F10010 45EF000C 5810C456 41000013   58F10010 05EFD20D C21DC46E D205C251   .1.........D..... .1....K.B.D.K.B.
004160   C1BADE05 C251C303 D205C25A C1BADE05   C25AC306 D205C265 C1BADE05 C265C309   A...B.C.K.B.A... B.C.K.B.A....B.C.
004180   D205C26D C1BADE05 C26DC30C D205C27A   C1BADE05 C27AC30F 5810C456 5800C466   K.B.A...B.C.K.B. A...B.C....D...D.
0041A0   58F10010 45EF000C 4110C44E 4500C1B6   F5404040 40404040 40404040 40404040   .1.........C...A. 5
0041C0   40404040 --SAME--
004200   50000400 00000000 1C00001C 4020205B   2020205B 2020205B 202120E2 E4D440C6   &............ ..$ ...$...$...SUM O
004220   C640D5E4 D4C2C5D9 E240C6D9 D6D440F1   40E3D640 F5404040 407AC2C3 D3D6E2C5   F NUMBERS FROM 1  TO 5    .BCLOSE
004240   00004080 0000417A 00404040 40404040   40404040 40404040 40404040 40404040   .. ......
004260   40404040 40400000 5B5BC2D6 D7C5D540   5B5BC2C3 D3D6E2C5 00004080 000041B0         ..$$BOPEN  $$BCLOSE.. .....
004280   000040B8 0000421B 1C044780 F04C9140   0A320000 0A320000 47F0F01A 0A32000C   .. ..........0).  .........00.....
0042A0   C9D1C3C6 E9C9E6F0 030A0A00 91801002   4710F026 0A0750E0 F07058E0 10209101   IJCFZIW0........ ..0...&.0.......
0042C0   10044780 F04C9140 10024710 F04658E0   F07047F0 F01A58E0 101C07FE D501F06A   ....0). .....0... 0..00.......N.0.
0042E0   E0004770 F05A47F0 F04650D0 F06C18D0   4400102C 98DEF06C 07FE615C 00005FC8   .....0...00.&.0... .......0.../*...Q
004300   80004026 F06C18D0 47F0F04C 47F0F05E   CA320000 47F0F01A C9D1C4C6 C3D7E9E6   .. .0....00).00.  .....00.IJDFCPZW
004320   F3F99180 10024710 F0240A07 90CEF098   58E01018 48C0102E 06C018D0 44C0F0A4   39......0......0. ...............0.
004340   98CEF098 D2001028 1017D200 10171016   CA0007FE 91801002 4710F056 0A074200   ..0.K......K..... ...........0.....
004360   10280A00 07FE9180 10024710 F0680A07   91011015 4780F07E 94FE1015 91021003   ............0...  .......0........
004380   078E47F0 F0849101 1004078E 12004780   F08E18F0 07FF928B 10280A00 07FE0000   ...00............ C..0............
0043A0   00000000 00000000 00000000 D200E000   D0000000 00000000 00000000 00000000   ...........K...  ................
0043C0   00000000 --SAME--                                                             ....
01F7E0   00000000 00000000 00000000 00000000   00000000 00000000 00000000 00000000   ................ ................
```

④ Limp ③ Inwork LIM ① Instruction causing interrupt

Figure 18-4 (*Concluded*)

Let's examine another exception. Figure 18-4 gives the listing from a data exception occurring during the execution of Program 5. In this problem, the limit of the series is entered as data on a punched card.

We find the instruction following the error in the OS listing at location $1D3DF4_{16}$. The ILC (bits 32–33 of the PSW) contains 11_2 indicating that the instruction in error contains three halfwords. We back up six bytes of storage to find the instruction in error at location $1D3DEE_{16}$ in the OS listing. DOS calculates the address for us. The instruction in error is found in location 004038_{16}(1) in the DOS listing. If we subtract the user entry point from this address (2) we obtain a location counter value of $00003E_{16}$ in the OS listing and 000038_{16} in the DOS listing. We see that the instruction causing the interrupt is

```
CP    CTR,LIMP
```

We now may assume that one of these fields does not contain valid packed data. Let's locate CTR and LIMP in storage.

Figure 18-5 shows two methods of locating data in storage. We may examine the generated code and locate the data by determining its effective address, or we may add the entry point to the location counter value. In both examples the answers agree.

Since we defined CTR as a packed constant, we might assume that it is not the item in error. Locating CTR at location $1D3F51_{16}$ in the OS/370 listing and at location 004209_{16} in the DOS listing, we see that it contains valid packed data.

But look at LIMP! It contains (4).

50	00	04

. . . certainly the cause of our problem! But how did this data become invalid? We must backtrack to the instruction

```
PACK    LIMP(3),LIM
```

The field LIM is entered from a punched card. Perhaps there was some error in our data. We locate INWORK at address $ID3EF8_{16}$ in the OS/370 listing and at location $0041BO_{16}$ in the DOS listing. LIM is defined as the first five bytes of this field (3). These bytes appear as

F5	40	40	40	40

But when the data is packed it appears as

50	00	04

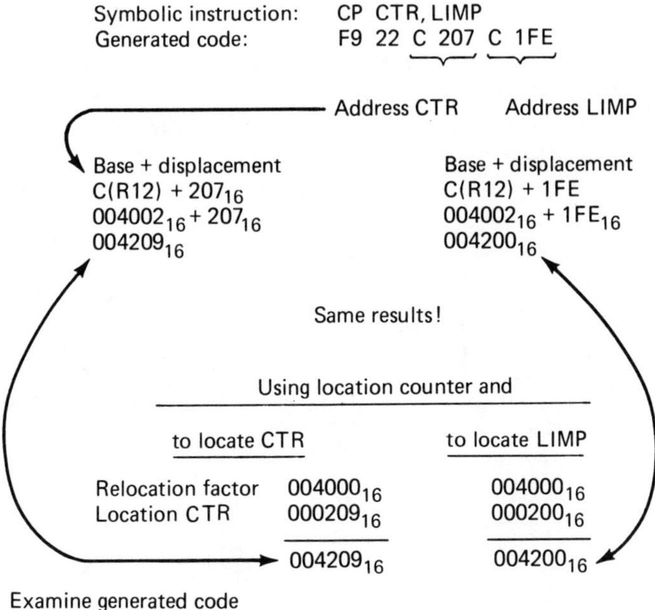

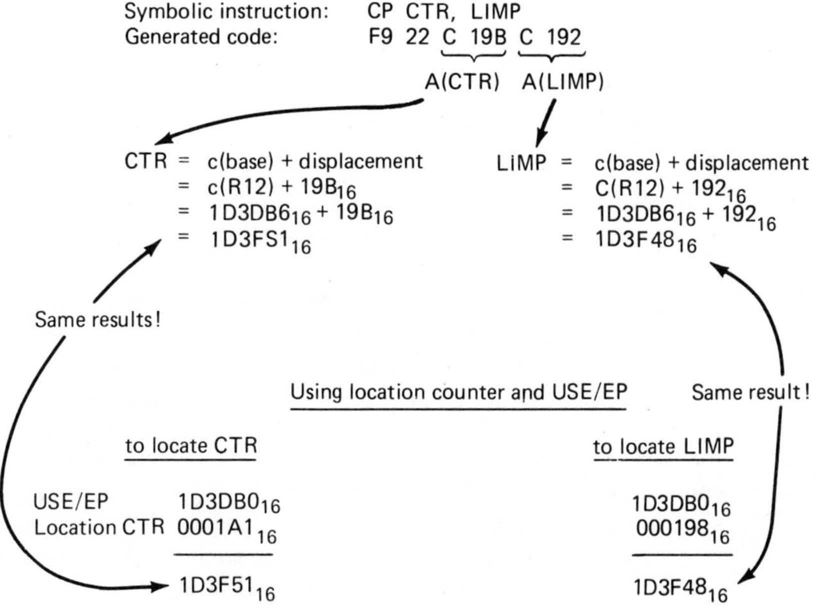

Figure 18-5 Locating data in storage. (a) DOS; (b) OS.

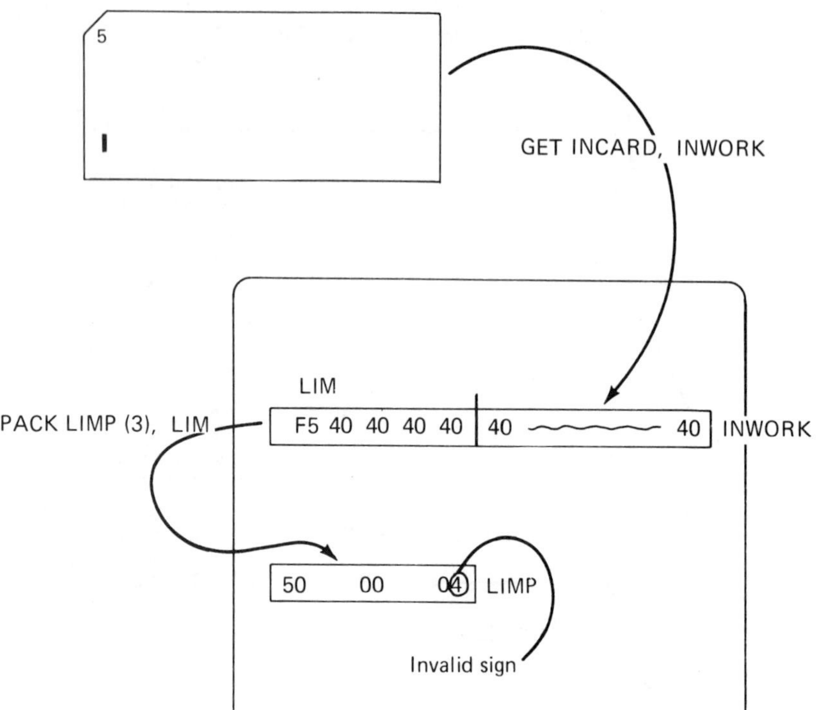

Figure 18-6 Incorrect data causing program check interrupt.

exactly the data found in LIMP! Our problem is caused by incorrect data. Figure 18-6 summarizes the error.

Errors Outside the User Program

Sometimes the PSW points to an instruction outside the user's program. This means that an error occurred in one of the operating system subroutines. "Quite out of my control," you might say. But this error is usually caused by the programmer. It is just a little harder to detect.

Figure 18-7 is an example of a program check occurring outside the user's program. The error is recognized by an invalid supervisor call 32 in the DOS program and an error at location 000001_{16} in the OS program—certainly out the user's program. But how did we get there? Remembering our linkage conventions, we might look at register 15. Whenever we enter an operating system routine—perhaps an I/O routine—the address of the routine is loaded into register 15. We see this code in the statements generated from the CNTRL macro. Similar code is generated from the GET and PUT macros.

Somehow the wrong address must have been loaded into register 15. But which macro caused the error? Again, the linkage conventions can help us. Register 14 is used to point to the return point in the calling program. But this time *we* are the calling program. Let's look at register 14.

Register 14 contains $500D95BE_{16}$ in the OS listing—certainly more valid than register 15. Subtracting the USE/01 (2) we calculate that the location counter value of the instruction *after* the BAL instruction is $00002E_{16}$. Thus the macro causing the error was the CNTRL macro in statement 21. We now must find out what was wrong with the macro.

Actually the macro is not in error. The problem is with the DCB for PRINT. In the MACRF keyword the programmer neglected to code the entry for CNTRL. He (or she) coded

```
MACRF = PM,
```

instead of

```
MACRF = PMC
```

The DCB must be corrected and the program must be reassembled.

Register 14 in the DOS listing contains 004024_{16}—the address of an instruction within our program. Subtracting the load address (2) of 004000_{16}, we calculate that the location counter value of the instruction *after* the BALR instruction is 000024_{16}. Thus the macro causing the error is the CNTRL macro. The macro is not in error. The problem is with the DTFPR. The programmer omitted the keyword entry

```
CONTROL = YES
```

The DTFPR must be corrected and the program reassembled.

```
LOC    OBJECT CODE    ADDR1 ADDR2  STMT   SOURCE STATEMENT                                          F04MAR74  6/17/76

                                     1 *
                                     2 * USE OF PRTOV AND  CNTRL MACROS
                                     3 * IN PROGRAM 1
                                     4 *
000000                               5          START
                                     6 FIRST    SAVE   (14,12)                                 SAVE REGISTERS
000000                               7+FIRST    DS     0H
000000 90EC D00C           0000C     8+         STM    14,12,12(13) SAVE REGISTERS
000004 05C0                          9          BALR   12,0                                    LOAD BASE
000006                              10          USING  *,12
000006 50D0 C226           0022C    11          ST     13,SAVEAREA+4                           FOLLOW R13 CONVENTIONS
00000A 41D0 C222           00228    12          LA     13,SAVEAREA                             DISCUSSED IN CH 16
                                    13          OPEN   (INCARD,,PRINT,OUTPUT)                  OPEN FILES
00000E 0700                         14+         CNOP   0,4 ALIGN LIST TO FULLWORD
000010 4510 C016           0001C    15+         BAL    1,*+12 LOAD REG1 W/LIST ADDR.
000014 00                           16+         DC     AL1(0) OPTION BYTE
000015 0000A0                       17+         DC     AL3(INCARD) DCB ADDRESS
000018 8F                           18+         DC     AL1(143) OPTION BYTE
000019 000100                       19+         DC     AL3(PRINT) DCB ADDRESS
00001C 0A13                         20+         SVC    19 ISSUE OPEN SVC
                                    21          CNTRL  PRINT,SK,1                              SKIP TO TOP OF PAGE
00001E 4110 C0FA           00100    22+         LA     1,PRINT LOAD PARAMETER REG 1
000022 4100 0001           00001    23+         LA     0,1(0,0) LOAD PARAMETER REG 0
000026 1300                         24+         LCR    0,0 INDICATE SK ACTION
000028 58F1 0054           00054    25+         L      15,84(1,0) LOAD CONTROL ROUT.ADDR
00002C 05EF                         26+         BALR   14,15 LINK TO CONTROL ROUT.
                                    27 READRT   GET    INCARD,INWORK                           GET RECORD
00002E 4110 C09A           000A0    28+READRT   LA     1,INCARD LOAD PARAMETER REG 1
000032 4100 C15A           00160    29+         LA     0,INWORK LOAD PARAMETER REG 0
000036 58F0 1030           00030    30+         L      15,48(0,1) LOAD GET ROUTINE ADDR.
00003A 05EF                         31+         BALR   14,15 LINK TO GET ROUTINE
00003C D205 C1B4 C15A 001BA 00160   32          MVC    NUMOUT(6),NUMIN
000042 D213 C1C4 C160 001CA 00166   33          MVC    NAMEOUT(20),NAMEIN                      MOVE EMP NAME
000048 D207 C1E2 C18C 001E8 00192   34          MVC    GROSSOUT(8),GROSSIN                     MOVE GROSS
                                    35          PUT    PRINT,PRINTBLD                          WRITE RECORD
00004E 4110 C0FA           00100    36+         LA     1,PRINT LOAD PARAMETER REG 1
000052 4100 C1AA           001B0    37+         LA     0,PRINTBLD LOAD PARAMETER REG 0
000056 58F0 1030           00030    38+         L      15,48(0,1) LOAD PUT ROUTINE ADDR.
00005A 05EF                         39+         BALR   14,15 LINK TO PUT ROUTINE
                                    40          CNTRL  PRINT,SP,2                              SPACE TWO
00005C 4110 C0FA           00100    41+         LA     1,PRINT LOAD PARAMETER REG 1
000060 4100 0002           00002    42+         LA     0,2(0,0) LOAD PARAMETER REG 0
000064 58F1 0054           00054    43+         L      15,84(1,0) LOAD CONTROL ROUT.ADDR
000068 05EF                         44+         BALR   14,15 LINK TO CONTROL ROUT.
                                    45          PRTOV  PRINT,12                                TEST FOR END OF PAGE
00006A 4110 C0FA           00100    46+         LA     1,PRINT LOAD DCB ADDR
00006E 9148 1011     00011          47+         TM     17(1),X'48' IS DEVICE A PRINTER
000072 47E0 C07C           00082    48+         BC     14,*+16 IF NOT BRANCH AROUND
000076 9180 1011     00011          49+         TM     17(1),X'80' FURTHER TESTING FOR PRINTER
00007A 4770 C07C           00082    50+         BNZ    *+8 IF NOT BR AROUND
00007E 9610 1012     00012          51+         OI     18(1),16 SET BIT ON IN DCB
000082 47F0 C028           0002E    52          B      READRT                                  LOOP BACK
                                    53 EOJRT    CLOSE  (INCARD,,PRINT)                         CLOSE FILES
000086 0700                         54+         CNOP   0,4 ALIGN LIST TO FULLWORD
000088 4510 C03E           00094    55+EOJRT    BAL    1,*+12 LOAD REG1 W/LIST ADDR
```

Handwritten annotations: "Code to link to subroutine" (bracketing statements 22–26); "Branch to I/O substitute" (at statement 26, 05EF); "R14 points here" (at statement 28).

Figure 18-7.

```
                                                                                                PAGE    2
  LOC   OBJECT CODE     ADDR1 ADDR2  STMT    SOURCE STATEMENT                             F04MAR74   6/17/76
000C8C 00                             56+           CC     AL1(0) OPTION BYTE
000C8D 0000A0                         57+           CC     AL3(INCARD) DCB ADDRESS
000C90 80                             58+           DC     AL1(128) OPTION BYTE
000C91 000100                         59+           DC     AL3(PRINT) DCB ADDRESS
000C94 0A14                           60+           SVC    20 ISSUE CLOSE SVC
000C96 58D0 C226             0022C    61            L      13,SAVEAREA+4                 RESTORE R13 POINTER
                                      62            RETURN (14,12)                       RETURN
000C9A 98EC D00C             0000C    63+           LM     14,12,12(13) RESTORE THE REGISTERS
000C9E 07FE                           64+           BR     14 RETURN
                                      65 *
                                      66 * DATA AREAS
                                      67 *
                                      68            PRINT  NOGEN
                                      69 INCARD     DCB    DSORG=PS,                                      C
                                                           MACRF=GM,                                      C
                                                           DDNAME=SYSIN,                                  C
                                                           BLKSIZE=80,                                    C
                                                           LRECL=80,                                      C
                                                           EODAD=EOJRT
                                     123 PRINT      DCB    DSORG=PS,                                      C
                                                           MACRF=PM,  ——MACRF should be PM                C
                                                           DDNAME=SYSOUT,                                 C
                                                           BLKSIZE=120,                                   C
                                                           LRECL=120
000C160                              177 INWORK     DS     0CL80
000C160                              178 NUMIN      DS     CL6
000C166                              179 NAMEIN     DS     CL20
000C17A                              180            DS     CL24
000192                               181 GROSSIN    DS     CL8
000C19A                              182            DS     CL22
0001B0                               183 PRINTBLD   DS     0CL120
000C1B0                              184            DS     CL10
000C1BA                              185 NUMOUT     DS     CL6
0001C0                               186            DS     CL10
000C1CA                              187 NAMEOUT    DS     CL20
0001DE                               188            DS     CL10
000C1E8                              189 GROSSOUT   DS     CL8
0001F0                               190            DS     CL56
000228                               191 SAVEAREA   DS     18F
000000                               192            END    FIRST
```

Figure 18-7 *(Continued)*

```
JOB CH16I              STEP GO                 TIME 093439    DATE 76169                                          PAGE 0001

COMPLETION CODE        SYSTEM = 0C6

PSW AT ENTRY TO ABEND  FF75000D 50000003

TCB  029360   RBP   00014870   PIE      00000000   DEB  0002981C   TIO 00029668   CMP    800C6000   TRN  00000000
              MSS   02031CE8   PK-FLG 70852400     FLG  00007F7B   LLS 00018AB0   JLB    00000000   JPQ  00016D18
              FSA   010FDF68   TCB      00000000   TME  00000000   JST 00029360   NTC    00000000   OTC  0002CE68
              LTC   00000000   IQE      00000000   ECB  000295AC   TSF 20000000   D-PQE  0002FFC8   SQS  00028F78
              NSTAE 00000000   TCT      800294A8   USER 00000000   DAR 00000000   RESV   00000000   JSCB 8702BE28
              RESV  00000000   IOB      00000000

ACTIVE RBS

PRB  0159D0   RESV    00000000   APSW    50000003   WC-SZ-STAB 00040082   FL-CDE 00016EB0   PSW FF75000D 50000003
              Q/TTR   00000000   WT-LNK 00029360

SVRB 0142D0   TAB-LN 00380220   APSW    F9F0F1C3   WC-SZ-STAB 0012D002   TQN     00000000   PSW 00040033 500089BA
              Q/TTR   00005212   WT-LNK 000159D0
              RG 0-7   FFFFFFFF   000D9690   00028790   5C0295B0   0002CBF0   0002CE68   000296D4   0002E3B8
              RG 8-15  00029588   000294A8   000295B0   00000000   400D9596   000D9788   500D95BE   00000001
              EXTSA    000021BE   8F0FDCA0   00000000   00000000   FF030000   0001434C   00014354   E2E8E2C9
                       C5C1F0F1   C9C5C160   C1C2C5D5   C4F90C60

SVRB 014870   TAB-LN 007803D8   APSW    F1F0F5C1   WC-SZ-STAB 0012D002   TQN     00000000   PSW FF04000C 400FD7A6
              Q/TTR   00005321   WT-LNK 000142D0
              RG 0-7   00105880   00014330   800088D2   0000AA50   00029360   000142D0   04029360   000142D0
              RG 8-15  00029360   4000881A   00029360   8F0FDCA0   000296AC   00014354   400085DC   00000000
              EXTSA    E2E8E2C9   C5C1F0F1   C9C7C3F5   F4F0F3C4   00014750   00000000   E2E3C1C5   0A2207FE
                       000CE2E3   C1C54040   00000000   404007FE

LOAD LIST

         NE 00018B48   RSP-CDE 02016D18        NE 00018B50   RSP-CDE 01015E00        NE 00018B00   RSP-CDE 01015E18
         NE 00018D98   RSP-CDE 01015D88        NE 00018AB8   RSP-CDE 01015DA0        NE 00018AD0   RSP-CDE 01015DE8
         NE 00018B40   RSP-CDE 01015E18        NE 00018B30   RSP-CDE 01015D28        NE 00018BB8   RSP-CDE 01015D58
         NE 00018B38   RSP-CDE 01015CC8        NE 00018B08   RSP-CDE 01015CF8        NE 00018B20   RSP-CDE 01015FF8
         NE 00000000   RSP-CDE 01015CE0

CDE

      016EB0     ATR1 0B   NCDE 000000   ROC-RB 000159D0   NM GO         USE 01   EPA 0D9590   ATR2 20   XL/MJ 017F50
      016D18     ATR1 30   NCDE 016EB0   ROC-RB 00000000   NM IGC0A05A   USE 02   EPA 0FD058   ATR2 28   XL/MJ 017E30
      015E00     ATR1 B0   NCDE 015DE8   ROC-RB 00000000   NM IGG019CF   USE 02   EPA 27C3F0   ATR2 20   XL/MJ 017470
      015E18     ATR1 B0   NCDE 015E00   ROC-RB 00000000   NM IGG019CL   USE 02   EPA 27E818   ATR2 20   XL/MJ 017480
      015D88     ATR1 B1   NCDE 015D70   ROC-RB 00000000   NM IGG019BA   USE 02   EPA 27D018   ATR2 28   XL/MJ 017420
      015DA0     ATR1 B0   NCDE 015D88   ROC-RB 00000000   NM IGG019BB   USE 02   EPA 27C988   ATR2 20   XL/MJ 017430
      015DE8     ATR1 B0   NCDE 015DD0   ROC-RB 00000000   NM IGG019CE   USE 02   EPA 27C660   ATR2 20   XL/MJ 017460
      015D28     ATR1 F0   NCDE 015D10   ROC-RB 00000000   NM IGG019CC   USE 02   EPA 27D228   ATR2 20   XL/MJ 0173E0
      015D58     ATR1 B1   NCDE 015D40   ROC-RB 00000000   NM IGG019CI   USE 02   EPA 27CD90   ATR2 28   XL/MJ 017400
```

Invalid instruction causes a specification error- instruction is outside user program

② *Entry point*

Figure 18-7 *(Continued)*

```
   FLTR 0-6      00029428000000E8     4000780800000000              0000000000000000    0000000000000000

   REGS 0-7      FFFFFFFF  000D9690  00028790  5C0295B0             0002CBF0  0002CE68  000296D4  0002E3B8
   REGS 8-15     00029588  000294A8  000295B0  00000000             400D9596  000D97B8  500D95BE  00000001

LOAD MODULE    GO

0D9580                                                 90ECD00C 05C050D0 C22641D0 C2220700   *........B....0B..........B...B...*
0D95A0   4510C016 000D9630 8F0D9690 0A134110           C0FA4100 00011300 58F10054 05EF4110   *.........................1.......*
0D95C0   C09A4100 C15A58F0 103005EF D205C1B4           C15AD213 C1C4C160 D207C1E2 C18C4110   *....A..0....K.A.A.K.ADA.K.ASA....*
0D95E0   C0FA4100 C1AA58F0 103005EF 4110C0FA           41000002 58F10054 05EF4110 C0FA9148   *....A..0................1........*
0D9600   101147E0 C07C91B0 10114770 C07C9610           101247F0 C0280700 4510C08E 000D9630   *....................0............*
0D9620   800D9690 0A1458D0 C22698EC D00C07FE           00000000 00000000 00000000 00000000   *........B........................*
0D9640   00410000 020FDEC0 00004000 00000001           040D9618 90000000 00545000 0002916C   *.........  ......................*
0D9660   12276098 0027E160 06000001 00090050           28022828 000FDD68 00000000 00000000   *.................................*
0D9680   00000050 00000001 00000000 0027D228           00000000 00000000 00000000 00000000   *................K................*
0D96A0   00480000 020FDDC8 00004000 00000001           04000001 00000000 002C0050 000290EC   *........H..  ....................*
0D96C0   9227E2D8 0027E050 07000001 00090078           28022828 420FDCF8 000FDE48 000FDDD0   *..SQ...............8.............*
0D96E0   00000078 00000001 00000000 0027C660           00000000 00000000 00000000 00000000   *..............F..................*
0D9700   00000000 00000000 00000000 00000000           00000000 00000000 00000000 00000000   *.................................*
      LINES 0D9720-0D9780 SAME AS ABOVE
0D97A0   00000000 00000000 00000000 00000000           00000000 00000000 00000000 000FDF68   *.................................*
0D97C0   00000000 00000000 00000000 00000000           00000000 00000000 00000000 00000000   *.................................*
      LINE 0D97E0 SAME AS ABOVE

LOAD MODULE    IGC0A05A

0FD040                                                                   4180D099 1B114313   *.................................*
0FD060   00001A81 41330001 95FF3000 47806068           1BEE1BFF 1B001B11 43E30000 43030001   *.........................T.......*
0FD080   8CE00004 88F0001C 8C000004 8810001C           1A2044E0 60701A1E 41818001 44F06076   *......0.........................0..*
0FD0A0   F384D069 D069DC07 D06962C6 41FFF001           44F0607C 47F066F8 413E3003 47F06010   *3.............F..0...0..8.....0..*
0FD0C0   41330001 47F060E2 D2008000 3002D200           D0692000 D2008000 D0695050 D08C5000   *......0.SK.....K.....K...........*
0FD0E0   D12094FC D1235B00 D1201A10 5800D120           41110003 5010D064 94FCD067 D703D06C   *J....J....J.......J.............P...*
0FD100   D06C1810 54006290 19014780 60BC1B10           4010D06C 5810D064 4A10D06C 1B005D00   *...............  ...............*
0FD120   66804000 D06A1211 4770611C 4810D06A           12114770 60E85850 D08C5860 D12407F5   *..  ......................Y.......J..5*
0FD140   4120D121 45B06236 5820D120 413062C4           48A0D06A 4BA0D06C 88A00002 45B0623E   *..J..........J.....D.............*
0FD160   46A06104 9640D112 455062DA 94BFD112           47F060DE 18A15810 D1204B10 D06C5010   *........ J.......J..0........J...*
0FD180   D0704120 D07145B0 62364810 D06C8810           00011A31 5820D120 45B0623E 5020D120   *.........................J.......J.*
0FD1A0   9640D112 455062DA 94BFD112 4810D06C           12114770 61984700 615E4110 0001191A   *. J........J.....................*
0FD1C0   47B061A6 18125B10 6680D51F 10002000           477061A6 4810D06E 41110001 4010D06E   *..........N..................  ...*
0FD1E0   41220020 5020D120 46A0615E 47F061B0           1B114010 D06C46A0 611E47F0 60D44810   *.........J.......0.... .........0.M..*
0FD200   D06E1211 4780619E 5810D120 4800D06E           89000005 1B105010 D0704120 D0714810   *..........J......................*
0FD220   D06E0610 12114770 6202D203 D09F629D           41306294 45B0623E D20DD0AA 62A29640   *..........K..............K......  *
0FD240   D1124550 62DA94BF D112D701 D06ED06E           12AA4780 60D447F0 619ED204 D09F629D           *J.........J.P...........M..0...K......*
0FD260   41306297 45B0623E 9260D0AB 5810D120           5B106680 5010D070 4120D071 4130629A   *...................J.............*
0FD280   45B0623E D20DD0B2 62A247F0 61E64130           62B047F0 65744180 D09995FF 30004780   *.....K.......0.W......0..........*
0FD2A0   627C1B00 43030000 1B114313 00011A80           44106284 F384D070 D070DC07 D07062C6   *.........................3..........F*
0FD2C0   41111001 4410628A 41330002 41220004           47F0623E 41330001 07FBD078 D200D070   *.....................0..........K....*
0FD2E0   2000D200 8000D070 FFFFFFE0 0B02FF0C           02FF1302 FFD3C9D5 C5E240E2 C1D4C540   *..K......................LINES SAME *
0FD300   C1E240C1 C2D6E5C5 0002FF09 0312031B           03240330 03390342 034B03FF 0903FF12   *AS ABOVE.........................*
0FD320   03FF1B03 FF2403FF 3003FF39 03FF4203           FF0098E0 D08012EE 47806310 D27CF000   *.............................K.0..*
0FD340   D09441FF 007D50F0 D084411F 007D1910           47D06332 1BFE40F0 D090D203 E000D090   *.........0................ 0..K.......*
0FD360   41FE0004 50F0D084 47F06722 92201005           58F10008 58F0F030 05EF5817 000058E0   *......0...0..........1...00.........*
0FD380   100858F0 E03405EF 0A030700 47F06770           9560D098 47406348 47206346 1A011A01   *...0..........0.......  .........*
```

Branch to invalid address in R15 caused error

Address in R14 shows return point in user program

Figure 18-7 (*Continued*)

Branch instruction to address in R15

Instruction after branch to subroutine


```
  LOC  OBJECT CODE    ADDR1 ADDR2 STMT   SOURCE STATEMENT                                       FDOS CL3-9 05/30/74

                                    1 *
                                    2 * USE OF PRTUV AND  CNTRL MACROS
                                    3 * IN PROGRAM 1
                                    4 *
000000                              5           START
000000 05C0                         6 FIRST     BALR  12,0                                ESTABLISH BASE
000002                              7           USING *,12
                                    8           OPEN  INCARD,PRINT
                                    9+* 360N-CL-453 OPEN      CHANGE LEVEL 3-3                                3-3
000002 0700                        10+          CNOP  0,4
000004                             11+          DC    OF'0'
000004 4110 C286            00288  12+          LA    1,=C'$$BOPEN '
000008 4500 C012            00014  13+IJJ00001 BAL    0,*+4+4*(3-1)
00000C 00000090                    14+          DC    A(INCARD)
000010 000000C8                    15+          DC    A(PRINT)
000014 0A02                        16+          SVC   2
                                   17           CNTRL PRINT,SK,1                          SKIP TO TOP OF PAGE
                                   18+* 360N-CL-453       CNTRL      CHANGE LEVEL 3-9                         3-9
000016 5810 C296            00298  19+          L     1,=A(PRINT) GET DTF TABLE ADDRESS
00001A 4100 008B            0008B  20+          LA    0,139 GET OPERATION CODE
00001E 58F1 0010            00010  21+          L     15,16(1) GET LOGIC MODULE ADDRESS
000022 05EF                        22+          BALR  14,15 BRANCH TO CNTRL ROUTINE
                                   23 READRT    GET INCARD,INWORK                         GET RECORD
                                   24+* 360N-CL-453 GET        CHANGE LEVEL 3-0
000024 5810 C29A            0029C  25+READRT    L     1,=A(INCARD) GET DTF TABLE ADDRESS
000028 5800 C29E            002A0  26+          L     0,=A(INWORK) GET WORK AREA ADDRESS
00002C 58F1 0010            00010  27+          L     15,16(1) GET LOGIC MODULE ADDRESS
000030 45EF 0008            00008  28+          BAL   14,8(15) BRANCH TO GET ROUTINE
000034 D205 C218 C1BE 0021A 001C0  29           MVC   NUMOUT(6),NUMIN
00003A D213 C228 C1C4 0022A 001C6  30           MVC   NAMEOUT(20),NAMEIN                  MOVE EMP NAME
000040 D207 C246 C1F0 00248 001F2  31           MVC   GROSSOUT(8),GROSSIN                 MOVE GROSS
                                   32           PUT   PRINT,PRINTBLD                      WRITE RECORD
                                   33+* 360N-CL-453 PUT           CHANGE LEVEL 3-5                            3-5
000046 5810 C296            00298  34+          L     1,=A(PRINT) GET DTF TABLE ADDRESS
00004A 5800 C2A2            002A4  35+          L     0,=A(PRINTBLD) GET WORK AREA ADDRESS
00004E 58F1 0010            00010  36+          L     15,16(1) GET LOGIC MODULE ADDRESS      3-5
000052 45EF 000C            0000C  37+          BAL   14,12(15) BRANCH TO PUT ROUTINE          3-5
                                   38           CNTRL PRINT,SP,2                          SPACE TWO
                                   39+* 360N-CL-453       CNTRL      CHANGE LEVEL 3-9                         3-9
000056 5810 C296            00298  40+          L     1,=A(PRINT) GET DTF TABLE ADDRESS
00005A 4100 0013            00013  41+          LA    0,19 GET OPERATION CODE
00005E 58F1 0010            00010  42+          L     15,16(1) GET LOGIC MODULE ADDRESS
000062 05EF                        43+          BALR  14,15 BRANCH TO CNTRL ROUTINE
                                   44           PRTOV PRINT,12                            TEST FOR END OF P\G+
                                   45+* 360N-CL-453 PRTOV     CHANGE LEVEL 3-0
000064 5810 C296            00298  46+          L     1,=A(PRINT) GET DTF TABLE ADDRESS
000068 1B00                        47+          SR    0,0 DESIGNATES NO USER ROUTINE ADDRESS
00006A 58F1 0010            00010  48+          L     15,16(1) GET LOGIC MODULE ADDRESS
00006E 45EF 0004            00004  49+          BAL   14,4(15) BRANCH TO PRTOV ROUTINE
000072 47F0 C022            00024  50           B     READRT                              LOOP BACK
                                   51 EOJRT     CLOSE INCARD,PRINT
```

Macro causing error

Figure 18-7 (*Continued*)

```
                                                                                   PAGE
  LOC  OBJECT CODE    ADDR1 ADDR2  STMT    SOURCE STATEMENT                                  FDOS CL3-9 05/30/74

                                    52+* 360N-CL-453 CLOSE      CHANGE LEVEL 3-3              3-3
000076 0700                         53+           CNOP  0,4
000078                              54+EOJRT      DC    0F'0'
000078 4110 C28E           00290    55+           LA    1,=C'$$BCLOSE'
00007C 4500 C086           00088    56+IJJC0007   BAL   0,*+4+4*(3-1)
000080 00000090                     57+           DC    A(INCARD)
000084 000000C8                     58+           DC    A(PRINT)
000088 0A02                         59+           SVC   2
                                    60            EOJ
                                    61+* 360N-CL-453 EOJ        CHANGE LEVEL 3-0
00008A 0A0E                         62+           SVC   14
                                    63 *
                                    64 * DATA AREAS
                                    65 *
                                    66            PRINT NOGEN
                                    67 INCARD     DTFCD DEVADDR=SYS004,                                 C
                                                        EOFADDR=EOJRT,                                  C
                                                        IOAREA1=AREA1,                                  C
                                                        BLKSIZE=80,                                     C
                                                        RECFORM=FIXUNB,                                 C
                                                        WORKA=YES,                                      C
                                                        TYPEFLE=INPUT
                                    87 PRINT      DTFPR DEVADDR=SYS005,                                 C
                                                        IOAREA1=OUT1,                                   C
                                                        BLKSIZE=120,                                    C
                                                        WORKA=YES,                                      C
                                                        DEVICE=1403,                                    C
                                                        RECFORM=FIXUNB
0000F8                              108 AREA1     DS    CL80
000148                              109 OUT1      DS    CL120
0001C0                              110 INWORK    DS    0CL80
0001C0                              111 NUMIN     DS    CL6
0001C6                              112 NAMEIN    DS    CL20
0001DA                              113           DS    CL24
0001F2                              114 GROSSIN   DS    CL8
0001FA                              115           DS    CL22
000210                              116 PRINTBLD  DS    0CL120
000210                              117           DS    CL10
00021A                              118 NUMOUT    DS    CL6
000220                              119           DS    CL10
00022A                              120 NAMEOUT   DS    CL20
00023E                              121           DS    CL10
000248                              122 GROSSOUT  DS    CL8
000250                              123           DS    CL56
000000                              124           END   FIRST
000288 5B5BC2D6D7C5D540             125                 =C'$$BOPEN '
000290 5B5BC2C3D3D6E2C5             126                 =C'$$BCLOSE'
000298 000000C8                     127                 =A(PRINT)
00029C 00000090                     128                 =A(INCARD)
0002A0 000001C0                     129                 =A(INWORK)
0002A4 00000210                     130                 =A(PRINTBLD)
```

No control = Yes parameter in the DTFPR

Figure 18-7 *(Continued)*

```
                                        RELOCATION DICTIONARY                                  PAGE    1

   POS.ID    REL.ID    FLAGS    ADDRESS                                                        05/30/74

     01        01        0C      00000C
     01        01        0C      000010
     01        01        0C      000080
     01        01        0C      000084
     01        01        0C      000098
     01        02        18      0000A1
     01        01        0C      0000A8
     01        01        0C      0000AC
     01        01        08      0000B1
     01        01        0C      0000D0
     01        03        18      0000D9
     01        01        0C      0000E0
     01        01        08      0000F1
     01        01        0C      000298
     01        01        0C      00029C
     01        01        0C      0002A0
     01        01        0C      0002A4
```

```
                                        CROSS-REFERENCE                                        PAGE    1

 SYMBOL     LEN   VALUE   DEFN      REFERENCES                                                 05/30/74

 AREA1     00080 0000F8 00108     0081  0083
 EOJRT     00004 000078 00054     0082
 FIRST     00002 000000 00006     0124
 GROSSIN   00008 0001F2 00114     0031
 GROSSOUT  00008 000248 00122     0031
 IJCX0009  00008 0000B0 00083     0073
 IJJC0007  00004 00007C 00056
 IJJD0001  00004 000008 00013
 IJJZ0009  00001 0000C2 00086
 IJJZ0010  00001 0000F8 00107
 INCARD    00006 000090 00070     0014  0025  0057  0128
 INWORK    00080 0001C0 00110     0026  0129
 NAMEIN    00020 0001C6 00112     0030
 NAMEOUT   00020 00022A 00120     0030
 NUMIN     00006 0001C0 00111     0029
 NUMOUT    00006 00021A 00118     0029
 OUT1      00120 000148 00109     0101  0106
 PRINT     00006 0000C8 00090     0015  0019  0034  0040  0046  0058  0127
 PRINTBLD  00120 000210 00116     0035  0130
 READRT    00004 000024 00025     0050


 NO STATEMENTS FLAGGED IN THIS ASSEMBLY
```

```
// EXEC LNKEDT
```

Figure 18-7 *(Continued)*

```
JOB   OUTCORE   05/30/74   DISK LINKAGE EDITOR DIAGNOSTIC OF INPUT

ACTION TAKEN  MAP
LIST    AUTOLINK    IJCFZIWO
LIST    AUTOLINK    IJDFZZZW
LIST    ENTRY
```

```
05/30/74    PHASE   XFR-AD  LOCORE  HICORE  DSK-AD   ESD TYPE  LABEL     LOADED  REL-FR (2)

         PHASE***  004000  004000  004371  56 07 4  CSECT               004000  004000

                                                    CSECT     IJCFZIWO  0042A8  0042A8

                                                    CSECT     IJDFZZZW  004320  004320
```



```
//ASSGN SYS004,X'00C'
1S01D  INVALID STATEMENT.
// ASSGN SYS004,X'00C'
// ASSGN SYS006,X'00D'
// ASSGN SYS005,X'00E'
// EXEC
```

```
0S04I ILLEGAL SVC - HEX LOCATION 004320 - SVC CODE 32
0S00I JOB OUTCORE  CANCELED
```


Figure 18-7 (*Continued*)

```
        OUTCORE          05/30/74                                                     00.10.33                      PAGE  1

GR 0-7  0000008B 000040C8 0001F7FF 00004000   0001F784 FFFFFF7C 00004000 00003F98
GR 8-F  00005B0A 0A0407F1 00004010 00004010   40004002 00005FD8 40004024 [00004320]—— Branch to this address
FP REG  00000000 00000000 00000000 00000000   00000000 00000000 00000000 00000000     caused error
COMREG  BG ADDR IS 0002D0

000000  00000000 00000000 00000000 00000000   00000000 000002D0 FF050000 00000000   ................  ................
000020  FF050007 40003B66 00000000 00000000   5B5BC2C5 D6D1F440 FF05000E 80004C28   .... ...........  $$BEOJ4 .......).
000040  00003C68 08000000 00003C78 00000000   FBF17600 00FED8FA 00040000 0F001FEA   ................  .1....Q.........
000060  00040000 0000003FE 00040000 00001EAA  00000000 00000E1C 00040000 000003A4   ................  ................
000080  00000000 00000000 00000000 00000003   00050003 06B006B0 06B041BB 00734570   ................  ................
0000A0  0168940F BEAB41A0 CF1C4570 0DEA18A8   419001A8 92FFB583 458000EA 9200B593   ................  ................
0000C0  47F0BCC0 06B006B0 06B006B0 06B006B0   06B006B0 06B006B0 06B041BB 001741BB   .0..............  ................
0000E0  00504570 01684180 01A89640 A0019120   A00C4710 00FA9261 A0019604 A00F95F2   ............ ....  ......./........S
000100  A0024780 B0EC95C1 A0024780 B0EC9561   A0024780 01229104 A0004780 01229203   .......A......./  ................
000120  008F9281 A0004BA0 032A487A CE0C49A0   036C41AA CF0C0778 94F9703B D7017058   ................  ..........9..P...
000140  70589283 A00095FF B5829200 B5820788   9680A001 440004FC 4780BBA0 947FA001   ................  ................
000160  92F0BB3D 47F0BBA0 42B000F7 58B002B8   9180A000 07175890 A0044880 02445000   .0...0.....7....  ...............&.
000180  902C6000 90586020 90606040 90686060   9070D21B 90100298 D2079008 80009680   ..-...-..-- ..--  ..K......K.......
0001A0  A00007F7 45700170 D20EB562 B57258E0   02C4DC0E B562CF0C 1BAADD0F B562000C   ...7....K.......  .D..............
0001C0  43A10010 42A0036F 4AA0034C D20002FF   A00D5AA0 03644400 A0045890 A0044220   .............)K...  ................
0001E0  A0009140 A0014710 CB96D207 02989008   9560036F 47200270 68009058 68209060   ... .......K.....  .-..............-
000200  68409068 68609070 4BA0032A 41AACE0C   D2010016 A0009898 90108200 02984400   . ...-...........  K...............
000220  A0049500 A0014780 02364400 04FC4780   023647F0 01A45890 A0049818 9030989F   ................  ...0............
000240  02983200 00389284 CF6CD207 0298B698   9890B6A0 82000298 9680A000 41100030   ...........K.....  ................
000260  47F0BAF0 96030039 96010038 82000038   92FF0298 96050299 440004FC 478001F8   .0.0............  ...............8
000280  D3000299 02FF47F0 01F8615C 40615040   44F00000 00000000 FF050007 40003B66   L.......C.8/* /&  .0........... ...
0002A0  00001000 00002000 00003000 00004000   000038B0 8000197A 00001000 00002000   ............... .  ................
0002C0  00003000 00004000 30420000 00000000   F0F561F3 F061F7F4 40004000 00000000   ...... .........  05/30/74 . .....
0002E0  00000000 00000000 D6E4E3C3 D6D9C540   0001F7FF 00004371 00004371 00000010   .........OUTCORE  ..7.............
000300  0003FFFF FC777CD0 A8A07CD0 0097319D   31A43295 32963310 34403444 344838F0   ......'...'.....  .......... ......0
000320  F5F3F0F7 F4F1F5F0 00002F0C 0000001E   139014CA 157C15F4 15FC0010 31240010   53074150........  .....'.4.........
000340  5B5BC2D6 0007000A 020016E0 2E0C0000   00000000 02D00080 0000035C 00000000   $$BO............  .............*....
000360  0000357C 00000100 00001614 00100010   0000317E 00001572 00000000 00000000   ...'............  ................
000380  00000000 00000000 00000000 00000000   00000000 00000000 00003028 00003C78   ................  ................
0003A0  000037D4 92380245 909F0298 98BE02B8   41900A14 48A0036E 4AA0032A 9180A000   ...M............  ................
0003C0  47100302 58B0A004 9018B030 98BE02B8   07F99601 A00098BE 02B895FF A00F0789   ...K............  .9..............
0003E0  5000B6BC 48E00244 D207B698 E00058E0   02C494FD B699D21B B6A00298 07F9909F   &........K.......  .D....K.......9..
000400  02989220 02454590 03844190 021E9500   00234780 04E89535 002347B0 00CE4860   ................  .....Y..........-
000420  00221A66 487002C8 48667000 07F6181F   1B664121 000F4570 B2304860 B4D81B22   ........H.....6..  ............-.Q..
000440  43201007 4130003D 1B234740 04584130   003D1B23 4780045A 1A234220 05F54320   ............ ....  ..............5..
000460  1007950B 10074780 049847F0 055E4720   00DA4230 05F54320 036E4322 CE0F1A23   .............0....  .....5..........
000480  950B1007 47800490 950B1007 47F0055A   437002FE 47F0049E 1B774370 BA648870   ...............0..  .....0..........
0004A0  00031177 4337CE0C 47F0056A 472000D8   96801002 960C1004 07F91858 41430002   ..........0.....Q  .........9......
0004C0  43540000 41455000 1A444A40 B4D095FF   40004770 04C04284 000007F9 95FF05B7   .......&.... ....  ...........9....
0004E0  07891B00 5000B6BC 95FF05B7 4780BBEA   4860036E 9560036F 4780042E D502A005   ....&...........  .-...-.......N...
000500  03494770 05144111 00004910 B2AE47B0   05141B66 4121000F 4570B230 D5021009   ................  ..............N...
000520  03014780 00D64400 06145870 039CD502   70010301 4780DD6 1B334330 10079501   .....O..........N.  ........O.......
000540  10064770 046E92FF 05F5D200 0553A00D   4123000B D5001007 A00E47B0 00DA4182   ..........5K......  ....N...........
000560  20004870 031C4338 7000D403 1002CF78   4930B2AC 47B004AC 89300003 4A300310   ..........M......  ................
000580  91F03004 4780C070 D5010022 C5CC4780   C356D501 B4C8B4D6 472005B4 4930B4F0   .0.......N...E...  C.N..H.O........0
0005A0  477005B4 950F0023 478005B4 91103006   4780BBEA 41800000 41488000 1A444A40   ................  ...............
0005C0  B4D01858 4A50033C D20005B7 40005010   400092FF 40004220 50004260 505A4260   .....&..K... .&.   ... ...&..-&..-
0005E0  501E91F0 501E4780 05F44A60 034CD200   501E600D 9203503C 91F03004 4780C090   &..0&....4.-.)K.  &.-...&..O......
```

Figure 18-7 (*Continued*)

```
0036E0  D5D640D5 C1D4C540 0003FFFF 00003F10   00003F10 00000030 0003FFFF FC777CDC   NO NAME ........  .............'.
003700  80007C50 0097319D 31A43295 32963310   34403444 344838F0 F5F3F0F7 F4F1F5F0   ..'&............  . .....053074150
003720  00002F0C 0000001E 145014CA 157C15F4   15FC0010 31240030 00000000 00000000   .........&...'.4  ...............
003740  00000000 2E0C0000 00000000 02000080   00003794 00000000 0000357C 00000100   ................  ............'....
003760  00001614 00200020 0000317E 00001572   00000000 00000000 00000000 00000000   ................  ...............
003780  00000000 00000000 00000000 00000000   00003031 00000000 0000357C 00000100   ................  ..........'....
0037A0  00001614 00300030 0000317E 00001572   00000000 00000000 00000000 00000000   ................  ...............
0037C0  00000000 00000000 00000000 00000000   0000303A 00000700 FF000000 00FF0000   ................  ...............
0037E0  0000FF00 000000FF 00000000 FF000000   00FF0000 0000FF00 000000FF 00000000   ................  ...............
003800  FF000000 00FF0000 0000FF00 000000FF   00000000 FF000000 00FF0000 0000FF00   ................  ...............
003820  000000FF FF000000 00000000 00000000   00000000 00000000 00000000 00000000   ................  ...............
003840  00000000 --SAME--                                                           ....
0038A0  00000000 00000000 00000000 00000000                                         ................

LBLTYP  HEX LENGTH IS 0000
--BG--
003F80                    D5D640D5 C1D4C540   FF150032 40004322 0A0407F1 00004010          NO NAME  .... ......1.. .
003FA0  00004010 40004002 00005FD8 40004024   000C4320 0000008B 000040C8 0001F7FF   .. . . ....Q . .  .......... H..7.
003FC0  00004000 0001F784 FFFFFF7C 00004000   00003F98 00005B0A 00000000 0002586F   .. ...7....'.. .  ......$.........
003FE0  00000000 --SAME--                                                           ....
004000  05C00700 4110C286 4500C012 00004090   000040C8 0A025810 C2964100 00B858F1   ......B....... .  .. H....B......1
004020  001005EF 5810C29A 5800C29E 58F10010   45EF0008 D205C218 C1BED213 C228C1C4   ......B...B..1..  ....K.B.A.K.B.AD
004040  D207C246 C1F05810 C2965800 C2A258F1   C01045EF 000C5810 C2964100 001358F1   K.B.A0..B...B..1  ........B......1
004060  001005EF 5810C296 180058F1 001045EF   000447F0 C0220700 4110C28E 4500C086   ......B....1....  ...0.......B.....
004080  00004090 000040C8 0A020A0E 00000000   00008000 00000104 000040B0 00000000   .. ... H........  .......... .....
0040A0  000042A8 02810202 000040F8 00004078   020040F8 20000050 47000000 D24FD000   .......... 8.. .  .. 8...&....K...
0040C0  E0000000 00000000 00008000 0C000105   000040F0 00003AD8 00004320 08920909   ................  .. 0...Q.......
0040E0  00004148 00000000 07004700 00000000   09004148 20000078 4740C04C 5810C456   ................  .......... .)..D.
004100  4100008B 58F10010 05EF5810 C4565800   C45A58F1 001045FF 000C5810 C4564100   .....1.......D...  D..1.........D...
004120  001358F1 001005EF D201C1C0 C46A47F0   C04CD277 C213C212 5810C456 5800C466   ...1....K.A.D..0  .)K.B.B...D...D.
004140  58F10010 45EF000C 5810C456 41000013   58F10010 05EFD20D C21DC46E D205C251   .1.........D.....  .1....K.B.D.K.B.
004160  C1BADE05 C251C303 D205C25A C1BADE05   C25AC306 D205C265 C1BADE05 C265C309   A...B.C.K.B.A...  B.C.K.B.A...B.C.
004180  D205C26D C1BADE05 C26DC30C D205C27A   C1BADE05 C27AC30F 5810C456 5800C466   K.B.A...B.C.K.B.  A...B.C...D...D.
0041A0  58F10010 45EF000C 4110C44E 4500C186   00004318 00004350 0A020A0E 40202020   .1........D...A.  .......&..... ...
0041C0  2120001C 40202020 2120001C 00000000   00000C00 001C4020 205B2020 205B2020   .... ..........  ...... ..$...$..
0041E0  205B2021 20E2E4D4 40D6C640 D5E4D4C2   C5D9E240 C6D9D6D4 40F140E3 D640F0CA   .$...SUM OF NUMB  ERS FROM 1 TO 0.
004200  9500E07A 4770F0A2 9610D048 92FFE000   47F0F040 40404040 40404040 40404040   ......0.........  .00
004220  40404040 40404040 40404040 40404040   5B5BC2D6 D7C5D540 5B5BC2C3 D3D6E2C5                     $$BOPEN $$BCLOSE
004240  00004080 0000417A 00000000 000041E5   1C004070 000041A0 0A320000 0A320000   .. ...........V  .. ............
004260  47F0F01A 0A320000 C9D1C3C6 E9C9E6F0   030A0A00 91801002 4710F026 0A0750E0   .00.....IJCFZIWO  ..........0...&.
004280  F07058E0 10209101 5B5BC2D6 D7C5D540   5B5BC2C3 D3D6E2C5 000040C8 00004090   0.......$$BOPEN   $$BCLOSE.. H.. .
0042A0  000041C0 00004210 0A320000 0A320000   47F0F01A 0A320000 C9D1C3C6 E9C9E6F0   ................  .00.....IJCFZIWO
0042C0  030A0A00 91801002 4710F026 0A0750E0   F07058E0 10209101 10044780 F04C9140   ..........0...&.  0...........0).
0042E0  10024710 F04658E0 F07047F0 F01A58E0   101C07FE D501F06A E0004770 F05A47F0   ....0...0..00...  ....N.0......0..0
004300  F04650D0 F06C18D0 4400102C 98DEF06C   07FE615C 00000000 00000000 00000104   0.&.0.........0.  ../*...........
004320  0A320000 0A320000 0A320000 47F0F01A   C9D1C4C6 E9E9E9E6 F3F99180 10024710   .............00.  IJDFZZZW39......
004340  F0240A07 90CEF040 58E01018 48C0102E   06C018D0 44C0F04C 98CEF040 0A0007FE   0.....0 ........  ......0)..0 ....
004360  00000000 00000000 00000000 D200E000   00000000 00000000 00000000 00000000   ............K...  ...............
004380  00000000 --SAME--                                                           ....
01F7E0  00000000 00000000 00000000 00000000   00000000 00000000 00000000 00000000   ................  ...............
```

Figure 18-7 (*Concluded*)

Appendices

Appendices

A

IBM S/370 Reference Data

System/370 Reference Summary

GX20-1850-2

Third Edition (March 1974)

This edition supersedes GX20-1850-1. It includes new machine instructions and control register functions associated with multiprocessing, and the new instructions CS, CDS, CLRIO, IPK, and SPKA. To the extent that space allows, additional non-TP devices most often attached to System/370s have been added to the I/O command code tables.

The card is intended primarily for use by S/370 assembler language programmers. It contains basic machine information on Models 115 through 168 summarized from the *System/370 Principles of Operation* (GA22-7000), frequently used information from *OS/VS and DOS/VS Assembler Language* (GC33-4010), command codes for various I/O devices, and a multi-code translation table. The card will be updated from time to time. However, the above manuals and others cited on the card are the authoritative reference sources and will be first to reflect changes.

The names of instructions essentially new with S/370 are shown in italics. Some machine instructions are optional or not available for some models. For those that are available on a particular model, the user is referred to the appropriate functional characteristics manual. For a particular installation, one must ascertain which optional hardware features and programming system(s) have been installed. The floating-point and extended floating-point instructions, as well as the instructions listed below, are not standard on every model. Monitoring (the MC instruction) is not available on the Model 165.

Conditional swapping	CDS, CS
CPU timer and clock comparator	SCKC, SPT, STCKC, STPT
Direct control	RDD, WRD
Dynamic address translation	LRA, PTLB, RRB, STNSM, STOSM
Input/output	CLRIO, SIOF
Multiprocessing	SIGP, SPX, STAP, STPX
PSW key handling	IPK, SPKA

Comments about this publication may be sent to the address below. All comments and suggestions become the property of IBM.

IBM Corporation, Technical Publications/Systems, Dept. 824, 1133 Westchester Avenue, White Plains, N. Y. 10604

MACHINE INSTRUCTIONS ②

NAME	MNEMONIC	OP CODE	FOR MAT	OPERANDS
Add (c)	AR	1A	RR	R1,R2
Add (c)	A	5A	RX	R1,D2(X2,B2)
Add Decimal (c)	AP	FA	SS	D1(L1,B1),D2(L2,B2)
Add Halfword (c)	AH	4A	RX	R1,D2(X2,B2)
Add Logical (c)	ALR	1E	RR	R1,R2
Add Logical (c)	AL	5E	RX	R1,D2(X2,B2)
AND (c)	NR	14	RR	R1,R2
AND (c)	N	54	RX	R1,D2(X2,B2)
AND (c)	NI	94	SI	D1(B1),I2
AND (c)	NC	D4	SS	D1(L,B1),D2(B2)
Branch and Link	BALR	05	RR	R1,R2
Branch and Link	BAL	45	RX	R1,D2(X2,B2)
Branch on Condition	BCR	07	RR	M1,R2
Branch on Condition	BC	47	RX	M1,D2(X2,B2)
Branch on Count	BCTR	06	RR	R1,R2
Branch on Count	BCT	46	RX	R1,D2(X2,B2)
Branch on Index High	BXH	86	RS	R1,R3,D2(B2)
Branch on Index Low or Equal	BXLE	87	RS	R1,R3,D2(B2)
Clear I/O (c,p)	CLRIO	9D01	S	D2(B2)
Compare (c)	CR	19	RR	R1,R2
Compare (c)	C	59	RX	R1,D2(X2,B2)
Compare and Swap (c)	CS	BA	RS	R1,R3,D2(B2)
Compare Decimal (c)	CP	F9	SS	D1(L1,B1),D2(L2,B2)
Compare Double and Swap (c)	CDS	BB	RS	R1,R3,D2(B2)
Compare Halfword (c)	CH	49	RX	R1,D2(X2,B2)
Compare Logical (c)	CLR	15	RR	R1,R2
Compare Logical (c)	CL	55	RX	R1,D2(X2,B2)
Compare Logical (c)	CLC	D5	SS	D1(L,B1),D2(B2)
Compare Logical (c)	CLI	95	SI	D1(B1),I2
Compare Logical Characters under Mask (c)	CLM	BD	RS	R1,M3,D2(B2)
Compare Logical Long (c)	CLCL	0F	RR	R1,R2
Convert to Binary	CVB	4F	RX	R1,D2(X2,B2)
Convert to Decimal	CVD	4E	RX	R1,D2(X2,B2)
Diagnose (p)		83		Model-dependent
Divide	DR	1D	RR	R1,R2
Divide	D	5D	RX	R1,D2(X2,B2)
Divide Decimal	DP	FD	SS	D1(L1,B1),D2(L2,B2)
Edit (c)	ED	DE	SS	D1(L,B1),D2(B2)
Edit and Mark (c)	EDMK	DF	SS	D1(L,B1),D2(B2)
Exclusive OR (c)	XR	17	RR	R1,R2
Exclusive OR (c)	X	57	RX	R1,D2(X2,B2)
Exclusive OR (c)	XI	97	SI	D1(B1),I2
Exclusive OR (c)	XC	D7	SS	D1(L,B1),D2(B2)
Execute	EX	44	RX	R1,D2(X2,B2)
Halt I/O (c,p)	HIO	9E00	S	D2(B2)
Halt Device (c,p)	HDV	9E01	S	D2(B2)
Insert Character	IC	43	RX	R1,D2(X2,B2)
Insert Characters under Mask (c)	ICM	BF	RS	R1,M3,D2(B2)
Insert PSW Key (p)	IPK	B20B	S	
Insert Storage Key (p)	ISK	09	RR	R1,R2
Load	LR	18	RR	R1,R2
Load	L	58	RX	R1,D2(X2,B2)
Load Address	LA	41	RX	R1,D2(X2,B2)
Load and Test (c)	LTR	12	RR	R1,R2
Load Complement (c)	LCR	13	RR	R1,R2
Load Control (p)	LCTL	B7	RS	R1,R3,D2(B2)
Load Halfword	LH	48	RX	R1,D2(X2,B2)
Load Multiple	LM	98	RS	R1,R3,D2(B2)
Load Negative (c)	LNR	11	RR	R1,R2
Load Positive (c)	LPR	10	RR	R1,R2
Load PSW (n,p)	LPSW	82	S	D2(B2)
Load Real Address (c,p)	LRA	B1	RX	R1,D2(X2,B2)
Monitor Call	MC	AF	SI	D1(B1),I2
Move	MVI	92	SI	D1(B1),I2
Move	MVC	D2	SS	D1(L,B1),D2(B2)
Move Long (c)	MVCL	0E	RR	R1,R2
Move Numerics	MVN	D1	SS	D1(L,B1),D2(B2)
Move with Offset	MVO	F1	SS	D1(L1,B1),D2(L2,B2)
Move Zones	MVZ	D3	SS	D1(L,B1),D2(B2)
Multiply	MR	1C	RR	R1,R2
Multiply	M	5C	RX	R1,D2(X2,B2)
Multiply Decimal	MP	FC	SS	D1(L1,B1),D2(L2,B2)
Multiply Halfword	MH	4C	RX	R1,D2(X2,B2)
OR (c)	OR	16	RR	R1,R2

MACHINE INSTRUCTIONS (Contd) ③

NAME	MNEMONIC	OP CODE	FOR MAT	OPERANDS
OR (c)	O	56	RX	R1,D2(X2,B2)
OR (c)	OI	96	SI	D1(B1),I2
OR (c)	OC	D6	SS	D1(L,B1),D2(B2)
Pack	PACK	F2	SS	D1(L1,B1),D2(L2,B2)
Purge TLB (p)	PTLB	B20D	S	
Read Direct (p)	RDD	85	SI	D1(B1),I2
Reset Reference Bit (c,p)	RRB	B213	S	D2(B2)
Set Clock (c,p)	SCK	B204	S	D2(B2)
Set Clock Comparator (p)	SCKC	B206	S	D2(B2)
Set CPU Timer (p)	SPT	B208	S	D2(B2)
Set Prefix (p)	SPX	B210	S	D2(B2)
Set Program Mask (n)	SPM	04	RR	R1
Set PSW Key from Address (p)	SPKA	B20A	S	D2(B2)
Set Storage Key (p)	SSK	08	RR	R1,R2
Set System Mask (p)	SSM	80	S	D2(B2)
Shift and Round Decimal (c)	SRP	F0	SS	D1(L1,B1),D2(B2),I3
Shift Left Double (c)	SLDA	8F	RS	R1,D2(B2)
Shift Left Double Logical	SLDL	8D	RS	R1,D2(B2)
Shift Left Single (c)	SLA	8B	RS	R1,D2(B2)
Shift Left Single Logical	SLL	89	RS	R1,D2(B2)
Shift Right Double (c)	SRDA	8E	RS	R1,D2(B2)
Shift Right Double Logical	SRDL	8C	RS	R1,D2(B2)
Shift Right Single (c)	SRA	8A	RS	R1,D2(B2)
Shift Right Single Logical	SRL	88	RS	R1,D2(B2)
Signal Processor (c,p)	SIGP	AE	RS	R1,R3,D2(B2)
Start I/O (c,p)	SIO	9C00	S	D2(B2)
Start I/O Fast Release (c,p)	SIOF	9C01	S	D2(B2)
Store	ST	50	RX	R1,D2(X2,B2)
Store Channel ID (c,p)	STIDC	B203	S	D2(B2)
Store Character	STC	42	RX	R1,D2(X2,B2)
Store Characters under Mask	STCM	BE	RS	R1,M3,D2(B2)
Store Clock (c)	STCK	B205	S	D2(B2)
Store Clock Comparator (p)	STCKC	B207	S	D2(B2)
Store Control (p)	STCTL	B6	RS	R1,R3,D2(B2)
Store CPU Address (p)	STAP	B212	S	D2(B2)
Store CPU ID (p)	STIDP	B202	S	D2(B2)
Store CPU Timer (p)	STPT	B209	S	D2(B2)
Store Halfword	STH	40	RX	R1,D2(X2,B2)
Store Multiple	STM	90	RS	R1,R3,D2(B2)
Store Prefix (p)	STPX	B211	S	D2(B2)
Store Then AND System Mask (p)	STNSM	AC	SI	D1(B1),I2
Store Then OR System Mask (p)	STOSM	AD	SI	D1(B1),I2
Subtract (c)	SR	1B	RR	R1,R2
Subtract (c)	S	5B	RX	R1,D2(X2,B2)
Subtract Decimal (c)	SP	FB	SS	D1(L1,B1),D2(L2,B2)
Subtract Halfword (c)	SH	4B	RX	R1,D2(X2,B2)
Subtract Logical (c)	SLR	1F	RR	R1,R2
Subtract Logical (c)	SL	5F	RX	R1,D2(X2,B2)
Supervisor Call	SVC	0A	RR	I
Test and Set (c)	TS	93	S	D2(B2)
Test Channel (c,p)	TCH	9F00	S	D2(B2)
Test I/O (c,p)	TIO	9D00	S	D2(B2)
Test under Mask (c)	TM	91	SI	D1(B1),I2
Translate	TR	DC	SS	D1(L,B1),D2(B2)
Translate and Test (c)	TRT	DD	SS	D1(L,B1),D2(B2)
Unpack	UNPK	F3	SS	D1(L1,B1),D2(L2,B2)
Write Direct (p)	WRD	84	SI	D1(B1),I2
Zero and Add Decimal (c)	ZAP	F8	SS	D1(L1,B1),D2(L2,B2)

Floating-Point Instructions

NAME	MNEMONIC	OP CODE	FOR MAT	OPERANDS
Add Normalized, Extended (c,x)	AXR	36	RR	R1,R2
Add Normalized, Long (c)	ADR	2A	RR	R1,R2
Add Normalized, Long (c)	AD	6A	RX	R1,D2(X2,B2)
Add Normalized, Short (c)	AER	3A	RR	R1,R2
Add Normalized, Short (c)	AE	7A	RX	R1,D2(X2,B2)
Add Unnormalized, Long (c)	AWR	2E	RR	R1,R2
Add Unnormalized, Long (c)	AW	6E	RX	R1,D2(X2,B2)
Add Unnormalized, Short (c)	AUR	3E	RR	R1,R2
Add Unnormalized, Short (c)	AU	7E	RX	R1,D2(X2,B2)

c. Condition code is set.
n. New condition code is loaded.
p. Privileged instruction.
x. Extended precision floating-point.

Floating-Point Instructions (Contd) ④

NAME	MNEMONIC	OP CODE	FOR MAT	OPERANDS
Compare, Long (c)	CDR	29	RR	R1,R2
Compare, Long (c)	CD	69	RX	R1,D2(X2,B2)
Compare, Short (c)	CER	39	RR	R1,R2
Compare, Short (c)	CE	79	RX	R1,D2(X2,B2)
Divide, Long	DDR	2D	RR	R1,R2
Divide, Long	DD	6D	RX	R1,D2(X2,B2)
Divide, Short	DER	3D	RR	R1,R2
Divide, Short	DE	7D	RX	R1,D2(X2,B2)
Halve, Long	HDR	24	RR	R1,R2
Halve, Short	HER	34	RR	R1,R2
Load and Test, Long (c)	LTDR	22	RR	R1,R2
Load and Test, Short (c)	LTER	32	RR	R1,R2
Load Complement, Long (c)	LCDR	23	RR	R1,R2
Load Complement, Short (c)	LCER	33	RR	R1,R2
Load, Long	LDR	28	RR	R1,R2
Load, Long	LD	68	RX	R1,D2(X2,B2)
Load Negative, Long (c)	LNDR	21	RR	R1,R2
Load Negative, Short (c)	LNER	31	RR	R1,R2
Load Positive, Long (c)	LPDR	20	RR	R1,R2
Load Positive, Short (c)	LPER	30	RR	R1,R2
Load Rounded, Extended to Long (x)	LRDR	25	RR	R1,R2
Load Rounded, Long to Short (x)	LRER	35	RR	R1,R2
Load, Short	LER	38	RR	R1,R2
Load, Short	LE	78	RX	R1,D2(X2,B2)
Multiply, Extended (x)	MXR	26	RR	R1,R2
Multiply, Long	MDR	2C	RR	R1,R2
Multiply, Long	MD	6C	RX	R1,D2(X2,B2)
Multiply, Long/Extended (x)	MXDR	27	RR	R1,R2
Multiply, Long/Extended (x)	MXD	67	RX	R1,D2(X2,B2)
Multiply, Short	MER	3C	RR	R1,R2
Multiply, Short	ME	7C	RX	R1,D2(X2,B2)
Store, Long	STD	60	RX	R1,D2(X2,B2)
Store, Short	STE	70	RX	R1,D2(X2,B2)
Subtract Normalized, Extended (c,x)	SXR	37	RR	R1,R2
Subtract Normalized, Long (c)	SDR	2B	RR	R1,R2
Subtract Normalized, Long (c)	SD	6B	RX	R1,D2(X2,B2)
Subtract Normalized, Short (c)	SER	3B	RR	R1,R2
Subtract Normalized, Short (c)	SE	7B	RX	R1,D2(X2,B2)
Subtract Unnormalized, Long (c)	SWR	2F	RR	R1,R2
Subtract Unnormalized, Long (c)	SW	6F	RX	R1,D2(X2,B2)
Subtract Unnormalized, Short (c)	SUR	3F	RR	R1,R2
Subtract Unnormalized, Short (c)	SU	7F	RX	R1,D2(X2,B2)

EXTENDED MNEMONIC INSTRUCTIONS[†]

Use	Extended Code* (RX or RR)	Meaning	Machine Instr.* (RX or RR)
General	B or BR	Unconditional Branch	BC or BCR 15,
	NOP or NOPR	No Operation	BC or BCR 0,
After Compare Instructions (A:B)	BH or *BHR*	Branch on A High	BC or BCR 2,
	BL or *BLR*	Branch on A Low	BC or BCR 4,
	BE or *BER*	Branch on A Equal B	BC or BCR 8,
	BNH or *BNHR*	Branch on A Not High	BC or BCR 13,
	BNL or *BNLR*	Branch on A Not Low	BC or BCR 11,
	BNE or *BNER*	Branch on A Not Equal B	BC or BCR 7,
After Arithmetic Instructions	BO or *BOR*	Branch on Overflow	BC or BCR 1,
	BP or *BPR*	Branch on Plus	BC or BCR 2,
	BM or *BMR*	Branch on Minus	BC or BCR 4,
	BNP or *BNPR*	Branch on Not Plus	BC or BCR 13,
	BNM or *BNMR*	Branch on Not Minus	BC or BCR 11,
	BNZ or *BNZR*	Branch on Not Zero	BC or BCR 7,
	BZ or *BZR*	Branch on Zero	BC or BCR 8,
After Test under Mask Instruction	BO or *BOR*	Branch if Ones	BC or BCR 1,
	BM or *BMR*	Branch if Mixed	BC or BCR 4,
	BZ or *BZR*	Branch if Zeros	BC or BCR 8,
	BNO or *BNOR*	Branch if Not Ones	BC or BCR 14,

*Second operand not shown; in all cases it is D2(X2,B2) for RX format or R2 for RR format.

[†]For OS/VS and DOS/VS; source: GC33-4010.

EDIT AND EDMK PATTERN CHARACTERS (in hex)

20—digit selector	40—blank	5C—asterisk
21—start of significance	4B—period	6B—comma
22—field separator	5B—dollar sign	C3D9—CR

CONDITION CODES (5)

Condition Code Setting	0	1	2	3
Mask Bit Value	8	4	2	1
General Instructions				
Add, Add Halfword	zero	<zero	>zero	overflow
Add Logical	zero, no carry	not zero, no carry	zero, carry	not zero, carry
AND	zero	not zero	–	–
Compare, Compare Halfword	equal	1st op low	1st op high	–
Compare and Swap/Double	equal	not equal	–	–
Compare Logical	equal	1st op low	1st op high	–
Exclusive OR	zero	not zero	–	–
Insert Characters under Mask	all zero	1st bit one	1st bit zero	–
Load and Test	zero	<zero	>zero	–
Load Complement	zero	<zero	>zero	overflow
Load Negative	zero	<zero	–	–
Load Positive	zero		>zero	overflow
Move Long	count equal	count low	count high	overlap
OR	zero	not zero	–	–
Shift Left Double/Single	zero	<zero	>zero	overflow
Shift Right Double/Single	zero	<zero	>zero	–
Store Clock	set	not set	error	not oper
Subtract, Subtract Halfword	zero	<zero	>zero	overflow
Subtract Logical	–	not zero, no carry	zero, carry	not zero, carry
Test and Set	zero	one	–	–
Test under Mask	zero	mixed	–	ones
Translate and Test	zero	incomplete	complete	–
Decimal Instructions				
Add Decimal	zero	<zero	>zero	overflow
Compare Decimal	equal	1st op low	1st op high	–
Edit, Edit and Mark	zero	<zero	>zero	–
Shift and Round Decimal	zero	<zero	>zero	overflow
Subtract Decimal	zero	<zero	>zero	overflow
Zero and Add	zero	<zero	>zero	overflow
Floating-Point Instructions				
Add Normalized	zero	<zero	>zero	–
Add Unnormalized	zero	<zero	>zero	–
Compare	equal	1st op low	1st op high	–
Load and Test	zero	<zero	>zero	–
Load Complement	zero	<zero	>zero	–
Load Negative	zero	<zero	–	–
Load Positive	zero	–	>zero	–
Subtract Normalized	zero	<zero	>zero	–
Subtract Unnormalized	zero	<zero	>zero	–
Input/Output Instructions				
Clear I/O	no oper in progress	CSW stored	chan busy	not oper
Halt Device	interruption pending	CSW stored	channel working	not oper
Halt I/O	interruption pending	CSW stored	burst op stopped	not oper
Start I/O, SIOF	successful	CSW stored	busy	not oper
Store Channel ID	ID stored	CSW stored	busy	not oper
Test Channel	available	interruption pending	burst mode	not oper
Test I/O	available	CSW stored	busy	not oper
System Control Instructions				
Load Real Address	translation available	ST entry invalid	PT entry invalid	length violation
Reset Reference Bit	R=0, C=0	R=0, C=1	R=1, C=0	R=1, C=1
Set Clock	set	secure	–	not oper
Signal Processor	accepted	stat stored	busy	not oper

CNOP ALIGNMENT

DOUBLEWORD							
WORD				WORD			
HALFWORD		HALFWORD		HALFWORD		HALFWORD	
BYTE	BYTE	BYTE	BYTE	BYTE	BYTE	BYTE	BYTE
0,4		2,4		0,4		2,4	
0,8		2,8		4,8		6,8	

ASSEMBLER INSTRUCTIONS† (6)

Function	Mnemonic	Meaning
Data definition	DC	Define constant
	DS	Define storage
	CCW	Define channel command word
Program sectioning and linking	START	Start assembly
	CSECT	Identify control section
	DSECT	Identify dummy section
	DXD*	Define external dummy section
	CXD*	Cumulative length of external dummy section
	COM	Identify blank common control section
	ENTRY	Identify entry-point symbol
	EXTRN	Identify external symbol
	WXTRN	Identify weak external symbol
Base register assignment	USING	Use base address register
	DROP	Drop base address register
Control of listings	TITLE	Identify assembly output
	EJECT	Start new page
	SPACE	Space listing
	PRINT	Print optional data
Program Control	ICTL	Input format control
	ISEQ	Input sequence checking
	PUNCH	Punch a card
	REPRO	Reproduce following card
	ORG	Set location counter
	EQU	Equate symbol
	OPSYN*	Equate operation code
	*PUSH**	Save current PRINT or USING status
	*POP**	Restore PRINT or USING status
	LTORG	Begin literal pool
	CNOP	Conditional no operation
	COPY	Copy predefined source coding
	END	End assembly
Macro definition	MACRO	Macro definition header
	MNOTE	Request for error message
	MEXIT	Macro definition exit
	MEND	Macro definition trailer
Conditional assembly	ACTR	Conditional assembly loop counter
	AGO	Unconditional branch
	AIF	Conditional branch
	ANOP	Assembly no operation
	GBLA	Define global SETA symbol
	GBLB	Define global SETB symbol
	GBLC	Define global SETC symbol
	LCLA	Define local SETA symbol
	LCLB	Define local SETB symbol
	LCLC	Define local SETC symbol
	SETA	Set arithmetic variable symbol
	SETB	Set binary variable symbol
	SETC	Set character variable symbol

SUMMARY OF CONSTANTS†

TYPE	IMPLIED LENGTH, BYTES	ALIGNMENT	FORMAT	TRUNCATION/PADDING
C	–	byte	characters	right
X	–	byte	hexadecimal digits	left
B	–	byte	binary digits	left
F	4	word	fixed-point binary	left
H	2	halfword	fixed-point binary	left
E	4	word	short floating-point	right
D	8	doubleword	long floating-point	right
L	16	doubleword	extended floating-point	right
P	–	byte	packed decimal	left
Z	–	byte	zoned decimal	left
A	4	word	value of address	left
Y	2	halfword	value of address	left
S	2	halfword	address in base-displacement form	–
V	4	word	externally defined address value	left
Q*	4	word	symbol naming a DXD or DSECT	left

†For OS/VS and DOS/VS; source: GC33-4010.
*OS/VS only.

I/O COMMAND CODES ⑦

Standard Command Code Assignments (CCW bits 0-7)

xxxx 0000	Invalid	tttt tt01	Write
tttt 0100	Sense	tttt tt10	Read
xxxx 1000	Transfer in Channel	tttt tt11	Control
tttt 1100	Read Backward	0000 0011	Control No Operation

x—Bit ignored. †Modifier bit for specific type of I/O device

CONSOLE PRINTERS

Write, No Carrier Return	01	Sense	04
Write, Auto Carrier Return	09	Audible Alarm	0B
Read Inquiry	0A		

3504, 3505 CARD READERS/3525 CARD PUNCH

Source: GA21-9124

Command	Binary	Hex
Sense	0000 0100	04
Feed, Select Stacker	SS10 F011	
Read Only*	11D0 F010	
Diagnostic Read	1101 0010	D2
Read, Feed, Select Stacker*	SSD0 F010	
Write RCE Format*	0001 0001	11
<u>3504, 3505 only</u>		
Write OMR Format†	0011 0001	31
<u>3525 only</u>		
Write, Feed, Select Stacker	SSD0 0001	
Print Line*	LLLL L101	

Bit Meanings	
<u>SS</u>	<u>Stacker</u>
00	1
01/10	2
<u>F</u>	<u>Format Mode</u>
0	Unformatted
1	Formatted
<u>D</u>	<u>Data Mode</u>
0	1—EBCDIC
1	2—Card image
<u>L</u>	<u>Line Position</u>
5-bit binary value	

*Special feature on 3525. †Special feature.

PRINTERS: 3211/3811 (GA24-3543), 3203/IPA, 1403*/2821 (GA24-3312)

	After Write	Immed
Space 1 Line	09	0B
Space 2 Lines	11	13
Space 3 Lines	19	1B
Skip to Channel 0†	–	83
Skip to Channel 1	89	8B
Skip to Channel 2	91	93
Skip to Channel 3	99	9B
Skip to Channel 4	A1	A3
Skip to Channel 5	A9	AB
Skip to Channel 6	B1	B3
Skip to Channel 7	B9	BB
Skip to Channel 8	C1	C3
Skip to Channel 9	C9	CB
Skip to Channel 10	D1	D3
Skip to Channel 11	D9	DB
Skip to Channel 12	E1	E3

Write without spacing	01
Sense	04
Load UCSB without folding	FB
Fold†	43
Unfold†	23
Load UCSB and Fold (exc. 3211)	F3
UCS Gate Load (1403 only)	EB
Load FCB†	63
Block Data Check	73
Allow Data Check	7B
Read PLB†	02
Read UCSB†	0A
Read FCB†	12
Diag. Check Read (exc. 3203)	06
Diagnostic Write†	05
Raise Cover†	6B
Diagnostic Gate†	07
Diagnostic Read (1403 only)	02

*UCS special feature; IPA diagnostics are model-dependent. †3211 only.

3420/3803, 3410/3411 MAGNETIC TAPE

(**Indicates 3420 only)

See GA32-0020, -0021, -0022 for special features and functions of specific models.

Write	01
Read Forward	02
Read Backward	0C
Sense	04
Sense Reserve**	F4
Sense Release**	D4
Request Track-in-Error	1B
Loop Write-to-Read**	8B
Set Diagnose**	4B
Rewind	07
Rewind Unload	0F
Erase Gap	17
Write Tape Mark	1F
Backspace Block	27
Backspace File	2F
Forward Space Block	37
Forward Space File	3F
Data Security Erase **	97
Diagnostic Mode Set **	0B

	Density	Parity	DC	Trans	Cmd
Mode Set 1 (7-track)	200	odd	on	off	13
			off	off	33
				on	3B
		even	off	off	23
				on	2B
	556	odd	on	off	53
			off	off	73
				on	7B
		even	off	off	63
				on	6B
	800	odd	on	off	93
			off	off	B3
				on	BB
		even	off	off	A3
				on	AB
Mode Set 2 (9-track), 800 bpi					CB
Mode Set 2 (9-track), 1600 bpi					C3
Mode Set 2 (9-track), 6250 bpi**					D3

I/O COMMAND CODES (Contd) ⑧

DIRECT ACCESS STORAGE DEVICES:

3330-3340 SERIES (GA26-1592, -1617, -1619, -1620); **2305/2835** (GA26-1589); **2314, 2319** (GA26-3599, -1606)

	Command	MT Off	MT On*	Count
Control	Orient (c)	2B		Nonzero
	Recalibrate	13		Nonzero
	Seek	07		6
	Seek Cylinder	0B		6
	Seek Head	1B		6
	Space Count	0F		3 (a); nonzero (d)
	Set File Mask	1F		1
	Set Sector (a,f)	23		1
	Restore (executes as a no-op)	17		Nonzero
	Vary Sensing (c)	27		1
	Diagnostic Load (a)	53		1
	Diagnostic Write (a)	73		512
Search	Home Address Equal	39	B9	4
	Identifier Equal	31	B1	5
	Identifier High	51	D1	5
	Identifier Equal or High	71	F1	5
	Key Equal	29	A9	KL
	Key High	49	C9	KL
	Key Equal or High	69	E9	KL
	Key and Data Equal (d)	2D	AD	Number of bytes (including mask bytes) in search argument
	Key and Data High (d)	4D	CD	
	Key and Data Eq. or Hi (d)	6D	ED	
Continue Scan	Search Equal (d)	25	A5	
	Search High (d)	45	C5	
	Search High or Equal (d)	65	E5	
	Set Compare (d)	35	B5	
	Set Compare (d)	75	F5	
	No Compare (d)	55	D5	
Read	Home Address	1A	9A	5
	Count	12	92	8
	Record 0	16	96	Number of bytes to be transferred
	Data	06	86	
	Key and Data	0E	8E	
	Count, Key and Data	1E	9E	
	IPL	02		
	Sector (a,f)	22		1
Sense	Sense I/O	04		24 (a); 6 (d)
	Read, Reset Buffered Log (b)	A4		24
	Read Buffered Log (c)	24		128
	Device Release (e)	94		24 (a); 6 (d)
	Device Reserve (e)	B4		24 (a); 6 (d)
	Read Diagnostic Status 1 (a)	44		16 or 512
Write	Home Address	19		5 (exc. 7 on 3340)
	Record 0	15		8+KL+DL of R0
	Erase	11		8+KL+DL
	Count, Key and Data	1D		8+KL+DL
	Special Count, Key and Data	01		8+KL+DL
	Data	05		DL
	Key and Data	0D		KL+DL

* Code same as MT Off except as listed.
a. Except 2314, 2319.
b. 3330-3340 Series only; manual reset on 3340.
c. 2305/2835 only.
d. 2314, 2319 only.
e. String switch or 2-channel switch feature required; standard on 2314 with 2844.
f. Special feature required on 3340.

IBM

International Business Machines Corporation
Data Processing Division
1133 Westchester Avenue, White Plains, New York 10604
(U.S.A. only)

IBM World Trade Corporation
821 United Nations Plaza, New York, New York 10017
(International)

Printed in U.S.A. GX20-1850-2

CODE TRANSLATION TABLE ⑨

Dec.	Hex	Instruction (RR)	Graphics and Controls BCDIC	EBCDIC(1)	ASCII	7-Track Tape BCDIC(2)	EBCDIC Card Code	Binary
0	00			NUL	NUL		12-0-1-8-9	0000 0000
1	01			SOH	SOH		12-1-9	0000 0001
2	02			STX	STX		12-2-9	0000 0010
3	03			ETX	ETX		12-3-9	0000 0011
4	04	SPM		PF	EOT		12-4-9	0000 0100
5	05	BALR		HT	ENQ		12-5-9	0000 0101
6	06	BCTR		LC	ACK		12-6-9	0000 0110
7	07	BCR		DEL	BEL		12-7-9	0000 0111
8	08	SSK			BS		12-8-9	0000 1000
9	09	ISK			HT		12-1-8-9	0000 1001
10	0A	SVC		SMM	LF		12-2-8-9	0000 1010
11	0B			VT	VT		12-3-8-9	0000 1011
12	0C			FF	FF		12-4-8-9	0000 1100
13	0D			CR	CR		12-5-8-9	0000 1101
14	0E	MVCL		SO	SO		12-6-8-9	0000 1110
15	0F	CLCL		SI	SI		12-7-8-9	0000 1111
16	10	LPR		DLE	DLE		12-11-1-8-9	0001 0000
17	11	LNR		DC1	DC1		11-1-9	0001 0001
18	12	LTR		DC2	DC2		11-2-9	0001 0010
19	13	LCR		TM	DC3		11-3-9	0001 0011
20	14	NR		RES	DC4		11-4-9	0001 0100
21	15	CLR		NL	NAK		11-5-9	0001 0101
22	16	OR		BS	SYN		11-6-9	0001 0110
23	17	XR		IL	ETB		11-7-9	0001 0111
24	18	LR		CAN	CAN		11-8-9	0001 1000
25	19	CR		EM	EM		11-1-8-9	0001 1001
26	1A	AR		CC	SUB		11-2-8-9	0001 1010
27	1B	SR		CU1	ESC		11-3-8-9	0001 1011
28	1C	MR		IFS	FS		11-4-8-9	0001 1100
29	1D	DR		IGS	GS		11-5-8-9	0001 1101
30	1E	ALR		IRS	RS		11-6-8-9	0001 1110
31	1F	SLR		IUS	US		11-7-8-9	0001 1111
32	20	LPDR		DS	SP		11-0-1-8-9	0010 0000
33	21	LNDR		SOS	! !		0-1-9	0010 0001
34	22	LTDR		FS	"		0-2-9	0010 0010
35	23	LCDR			#		0-3-9	0010 0011
36	24	HDR		BYP	$		0-4-9	0010 0100
37	25	LRDR		LF	%		0-5-9	0010 0101
38	26	MXR		ETB	&		0-6-9	0010 0110
39	27	MXDR		ESC	'		0-7-9	0010 0111
40	28	LDR			(		0-8-9	0010 1000
41	29	CDR			)		0-1-8-9	0010 1001
42	2A	ADR		SM	*		0-2-8-9	0010 1010
43	2B	SDR		CU2	+		0-3-8-9	0010 1011
44	2C	MDR			,		0-4-8-9	0010 1100
45	2D	DDR		ENQ	-		0-5-8-9	0010 1101
46	2E	AWR		ACK	.		0-6-8-9	0010 1110
47	2F	SWR		BEL	/		0-7-8-9	0010 1111
48	30	LPER			0		12-11-0-1-8-9	0011 0000
49	31	LNER			1		1-9	0011 0001
50	32	LTER		SYN	2		2-9	0011 0010
51	33	LCER			3		3-9	0011 0011
52	34	HER		PN	4		4-9	0011 0100
53	35	LRER		RS	5		5-9	0011 0101
54	36	AXR		UC	6		6-9	0011 0110
55	37	SXR		EOT	7		7-9	0011 0111
56	38	LER			8		8-9	0011 1000
57	39	CER			9		1-8-9	0011 1001
58	3A	AER			:		2-8-9	0011 1010
59	3B	SER		CU3	;		3-8-9	0011 1011
60	3C	MER		DC4	<		4-8-9	0011 1100
61	3D	DER		NAK	=		5-8-9	0011 1101
62	3E	AUR			>		6-8-9	0011 1110
63	3F	SUR		SUB	?		7-8-9	0011 1111

1. Two columns of EBCDIC graphics are shown. The first gives standard bit pattern assignments. The second shows the T-11 and TN text printing chains (120 graphics).
2. Add C (check bit) for odd or even parity as needed, except as noted.
3. For even parity use CA.

TWO-CHARACTER BSC DATA LINK CONTROLS

Function	EBCDIC	ASCII
ACK-0	DLE,X'70'	DLE,0
ACK-1	DLE,X'61'	DLE,1
WACK	DLE,X'6B'	DLE, ;
RVI	DLE,X'7C'	DLE,<

CODE TRANSLATION TABLE (Contd) ⑩

Dec.	Hex	Instruction (RX)	Graphics and Controls BCDIC	EBCDIC(1)	ASCII	7-Track Tape BCDIC(2)	EBCDIC Card Code	Binary
64	40	STH		Sp Sp	@	(3)	no punches	0100 0000
65	41	LA			A		12-0-1-9	0100 0001
66	42	STC			B		12-0-2-9	0100 0010
67	43	IC			C		12-0-3-9	0100 0011
68	44	EX			D		12-0-4-9	0100 0100
69	45	BAL			E		12-0-5-9	0100 0101
70	46	BCT			F		12-0-6-9	0100 0110
71	47	BC			G		12-0-7-9	0100 0111
72	48	LH			H		12-0-8-9	0100 1000
73	49	CH			I		12-1-8	0100 1001
74	4A	AH		¢ ¢	J		12-2-8	0100 1010
75	4B	SH	.	. .	K	B A 8 2 1	12-3-8	0100 1011
76	4C	MH	⌑)	< <	L	B A 8 4	12-4-8	0100 1100
77	4D		[	((	M	B A 8 4 1	12-5-8	0100 1101
78	4E	CVD	<	+ +	N	B A 8 4 2	12-6-8	0100 1110
79	4F	CVB	‡	¦ ¦	O	B A 8 4 2 1	12-7-8	0100 1111
80	50	ST	& +	& &	P	B A	12	0101 0000
81	51				Q		12-11-1-9	0101 0001
82	52				R		12-11-2-9	0101 0010
83	53				S		12-11-3-9	0101 0011
84	54	N			T		12-11-4-9	0101 0100
85	55	CL			U		12-11-5-9	0101 0101
86	56	O			V		12-11-6-9	0101 0110
87	57	X			W		12-11-7-9	0101 0111
88	58	L			X		12-11-8-9	0101 1000
89	59	C			Y		11-1-8	0101 1001
90	5A	A		! !	Z		11-2-8	0101 1010
91	5B	S	$	$ $	[	B 8 2 1	11-3-8	0101 1011
92	5C	M	*	* *	\	B 8 4	11-4-8	0101 1100
93	5D	D	]	))	]	B 8 4 1	11-5-8	0101 1101
94	5E	AL	;	; ;	¬ ^	B 8 4 2	11-6-8	0101 1110
95	5F	SL	Δ	¬ ¬	_	B 8 4 2 1	11-7-8	0101 1111
96	60	STD	-	- -	`	B	11	0110 0000
97	61		/	/ /	a	A 1	0-1	0110 0001
98	62				b		11-0-2-9	0110 0010
99	63				c		11-0-3-9	0110 0011
100	64				d		11-0-4-9	0110 0100
101	65				e		11-0-5-9	0110 0101
102	66				f		11-0-6-9	0110 0110
103	67	MXD			g		11-0-7-9	0110 0111
104	68	LD			h		11-0-8-9	0110 1000
105	69	CD			i		0-1-8	0110 1001
106	6A	AD		¦	j		12-11	0110 1010
107	6B	SD	,	, ,	k	A 8 2 1	0-3-8	0110 1011
108	6C	MD	% (	% %	l	A 8 4	0-4-8	0110 1100
109	6D	DD	¥	_ _	m	A 8 4 1	0-5-8	0110 1101
110	6E	AW	\	> >	n	A 8 4 2	0-6-8	0110 1110
111	6F	SW	⧻	? ?	o	A 8 4 2 1	0-7-8	0110 1111
112	70	STE			p		12-11-0	0111 0000
113	71				q		12-11-0-1-9	0111 0001
114	72				r		12-11-0-2-9	0111 0010
115	73				s		12-11-0-3-9	0111 0011
116	74				t		12-11-0-4-9	0111 0100
117	75				u		12-11-0-5-9	0111 0101
118	76				v		12-11-0-6-9	0111 0110
119	77				w		12-11-0-7-9	0111 0111
120	78	LE			x		12-11-0-8-9	0111 1000
121	79	CE			y		1-8	0111 1001
122	7A	AE	ƀ	: :	z	A	2-8	0111 1010
123	7B	SE	# =	# #	{	8 2 1	3-8	0111 1011
124	7C	ME	@ '	@ @	¦	8 4	4-8	0111 1100
125	7D	DE	:	' '	}	8 4 1	5-8	0111 1101
126	7E	AU	>	= =	~	8 4 2	6-8	0111 1110
127	7F	SU	√	" "	DEL	8 4 2 1	7-8	0111 1111

CODE TRANSLATION TABLE (Contd)

(11)

Dec.	Hex	Instruction and Format	Graphics and Controls BCDIC	EBCDIC(1)	ASCII	7-Track Tape BCDIC(2)	EBCDIC Card Code	Binary
128	80	SSM -S					12-0-1-8	1000 0000
129	81			a	a		12-0-1	1000 0001
130	82	LPSW -S		b	b		12-0-2	1000 0010
131	83	Diagnose		c	c		12-0-3	1000 0011
132	84	WRD } SI		d	d		12-0-4	1000 0100
133	85	RDD } SI		e	e		12-0-5	1000 0101
134	86	BXH		f	f		12-0-6	1000 0110
135	87	BXLE		g	g		12-0-7	1000 0111
136	88	SRL		h	h		12-0-8	1000 1000
137	89	SLL		i	i		12-0-9	1000 1001
138	8A	SRA					12-0-2-8	1000 1010
139	8B	SLA RS			{		12-0-3-8	1000 1011
140	8C	SRDL			≤		12-0-4-8	1000 1100
141	8D	SLDL			(		12-0-5-8	1000 1101
142	8E	SRDA			+		12-0-6-8	1000 1110
143	8F	SLDA			+		12-0-7-8	1000 1111
144	90	STM					12-11-1-8	1001 0000
145	91	TM } SI		j	j		12-11-1	1001 0001
146	92	MVI } SI		k	k		12-11-2	1001 0010
147	93	TS -S		l	l		12-11-3	1001 0011
148	94	NI		m	m		12-11-4	1001 0100
149	95	CLI		n	n		12-11-5	1001 0101
150	96	OI } SI		o	o		12-11-6	1001 0110
151	97	XI		p	p		12-11-7	1001 0111
152	98	LM -RS		q	q		12-11-8	1001 1000
153	99			r	r		12-11-9	1001 1001
154	9A						12-11-2-8	1001 1010
155	9B				}		12-11-3-8	1001 1011
156	9C	SIO, SIOF			⌑		12-11-4-8	1001 1100
157	9D	TIO, CLRIO } S			)		12-11-5-8	1001 1101
158	9E	HIO, HDV			±		12-11-6-8	1001 1110
159	9F	TCH			■		12-11-7-8	1001 1111
160	A0				-		11-0-1-8	1010 0000
161	A1			~	°		11-0-1	1010 0001
162	A2			s	s		11-0-2	1010 0010
163	A3			t	t		11-0-3	1010 0011
164	A4			u	u		11-0-4	1010 0100
165	A5			v	v		11-0-5	1010 0101
166	A6			w	w		11-0-6	1010 0110
167	A7			x	x		11-0-7	1010 0111
168	A8			y	y		11-0-8	1010 1000
169	A9			z	z		11-0-9	1010 1001
170	AA						11-0-2-8	1010 1010
171	AB				└		11-0-3-8	1010 1011
172	AC	STNSM } SI			┌		11-0-4-8	1010 1100
173	AD	STOSM } SI			[		11-0-5-8	1010 1101
174	AE	SIGP -RS			≥		11-0-6-8	1010 1110
175	AF	MC -SI			●		11-0-7-8	1010 1111
176	B0				0		12-11-0-1-8	1011 0000
177	B1	LRA -RX			1		12-11-0-1	1011 0001
178	B2	See below			2		12-11-0-2	1011 0010
179	B3				3		12-11-0-3	1011 0011
180	B4				4		12-11-0-4	1011 0100
181	B5				5		12-11-0-5	1011 0101
182	B6	STCTL } RS			6		12-11-0-6	1011 0110
183	B7	LCTL } RS			7		12-11-0-7	1011 0111
184	B8				8		12-11-0-8	1011 1000
185	B9				9		12-11-0-9	1011 1001
186	BA	CS } RS					12-11-0-2-8	1011 1010
187	BB	CDS } RS			┘		12-11-0-3-8	1011 1011
188	BC				┐		12-11-0-4-8	1011 1100
189	BD	CLM			]		12-11-0-5-8	1011 1101
190	BE	STCM } RS			≠		12-11-0-6-8	1011 1110
191	BF	ICM			—		12-11-0-7-8	1011 1111

Op code (S format)

B202 - STIDP	B207 - STCKC	B20D - PTLB
B203 - STIDC	B208 - SPT	B210 - SPX
B204 - SCK	B209 - STPT	B211 - STPX
B205 - STCK	B20A - SPKA	B212 - STAP
B206 - SCKC	B20B - IPK	B213 - RRB

CODE TRANSLATION TABLE (Contd)

(12)

Dec.	Hex	Instruction (SS)	Graphics and Controls BCDIC	EBCDIC(1)	ASCII	7-Track Tape BCDIC(2)	EBCDIC Card Code	Binary
192	C0		?	{		B A 8 2	12-0	1100 0000
193	C1		A	A	A	B A 1	12-1	1100 0001
194	C2		B	B	B	B A 2	12-2	1100 0010
195	C3		C	C	C	B A 2 1	12-3	1100 0011
196	C4		D	D	D	B A 4	12-4	1100 0100
197	C5		E	E	E	B A 4 1	12-5	1100 0101
198	C6		F	F	F	B A 4 2	12-6	1100 0110
199	C7		G	G	G	B A 4 2 1	12-7	1100 0111
200	C8		H	H	H	B A 8	12-8	1100 1000
201	C9		I	I	I	B A 8 1	12-9	1100 1001
202	CA						12-0-2-8-9	1100 1010
203	CB						12-0-3-8-9	1100 1011
204	CC			⑀			12-0-4-8-9	1100 1100
205	CD						12-0-5-8-9	1100 1101
206	CE			Ψ			12-0-6-8-9	1100 1110
207	CF						12-0-7-8-9	1100 1111
208	D0		!	}		B 8 2	11-0	1101 0000
209	D1	MVN	J	J	J	B 1	11-1	1101 0001
210	D2	MVC	K	K	K	B 2	11-2	1101 0010
211	D3	MVZ	L	L	L	B 2 1	11-3	1101 0011
212	D4	NC	M	M	M	B 4	11-4	1101 0100
213	D5	CLC	N	N	N	B 4 1	11-5	1101 0101
214	D6	OC	O	O	O	B 4 2	11-6	1101 0110
215	D7	XC	P	P	P	B 4 2 1	11-7	1101 0111
216	D8		Q	Q	Q	B 8	11-8	1101 1000
217	D9		R	R	R	B 8 1	11-9	1101 1001
218	DA						12-11-2-8-9	1101 1010
219	DB						12-11-3-8-9	1101 1011
220	DC	TR					12-11-4-8-9	1101 1100
221	DD	TRT					12-11-5-8-9	1101 1101
222	DE	ED					12-11-6-8-9	1101 1110
223	DF	EDMK					12-11-7-8-9	1101 1111
224	E0		‡	\		A 8 2	0-2-8	1110 0000
225	E1						11-0-1-9	1110 0001
226	E2		S	S	S	A 2	0-2	1110 0010
227	E3		T	T	T	A 2 1	0-3	1110 0011
228	E4		U	U	U	A 4	0-4	1110 0100
229	E5		V	V	V	A 4 1	0-5	1110 0101
230	E6		W	W	W	A 4 2	0-6	1110 0110
231	E7		X	X	X	A 4 2 1	0-7	1110 0111
232	E8		Y	Y	Y	A 8	0-8	1110 1000
233	E9		Z	Z	Z	A 8 1	0-9	1110 1001
234	EA						11-0-2-8-9	1110 1010
235	EB						11-0-3-8-9	1110 1011
236	EC			⑁			11-0-4-8-9	1110 1100
237	ED						11-0-5-8-9	1110 1101
238	EE						11-0-6-8-9	1110 1110
239	EF						11-0-7-8-9	1110 1111
240	F0	SRP	0	0	0	8 2	0	1111 0000
241	F1	MVO	1	1	1	1	1	1111 0001
242	F2	PACK	2	2	2	2	2	1111 0010
243	F3	UNPK	3	3	3	2 1	3	1111 0011
244	F4		4	4	4	4	4	1111 0100
245	F5		5	5	5	4 1	5	1111 0101
246	F6		6	6	6	4 2	6	1111 0110
247	F7		7	7	7	4 2 1	7	1111 0111
248	F8	ZAP	8	8	8	8	8	1111 1000
249	F9	CP	9	9	9	8 1	9	1111 1001
250	FA	AP		|			12-11-0-2-8-9	1111 1010
251	FB	SP					12-11-0-3-8-9	1111 1011
252	FC	MP					12-11-0-4-8-9	1111 1100
253	FD	DP					12-11-0-5-8-9	1111 1101
254	FE						12-11-0-6-8-9	1111 1110
255	FF			EO			12-11-0-7-8-9	1111 1111

ANSI-DEFINED PRINTER CONTROL CHARACTERS

(A in RECFM field of DCB)

Code	Action before printing record
blank	Space 1 line
0	Space 2 lines
-	Space 3 lines
+	Suppress space
1	Skip to line 1 on new page

MACHINE INSTRUCTION FORMATS (13)

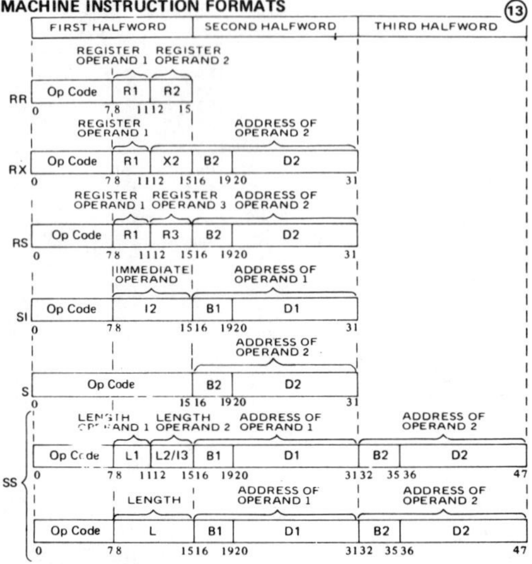

CONTROL REGISTERS

CR	Bits	Name of field	Associated with	Init.
0	0	Block-multiplex'g control	Block-multiplex'g	0
	1	SSM suppression control	SSM instruction	0
	2	TOD clock sync control	Multiprocessing	0
	8-9	Page size control		0
	10	Unassigned (must be zero)	Dynamic addr. transl.	0
	11-12	Segment size control		0
	16	Malfunction alert mask		0
	17	Emergency signal mask	Multiprocessing	0
	18	External call mask		0
	19	TOD clock sync check mask		0
	20	Clock comparator mask	Clock comparator	0
	21	CPU timer mask	CPU timer	0
	24	Interval timer mask	Interval timer	1
	25	Interrupt key mask	Interrupt key	1
	26	External signal mask	External signal	1
1	0-7	Segment table length	Dynamic addr. transl.	0
	8-25	Segment table address		0
2	0-31	Channel masks	Channels	1
8	16-31	Monitor masks	Monitoring	0
9	0	Successful branching event mask		0
	1	Instruction fetching event mask		0
	2	Storage alteration event mask	Program-event record'g	0
	3	GR alteration event mask		0
	16-31	PER general register masks		0
10	8-31	PER starting address	Program-event record'g	0
11	8-31	PER ending address	Program-event record'g	0
14	0	Check-stop control	Machine-check handling	1
	1	Synch. MCEL control		1
	2	I/O extended logout control	I/O extended logout	0
	4	Recovery report mask		0
	5	Degradation report mask		0
	6	Ext. damage report mask	Machine-check handling	1
	7	Warning mask		0
	8	Asynch. MCEL control		0
	9	Asynch. fixed log control		0
15	8-28	MCEL address	Machine-check handling	512

PROGRAM STATUS WORD (BC Mode) (14)

Channel masks	E	Protect'n key	CMWP	Interruption code
0–6	7	8–11	12–15	16–23, 24–31

ILC	CC	Program mask	Instruction address
32–33	34–35	36–39	40–47, 48–55, 56–63

0–5 Channel 0 to 5 masks
6 Mask for channel 6 and up
7 (E) External mask
12 (C=0) Basic control mode
13 (M) Machine-check mask
14 (W=1) Wait state
15 (P=1) Problem state
32–33 (ILC) Instruction length code
34–35 (CC) Condition code
36 Fixed-point overflow mask
37 Decimal overflow mask
38 Exponent underflow mask
39 Significance mask

PROGRAM STATUS WORD (EC Mode)

0R00 0TIE	Protect'n key	CMWP	00	CC	Program mask	0000 0000
0–7	8–11	12–15	16–17	18–19	20–23	24–31

0000 0000	Instruction address
32–39	40–47, 48–55, 56–63

1 (R) Program event recording mask
5 (T=1) Translation mode
6 (I) Input/output mask
7 (E) External mask
12 (C=1) Extended control mode
13 (M) Machine-check mask
14 (W=1) Wait state
15 (P=1) Problem state
18–19 (CC) Condition code
20 Fixed-point overflow mask
21 Decimal overflow mask
22 Exponent underflow mask
23 Significance mask

CHANNEL COMMAND WORD

Command code	Data address
0–7	8–15, 16–23, 24–31

Flags	00	(unused)	Byte count
32–37	38–39	40–47	48–55, 56–63

CD–bit 32 (80) causes use of address portion of next CCW.
CC–bit 33 (40) causes use of command code and data address of next CCW.
SLI–bit 34 (20) causes suppression of possible incorrect length indication.
Skip–bit 35 (10) suppresses transfer of information to main storage.
PCI–bit 36 (08) causes a channel program controlled interruption.
IDA–bit 37 (04) causes bits 8–31 of CCW to specify location of first IDAW.

CHANNEL STATUS WORD (hex 40)

Key	0	L	CC	CCW address
0–3	4	5	6–7	8–15, 16–23, 24–31

Unit status	Channel status	Byte count
32–39	40–47	48–55, 56–63

5 Logout pending
6–7 Deferred condition code
32 (80) Attention
33 (40) Status modifier
34 (20) Control unit end
35 (10) Busy
36 (08) Channel end
37 (04) Device end
38 (02) Unit check
39 (01) Unit exception
40 (80) Program-controlled interruption
41 (40) Incorrect length
42 (20) Program check
43 (10) Protection check
44 (08) Channel data check
45 (04) Channel control check
46 (02) Interface control check
47 (01) Chaining check
48–63 Residual byte count for the last CCW used

PROGRAM INTERRUPTION CODES

Code	Exception	Code	Exception
0001	Operation exception	000C	Exponent overflow excp
0002	Privileged operation excp	000D	Exponent underflow excp
0003	Execute exception	000E	Significance exception
0004	Protection exception	000F	Floating-point divide excp
0005	Addressing exception	0010	Segment translation excp
0006	Specification exception	0011	Page translation exception
0007	Data exception	0012	Translation specification excp
0008	Fixed-point overflow excp	0013	Special operation exception
0009	Fixed-point divide excp	0040	Monitor event
000A	Decimal overflow exception	0080	Program event (code may be combined with another code)
000B	Decimal divide exception		

FIXED STORAGE LOCATIONS

(15)

Area, dec.	Hex addr	EC only	Function
0- 7	0		Initial program loading PSW, restart new PSW
8- 15	8		Initial program loading CCW1, restart old PSW
16- 23	10		Initial program loading CCW2
24- 31	18		External old PSW
32- 39	20		Supervisor Call old PSW
40- 47	28		Program old PSW
48- 55	30		Machine-check old PSW
56- 63	38		Input/output old PSW
64- 71	40		Channel status word (see diagram)
72- 75	48		Channel address word [0-3 key, 4-7 zeros, 8-31 CCW address]
80- 83	50		Interval timer
88- 95	58		External new PSW
96-103	60		Supervisor Call new PSW
104-111	68		Program new PSW
112-119	70		Machine-check new PSW
120-127	78		Input/output new PSW
132-133	84		CPU address assoc'd with external interruption, or unchanged
132-133	84	X	CPU address assoc'd with external interruption, or zeros
134-135	86	X	External interruption code
136-139	88	X	SVC interruption [0-12 zeros, 13-14 ILC, 15:0, 16-31 code]
140-143	8C	X	Program interrupt. [0-12 zeros, 13-14 ILC, 15:0, 16-31 code]
144-147	90	X	Translation exception address [0-7 zeros, 8-31 address]
148-149	94		Monitor class [0-7 zeros, 8-15 class number]
150-151	96	X	PER interruption code [0-3 code, 4-15 zeros]
152-155	98	X	PER address [0-7 zeros, 8-31 address]
156-159	9C		Monitor code [0-7 zeros, 8-31 monitor code]
168-171	A8		Channel ID [0-3 type, 4-15 model, 16-31 max. IOEL length]
172-175	AC		I/O extended logout address [0-7 unused, 8-31 address]
176-179	B0		Limited channel logout (see diagram)
185-187	B9	X	I/O address [0-7 zeros, 8-23 address]
216-223	D8		CPU timer save area
224-231	E0		Clock comparator save area
232-239	E8		Machine-check interruption code (see diagram)
248-251	F8		Failing processor storage address [0-7 zeros, 8-31 address]
252-255	FC		Region code*
256-351	100		Fixed logout area*
352-383	160		Floating-point register save area
384-447	180		General register save area
448-511	1C0		Control register save area
512†	200		CPU extended logout area (size varies)

*May vary among models; see system library manuals for specific model.
†Location may be changed by programming (bits 8-28 of CR 15 specify address).

LIMITED CHANNEL LOGOUT (hex B0)

0	SCU id	Detect	Source	000	Field validity flags	TT	00	A	Seq.
0	1 3	4 7	8 12	13 15	16 23	24	26	28	29 31

4 CPU
5 Channel
6 Main storage control
7 Main storage
8 CPU
9 Channel
10 Main storage control
11 Main storage

12 Control unit
16 Interface address
17-18 Reserved (00)
19 Sequence code
20 Unit status
21 Cmd. addr. and key
22 Channel address
23 Device address

24-25 Type of termination
00 Interface disconnect
01 Stop, stack or normal
10 Selective reset
11 System reset
28(A) I/O error alert
29-31 Sequence code

MACHINE-CHECK INTERRUPTION CODE (hex E8)

MC conditions	000 00	Time	Stg. error	0	Validity indicators
0 8	9 13	14	16 18	19	20 31

0000 0000	0000 00	Val.	MCEL length
32 39	40 45	46	48 55 56 63

0 System damage
1 Instr. proc'g damage
2 System recovery
3 Timer damage
4 Timing facil. damage
5 External damage
6 Not assigned (0)
7 Degradation
8 Warning

14 Backed-up
15 Delayed
16 Uncorrected
17 Corrected
18 Key uncorrected
20 PSW bits 12-15
21 PSW masks and key
22 Prog. mask and CC
23 Instruction address

24 Failing stg. address
25 Region code
27 Floating-pt registers
28 General registers
29 Control registers
30 CPU ext'd logout
31 Storage logical
46 CPU timer
47 Clock comparator

DYNAMIC ADDRESS TRANSLATION

(16)

VIRTUAL (LOGICAL) ADDRESS FORMAT

Segment Size	Page Size		Segment Index	Page Index	Byte Index
64K	4K	Bits	8 - 15	16 - 19	20 - 31
64K	2K	0 - 7	8 - 15	16 - 20	21 - 31
1M	4K	are	8 - 11	12 - 19	20 - 31
1M	2K	ignored	8 - 11	12 - 20	21 - 31

SEGMENT TABLE ENTRY

PT length	0000*	Page table address	00*	I
0 3	4 7	8 28	29	31

*Normally zeros; ignored on some models. 31 (I) Segment-invalid bit.

PAGE TABLE ENTRY (4K)

Page address	I	00	/
0 11	12	13	15

12 (I) Page-invalid bit.

PAGE TABLE ENTRY (2K)

Page address	I	0	/
0 12	13	14	15

13 (I) Page-invalid bit.

HEXADECIMAL AND DECIMAL CONVERSION

From hex: locate each hex digit in its corresponding column position and note the decimal equivalents. Add these to obtain the decimal value.

From decimal: (1) locate the largest decimal value in the table that will fit into the decimal number to be converted, and (2) note its hex equivalent and hex column position. (3) Find the decimal remainder. Repeat the process on this and subsequent remainders.

Note: Decimal, hexadecimal, (and binary) equivalents of all numbers from 0 to 255 are listed on panels 9 - 12.

HEXADECIMAL COLUMNS

6		5		4		3		2		1	
HEX	= DEC	HEX	= DEC	HEX	= DEC	HEX	= DEC	HEX	= DEC	HEX	= DEC
0	0	0	0	0	0	0	0	0	0	0	0
1	1,048,576	1	65,536	1	4,096	1	256	1	16	1	1
2	2,097,152	2	131,072	2	8,192	2	512	2	32	2	2
3	3,145,728	3	196,608	3	12,288	3	768	3	48	3	3
4	4,194,304	4	262,144	4	16,384	4	1,024	4	64	4	4
5	5,242,880	5	327,680	5	20,480	5	1,280	5	80	5	5
6	6,291,456	6	393,216	6	24,576	6	1,536	6	96	6	6
7	7,340,032	7	458,752	7	28,672	7	1,792	7	112	7	7
8	8,388,608	8	524,288	8	32,768	8	2,048	8	128	8	8
9	9,437,184	9	589,824	9	36,864	9	2,304	9	144	9	9
A	10,485,760	A	655,360	A	40,960	A	2,560	A	160	A	10
B	11,534,336	B	720,896	B	45,056	B	2,816	B	176	B	11
C	12,582,912	C	786,432	C	49,152	C	3,072	C	192	C	12
D	13,631,488	D	851,968	D	53,248	D	3,328	D	208	D	13
E	14,680,064	E	917,504	E	57,344	E	3,584	E	224	E	14
F	15,728,640	F	983,040	F	61,440	F	3,840	F	240	F	15
0123		4567		0123		4567		0123		4567	
BYTE				BYTE				BYTE			

POWERS OF 2

2^n	n
256	8
512	9
1 024	10
2 048	11
4 096	12
8 192	13
16 384	14
32 768	15
65 536	16
131 072	17
262 144	18
524 288	19
1 048 576	20
2 097 152	21
4 194 304	22
8 388 608	23
16 777 216	24

$2^0 = 16^0$
$2^4 = 16^1$
$2^8 = 16^2$
$2^{12} = 16^3$
$2^{16} = 16^4$
$2^{20} = 16^5$
$2^{24} = 16^6$
$2^{28} = 16^7$
$2^{32} = 16^8$
$2^{36} = 16^9$
$2^{40} = 16^{10}$
$2^{44} = 16^{11}$
$2^{48} = 16^{12}$
$2^{52} = 16^{13}$
$2^{56} = 16^{14}$
$2^{60} = 16^{15}$

POWERS OF 16

16^n	n
1	0
16	1
256	2
4 096	3
65 536	4
1 048 576	5
16 777 216	6
268 435 456	7
4 294 967 296	8
68 719 476 736	9
1 099 511 627 776	10
17 592 186 044 416	11
281 474 976 710 656	12
4 503 599 627 370 496	13
72 057 594 037 927 936	14
1 152 921 504 606 846 976	15

B

Reference Tables

Table B-1 Condition-Code Settings

INSTRUCTION	CONDITION CODE 0	1	2	3
<u>General Instructions</u>				
ADD (and ADD HALFWORD)	zero	< zero	> zero	overflow
ADD LOGICAL	zero, no carry	not zero, no carry	zero, carry	not zero, carry
AND	zero	not zero	--	--
COMPARE (and COMPARE HALFWORD)	equal	low	high	--
COMPARE AND SWAP	equal	not equal	--	--
COMPARE DOUBLE AND SWAP	equal	not equal	--	--
COMPARE LOGICAL	equal	low	high	--
COMPARE LOGICAL CHARACTERS UNDER MASK	equal	low	high	--
COMPARE LOGICAL LONG	equal	low	high	--
EXCLUSIVE OR	zero	not zero	--	--
INSERT CHARACTERS UNDER MASK	zero	1st bit one	1st bit zero	--
LOAD AND TEST	zero	< zero	> zero	--
LOAD COMPLEMENT	zero	< zero	> zero	overflow
LOAD NEGATIVE	zero	< zero	--	--
LOAD POSITIVE	zero	--	> zero	overflow
MOVE LONG	count equal	count low	count high	destr. overlap
OR	zero	not zero	--	--
SHIFT LEFT DOUBLE	zero	< zero	> zero	overflow
SHIFT LEFT SINGLE	zero	< zero	> zero	overflow
SHIFT RIGHT DOUBLE	zero	< zero	> zero	--
SHIFT RIGHT SINGLE	zero	< zero	> zero	--
STORE CLOCK	set	not set	error	not operational
SUBTRACT (and SUBTRACT HALFWORD)	zero	< zero	> zero	overflow
SUBTRACT LOGICAL	--	not zero, no carry	zero, carry	not zero, carry
TEST AND SET	zero	one	--	--
TEST UNDER MASK	zero	mixed	--	ones
TRANSLATE AND TEST	zero	incomplete	complete	--
<u>Decimal Instructions</u>				
ADD DECIMAL	zero	< zero	> zero	overflow
COMPARE DECIMAL	equal	low	high	--
EDIT	zero	< zero	> zero	--
EDIT AND MARK	zero	< zero	> zero	--
SHIFT AND ROUND DECIMAL	zero	< zero	> zero	overflow
SUBTRACT DECIMAL	zero	< zero	> zero	overflow
ZERO AND ADD	zero	< zero	> zero	overflow
<u>Floating-Point Instructions</u>				
ADD NORMALIZED	zero	< zero	> zero	--
ADD UNNORMALIZED	zero	< zero	> zero	--
COMPARE	equal	low	high	--
LOAD AND TEST	zero	< zero	> zero	--
LOAD COMPLEMENT	zero	< zero	> zero	--
LOAD NEGATIVE	zero	< zero	--	--
LOAD POSITIVE	zero	--	> zero	--
SUBTRACT NORMALIZED	zero	< zero	> zero	--
SUBTRACT UNNORMALIZED	zero	< zero	> zero	--

Table B-1 (*Continued*)

INSTRUCTION (Continued)	CONDITION CODE 0	1	2	3
Input/Output Instructions				
CLEAR I/O	no operation in progress	CSW stored	channel busy	not operational
HALT DEVICE	interruption pending,or busy	CSW stored	channel working	not operational
HALT I/O	interruption pending	CSW stored	burst op. stopped	not operational
START I/O	successful	CSW stored	busy	not operational
START I/O FAST RELEASE	successful	CSW stored	busy	not operational
STORE CHANNEL ID	ID stored	CSW stored	busy	not operational
TEST CHANNEL	available	interruption pending	burst mode	not operational
TEST I/O	available	CSW stored	busy	not operational
System Control Instructions				
LOAD REAL ADDRESS	translation available	ST entry invalid	PT entry invalid	length violation
RESET REFERENCE BIT	R bit zero, C bit zero	R bit zero, C bit one	R bit one, C bit zero	R bit one, C bit one
SET CLOCK	set	secure	--	not operational
SIGNAL PROCESSOR	order code accepted	status stored	busy	not operational

Explanation:

> zero	Result is greater than zero
high	First operand compares high
< zero	Result is less than zero
low	First operand compares low

NOTE: The condition code may also be changed by LOAD PSW, SET PROGRAM MASK, and DIAGNOSE, and by an interruption.

Table B-2 Summary of Constants

TYPE	IMPLIED LENGTH (BYTES)	ALIGN-MENT	LENGTH MODI-FIER RANGE	SPECIFIED BY	NUMBER OF CON-STANTS PER OPERAND	RANGE FOR EX-PONENTS	RANGE FOR SCALE	TRUN-CATION/ PADDING SIDE
C	as needed	byte	.1 to 256 (1)	characters	one			right
X	as needed	byte	.1 to 256 (1)	hexadecimal digits	one			left
B	as needed	byte	.1 to 256	binary digits	one			left
F	4	word	.1 to 8	decimal digits	multi-ple	-78 to +75	-187 to +346	left (4)
H	2	half word	.1 to 8	decimal digits	multi-ple	-78 to +75	-187 +346	left (4)
E	4	word	.1 to 8	decimal digits	multi-ple	-78 to +75	0-14	right (4)
D	8	double word	.1 to 8	decimal digits	multi-ple	-78 to +75	0-14	right (4)
L (3)	16	double word	.1 to 16	decimal digits	multi-ple	-78 to +75	0-28	right (4)
P	as needed	byte	.1 to 16	decimal digits	multi-ple			left
Z	as needed	byte	.1 to 16	decimal digits	multi-ple			left
A	4	word	.1 to 4 (2)	any expression	multi-ple			left
Q (3)	4	word	1-4	symbol nam-ing a DXD or DSECT	multi-ple			left
V	4	word	3 or 4	relocatable symbol	multi-ple			left
S	2	half word	2 only	one absolute or relocatab-le expression or two absol-ute express-ions: exp (exp)	multi-ple			
Y	2	half word	.1 to 2 (2)	any expression	multi-ple			left

(1) In a DS assembler instruction C and X type constants may have length specification to 65535.
(2) Bit length specification permitted with absolute expressions only. Relocatable A-type constants, 3 or 4 bytes only; relocatable Y-type constants, 2 bytes only.
(3) Assembler F only.
(4) Errors will be flagged if significant bits are truncated or if the value specified cannot be contained in the implied length of the constant.

C

Problem Statements

Program 1 A payroll file resides on punched cards. Each punched card contains the payroll record of an employee. Write a program to print the employee number, employee name, and gross pay. All other fields are ignored. The input/output specifications are given below.

input positions	field	output positions
1–6	Employee Number	11–16
7–26	Employee Name	27–46
51–58	Gross Pay	57–64

Program 2 Find the sum of four constants in storage. Store the sum in an area of storage called RESULT. Solve this problem for:

1. Four zoned decimal constants with a length of 4 bytes
2. Four fullword binary constants
3. Four double word binary constants

Program 3 Find the average of four constants in storage. Store the quotient in an area of storage called RESULT. You may ignore the remainder. Solve this problem for:

1. Four zoned decimal constants with a length of 4 bytes
2. Four fullword binary constants

Program 4 The formula for the volume of a sphere is $(4/3)\pi R^3$. Write a program to find the volume of a sphere. Solve this program. for:

1. Decimal numbers—radius $= 10$, $\pi = 3$
2. Binary numbers—radius $= 10$, $\pi = 3$
3. Decimal numbers—radius $= 10.12$, $\pi = 3.14$
4. Binary numbers—radius $= 10.12$, $\pi = 3.14$

Program 5 Find the sum of the numbers from 1–5. Store the answer in an area of storage called RESULT. Solve this problem using (a) decimal instructions and (b) binary instructions.

Program 6 A payroll file is recorded on punched cards. The file is sequenced by employee number.

a. Find the total earnings for all the employees in Department A30. Store the total earnings in an area of storage called TOTGROSS.

input positions	field
1–6	Employee Number
1–3	Department Number
4–6	Employee Within Department
51–58	Gross Pay

b. Summarize the gross employee earnings within each department. Use the following I/O specifications.

input positions	field	output positions
1–6	Employee Number	
1–3	Department Number	1–3
4–6	Person Number	
51–58	Gross Pay	4–16

c. Code Program 6 to print a report summarizing earnings by department. Print a detail line for each input card, and a department total line for each department. The I/O specifications follow.

input positions	field	output positions detail line	output positions total line
1–3	Department Number	1–3	1–3
4–6	Person Number	16–18	
7–26	Employee Name	27–46	
51–58	Gross Pay	41–53	39–53

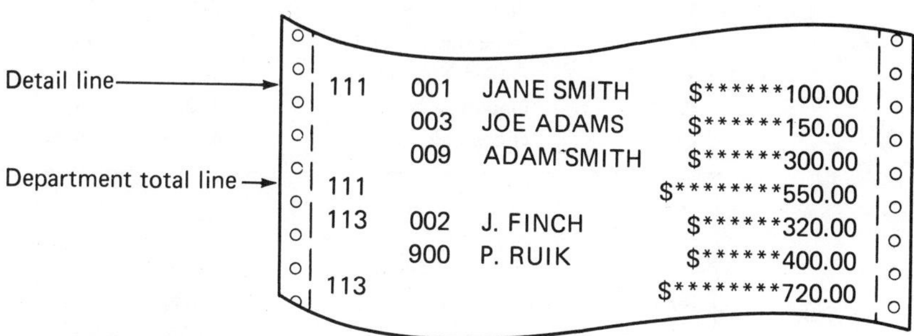

Output Report

d. Code Program 6 to print the Employee Payroll Report in employee number sequence within department. Within this sequence, each employee will have only one card. Develop department and final totals on gross earnings. The I/O specifications are:

input positions	field	output positions detail line	output positions total line
1–3	Department Number	1–3	1–3
4–6	Person Number	9–11	
7–26	Employee Name	17–36	
51–58	Gross Pay	41–53	39–53

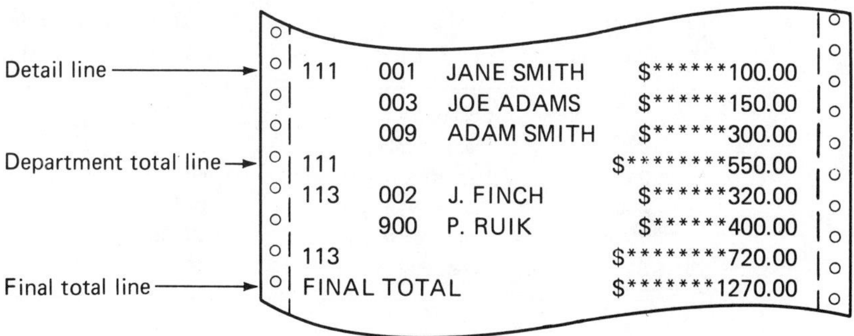

e. Assume that the employee number reflects employee within department within plant. Write a program to print the Employee Payroll Report in employee number sequence within department within plant. Develop department, plant, and final totals on gross earnings, using the following I/O specifications.

input positions	field	output positions detail line	total line
1–2	Plant Number	1–2	1–2
3	Department Number	5	5
4–6	Person Number	9–11	
7–26	Employee Name	7–26	
51–58	Gross Pay	41–53	39–53

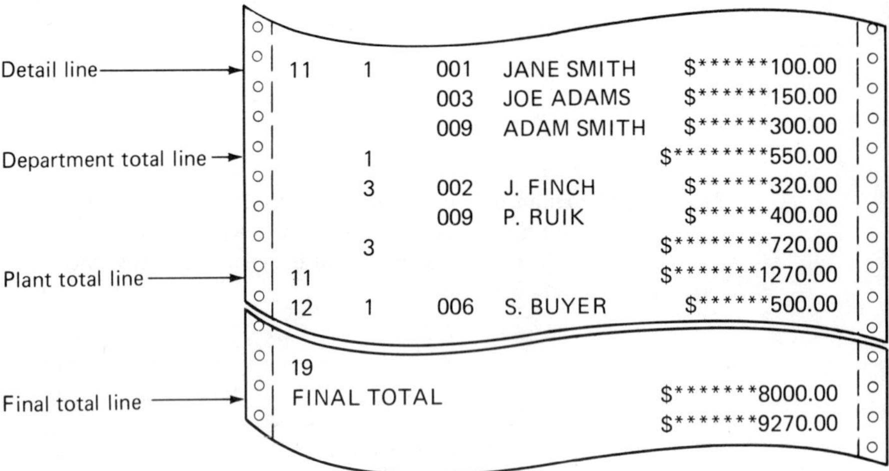

f. Code Program 6 to print the Employee Payroll Report in employee number sequence within department within plant within location. Develop department, plant, and location totals on gross earnings. The I/O specifications follow.

input positions	field	output positions detail line	total line
1	Location	1	1
2	Plant Number	3	3
3	Department Number	5	5
4–6	Person Number	9–11	
7–26	Employee Name	17–36	
51–58	Gross Pay	41–53	39–53

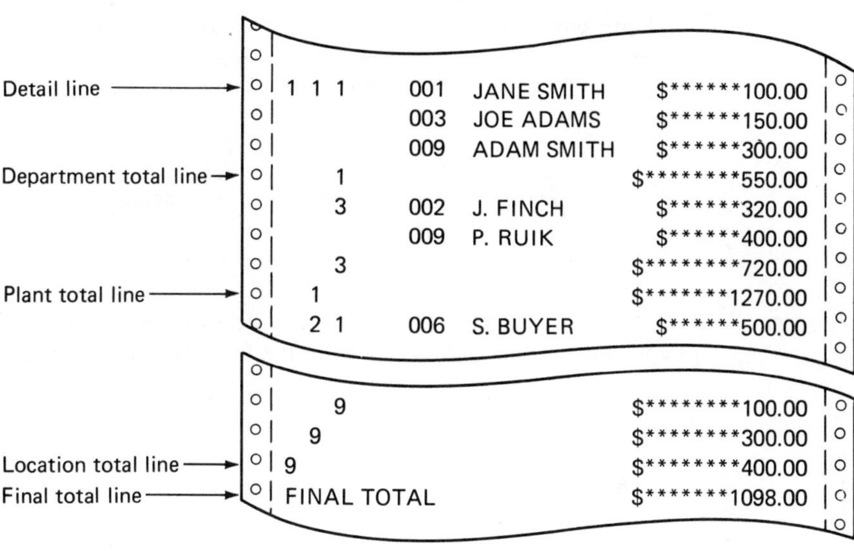

g. Code the preceding four problems developing net pay for each detail record. Maintain appropriate totals on net pay. The I/O specifications are:

input positions	field	output positions detail line	output positions total line
1–6	Employee Number		
1	Location	reference	
2	Plant Number	previous	
3	Department Number	specifications	
4–6	Employee Number	9–11	
7–26	Employee Name	17–36	
51–58	Gross Pay	41–53	39–53
	Net Pay	61–63	59–63
59–65	FICA Withheld		
66–72	Federal Tax Withheld		
73–78	State Tax Withheld		

Net pay is calculated by subtracting total amounts withheld from gross earnings.

h. Develop a program to print the Employee Hours-Worked Report in employee number sequence. Each employee must have a payroll card (1 in 80) followed by a cumulative time card (2 in 80). Information from each of these cards is needed to print a single detail line.

input positions	field	output positions
1–6	Employee Number	1–6
7–26	Employee Name	10–29
80	1 in 80	
1–6	Employee Number	
7–10	Hours Worked	35–38
80	2 in 80	

Program 7 Find the sum of a variable number of fullword binary constants. The number of constants in the table is placed in the first fullword of the table.

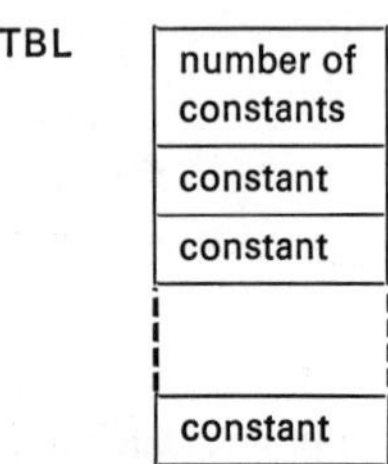

Place the sum in an area of storage called RESULT.

Program 8 Write a program to select male employees who are college graduates with a second language. List employees with any of these characteristics. Use an asterisk to flag employees with all the specified characteristics. The I/O specifications are:

input positions	field	output positions
1–6	Employee Number	11–16
7–26	Employee Name	21–40
80	Profile	
	BIT	
	0 1—MALE,0-FEMALE	
	1 1—GRADUATE SCHOOL	
	2 1—COLLEGE	
	3 1—HIGH SCHOOL	
	4 1—LANGUAGE	
	5 1—PHYSICS	
	6 1—VETERAN	
	7 1—21 OR OVER	
	Flag	42

Program 9 A table of employee names and addresses resides in storage.

ALP code			table
DATATBL	DC	CL16'PRISCILLA STRONG;'	PRISCILLA STRONG;
	DC	CL17'128 EAST 6 STREET;'	128 EAST 6 STREET;
	DC	CL12'NEW YORK, NY:;	NEW YORK, NY:
	DC	CL12'MARY MICHAEL'	MARY MICHAEL;
	DC	CL11'883 HUGO RD;'	883 HUGO RD;
	DC	CL12'CHICAGO, ILL;	CHICAGO, ILL:
	↓		
	DC	X'FF'	FF

An FF_{16} marks the end of the table. The entries within the table are separated by colons. The fields within each entry are separated by semicolons. The maximum length of any field is 20 bytes. Use the information in this table to print name and address labels. Following are the output specifications.

field	output positions
Name	1–20
Street Address	1–20
City and State	1–20

Program 10 Write a program to convert a deck of cards punched in the BCD code to the correct S/370 EBCDIC code. Convert the following special characters.

desired graphic	BCD punch	internal code	EBCDIC interpretation
>	6-8	X'7E'	=
<	12-6-8	X'4E'	+
(	0-4-8	X'6C'	%
=	3-8	X'7B'	#

D

The HSKPING Macro

```
         MACRO
&NAME    HSKPING &CARDID=,&PUNCHID=,&PRINTID=,&EOFID=
&NAME    SAVE   (14,12)
         BALR   12,0
         USING  *,12
         AIF    ('&CARDID' EQ '' AND '&PUNCHID' EQ '' AND '&PRINTID' E
                '').EXIT
         ST     13,SAVE&SYSNDX+4
         LA     13,SAVE&SYSNDX
         B      AB&SYSNDX
SAVE&SYSNDX DS  18F
AB&SYSNDX EQU   *
         AIF ('&CARDID' EQ '').PRINT
         OPEN   (&CARDID,INPUT)
         B      A&SYSNDX
         AIF    ('&EOFID' EQ '').NEXT2
&CARDID  DCB    DSORG=PS,
                MACRF=GM,
                LRECL=80,
                BLKSIZE=80,
                DDNAME=SYSIN,
                EODAD=&EOFID
         AGO    .AEXIT
.NEXT2   ANOP
&CARDID  DCB    DSORG=PS,
                MACRF=GM,
                LRECL=80,
                BLKSIZE=80,
                DDNAME=SYSIN,
                EODAD=EOJRT
EOJRT    CLOSE  (&CARDID)
         AIF    ('&PUNCHID' EQ '').NEXT3
         CLOSE  (&PUNCHID)
.NEXT3   AIF    ('&PRINTID' EQ '').NEXT4
         CLOSE  (&PRINTID)
.NEXT4   ANOP
         L      13,4(13)
         RETURN (14,12)
.AEXIT   ANOP
A&SYSNDX EQU    *
.PRINT   ANOP
         AIF    ('&PRINTID' EQ '').PUNCH
         OPEN   (&PRINTID,OUTPUT)
         B      B&SYSNDX
&PRINTID DCB    DSORG=PS,
                MACRF=PMC,
                LRECL=120,
                BLKSIZE=120,
                DDNAME=SYSOUT
B&SYSNDX EQU    *
.PUNCH   ANOP
         AIF    ('&PUNCHID' EQ '').EXIT
         OPEN   (&PUNCHID,OUTPUT)
         B      EXIT&SYSNDX
&PUNCHID DCB    DSORG=PS,
                MACRF=PM,
                LRECL=80,
                BLKSIZE=80,
                DDNAME=SYSOUT
.EXIT    ANOP
EXIT&SYSNDX EQU *
         MEND
&&
//
```

Figure D-1 HSKPING macro for OS/370.

```
         MACRO
&NAME    HSKPING &CARDID=,&PUNCHID=,&PRINTID=,&EOFID=
&NAME    SAVE  (14,12)
         BALR  12,0
         USING *,12
         AIF   ('&CARDID' EQ '' AND '&PUNCHID' EQ '' AND '&PRINTID' EQ C
               '').EXIT
         ST    12,SAVE&SYSNDX+4
         LA    13,SAVE&SYSNDX
         AIF   ('&CARDID' EQ '').PRINT
         OPEN  &CARDID
         B     A&SYSNDX
SAVE&SYSNDX DS   18F
AREA1    DS    CL80
         AIF   ('&EOFID' EQ '').NEXT2
&CARDID  DTFCD DEVADDR=SYSOO4,                                         C
               IOAREA1=AREA1.                                          C
               BLKSIZE=80,                                             C
               DEVICE=2540,                                            C
               EOFADDR=&EOFID,                                         C
               RECFORM=FIXUNB,                                         C
               WORKA=YES,                                              C
               TYPEFLE=INPUT
         AGO   .AEXIT
.NEXT2   ANOP
&CARDID  DTFCD DEVADDR=SYS004,                                         C
               IOAREA1=AREA1,                                          C
               BLKSIZE=80,                                             C
               DEVICE=2540,                                            C
               EOFADDR=EOJRT,                                          C
               RECFORM=FIXUNB,                                         C
               WORKA=YES,                                              C
               TYPEFLE=INPUT
EOJRT    CLOSE &CARDID
         AIF   ('&PUNCHID' EQ '').NEXT3
         CLOSE &PUNCHID
.NEXT3   AIF   ('&PRINTID' EQ '').NEXT4
         CLOSE &PRINTID
.NEXT4   ANOP
         L     13,4(13)
         RETURN (14,12)
.AEXIT   ANOP
A&SYSNDX EQU   *
.PRINT   ANOP
         AIF   ('&PRINTID' EQ '').PUNCH
         OPEN  &PRINTID
         B     B&SYSNDX
&PRINTID DTFPR   DEVADDR=SYS005,                                       C
               BLKSIZE=120,                                            C
               IOAREA1=120,                                            C
               CONTROL=YES,                                            C
               PRINTOV=YES,                                            C
               WORKA=YES,                                              C
```

Figure D-2 HSKPING macro for DOS/370.

```
                    RECFORM=FIXUNB,                                         C
                    DEVICE=1403
OUT1       DS       CL120
B&SYSNDX   EQU      *
.PUNCH     ANOP
           AIF      ('&PUNCHID' EQ '').EXIT
           OPEN     &PUNCHID
           B        EXIT&SYSNDX
&PUNCHID   DTFCD    DEVADDR=SYS006,                                         C
                    IOAREA1=OUT2,                                           C
                    BLKSIZE=80,                                             C
                    WORKA=YES,                                              C
                    RECFORM=FIXUNB,                                         C
                    DEVICE=2540
OUT2       DS       CL80
.EXT       ANOP
EXIT&SYSNDX EQU     *
           MEND
```

Figure D-2 (*Concluded*)

E

Operating System Formats

Table E-1 OS/370 Declarative Macros

name	operation	operands
dcbname	DCB	DSORG=PS or PSU, MACRF= { (GM or GL or GT or GMC or GLC or GTC) / (PM or PL or PT or PMC or PLC or PTC) / (GM or GL or GT or GMC or GLC or GTC, PM or PL or PT or PMC or PLC or PTC) }
		[, DDNAME=name of DD statement]
		[, DEVD= { DA / TA[, DEN=0 or 1 or 2][, TRTCH=C or E or T or ET] / PT[, CODE=I or F or F or B or C or A or T or N] / PR[, PRTSP=0 or 1 or 2 or 3] / PC or RD[, MODE=C or E][, STACK=1 or 2] }
		[, OPTCD=W or C or WC]
		[, RECFM= { U [T] [A or M] / V [B or T] [A or M] / F [B or S or T or BS or BT or BST or ST][A or M] }
		[, LRECL=1 to 32, 760 bytes in format-F record or maximum bytes in format-V record]
		[, BLKSIZE=1 to 32, 760 maximum bytes in block]
		[, BFTEK=S or E][, BUFNO=1 to 255 buffers][, BFALN=F or D]
		[, BUFL=1 to 32, 760 bytes per buffer][, BUFCB=address of buffer pool]
		[, EODAD=address of user's end-of-data set routine for input data sets]
		[, EXLST=address of exit list][, EROPT=ACC or SKP or ABE]
		[, SYNAD=address of user's routine for uncorrectable input/output errors]

Table E-2 OS/370 Imperative Macros

name	operation	operands
[label]	OPEN	(address of data control block, [({INPUT / OUTPUT / INOUT / OUTIN / RDBACK / UPDAT} [, DISP / REREAD / LEAVE])] [, address of data control block, [({INPUT / OUTPUT / INOUT / OUTIN / RDBACK / UPDAT} [, DISP / REREAD / LEAVE])]] . . .)
[label]	CLOSE	(address of data control bloc, [DISP / REREAD / LEAVE] [, address of data control block, [DISP / REREAD / LEAVE]] . . .)
[label]	GET	{(1) / dcbaddress} [, {(0) / workaddress}]
[label]	PUT	{(1) / dcbaddress} [, {(0) / workaddress}]

Table E-3 OS/370 Job Control Cards—the JOB Statement

name	operation	operand
//jobname	JOB	[(acct#] [,acctg information])] [programmer's name] [MSGLEVEL = ([0 / 1 / 2] [,0 / ,1])] [COND=((condition), . . .)] [additional options]

Legend:
{} Choose one.
[] Optional; if more than one line is enclosed, choose one or none.

Table E-4 OS/370 Job Control Cards—The EXEC Statement

name	operation	operand
//[stepname]	EXEC	{PGM=program name PGM=*.stepname.ddname PGM=*.stepname.procstepname.ddname [PROC=] procedure name}
		[PARM=value PARM.procstepname=value]

Legend:
{} Choose one.
[] Optional; if more than one line is enclosed, choose one or none.

Table E-5 OS/370 Job Control Cards—The DD Statement

name	operation	operand	comments
//[ddname procstepname. ddname]	DD	[DSNAME=identification DSN=identification]	See Table E-6 for subparameters
		[UNIT=(unit information)]	See Table E-6 for subparameters
		[VOLUME=(volume information) VOL=(volume information)]	See Table E-6 for subparameters
		[DCB=(attributes) DCB=({dsname *.stepname.ddname *.stepname.procstep.ddname} [,attributes])]	
		[DISP=([status] [,disposition])]	See Table E-6 for subparameters
		[SPACE=(direct access space)]	See Table E-6 for subparameters
		[* DATA] [,DCB=([BLKSIZE=block] [,BUFNO=number])]	To define a data set in the input stream (DCB subparameters only for systems with MFT or MVT)

Legend:
{} Choose one.
[] Optional; if more than one line is enclosed, choose one or none.

Table E-6 OS/370 Job Control Card Subparameters

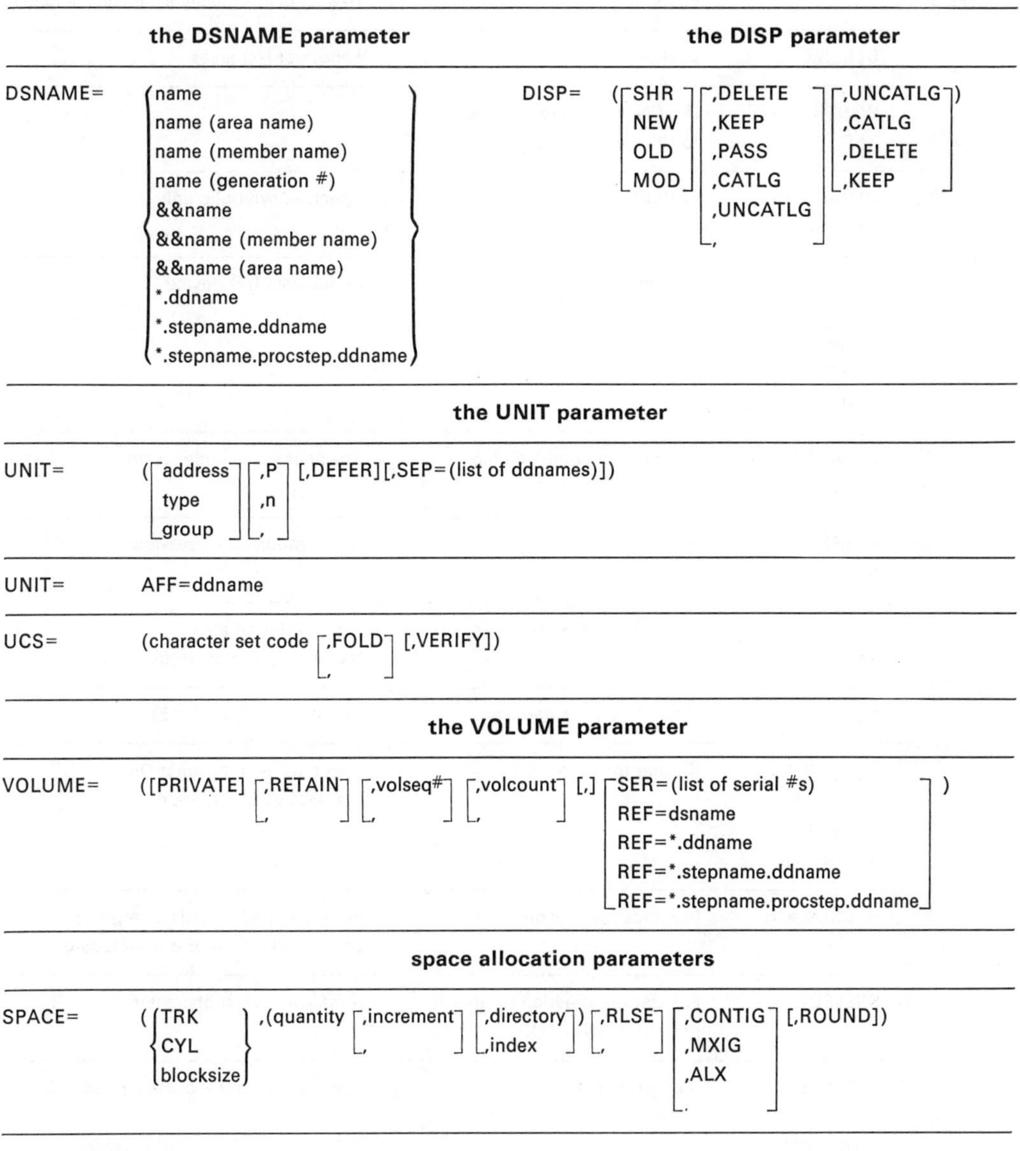

```
              the DSNAME parameter                            the DISP parameter

DSNAME=   (name                          )   DISP=  ([SHR ] [,DELETE  ] [,UNCATLG])
          (name (area name)              )           [NEW ] [,KEEP    ] [,CATLG  ]
          (name (member name)            )           [OLD ] [,PASS    ] [,DELETE ]
          (name (generation #)           )           [MOD ] [,CATLG   ] [,KEEP   ]
          (&&name                        )                  [,UNCATLG ]
          (&&name (member name)          )                  [,        ]
          (&&name (area name)            )
          (*.ddname                      )
          (*.stepname.ddname             )
          (*.stepname.procstep.ddname    )

                              the UNIT parameter

UNIT=     ([address] [,P] [,DEFER][,SEP=(list of ddnames)])
           [type   ] [,n]
           [group  ] [, ]

UNIT=     AFF=ddname

UCS=      (character set code [,FOLD] [,VERIFY])
                              [,    ]

                              the VOLUME parameter

VOLUME=   ([PRIVATE] [,RETAIN] [,volseq#] [,volcount] [,] [SER=(list of serial #s)        ] )
                     [,      ] [,       ] [,        ]     [REF=dsname                     ]
                                                          [REF=*.ddname                   ]
                                                          [REF=*.stepname.ddname          ]
                                                          [REF=*.stepname.procstep.ddname ]

                              space allocation parameters

SPACE=    ({TRK      } ,(quantity [,increment] [,directory]) [,RLSE] [,CONTIG] [,ROUND])
           {CYL      }            [,         ] [,index    ]  [,    ] [,MXIG  ]
           {blocksize}                                               [,ALX   ]
                                                                     [,      ]
```

Legend:

{} Choose one.

[] Optional; if more than one line is enclosed, choose one or none.

Table E-7 DOS/370 Declarative Macros

operation	operand	must be included	remarks
DTFCD		Each file	Header card. Specify symbolic file name.
	BLKSIZE=n	Each file	Length of I/O areas
	CONTROL= YES	If a CNTRL macro is issued to the file	
	DEVADDR= SYSnnn	Each file	Specifies symbolic unit
	DEVICE= 2540 1442 2520 2501	For device other than 2540.	To indicate I/O device
	EOFADDR= name	For input or combined file	Specifies end-of-file routine
	IOAREA1= name	Each file	Name=address expression
	IOAREA2= name	Combined file output area	Second output area Name=address expression
	IOREG=(r)	If two I/O areas are used.	Specify r (register 2-12)
	RECFORM= FIXUNB UNDEF VARUNB	If other than FIXUNB.	Specifies record format Only FIXUNB valid for input.
	RECSIZE=(r)	For undefined records	For undefined records, r=register containing length of output record
	SSELECT=n	For stacker selection to pocket other than NR or NP	n=stacker select character
	TYPEFLE= INPUT OUTPUT CMBND	If other than input	Specifies an input, output, or combined file
	WORKA=YES		If I/O records are processed in work areas, answer YES

Table E-7 (*Continued*)

operation	operand	must be included	remarks
DTFPR		Each file	Specifies header card. Specifies symbolic file name
	BLKSIZE=n	If other than 121	n=length of I/O area. If the record is not fixed, enter the length of the longest record.
	CONTROL= YES	If a CNTRL macro will be used	
	DEVADDR= SYSnnn	Each file	Symbolic unit
	DEVICE= 1403 1404 1443 1445	For file other than 1403.	Actual device
	IOAREA1= name	Each file	Specifies name as output area
	IOAREA2= name	If two I/O areas are specified	Second name output area
	IOREG=(r)	For two output areas	r=register 2-12
	PRINTOV= YES	If PRTOV macro is used	
	RECFORM= FIXUNB UNDEF VARUNB	If record is not FIXUNB	
	RECSIZE=(r)	For undefined records	r=register 2-12 containing length of output record
	WORKA=YES	If records are processed in work areas	

Table E-7 (*Continued*)

operation	operand	must be included	remarks
DTFMT		Each file	Specifies header card and symbolic file name.
	*BLKSIZE=n	Each file	n=length of the I/O area. If the record is not fixed enter the length of the longest record.
	*DEVADDR= SYSnnn	Each file	Specifies symbolic unit
	*EOFADDR= name	Input or work files	Specifies name of user's end-of-file routine.
	FILABL= STD NSTD NO	Each file	Specifies the type of labels.
	IOAREA1= name	Each file	Specifies I/O area. Name=address expression.
	IOAREA2= name	If two I/O areas are specified	Specifies a second I/O area. Name= address expression
	IOREG=(r)		r=register (2-12) if records are blocked or processed in the I/O area.
	*RECFORM= * FIXUNB FIXBLK VARUNB VARBLK * UNDEF	For other than FIXUNB	
	RECSIZE=n or (r)	For FIXBLK or UNDEF	n=number of characters in each record for fixed-length blocked records. r=register (2-12) containing record length for undefined records.
	*TYPEFLE= INPUT OUTPUT *WORK	For output or work files	Specifies whether file is input or output or if a work file is specified.
	WORKA=YES	If records are processed in work areas	

*Entries for work files

Table E-8 DOS/370 Imperative Macros—Card

name	operation	operands
[label]	OPEN [R]	{Filename 1 / (r1)} [,{Filename 2 / (r2)}, . . . Filename 16 Maximum
[label]	CLOSE [R]	{Filename 1 / (r1)} [,{Filename 2 / (r2)}, . . . Filename 16 Maximum
[label]	GET	{Filename / (1)}
[label]	GET	{Filename / (1)} [,{Workname / (0)}]
[label]	PUT	{Filename / (1)}
[label]	PUT	{Filename / (1)} [,{Workname / (0)}]
[label]	CNTRL	{Filename / (1)} ,code [,n] [,m]

Table E-9 DOS/370 Imperative Macros—Printer

name	operation	operands
[label]	OPEN [R]	{Filename 1 / (r1)} [,{Filename 2 / (r2)}, . . . Filename 16 Maximum
[label]	PUT	{Filename / (1)}
[label]	PUT	{Filename / (1)} [,{Workname]}
[label]	CNTRL	{Filename / (1)} ,code [,n] [,m]
[label]	PRTOV	{Filename / (1)} ,{9 / 12} [,{Routine-name / (0)}]}
[label]	CLOSE [R]	{Filename 1 / (r1)} [,{Filename 2 / (r2)}, . . . Filename 16 Maximum

Table E-10 DOS/370 Imperative Macros—Tape

name	operation	operands
[label]	OPEN [R]	{Filename 1 / (r1)} [,{Filename 2 / (r2)}, . . . Filename 16 Maximum]
[label]	CLOSE [R]	{Filename 1 / (r1)} [,{Filename 2 / (r2)}, . . . Filename 16 Maximum]
[label]	LBRET	{1 / 2} Used if DTFMT LABADDR specified.
[label]	GET	{Filename / (1)}
[label]	GET	{Filename / (1)} [,{Workname / (0)}]
[label]	PUT	{Filename / (1)}
[label]	PUT	{Filename / (1)} [,{Workname / (0)}]
[label]	CNTRL	{Filename / (1)} ,code
[label]	FEOV	{Filename / (1)}
[label]	RELSE	{Filename / (1)}
[label]	TRUNC	{Filename / (1)}

Table E-11 DOS/370 Job Control Cards—Job Control Statements

name	operation	operand	72	remarks
//	JOB	jobname	ƀ	jobname: one to eight alphameric characters
//	EXEC	[progname]	ƀ	progname: one to eight alphameric characters. Used only if the program is in the core image library.
//	ASSGN	SYSxxx, address [{,X'ss' / ,ALT}]	ƀ	SYSxxx: can be SYSRDR SYSIPT SYSIN SYSPCH SYSLST SYSLOG SYSLNK SYS000-SYS244 address: can be X'cuu', UA, or IGN X'cuu': c = 0–6 uu = 00–FE(0–254) in hex UA: unassign IGN: unassign and igmore X'ss:' used for magnetic tape only ALT: specifies alternate unit
//	OPTION	optional [option 2, ...]	ƀ	option: can be any of the following LOG Log control statements on SYSLST NOLOG Suppress LOG option DUMP Dump registers and main storage on SYSLST in the case of abnormal program end NODUMP Suppress DUMP option LINK Write output of language translator on SYSLNK for linkage editing NOLINK Suppress LINK option DECK Output object module on SYSPCH NODECK Suppress DECK option LIST Output listing of source module on SYSLST NOLIST Suppress LIST option LISTX Output listing of object module on SYSLST NOLISTX Suppress LISTX option

Table E-11 (*Continued*)

name	operation	operand	72	remarks	
				SYM	Punch symbol deck on SYSPCH
				NOSYM	Suppress SYM option
				XREF	Output symbolic cross-reference list on SYSLST
				NOXREF	Suppress XREF option
				ERRS	Output listing of all errors in source program on SYSLST
				NOERRS	Suppress ERRS option
				CATAL	Catalog program or phase in core image library after completion of Linkage Editor run
				STDLABEL	Causes all sequential disk or tape labels to be written on the standard label track
				USRLABEL	Causes all sequential disk or tape labels to be written on the user label track
				48C	48-character set
				60C	60-character set
//	PAUSE	[comments]	b	PAUSE statement is always printed on 1052 (SYSLOG). If no 1052 is available, the statement is ignored.	
/*	ignored	ignored	b	Columns 1 and 2 are the only columns checked.	
/&	ignored	ignored	b	Columns 1 and 2 are the only columns checked.	
*		comments	b	Column 2 must be blank.	

Index